1995

# THE RIGHT TO DIE
## SECOND EDITION
### VOLUME 2

# THE RIGHT TO DIE
## SECOND EDITION
### VOLUME 2

ALAN MEISEL

Dickie, McCamey & Chilcote Professor of Bioethics, Law, and Psychiatry
School of Law and School of Medicine
Director, Center for Medical Ethics
University of Pittsburgh
Pittsburgh, Pennsylvania

Wiley Law Publications
JOHN WILEY & SONS, INC.
New York · Chichester · Brisbane · Toronto · Singapore

*Library of Congress Cataloging-in-Publication Data*

ISBN 0-471-04672-8   (set)
ISBN 0-471-04782-5   (vol. 1)
ISBN 0-471-04674-4   (vol. 2)

Printed in the United States of America

10 9 8 7 6 5 4 3 2 1

# SUMMARY CONTENTS

# SUMMARY CONTENTS

# DETAILED CONTENTS

**Volume 1**

**Volume 2**

# SHORT REFERENCE LIST

| Short Reference | Full Reference |
|---|---|
| EMTALA | Emergency Medical Treatment and Active Labor Act, 42 U.S.C.A. § 1395dd (West 1992) |
| Hastings Center Guidelines | Hastings Center, Guidelines on the Termination of Life-Sustaining Treatment and Care of the Dying (1987) |
| PSDA | Patient Self-Determination Act, Pub. L. No. 101-508, §§ 4206, 4751 (OBRA), 104 Stat. 1388-115 to -117, 1388-204 to -206 (1990) (codified at 42 U.S.C.A. § 1395cc(f)(1) & *id.* § 1396a(a) (West Supp. 1994)) |
| President's Commission, Deciding to Forego Life-Sustaining Treatment | President's Commission for the Study of Ethical Problems in Medicine and Biomedical and Behavioral Research, Deciding to Forego Life-Sustaining Treatment (1983) |
| President's Commission, Making Health Care Decisions | President's Commission for the Study of Ethical Problems in Medicine and Biomedical and Behavioral Research, Making Health Care Decisions: The Ethical and Legal Implications of Informed Consent in the Patient-Practitioner Relationship (1982) |
| UHCDA | Uniform Health-Care Decisions Act, 9 U.L.A. pt. I at 93 (West Supp. 1994) |
| UMHCCA | Uniform Model Health-Care Consent Act, 9 U.L.A. pt. I at 453 (West 1988 & Supp. 1994) |
| URTIA | Uniform Rights of the Terminally Ill Act, 9B U.L.A. 127 (West Supp. 1994) |

# PART IV

# ADVANCE DIRECTIVES

# CHAPTER 10

# LEGAL STATUS OF ADVANCE DIRECTIVES

3

# § 10.1   Scope of Part IV

**Chapters 10** through **13** examine the meaning, current legal status, and some practical problems in the drafting, use, and administration of advance directives.[1] This chapter discusses the relationship of advance directives to general issues of end-of-life decisionmaking, and focuses on nonstatutorily-based advance directives. **Chapters 11** and **12** discuss the two different types of statutory advance directives, living wills (**Chapter 11**) and health care powers of attorney (**Chapter 12**). **Chapter 13** addresses problems in drafting advance directives and issues for health care providers in implementing and administering advance directives. Because relatively few people have advance directives, state legislatures have begun, especially after the United States Supreme Court's decision in *Cruzan*,[2] to enact legislation to prescribe procedures for decisionmaking in the absence of advance directives. These are usually referred to as *surrogate decisionmaking statutes,* or sometimes as *family decisionmaking statutes* because they ordinarily authorize family members to make decisions on behalf of patients who have not written a living will or appointed a health care proxy. This legislation is discussed in **Chapter 14.**

---

[1] *See* McCarrick, Living Wills and Durable Powers of Attorney: Advance Directive Legislation and Issues (National Reference Ctr. for Bioethics Literature, Kennedy Inst. of Ethics, Geo. U. 1991) (scope note 2) (annotated bibliography of advance directives); Thomas, Treatment and Appointment Directives: Living Wills, Powers of Attorney, and Other Advance Medical Care Documents (Congressional Research Serv. No. 91-87A, Jan. 14, 1991) (collection of advance directive statutes). See §§ **5.61** and **7.4.**

[2] Cruzan v. Director, 497 U.S. 261 (1990).

## § 10.2   Background

Advance directives are a mechanism by which competent individuals plan for medical decisionmaking at some future time when they might no longer possess decisionmaking capacity. That is, they are *directions* to others about health care issued in *advance* of the need for that care.

The hallmark of advance directives is that they are a form of *anticipatory* medical decisionmaking. This stands in contrast to the ordinary medical decisionmaking process for competent patients, which is *contemporaneous.* Although advance directives are usually discussed in the context of decision-making about life-sustaining treatment, they need not be thus confined.[3] Advance directives may pertain to decisionmaking about any kind of health care. They are also usually thought of as a device to direct the *forgoing* of treatment, but advance directives can equally direct the *administration* of treatment[4] (though whether directions to administer treatment are enforceable is open to question[5]). An advance directive may be issued by one who is in good or poor health, but it must be issued by one who possesses decisionmaking capacity.[6]

The term *advance directive* is not one that is generally familiar to attorneys, health care professionals, or the lay public, though it is becoming more familiar, especially after the passage of the federal Patient Self-Determination Act,[7] mandating that patients entering health care institutions be given certain information about advance directives. Many people are more familiar with the term *living will,* which is a particular kind of advance directive.[8] Although there has been a great deal of public discussion of living wills in recent years, still "[s]urveys show that the overwhelming majority of Americans have not executed such written instructions."[9]

---

[3] *See* Uniform Health-Care Decisions Act, 9 U.L.A. pt. I at 93 (West Supp. 1994); Uniform Model Health-Care Consent Act, 9 U.L.A. 453 (West 1988 & Supp. 1994). See **§§ 10.18–10.20.**

[4] See **§ 11.1.**

[5] See **Ch. 19.**

[6] See **§§ 11.8, 12.9,** and **13.18.**

[7] See **§ 10.21.**

[8] See **§ 10.5.**

[9] Cruzan v. Director, 497 U.S. 261, 323 n.21 (1990) (Brennan, J., dissenting) (citing Emanuel & Emanuel, *The Medical Directive: A New Comprehensive Advance Care Document,* 261 JAMA 3288 (1989) (9% of Americans execute advance directives); American Medical Ass'n Surveys of Physician and Public Opinion on Health Care Issues 29–30 (1988) (15% of those surveyed had executed living wills); President's Commission for the Study of Ethical Problems in Medicine & Biomedical & Behavioral Research, Making Health Care Decisions 241–42 (1982) (23% of those surveyed said that they had put treatment instructions in writing)). *See also* Gamble et al., *Knowledge, Attitudes, and Behavior of Elderly Persons Regarding Living Wills,* 151 Archives Internal Med. 277 (1991) (although 52% of 75 elderly persons knew about living wills, none had executed one, and only two had discussed their preference for limiting treatment with their physician).

## § 10.3  Purposes of Advance Directives

Advance directives have three general and interrelated purposes. The first and most important from the perspective of those who issue the directives ("declarants") is to provide a means of exercising some degree of control over medical care if they lack the capacity to do so at the time that treatment decisions need to be made. Advance directives are intended to effectuate the patient's own choice, thereby honoring self-determination even when individuals no longer possess the capacity for self-determination.[10]

The utility as well as the legitimacy of advance directives is based on the assumption that the preferred manner of decisionmaking for patients lacking decisionmaking capacity is that which reflects as nearly as possible the patient's own views, that is, a subjective standard.[11] Implementing this standard requires the surrogate to know the patient's wishes about treatment. Advance directives are crucial to implementing the subjective standard,[12] and though not quite as crucial in implementing the substituted judgment standard, they can play an important role there too.[13] Even if not legally binding, advance directives are often the best evidence of the patient's wishes,[14] and without them, health care professionals and surrogate decisionmakers might be compelled to rely on less trustworthy evidence of the patient's wishes about treatment.

The second general purpose of advance directives is to avoid some of the more serious procedural problems associated with making decisions for patients who lack decisionmaking capacity, primarily by forestalling recourse to the judicial process. When patients lack decisionmaking capacity, and especially when the therapy in question is life-sustaining, a great deal of confusion can arise in the clinical setting concerning how decisionmaking is to proceed. Because living wills provide health care personnel with guidance about the patient's wishes and health care powers of attorney provide guidance about who

---

[10] **IN:** *In re* Lawrance, 579 N.E.2d 32, 39 (Ind. 1991) ("The Living Will Act . . . demonstrates respect for patient autonomy.").

[11] See §§ **7.4–7.6.**

[12] **AZ:** Rasmussen v. Fleming, 741 P.2d 674, 689 n.21 (Ariz. 1987).

  **MO:** Cruzan v. Harmon, 760 S.W.2d 408 (Mo. 1988).

  **NJ:** *In re* Conroy, 486 A.2d 1209, 1229–30 (N.J. 1985).

  **NY:** *In re* Westchester County Medical Center (O'Connor), 531 N.E.2d 607 (N.Y. 1988).

[13] See §§ **7.7–7.10.**

[14] **FL:** John F. Kennedy Memorial Hosp. v. Bludworth, 452 So. 2d 921, 926 (Fla. 1984).

  **NJ:** *In re* Peter, 529 A.2d 419, 430 (N.J. 1987) (Handler, J., concurring) ("Ms. Peter's granting of a durable power of attorney to Mr. Johanning, combined with the fact that he was a close friend to Ms. Peter, is sufficient evidence that the treatment decision made for Ms. Peter now that she is incompetent is one with which she would have been content."); *In re* Conroy, 486 A.2d at 1229 n.5; *In re* Clark, 510 A.2d 136, 142 (N.J. Super. Ct. Ch. Div. 1986) ("In this case, there is little subjective evidence as to his wishes. Clark has made no living will, nor signed a power of attorney authorizing another person to make decisions on his behalf.").

has the authority to speak for the patient, advance directives promote a greater willingness on the part of health care professionals to avoid a judicial resolution to end-of-life decisionmaking for incompetent patients. The use of an advance directive for designating a proxy[15] to make decisions for an individual when that person loses medical decisionmaking capacity will ordinarily obviate the need for either the clinical designation of a surrogate or the judicial appointment of a guardian.[16] Advance directives will not always avoid judicial proceedings. When an advance directive does not designate a proxy but merely gives instructions, a surrogate will still need to be designated through either the clinical or judicial approach if the instructions do not adequately address the issues requiring resolution. If a third party (for example, a family member or friend of the patient, or a health care professional) is dissatisfied with the patient's designation of a proxy through an advance directive, perhaps arising from the belief that the proxy does not represent the patient's true wishes or best interests, the appropriate remedy is a judicial hearing.[17]

The third general purpose of advance directives, and perhaps the most important from the perspective of health care providers, is to provide immunity from civil and criminal liability. All advance directive statutes contain provisions conferring immunity on health care providers if stated conditions are met.[18] Because most litigated right-to-die cases wind up in court because of the fear of liability, these statutory immunity provisions also serve to facilitate decisionmaking by providing another reason for keeping cases in the clinical setting.

It has also been suggested that the widespread use of advance directives would help to lower the costs of providing medical treatment to those who are not likely to benefit significantly from it. It has been proposed that individuals having advance directives could be charged lower premiums for health insurance—though the nondiscrimination provisions of many advance directive statutes[19] would need to be amended to permit this—or even that the issuance of health insurance be made contingent upon the execution of an advance directive (overlooking the fact that advance directives may request treatment as well as request to forgo treatment). It is not at all clear, however, that it costs less to treat patients near the ends of their lives who have advance directives than to treat those who do not.[20]

---

[15] See **Ch. 12.**

[16] **PA:** *Cf. In re* Aston, 37 Cumb. L.J. 198, 7 Fiduc. Rep. 2d 171 (C.P. Cumberland County, Pa. 1987) (existence of durable power of attorney designating an attorney in fact to handle principal's financial affairs obviates need for appointment of guardian of estate, but adjudication of incompetence necessary for appointment of guardian of the person because durable power of attorney did not grant authority to make health care decisions).

[17] **FL:** Browning v. Herbert, 568 So. 2d 4, 16 (Fla. 1990).

**PA:** Leader Nursing v. McCracken, 8 Fiduc. Rep. 2d 37 (C.P. Cumberland County, Pa. 1988).

[18] See §§ **10.15** and **11.17.**

[19] See §§ **11.20** and **12.49.**

[20] *See* Schneiderman et al., *Effects of Offering Advance Directives on Medical Treatments and Costs,* 117 Annals Internal Med. 599 (1992).

## § 10.4   Types of Advance Directives

There are two general types of advance directives, living wills and health care powers of attorney. Advance directives may give instructions, appoint a proxy to serve as a surrogate, or do both.

**Living Wills.**   Living wills are documents that give instructions to health care providers about particular kinds of medical care that an individual would or would not want to have to prolong life. Most states now have detailed statutes concerning living wills.[21]

Living wills were originally intended to give instructions to limit, withhold, or withdraw treatment, but they can also be used to give instructions about what kind of treatment an individual might wish to have administered rather than forgone. Many living will statutes explicitly provide for such an option.[22] Although there are no reported cases involving living wills in which an individual has requested the administration of treatment, it is likely that they will begin to arise as the debate about "futile" medical treatment continues and expands.[23]

Traditionally, most people who have been concerned enough to issue an advance directive have feared that they would "be kept alive as vegetables" or would be subjected to painful and degrading medical procedures long after they offered any benefit. Motivated by such concerns, an individual might draft a written advance directive or make oral statements aimed at instructing health care professionals not to administer any "extraordinary treatment," "heroic treatment," "artificial treatment," or "life-support" in the event of terminal illness.[24] Although the motivation behind such a directive is understandable, unappreciated dangers lurk in its interpretation and application. Did the individual, for example, mean to direct physicians not to administer cardiopulmonary resuscitation not only if the individual were terminally ill from cancer yet still functioning quite well on a day-to-day basis but also if he were to have a heart attack at work?

If a living will intended to limit therapy is too general, there is the danger that therapy will be withheld prematurely or in circumstances that the patient did not anticipate and could not have contemplated. Similarly, there is the related risk that, because of vagueness, treatment may be administered when the patient would not have wanted it.[25] On the other hand, if a living will is too specific, it

---

[21] See **Ch. 11.**

[22] See § **11.1.**

[23] See **Ch. 19.**

[24] See **Ch. 9.**

[25] **NY:** *See* Elbaum v. Grace Plaza of Great Neck, Inc., 544 N.Y.S.2d 840, 846 (App. Div. 1989) ("'[I]nfirmities [patient] was concerned with and the procedures she eschewed'" must "not [be] 'qualitatively different than those now presented.'") (quoting *O'Connor*); *In re* Westchester County Medical Ctr. (O'Connor), 531 N.E.2d 607, 614 (N.Y. 1988) (patient's "comments— that she would never want to lose her dignity before she passed away, that nature should be permitted to take its course, that it is 'monstrous' to use life support machinery—" did not contemplate death from forgoing artificial nutrition and hydration).

might not apply to situations that actually arise that the patient did not foresee and could not have contemplated, but in which the patient might have wished to have had treatment withheld or administered had he been specifically asked.

One of the reasons that advance directives can fail in achieving the declarant's purpose is that it is impossible to know in advance what illness or injury might befall someone and thus what realistic therapeutic options may be available. Indeed, a living will anticipates and plans for an event that might never occur. Even if it does occur in a general way—such as when the declarant loses decisionmaking capacity and requires treatment—the kind of situation that the patient most feared and that was the motivating factor in issuing the advance directive may differ significantly from what actually materializes.

**Proxy Directives.**   The recognition of the difficulties inherent in living wills is probably responsible for an increased emphasis on proxy directives. This has been manifested in the enactment of health care power of attorney statutes, which authorize and regulate proxy directives (also known as health care powers of attorney). These directives permit individuals to appoint someone to make medical decisions for them when they are no longer able to do so for themselves. Most states have enacted statutes to provide an explicit basis for the issuance of health care powers of attorney.[26]

Through a proxy directive, one may appoint another to act as his surrogate decisionmaker, making it an extremely useful and powerful tool for avoiding one of the major pitfalls in decisionmaking for incompetent patients—unclarity as to who has the authority to serve as the patient's surrogate.[27] One of the significant advantages that a proxy directive has over a living will is that it provides a means for decisionmaking even when the situation that actually arises is not one that the patient might have contemplated and to which, therefore, a living will might be inapplicable or might lead to results that the patient would not have wanted.

Appointing a proxy for medical decisionmaking provides a great deal more flexibility than can ever be incorporated in any meaningful, simple, and sensible way in an instruction directive because it is simply not possible to anticipate in advance all of the different medical decisions that might need to be made and the circumstances under which they might arise. Nor is it possible to anticipate all of the subtleties of medical decisionmaking even for a patient who is clearly dying from a particular disease. Rather than attempting to decide all things in advance, one who executes a proxy directive implicitly acknowledges that such detailed advance planning is either not possible or, if possible, not desirable because it is too inflexible. The proxy directive is, in effect, interstitial decision-making in the form of a statement by the person who executes it that he entrusts decisionmaking about his future medical care, should he be unable to participate in the decisionmaking process himself, to someone he trusts to represent him.

---

[26] See **Ch. 12.**

[27] See **Ch. 5.**

However, there are pitfalls in proxy directives, too, the potentially most serious ones being that the proxy might act contrary to the patient's wishes or have no idea what medical treatment the patient would have wanted. Although proxy directives are advantageous to health care professionals because they provide them with knowledge of who is to serve as the surrogate decisionmaker, a proxy directive may merely shift the burden of the uncertainty concerning the patient's wishes from health care professionals to the surrogate.

**Combination Directives.**    The respective advantages of living wills and proxy directives can be combined into a single advance directive that both appoints a proxy decisionmaker and gives instructions to that proxy concerning the patient's preferences about health care. A combination directive possesses the virtues of a living will and a proxy directive while avoiding most of the pitfalls of each. If the instructions are too general, the proxy has the authority to determine whether the instructions should be applied to the particular circumstances. If the instructions are too specific and do not by their terms apply to the existing medical situation, the proxy has the discretion to apply them or not. When the declarant issues only a proxy directive, the proxy lacks any formal guidance from the declarant as to the declarant's actual wishes about treatment. By including instructions, however, the proxy's discretion can be guided in such a way that it is the declarant's will that is being applied rather than a fictionalized version of the declarant's will, as might occur when some versions of the substituted judgment standard are applied.[28] A combination directive permits the spirit of the declarant's instructions to govern, with the interstices filled in by the proxy.

A declarant may provide oral instructions to a person named as proxy in a proxy directive,[29] thereby making a proxy directive more useful than it would be without any written or oral directions. However, if the instructions are provided in writing in the directive, the proxy's authority might be less subject to challenge by other members of the patient's family or by the attending physician.[30] Nonetheless, a discussion between the declarant and the proxy, whether there is a proxy directive or a combination directive, is always advisable, as is a discussion between the declarant and the declarant's physician if logistically possible, regardless of the kind of directive.

---

[28] See **Ch. 7.**

[29] **NJ:** *See In re* Peter, 529 A.2d 419, 426 (N.J. 1987) (Ms. Peter's appointed proxy "explain[ed] that Ms. Peter directed him to refuse life-sustaining treatment on her behalf in a situation like this.").

[30] **NY:** *In re* Westchester County Medical Ctr. (O'Connor), 531 N.E.2d 607, 613 (N.Y. 1988) ("existence of a writing suggests the author's seriousness of purpose"). *See also* Mower & Baraff, *Advance Directives: Effect of Type of Directive on Physicians' Therapeutic Decisions,* 153 Archives Internal Med. 375 (1993) (physicians are more likely to honor combination directive than living will or proxy directive alone).

A number of states have a single advance directive statute that coordinates the issuance of a directive that both gives instructions and appoints a proxy.[31] Even in the absence of such legislation, there is no reason why one cannot combine the living will and proxy directive into a single document.

## § 10.5 Terminology

A variety of different terms are employed to refer to the concepts and instruments involved in anticipatory health care decisionmaking. The President's Commission for the Study of Ethical Problems in Medicine and Biomedical and Behavioral Research adopted the phrase "advance directive."[32] The imprimatur thus placed on this phrase has helped to make it more familiar among health care professionals, and courts and legislatures have gradually come to use it. Nonetheless, a number of other terms continue to be used, and the long-used popular term *living will* is unlikely to be superseded any time soon.

**Advance Directive.** The term *advance directive* itself is used to denote several different things. First, it is sometimes used to designate the concept of anticipatory health care decisionmaking. At other times, it is used to refer to the content of an oral or written statement made by an individual (declarant) to become effective under stated conditions. The term can also be used to refer to a vehicle for embodying such a statement, such as a living will or durable power of attorney. Different forms of advance directives have certain advantages and disadvantages, such as specificity, clarity, and likelihood of enforceability in a medical setting and, if necessary, by a court.

**Living Will.** The term *living will* is the popular name used to refer generically to written advance directives. The term should be used to refer to advance directives that give instructions, not to a *health care power of attorney* or *health care proxy,* but that is not always the case in practice. A living will might be

---

[31] **AZ:** Ariz. Rev. Stat. Ann. §§ 36-3201 to -3262.

   **CT:** Conn. Gen. Stat. Ann. §§ 19a-570 to -580c.

   **FL:** Fla. Stat. Ann. §§ 765.101–.401.

   **KY:** Ky. Rev. Stat. Ann. §§ 311.621–.643.

   **MD:** Md. Code Ann., Health-Gen. §§ 5-601 to -618.

   **NJ:** N.J. Stat. Ann. §§ 26:2H-53 to -78.

   **OK:** Okla. Stat. Ann. tit. 63, §§ 3101.1–.16.

   **OR:** Or. Rev. Stat. §§ 127.505–.660, .995.

   **VA:** Va. Code Ann. §§ 54.1-2981 to -2993.

[32] President's Comm'n for the Study of Ethical Problems in Medicine & Biomedical & Behavioral Research, Deciding to Forego Life-Sustaining Treatment 136–53 (1983).

custom-drafted by or for the declarant, or it might be based on a form. Many living will statutes contain form living wills,[33] and generic living will forms have been drafted and are disseminated by some organizations concerned with the rights of terminally ill persons.[34]

**Statutory Advance Directives.** A *statutory advance directive* is an advance directive drafted pursuant to a living will statute or health care power of attorney statute.

**Nonstatutory Advance Directive.** An advance directive need not necessarily be drafted in accordance with a statute. Most advance directive statutes contain provisions stating that they are not intended to preempt any preexisting rights, and courts have held that there is a common-law and/or constitutional right to issue enforceable instructions about one's medical care or to appoint another to make such decisions in the event of future incapacity.[35] Such nonstatutory advance directives are sometimes referred to as *common-law advance directives*.

**Health Care Proxy or Power of Attorney.** An individual who wishes to appoint another person to make health care decisions for him in the event of future incapacity may do so instead of or in addition to executing a living will. The means for doing so is often referred to as a health care proxy, a health care power of attorney, or a durable power of attorney for health care,[36] though an oral statement might be used.[37]

The person making the appointment is usually referred to as the principal but may also be referred to as a grantor, settlor, creator, declarant, or patient (though the individual need not be under medical care to execute a proxy directive). A health care directive is usually embodied in a document known as a health care proxy or health care power of attorney. The individual upon whom these decisionmaking powers are conferred is a surrogate, but when appointed by the patient is usually referred to as a *health care proxy,* but sometimes as a *health care agent* or simply as a *surrogate*.

One need not necessarily use any particular formalities to designate a health care proxy. However, most states have enacted special statutes for this purpose that are referred to as health care proxy or health care power of attorney statutes. The term *health care power of attorney* should be used to refer to the instrument

---

[33] See § **11.3.**

[34] **NY:** Saunders v. State, 492 N.Y.S.2d 510, 512–13 (Sup. Ct. Nassau County 1985) ("A variety of organizations concerned with the rights of individuals to forgo life-sustaining treatment . . . have drafted forms for issuing instructions.").

[35] See §§ **10.11–10.16.**

[36] *See, e.g.,* Or. Rev. Stat. § 127.505(10) (durable power of attorney for health care is "a power of attorney that authorizes an agent to make health care decisions for the principal when the principal is incapable").

[37] See § **10.16.**

used to appoint someone to make health care decisions for another, and *health care proxy* should be used to refer to the person so designated. However, not all statutes follow this logic in their terminology.[38]

Because health care powers of attorneys had their origins in *durable powers of attorney,* they are sometimes referred to as such, or as *durable powers of attorney for health care.* Durable powers of attorney are used for far more purposes than for creating advance directives and were not originally enacted with such a use in mind.[39] A durable power of attorney is not an advance directive; rather, it is one of the vehicles for creating and embodying an advance directive, like a living will form, an oral statement, or a holographic document.[40]

**Declarant, Principal, Declaration.**  An individual who issues a living will is frequently referred to in advance directive statutes as a *declarant,* and the advance directive is sometimes referred to as a *declaration.* However, in health care power of attorney statutes, the declarant is usually referred to as the *principal.* These two terms should be considered interchangeable.

**Proxy, Agent, Attorney in Fact.**  The person who is appointed by a health care power of attorney to make decisions for the principal is usually referred to as a *proxy* or an *agent,* and sometimes as an *attorney in fact.* At least one statute uses the term *surrogate,* but this term is probably better reserved for the more general purpose of referring to any person, however designated, who makes decisions for another, including a person appointed by a health care power of attorney, but also for referring to a guardian, to a person designated under a surrogate decisionmaking statute, or to a common-law surrogate.

## VALIDITY AND ENFORCEABILITY OF ADVANCE DIRECTIVES

## § 10.6  Background

For a long time, there had been a great deal of uncertainty about the enforceability of advance directives. This has gradually disappeared as most states

---

[38] **FL:** *See, e.g.,* Fla. Stat. Ann. §§ 765.101(15) ("'Proxy' means a competent adult who has not been expressly designated to make health care decisions for a particular incapacitated individual, but who, nevertheless, is authorized" by statute to do so."), 765.101(16) ("'Surrogate' means any competent adult expressly designated by a principal to make health care decisions on behalf of the principal upon the principal's incapacity.").

**KY:** Ky. Rev. Stat. Ann. § 311.625 (surrogate).

**MA:** Mass. Gen. Laws. Ann. ch. 201D, § 1 (referring to document as "health care proxy").

[39] **NY:** *In re* Westchester County Medical Ctr. (O'Connor), 531 N.E.2d 607, 612 n.2 (N.Y. 1988).

[40] See § **12.2.**

enacted a statutory basis first for living wills and then for health care powers of attorney.[41] The Supreme Court's decision in *Cruzan v. Director,*[42] while not holding that the constitution requires an advance directive for the termination of life support, provides an impetus for individuals to draft them, especially living wills, in the event that the state in which they live might come to require them. The passage by Congress of the Patient Self-Determination Act[43] shortly after *Cruzan* was decided gave further impetus to the momentum for advance directives.

Consequently, the debate about the validity and enforceability of advance directives is gradually shifting to the question of the validity of advance directives not drafted in conformance with and pursuant to a living will or health care power of attorney statute. A related question is whether or not some of the restrictive provisions in advance directive legislation apply to advance directives that do not conform to the statute.

Insistence on using and enforcing only advance directives that comply strictly with state statutes can seriously frustrate the wishes of declarants and pose significant barriers to end-of-life decisionmaking because most people have not executed an advance directive.[44] In one case, even a patient described as having "been an active member of the Euthanasia Council of Delaware" who "had made statements to the effect that she wanted to make a 'living will' and that she did not want to be kept alive as a 'vegetable' or by extraordinary means" nevertheless had not actually executed a written living will.[45]

Insistence on formal compliance also runs the risk of discriminating against the less sophisticated members of society, as Justice Brennan observed in *Cruzan:*

> Too few people execute living wills or equivalently formal directives for such an evidentiary rule to ensure adequately that the wishes of incompetent persons will be honored [footnote omitted]. While it might be a wise social policy to encourage people to furnish such instructions, no general conclusion about a patient's choice can be drawn from the absence of formalities. The probability of becoming irreversibly vegetative is so low that many people may not feel an urgency to marshal formal evidence of their preferences. Some may not wish to dwell on their own physical deterioration and mortality. Even someone with a resolute determination to avoid life-support under circumstances such as Nancy's would still need to know that such things as living wills exist and how to execute one. Often legal help would be necessary, especially given the majority's apparent willingness to permit

---

[41] See **Chs. 11** and **12.**

[42] Cruzan v. Director, 497 U.S. 261 (1990).

[43] See § **10.21.**

[44] **CA:** *See* Barber v. Superior Court, 195 Cal. Rptr. 484, 489 (Ct. App. 1983) ("The lack of generalized public awareness of the statutory scheme and the typically human characteristics of procrastination and reluctance to contemplate the need for such arrangements however makes this a tool which will all too often go unused by those who might desire it.").

[45] **DE:** Severns v. Wilmington Medical Ctr., Inc., 421 A.2d 1334, 1338 n.2 (Del. 1980).

States to insist that a person's wishes are not truly known unless the particular medical treatment is specified.[46]

## § 10.7  Advance Directives and Informed Consent

Medical decisionmaking by competent patients, whether it concerns life-sustaining or other treatment, ordinarily requires informed consent.[47] Advance directives are based on the concept of informed consent and they share certain similarities, most notably that they are both forms of decisionmaking about medical care. However, there are also important differences.

Informed consent is obtained more or less contemporaneously with the administration of treatment. Although there may be some time delay between a physician's disclosure of information to a patient and the patient's decision on the one hand and treatment on the other, the process of obtaining informed consent is usually undertaken in contemplation of administering some particular treatment or performing some diagnostic procedure in the not-too-distant future. It usually involves individuals who are ill or injured and are currently contemplating medical treatment (though they may ultimately decide to forgo it). The duration of the decisionmaking and treatment processes might be protracted, but these processes all occur in the context of the contemporaneous need for decisionmaking and therapy.

Although informed consent is ordinarily not a hypothetical exercise contingent upon the happening of some event, it may occasionally be partially so. For example, a patient suffering from amyotrophic lateral sclerosis, which is a slow, progressively degenerative disease,[48] will learn that the ability to swallow food or breathe spontaneously will eventually be lost and might therefore decide in advance that when this happens the use of a mechanical ventilator or artificial nutrition and hydration should not be begun.[49] Although the patient made the decision in advance of the need for the treatment in question, it is not an advance directive if at the time the decision is made the patient is still competent. Of course, if that is the case, the patient may also change his mind at that time if he is still competent. That is precisely what happened in *State*

---

[46] US: Cruzan v. Director, 497 U.S. at 323 (Brennan, J., dissenting).

  WI: *Accord* L.W. v. L.E. Phillips Career Dev. Ctr., 482 N.W.2d 60, 67–68 (Wis. 1992) ("Relatively few individuals provide explicit written or oral instructions concerning their treatment preferences should they become incompetent [footnote omitted]. The reasons for this are undoubtedly myriad: ignorance, superstition, carelessness, sloth, procrastination or the simple refusal to believe it could happen to oneself.").

[47] See **Ch. 3.**

[48] See **§ 9.44.**

[49] *See, e.g., In re* Requena, 517 A.2d 886 (N.J. Super. Ct. Ch. Div.), *aff'd,* 517 A.2d 869 (N.J. Super. Ct. App. Div. 1986).

*v. McAfee.*[50] The patient's decision to have his ventilator disconnected was approved by the Georgia Supreme Court. After the court's opinion was handed down, Mr. McAfee came to symbolize the plight of severely handicapped persons. The publicity surrounding the case served to mobilize private and public resources for the handicapped, and when adequate social services were made available, Mr. McAfee chose not to exercise his right to have his ventilator disconnected.[51]

An advance directive, by contrast, is a kind of anticipatory and contingent decisionmaking.[52] At the time of making it, the declarant is often (though not always) someone in good health. The time at which the directive is to go into effect cannot be specified, so it is made contingent on the happening of some event, usually the need for some kind of medical treatment. The decision is usually made in fairly general terms because the precise kind of medical treatment cannot be specified without making the advance directive so specific that it runs the risk of failing to apply to various possible situations. Finally, the patient states his preference for the type of medical treatment he should receive if these conditions occur.

An advance directive not only goes into effect at some future time when a decision needs to be made about administering or forgoing medical treatment, but also goes into effect only if the patient has lost the capacity to make a decision about treatment at that time. If the patient is still in possession of decisionmaking capacity, the patient's decision governs, not the patient's prior oral instructions or prior written statements (whether in a common-law or statutory living will) or the decision of a family member or other interested person, even if that person was previously designated as the patient's proxy in a health care power of attorney or other writing.[53]

---

[50] **GA:** State v. McAfee, 385 S.E.2d 651 (Ga. 1989) (living will act does not apply to a competent patient still capable of making his own medical decisions, who has not executed a living will, and is not terminally ill).

[51] Applebome, *An Angry Man Fights to Die, Then Tests Life,* N.Y. Times, Feb. 7, 1990, at 1, col. 2 (late ed.). *See also* Sehgal et al., *How Strictly Do Dialysis Patients Want Their Advance Directives Followed?,* 267 JAMA 59 (1992) (patients in outpatient hemodialysis clinic were willing to accord varying degrees of leeway to their surrogates in varying from their living wills should they become incompetent).

[52] **FL:** Browning v. Herbert, 568 So. 2d 4 (Fla. 1990).

**MD:** 73 Md. Op. Att'y Gen. 253, 276–77 (Op. No. 88-046, Oct. 17, 1988) (recognizing advance directives as contingent decisionmaking).

**NJ:** *In re* Jobes, 529 A.2d 434, 456 n.9 (N.J. 1987) (Handler, J., concurring and dissenting) ("[T]here is a difference between even the most considered judgment about a hypothetical decision and actually deciding in the face of the particular circumstances. This may be especially true when, as here, the decision touches upon basic factors: if one is to go on living and in what manner.").

**NY:** *In re* Westchester County Medical Ctr. (O'Connor), 531 N.E.2d 607 (N.Y. 1988).

[53] *See In re* Dubreuil, 603 So. 2d 538, 541 (Fla. Dist. Ct. App. 1992) (a patient's "constitutional right to refuse treatment was [not] in any way dependent upon the consent of her husband"). See § **10.14.**

Right-to-die cases involving competent patients who have declined life-sustaining treatment[54] should not be treated as involving advance directives because they involve contemporaneous, rather than anticipatory, decision-making.[55] However, the distinction is not always clear. For example, *In re Lydia E. Hall Hospital*[56] involved a mix of informed consent and advance directive. When the patient initially declined treatment, he was competent and fully informed that he would die if dialysis were discontinued and that there were no other treatments available. A judicial proceeding was initiated to compel him to submit to dialysis, but by the time the hearing could be held, the patient had lapsed into a coma and become incompetent. Thus, the decision of the court to permit the termination of treatment based on the patient's earlier oral and written statements about dialysis was, in effect, the judicial enforcement of an advance directive.

Some courts have suggested that for advance directives to be enforceable they should essentially be the equivalent of anticipatory informed consent.[57] That is,

---

[54] **DDC:** *See, e.g.,* Tune v. Walter Reed Army Medical Hosp., 602 F. Supp. 1452 (D.D.C. 1985).

**CA:** *See, e.g.,* Bouvia v. Superior Court (Glenchur), 225 Cal. Rptr. 297 (Ct. App. 1986); Bartling v. Superior Court, 209 Cal. Rptr. 220 (Ct. App. 1984).

**FL:** *See, e.g.,* Wons v. Public Health Trust, 541 So. 2d 96 (Fla. 1989); Satz v. Perlmutter, 379 So. 2d 359 (Fla. 1980); St. Mary's Hosp. v. Ramsey, 465 So. 2d 666 (Fla. Dist. Ct. App. 1985).

**GA:** *See, e.g.,* State v. McAfee, 385 S.E.2d 651 (Ga. 1989).

**NV:** *See, e.g.,* McKay v. Bergstedt, 801 P.2d 617 (Nev. 1990).

**NJ:** *See, e.g., In re* Farrell, 529 A.2d 404 (N.J. 1987).

**NY:** Fosmire v. Nicoleau, 551 N.E.2d 77 (N.Y. 1990).

**PA:** *See, e.g.,* Pocono Medical Ctr. v. Harley, 11 Fiduc. Rep. 2d 128, 129 (C.P. Monroe County, Pa. 1990) (patient, while competent, made oral refusal of kidney dialysis, which her physician told her there was "imminent prospect" of her needing); *In re* Doe, 45 Pa. D. & C.3d 371 (C.P. Phila. County 1987).

[55] *See, e.g.,* A.B. v. C., 477 N.Y.S.2d 281, 284 (Sup. Ct. 1984) (if petitioner were "to be admitted to the hospital and if she is still competent and able to communicate her thoughts, she has right to refuse medical treatment without having executed an advance directive) (dictum).

[56] 455 N.Y.S.2d 706 (Sup. Ct. Nassau County 1982).

[57] **FL:** *But see* Browning v. Herbert, 568 So. 2d 4, 13 (Fla. 1990) (While, "[u]nfortunately, human limitations preclude absolute knowledge of the wishes of someone in Mrs. Browning's condition," one "cannot avoid making a decision in these circumstances, for even the failure to act constitutes a choice.").

**ME:** *See, e.g., In re* Gardner, 534 A.2d 947, 957 (Me. 1987) (Clifford, J., dissenting) ("[T]he decision to refuse medical treatment, especially where certain death will result, should be at least as informed as the decision to consent to treatment.").

**MI:** *Cf.* Werth v. Taylor, 475 N.W.2d 426 (Mich. Ct. App. 1991).

**NJ:** *Cf. In re* Quinlan, 348 A.2d 801, 819 (N.J. 1975) (living wills are based on the concept of informed consent), *rev'd,* 355 A.2d 647 (N.J.), *cert. denied,* 429 U.S. 922 (1976); *In re* Hughes, 611 A.2d 1148 (N.J. Super. Ct. App. Div. 1992).

**NY:** *Cf. In re* Westchester County Medical Ctr. (O'Connor), 531 N.E.2d 607, 619 (N.Y. 1988) (Hancock, J., concurring) (characterizes majority's position as requiring application of *specific-subjective-intent rule* or a patient's *actual intent* rule which requires "clear expression of a

the patient should decide anticipatorily to refuse or consent to treatment only after having been adequately informed about the therapeutic options. However desirable it might be to invalidate an advance directive in a medical emergency for this reason,[58] it should have no applicability in nonemergencies. A requirement that an advance directive meet the standards of information and understanding required of contemporaneous informed consent would render advance directives useless.

Thus, insistence that an advance directive be as informed as informed consent would effectively preclude individuals from anticipatorily making their own post-incompetence decisions about medical care, except for those (probably few) who guess correctly what kind of illnesses they will suffer from and what kind of treatment they will need and wish to forgo, and who take the trouble to be certain that they are adequately informed about the therapeutic options under such circumstances as well as the risks and benefits of those options. For the remainder of patients—the vast majority in all likelihood—decisionmaking will have to be made on the basis of less reliable information or will have to be made in the absence of any information at all about what the particular patient would have wanted. Exceedingly stringent requirements for advance directives can thwart patients' desires.[59]

Closely related to the concern of some courts that an advance directive meet the standards for informed consent is that when an advance directive is given effect, there can be no guarantee that the patient has not had a change of mind

---

present intention to forego" the treatment in question); Saunders v. State, 492 N.Y.S.2d 510 (Sup. Ct. 1985) (refusing in the case of a currently competent patient to recognize the validity of a living will but treating it as an anticipatory informed consent).

**OH:** *See, e.g.,* Estate of Leach v. Shapiro, 469 N.E.2d 1047, 1053 (Ohio Ct. App. 1984) (anticipatory refusal "must satisfy the same standards of knowledge and understanding required for informed consent"). *Cf.* University of Cincinnati Hosp. v. Edmond, 506 N.E.2d 299 (C.P. Hamilton County, Ohio 1986).

**PA:** *Cf. In re* Estate of Dorone, 534 A.2d 452 (Pa. 1987).

[58] **MI:** Werth v. Taylor, 475 N.W.2d 426 (Mich. Ct. App. 1991) (in context of refusal of health-restoring, not death-postponing, treatment).

**OH:** Estate of Leach v. Shapiro, 469 N.E.2d 1047, 1053 (Ohio Ct. App. 1984) (before anticipatory refusal of treatment can controvert implied consent arising from a medical emergency, it must satisfy the standards of knowledge and understanding required for informed consent).

**PA:** *In re* Estate of Dorone, 502 A.2d 1271 (Pa. Super. Ct. 1985), *aff'd,* 534 A.2d 452 (Pa. 1987).

[59] **MI:** *Cf.* Werth v. Taylor, 475 N.W.2d 426 (Mich. Ct. App. 1991).

**MO:** *Compare* Cruzan v. Harmon, 760 S.W.2d 408 (Mo. 1988), *with* Cruzan v. Director, 497 U.S. 261, 323 n.19 (1990) (Brennan, J., dissenting) (recitation of trial court evidence of patient's wishes).

**NJ:** *Cf. In re* Hughes, 611 A.2d 1148.

**NY:** *See, e.g., In re* Westchester County Medical Ctr. (O'Connor), 531 N.E.2d 607 (N.Y. 1988).

**PA:** *Cf. In re* Estate of Dorone, 534 A.2d 452.

between the time of decisionmaking and the time of implementation of the decision.[60] This concern has caused the New York Court of Appeals to be extremely wary about giving effect to an advance directive, especially an oral one that may lack the indicia of solemnity that attach to a written statement. While not altogether rejecting oral advance directives,[61] the court refused in the *O'Connor* case to give effect to an advance directive when the patient's statements, although consistent and made over a course of years to a number of different people, indicated that

> there is nothing, other than speculation, to persuade the fact finder that her expressions were more than immediate reactions to the unsettling experience of seeing or hearing of another's unnecessarily prolonged death. Her comments . . . are, in fact, no different than those that many of us might make after witnessing an agonizing death. Similarly, her statements to the effect that she would not want to be a burden to anyone are the type of statements that older people frequently, almost invariably make after witnessing an agonizing death.[62]

The position of the New York court is likely to either lead to subterfuge (such as transferring patients to other jurisdictions) if not outright perjury, in order to effectuate what their families believe was their clear intent, or lead to a great deal of suffering. Alternatively, the lower courts might decide to apply the *actual intent* rule liberally, as was the case in *Elbaum v. Grace Plaza of Great Neck, Inc.,*[63] in which the court gave effect to an oral advance directive similar to the one in *O'Connor.*[64]

The Florida Supreme Court has resolved this problem in a more practical fashion than the New York court. While acknowledging the existence of the problem—"human limitations preclude absolute knowledge of the wishes of someone in Mrs. Browning's condition"—it concluded that it could not "avoid making a decision in these circumstances, for even the failure to act constitutes a choice. That choice must be the patient's choice whenever possible."[65]

---

[60] **FL:** Browning v. Herbert, 568 So. 2d 4 .

**NY:** *In re* Westchester County Medical Ctr. (O'Connor), 531 N.E.2d 607.

*See also* Sehgal et al., *How Strictly Do Dialysis Patients Want Their Advance Directives Followed?,* 267 JAMA 59 (1992) (patients in outpatient hemodialysis clinic were willing to accord varying degrees of leeway to their surrogates in varying from their living wills should they become incompetent).

[61] *See, e.g.,* Eichner v. Dillon, 420 N.E.2d 64 (N.Y. 1981).

[62] **NY:** *In re* Westchester County Medical Ctr. (O'Connor), 531 N.E.2d at 614.

**KY:** *Accord* DeGrella v. Elston, 858 S.W.2d 698, 713 (Ky. 1993) (Wintersheimer, J., dissenting) ("the obvious impossibility to really know whether the patient ever had a change of heart, either expressed or unexpressed when actually faced with a life or death decision").

[63] 544 N.Y.S.2d 840 (App. Div. 1989).

[64] See §§ **7.4–7.7.**

[65] Browning v. Herbert, 568 So. 2d 4, 13 (Fla. 1990).

The value of advance directives lies in their allowing patients to direct the course of their medical treatment if they lose decisionmaking capacity at some future time. Human foresight being what it is, it is impossible for individuals to specify with precision all the events that might arise and what sorts of treatment they would or would not want if those conditions were to materialize. Of necessity, directions must be somewhat general and imprecise.[66]

The solution, then—if the right of self-determination is to be respected not only in the present when a person is competent but also in the future when decisionmaking capacity is absent—is for advance directives to be recognized without the degree of particularity that contemporaneous informed consent requires. (It would be ironic for courts to insist on such high levels of informed consent for advance directives when they frequently neglect to do so for contemporaneous medical decisionmaking.)

If written advance directives are to be useful, it is necessary in drafting them to strike a balance between generality and specificity in order to avoid the dual risks of having the directive so precisely drafted that it fails to cover the contingency that has in fact arisen and having it so broadly drafted that it is unclear what decision the declarant would make if currently capable of doing so. In turn, the risks of the latter kind of situation are that a patient will receive treatment that he would have refused or will fail to receive treatment that he would have approved. The failure of courts to recognize this reality might eventually undermine the preference accorded to subjective standards for surrogate decisionmaking and will force a decision to be made in accordance with objective standards instead.

## § 10.8  Legal Basis for Advance Directives

Legislative and judicial developments continually clarify the legal status of advance directives in the context of somewhat murky legal origins. The widespread enactment of advance directive legislation provides a high degree of assurance that an advance directive drafted in conformance with this legislation will be valid and enforceable. However, some advance directive legislation imposes restrictions on the circumstances under which an advance directive is effective and the types of decisions that can be made through an advance directive. Under many statutes, advance directives are not effective unless the patient is terminally ill or permanently unconscious,[67] are not effective if the patient is pregnant,[68] restrict the forgoing of certain types of treatment such as

---

[66] **NY:** *In re* Westchester County Medical Ctr. (O'Connor), 531 N.E.2d at 614 ("human beings are not capable of foreseeing either their own medical condition or advances in medical technology").

[67] See §§ **11.9** and **12.17.**

[68] See §§ **11.11** and **12.27.**

artificial nutrition and hydration,[69] and require compliance with many formalities of execution and implementation. As a consequence, individuals wishing to engage in future planning through the use of advance directives might wish to issue directives that are more permissive than the statutes contemplate. This raises the issue of whether a directive that is not in conformance with statutory requirements is nonetheless valid and enforceable. Closely related to this issue is the question of whether or not one can create a valid and enforceable advance directive in the absence of an advance directive statute.

The conceptual legal basis of advance directives is closely related to the core concepts underpinning the right to die: self-determination for competent patients and substituted judgment for incompetent patients. Advance directives are a mechanism for the exercise of self-determination, albeit anticipatorily. The substituted judgment standard is premised on the notion that the surrogate is to attempt insofar as possible to implement an incompetent patient's wishes, expressed while the patient still had decisionmaking capacity. Even more so than the substituted judgment standard, the subjective standard is completely dependent on the validity and enforceability of advance directives. If a court insists on applying a subjective standard but refuses to honor advance directives because the declarant is not as informed as when making a contemporaneous decision, that court has in effect held that life-sustaining treatment cannot be withheld or withdrawn from incompetent patients. This is what the Missouri Supreme Court did in *Cruzan*. The court stated that

> [a] decision to refuse treatment, when that decision will bring about death, should be as informed as a decision to accept treatment. If offered to show informed refusal, the evidence offered here would be woefully inadequate. It is all the more inadequate to support a refusal that will result in certain death.[70]

However, it also concluded that

> it is definitionally impossible for a person to make an informed decision—either to consent or to refuse—under hypothetical circumstances; under such circumstances, neither the benefits nor the risks of treatment can be properly weighed or fully appreciated.[71]

In addition to the conceptual underpinnings of advance directives—self-determination and substituted judgment—there are a number of judicial decisions

---

[69] See §§ **11.12** and **12.26.**

[70] Cruzan v. Harmon, 760 S.W.2d 408, 424 (Mo. 1988).

[71] **MO:** 760 S.W.2d at 417.

**OH:** *Accord* Couture v. Couture, 549 N.E.2d 571 (Ohio Ct. App. 1989) ("It is not necessary that evidence show exactly what the ward would do in the precise circumstances at hand. Application of such a standard would impose impossible burdens as it could almost never be shown that the precise circumstances were anticipated.").

specifically approving of nonstatutory advance directives.[72] Finally, almost all jurisdictions now have a living will statute or a health care power of attorney statute, and most have both.

## § 10.9   Statutory Advance Directives

The controversy and long litigation surrounding the *Quinlan* case[73] was instrumental in the enactment in California in 1976 of the Natural Death Act,[74] intended to forestall similar litigation by expressly legitimizing living wills and thereby imparting greater certainty to the decisionmaking process for incompetent patients. Since the California enactment, almost all other states have passed similar legislation. Their formal names vary, but these statutes are referred to generically as *living will statutes*. Beginning somewhat later, most state legislatures also began to enact *health care power of attorney statutes,* providing an explicit legal basis for the designation of an agent to make medical decisions.

A directive that meets the requirements of a state's legislation is valid and enforceable. As a result, some end-of-life decisions that would have reached an impasse and would possibly have resulted in litigation are resolved in the clinical context. Others, though litigated, may be quickly and simply resolved at the trial level by a judicial order enforcing the directive, an order that might not have been so easily forthcoming without the authorizing legislation.

## § 10.10   Relationship Between Advance Directive Statutes and Case Law

There were advance directives long before there were advance directive statutes.[75] Until a particular jurisdiction enacts an advance directive statute, uncertainty exists as to the validity and enforceability of, what might be called, prestatutory or nonstatutory advance directives. However, the widespread enactment of advance directive statutes, rather than mooting the question of the validity and enforceability of nonstatutory advance directives, has led to its reformulation: Are advance directives that deviate from statutory requirements legally valid and effective?

In addition, there are a number of related questions. One is whether or not any of the provisions of advance directive statutes apply to persons who have not

---

[72] See §§ **10.11** and **10.16.**

[73] *In re* Quinlan, 355 A.2d 647 (N.J. 1976).

[74] Cal. Health & Safety Code §§ 7185–7195 (West Supp. 1988) (amended).

[75] *See* Kutner, *Due Process and Euthanasia: The Living Will, A Proposal,* 44 Ind. L.J. 539 (1969).

executed an advance directive ("nondeclarants").[76] Another is whether or not any of the provisions of advance directive statutes apply to individuals who have executed an advance directive but still possess decisionmaking capacity.[77] Yet another is whether or not the immunity provisions of advance directive statutes apply to directives that do not conform to the statute.[78]

Most advance directive statutes contain provisions that bear on the resolution of these questions, though not always clearly and directly. Although there has not been a great deal of litigation about advance directives in general and the questions about the relationship between advance directive statutes and the case law in particular, what little litigation that has occurred has dealt primarily with nonstatutory advance directives. These cases have resulted in a rather uniform, though thin, body of case law providing support for both written and oral nonstatutory advance directives.

## § 10.11   —Advance Directives Created in Absence of Statute (Nonstatutory Advance Directives)

Although every jurisdiction has some kind of advance directive statute, there are a few jurisdictions that provide statutory recognition only for living wills or only for health care powers of attorney, but not both. There is no reason to believe that an advance directive executed in the absence of a statutory basis is invalid. Although nonstatutory written advance directives have been the subject of very little litigation, courts have taken notice of their existence and their potential use in decisionmaking for incompetent patients,[79] and the judicial decisions are in

---

[76] See § 10.13.

[77] See § 10.14.

[78] See § 10.15.

[79] **CA:** *See, e.g.,* Bartling v. Superior Court, 209 Cal. Rptr. 220 (Ct. App. 1984); Barber v. Superior Court, 195 Cal. Rptr. 484, 493 (Ct. App. 1983).

**DE:** *See, e.g.,* Severns v. Wilmington Medical Ctr., Inc., 421 A.2d 1334 (Del. 1980).

**DC:** *See, e.g., In re* N., 406 A.2d 1275, 1282 (D.C. 1979).

**FL:** *See, e.g.,* Browning v. Herbert, 568 So. 2d 4 (Fla. 1990) (enforcing written living will and designation of agent for decisionmaking); John F. Kennedy Memorial Hosp. v. Bludworth, 452 So. 2d 921 (Fla. 1994).

**GA:** *Cf. In re* L.H.R., 321 S.E.2d 716 (Ga. 1984).

**NJ:** *See, e.g., In re* Peter, 529 A.2d 419 (N.J. 1987); *In re* Conroy, 486 A.2d 1209 (N.J. 1985).

**NY:** *See, e.g., In re* Westchester County Medical Ctr. (O'Connor), 531 N.E.2d 607 (N.Y. 1988); Eichner v. Dillon, 420 N.E.2d 64 (N.Y. 1981); Saunders v. State, 492 N.Y.S.2d 510 (Sup. Ct. Nassau County 1985); A.B. v. C., 477 N.Y.S.2d 281 (Sup. Ct. Schenectady County 1984); *In re* Lydia E. Hall Hosp., 455 N.Y.S.2d 706 (Sup. Ct. Nassau County 1982).

**OH:** *See, e.g.,* Leach v. Akron Gen. Medical Ctr., 426 N.E.2d 809 (P. Ct. Summit County, Ohio 1980); Estate of Leach v. Shapiro, 469 N.E.2d 1047 (Ohio Ct. App. 1984).

agreement that such advance directives are valid and enforceable.[80] The fact that courts accept evidence of patients' *oral* statements about their treatment preferences, made before they lost decisionmaking capacity, leads a fortiori to the conclusion that written statements—that is, living wills and health care powers of attorney—should be valid and enforceable.[81]

The first ruling on the validity of a nonstatutory living will was *John F. Kennedy Memorial Hospital v. Bludworth.*[82] The patient, Mr. Landy, had written a document denominated "Mercy Will and Last Testament." Signed by him and two witnesses, it stated that he "did not wish to be kept alive through the use of extraordinary life support equipment such as a respirator."[83] It was not written pursuant to any statute. At the time that the document was brought to the attention of his attending physician, Mr. Landy was suffering from acute respiratory failure and being kept alive by a respirator from which it was impossible to wean him. The Florida Supreme Court upheld the validity of the living will and concluded that "[i]n the case of a comatose and terminally ill individual who has executed a so-called 'living' or 'mercy' will . . . court approval was not necessary in order to relieve the consenting family members, the attending physicians, and the hospital and its administrators of civil and criminal liability."[84] Six years later, the Florida Supreme Court reaffirmed the validity of this holding in the *Browning* case.[85]

---

**PA:** *See, e.g., In re* E.L.K., 11 Fiduc. Rep. 2d 78, 82 (C.P. Berks County, Pa. 1991) (by implication) (The court in a jurisdiction without a living will statute observed that "[t]he best evidence as to intent is a living will. Mother never executed one, although she definitely knew of the concept and had the opportunity to have one drawn.").

**WA:** *See, e.g., In re* Ingram, 689 P.2d 1363 (Wash. 1984); *In re* Hamlin, 689 P.2d 1372, 1376 (Wash. 1984); *In re* Colyer, 660 P.2d 738, 741 (Wash. 1983).

*See also* American Medical Ass'n, Current Opinions of the Council on Ethical and Judicial Affairs § 2.21, at 13 (1989).

[80] **US:** *Cf.* Cruzan v. Director, 497 U.S. 261, 289 (1990) (O'Connor, J., concurring) (It "may well be constitutionally required [for a state to give effect to the decisions of a surrogate decision-maker] to protect the patient's liberty interest in refusing medical treatment.").

**NJ:** *Cf. In re* Peter, 529 A.2d 419 (enforcing durable power of attorney appointing proxy in absence of specific health care power of attorney statute); *In re* Conroy, 486 A.2d at 1229 (approving living wills and durable powers of attorney).

**NY:** *Cf.* Grace Plaza of Great Neck, Inc. v. Elbaum, 623 N.E.2d 513 (N.Y. 1993) ("decisions in cases such as this may now be facilitated by use of proxies or living wills"); *In re* Westchester County Medical Ctr. (O'Connor), 531 N.E.2d 607, 612 (N.Y. 1988) (since enactment of springing durable power of attorney legislation, there is "no longer any reason in principle why those wishing to appoint another to express their specific or general desires with respect to medical treatment, in the event they become incompetent, may not do so formally through a power of attorney").

[81] See § **10.16.**

[82] 452 So. 2d 921 (Fla. 1984).

[83] *Id.* at 922.

[84] *Id.*

[85] Browning v. Herbert, 568 So. 2d 4 (Fla. 1990).

Perhaps the clearest support for the enforcement of advance directives created in the absence of a statute are the right-to-die opinions of the New York Court of Appeals. That court requires that there be clear and convincing evidence that the patient made a decision to forgo life-sustaining treatment for treatment to be withheld or withdrawn.[86] Because New York has no living will statute, if such proof is required to forgo life-sustaining treatment, of necessity it must be supplied either by nonstatutory written advance directives or by oral statements. In fact, the court of appeals and other New York courts have found that such directives satisfy this standard.[87]

Other courts have spoken to this subject, though in dictum. In explaining the subjective standard for decisionmaking for incompetent patients,[88] the New Jersey Supreme Court stated in *Conroy* that a patient's "intent might be embodied in a written document, or 'living will,' stating the person's desire not to have certain types of life-sustaining treatment administered under certain circumstances."[89] It then observed that, although the legislature had not enacted a statute recognizing the validity of living wills or prescribing procedures for executing them, "advance directives are relevant evidence of the patient's intent."[90] Dicta in another New Jersey case, *Peter,*[91] and cases in other jurisdictions underscore the favorable judicial stance toward advance directives even without a legislative imprimatur.

## § 10.12  —Nonconforming or Conflicting Advance Directives

Despite the enactment of advance directive statutes providing a firm legal foundation for advance directives, there are reasons why individuals might wish to write advance directives that either do not conform to the statute or are plainly in conflict with it. Many advance directive statutes contain provisions that are more restrictive than the case law. For example, many living will and some health care power of attorney statutes require that a patient be in a terminal condition or permanently unconscious in order for the advance directive to go

---

[86] *In re* Westchester County Medical Ctr. (O'Connor), 531 N.E.2d 607 (N.Y. 1988); Eichner v. Dillon, 420 N.E.2d 64 (N.Y. 1981).

[87] Eichner v. Dillon, 420 N.E.2d 64; Elbaum v. Grace Plaza of Great Neck, Inc., 544 N.Y.S.2d 840 (App. Div. 1989); Delio v. Westchester County Medical Ctr., 516 N.Y.S.2d 677 (App. Div. 1987).

[88] See §§ 7.4–7.6.

[89] *In re* Conroy, 486 A.2d 1209, 1229 (N.J. 1985).

[90] *Id.* at 1229 n.5 (citing John F. Kennedy Memorial Hosp. v. Bludworth, 452 So. 2d 921 (Fla. 1994)).

[91] *In re* Peter, 529 A.2d 419, 426 (N.J. 1987) ("Clearly, the best evidence is a 'living will,' a written statement that specifically explains the patient's preferences about life-sustaining treatment.").

into effect.[92] Some advance directive statutes impose restrictions on the forgoing of nutrition and hydration,[93] though these restrictions have been eliminated or significantly loosened by most state legislatures after the United States Supreme Court's *Cruzan* decision.[94] A larger number of statutes also contain restrictions on the forgoing of treatment if the patient is pregnant,[95] but in practice the effect of this type of restriction is likely to be relatively infrequent. There are also restrictions in health care power of attorney statutes on the agent's power to authorize certain specific procedures,[96] and this can be viewed as a limitation of common-law rights, because the principal has the power to authorize these procedures if competent.[97] Finally, all advance directive statutes contain a variety of formalities that need to be complied with, most notably witnessing, making it more onerous for individuals to execute advance directives if they must precisely follow statutory requirements.[98]

As a result, people will, and probably already do, attempt to write advance directives that intentionally circumvent these restrictions. In addition to intentional noncompliance with statutory requirements, declarants may execute an advance directive in ignorance of the requirements—indeed in ignorance even of the existence—of the advance directive statute, or they may intend to comply with the statute but inadvertently fail to do so. Some declarants have executed advance directives prior to the enactment of an advance directive statute in their jurisdiction and have not revised them to conform to the statute. Also, health care providers and their attorneys are presented with advance directives that do not conform to the requirements of statutory law and are faced with the question of whether such advance directives are valid and enforceable and what kind of immunity, if any, exists if they are honored or dishonored. Consequently, courts will sometimes be required to reconcile these "nonconforming" advance directives and the advance directive statutes with which they appear to conflict.

Nonstatutory advance directives should be presumed to be valid even in a jurisdiction that has enacted advance directive legislation. The better view and

---

[92] See §§ **11.9** and **12.17.**

[93] See §§ **11.12** and **12.26.**

[94] Cruzan v. Director, 497 U.S. 261 (1990).

[95] See §§ **11.11** and **12.27.**

[96] See §§ **12.23–12.29.**

[97] **ID:** Idaho Code § 39-450(1).

   **IA:** Iowa Code Ann. § 144A.11.4.

   **LA:** La. Rev. Stat. Ann. § 40:1299.58.5(C).

   **MD:** Md. Code Ann., Health-Gen. § 5-605(D).

   **MA:** Mass. Gen. Laws Ann. ch. 201D, § 16.

   **NY:** N.Y. Pub. Health Law § 2989(1).

   **WV:** W. Va. Code § 16-30A-15(c).

   **WI:** Wis. Stat. Ann. § 155.70(8).

[98] See §§ **11.6–11.8** and **12.12–12.14.**

the one likely to prevail is that advance directive statutes were enacted not to *create* the right to make treatment decisions anticipatorily, for the existence of that right predated the enactment of the statute,[99] but rather they were enacted to provide assurance to health care providers seeking to honor such choices that they would not incur legal liability if they did so, and to provide them with a specific statutory grant of immunity if the advance directive conforms with statutory requirements. Advance directive statutes are cumulative and many so provide; that is, they are intended to preserve and supplement existing common-law and constitutional rights and not to supersede or limit them.[100] Advance directive

---

[99] **US:** Cruzan v. Director, 497 U.S. 261, 314 n.15 (1990) (Brennan, J., dissenting).

**AL:** Camp v. White, 510 So. 2d 166, 170 (Ala. 1987).

**CA:** Drabick v. Drabick, 245 Cal. Rptr. 840, 859–60 (Ct. App. 1988); Barber v. Superior Court, 195 Cal. Rptr. 484, 489 (Ct. App. 1983).

**FL:** Browning v. Herbert, 543 So. 2d 258, 265 (Fla. Dist. Ct. App. 1989), *aff'd,* 568 So. 2d 4 (Fla. 1990); Corbett v. D'Alessandro, 487 So. 2d 368, 370 (Fla. Dist. Ct. App. 1986).

**IL:** *In re* Estate of Greenspan, 558 N.E.2d 1194, 1203 (Ill. 1990).

**ME:** *In re* Gardner, 534 A.2d 947, 952 & n.3 (Me. 1987).

[100] **AL:** Ala. Code § 22-8A-9(d) ("Nothing in this chapter . . . impairs or supercedes any right or responsibility that a person has to effect the withholding or withdrawal of medical care in a lawful manner.").

**AK:** Alaska Stat. § 18.12.080(e) ("impair or supercede any legal right or legal responsibility").

**AR:** Ark. Code Ann. § 20-17-210(e).

**CA:** Cal. Health & Safety Code § 7191.5(e); Cal. Civ. Code § 2434(c).

**CO:** Colo. Rev. Stat. § 15-18-102(f) ("nothing in this article shall have the effect of modifying or changing currently practiced medical ethics or protocol with respect to any patient in the absence of a declaration").

**DC:** D.C. Code Ann. § 6-2429(a); D.C. Code Ann. § 21-2201 (statute intended "to affirm the right of all competent adults to control decisions relating to their own health care").

**FL:** Fla. Stat. Ann. § 765.106 (statute "is cumulative to the existing law regarding an individual's right to consent, or refuse to consent, to medical treatment and do[es] not impair any existing rights . . . under the common law or statutes of the State").

**GA:** Ga. Code Ann. § 31-32-11(a).

**HI:** Haw. Rev. Stat. § 327D-22.

**ID:** Idaho Code § 39-4509(1) ("nor . . . shall it affect the rights of any such persons . . . to give or refuse to give consent or withhold consent for any medical care").

**IL:** Ill. Ann. Stat. ch. 755, § 35/9(d) ("the withholding or withdrawal of death-delaying procedures").

**IN:** Ind. Code Ann. § 16-36-4-17(e).

**IA:** Iowa Code Ann. § 144A.11(5).

**KS:** Kan. Stat. Ann. § 65-28,108(d).

**KY:** Ky. Rev. Stat. Ann. § 311.637(5).

**LA:** La. Rev. Stat. Ann. § 40:1299.58.1(4) ("the legislature finds and declares that nothing in this Part shall be construed to be the exclusive means by which life-sustaining procedures may be withheld or withdrawn").

**ME:** Me. Rev. Stat. Ann. tit. 18-A, § 5-711(e).

statutes were enacted not to create substantive rights but merely to provide a mechanism for individuals to implement their wishes about life-sustaining medical treatment once they lacked the capacity to do so contemporaneously.[101]

There are a number of reasons why nonstatutory advance directives should be presumed to be valid even in a jurisdiction that has enacted advance directive legislation. Some of these reasons are based on the statutes themselves. The first is that the statutes generally include provisions preserving constitutional and/or common-law rights to make an advance directive.[102] Some are even more explicit, such as the provision in the Kentucky statute stating that the statute

---

**MD:** Md. Code Ann., Health-Gen. § 5-616 (advance directive statute does "not impair any existing rights . . . under the common law or statutes of this state").

**MN:** Minn. Stat. Ann. § 145B.17 ("to begin, continue, withhold or withdraw health care").

**MO:** Mo. Ann. Stat. § 459.055(2).

**MT:** Mont. Code Ann. § 50-9-205(5).

**NE:** Neb. Rev. Stat. § 20-412(5); Neb. Rev. Stat. § 30-3401(2).

**NV:** Nev. Rev. Stat. Ann. § 449.535–.690.

**NH:** N.H. Rev. Stat. Ann. § 137-H:12 ("to supplant any existing rights and responsibilities . . . in the absence of a living will").

**NJ:** N.J. Stat. Ann. § 26:2H-67(c).

**NM:** N.M. Stat. Ann. § 24-7-9 ("withholding or nonutilization of any maintenance medical treatment").

**NC:** N.C. Gen. Stat. § 90-320.

**ND:** N.D. Cent. Code § 23-06.4-11(5); N.D. Cent. Code § 23-06.5-01.

**OH:** Ohio Rev. Code Ann. § 1337.13(A)(2).

**OK:** Okla. Stat. Ann. tit. 63, § 3101.12(E).

**PA:** Pa. Cons. Stat. Ann. tit. 20, § 5412 ("shall not impair or supersede any existing rights or responsibilities not addressed in this chapter").

**RI:** R.I. Gen. Laws § 23-4.11-10(e).

**SC:** S.C. Code Ann. § 44-77-140.

**SD:** S.D. Codified Laws Ann. § 34-12D-18.

**TN:** Tenn. Code Ann. § 32-11-110(d).

**TX:** Tex. Health & Safety Code Ann. § 672.021.

**UT:** Utah Code Ann. § 75-2-1117(4).

**VA:** Va. Code Ann. § 54.1-2992.

**WA:** Wash. Rev. Code Ann. § 70.122.910 ("This chapter shall not be construed as providing the exclusive means by which individuals may make decisions regarding their health treatment.").

**WV:** W. Va. Code § 16-30-9(a); W. Va. Code § 16-30A-15(c) (any right a person who was designated as agent may have to participate in decisions apart from any agency is unaffected by statute).

**WI:** Wis. Stat. Ann. § 154.11(4).

**WY:** Wyo. Stat. § 35-22-108(d).

[101] Gelfand, *Living Will Statutes: The First Decade,* 1987 Wis. L. Rev. 737, 796–97.

[102] Uniform Rights of the Terminally Ill Act prefatory note & § 11(d), (e), 9B U.L.A. 127 (West Supp. 1994).

"shall not preclude or restrict the right of persons to make advance directives outside the provisions of" the statute.[103]

Second, most statutes provide that living will forms contained in the statutes need not be used or may be modified or that the immunity provisions of the statute apply to an advance directive that is *substantially* (but not precisely) in the same form as the statutory form.[104] A third reason is found in health care power of attorney statutes, which often confer on an agent the same decision-making authority the principal would have had if competent,[105] and the authority of the agent is governed by the substantive common and constitutional law of the jurisdiction.[106] Finally, there are no statutory provisions specifically requiring that advance directives comply with the provisions of advance directive statutes, nor are there any appellate cases requiring that advance directives comply with advance directive statutes. Courts have consistently upheld, in holdings and in dicta, that advance directive statutes are not intended to preempt common-law[107]

---

[103] **KY:** Ky. Rev. Stat. Ann. § 311.637(6).

**HI:** *Accord* Haw. Rev. Stat. § 327D-21 (absent a declaration, "ordinary standard of current medical practice will be followed. . . . Nothing in this chapter shall be construed to require a declaration in order for life-sustaining procedures to be provided, continued, withheld, or withdrawn.").

[104] **WA:** *Cf.* DiNino v. State *ex rel.* Gorton, 684 P.2d 1297 (Wash. 1984) (in action by woman who was neither pregnant nor terminally ill, challenging pregnancy provision, state conceded that provision in living will statute's optional sample living will could be deleted and living will would still be valid, but that a directive requiring termination of a pregnancy prior to removal of life support from mother would be invalid because it ignores state's potential interest in life of fetus). See §§ **9.55, 11.11,** and **12.27.**

[105] See § **12.14.**

[106] **KY:** *See, e.g.,* DeGrella v. Elston, 858 S.W.2d 698, 707 (Ky. 1993).

**WI:** *See, e.g.,* L.W. v. L.E. Phillips Career Dev. Ctr., 482 N.W.2d 60, 68 (Wis. 1992) ("[T]he stated legislative policy is to leave the decision, if not declared by the patient, to be determined as a matter of common law—and the common law, where the individual was never competent or where the conduct of the individual while competent never was of a kind from which one could draw a reasonable inference upon which to make a substituted judgment, requires that decision to be resolved by a surrogate decision maker acting in the best interests of the incompetent.").

[107] **AL:** *See* Camp v. White, 510 So. 2d 166 (Ala. 1987).

**CA:** *See* Bouvia v. Superior Court (Glenchur), 225 Cal. Rptr. 297, 302 (Ct. App. 1986); Bartling v. Superior Court, 209 Cal. Rptr. 220 (Ct. App. 1984) (construing Cal. Health & Safety Code § 7193); Barber v. Superior Court, 195 Cal. Rptr. 484 (Ct. App. 1983) (same).

**CT:** *See* McConnell v. Beverly Enters.-Conn., Inc., 553 A.2d 596, 605 n.15 (Conn. 1989) (1989) ("Under our act, this clear expression of Mrs. McConnell's wishes is legally operative even though it was not memorialized in the form of a written document. General Statutes § 19a-572.").

**FL:** *See* Corbett v. D'Alessandro, 487 So. 3d 368, 370 (Fla. Dist. Ct. App.), *review denied,* 492 So. 2d 1331 (Fla. 1986).

**KY:** *See* DeGrella v. Elston, 858 S.W.2d at 706–07.

**ME:** *See In re* Gardner, 534 A.2d 947, 952 (Me. 1987).

or state constitutional rights[108] to make advance directives and to have them enforced.

The clearest example of the view that advance directives may conflict with the advance directive statute and still be valid and enforceable is the Florida Supreme Court's decision in *Browning.* Mrs. Browning had executed a "generic" living will, created and distributed by a nonprofit organization, explicitly stating that if she was terminally ill, there was no hope for recovery, and death was imminent, she did not wish to have "'nutrition and hydration (food and water) provided by gastric tube or intravenously'" if it would only prolong the process of dying.[109] When the living will was executed and at the time that the case was decided, the Florida living will statute prohibited the enforcement of a directive to withhold or withdraw nutrition and hydration.[110] The court held that the living will was enforceable even though it conflicted with the statute because the Florida constitutional right of privacy[111] guaranteed the right to decline all forms of medical treatment.[112] Similarly, the Maine Supreme Court concluded, based on the common-law doctrine of informed consent, that the provision in its living will statute severely limiting the forgoing of nutrition and hydration was inapplicable in the case of an individual who had made oral statements that he would not want to be kept alive in this fashion.[113]

## § 10.13 —Applicability of Advance Directive Legislation to Nondeclarants

Another issue that looms over the use of advance directives for decisionmaking about life-sustaining treatment is whether the provisions of advance directive

---

**OH:** *See In re* Myers, 610 N.E.2d 663, 668 (P. Ct., Summit County, Ohio 1993) ("The statute is non-binding in that there are neither sanctions nor penalties, nor a mandate that its provisions must be followed. The only sanction provided is . . . where it is stated that, if its provisions are not followed, the specific statutory immunity or defense given under the statute cannot be raised in civil or criminal litigation. [The statute] was devised as a 'carrot' approach to legislation, as opposed to mandatory and binding law. While [it] may provide some guidance, this court is not bound, nor is its guardian bound, to follow the provisions of the statutes.").

**WA:** *See In re* Grant, 747 P.2d 445 (Wash. 1987), *modified,* 757 P.2d 534 (Wash. 1988).

**WI:** L.W. v. L.E. Phillips Career Dev. Ctr., 482 N.W.2d at 68 ("[T]he stated legislative policy is to leave the decision, if not declared by the patient, to be determined as a matter of common law.").

[108] **FL:** *See* Browning v. Herbert, 568 So. 2d 4 (Fla. 1990).

[109] *Id.* at 8.

[110] *See* Fla. Stat. Ann. § 765.03(3)(b) (West 1986) (repealed).

[111] Fla. Const. art. I, § 23.

[112] Browning v. Herbert, 568 So. 2d at 11–12.

[113] *In re* Gardner, 534 A.2d 947 (Me. 1987) (construing Me. Rev. Stat. Ann. tit. 22, § 2921(4) (Supp. 1986) (repealed)). *Cf.* Me. Rev. Stat. Ann. tit. 18-A, § 5-701(b)(4) (defining "life-sustaining treatment" to include artificial nutrition and hydration which may be forgone).

statutes apply to "nondeclarants," that is, to individuals who have not executed an advance directive. Logically, the formalities of such statutes cannot apply, but the substantive provisions could. Thus, for example, the statutory requirement that the patient be in a terminal condition or permanently unconscious before the advance directive becomes effective could be applied to patients without advance directives to prohibit the forgoing of life-sustaining treatment unless the nondeclarant patient were terminally ill or permanently unconscious as well.

The courts that have considered this question have made it abundantly clear, often based on a construction of a statutory provision to that effect, that advance directive statutes apply only to those who have actually executed an advance directive.[114] The only court squarely to hold otherwise is the Missouri Supreme Court in *Cruzan v. Harmon,* which concluded that the state's "living will statute is . . . an expression of the policy of this State with regard to the sanctity of life,"[115] and therefore a provision of the living will statute prohibiting the forgoing of nutrition and hydration was applicable to a patient who had not executed a living will and had not made sufficiently clear and convincing oral statements of her wish not to be kept alive by nutrition and hydration. This holding was reached despite the language in the Missouri living will statute that "no presumption concerning the intention of an individual who has not executed

---

[114] **DCO:** *See* Ross v. Hilltop Rehabilitation Hosp., 676 F. Supp. 1528 (D. Colo. 1987).

**AL:** *See* Camp v. White, 510 So. 2d 166 (Ala. 1987).

**AZ:** *See* Rasmussen v. Fleming, 741 P.2d 674 (Ariz. 1987).

**CA:** *See* Bartling v. Superior Court, 209 Cal. Rptr. 220, 224 n.5 (Ct. App. 1984); Barber v. Superior Court, 195 Cal. Rptr. 484 (Ct. App. 1983).

**CT:** *See* McConnell v. Beverly Enters.-Conn., Inc., 553 A.2d 596 (Conn. 1989).

**FL:** *See* Browning v. Herbert, 568 So. 2d 4 (Fla. 1990); Corbett v. D'Alessandro, 487 So. 2d 368 (Fla. Dist. Ct. App. 1986).

**IL:** *See In re* Austin, 615 N.E.2d 411, 417–18 (Ill. App. Ct. 1993) (living will and health care power of attorney statutes are irrelevant to persons who have not executed such respective documents).

**KY:** *See* DeGrella v. Elston, 858 S.W.2d 698 (Ky. 1993).

**ME:** *See In re* Gardner, 534 A.2d 947 (Me. 1987).

**MA:** *See* Commissioner v. Myers, 399 N.E.2d 452 (Mass. 1979) ("A corollary of this is that advance directive statutes apply only to those who have actually executed an advance directive.").

**OH:** *See In re* Myers, 610 N.E.2d 663 (P. Ct. Summit County, Ohio 1993).

**WA:** *See In re* Hamlin, 689 P.2d 1372 (Wash. 1984); *In re* Colyer, 660 P.2d 738 (Wash. 1983); *In re* Grant, 747 P.2d 445 (Wash. 1987), *modified,* 757 P.2d 534 (Wash. 1988).

**WI:** *See* L.W. v. L.E. Phillips Career Dev. Ctr., 482 N.W.2d 60, 68 (Wis. 1992) ("[T]he stated legislative policy is to leave the decision, if not declared by the patient, to be determined as a matter of common law.").

[115] **MO:** Cruzan v. Harmon, 760 S.W.2d 408, 420 (Mo. 1988).

**DCO:** *Accord* Ross v. Hilltop Rehabilitation Hosp., 676 F. Supp. 1528 (D. Colo. 1987) (living will statute not specifically applicable because patient did not execute declaration under its provisions; nevertheless, it provides guidance on right to refuse treatment).

a declaration to consent to the use or withholding of medical procedures shall be created,"[116] language which other courts have construed to mean that the advance directive statute was inapplicable.[117] The court's holding provoked Justice Brennan to remark, based on this provision, that "apparently not even Missouri's own legislature believes that a person who does not execute a living will fails to do so because he wishes continuous medical treatment under all circumstances."[118] According to the Florida District Court of Appeal, the Missouri *Cruzan* holding "is distinguishable because [it] relied upon the absence of a state right of privacy [in Missouri] to reach its result."[119]

It is possible that specific provisions of advance directive statutes, if not the entire enactment, might apply to decisionmaking for nondeclarants. For example, in the *Longeway* case, the Illinois Supreme Court stated that the living will statute "specifically includes intravenous feeding and tube feeding as death-delaying procedures which, under the direction of a living will, may be withdrawn. However, the Living Will Act provides that nutrition and hydration may not be withdrawn or withheld if the result be death solely from dehydration or starvation, rather than from the existing terminal condition."[120] The court specifically applied this statutory provision to a patient without a living will. However, in a subsequent case, *Greenspan,* the court stated that this provision of the living will statute did not apply to someone without a living will and that an agent appointed under a statutory health care power of attorney had the authority to withhold or withdraw artificial nutrition and hydration even if the patient had a living will. In such a case, the living will is not operative "so long as the agent under the power is available to act."[121]

Another example makes it clear that the applicability of particular provisions to nondeclarants might depend on the wording of that provision and how it should be construed in the context of the larger act providing that in general the act is not intended to abolish, limit, or supersede preexisting legal rights. For example, the Pennsylvania advance directive statute, like many others,[122] contains a provision restricting the forgoing of life-sustaining medical treatment

---

[116] Mo. Ann. Stat. § 459.055(3) (Vernon Supp. 1988).

[117] *See, e.g., In re* Gardner, 534 A.2d 947, 952 n.3 (Me. 1987) ("The legislature . . . expressly provided that the Act creates no presumption concerning the intention of a person who does not have a document that qualifies as a "living will" [citation omitted] and that the Act does not limit our power to read more broadly under Maine common law the right of a patient to make decisions concerning life-sustaining care."). *See also* Uniform Health-Care Decisions Act § 13(a).

[118] Cruzan v. Director, 497 U.S. 261, 325 (1990) (Brennan, J., dissenting).

[119] Browning v. Herbert, 543 So. 2d 258, 267 (Fla. Dist. Ct. App. 1989).

[120] Estate of Longeway v. Community Convalescent Ctr., 549 N.E.2d 292, 301 (Ill. 1989) (citing Ill. Rev. Stat. 1987, ch. 110-1/2, para. 702(d)).

[121] *In re* Estate of Greenspan, 558 N.E.2d 1194, 1203 (Ill. 1990).

[122] See §§ **11.11** and **12.27**.

if the patient is pregnant.[123] This section states in relevant part that "[n]ot-withstanding the existence of a declaration or direction to the contrary, life-sustaining treatment, nutrition and hydration must be provided to a pregnant woman who is incompetent and has a terminal condition or who is permanently unconscious unless" certain conditions are met.[124]

The scope of applicability of this section is not clear on its face. It might mean that it applies to all pregnant women who are in a terminal condition or permanently unconscious. Another interpretation is that it applies only to preg-nant women who have executed a declaration or otherwise directed the forgoing of life-sustaining treatment (that is, "to the contrary"). If the latter interpretation is correct, individuals who have *not* expressed their intent to have life-sustaining treatment withheld or withdrawn would be in a better position to have it withheld or withdrawn than someone who had expressed such an intention, because the statute would override the expressed intent. Not only is this inter-pretation illogical, but also it could be held to deny equal protection because it would treat otherwise similarly-situated declarants (that is, those who are pregnant, and in a terminal condition or permanently unconscious) and non-declarants differently without any compelling, or possibly even rational, reason for doing so. However, whether that would mean that the provision must apply to nondeclarants as well as declarants in order to preserve the constitutionality of the statute is uncertain. The other, and possibly stronger, interpretation is that the provision is unconstitutional, at least in the earlier stages of pregnancy, because it unreasonably burdens an individual's right to choose to terminate a pregnancy.[125]

The Pennsylvania statute also contains a section on the preservation of existing legal rights, which states that "[t]he provisions of this chapter shall not impair or supersede any existing rights or responsibilities not addressed in this chapter."[126] This language is narrower than that in many other advance directive statutes that state that the statute does not impair or supersede *any* existing rights (whether addressed in the statute or not). If that were the kind of provision contained in the Pennsylvania statute, then the restriction on forgoing life-sustaining treatment for pregnant patients (or other restrictions) could more reasonably be read to apply only to those who had executed an advance directive. However, this interpretation would also raise equal protection problems.

---

[123] Pa. Cons. Stat. Ann. tit. 20, § 5414.

[124] *Id.* § 5414(a).

[125] Planned Parenthood v. Casey, 505 U.S. ____, 112 S. Ct. 2791 (1992). *See generally* Dyke, Note, *A Matter of Life and Death: Pregnancy Clauses in Living Will Statutes,* 70 B.U. L. Rev. 867 (1990); Fouty, Note, *The Constitutionality of Pregnancy Clauses in Living Will Statutes,* 43 Vand. L. Rev. 1821 (1990); Goldberg, *Medical Choices During Pregnancy: Whose Deci-sion Is It Anyway,* 41 Rutgers L. Rev. 591 (1989); Mahoney, *Death with Dignity: Is There an Exception for Pregnant Women?,* 57 UMKC L. Rev. 221 (1989).

[126] Pa. Cons. Stat. Ann. tit. 20, § 5412.

Because the Pennsylvania provision preserves only existing rights that are *not* dealt with in the statute, it could be read as abolishing any common-law right of pregnant patients in a terminal condition or permanently unconscious to have life-sustaining treatment withheld or withdrawn. In other words, the statutory provision restricting forgoing life-sustaining treatment if the patient is pregnant could be construed to apply to all pregnant patients, not just those with a statutory declaration. This reading might also raise equal protection problems— though probably less serious ones—as between pregnant and nonpregnant patients.

## § 10.14 —Applicability of Advance Directive Legislation to Declarants Possessing Decisionmaking Capacity

Some health care professionals hold the mistaken notion that they need not obtain informed consent from a competent patient if that patient has a living will,[127] or that they need not obtain informed consent from a competent patient but may obtain it from the patient's proxy if the patient has appointed one through a health care power of attorney. An example is when a physician writes a do-not-resuscitate order for a hospitalized competent patient on the basis of the fact that the patient has an advance directive that states that he does not want CPR rather than on the basis of a contemporaneous discussion with the patient.

Although the courts have not had occasion to address these questions, some guidance can be intuited from the fundamental purpose of advance directives and from the probable intent of those who make them. The purpose of advance directives is to provide people with a means for influencing, if not directing, decisions about their medical treatment after they have lost the capacity to do so contemporaneously. As a general rule, doctors should assume that as long as a patient remains competent, his *decisions* govern, not his advance directive. The only exception should be where the patient has expressly stated in a health care power of attorney that it is his intent to transfer decisionmaking authority to a proxy upon execution rather than upon the patient's loss of decisionmaking capacity (a so-called springing power of attorney).[128] Even in that case, how-ever, it is better practice for the physician to specifically ask the patient whether the physician should deal with the patient or with the proxy. And the physician most certainly must observe the competent patient's objection to any decision made by a proxy. A physician who makes treatment decisions without obtaining

---

[127] **GA:** *But cf.* State v. McAfee, 385 S.E.2d 651 (Ga. 1989) (holding living will statute inappli-cable to competent patient who is not terminally ill, leaving implication that it would be applicable to competent patient if he were terminally ill).

[128] See § **12.16.**

informed consent from a competent patient (whether on the basis of a living will or otherwise) exposes himself to the possibility of liability.[129]

In addition, most advance directive statutes require that the patient be incompetent or lack decisionmaking capacity to trigger the operation of the advance directive[130] and therefore implicitly require that the physician continue to obtain informed consent from the patient when the patient still possesses decisionmaking capacity. In other words, a competent patient retains the authority to make his own decisions contemporaneously, and decisionmaking is not governed either by the patient's prior decisions expressed orally or in writing or by any proxy the patient might have designated.[131] The provisions in advance directive statutes preserving existing common-law and constitutional rights point to the same conclusion.

If a patient is incompetent at the time that a decision about treatment needs to be made but is able to express preferences nonetheless, at common law these preferences should at least be accorded some weight in the decisionmaking process.[132] It is not entirely clear that legislatures had this possibility in mind when drafting advance directive statutes. However, some do contain language that arguably supports such a construction, such as the provisions in some living will statutes that a qualified patient may make decisions regarding life-sustaining treatment as long as the patient is able to do so.[133] Whether "able to do so" means literally able, or able to render a decision in accordance with standards for establishing competence,[134] is unclear. A few more clearly permit the expressed

---

[129] See §§ 17.2–17.7, 17.11–17.12.

[130] See §§ 11.9 and 12.16.

[131] *Cf. In re* Dubreuil, 603 So. 2d 538 (Fla. Dist. Ct. App. 1992) (husband of competent patient has no authority to make decisions for patient while she is competent nor to overrule any decisions made while competent if she is now incompetent).

[132] See §§ 7.45–7.46.

[133] **AR:** *See* Ark. Code Ann. § 20-17-206(a).

**CA:** Cal. Health & Safety Code § 7189.5(a).

**IA:** Iowa Code Ann. § 144A.6.

**ME:** Me. Rev. Stat. Ann. tit. 18-A, § 5-706(a).

**MO:** Mo. Ann. Stat. § 459.055(2).

**MT:** Mont. Code Ann. § 50-9-202(1).

**NE:** Neb. Rev. Stat. § 20-408(1).

**NV:** Nev. Rev. Stat. Ann. § 449.624(1).

**ND:** N.D. Cent. Code § 23-06.4-12.5.

**OH:** Ohio Rev. Code Ann. § 2133.06(A).

**OK:** Okla. Stat. Ann. tit. 63, § 3101.8(A).

**RI:** R.I. Gen. Laws § 23-4.11-6(a).

[134] See **Ch. 4.**

contemporaneous desires of an incompetent patient to override a living will.[135] Furthermore, most include provisions for revoking a living will without regard to the patient's mental state,[136] in effect permitting a patient who lacks decision-making capacity but is able to communicate to invalidate a living will.

This leads to the curious, if not paradoxical, result that the patient's wishes as expressed in the living will are no longer to govern, yet the patient lacks the capacity to make a contemporaneous decision so that a surrogate must make decisions for the patient. The surrogate, however, is bound to attempt to effectuate what the patient would have wanted or what is in the patient's best interests.[137] Whether the patient's wishes and interests are to be discerned from the contents of the now-revoked living will or from the implication created by the revocation—that these previously expressed wishes are precisely what the patient no longer wants—is completely unclear.

---

[135] **AK:** Alaska Stat. § 18.12.020(a).

**AR:** Ark. Code Ann. § 20-17-204(a) ("A declaration may be revoked at any time and in any manner by the declarant, without regard to the declarant's mental or physical condition.").

**CA:** Cal. Health & Safety Code § 7188(a).

**CT:** Conn. Gen. Stat. Ann. § 19a-579a(a).

**DE:** Del. Code Ann. tit. 16, § 2504(a) ("A declarant may revoke his declaration at any time, without regard to his mental state or competency," but "[t]he desires of a declarant who is competent shall at all times supersede the effect of the declaration.").

**DC:** D.C. Code Ann. § 6-2424(a).

**ID:** Idaho Code § 39-4504 ("without regard to his mental state or competence").

**IL:** Ill. Ann. Stat. ch. 755, § 35/5.

**IA:** Iowa Code Ann. § 144A.4(2).

**KY:** *But see* Ky. Rev. Stat. Ann. § 311.627(2) ("An oral statement by a grantor with decisional capacity to revoke an advance directive shall override any previous . . . directive made.").

**LA:** La. Rev. Stat. Ann. § 40:1299.58.4 (without regard to mental state or competency).

**ME:** Me. Rev. Stat. Ann. tit. 18-A, § 5-704(a).

**MN:** Minn. Stat. Ann. § 145B.09(1).

**MO:** Mo. Ann. Stat. § 459.020(1).

**MT:** Mont. Code Ann. § 50-9-104(1).

**NE:** Neb. Rev. Stat. § 20-406(1).

**NV:** Nev. Rev. Stat. Ann. § 449.620(1).

**NJ:** N.J. Stat. Ann. § 26:2H-57(d) (an incompetent patient may suspend an advance directive).

**ND:** N.D. Cent. Code § 23-06.4-05(1) ("a declaration may be revoked at any time . . . provided the declarant is competent").

**OK:** Okla. Stat. Ann. tit. 63, § 3101.6(A) (without regard to declarant's mental or physical condition).

**WV:** W. Va. Code § 16-30-6(a) ("The desires of a qualified patient at all times supersede the effect of the declaration.").

[136] See § **11.13.**

[137] See **Ch. 4.**

## § 10.15   —Immunity and Nonconforming Advance Directives

Advance directive statutes generally confer immunity on health care professionals who make decisions to forgo or administer treatment in reliance on an advance directive that complies with the statute's requirements.[138] Indeed, one of the primary motivating forces in the enactment of advance directive legislation has been to provide immunity, in order to encourage health care professionals to comply with advance directives. The statutes do not ordinarily, by their terms, confer immunity on treatment decisions made on the basis of nonconforming advance directives. (In fact, the immunity provisions of most advance directive statutes confer immunity for actions taken in accordance with the statute.) Consequently, the absence of statutory immunity when a decision is made on the basis of a nonconforming directive—or indeed without any kind of advance directive—might seem to be a serious disadvantage of and disincentive to executing a nonconforming directive.

In fact, however, it might make little difference in terms of immunity whether a decision is made on the basis of a statutory directive or a nonconforming directive (or no directive at all) because the courts have held that health care professionals who comply with the decisions of surrogates in the absence of *any* advance directive are also presumed to be immune from liability.[139] Perhaps the clearest statement of this is from the Kentucky Supreme Court's opinion in *Degrella v. Elston,* in which the court specifically addressed this issue, stating that "[f]uture criminal sanctions or civil liability turn not on the existence or absence of a court order, but on the facts of the case. . . . No liability attaches to a decision to refuse or withdraw treatment in a case of this nature once the necessary facts are established and carefully documented by the parties involved."[140] The Florida Supreme Court's ruling in *John F. Kennedy Memorial Hospital v. Bludworth,*[141] a case involving the enforcement of a nonstatutory advance directive, that "court approval to terminate extraordinary life support systems was not necessary in this type of case in order to relieve the consenting family members, the attending physicians, and the hospital and its administrators of civil and criminal liability" is to the same effect.[142] "To be relieved of potential civil and criminal liability," the court held, "guardians, consenting family members, physicians, hospitals, or their administrators need only act in good faith."[143]

---

[138] See §§ **11.17** and **12.46.**

[139] See § **17.24.**

[140] 858 S.W.2d 698, 710 (Ky. 1993).

[141] 452 So. 2d 921 (Fla. 1984).

[142] John F. Kennedy Memorial Hosp. v. Bludworth, 452 So. 2d at 922.

[143] *Id.* at 926.

Compliance with a nonconforming advance directive should carry with it at least the same immunity as that available when an end-of-life decision is made in the absence of any advance directive, though it is possible that the presumption of immunity conferred by an advance directive statute is probably more difficult to overcome than is nonstatutory immunity. Further, since advance directive statutes generally provide that an advance directive "substantially" in the statutory form complies with the act and thereby acquires immunity, there is the question of how much an advance directive may deviate from the statutory form and still be considered a statutory advance directive, adherence to which clothes the physician with *statutory* immunity.

## § 10.16  —Nonstatutory Oral Directives

For a long time even before the enactment of advance directive legislation, *written* living wills were a matter of common knowledge among laypersons. It is therefore ironic that most of the case law involves *oral* rather than written advance directives and that there is a greater degree of precedent for enforcing oral advance directives. Of course, if oral advance directives are valid and enforceable, there is an even stronger case for the enforcement of nonstatutory *written* directives.[144]

Although a written advance directive is preferable,[145] especially under emergency circumstances,[146] courts view oral advance directives favorably (especially living wills, but occasionally proxy directives[147]) and have either enforced

---

[144] **PA:** *But see* Pocono Medical Ctr. v. Harley, 11 Fiduc. Rep. 2d 128 (C.P. Monroe County, Pa. 1990) (enforcing oral instruction directive in preference to written power of attorney that was not durable and did not specifically empower proxy to make decisions about principal's health care).

[145] **US:** *Cf.* Cruzan v. Director, 497 U.S. 261, 284 (1990) ("Most, if not all, States simply forbid oral testimony entirely in determining the wishes of parties in transactions.").

**FL:** Browning v. Herbert, 568 So. 2d 4, 16 (Fla. 1990) ("Oral evidence, considered alone, may constitute clear and convincing evidence.").

**MI:** Martin v. Martin, 504 N.W.2d 917, 923 (Mich. Ct. App. 1993).

**NJ:** McVey v. Englewood Hosp. Ass'n, 524 A.2d 450 (N.J. Super. Ct. App. Div.), *cert. denied,* 528 A.2d 12 (N.J. 1987) (hospital not liable for failure to honor purported oral advance directive of presently incompetent patient).

**NY:** *In re* Westchester County Medical Ctr. (O'Connor), 531 N.E.2d 607, 613 (N.Y. 1988) ("existence of a writing suggests the author's seriousness of purpose").

[146] **MI:** Werth v. Taylor, 475 N.W.2d 426 (Mich. Ct. App. 1991).

**NJ:** *In re* Hughes, 611 A.2d 1148 (N.J. Super. Ct. App. Div. 1992).

**OH:** University of Cincinnati Hosp. v. Edmond, 506 N.E.2d 299 (C.P. Hamilton County, Ohio 1986).

**PA:** *In re* Estate of Dorone, 502 A.2d 1271 (Pa. Super. Ct. 1985), *aff'd,* 534 A.2d 452 (Pa. 1987).

See §§ **10.22–10.24.**

[147] **FL:** *See* Browning v. Herbert, 568 So. 2d 4 (Fla. 1990) (discussing enforceability of oral appointments of a proxy).

them per se[148] or relied heavily on them in deciding that treatment should be forgone.[149] In other cases, there has been evidence of an oral advance directive, but it played a minor role, if any, in the resolution of the case. In these cases, too, courts have spoken approvingly of advance directives in general and oral advance directives in particular.[150] Despite the obvious evidentiary advantages

---

[148] **ME:** *See, e.g., In re* Gardner, 534 A.2d 947 (Me. 1987).

**NJ:** *See, e.g.,* McVey v. Englewood Hosp. Ass'n, 524 A.2d 450 (oral advance directive enforced by court, but hospital not liable for refusal to do so).

**NY:** *See, e.g.,* Elbaum v. Grace Plaza of Great Neck, Inc., 544 N.Y.S.2d 840 (App. Div. 1989); Eichner v. Dillon, 420 N.E.2d 64 (N.Y. 1981).

**PA:** *See, e.g.,* Ragona v. Preate, 11 Fiduc. Rep. 2d 1 (C.P. Lackawanna County, Pa. 1990).

[149] **DRI:** *See* Gray v. Romeo, 697 F. Supp. 580 (D.R.I. 1988).

**CT:** *See* McConnell v. Beverly Enters.-Conn., Inc., 553 A.2d 596 (Conn. 1989) (oral statements of patient prior to accident that if she were ever in a persistent vegetative state she would not want her life prolonged was adequate expression of her wishes to serve as basis for termination of artificial nutrition and hydration).

**KY:** *See* DeGrella v. Elston, 858 S.W.2d 698, 708–09 (Ky. 1993) ("[P]revious oral statements cannot be considered conclusive in nature. . . . But the fact that other evidentiary considerations, where available, may outweigh oral statements does not rule them out as reliable evidence to guide surrogate decision-making, where such statements have been made.").

**MD:** *See also* 73 Md. Op. Att'y Gen. 253, 276 (Op. No. 88-046, Oct. 17, 1988) (formal document unnecessary; competent patient may simply tell the attending physician).

**MI:** *See* Martin v. Martin, 504 N.W.2d 917, 923 (Mich. Ct. App. 1993) ("While a writing would be preferable, it is invariably recognized by other states that other evidence tending to demonstrate a person's intent with respect to medical treatment, including oral statements, may constitute sufficient evidence of intent.").

**NJ:** *See In re* Conroy, 486 A.2d 1209, 1229 (N.J. 1985) ("It might also be evidenced in an oral directive that the patient gave to a family member, friend, or health care provider.").

**NY:** *See* Delio v. Westchester County Medical Ctr., 516 N.Y.S.2d 677, 681 (App. Div. 1987) (treatment ordered forgone on basis of oral statements of patient and inferences drawn from patient's lifestyle). *But cf.* Workmen's Circle Home & Infirmary for the Aged v. Fink, 514 N.Y.S.2d 893 (Sup. Ct. Bronx County 1987) (oral advance directive "to terminate any life-reviving procedures where there is no hope of recovery" held to bar gastrostomy but not continuation of intravenous feeding and antibiotics).

**OH:** *See In re* McInnis, 584 N.E.2d 1389 (P. Ct. Stark County, Ohio 1991) ("[I]n the absence of advance directives the administration or the withdrawal of life-sustaining treatment should be based upon medical expertise, consistent with the patient's wishes, as they are expressed by the family members."). *Cf.* Couture v. Couture, 549 N.E.2d 571 (Ohio Ct. App. 1989) (oral advance directive is a "'legally significant' statement").

**PA:** *See* Pocono Medical Ctr. v. Harley, 11 Fiduc. Rep. 2d 128 (C.P. Monroe County, Pa. 1990); *In re* Yetter, 62 Pa. D. & C.2d 619 (C.P. Northampton County 1973) (upholding refusal of treatment for breast cancer based on oral advance directive).

*See also* National Ctr. for State Courts, Guidelines for State Court Decision Making in Life-Sustaining Medical Treatment Cases 83 (2d ed. 1992) (standard 14(A)).

[150] **CA:** *See, e.g.,* Barber v. Superior Court, 195 Cal. Rptr. 484, 493 (Ct. App. 1983) ("There was evidence that Mr. Herbert had, prior to his incapacitation, expressed to his wife his feeling that he would not want to be kept alive by machines or 'become another Karen Ann Quinlan.'").

of written advance directives,[151] courts have only infrequently been reluctant to enforce oral directives[152] because to require "a written expression in every case would be unrealistic . . . [and] would unfairly penalize those who lack the skills to place their feelings in writing."[153] Even when the legislature has enacted a statute providing a formal means for making advance directives, an oral advance directive has been held to be legally operative.[154]

---

**DE:** Severns v. Wilmington Medical Ctr., Inc., 421 A.2d 1334, 1338 n.2 (Del. 1980) (court considered fact that patient had said she did not want to be kept alive as a "vegetable" or by extraordinary means).

**NJ:** *In re* Conroy, 486 A.2d at 1229–30 (intent might be evidenced in an oral directive).

**NY:** *In re* Beth Israel Medical Ctr., 519 N.Y.S.2d 511, 513, 517–18 (Sup. Ct. N.Y. County 1987) (views of patient's sister, who can state unequivocally that patient would refuse surgery, although not definitive, are consistent with tenor of patient's life). *But see* Vogel v. Forman, 512 N.Y.S.2d 622, 623 (Sup. Ct. Nassau County 1986) (refusing to withdraw nasogastric feeding despite testimony of several witnesses that "he did not wish to be kept alive by having tubes inserted into his body").

**PA:** Pocono Medical Ctr. v. Harley, 11 Fiduc. Rep. 2d at 129 (On the day of admission, the attending physician discussed the "serious stage of [the patient's] rectal cancer and the imminent prospect of kidney failure which would require dialysis. The patient advised the doctor that she did not wish any extraordinary means to be utilized . . . and specifically rejected any resuscitation, dialysis, or use of a ventilator.").

**WA:** *In re* Hamlin, 689 P.2d 1372, 1381 (Wash. 1984) (Rosellini, J., dissenting) (patient's informal consent might be sufficient); *In re* Colyer, 660 P.2d 738, 748 (Wash. 1983) (oral advance directives probative in determining wishes of an incompetent patient).

[151] **NJ:** *In re* Peter, 529 A.2d 419, 426 (N.J. 1987) (best evidence is a living will). *Cf. In re* Conroy, 486 A.2d at 1230 ("dealing with the matter in advance in some sort of thoughtful and explicit way is best for all concerned").

[152] **MO:** *See, e.g.,* Cruzan v. Harmon, 760 S.W.2d 408 (Mo. 1988).

**NJ:** *See, e.g., In re* Quinlan, 355 A.2d 647 (N.J. 1976), *recanted in In re* Conroy, 486 A.2d at 1230; *In re* Peter, 529 A.2d 419.

**NY:** *See, e.g., In re* Westchester County Medical Ctr. (O'Connor), 531 N.E.2d 607.

[153] **NY:** *In re* Westchester County Medical Ctr. (O'Connor), 531 N.E.2d at 614.

**US:** *Accord* Cruzan v. Director, 497 U.S. 261, 323 n.21 (1990) (Brennan, J., dissenting) (few people execute advance directives).

[154] **CT:** *See* McConnell v. Beverly Enters.-Conn., Inc., 553 A.2d 596, 605 n.15 (Conn. 1989) (now embodied in Conn. Gen. Stat. Ann. § 19a-571(a) (West Supp. 1991)) ("If the wishes of the patient have not been expressed in a living will the attending physician shall determine the wishes of the patient by consulting any statement made by the patient directly to the attending physician and, if available, the patient's health care agent, the patient's next of kin, the patient's legal guardian or conservator, if any, and any other person to whom the patient has communicated his wishes, if the attending physician has knowledge of such person.").

**FL:** *Cf.* Browning v. Herbert, 568 So. 2d 4 (Fla. 1990).

**KY:** *See* DeGrella v. Elston, 858 S.W.2d 698, 713 (Ky. 1993) (Wintersheimer, J., dissenting) ("Matters of far less importance than death or life may not legally be based on purely oral expression.").

The first right-to-die case, *Quinlan*,[155] raised the issue of the enforceability of an oral advance directive. The court refused to do so not as a matter of general principle but because it considered the statements purported to have been made by the patient to have been "remote and impersonal" and therefore evidence concerning them to lack probative weight.[156] When the same court next considered the issue of advance directives, though not exclusively oral ones, it not only expressed a more favorable view toward them, it engaged in a confession of error not frequently seen in judicial opinions. Referring to "living wills," oral directives, and durable powers of attorney, the court stated in *Conroy* that

> [a]ny of the[se] . . . types of evidence, and any other information bearing on the person's intent, may be appropriate aids in determining what course of treatment the patient would have wished to pursue. In this respect, *we now believe we were in error in Quinlan* . . . to disregard evidence of statements that Ms. Quinlan made to friends concerning artificial prolongation of the lives of others who were terminally ill. . . . Such evidence is certainly relevant to shed light on whether the patient would have consented to the treatment if competent to make the decision.[157]

And two years later in the *Peter* case, the court again offered penance, stating that

> [i]n *Conroy* . . . we acknowledged that we were wrong . . . to disregard evidence of hearsay accounts of Ms. Quinlan's disapproval of certain uses of life-supporting treatment. Such evidence can shed light on whether a patient would consent to or refuse treatment. Hence we have considered similar evidence in this case.[158]

Even in *Cruzan,* in which the Missouri Supreme Court refused to permit the forgoing of artificial nutrition and hydration on the basis of testimony that the patient had made statements that she would not want to live in a vegetative state,[159] on remand, the trial court took additional testimony of oral statements that the patient had made to others and relied on them as the basis for finding that there *was* clear and convincing evidence that she would not want to be kept alive in this condition and authorized the termination of tube-feeding.[160]

The more specific an oral advance directive is, the more likely it is to be enforced.[161] *Eichner* is an excellent example at the other end of the spectrum

---

[155] *In re* Quinlan, 355 A.2d 647 (N.J. 1976).

[156] *Id.* at 653.

[157] *In re* Conroy, 486 A.2d 1209, 1230 (N.J. 1985) (emphasis added).

[158] *In re* Peter, 529 A.2d 419, 426 n.8 (N.J. 1987).

[159] *See* Cruzan v. Director, 497 U.S. 261, 323 (1990) (Brennan, J., dissenting) (recounting testimony at trial).

[160] *See* Cruzan v. Mouton, Estate No. CV384-9P (Mo. Cir. Ct. Jasper County Dec. 14, 1990), *reported in* 6 Issues L. & Med. 433 (1991).

[161] See § **10.31.**

from *Quinlan*. The patient in that case, Brother Fox, had expressed the view, in 1976 when his religious order discussed the moral implications of the *Quinlan* case, that he would want a respirator removed in similar circumstances. This was during formal discussions prompted by the religious community's mission to teach and promulgate Catholic moral principles. There was evidence that Brother Fox had expressed agreement with Catholic principles permitting the termination of extraordinary life-support systems when there is no reasonable hope for the patient's recovery and that he had stated that he would not "want any of this 'extraordinary business' done for him under those circumstances." There was additional evidence that several years later, and only a few months before his final hospitalization, he reiterated these views.[162] The New York Court of Appeals, in response to the state's argument that a decision to discontinue life-sustaining treatment could not be made by anyone other than the patient, and sympathetic to that argument itself,[163] held that treatment could be forgone "because here Brother Fox made the decision for himself before he became incompetent."[164] However, it was not merely that the patient's statement was specific. The New York court also appears to require that the directive be a "solemn pronouncement[]" rather than a "casual remark."[165] Other courts, however, have found less solemn oral statements made in similar contexts to be dispositive and enforceable.[166]

---

[162] **NY:** Eichner v. Dillon, 420 N.E.2d 64, 68 (N.Y. 1981). *See also* Elbaum v. Grace Plaza of Great Neck, Inc., 544 N.Y.S.2d 840, 843–44 (App. Div. 1989) (The patient "first expressed her views on extraordinary or artificial life-sustaining medical treatment in the context of the Karen Ann Quinlan case . . . remark[ing] 'how awful it must be for the parents to sit vigil over a virtually dead and comatose daughter' and she stated that if she were in a similar situation 'she would not want to be on any respirator or any other mechanical means, she wanted to die.'"); Delio v. Westchester County Medical Ctr., 516 N.Y.S.2d 677, 681–82 (App. Div. 1987) (patient's discussion with wife of *Quinlan* case).

**DRI:** *See also* Gray v. Romeo, 697 F. Supp. 580, 583 (D.R.I. 1988) ("Mr. Gray states that on one occasion Mrs. Gray required that he promise not to keep her alive by artificial means should she ever be in a circumstance similar to Karen Ann Quinlan.").

**CT:** *See also* McConnell v. Beverly Enters.-Conn., Inc., 553 A.2d 596, 605 (Conn. 1989) ("Another co-worker, Elisa Goosman, testified that Mrs. McConnell was quite familiar with feeding tubes as a means of sustaining life and that she stated that 'she never wanted to be a vegetable or a burden on her family.'").

**ME:** *See also* In re Swan, 569 A.2d 1202, 1205 (Me. 1990) (patient's reaction to *In re* Gardner, 534 A.2d 947 (Me. 1987)).

**MA:** *See also* Brophy v. New Eng. Sinai Hosp., Inc., 497 N.E.2d 626, 632 n.22 (1986) (patient's discussion of *Quinlan* case with wife).

[163] *See In re* Storar, 420 N.E.2d 64 (N.Y.), *cert. denied,* 454 U.S. 858 (1981).

[164] Eichner v. Dillon, 420 N.E.2d at 72.

[165] *Id. Cf. In re* Westchester County Medical Ctr. (O'Connor), 531 N.E.2d 607, 611 (N.Y. 1988) (The patient's daughter "described her mother's statements on this subject as less solemn pronouncements: 'it was brought up when we were together, at times when in conversations you start something, you know, maybe the news was on and maybe that was the topic that was brought up and that's how it came about.'").

[166] **ME:** *See, e.g., In re* Swan, 569 A.2d 1202; *In re* Gardner, 534 A.2d 947 (Me. 1987).

**NY:** *Cf.* Elbaum v. Grace Plaza of Great Neck, Inc., 544 N.Y.S.2d 840 (App. Div. 1989).

An oral advance directive, when used with other evidence, may constitute a portion of the basis for forgoing life-sustaining treatment. In a New York trial court case, the court permitted the forgoing of life-sustaining dialysis. There was testimony concerning oral statements the patient had made on a number of occasions to his family before he became incompetent, such as " 'I want this artificial means of keeping me alive ended' " and " 'I am ready to die. I am ready to stop dialysis.' "[167] There were also two written documents "evidencing a clear intention to discontinue dialysis treatment" as well as notes in the patient's hospital chart documenting instances in which he attempted to refuse treatment.[168]

In a similar case in Ohio, relatives and friends of the patient testified that she had several times in the past, and most recently only two days before entering the hospital, said that she did not want to be placed on "a life support system."[169] This oral advance directive proved to be the basis for the holding that the ventilator could be disconnected if certain procedural requirements were met. However, in a subsequent, related proceeding involving an action for damages against the attending physician and others for having refused to disconnect the life support, the trial court stated that, although a patient has the right to refuse treatment prospectively through an advance directive, "it must satisfy the same standards of knowledge and understanding required for informed consent."[170] The court's concern was that statements be "made in contemplation of the specific circumstances and the specific medical treatment required."[171] Although this is a reasonable requirement in general, if carried too far it would undermine the value of advance directives, whether written or oral.[172]

## § 10.17   Uniform Acts

There are three statutes drafted by the National Commissioners on Uniform State Laws that deal with medical decisionmaking: the Uniform Model Health-Care Consent Act, the Uniform Rights of the Terminally Ill Act, and the Uniform Health-Care Decisions Act. Only one—the Uniform Rights of the Terminally Ill Act—has had a substantial impact on advance directive legislation, but it was originally limited to living wills and neglected health care proxies. In 1993 the Commissioners approved a new act, the Uniform Health-Care Decisions Act, which not only includes provisions for living wills and proxies, but also addresses

---

[167] *In re* Lydia E. Hall Hosp., 455 N.Y.S.2d 706, 709 (Sup. Ct. Nassau County 1982).

[168] *Id.*

[169] **OH:** Leach v. Akron Gen. Medical Ctr., 426 N.E.2d 809, 811 (P. Ct. Summit County, Ohio 1980). *See also* Estate of Leach v. Shapiro, 469 N.E.2d 1047, 1053 (Ohio Ct. App. 1984).

**PA:** *Accord* Pocono Medical Ctr. v. Harley, 11 Fiduc. Rep. 2d 128 (C.P. Monroe County, Pa. 1990) (patient's conversation with attending physician and patient's sister's testimony about patient's views regarding treatment constituted clear and convincing evidence of patient's wish to have treatment forgone).

[170] Estate of Leach v. Shapiro, 469 N.E.2d at 1053.

[171] *Id.*

[172] See § 10.7.

the designation of surrogates for individuals who do not appoint a proxy and deals with all medical decisionmaking rather than being limited to end-of-life decisionmaking. This uniform act has not yet had an impact on any state legislation.

## § 10.18 —Uniform Health-Care Decisions Act (UHCDA)

The Uniform Health-Care Decisions Act (UHCDA)[173] is a comprehensive statute for dealing with procedural aspects of decisionmaking for incompetent patients.[174] It includes provisions for giving instructions (that is, living wills), for appointing an agent for decisionmaking (that is, health care powers of attorney), and for making decisions for incompetent patients who have neither given instructions nor designated an agent, both patients with family members to serve as a surrogate (surrogate decisionmaking provisions)[175] and patients who do not have family members to serve as surrogates (guardianship provisions). The Act also includes provisions for making donations of tissues and organs.

The Act is intended to supplant existing uniform legislation dealing with health care decisionmaking—that is, the 1985 and 1989 versions of the Uniform Rights of the Terminally Ill Act and the Model Health-Care Consent Act—as well as other state-specific advance directive statutes and surrogate decision-making statutes, and to do it with one integrated statutory scheme, rather than the two or three acts that many states now have.[176] Furthermore, the UHCDA deals not merely with decisionmaking about life-sustaining treatment but also about all forms of health care decisionmaking for patients who lack decision-making capacity.

Many existing advance directive and surrogate decisionmaking statutes do at least as much, if not more, to impede decisionmaking for incompetent patients than to facilitate it. This results especially from restrictive provisions about when an advance directive becomes effective, but also from restrictive provisions on forgoing artificial nutrition and hydration, restrictive provisions on decisionmaking for pregnant patients, and a host of execution formalities. Perhaps even more important is the fact that by conferring immunity on health care professionals who act in accordance with a statutorily-based advance directive, the statutes create the impression that an advance directive that does not conform to the statute is not "legal," despite the provisions in many statutes that clearly state or imply that the statutes are intended merely to provide a mechanism for drafting advance directives and not to limit existing constitutional (which no statute can do) or common-law rights to make decisions in

---

[173] 9 U.L.A. pt. I at 93 (West Supp. 1994).

[174] *See* English & Meisel, *The Uniform Health-Care Decisions Act,* 21 Est. Plan. 355 (1994).

[175] See **Ch. 14.**

[176] Uniform Health-Care Decisions Act prefatory note.

advance of losing decisionmaking capacity.[177] The UHCDA seeks to avoid these pitfalls of existing legislation.

**Triggering Conditions.** Most existing advance directive legislation restricts the operation of an advance directive to situations in which a patient is either in a "terminal condition" or "permanently unconscious." These provisions can severely limit the usefulness of an advance directive and can place serious roadblocks in the way of individuals who wish to have treatment forgone when they become severely demented, which may or may not qualify as a "terminal condition," depending on statutory definitions and on the progress of the particular individual's illness. The UHCDA does not dictate the circumstances in which the advance directive becomes effective.

**Execution Requirements.** The UHCDA has a minimum of execution requirements—such as witnesses and notarization—based primarily on the assumption that such requirements do little if anything to prevent fraud or enhance reliability. In addition, the complicated execution requirements found in some advance directive statutes work directly against the intent of the statutes by hampering rather than fostering their use. Under the UHCDA, a health care power of attorney must be in writing and signed by the principal but need not be witnessed or acknowledged.[178] Instructions may be either oral or written.[179]

**Decisionmaking for Patients Who Fail to Name an Agent.** A gradually increasing number of states have enacted statutes (known as surrogate decisionmaking or family decisionmaking statutes[180]) to provide for the nonjudicial appointment of a surrogate in the absence of a patient-appointed agent. The UHCDA contains such provisions, which are similar to the standard list of individuals contained in existing legislation. However, the UHCDA also recognizes the authority of an individual orally designated by the patient, and even gives such a surrogate first priority. Because of the uncertainty that inheres in oral statements, however, the UHCDA requires that, to be effective, such an appointment must be communicated by the patient, while competent, to his health care provider.[181]

**Substantive Standards for Decisionmaking.** In addition to prescribing decisionmaking procedures, unlike most existing legislation the UHCDA also takes on the equally important issue of substantive standards for the forgoing of life-sustaining treatment for patients who lack decisionmaking capacity.[182] The

---

[177] See §§ **10.11–10.16.**

[178] Uniform Health-Care Decisions Act § 2(b).

[179] *Id.* § 2(a).

[180] See **Ch. 14.**

[181] Uniform Health-Care Decisions Act § 5(b).

[182] See **Ch. 7.**

UHCDA follows the general trend of the case law by giving primacy to the subjective standard in requiring a surrogate to comply with the patient's instructions if any have been given, and to comply with any other of the patient's oral or written wishes of which the agent is aware (which is roughly akin to the substituted judgment standard).[183] Frequently, however, the principal's wishes are unknown. The UHCDA then follows the dominant (though not quite as uniform) trend in the case law, requiring that the surrogate act in the patient's best interest, as determined in light of the patient's personal values to the extent they are known.[184]

## § 10.19    —Uniform Rights of the Terminally Ill Act (URTIA)

The Uniform Rights of the Terminally Ill Act (URTIA) was approved by the National Commissioners on Uniform State Laws in 1985[185] and completely revised in 1989.[186] The 1985 version was enacted in several states[187] (some of which have since been repealed[188]). This version is superseded by the 1989 version, which has been adopted, sometimes with revisions, in several states. The Act authorizes adults to control decisions about life-sustaining treatment through an instruction directive but neither establishes nor limits the rights of individuals who have not executed one. The URTIA is designed to be narrow in scope and is intended to be limited to life-prolonging treatment and to patients who are in an incurable and irreversible terminal condition whose death will soon occur, and who are unable to participate in the treatment decision.

**Execution Requirements.**    The Act contains minimal execution requirements. A declaration may be signed either by the declarant or by another at the declarant's direction, and a declarant must be of sound mind and 18 years of age or older.[189] The Act contains a sample form for a declaration.[190]

---

[183] Uniform Health-Care Decisions Act § 2(e). See §§ **7.4–7.10.**

[184] See §§ **7.11–7.25.**

[185] 9B U.L.A. 609 (West 1987).

[186] *See* 9B U.L.A. 127 (West Supp. 1994).

[187] **AK:** Alaska Stat. §§ 18.12.010–.100.

   **AR:** Ark. Code Ann. §§ 20-17-210 to -218.

   **IA:** Iowa Code Ann. §§ 144A.1–.11.

   **MO:** Mo. Ann. Stat. §§ 459.010–.055.

   **ND:** N.D. Cent. Code §§ 23-06.4-01 to -14.

[188] **ME:** Me. Rev. Stat. Ann. tit. 22, §§ 2921–2931.

   **MT:** Mont. Code Ann. §§ 50-9-101 to -206.

   **OK:** Okla. Stat. Ann. tit. 63, §§ 3101–3111.

[189] Uniform Rights of the Terminally Ill Act § 2(a)

[190] *Id.* § 2(b).

**When Declaration Becomes Effective.**  A declaration becomes effective when it is communicated to the declarant's attending physician and when the attending physician determines that the declarant is in a terminal condition and no longer possesses decisionmaking capacity.[191] A *terminal condition* is defined as "an incurable and irreversible condition, that, without the administration of life-sustaining treatment, will, in the opinion of the attending physician, result in death within a relatively short time."[192] Individuals who are over 18, have executed a declaration, and are in a terminal condition are referred to as "qualified patient[s],"[193] and remain entitled to make their own treatment decisions "as long as they are able to do so."[194]

**Revocation.**  A declaration may be revoked at any time and in any manner regardless of the declarant's physical and mental condition. The revocation is effective when it is communicated to the physician by either the declarant or a witness to the revocation.[195]

**Appointment of Proxy.**  The declarant may also designate a surrogate in the declaration. The Act contains a sample form for doing so.[196] It also provides that a proxy may be appointed pursuant to the Uniform Durable Power of Attorney Act or the Model Health-Care Consent Act.[197]

**Rights of Nondeclarants.**  The Act makes clear in several ways that its provisions apply only to those who have executed a declaration under the Act,[198] and that its provisions do not apply to declarants who are still in possession of decisionmaking capacity.[199] The Act contains a rather oblique section (§ 7) that authorizes decisionmaking on behalf of individuals who have not executed a declaration. It is so oblique that it is difficult to understand how this section is to

---

[191] *Id.* § 3.

[192] *Id.* § 1(9)

[193] *Id.* § 1(7).

[194] *Id.* § 6(a).

[195] Uniform Rights of the Terminally Ill Act § 4(a).

[196] *Id.* § 2(c).

[197] *Id.* § 2(d).

[198] *Id.* § 11(d) ("This [Act] creates no presumption concerning the intention of an individual who has revoked or has not executed a declaration."). *Cf. id.* § 1(2) ("'Declaration' means a writing executed in accordance with the requirements of Section 2(a)."); *id.* § 2(b) ("A declaration directing a physician to withhold or withdraw life-sustaining treatment may, but need not, be in the following form."). See §§ **10.12** and **10.13**.

[199] Uniform Rights of the Terminally Ill Act § (3) ("A declaration becomes operative when . . . the declarant is determined . . . to be . . . no longer able to make decisions."); *id.* § (6) ("A qualified patient may make decisions regarding life-sustaining treatment so long as the patient is able to do so."); *id.* § 11(e) ("This [Act] does not affect the right of a patient to make decisions regarding use of a life-sustaining treatment, so long as the patient is able to do so."). See § **10.14**.

operate without resort to the drafter's comments. The comments state that this section "provides a procedure by which an attending physician may obtain consent to the withholding or withdrawal of life-sustaining treatment in the absence of an effective declaration." In the absence of an effective declaration, the attending physician may rely on consent from persons on a list to forgo life-sustaining treatment.[200]

**Artificial Nutrition and Hydration.**   The Act skirts the controversial issue of forgoing artificial nutrition and hydration by stating that "[t]his [Act] does not affect the responsibility of the attending physician or other health-care provider to provide treatment, including nutrition and hydration, for a patient's comfort care or alleviation of pain."[201] Thus, the Act leaves it to nonstatutory state law for a determination of whether artificial nutrition and hydration may be forgone at all.[202] The Act does not even take a position on whether artificial nutrition and hydration must be administered for comfort care, whereas many existing advance directive statutes require that artificial nutrition and hydration be provided if necessary for comfort care.[203]

**Pregnancy.**   A physician may not withhold or withdraw treatment from a declarant known to be pregnant if it is likely that the fetus will develop to the point of live birth if continued life-sustaining treatment is administered.[204] This is consistent with the majority of advance directive statutes.[205]

**Obligation to Comply or Transfer.**   An attending physician or health care provider must either comply with the declaration or "take all reasonable steps as promptly as practicable" to transfer the patient to a physician or provider who will comply.[206] The commentary envisions that this provision will apply if the physician is unwilling to denominate the patient as terminally ill or if the physician or provider has "personal convictions or policies unrelated to medical judgment" about complying with the declaration.

**Miscellaneous Provisions.**   The Act contains provisions conferring immunities for health care providers and surrogates,[207] prescribing penalties for a variety of acts with respect to advance directives,[208] stating that death resulting

---

[200] See **Ch. 14.**

[201] Uniform Rights of the Terminally Ill Act §  6(b).

[202] See §§  **9.39–9.40.**

[203] See §§  **11.12** and **12.26.**

[204] Uniform Rights of the Terminally Ill Act §  7(f).

[205] See §§  **11.11** and **12.27.**

[206] Uniform Rights of the Terminally Ill Act §  8.

[207] *Id.* §  9.

[208] *Id.* §  10.

from compliance with an advance directive is not suicide or homicide,[209] concerning the effect of a declaration on life insurance or health insurance and health services,[210] and concerning portability.[211]

## § 10.20   —Uniform Model Health-Care Consent Act (UMHCCA)

The Uniform Model Health-Care Consent Act[212] was approved by the National Conference on Uniform State Laws in 1982 but has been adopted only in Indiana and with some textual variations.[213] The primary purpose of this Act is to create a statutory mechanism for individuals to appoint a surrogate, referred to in the Act as a "health-care representative,"[214] and in the absence of such an appointment (or the unwillingness or inability of an appointed surrogate to serve), to specify who has the authority to make health care decisions. The Act also addresses the issue of who has the authority to make medical decisions for minors.[215]

The Act is "procedural in nature and is purposely narrow in scope."[216] It also provides that it does not alter state law in any substantive manner.[217] Despite the Act's use of the term "consent" rather than decisionmaking, the Act was construed by the Indiana Supreme Court in the *Lawrance* case to permit the *forgoing* of treatment.[218] *Lawrance* held that its provisions apply to end-of-life decisionmaking and specifically that judicial proceedings are not necessary when close relatives, of the degree of relationship specified in the Act, are available to make such decisions.

**Triggering Conditions.**   The provisions of the Act become effective if, in the opinion of the health care provider, the individual is not capable of making a health care decision.[219]

**Execution Requirements.**   The appointment of a health care representative must be in writing, signed, witnessed, and "accepted in writing by the health

---

[209] *Id.* § 11(a).

[210] *Id.* § 11(b), (c).

[211] *Id.* § 13.

[212] Uniform Model Health-Care Consent Act § 2(2)(i), 9 U.L.A. pt. I at 453 (West 1988 & Supp. 1994).

[213] *See* Ind. Code Ann. §§ 16-36-1-1 to -14.

[214] Uniform Model Health-Care Consent Act § 6(a).

[215] *Id.* § 2.

[216] 9 U.L.A. pt. I at 453 (1988) (prefatory note).

[217] Uniform Model Health-Care Consent Act § 11.

[218] *In re* Lawrance, 579 N.E.2d 32 (Ind. 1991).

[219] Uniform Model Health-Care Consent Act § 3.

care representative."[220] The person making the directive may specify terms and conditions, such as authorizing the health care representative to delegate authority to another person[221] or specifying when the writing becomes effective.[222] Unless specified in the writing, the surrogate appointed in this fashion has priority to make health care decisions for the individual.[223] In order to serve as a health care representative, an individual must be one who would be authorized to consent to his own health care under the Act,[224] namely, a competent adult or an emancipated minor.[225] Comments to the Act also provide a suggested form for the appointment of a health care representative.[226]

An individual who is competent to make his own health care decisions may, by a signed writing, disqualify other individuals who would otherwise be qualified to act as surrogate from so acting.[227] A health care provider who knows of the disqualification may not rely on consent from the disqualified individual, and an individual who knows he has been disqualified may not act as a surrogate.[228]

**Substantive Standards for Decisionmaking.**   Because the Act is largely procedural, it does not clearly articulate standards for decisionmaking by a health care representative. However, there are implicit standards because under the Act, a surrogate must act in good faith and in the best interest of the individual. On the basis of this provision, the Indiana Supreme Court in *Lawrance* applied a best interests standard for determining whether life-sustaining medical treatment must be continued or could be withdrawn.[229]

**Decisionmaking for Persons Who Fail to Name a Health Care Representative.**   If a health care representative has not been appointed or declines to serve, the Act authorizes specified family members (a person's spouse, parent, adult child, or adult sibling) to serve unless they have been disqualified by the patient.[230] A person's guardian, appointed under the Act or under any other state law, may also make decisions about treatment.[231]

---

[220] *Id.* § 6(c).

[221] *Id.* § 6(d).

[222] *Id.* § 6(e), (f).

[223] *Id.* § 6(g).

[224] *Id.* § 6(j).

[225] Uniform Model Health-Care Consent Act § 2.

[226] *Id.* § 6 cmts.

[227] *Id.* § 8.

[228] *Id.*

[229] *Id.* § 4(c). *See In re* Lawrance, 579 N.E.2d 32 (Ind. 1991).

[230] Uniform Model Health-Care Consent Act § 4(a).

[231] *Id.* § 7(d).

**Immunity.**   The Act limits or provides immunity from civil and criminal liability and from professional disciplinary action for health care providers who act, or decline to act, in reliance on a person who they believe is authorized by the Act to consent to health care.[232] The Act also provides immunity for health care providers who fail to follow an individual's direction when they believe that person is incapable of consenting.[233] Immunity is also conferred on a surrogate who believes in good faith that he is entitled to consent for another.[234]

**Miscellaneous Provisions.**   A surrogate has the same right of access to medical records as the individual for whom he is acting.[235] The Act has several other miscellaneous provisions regarding effect on existing state law,[236] severability,[237] and construction.[238]

## § 10.21   Patient Self-Determination Act (PSDA)

The federal Omnibus Budget Reconciliation Act of 1990 (OBRA)[239] contains provisions imposing responsibilities on institutional health care providers with respect to advance directives. These provisions grew out of earlier legislative efforts to enact the Patient Self-Determination Act of 1989,[240] and therefore are sometimes referred to by this name even though the name itself is not used in OBRA. An interim final rule for the implementation of the Act was promulgated by the Health Care Financing Administration.[241]

The Patient Self-Determination Act (PSDA) requires, as a condition of participation in Medicare and/or Medicaid programs, that certain institutional health care providers (hospitals, skilled nursing facilities, home health agencies, hospice programs, and prepaid health care organizations) furnish patients with information about advance directives. The central right that this legislation creates is the right of patients to be provided with certain information. The content of the information itself is governed by state law and by the policies of

---

[232] *Id.* § 9(a).

[233] *Id.* § 9 (b).

[234] *Id.* § 9(c).

[235] *Id.* § 10.

[236] Uniform Model Health-Care Consent Act § 11.

[237] *Id.* § 12.

[238] *Id.* § 13.

[239] Pub. L. No. 101-508, §§ 4206, 4751 [hereinafter OBRA], 104 Stat. 1388-115 to -117, 1388-204 to -206 (codified at 42 U.S.C.A. § 1395cc(f)(1) & *id.* § 1396a(a) (West Supp. 1994)).

[240] S. 1766, 101st Cong., 1st Sess. (1989).

[241] *See* U.S. Dep't of Health & Hum. Servs., *Medicare and Medicaid Programs; Advance Directives,* 57 Fed. Reg. 8194 (Mar. 6, 1992) (interim final rule).

particular health care organizations. Some state advance directive statutes mirror the requirements of the Patient Self-Determination Act.[242]

The key provisions of the legislation are as follows:

1.  *Applicability.* The PSDA applies to hospitals, skilled nursing facilities, home health agencies, hospices,[243] and prepaid health care organizations.[244]

2.  *Maintenance of Written Policies and Procedures.* Health care providers must "maintain written policies and procedures" applicable to "all adult individuals receiving medical care." These policies and procedures are to describe "an individual's rights under State law . . . to make decisions concerning [his] medical care, including the right to accept or refuse [treatment] . . . and the right to formulate advance directives."[245] Thus, the PSDA does not apply solely to information about advance directives but rather applies to a patient's medical decisionmaking rights in general.

3.  *Provision of Written Information to Patients.* Patients must be given written information about their state-law rights to make decisions concerning their medical care, the right to accept or refuse treatment, the right to formulate advance directives, and "the written policies of the provider or organization respecting the implementation of such rights."[246] This information must be provided at the time of admission to a hospital as an inpatient, by a skilled nursing home at the time of admission as a resident, by a home health agency "in advance of the individual coming under the care of the agency," by a hospice "at the time of initial receipt of hospice care by the individual," and by a prepaid health care plan at the time of enrollment in the plan.[247] These requirements seem only to apply to hospital *inpatients,* though this is not entirely clear because of the language in the requirement that health care providers must "maintain written policies and procedures" applicable to "all adult individuals receiving medical care,"[248] which could be construed to apply to patients treated in hospital outpatient clinics.

---

[242] *See, e.g.,* N.J. Stat. Ann. § 26:2H-65(1), (2) (requiring health care institutions to adopt policies and practices "as are necessary to provide for routine inquiry, at the time of admission and at . . . other . . . appropriate [times] . . . concerning the existence and location of an advance directive," and "appropriate informational materials concerning advance directives to all interested patients . . . , to assist patients in discussing and executing an advance directive").

[243] OBRA § 4206(a), 42 U.S.C. § 1395cc(f)(2); OBRA § 4751(a)(2), 42 U.S.C. § 1396a(w)(2).

[244] OBRA § 4206(b), 42 U.S.C. §§ 1395mm(c)(8) & 1395l(r); OBRA § 4751(a)(2), 42 U.S.C. § 1396a(w)(2)(E).

[245] OBRA § 4206(a)(2), 42 U.S.C. § 1395cc(f)(1); OBRA § 4751(a)(2), 42 U.S.C. § 1396a(w)(1).

[246] OBRA § 4206(a)(2), 42 U.S.C. § 1395cc(f)(1)(a)(i), (ii); OBRA § 4751(a)(2), 42 U.S.C. § 1396a(w)(1)(A).

[247] OBRA § 4206(a)(2), 42 U.S.C. § 1395cc(f)(2)(A)–(E); OBRA § 4751(a)(2), 42 U.S.C. § 1396a(w)(2)(A)–(E).

[248] OBRA § 4206(a)(2), 42 U.S.C. § 1395cc(f)(1); OBRA § 4751(a)(2), 42 U.S.C. § 1396a(w)(1).

4. *Documentation.* Health care providers must document in the patient's medical record whether or not the patient has executed an advance directive.[249]

5. *Nondiscrimination.* Health care providers are prohibited from conditioning the provision of care "or otherwise discriminat[ing] against an individual based on whether or not the individual has executed an advance directive."[250] Further, this provision is not to be "construed as requiring the provision of care which conflicts with an advance directive."[251]

6. *Compliance with State Law.* The Act requires health care providers to "ensure compliance with requirements of State law ... respecting advance directives."[252]

7. *Provider Education About Advance Directives.* Health care providers are required to conduct education for their staff and for the community on advance directives.[253]

8. *Conscientious Objection.* The Act is not to be construed to require the implementation of an advance directive by "any health care provider or any agent of such provider" if state law permits an objection to doing so as "a matter of conscience."[254]

9. *Written Description of State Law.* The Act also requires states to "develop a written description of the law of the State (whether statutory or as recognized by the courts of the State) concerning advance directives," which is to be distributed to patients by health care providers.[255] The Commission on Legal Problems of the Elderly of the American Bar Association has published a guide to assist states in carrying out this responsibility.[256] It is essential to note that when the Act refers to "state law," it is referring not merely to a state's advance directive statutes but also to the corpus of case law concerning medical decisionmaking— case law concerning consent to treatment, informed consent, and end-of-life decisionmaking.

---

[249] OBRA § 4206(a)(2), 42 U.S.C. § 1395cc(f)(1)(B); OBRA § 4751(a)(2), 42 U.S.C. § 1396a(w)(1)(B).

[250] OBRA § 4206(a)(2), 42 U.S.C. § 1395cc(f)(1)(C); OBRA § 4751(a)(2), 42 U.S.C. § 1396a(w)(1)(C).

[251] OBRA § 4206(a)(2), 42 U.S.C. § 1395cc(f)(1); OBRA § 4751(a)(2), 42 U.S.C. § 1396a(w)(1).

[252] OBRA § 4206(a)(2), 42 U.S.C. § 1395cc(f)(1)(D); OBRA § 4751(a)(2), 42 U.S.C. § 1396a(w)(1)(D).

[253] OBRA § 4206(a)(2), 42 U.S.C. § 1395cc(f)(1)(E); OBRA § 4751(a)(2), 42 U.S.C. § 1396a(w)(1)(E).

[254] OBRA § 4206(c); OBRA § 4751(a)(2), 42 U.S.C. § 1396a(w)(3). See § **17.23.**

[255] OBRA § 4751(a)(1), 42 U.S.C. § 1396a(a)(58).

[256] *See* Commission on Legal Problems of the Elderly, American Bar Ass'n, Patient Self-Determination Act State Law Guide (1991).

10. *Public Education Campaign.* The Department of Health and Human Services is required to "develop and implement a national campaign to inform the public of the option to execute advance directives and of a patient's right to participate and direct health care decisions."[257] The department must also "develop or approve nationwide informational materials" to be distributed by providers.[258] These materials must be directed not only to patients but also to "the medical and legal profession."[259] They must contain information about the right to make decisions about medical care, "including the right to accept or refuse medical or surgical treatment," and about advance directives.[260] The Department must send information about the PSDA by mail to Social Security recipients and add information about it to the Medicare handbook.[261] The Department is also required to provide assistance to the states and/or private organizations in developing "State-specific documents" to be distributed by health care providers under the Act.[262]

The concern has been expressed that the PSDA is "motivated less by a genuine respect for actual informed patient choice than by the feeling that physicians and hospitals now need not trouble themselves in making truly critical and sometimes agonizing decisions."[263] Anecdotal evidence suggests that the statute has not had the effect of encouraging physicians to initiate end-of-life discussions with patients.[264]

## § 10.22  Enforcement in Medical Emergencies

Whether to honor an advance directive in a medical emergency is a particularly vexing question for health care personnel. This is especially so when emergency medical technicians are transporting patients to hospitals from their homes or nursing homes, but it also arises in health care institutions. The major concern is that a patient not be permitted to die from withholding treatment on the mistaken assumption that that is what the patient would have wanted had he been competent to make a contemporaneous decision.[265] Although this is a problem

---

[257] OBRA § 4751(d)(1).

[258] *Id.* § 4751(d)(2).

[259] *Id.*

[260] *Id.*

[261] OBRA § 4751(d)(4).

[262] *Id.* § 4751(d)(3).

[263] Loewy, *Advance Directives and Surrogate Laws: Ethical Instruments or Moral Cop-out?,* 152 Archives Internal Med. 1973, 1973 (1992).

[264] *See* Gianelli, *Many Say Doctors Aren't Living Up to Expectations of Living Will Law,* Am. Med. News, May 17, 1993, at 1.

[265] **RI:** *Cf.* Miller v. Rhode Island Hosp., 625 A.2d 778, 783 (R.I. 1993) ("In this sea of competing interests, the case at bar compels us to chart a course between the perils of insufficient emergency medical care and violation of a patient's individual liberty.").

with advance directives under all circumstances, under nonemergency circumstances there is time to attempt to ascertain whether the prevailing medical circumstances are those actually contemplated by the patient. In an emergency, this is usually not possible, unless perhaps the patient has very clearly and specifically drafted a directive with such an emergency in mind or the health care personnel involved are familiar with the patient's wishes through previous experience with this patient under similar circumstances. Even then, however, courts seem loath to permit the forgoing of treatment, especially when that treatment is virtually certain to restore the patient to health, as opposed to postponing the process of dying, which is frequently the case with religiously motivated refusals of treatment by competent adults.[266]

The black-letter law is that in a bona fide medical emergency neither the informed consent nor the simple consent of the patient need be obtained. It is said that in such situations consent is implied, although the better explanation is that physicians are privileged to render treatment in the absence of consent.[267] Indeed, the law requires physicians (and other health care personnel under their control, such as emergency medical technicians) to exercise their best professional judgment to provide treatment in a life-threatening emergency.[268] In the absence of an advance directive, however, if a patient possesses decisionmaking capacity and expressly refuses treatment in an emergency, that refusal must be respected. Furthermore, consent is not implied in an emergency if the patient has previously stated that he would not consent under such circumstances,[269] so that it is not permissible for health care providers to wait until an emergency

---

[266] **MI:** *See, e.g.,* Werth v. Taylor, 475 N.W.2d 426 (Mich. Ct. App. 1991) (physicians entitled to administer blood transfusion in emergency to patient of Jehovah's Witness faith who had previously refused transfusion).

**NJ:** *See, e.g., In re* Hughes, 611 A.2d 1148 (N.J. Super. Ct. App. Div. 1992) (same).

**OH:** *See, e.g.,* University of Cincinnati Hosp. v. Edmond, 506 N.E.2d 299 (C.P. Hamilton County, Ohio 1986) (same).

**PA:** *See, e.g., In re* Estate of Dorone, 534 A.2d 452 (Pa. 1987) (same).

[267] See § **3.23.**

[268] **CA:** Drabick v. Drabick, 245 Cal. Rptr. 840, 846 (Ct. App. 1988) ("The decision to keep William alive immediately after his accident was the ordinary one that emergency care physicians make—to buy time in the hope that the patient can be cured.").

**OH:** Estate of Leach v. Shapiro, 469 N.E.2d 1047, 1053 (Ohio Ct. App. 1984).

[269] **MI:** *But see* Werth v. Taylor, 475 N.W.2d at 430 ("We agree with the principle in *Dorone* that it is the patient's fully informed, contemporaneous decision which alone is sufficient to override evidence of medical necessity.").

**NJ:** *But see In re* Hughes, 611 A.2d 1148.

**NY:** Fosmire v. Nicoleau, 551 N.E.2d 77, 80 (N.Y. 1990) (emergency exception inapplicable when "patient clearly stated before admission to the hospital and throughout her stay that she would not consent to blood transfusions"); Eichner v. Dillon, 420 N.E.2d 64, 70 (N.Y. 1981) (citing Restatement (Second) of Torts § 62 illus. 5 (1965)).

**OH:** Anderson v. St. Francis-St. George Hosp., 614 N.E.2d 841, 844 (Ohio Ct. App. 1992); Estate of Leach v. Shapiro, 469 N.E.2d at 1053.

**PA:** *But see In re* Estate of Dorone, 534 A.2d at 456 (same).

develops and then invoke the emergency exception to obtaining informed consent to override the patient's previously expressed wishes.[270]

The logistical difficulties associated with implementing these settled rules of law can be daunting. In a true emergency, it can be very difficult if not impossible to ascertain quickly enough whether the patient's life or health are compromised, whether the patient is competent, whether an advance directive exists and what its terms are,[271] and whether the facts of the current situation are those that the declarant contemplated in an advance directive. In other words, questions about the veracity, accuracy, and enforceability of the advance directive cannot even be raised, let alone resolved, in most emergencies. These are questions that in less exigent circumstances could be explored in a reflective manner, thereby permitting health care personnel to avoid (or at least reduce the risk of) the dual pitfalls of invading the patient's interests by withholding medically indicated treatment on the basis of an inaccurate understanding of his wishes or invading the patient's interests by administering unwanted treatment.

It is not difficult to understand why, in emergencies, health care personnel are inclined to resolve dilemmas by erring on the side of providing treatment rather than withholding it. Withholding treatment means that a patient will die, which, in addition to not being what the patient might want, might entail serious adverse consequences of an emotional, professional, and legal nature for the responsible health care professional. Furthermore, withholding treatment in an emergency is inconsistent with the strongly conditioned responses of health care professionals as well as with the ethos and ethics of the health care professions. By contrast, if the provision of treatment saves the life of a patient who would have preferred death, the patient's will is temporarily thwarted, albeit at the expense of the

---

UT: Lounsbury v. Capel, 836 P.2d 188, 199 (Utah 1992) (doctor "may not rely on the temporary incapacity of [patient], induced by preoperative medication, as a reason to resort to obtaining consent from [patient's wife]"; "spousal consent is particularly suspect in a case such as this where, taking [patient's] version of the facts as true, [spousal] consent followed on the heels of [patient's] own repeated refusals to consent").

[270] DIL: *Cf.* Holmes v. Silver Cross Hosp., 340 F. Supp. 125 (N.D. Ill. 1972) (hospital acted improperly in waiting until patient became unconscious to have him declared incompetent).

OH: *See* Anderson v. St. Francis-St. George Hosp., 614 N.E.2d 841 (Ohio Ct. App. 1992); Estate of Leach v. Shapiro, 469 N.E.2d at 1053.

UT: *Cf.* Lounsbury v. Capel, 836 P.2d at 199 (doctor "may not rely on the temporary incapacity of [patient], induced by preoperative medication, as a reason to resort to obtaining consent from [patient's wife]"; "spousal consent is particularly suspect in a case such as this where, taking [patient's] version of the facts as true, [spousal] consent followed on the heels of [patient's] own repeated refusals to consent").

Hastings Ctr., Guidelines on the Termination of Life-Sustaining Treatment and the Care of the Dying 46 (1987) (Part Two, § B.I) [hereinafter Hastings Center Guidelines].

[271] MI: *See, e.g.,* Werth v. Taylor, 475 N.W.2d 426.

NJ: *See, e.g., In re* Hughes, 611 A.2d 1148.

OH: *See, e.g.,* University of Cincinnati Hosp. v. Edmond, 506 N.E.2d 299 (C.P. Hamilton County, Ohio 1986).

PA: *See, e.g., In re* Estate of Dorone, 534 A.2d 452.

patient's dignity and any other burdens associated with the treatment, but treatment may later be terminated.

The resolution of these questions is further complicated by the fact that the issues present themselves in a variety of fact patterns; consequently, there is no single solution that fits all situations.[272] Ideally, health care personnel should attempt to distinguish between quite different cases, such as the

> terminally ill patient fully advised of an impending crisis [who] might then be able to refuse treatments which would only prolong suffering, [and] a patient afflicted with a disease which would be terminal in several years and who had generally expressed the desire to die peacefully ... [who is now suffering from] injuries sustained in an automobile crash.[273]

Health care personnel do not always have a studied opportunity to make such distinctions, but sometimes they do. At one end of the spectrum are what might be referred to as "anticipatable" emergencies, exemplified by chronically ill patients, often but not always elderly.[274] When a patient in such a situation has anticipatorily refused care—for example, cardiopulmonary resuscitation via a do-not-resuscitate order[275] or hospitalization via a do-not-hospitalize (or do-not-transport) order[276]—the emergency exception, based on the doctrine of implied consent, cannot legitimately be invoked.[277] Members of the Jehovah's Witness

---

[272] **NY:** *In re* Westchester County Medical Ctr. (O'Connor), 531 N.E.2d 607, 612–13 (N.Y. 1988) ("It would, of course, be unrealistic for us to attempt to establish a rigid set of guidelines to be used in all cases requiring an evaluation of a now-incompetent patient's previously expressed wishes. The number and variety of situations in which the problem of terminating artificial life supports arises preclude any attempt to anticipate all of the possible permutations.").

[273] Estate of Leach v. Shapiro, 469 N.E.2d at 1053.

[274] **CA:** *See, e.g.,* Bartling v. Superior Court, 209 Cal. Rptr. 220, 222 (Ct. App. 1984) (the advance directive stated in part, "'I am aware that impairment, incapacity and unconscious ness may occur as a result of my refusal of ventilation, but I desire that none of these be deemed to be a medical emergency.'").

**OH:** *See, e.g.,* Anderson v. St. Francis-St. George Hosp., 614 N.E.2d 841.

[275] **CA:** *See, e.g.,* Bartling v. Glendale Adventist Medical Ctr., 229 Cal. Rptr. 360 (Ct. App. 1986).

**OH:** *See, e.g.,* Anderson v. St. Francis-St. George Hosp., 614 N.E.2d 841.

See §§ **9.4–9.32.**

[276] **AZ:** *Cf.* Rasmussen v. Fleming, 741 P.2d 674 (Ariz. 1987) (physician of nursing home patient had written do-not-hospitalize order).

[277] **DIL:** *Cf.* Holmes v. Silver Cross Hosp., 340 F. Supp. 125 (N.D. Ill. 1972) (hospital acted improperly in waiting until patient became unconscious to have him declared incompetent).

**OH:** *Cf.* Anderson v. St. Francis-St. George Hosp., 614 N.E.2d 841; Estate of Leach v. Shapiro, 469 N.E.2d at 1053.

**UT:** *Cf.* Lounsbury v. Capel, 836 P.2d 188, 199 (Utah 1992) (doctor "may not rely on the temporary incapacity of [patient], induced by preoperative medication, as a reason to resort to obtaining consent from [patient's wife]"; "spousal consent is particularly suspect in a case such as this where, taking [patient's] version of the facts as true, [spousal] consent followed on the heels of [patient's] own repeated refusals to consent").

Hastings Center Guidelines (Part Two, § B.I).

faith who make it known that their religious beliefs preclude their acceptance of a blood transfusion should it be needed are in the same sort of situation, with the exception that the treatment that they are refusing will often restore their health, and as a consequence courts are reluctant to enforce their wishes in such circumstances.[278]

Toward the middle of the spectrum are patients who have made some sort of general advance directive to the effect that they do not wish any extraordinary treatment, and others who have experienced the same sort of emergency before and who have expressed opposition to this very kind of treatment (such as cardiopulmonary resuscitation) again in the future should the occasion arise. At the other end of the spectrum are ordinary, healthy individuals suffering from no acute or chronic illnesses who have executed a written advance directive or made oral statements of a general type that they do not wish extraordinary treatment should they become terminally ill, or possibly a more specific directive prohibiting the administration of some particular form of care. Such individuals might then suffer an acute illness or injury and become incompetent as a result, which might lead family members to produce the patient's written advance directive or to relate an account of the patient's oral advance directive.[279]

A difficult situation between the extremes is the patient who is conscious and is actively protesting the administration of treatment or transport to a hospital under emergency conditions but whose decisionmaking capacity is uncertain. It is even more difficult for emergency medical technicians and other health care personnel to know what to do in an emergency when some other party, who appears to be a responsible person in general and responsible in particular for the patient (such as a family member or nursing home personnel), claims that the patient has previously stated that he does not wish to be treated or transported.[280]

---

[278] **MI:** *See, e.g.,* Werth v. Taylor, 475 N.W.2d 426 (Mich. Ct. App. 1991).

**NJ:** *See, e.g., In re* Hughes, 611 A.2d 1148 (N.J. Super. Ct. App. Div. 1992).

**OH:** *See, e.g.,* University of Cincinnati Hosp. v. Edmond, 506 N.E.2d 299 (C.P. Hamilton County, Ohio 1986).

**PA:** *See, e.g., In re* Estate of Dorone, 534 A.2d 452 (Pa. 1987).

[279] **FL:** *See, e.g.,* Browning v. Herbert, 568 So. 2d 4 (Fla. 1990).

**ME:** *See, e.g., In re* Swan, 569 A.2d 1202 (Me. 1990); *In re* Gardner, 534 A.2d 947 (Me. 1987).

**MO:** *See, e.g.,* Cruzan v. Harmon, 760 S.W.2d 408 (Mo. 1988).

**NJ:** *See, e.g., In re* Quinlan, 355 A.2d 647 (N.J. 1976); McVey v. Englewood Hosp. Ass'n, 524 A.2d 450 (N.J. Super. Ct. App. Div. 1987).

**NY:** *See, e.g., In re* Westchester County Medical Ctr. (O'Connor), 531 N.E.2d 607 (N.Y. 1988); Eichner v. Dillon, 420 N.E.2d 64 (N.Y. 1981); Elbaum v. Grace Plaza of Great Neck, Inc., 544 N.Y.S.2d 840 (App. Div. 1989); Delio v. Westchester County Medical Ctr., 516 N.Y.S.2d 677 (App. Div. 1987).

[280] *See* Miles & Crimmins, *Orders to Limit Emergency Treatment for an Ambulance Service in a Large Metropolitan Area,* 254 JAMA 525 (1985); Sachs et al., *Emergencies and Advance Directives,* 20 Hastings Center Rep. No. 6, at 42 (Nov.–Dec. 1990); *Prehospital DNR Orders,* 19 Hastings Center Rep. No. 6, at 17 (Nov.–Dec. 1989); Siner, *Advance Directives in Emergency Medicine: Medical, Legal, and Ethical Implications,* 18 Annals Emergency Med. 136

Another kind of situation between the extremes involves individuals who are terminally ill with a life expectancy of some years or months who are leading a reasonably normal life but suffer an accident or acute illness, perhaps unrelated to the terminal illness. If they have an advance directive that states that they do not wish to be kept alive by artificial or extraordinary means, the question might arise as to whether it should be applied in circumstances such as these.[281]

It can often be anticipated that a patient who is terminally ill and on a long, downward course will lose decisionmaking capacity long before he actually does and long before any urgent treatment decisions need to be made. In many cases, these decisions are likely to include cardiopulmonary resuscitation and artificial hydration and nutrition. Other treatment decisions specific to particular medical conditions, such as hospitalization, can also be anticipated.

Attending physicians should advise chronically ill patients with life-threatening diseases or injuries of the possibility that emergencies might arise. They should take the initiative, if the patient or family members do not, to ascertain the patient's wishes about the likely kinds of treatment decisions that will need to be made in an emergency. Through conversation between the attending physician and patient, an understanding—which might be referred to as a negotiated advance directive—can sometimes be reached about administering life-sustaining treatment in an emergency. (This is not unlike the issue of "required reconsideration" of DNR orders for a patient undergoing palliative surgery.[282]) Nonetheless, logistical considerations are sometimes such that emergency medical technicians will remain unaware of these agreements. Reducing them to writing, as for example through drafting or modifying a written advance directive, also will not always work because of the exigent nature of the circumstances under which decisions need to be made.

Whether dishonoring an advance directive is wrongful depends in large part on the reasons for doing so. First, it may result from oversight—for example, the attending physician is not present and the health care personnel who respond to the emergency are unaware of the advance directive. If this results from a physician's failure to properly ensure that other health care personnel are aware of the existence and the content of the advance directive, there could be liability for negligence.[283] In a genuine emergency, however, what would otherwise be negligent conduct may not be.

An advance directive might also be ignored because the attending physician believes that the emergency situation that actually arises is not the sort

---

(1989); Emergency Medical Servs. Comm., American College of Emergency Physicians, *Guidelines for "Do Not Resuscitate" Orders in the Prehospital Setting,* 17 Annals Emergency Med. 1106 (1988); Miles, *Advanced [sic] Directives to Limit Treatment: The Need for Portability,* 35 J. Am. Geriatrics Soc'y 74 (1987). *See also* Hastings Center Guidelines 51 (Part Two, § B.II(9)(e)).

[281] **OH:** *Cf.* Estate of Leach v. Shapiro, 469 N.E.2d at 1053 ("[T]he prospect of refusing to act in an emergency because the patient at some time voiced vague wishes not to be kept alive on machines is . . . unacceptable.").

[282] See § 9.31.

[283] **OH:** Anderson v. St. Francis-St. George Hosp., 614 N.E.2d 841 (Ohio Ct. App. 1992).

envisioned by the agreement. The legitimacy of the administration of treatment under such circumstances depends in part on the content of the advance directive. The more specific a patient's statement refusing treatment, the more binding it should be on those who know or should have known of it. However, to require, as some courts have done,[284] that an advance directive meet the same standards of knowledge and understanding as would be required to give an informed consent could effectively make advance directives worthless.[285] Although health care professionals must be free to exercise their best medical judgment in treating a life-threatening emergency, the doctrine of implied consent can, if construed too broadly, effectively nullify a patient's right of self-determination.

## § 10.23  —Statutory Provisions for Implementing Advance Directives in Emergencies

Many states have provisions in advance directive statutes or have enacted freestanding legislation addressing the problem of implementing advance directives in an emergency. Many of these statutes apply only to cardiopulmonary resuscitation, but some are of more general applicability and apply to other forms of treatment as well.[286]

## § 10.24  Enforcement in Other Jurisdictions ("Portability")

Whether an advance directive that is valid and enforceable in the jurisdiction in which it was executed is valid and enforceable in other jurisdictions—that is, whether the advance directive is "portable"—is an issue as complex as it is unresolved. Some advance directive statutes have provisions addressing this issue, and most portability provisions provide that an advance directive from another jurisdiction is valid and enforceable if it is in compliance with the law of the state where it was executed or the state where it is to be enforced.[287]

These provisions do not settle all questions. One immediate problem is that health care professionals will sometimes need to make a determination of whether an advance directive complies with the law of another state, which can

---

[284] **MI:** Werth v. Taylor, 475 N.W.2d 426 (Mich. Ct. App. 1991).

  **NJ:** *In re* Hughes, 611 A.2d 1148 (N.J. Super. Ct. App. Div. 1992).

  **OH:** Estate of Leach v. Shapiro, 469 N.E.2d at 1053.

  **PA:** *In re* Estate of Dorone, 534 A.2d 452 (Pa. 1987).

[285] See § **10.7.**

[286] See §§ **9.7–9.30.**

[287] See §§ **10.24** and **11.21.**

be difficult for lawyers and certainly is no easy task for people not trained in the law. Second, the advance directive might not comply with the statutory law of another jurisdiction, but it might comply with the requisites for decisionmaking for incompetent patients set forth in the *case law* of the jurisdiction in which it was executed, a determination that is even more difficult to make. Furthermore, if the advance directive does not conform to (and perhaps even conflicts with) the law of the jurisdiction in which it was drafted, it might still be in conformance with the case law of the jurisdiction in which it is sought to be enforced.

Even if a directive meets the requisite formalities of execution of the sending jurisdiction, the receiving jurisdiction, or both, it may request conduct which is legal in the jurisdiction of execution but is illegal or of questionable or unsettled legality in the jurisdiction of enforcement. For instance, a directive stating that the declarant does not wish to be kept alive by a feeding tube, executed in a state that does not proscribe such a request, might encounter opposition from health care personnel in a jurisdiction in which there is no judicial precedent for honoring it or a precedent against implementing it.[288]

In the final analysis, many of these potentially difficult questions can be sidestepped by the rather simple expedient of treating an advance directive from another jurisdiction as evidence of the declarant's wishes. In other words, the directive is enforced as such, and thus it does not matter whether it is valid in the jurisdiction in which it was drafted. This evidence should be taken into account by the appropriate decisionmakers (attending physician and surrogate, or court and/or guardian if judicial review has been sought) under the appropriate substantive standard for surrogate decisionmaking. Only if the directive requests conduct specifically proscribed by the case or statutory law in the jurisdiction of enforcement should there be any concern about its implementation.

## JUDICIAL REVIEW

## § 10.25   Judicial Administration of Advance Directives

Advance directives are intended to simplify decisionmaking for patients who lack decisionmaking capacity, in part by avoiding recourse to the judicial process for making end-of-life decisions for incompetent patients. However, advance directives can also be a *source* of litigation, rather than a means of avoiding it. Disputes can arise about the meaning and applicability of an advance directive. They can arise because of a conflict between the terms of an advance directive and the decision made by a patient's proxy. Or they can arise

---

[288] See **Table 9–2** in **§ 9.39.**

because the advance directive might request an action thought not to be legally permissible under the advance directive statute[289] or the case law.

Few advance directive statutes address this issue,[290] and judicial attention has also been scant. On balance, the law in this area is developing along much the same lines as it is with respect to judicial review of other aspects of end-of-life decisionmaking for incompetent patients. As is the case with determining decisionmaking incapacity, designating a surrogate, and reviewing surrogate decisions, courts are inclined to permit advance directives to be carried out privately without any requirement of judicial review or oversight.[291] However, as is also true in these related areas, the courts are available for reviewing advance directives when so requested by any of the participants in the decisionmaking process, and review may even be necessary when certain conditions exist.

No court has held that judicial review of an advance directive is a categorical prerequisite to its validity and enforceability. Nor are there any statutory requirements that nonstatutory advance directives be subjected to judicial review before they may be enforced.[292] Indeed, requiring judicial review would go a long way in undermining an essential purpose of advance directives and one of the strong motivations for individuals to execute advance directives, namely, avoiding protracted judicial proceedings to forgo life-sustaining treatment.

## § 10.26   Review Not Required

The Florida Supreme Court took the lead in establishing that there is ordinarily no need for judicial review of an advance directive. In *John F. Kennedy Memorial Hospital v. Bludworth,*[293] the court responded in the negative to a certified question asking, "[i]n the case of a comatose and terminally ill individual who has executed a so-called 'living' or 'mercy' will, is it necessary that a court appointed guardian of his person obtain the approval of a court of competent jurisdiction before terminating extraordinary life support systems?"[294] The court rejected the state's argument that judicial approval was needed to terminate treatment even when an advance directive existed, because requiring judicial approval in this kind of case is "too burdensome, is not necessary to

---

[289] *See, e.g.,* Browning v. Herbert, 568 So. 2d 4 (Fla. 1990) (requesting forgoing of tube-feeding).

[290] See § **12.51.**

[291] See §§ **5.25–5.44.**

[292] *But see* Ohio Rev. Code Ann. §§ 1337.16(D), 2133.05(B) (requiring judicial review of a health care power of attorney and living will if certain specified persons object to forgoing of life-sustaining treatment).

[293] 452 So. 2d 921 (Fla. 1984).

[294] *Id.* at 922.

protect the state's interests or the interests of the patient, and could render the rights of the incompetent a nullity."[295] The court did not, however, hold that the living will must be followed, but only that it should be given "great weight" by the surrogate decisionmaker.[296]

This court reiterated and expanded on this position in *Browning v. Herbert*,[297] in which it laid down a set of rules for surrogates to follow when implementing an advance directive without judicial guidance. In such situations,

1.  The surrogate must be satisfied that the patient executed any document knowingly, willingly, and without undue influence, and that the evidence of the patient's oral declarations is reliable;

2.  The surrogate must be assured that the patient does not have a reasonable probability of recovering competency so that the right could be exercised directly by the patient; and

3.  The surrogate must take care to assure that any limitations or conditions expressed either orally or in the written declaration have been carefully considered and satisfied.[298]

However, the court added that the "courts are always open to adjudicate legitimate questions pertaining to the written or oral instructions."[299]

The court also recognized that "interested parties" are entitled to use the courts to challenge the surrogate's decision, but only on the question of the patient's wishes. The reasons for such a challenge might include claims that:

- "the declaration was not executed knowingly, willingly, and without undue influence";
- "the patient had changed his or her mind after executing the declaration";
- "the declaration was ambiguous";
- "the conditions or limitations contained in the declaration were not satisfied";
- "the surrogate or proxy was [not] the one actually designated";
- "there was a reasonable probability that the patient would regain competency."[300]

---

[295] *Id.* at 925.

[296] *Id.* at 926. See § **10.23.**

[297] 568 So. 2d 4 (Fla. 1990).

[298] *Id.* at 15–16.

[299] **FL:** Browning v. Herbert, 568 So.2d at 16.

  **NY:** *Accord* A.B. v. C., 477 N.Y.S.2d 281, 284 (Sup. Ct. Schenectady County 1984) (if a declarant becomes incompetent, guardian could seek "judicial approval that no medical care or nourishment be given in accordance with [declarant's] stated wishes") (dictum).

[300] Browning v. Herbert, 568 So. 2d at 16.

Finally, "[w]hen the only evidence of intent is an oral declaration, the accuracy and reliability of the declarant's oral expression of intent also may be challenged."[301]

The only other reported case involving the application of a written advance directive is *In re Peter*,[302] in which the advance directive was a proxy directive rather than an instruction directive. Although the court did not specifically comment on the need for judicial review of advance directives, it held (consistent with other New Jersey cases) that judicial review is not necessary for the forgoing of life-sustaining treatment.[303] By implication, all of the cases applying oral advance directives and not requiring judicial review[304] are also authority for the view that there need not be judicial review of advance directives.

## § 10.27   Review Desirable

Judicial review of advance directives is desirable under the same conditions that make judicial review of other aspects of the decisionmaking process about life-sustaining treatment advisable.[305] The primary indicium of seeking judicial review of an advance directive is irreconcilable disagreement among participants in the decisionmaking process about whether the directive should be implemented.

Disagreement about implementing an advance directive may arise for a number of other reasons. First, there may be questions about the authenticity of a written instrument, such as whether it is a forgery or has been subjected to unauthorized alteration.[306] In the case of an oral advance directive, there may be analogous questions about whether the directive actually was given and about its content. For this reason it has been suggested, but never required, that judicial review should always be required in the absence of a written living will.[307] Whether the directive is written or oral, in a particular case there may be reason

---

[301] *Id.*

[302] 529 A.2d 419 (N.J. 1987).

[303] N.J. Stat. Ann. § 26:2H-66.a (codifying case law; "In the event of disagreement among the patient, health care representative, and attending physician concerning the patient's decision making capacity or the appropriate interpretation and application of the terms of an advance directive to the patient's course of treatment, the parties may seek to resolve the disagreement by means of procedures and practices established by the health care institution, including but not limited to, consultation with an institutional ethics committee, or with a person designated by the health care institution for this purpose or may seek resolution by a court of competent jurisdiction.").

[304] See **Ch. 8** and § **10.16.**

[305] See **Ch. 5.**

[306] See §§ **11.19** and **12.48.**

[307] **FL:** Browning v. Herbert, 568 So. 2d 4, 18 (Fla. 1990) (Overton, J., concurring and dissenting).

to question the voluntariness of the directive.[308] In cases in which an advance directive appoints a proxy but gives no instructions, there may also be reason to question the degree of knowledge that the proxy has of the declarant's wishes.[309]

Second, it may be uncertain whether general language of an advance directive, either written or oral, is intended to cover the facts of the patient's current medical situation. For example, when the declarant stated that he did not want any extraordinary treatment, did he mean to include the particular treatment now in question, such as a nasogastric tube? Or when a declarant designated a proxy through a durable power of attorney to make " 'all medical decisions' for her and 'to be given full and complete authority to manage and direct her medical care,' "[310] did she intend to include decisions to forgo life-sustaining treatment?

Third, there may be disagreement about whether a particular decision the directive clearly contemplates is legally permissible. A clear directive that a patient wishes not to be kept alive by tube-feeding, in a jurisdiction in which the case law has not yet considered whether it is legal to forgo artificial nutrition and hydration, might cause a great deal of concern among health care personnel despite the fact that authority in other jurisdictions overwhelmingly holds that the forgoing of artificial nutrition and hydration is to be treated the same as any other medical procedure. Another type of directive that might warrant recourse to the courts—though it could probably be safely ignored without seeking judicial review—is a directive requesting a clearly illegal act, such as affirmative intervention to end a patient's life.

Should any of these or other conditions create irresolvable disagreement between participants in the decisionmaking process, the attending physician or health care administrators should seriously consider seeking judicial review before abiding by an advance directive.[311] However, when none of these concerns exists, or when the law is reasonably clear that the action contemplated by

---

[308] *Id.* at 15 ("surrogate must be satisfied that the patient executed any document knowingly, willing, and without undue influence"). See **§ 3.18.**

[309] **NJ:** *In re* Jobes, 529 A.2d 419, 457 n.10 (N.J. 1987) (Handler, J., concurring) ("[I]t is not the mere signing over of authority that makes the resulting decision an expression of the patient's right of self-determination. It is important that the durable power of attorney was given by the patient to someone who knows her well.").

[310] **NJ:** *In re* Peter, 529 A.2d 419, 426 (N.J. 1987).

**NY:** *Accord In re* Westchester County Medical Ctr. (O'Connor), 531 N.E.2d 607, 615 (N.Y. 1987).

[311] *See, e.g.,* N.J. Stat. Ann. § 26:2H-66.a ("In the event of disagreement among the patient, health care representative, and attending physician concerning the patient's decision making capacity or the appropriate interpretation and application of the terms of an advance directive to the patient's course of treatment, the parties may seek to resolve the disagreement by means of procedures and practices established by the health care institution, including but not limited to, consultation with an institutional ethics committee, or with a person designated by the health care institution for this purpose or may seek resolution by a court of competent jurisdiction.").

the advance directive is permissible, the failure to abide by an advance directive could be grounds for liability for unauthorized treatment.[312]

## EVIDENTIARY CONSIDERATIONS

### § 10.28   Need for Evidentiary Rules

The mere existence of an advance directive does not mean that it should be blindly followed. This is especially so if the purported advance directive is oral and there are doubts about whether it was actually made or was intended to apply to the circumstances in question.[313] Few advance directives automatically resolve all the major issues of decisionmaking. Whether implemented purely in the clinical setting or with some judicial oversight, a number of evidentiary rules are necessary to guide those who must interpret and apply the terms of advance directives. Courts have only occasionally addressed these concerns, and therefore lawyers, whether in the litigation process or in counseling health care clients, should be guided by established rules of evidence when the courts have been silent on these issues in the context of advance directives.[314]

The need for evidentiary rules is perhaps greater when an advance directive is enforced in the clinical setting than it is in a court because in the latter, the judge can be assumed to know and apply rules of evidence. Perhaps with this in mind, the Florida Supreme Court in *Browning v. Herbert,*[315] set forth a number of evidentiary rules to be followed in the clinical implementation of advance directives so that there need not be routine recourse to the courts, yet there can be an assurance of accurate and reliable decisionmaking:

Before exercising the incompetent's right to forego treatment, the surrogate must satisfy the following conditions:

  1. The surrogate must be satisfied that the patient executed any document knowingly, willing, and without undue influence, and that the evidence of the patient's oral declarations is reliable;

---

[312] See **Ch. 17.**

[313] **NJ:** *See, e.g.,* McVey v. Englewood Hosp. Ass'n, 524 A.2d 450 (N.J. Super. Ct. App. Div. 1987).

  **NY:** *See, e.g., In re* Westchester County Medical Ctr. (O'Connor), 531 N.E.2d 607 (N.Y. 1988).

[314] *See generally* Gorby, *Admissibility and Weighing Evidence of Intent in Right to Die Cases,* 6 Issues L. & Med. 33 (1990).

[315] 568 So. 2d 4 (Fla. 1990).

2. The surrogate must be assured that the patient does not have a reasonable probability of recovering competency so that the right could be exercised directly by the patient; and

3. The surrogate must take care to assure that any limitations or conditions expressed either orally or in the written declaration have been carefully considered and satisfied.[316]

Further, when decisionmaking is to be made by a proxy designated by the patient but without explicit instructions from the patient, the proxy must satisfy the following conditions:

1. The proxy must be satisfied that the patient executed the written designation of proxy knowingly, willingly, and without undue influence; and

2. The proxy must be assured that the patient does not have a reasonable probability of recovering competency so that the right could be exercised directly by the patient.[317]

## § 10.29   Relevance

From an early position of distrusting statements patients were said to have made while competent,[318] most courts now exhibit a willingness to admit such evidence,[319] subject to the caution that its probative value may vary. It is now generally acknowledged, as the Washington Supreme Court has held, that "prior statements may be probative in determining the wishes of an incompetent patient, with the age and maturity of the patient, the context of the statements, and the connection of the statements to the debilitating event being factors to be weighed by the guardian."[320] The holdings of those courts that have rested their decisions to permit the forgoing of life-sustaining medical treatment on advance

---

[316] *Id.* at 15.

[317] *Id.* at 15–16.

[318] **NJ:** *See In re* Quinlan, 355 A.2d 647, 653 (N.J. 1976) (statements were "remote and impersonal" and therefore lacking in probative weight).

**NY:** *See In re* Westchester County Medical Ctr. (O'Connor), 531 N.E.2d 607, 613 (N.Y. 1988) ("[T]here always exists the possibility that, despite his or her clear expressions in the past, the patient has since changed his or her mind.").

[319] **MO:** *But see* Cruzan v. Harmon, 760 S.W.2d 408 (Mo. 1988).

**NY:** *In re* Westchester County Medical Ctr. (O'Connor), 531 N.E.2d at 612 (oral statements must be "solemn pronouncements and not casual remarks").

[320] **WA:** *In re* Colyer, 660 P.2d 738, 740 (Wash. 1983). *Accord In re* Grant, 747 P.2d 445, 457 (Wash. 1987).

**NJ:** *Accord In re* Conroy, 486 A.2d 1209, 1230 (N.J. 1985).

directives, whether written or oral, are authority for the relevance of advance directives in general in end-of-life decisionmaking.[321]

Any evidence that will shed light on what the incompetent patient would choose if he were able to do so is relevant to the decisionmaking process.[322] This is true whether decisionmaking takes place in a clinical or judicial forum.[323] However, some varieties of the subjective standard are extremely exacting,[324] and thus evidence that is "remote, general, spontaneous, and made in casual circumstances" may not be satisfactory under this standard.[325] If an objective standard is applied, the surrogate may consider evidence that "would be too vague, casual, or remote to constitute the clear proof of the patient's subjective intent that is necessary to satisfy the subjective test—for example, informally expressed reactions to other people's medical conditions and treatment."[326]

## § 10.30   Probative Value (Weight)

The *relevance* of information goes only to the issue of whether it should be taken into account in the decisionmaking process. However, regardless of whether the decisionmaking process takes place exclusively in a clinical setting or is also subject to judicial oversight, consideration must be given to how much probative value or *weight* should be accorded the evidence. A written instruction directive should be given "great weight"[327] because it is "evidence of the most

---

[321] See §§ 10.10–10.16.

[322] **NJ:** *In re* Conroy, 486 A.2d at 1230 ("[A]ll evidence tending to demonstrate a person's intent with respect to medical treatment should properly be considered.").

**NY:** *But see In re* Westchester County Medical Ctr. (O'Connor), 531 N.E.2d at 612 (oral statements must be "solemn pronouncements and not casual remarks").

**WA:** *In re* Colyer, 660 P.2d at 748.

[323] **NJ:** *In re* Conroy, 486 A.2d at 1230 (such evidence may be considered "by surrogate decision-makers, or by a court in the event of judicial proceedings").

**NY:** Saunders v. State, 492 N.Y.S.2d 510, 517 (Sup. Ct. Nassau County 1985) ("The document executed by the petitioner . . . should be given great weight by the hospital authorities *and treating physicians* attending her.") (emphasis added).

[324] See § 7.6.

[325] **NJ:** *In re* Jobes, 529 A.2d 419, 443 (N.J. 1987).

**MO:** *Accord* Cruzan v. Harmon, 760 S.W.2d 408, 424 (Mo. 1988).

**NY:** *Accord In re* Westchester County Medical Ctr. (O'Connor), 531 N.E.2d 607.

[326] *In re* Conroy, 486 A.2d at 1232.

[327] **FL:** John F. Kennedy Memorial Hosp. v. Bludworth, 452 So. 2d 921, 926 (Fla. 1994), *rev'g* John F. Kennedy Memorial Hosp. v. Bludworth, 432 So. 2d 611, 620 (Fla. Dist. Ct. App. 1983) (living will "shall be given such weight . . . as the trial court deems appropriate having considered the timeliness of its execution, the circumstances under which it was executed, its contents and any evidence of a contrary intention"). *Accord* Browning v. Herbert, 568 So. 2d 4, 16 (Fla. 1990) ("written declaration or designation of proxy, in the absence of any evidence of intent to the contrary, establishes a rebuttable presumption that constitutes clear and convincing evidence of the patient's wishes").

**NY:** *Accord* Saunders v. State, 492 N.Y.S.2d 510, 517 (Sup. Ct. Nassau County 1985).

persuasive quality."[328] Oral advance directives are also "probative in determining the wishes of an incompetent patient."[329] In addition to considering the patient's oral or written directive, courts consider other information relevant to determining the patient's wishes.[330] For example, in *McConnell v. Beverly Enterprises-Connecticut, Inc.,*[331] the Connecticut Supreme Court considered the patient's work experience as a nurse caring for brain-damaged patients in addition to her oral statement that she would never want to be kept alive in a persistent vegetative state.

The probative value of an advance directive is affected by a number of factors, such as the consistency of the declarant's views,[332] the maturity of the declarant at the time the advance directive was issued,[333] the specificity of the declaration,[334] how long ago the declaration was made,[335] and the "thoughtfulness" or seriousness of the declarant in making the statements.

> Thus, for example, an offhand remark about not wanting to live under certain circumstances made by a person when young and in the peak of health would not in itself constitute clear proof twenty years later that he would want life-sustaining treatment withheld under those circumstances. In contrast, a carefully considered position, especially if written, that a person had maintained over a number of years or that he had acted upon in comparable circumstances might be clear evidence of his intent.[336]

---

[328] Saunders v. State, 492 N.Y.S.2d at 517.

[329] **WA:** *In re* Colyer, 660 P.2d 738, 748 (Wash. 1983).

**FL:** *Accord* Browning v. Herbert, 568 So. 2d at 15.

**ME:** *But see In re* Gardner, 534 A.2d 947, 957 (Me. 1987) (Clifford, J., dissenting) ("The court relied in large measure upon Gardner's active life-style in finding that he would want the feeding tube removed. That type of evidence, if offered to support a decision of informed consent, would be woefully inadequate. It is all the more inadequate to support a refusal that will result in certain death.").

See § **10.16.**

[330] **FL:** Browning v. Herbert, 543 So. 2d 258, 272 (Fla. Dist. Ct. App. 1989), *aff'd,* 568 So. 2d 4 (Fla. 1990) ("The surrogate may also consider character evidence from close family members and friends which is relevant concerning the decision the patient would have made under these circumstances."). *See also* National Ctr. for State Courts, Guidelines for State Court Decision Making in Life-Sustaining Medical Treatment Cases 81–82 (2d ed. 1992) (standard 13).

[331] 553 A.2d 596 (Conn. 1989).

[332] **MI:** Martin v. Martin, 504 N.W.2d 917, 923 n.3 (Mich. Ct. App. 1993).

**NJ:** *In re* Jobes, 529 A.2d 419, 443 n.8 (N.J. 1987); *In re* Conroy, 486 A.2d 1209, 1230 (N.J. 1985).

[333] **MI:** Martin v. Martin, 504 N.W.2d at 923 n.3.

**NJ:** *In re* Jobes, 529 A.2d at 443 n.8; *In re* Conroy, 486 A.2d at 1230.

[334] See § **10.31.**

[335] See § **10.32.**

[336] *In re* Conroy, 486 A.2d at 1230.

When the advance directive is oral, even if it is assumed that witnesses are acting in the best of faith, there is still a need to be concerned about their ability to recall what was said.[337]

## § 10.31 —Specificity of the Directive

*Specificity* refers to the degree to which statements that the declarant made before losing decisionmaking capacity relate to his current medical situation. The specificity of an advance directive affects its probative value.[338] The more specific an advance directive is, the greater its weight; the more general a patient's statements, the less probative value ought to be accorded to them.[339] Thus, "any details about the level of impaired functioning and the forms of medical treatment that one would find tolerable should be incorporated into advance directives to enhance their later usefulness as evidence."[340]

For example, an instruction directive, either written or oral, in which a patient states that he does not want any "extraordinary treatment" is of less probative value than a directive in which a patient states that he would not wish to be kept alive in a persistent vegetative state on a ventilator. In the *Eichner* case, in which the patient had specifically stated that he would not "want any of this 'extraordinary business' done for him under those circumstances," and had repeated it only a few months before his final hospitalization in a context in which the court could see that these were "obviously solemn pronouncements and not casual remarks," the court found the proof of the declarant's intent compelling.[341] Similarly, in a proxy directive, the declarant should specifically

---

[337] **FL:** *Cf.* Browning v. Herbert, 568 So. 2d 4, 16 (Fla. 1990) (surrogate may rely on oral statements but "presumption of clear and convincing evidence that attaches to a written declaration does not attach to purely oral declarations").

**NJ:** *In re* Jobes, 529 A.2d at 442 n.7 (testimony of witnesses "should be treated with suspicion because of the length of time that had elapsed since the time of the conversations and because post-event information could have affected their memories").

[338] **NJ:** *In re* Conroy, 486 A.2d 1209, 1230 (N.J. 1985).

[339] **MI:** Martin v. Martin, 504 N.W.2d 917, 923 n.3 (Mich. Ct. App. 1993).

**NJ:** *In re* Conroy, 486 A.2d at 1231 n.7 (probative value may vary depending on the "thoughtfulness" of prior statements).

**NY:** Eichner v. Dillon, 420 N.E.2d 64, 72 (N.Y. 1981) (oral directive enforceable where "[w]hat occurred to [declarant] was identical to what happened in the Karen Ann Quinlan case, which had originally prompted his decision").

**WA:** *In re* Colyer, 660 P.2d 738, 748 (Wash. 1983) ("[P]rior statements may be probative in determining the wishes of an incompetent patient, with . . . the connection of the statements to the debilitating event being factors to be weighed by the guardian.").

[340] *In re* Conroy, 486 A.2d at 1230–31.

[341] Eichner v. Dillon, 420 N.E.2d at 72.

authorize the proxy to forgo life-sustaining treatment in appropriate circumstances and, even better, specify those circumstances.[342]

Nonetheless, general statements are relevant and should be given due consideration by the patient's attending physician in the clinical setting or by the courts. A durable power of attorney appointing a proxy and authorizing him "to make 'all medical decisions' for her and 'to be given full and complete authority to manage and direct her medical care' "[343] is possibly too general to permit by itself the forgoing of life-sustaining treatment. However, in conjunction with the proxy's explanation of the declarant's oral directions to refuse life-sustaining treatment on her behalf in a situation such as the current one and with other reliable evidence of the declarant's disinclination for the kind of treatment sought to be forgone, life-sustaining treatment has been discontinued.[344]

In advance directives, declarants should be as specific as possible both about the level of impairment and about the forms of treatment that they wish to avoid.[345] However, there is a danger in making them so specific that the directive will not apply to the circumstances that actually exist. One may state in a living will that one wishes not to be kept alive in a persistent vegetative state on a feeding tube. Such a statement is not necessarily useful, however, if one is instead in a locked-in state being kept alive by a feeding tube.[346] A court could liberally construe such a directive as a general prohibition[347] on the use of feeding tubes, thereby finding that artificial nutrition and hydration should be terminated. However, such an interpretation in this and analogous situations is not a certainty. Another reasonable interpretation is that the declarant did not wish to be kept alive in a state in which he has no cognition and awareness of the environment but would not necessarily object if cognition might be intact and experience of the environment possible, even if he could not communicate

---

[342] **NJ:** *In re* Peter, 529 A.2d 419, 426 (N.J. 1987) ("It would have been better if Ms. Peter had specifically provided in her power of attorney . . . the authority to terminate life-sustaining treatment.").

[343] *Id.*

[344] *Id.* n.7.

[345] **NJ:** *In re* Conroy, 486 A.2d at 1230–31. *See also In re* Peter, 529 A.2d at 426 ("The best evidence is a 'living will,' a written statement that *specifically* explains the patients preferences about life sustaining treatment.") (emphasis added).

[346] **ME:** *See, e.g., In re* Gardner, 534 A.2d 947 (Me. 1987).

**MA:** *See, e.g.,* Brophy v. New Eng. Sinai Hosp., Inc., 497 N.E.2d 626 (Mass. 1986).

[347] **NY:** *But see In re* Westchester County Medical Ctr. (O'Connor), 531 N.E.2d 607 (N.Y. 1988) (prior oral statements too general to construe as authorizing cessation of artificial nutrition and hydration).

**OH:** Estate of Leach v. Shapiro, 469 N.E.2d 1047, 1053 (Ohio Ct. App. 1984) (general statements by a patient can be considered by a court).

with others.[348] Advance directives can and should be drafted to minimize these problems.[349]

## § 10.32 —Remoteness of Execution of the Directive

An advance directive can be a two-edged sword. If it is too specific in identifying the kinds of treatment to be forgone or the conditions for which treatment should not be administered, patients may receive other treatments they would have declined if they had given consideration to them or if they had the present capacity to forgo them. On the other hand, if an advance directive is too general, it may result in the forgoing of treatment that the patient would have wanted administered or the administration of treatment that the patient would have forgone.

A similar problem can arise from temporal factors. If the directive was made years before the time it is sought to be implemented, a variety of factors may be different from those the declarant contemplated at the time of declaration.[350] These factors fall into two general categories: changes in the declarant's life circumstances and changes in the forms of medical treatment.

Objective circumstances of an individual's life change over time. Marriage, the birth of children, a change in economic well-being, and similar circumstances may lead to a change in attitude about the kinds of treatment that an individual would wish to have. In addition, the mere passage of time—the processes of maturation and aging—may lead to a change in attitude about the conditions under which one might wish to live or die.

Medical practice is also subject to constant change. Particular diseases viewed as hopeless at the time an advance directive was made may not be fatal when the declarant is later being treated for that illness. New treatments may be developed that reduce the burdens of a particular illness or that are themselves less burdensome than previous treatments for that illness. Thus, because of changing circumstances, a person's will expressed today may not be the same tomorrow.[351] And the greater the time between the advance directive and its implementation,

---

[348] **MI:** *Cf.* Martin v. Martin, 504 N.W.2d 917 (Mich. Ct. App. 1993).

[349] See **Ch. 13.**

[350] **FL:** Browning v. Herbert, 568 So. 2d 4, 13 (Fla. 1990) (state's argument that patient might have changed her mind after executing advance directive rejected because "human limitations preclude absolute knowledge of the wishes of someone" who is permanently unconscious).

**NY:** *In re* Westchester County Medical Ctr. (O'Connor), 531 N.E.2d 607, 613 (N.Y. 1988) ("[T]he trier of fact must be convinced, as far as is humanly possible, that the strength of the individual's beliefs and the durability of the individual's commitment to those beliefs . . . makes a recent change of heart unlikely.").

[351] **NY:** *In re* Westchester County Medical Ctr. (O'Connor), 531 N.E.2d at 614 ("human beings are not capable of foreseeing either their own medical condition or advances in medical technology").

the greater is the uncertainty about whether the earlier desire and the current one are identical.

The courts have had little occasion to address this issue. A few have stated in dictum that the temporal remoteness of a document should affect its probative value.[352] However, this is merely one factor to be weighed by the surrogate decisionmaker[353] rather than a matter rendering the directive irrelevant. It is to be weighed along with related factors, such as "the age and maturity of the patient [when the declaration was made], the context of the statements, and the connection of the statements to the debilitating event."[354]

## § 10.33 Hearsay Exception

Instruction directives, whether written or oral, are hearsay and thus technically inadmissible in judicial proceedings unless they fall within one of the recognized exceptions to the hearsay rule. Some courts have found that instruction directives are admissible under the exception for the declarant's "existing state of mind."[355]

An example is the patient's statement in the *Eichner* case "that he personally would not want any of this 'extraordinary business' done for him under such circumstances."[356] This statement was admitted to show the patient's state of

---

[352] **FL:** Browning v. Herbert, 543 So. 2d 258, 271 (Fla. Dist. Ct. App. 1989), *aff'd*, 568 So. 2d 4 (Fla. 1990) ("When the surrogate decisionmaker decides to forego life-sustaining treatment, he or she must have adequate, up-to-date evidence."); John F. Kennedy Memorial Hosp. v. Bludworth, 432 So. 2d 611, 620 (Fla. Dist. Ct. App. 1983) (weight to be accorded a living will should take into account, among other things, "timeliness of its execution").

    **MI:** Martin v. Martin, 504 N.W.2d 917, 923 n.3 (Mich. Ct. App. 1993).

    **NJ:** *In re* Conroy, 486 A.2d 1209, 1230 (N.J. 1985); *In re* Clark, 510 A.2d 136, 143 (N.J. Super. Ct. Ch. Div. 1986) (oral statement, in addition to being vague, was made five years ago and is remote and unenforceable).

    **WA:** *In re* Colyer, 660 P.2d 738, 748 (Wash. 1983).

[353] **MI:** *Cf.* Martin v. Martin, 504 N.W.2d at 923 n.3 ("A nonexclusive list of factors that may be considered in evaluating the weight and probative value of other evidence of a person's medical treatment preferences include: the remoteness . . . of the person's prior statements or actions.").

    **WA:** *In re* Colyer, 660 P.2d at 748.

[354] *In re* Colyer, 660 P.2d at 758.

[355] **KY:** DeGrella v. Elston, 858 S.W.2d 698, 709 (Ky. 1993) (oral statement by patient prior to losing decisionmaking capacity "falls within the parameters of the exception to the hearsay rule now codified in the Kentucky Rules of Evidence, KRE 803(3), recognizing the admissibility of a 'statement of the declarant's then existing state of mind, emotion, sensation, or physical condition" where relevant to the issue at hand'").

    **NJ:** *In re* Conroy, 486 A.2d 1209, 1230 n.6 (N.J. 1985).

    **NY:** Eichner v. Dillon, 426 N.Y.S.2d 517, 547 (App. Div. 1980).

[356] *In re* Eichner, 423 N.Y.S.2d 580, 586 (Sup. Ct. Nassau County 1979), *aff'd*, 426 N.Y.S.2d 517 (App. Div. 1980), *modified*, 420 N.E.2d 64 (N.Y. 1981).

mind about extraordinary treatment rather than to show that he would not in fact agree to such treatment if he were in that condition, which would be prohibited by the hearsay rule because it would tend to show the truth of the matter asserted in the statement.

However, in this sort of situation, the "truth of the matter asserted" and the declarant's "state of mind" are essentially identical. The issue to which this statement was relevant was whether the patient's extraordinary treatment should be discontinued. The substantive law allowed treatment to be discontinued only if the patient would have consented to its discontinuance had he been competent to do so.[357] The reason his statement was sought to be introduced was to show what he would have decided about continuing or discontinuing treatment. The statement "I would not want any of this 'extraordinary business' done for me" did provide evidence of the declarant's state of mind—that is, that he did not believe in extraordinary treatment under certain circumstances—but it also tended to prove the truth of the matter asserted, namely, that he would not want such treatment himself. Indeed, if it had not been probative of the ultimate issue (his wishes), it would not have provided the clear and convincing evidence that the New York courts require for forgoing life-sustaining treatment for incompetent patients, but would merely have constituted casual, offhand remarks.[358]

Irrespective of the technicalities of evidence law, the hearsay rule has not proved to be a barrier to the admissibility of advance directives, in part because of the general trend toward a liberal view of the admissibility of "reliable" hearsay.[359] A declaration of state of mind provides a special assurance of reliability because of its spontaneity and probable sincerity. McCormick states that "[t]his has been assured by the requirements that the statements must purport to relate to a condition of mind or emotion existing at the time of the statement and, as sometimes stated, must have been made under circumstances indicating apparent sincerity."[360]

A court should consider an advance directive, even if hearsay, because it is relevant to "shed light on whether a patient would consent to or refuse treatment."[361] Courts have even been willing to consider "double hearsay." For

---

[357] Eichner v. Dillon, 420 N.E.2d 64 (N.Y. 1981).

[358] *See In re* Westchester County Medical Ctr. (O'Connor), 531 N.E.2d 607, 612 (N.Y. 1988).

[359] McCormick on Evidence § 245, at 728–29 (E. Cleary ed., 3d ed. 1984).

[360] *Id.* § 294, at 844.

[361] **NJ:** *In re* Peter, 529 A.2d 419, 426 n.8 (N.J. 1987). *Accord In re* Conroy, 486 A.2d 1209, 1230 (N.J. 1985) ("all evidence tending to demonstrate a person's intent with respect to medical treatment should properly be considered by surrogate decision-makers, or by a court in the event of judicial proceedings").

**NY:** Saunders v. State, 492 N.Y.S.2d 510, 517 (Sup. Ct. Nassau County 1985) ("The document executed by the petitioner . . . should be given great weight by the hospital authorities and treating physicians attending her.").

example, in *Peter,* the New Jersey Supreme Court took into account oral statements that the patient had made that were reported in interviews the Ombudsman had with participants in these conversations.[362] In so doing, it belatedly rejected the state's objection in *Quinlan* to the admission of statements Karen Quinlan reputedly made prior to becoming incompetent that such evidence was inadmissible hearsay.[363]

The same is true of parol evidence. Under a strict application of the parol evidence rule, when a written advance directive exists, there should be limited, if any, oral evidence admitted to explain it. This has not been the case, however, in end-of-life decisionmaking cases. For example, the written living will involved in *Browning*[364] was ambiguous, and the court permitted the admission of oral evidence to clarify it. The Florida Supreme Court observed that "[e]specially when the language of the living will is prepared by a third party, parol evidence should be considered to understand the true intent of the patient."[365]

Given the receptive attitude of courts toward advance directives and the holdings refusing to find the hearsay rule to be a barrier to their consideration, there is even less reason to be concerned about the fact that advance directives are hearsay when the clinical approach to decisionmaking is used.

## § 10.34  Standard of Proof

As is so with most other matters needed to be proved in a right-to-die case,[366] the courts generally agree that an advance directive must be proved by clear and convincing evidence.[367] Thus,

---

[362] *In re* Peter, 529 A.2d at 426 n.9.

[363] *See In re* Quinlan, 355 A.2d 647, 653 (N.J. 1976) (court declined to consider whether statements were admissible, because even if admissible they "lacked significant probative weight").

[364] Browning v. Herbert, 543 So. 2d 258 (Fla. Dist. Ct. App. 1989), *aff'd,* 568 So. 2d 4 (Fla. 1990).

[365] **FL:** Browning v. Herbert, 543 So. 2d at 272.

**US:** *But cf.* Cruzan v. Director, 497 U.S. 261, 284 (1990) (parol evidence rule bars evidence to vary the terms of a written contract by oral testimony, and statute of frauds makes unenforceable oral contracts to leave property by will).

[366] Elbaum v. Grace Plaza of Great Neck, Inc., 544 N.Y.S.2d 840, 843–44 (App. Div. 1989).

[367] **CT:** McConnell v. Beverly Enters.-Conn., Inc., 553 A.2d 596, 604 (Conn. 1989).

**FL:** John F. Kennedy Memorial Hosp. v. Bludworth, 432 So. 2d 611, 620 (Fla. Dist. Ct. App. 1983). *Cf.* Browning v. Herbert, 543 So. 2d 258, 273 (Fla. Dist. Ct. App. 1989), *aff'd,* 568 So. 2d 4, 15 (Fla. 1990).

**ME:** *In re* Gardner, 534 A.2d 947, 953 (Me. 1987).

**NJ:** *In re* Peter, 529 A.2d 419, 425 (N.J. 1987); *In re* Conroy, 486 A.2d 1209, 1242–43 (N.J. 1985).

a general statement . . . in which someone may have said . . . in writing merely that he would not want to be "artificially sustained" by "heroic measures" if his condition was "hopeless," or that he would not want to have doctors applying life-sustaining procedures "that would serve only to artificially prolong the dying process" if he were "terminally ill" . . . might not in itself provide clear guidance to a surrogate decision-maker in all situations.[368]

When this standard has been met, oral advance directives have been implemented.[369] However, when "the proofs do not meet a standard clear enough to have the probative weight sufficient to convince the court that [the patient], in full command of the facts, would favor death," relief has been denied.[370] Thus, a trial court's finding that the testimony of the patient's husband, sister, son, and daughter about six different occasions on which the patient evidenced a desire not to have life-sustaining treatment did not meet the clear and convincing standard was reversed.[371]

---

**NY:** *In re* Westchester County Medical Ctr. (O'Connor), 531 N.E.2d 607, 612 (N.Y. 1988) ("Nothing less than unequivocal proof will suffice when the decision to terminate life support is at issue."); Eichner v. Dillon, 420 N.E.2d 64, 72 (N.Y. 1981); Workmen's Circle Home & Infirmary for the Aged v. Fink, 514 N.Y.S.2d 893, 895 (Sup. Ct. Bronx County, N.Y. 1987); Saunders v. State, 492 N.Y.S.2d 510, 517 (Sup. Ct. Nassau County 1985); *In re* Lydia E. Hall Hosp., 455 N.Y.S.2d 706, 712 (Sup. Ct. Nassau County 1982).

**PA:** Pocono Medical Ctr. v. Harley, 11 Fiduc. Rep. 2d 128 (C.P. Monroe County, Pa. 1990) (by implication); *In re* E.L.K., 11 Fiduc. Rep. 2d 78, 82–83 (C.P. Berks County, Pa. 1991) (by implication) ("hypothetical discussion" with friend in which patient said she did not want to be kept alive by artificial means, "occurring prior to her illness when the need for such a decision was not on the horizon," in combination with fact that when patient did become ill and "was presented with the question, she had no answer" and "informed her physician that she wanted to discuss the matter with a rabbi" is not sufficient proof of patient's intent to refuse cardiopulmonary resuscitation); Ragona v. Preate, 11 Fiduc. Rep. 2d 1 (C.P. Lackawanna County, Pa. 1990).

[368] **NJ:** *In re* Conroy, 486 A.2d at 1231 n.7.

**NY:** *Accord In re* Westchester County Medical Ctr. (O'Connor), 531 N.E.2d 607 (N.Y. 1988).

[369] **NJ:** *In re* Quinlan, 355 A.2d 647 (N.J. 1976).

**NY:** *See, e.g.,* Elbaum v. Grace Plaza of Great Neck, Inc., 544 N.Y.S.2d 840 (App. Div. 1989); Eichner v. Dillon, 420 N.E.2d 64 (N.Y. 1981).

[370] **NJ:** *In re* Quinlan, 348 A.2d 801, 822 (N.J. Super. Ct. Ch. Div. 1975).

**MO:** *Accord* Cruzan v. Harmon, 760 S.W.2d 408 (Mo. 1988).

**NY:** *Accord In re* Westchester County Medical Ctr. (O'Connor), 531 N.E.2d 607.

[371] **NY:** *See* Elbaum v. Grace Plaza of Great Neck, Inc., 544 N.Y.S.2d 840. *But cf. In re* Westchester County Medical Ctr. (O'Connor), 531 N.E.2d 607 (testimony of several family members that patient made statements over the course of several years that she would not want treatment do not constitute clear and convincing evidence of her wish not to be kept alive by artificial nutrition and hydration).

**PA:** *See also* Ragona v. Preate, 11 Fiduc. Rep. 2d 1, 8 (C.P. Lackawanna County, Pa. 1990) (testimony by patient's husband and son regarding patient's conduct and statements over six-year period constituted clear and convincing evidence of her wish not to be kept alive in persistent vegetative state by artificial nutrition and hydration).

Although ordinarily a preponderance of evidence standard is applied in civil cases, such a standard is inappropriate in cases involving "life-or-death issues and in . . . instances involv[ing] personal interests more important than those found in the typical civil dispute where private litigants squabble over a sum of money."[372] This is appropriate to ensure that any errors that might occur favor life.[373] It "requires proof sufficient to persuade the trier of fact that the patient held a firm and settled commitment to the termination of life supports under the circumstances like those presented."[374] Furthermore, requiring proof of an advance directive by clear and convincing evidence does not contravene the Fourteenth Amendment's guarantee of liberty.[375] In jurisdictions requiring that the subjective standard of surrogate decisionmaking be met, it is unclear whether or not "only a living will or equivalently formal directive" will satisfy the clear and convincing evidence standard.[376] It should be recalled, however, that the "clear and convincing evidence" standard is a *standard of proof* and not a substantive standard for determining when it is legal to forgo life-sustaining treatment. As a standard of proof, it can be applied to the highest standard for forgoing life-sustaining treatment, namely, the subjective standard requiring proof of the patient's actual intent, but it can also be applied to the other, more easily satisfied, substituted judgment and best interests standards.[377]

The argument has been made that because the granting of relief may result in the patient's death, the higher *reasonable doubt* standard of proof should be utilized.[378] It has been rejected on the ground that such a standard is "traditionally reserved for criminal cases where involuntary loss of liberty and possible stigmatization are at issue . . . and is inappropriate in cases where the purpose of granting the relief is to give effect to an individual's right by carrying out his stated intentions."[379]

---

[372] Eichner v. Dillon, 420 N.E.2d 64, 72 (N.Y. 1981). *Accord In re* Westchester County Medical Ctr. (O'Connor), 531 N.E.2d at 614 n.4 ("[I]t cannot be seriously urged that it would be 'unrealistic' for the law to accord the same protections to the individual's life and right to survive, as have long been accorded to the individual's land and pocketbook.").

[373] **NY:** *In re* Westchester County Medical Ctr. (O'Connor), 531 N.E.2d at 613.

[374] **DNY:** *In re* Department of Veterans Affairs Medical Ctr., 749 F. Supp. 495 (S.D.N.Y.), *aff'd,* 914 F.2d 239 (2d Cir. 1990) (wife's claim that husband had said while competent that he would not want amputation is not credible because of wife's hostility toward doctors and because of her denial of the severity of husband's illness).

   **NY:** *In re* Westchester County Medical Ctr. (O'Connor), 531 N.E.2d at 613.

[375] **US:** Cruzan v. Director, 497 U.S. 261 (1990).

[376] *Id.* at 323 (Brennan, J., dissenting) (citing Cruzan v. Harmon, 760 S.W.2d 408, 424–25 (Mo. 1988)).

[377] See §§ **5.61–5.62.**

[378] **KY:** DeGrella v. Elston, 858 S.W.2d 698, 716 (Ky. 1993) (Wintersheimer, J., dissenting).

   **NY:** Eichner v. Dillon, 420 N.E.2d at 72 (rejecting state's argument that beyond-reasonable-doubt standard is required).

[379] Eichner v. Dillon, 420 N.E.2d at 72 (citing Addington v. Texas, 441 U.S. 418 (1979)).

The Florida Supreme Court, although insisting that the clear and convincing evidence standard be met, has held that "a written declaration or designation of proxy, in the absence of any evidence of intent to the contrary, establishes a rebuttable presumption that constitutes clear and convincing evidence of the patient's wishes."[380] Although oral evidence alone can satisfy the clear and convincing evidence standard, no presumption attaches to oral evidence, and the surrogate must "bear the burden of proof if a decision based on purely oral evidence is challenged."[381]

---

[380] Browning v. Herbert, 568 So. 2d 4, 16 (Fla. 1990).

[381] *Id.*

# Bibliography

Alexander, G. "Death by Directive." *Santa Clara Law Review* 28 (1988): 87.

American Bar Association Commission on Legal Problems of the Elderly, *Patient Self-Determination Act State Law Guide.* Washington: American Bar Association Commission on Legal Problems of the Elderly, 1991.

Barnett, T. *Living Wills and More—Everything You Need to Know to Ensure That All Your Medical Wishes Are Followed.* New York: John Wiley & Sons, Inc., 1993.

Cantor, N. *Advance Directives and the Pursuit of Death.* Bloomington: Indiana University Press, 1993.

Cate, F., and B. Gill. *The Patient Self-Determination Act: Implementation Issues and Opportunities.* Washington: Annenberg Washington Program, 1991.

Condie, C. Comment. "Comparison of the Living Will Statutes of the Fifty States." *Journal of Contemporary Law* 14 (1988): 105.

Doukas, D. and W. Reichel. *Planning for Uncertainty—A Guide to Living Wills and Other Advance Directives for Health Care.* Baltimore: Johns Hopkins University Press, 1993.

Emergency Medical Services Committee. American College of Emergency Physicians. "Guidelines for 'Do Not Resuscitate' Orders in the Prehospital Setting." *Annals of Emergency Medicine* 17 (1988): 1106.

Francis, L. "The Evanescence of Living Wills." *Journal of Contemporary Law* 14 (1988): 27.

Gelfand, G. "Living Will Statutes: The First Decade." *Wisconsin Law Review,* 1987, no. 5: 737.

Hackler, C., et al. *Advance Directives in Medicine.* New York: Praeger, 1989.

Iserson, K. "Foregoing Prehospital Care: Should Ambulance Staff Always Resuscitate?" *Journal of Medical Ethics* 17 (1991): 19.

King, N. *Making Sense of Advance Directives.* Boston: Kluwer Academic Publishers, 1991.

Kutner, L. "Euthanasia: Due Process for Death with Dignity; The Living Will." *Indiana Law Journal* 54 (1979): 201.

Lieberson, A. *Advance Medical Directives.* Deerfield, IL: Clark Boardman Callaghan, 1992.

Marzen, T. "The 'Uniform Rights of the Terminally Ill Act': A Critical Analysis." *Issues in Law and Medicine* 1 (1986): 441.

McCarrick, P. Living Wills and Durable Powers of Attorney: Advance Directive Legislation and Issues, scope note 2 (annotated bibliography of advance directives). (National Reference Center for Bioethics Literature, Kennedy Institute of Ethics, Georgetown University, 1991.

New Jersey Commission on Legal and Ethical Problems in the Delivery of Health Care. *The New Jersey Advance Directives for Health Care Act: A Guidebook for Health Care Professionals.* Trenton: New Jersey Bioethics Commission, 1992.

New Jersey Commission on Legal and Ethical Problems in the Delivery of Health Care. *The New Jersey Advance Directives for Health Care and Declaration of Death Acts: Statutes, Commentaries and Analyses.* Trenton: New Jersey Bioethics Commission, 1991.

New York State Task Force on Life and the Law. *Life-Sustaining Treatment: Making Decisions and Appointing a Health Care Agent.* New York: New York State Task Force on Life and the Law, 1987.

Redleaf, D. Note. "California Natural Death Act: An Empirical Study of Physicians' Practices." *Stanford Law Review* 31 (1979): 913.

Refolo, M. Comment. "The Patient Self-Determination Act of 1990: Health Care's Own Miranda." *Journal of Contemporary Health Law and Policy* 8 (1992): 455.

Sabatino, C., and V. Gottlich. "Seeking Self-Determination in the Patient Self-Determination Act." *Clearinghouse Review* 25 (1991): 639.

Sachs, G. "Emergencies and Advance Directives." *Hastings Center Report* 20 (November–December 1989): 42.

Shugrue, R. "The Patient Self-Determination Act." *Creighton Law Review* 26 (1993): 751.

Stoll, K. *Pregnancy Exclusions in State Living Will and Medical Proxy Statutes.* Washington, DC: Centre for Women Policy Studies.

Thomas, K. *Treatment and Appointment Directives: Living Wills, Powers of Attorney, and Other Advance Medical Care Documents,* No. 91-87A. Congressional Research Service, 1991.

Zinberg, J. "Decisions for the Dying: An Empirical Study of Physicians' Responses to Advance Directives." *Vermont Law Review* 13 (1989): 445.

# CHAPTER 11

# STATUTORY LIVING WILLS

## § 11.1  Purpose

Beginning with California in 1976,[1] almost all states have enacted living will statutes. See **Table 11–1** in **§ 11.22.** These statutes are intended to provide a firm legal basis for the issuance by competent persons of instructions about medical decisionmaking in the event that they later lose the capacity to make such decisions contemporaneously. (Some living will statutes also contain provisions for the appointment of a proxy to serve as a surrogate decisionmaker. These provisions are discussed in **Chapter 12.**) They are intended to provide assurance to individuals that their wishes will be respected and to provide assurance to health care providers that they will be immune from legal liability if they rely on these instructions.

The California legislature intended to forestall litigation similar to that in the *Quinlan* case.[2] The act's legislative findings and declaration of purpose are an early testimonial to themes that, ironically, would be struck repeatedly in the very litigation (both in and outside of California) that this kind of legislation was intended to prevent:

> The legislature . . . finds that, in the interest of protecting individual autonomy, such prolongation of life for persons with a terminal condition may cause loss of patient dignity and unnecessary pain and suffering, while providing nothing medically necessary or beneficial to the patient.
>
> The Legislature further finds that there exists considerable uncertainty in the medical and legal professions as to the legality of terminating the use or application of life-sustaining procedures where the patient has voluntarily and in sound mind evidenced a desire that such procedures be withheld or withdrawn.
>
> In recognition of the dignity and privacy which patients have a right to expect, the Legislature hereby declares that the laws of the State of California shall recognize the right of an adult person to make a written directive instructing his physician to withhold or withdraw life-sustaining procedures in the event of a terminal condition.[3]

Despite the lofty intentions of the California legislature, the act failed to achieve many of its goals. Indeed, there is even evidence that it produced some results contrary to those intended. Part of the reason had to do with the restrictive drafting of the act,[4] a problem that has been ameliorated in other jurisdictions and California as well.

---

[1] Cal. Health & Safety Code §§ 7185–7195 (West Supp. 1988).

[2] *See In re* Quinlan, 355 A.2d 647 (N.J.), *cert. denied,* 429 U.S. 922 (1976).

[3] Cal. Health & Safety Code § 7186, *revised* 1991 Cal. Stat. ch. 895 (S. 980) (statement of purpose largely unchanged, except for addition of persons in persistent vegetative state to those with terminal condition; *see* Cal. Health & Safety Code § 7185.5).

[4] *See* Note, *The California Living Will Statute: An Empirical Study of Physicians' Practices,* 31 Stan. L. Rev. 913 (1979).

Living will legislation has hardly solved all of the problems associated with decisionmaking for incompetent patients and has created new ones too. Some of the most intense litigation has occurred in states without living will legislation (for example, Massachusetts and New York), but there has also been extensive litigation in states that have long had living will legislation (for example, California, Florida, and Washington). Nonetheless, living will statutes probably do decrease the uncertainty surrounding the legitimacy of the clinical approach to decisionmaking for incompetent patients.[5] An advance directive that meets the requirements of a given state's living will statute or equivalent legislation is at least presumptively valid and enforceable. Consequently, some cases that would have reached an impasse, and therefore possibly would have resulted in litigation, are now resolved in the clinical context. Other cases, though litigated, may be resolved at the trial level—perhaps even in highly abbreviated proceedings—by the entry of a judicial order enforcing the directive, an order that might not have been so easily forthcoming in the absence of authorizing legislation.

Although ordinarily intended to provide a vehicle for refusing future treatment, like nonstatutory advance directives,[6] living will statutes may also be used to permit anticipatory *consent* to treatment, and some specifically provide for this use. For example, the Arizona statutory form directive permits a declarant to state that "I want my life to be prolonged to the greatest extent possible."[7]

---

[5] See § **5.4.**

[6] See § **10.11.**

[7] **AZ:** Ariz. Rev. Stat. Ann. § 36-3262.

**CO:** *Accord* Colo. Rev. Stat. § 15-18-102(e) (legislative declaration).

**DE:** *Accord* Del. Code Ann. tit. 16, § 2502(c).

**FL:** *Accord* Fla. Stat. Ann. § 765.302(1).

**HI:** *Accord* Haw. Rev. Stat. § 327D-1 (legislative intent).

**ID:** *Accord* Idaho Code § 39-4504 (form).

**IN:** *Accord* Ind. Code Ann. § 16-36-4-11.

**KY:** *Accord* Ky. Rev. Stat. Ann. § 311.625 (form).

**ME:** *Cf.* Me. Rev. Stat. Ann. tit. 18-A, § 5-702(b), (c) (enabling declarant to request administration of artificial nutrition and hydration).

**MD:** *Accord* Md. Code Ann., Health-Gen. § 5-603 (form).

**MN:** *Accord* Minn. Stat. Ann. § 145B.04 (form).

**NV:** *Cf.* Nev. Rev. Stat. Ann. § 449.610 (enabling declarant to request administration of artificial nutrition and hydration if by its withholding or withdrawing death would result from "starvation or dehydration").

**NH:** *Accord* N.H. Rev. Stat. Ann. § 137-H:1.

**ND:** *Accord* N.D. Cent. Code § 23-06.4-03(3) (form).

**OH:** *Accord* Ohio Rev. Code Ann. § 2133.02(A)(1).

**OR:** *Accord* Or. Rev. Stat. § 127.531 (form).

**PA:** *Accord* Pa. Cons. Stat. Ann. tit. 20, § 5404 (form).

Such provisions open up the possibility that advance directives will be used by families of incompetent patients as a mechanism for demanding treatment that physicians believe will be futile.[8]

There is also a substantive side to living will statutes: they can be seen as providing a statutory legal basis for forgoing life-sustaining treatment.[9] Under most living will statutes, this substantive purpose is implicit and limited, in that it is confined to persons who have made a living will in conformance with the statute.[10] A few acts, however, explicitly establish substantive rights, in language identical or similar to the following provision of the Iowa statute:

> Life-sustaining procedures may be withheld or withdrawn from a patient who is in a terminal condition and who is comatose, incompetent, or otherwise physically or mentally incapable of communication *and has not made a declaration in accordance with this chapter* if there is consultation and written agreement . . . between the attending physician and [certain designated individuals, including family members].[11]

---

SC: *Cf.* S.C. Code Ann. § 44-77-50 (form directive; artificial nutrition and hydration; persistent vegetative state).

SD: *Accord* S.D. Codified Laws Ann. § 34-12D-3 (form).

UT: *Accord* Utah Code Ann. § 75-2-1102 (legislative intent statement); Utah Code Ann. § 75-2-1105 (form).

VT: *Accord* Vt. Stat. Ann. tit. 18, § 5251 (purpose and policy section).

VA: *Accord* Va. Code Ann. § 54.1-2984 (form).

WI: *Accord* Wis. Stat. Ann. § 154.03 (form).

[8] See **Ch. 19.**

[9] See § **2.10.**

[10] See §§ **10.11–10.14.**

[11] **IA:** Iowa Code Ann. § 144A.7.

FL: *Accord* Fla. Stat. Ann. § 765.401.

LA: *Cf.* La. Rev. Stat. Ann. § 40:1299.58.5 (When a person is certified as a qualified patient, and has not previously made a declaration, any of the priority individuals may make a declaration in the qualified patient's behalf.).

ME: *Cf.* Me. Rev. Stat. Ann. tit. 18-A, § 5-707 ("[I]f written consent to withholding or withdrawal of treatment is given to the attending physician, the attending physician may withhold or withdraw life-sustaining treatment from an individual who . . . has no effective declaration.").

MT: *Cf.* Mont. Code Ann. § 50-9-106 ("[I]f written consent to withholding or withdrawal of treatment is given to the attending physician, the attending physician may withhold or withdraw life-sustaining treatment from an individual who . . . has no effective declaration.").

NM: *Accord* N.M. Stat. Ann. § 24-7-8.1.

NC: *Accord* N.C. Gen. Stat. § 90-322.

OR: *Accord* Or. Rev. Stat. § 127.635(2).

## § 11.2  Relationship to Common-Law Rights

Most living will statutes contain one or more provisions making clear that the statutes are not intended to supersede common-law decisionmaking rights or to be the sole means by which an advance directive can be executed. Further, most courts that have considered the issue have held that living will statutes are not intended to preempt common-law or state constitutional rights to make advance directives.[12]

# REQUIREMENTS FOR EXECUTION

## § 11.3  Statutory Living Will Form

All living will statutes except those in Delaware, New Jersey, New Mexico, and Ohio provide a living will form that the declarant may, but is ordinarily not required to, use.[13] However, the failure to use, or to substantially comply with,

---

**TX:** *Accord* Tex. Health & Safety Code Ann. § 672.009.

**UT:** *Accord* Utah Code Ann. § 75-2-1107.

**VA:** *Accord* Va. Code Ann. § 54.1-2986(A).

**WY:** *Accord* Wyo. Stat. § 35-22-105(b).

[12] See §§ **10.10–10.12.**

[13] **AL:** Ala. Code § 22-8A-4(c) ("substantially in the following form").

**AK:** Alaska Stat. § 18.12.010(c) ("may but need not, be in the following form").

**AZ:** Ariz. Rev. Stat. Ann. § 36-3262 ("form is offered as a sample only and does not prevent a person from using other language or another form").

**AR:** Ark. Code Ann. § 20-17-202(b) ("may, but need not, be in the following form").

**CA:** Cal. Health & Safety Code § 7186.5 ("declaration shall substantially contain the following provisions").

**CO:** Colo. Rev. Stat. § 15-18-104(3) ("may, but need not, be in the following form").

**CT:** Conn. Gen. Stat. Ann. § 19a-578 ("may, but need not be in substantially the following form").

**DC:** D.C. Code Ann. § 6-2422(c) ("shall be substantially in the following form").

**FL:** Fla. Stat. Ann. § 765.303(1) ("may, but need not, be in the following form").

**GA:** Ga. Code Ann. § 31-32-3(b) ("similar to the following form").

**HI:** Haw. Rev. Stat. § 327D-4 ("same form may be copied and used by filling in the blanks or may be changed . . . or an entirely different format may be used").

**ID:** Idaho Code § 39-4504 ("shall be in the following form or in another form that contains the elements set forth in this section").

**IL:** Ill. Ann. Stat. ch. 755, § 35/3(e) ("may, but need not, be in the following form").

**IN:** Ind. Code Ann. § 16-36-4-9 ("must be substantially in the form").

**IA:** Iowa Code Ann. § 144A.3 ("may, but need not, be in the following form").

**KS:** Kan. Stat. Ann. § 65-28,103(c) ("shall be substantially in the following form").

**KY:** Ky. Rev. Stat. Ann. § 311.625(1) ("shall be substantially in the following form, and may include other specific directives which are in accordance with accepted medical practice and not specifically prohibited by any other statute").

**LA:** La. Rev. Stat. Ann. § 40:1299.58.3(C)(1) ("may, but need not, be in the following illustrative form").

**ME:** Me. Rev. Stat. Ann. tit. 18-A, § 5-702(b) ("may, but need not, be in the following form").

**MD:** Md. Code Ann., Health-Gen. § 5-603.

**MN:** Minn. Stat. Ann. § 145B.04 ("must be substantially in the following form"; "Forms printed for public distribution must be substantially in the form in this section.").

**MS:** Miss. Code Ann. § 41-41-107 ("shall be in substantially the following form").

**MO:** Mo. Ann. Stat. § 459.015(3) ("may be in the following form, but it shall not be necessary to use this sample form").

**MT:** Mont. Code Ann. § 50-9-103(2) ("may, but need not, be in the following form").

**ND:** N.D. Cent. Code § 23-06.4-03.3 ("must be substantially in the form").

**NE:** Neb. Rev. Stat. § 20-404 ("may, but need not, be in the form provided in this subsection").

**NV:** Nev. Rev. Stat. Ann. § 449.610 ("may, but need not, be in the following form").

**NH:** N.H. Rev. Stat. Ann. § 137-H:3 ("may, but need not, be in form and substance substantially as follows").

**NC:** *Cf.* N.C. Gen. Stat. § 90-321(d) ("The following form is specifically determined to meet the requirements above.").

**ND:** N.D. Cent. Code § 23-06.4-03(3) ("declaration must be substantially in the following form").

**OK:** Okla. Stat. Ann. tit. 63, § 3101.4 ("shall be in substantially the following form").

**OR:** *But see* Or. Rev. Stat. § 127.531(1) ("The form of an advance directive executed by an Oregon resident must be the same as the form set forth in this section to be valid.").

**PA:** Pa. Cons. Stat. Ann. tit. 20, § 5404 ("may but need not be in the following form").

**SC:** S.C. Code Ann. § 44-77-50 ("declaration must be substantially in the following form").

**SD:** S.D. Codified Laws Ann. § 34-12D-3 ("A declaration may, but need not, be in the following form.").

**TN:** Tenn. Code Ann. § 32-11-105 ("may be substantially in the following form, but not to the exclusion of other written and clear expressions of intent").

**TX:** Tex. Rev. Civ. Stat. Ann. art. 4590h, § 3(d) ("A written directive may be in the following form.").

**UT:** Utah Code Ann. § 75-2-1104 ("shall be in substantially the following form").

**VT:** Vt. Stat. Ann. tit. 18, § 5253 ("may, but need not, be in form and substance substantially as follows").

**VA:** Va. Code Ann. § 54.1-2984 ("may, but need not be in the following form").

**WA:** Wash. Rev. Code Ann. § 70.122.030 ("may be in the following form").

**WV:** W. Va. Code § 16-30-3(3) ("may, but need not, be in the following form").

**WI:** *But see* Wis. Stat. Ann. § 154.03(2) ("shall be in the following form").

**WY:** Wyo. Stat. § 35-22-102(d) ("may be substantially in the following form").

Uniform Health-Care Decisions Act § 4 ("optional form") [hereinafter UHCDA].

the form directive might render the statutory immunity provisions inapplicable.[14]

## § 11.4  Execution for Incompetent

In most jurisdictions, a directive may only be executed by a competent patient. However, in a few states, a directive may be executed by specified family members or by a legal guardian on behalf of an incompetent patient.[15] Because such a directive is not the actual will of the patient, provisions providing for their validity are in effect surrogate decisionmaking statutes.[16]

## § 11.5  Execution by or for Minor

A small number of states permit the execution of a directive for a minor by a spouse or parent or guardian.[17] However, New Mexico requires judicial review of a directive so executed.[18] Illinois permits emancipated minors to execute their own directives.[19] Like a directive executed for an incompetent adult,[20] a directive executed by another for a minor is not truly an advance directive but a form of surrogate decisionmaking. Because the oral statements of mature minors have been given effect by courts under the subjective and substituted judgment standards, there is no reason why written advance directives by mature minors should not also be considered to be valid and enforceable.[21]

## § 11.6  Witnesses

**Number of Witnesses.**  Generally, living will statutes require declarations to be witnessed by two persons. However, Missouri requires no witnesses if the

---

[14] See §§ **10.15, 11.17,** and **17.24.**

[15] **AR:** Ark. Code Ann. § 20-17-214.

  **LA:** La. Rev. Stat. Ann. § 40:1299.58.5 (When a person is certified as a qualified patient, and has not previously made a declaration, any of the priority individuals may make a declaration in the qualified patient's behalf.).

[16] See **Ch. 14.**

[17] **AR:** Ark. Code Ann. § 20-17-214.

  **LA:** La. Rev. Stat. Ann. § 40:1299.58.6.

  **NM:** N.M. Stat. Ann. § 24-7-4.

  **TX:** Tex. Health & Safety Code Ann. § 672.006.

[18] N.M. Stat. Ann. § 24-7-4.D.

[19] Ill. Ann. Stat. ch. 755, § 35/3. *See also* UHCDA § 2(a), (b).

[20] See § **11.4.**

[21] See § **15.3.**

declaration is handwritten;[22] a few states require no witnesses if the declaration is notarized.[23]

**Who May Witness.** Most jurisdictions preclude anyone deemed to have or potentially to have a conflict of interest with the declarant from serving as a witness to a directive. Thus, most prohibit spouses or other close relatives from serving,[24] although some states permit one of the two witnesses to be a spouse

---

[22] Mo. Ann. Stat. § 459.015(1)(4).

[23] **KY:** Ky. Rev. Stat. Ann. § 311.625(2).

**MN:** Minn. Stat. Ann. § 145B.03(2).

**NJ:** N.J. Stat. Ann. § 26:2H-56.

[24] **AL:** Ala. Code § 22-8A-4(a) (related to the declarant neither by blood nor by marriage).

**AK:** Alaska Stat. § 18.12.010(a).

**AZ:** Ariz. Rev. Stat. Ann. § 36-3221(D) (witness may not be related to principal by blood, marriage, or adoption if there is only one witness).

**DE:** Del. Code Ann. tit. 16, § 2503(b)(1).

**DC:** D.C. Code Ann. § 6-2422(b).

**GA:** Ga. Code Ann. § 31-32-3(a)(1).

**HI:** Haw. Rev. Stat. § 327D-3(b)(4)(B).

**IN:** Ind. Code Ann. § 16-36-4-8(c)(2).

**KS:** Kan. Stat. Ann. § 65-28,103(a)(4).

**KY:** Ky. Rev. Stat. Ann. § 311.625(2)(a).

**LA:** La. Rev. Stat. Ann. § 40:1299.58.2(1).

**MS:** Miss. Code Ann. § 41-41-107(1) (form declaration).

**NV:** Nev. Rev. Stat. Ann. § 449.600(1).

**NH:** N.H. Rev. Stat. Ann. § 137-H:4.

**NC:** N.C. Gen. Stat. § 90-321(c)(3).

**ND:** N.D. Cent. Code § 23-06.4-3.1.a.

**OH:** Ohio Rev. Code Ann. § 2133.02(B)(1).

**OR:** Or. Rev. Stat. § 127.610(2)(a).

**RI:** R.I. Gen. Laws § 23-4.11-3(a).

**SC:** S.C. Code Ann. § 44-77-40(2).

**TN:** Tenn. Code Ann. § 32-11-104(a).

**TX:** Tex. Health & Safety Code Ann. § 672.003(c)(1).

**UT:** Utah Code Ann. § 75-2-1104(3)(b).

**VA:** Va. Code Ann. § 54.1-2982.

**VT:** Vt. Stat. Ann. tit. 18, § 5254.

**WA:** Wash. Rev. Code Ann. § 70.122.030(1).

**WV:** W. Va. Code § 16-30-3(b)(2).

**WI:** Wis. Stat. Ann. § 154.03(1)(a).

**WY:** Wyo. Stat. § 35-22-102(a)(ii).

or close relative.[25] This limitation runs contrary to the clear trend in the courts of strongly approving the practice of close family members making decisions to forgo life-sustaining treatment for incompetent patients without any judicial review.[26]

Many statutes also do not accept as a witness an heir or claimant of the declarant's estate,[27] the declarant's physician or anyone employed by the declarant's

---

[25] **FL:** Fla. Stat. Ann. § 765.302(1).

**IA:** Iowa Code Ann. § 144A.3(2)(a).

[26] See §§ **7.32** and **7.34.**

[27] **AL:** Ala. Code § 22-8A-4(a).

**AZ:** Ariz. Rev. Stat. Ann. § 36-3221(D) (witness may not be entitled to any part of principal's estate if there is only one witness).

**CA:** Cal. Health & Safety Code § 7186.5.

**CO:** Colo. Rev. Stat. § 15-18-106.

**DE:** Del. Code Ann. tit. 16, § 2503(b).

**DC:** D.C. Code Ann. § 6-2422(c).

**GA:** Ga. Code Ann. § 31-32-3(a)(2).

**IL:** Ill. Ann. Stat. ch. 755, § 35/3(3)(e).

**IN:** Ind. Code Ann. § 16-36-4-8(c)(3).

**KS:** Kan. Stat. Ann. § 65 28,103(a)(4).

**KY:** Ky. Rev. Stat. Ann. § 311.625(2)(b).

**LA:** La. Rev. Stat. Ann. § 40:1299.58-2(10).

**MD:** Md. Code Ann., Health-Gen. § 5-602(c)(2)(iii) (at least one of two needed witnesses cannot be heir to estate).

**MN:** Minn. Stat. Ann. § 145B.03(2).

**MS:** Miss. Code Ann. § 41-41-107(1).

**NH:** N.H. Rev. Stat. Ann. § 137-H:4.

**NC:** N.C. Gen. Stat. § 90-321(c)(3).

**ND:** N.D. Cent. Code § 23-06.4-03.1.b.

**OK:** Okla. Stat. Ann. tit. 63, § 3101.4(A).

**OR:** Or. Rev. Stat. § 127.610(2)(b).

**SC:** S.C. Code Ann. 44-77-40(2).

**TN:** Tenn. Code Ann. § 32-11-104(a).

**TX:** Tex. Health & Safety Code Ann. § 672.003(c)(2).

**UT:** Utah Code Ann. § 75-2-1104(3)(c).

**VT:** Vt. Stat. Ann. tit. 18, § 5254.

**WA:** Wash. Rev. Code Ann. § 70.122.030(1).

**WV:** W. Va. Code § 16-30-3(b)(3).

**WI:** Wis. Stat. Ann. § 154.03(1)(b).

**WY:** Wyo. Stat. § 35-22-102(a).

physician,[28] an employee of the health care facility in which the declarant is currently a patient,[29] a person responsible for the health care costs of the

---

[28] **AZ:** Ariz. Rev. Stat. Ann. § 36-3221(C)(2).

**CA:** Cal. Health & Safety Code § 7186.5.

**CO:** Colo. Rev. Stat. § 15-18-106.

**DC:** D.C. Code Ann. § 6-2422(e).

**GA:** Ga. Code Ann. § 31-32-3(a)(3).

**HI:** Haw. Rev. Stat. § 327D-3(b)(4)(C).

**IA:** Iowa Code Ann. § 144A.3(2)(a)(1), (2).

**KY:** Ky. Rev. Stat. Ann. § 311.625(2)(d).

**MD:** *But see* Md. Code Ann., Health-Gen. § 5-602(c)(2)(i) ("including an employee of a health care facility or physician caring for the declarant if acting in good faith").

**MS:** Miss. Code Ann. § 41-41-107(1).

**NH:** N.H. Rev. Stat. Ann. § 137-H:4.

**NC:** N.C. Gen. Stat. § 90-321(c)(3).

**ND:** N.D. Cent. Code § 23-06.4-03.1.3 (bars declarant's attending physician but not employee of attending physician).

**OH:** Ohio Rev. Code Ann. § 2133.02(B)(1).

**OR:** Or. Rev. Stat. § 127.610(2)(c).

**SC:** S.C. Code Ann. § 44-77-40(2).

**TN:** Tenn. Code Ann. § 32-11-104(a).

**TX:** Tex. Health & Safety Code Ann. § 672.003(c)(3), (4).

**VT:** Vt. Stat. Ann. tit. 18, § 5254.

**VA:** *But see* Va. Code Ann. § 54.1-2982 ("Employees of . . . physician's offices, who act in good faith, shall be permitted to serve as witnesses.").

**WA:** Wash. Rev. Code Ann. § 70.122.030(1).

**WV:** W. Va. Code § 16-30-3(b)(5).

**WI:** Wis. Stat. Ann. § 154.03(1)(d).

[29] **AZ:** Ariz. Rev. Stat. Ann. § 36-3221(C)(2) (if directly involved with provision of health care to declarant).

**CA:** Cal. Health & Safety Code § 7186.5.

**CO:** Colo. Rev. Stat. § 15-18-106.

**DE:** Del. Code Ann. tit. 16, § 2503(b)(5).

**DC:** D.C. Code Ann. § 6-2422(e).

**GA:** Ga. Code Ann. § 31-32-3(a)(3).

**HI:** Haw. Rev. Stat. § 327D-3(b)(4)(C).

**KY:** Ky. Rev. Stat. Ann. § 311.625(2)(c).

**MD:** *But see* Md. Code Ann.,Health-Gen § 5-602(c)(2)(i) ("including an employee of a health care facility . . . if acting in good faith").

**MS:** Miss. Code Ann. § 41-41-107(1).

**NE:** Neb. Rev. Stat. § 20-404(1) (no more than one witness to declaration shall be administrator or employee of health care provider).

declarant,[30] or a person designated by the declarant as a proxy.[31] The Nebraska statute disqualifies an employee of a life or health insurance provider from serving as a witness.[32]

Some statutes also have special witnessing provisions for nursing home residents. These statutes recognize that patients in skilled nursing facilities may, by virtue of the custodial nature of their care, be subject to subtle (or not-so-subtle) pressures, and thus special assurance is warranted in ascertaining that they are capable of intentionally and voluntarily executing a directive. The California statute, for example, provides that a declaration shall have no force

---

**NH:** N.H. Rev. Stat. Ann. § 137-H:4 (no more than one witness may be health care provider or health care provider's employee).

**NC:** N.C. Gen. Stat. § 90-321(c)(3).

**OR:** Or. Rev. Stat. § 127.610(2)(c).

**SC:** S.C. Code Ann. § 44-77-40(2) (one witness may be employed by facility).

**TN:** Tenn. Code Ann. § 32-11-104(a).

**TX:** Tex. Health & Safety Code Ann. § 672.003(c)(5) (employee of health care facility not barred if not providing direct patient care).

**UT:** Utah Code Ann. § 75-2-1104(3)(e).

**VA:** *But see* Va. Code Ann. § 54.1-2982 ("Employees of health care facilities . . . who act in good faith, shall be permitted to serve as witnesses.").

**WA:** Wash. Rev. Code Ann. § 70.122.030(1).

**WV:** W. Va. Code § 16-30-3(b)(5).

**WI:** Wis. Stat. Ann. § 154.03(1)(d).

[30] **AL:** Ala. Code § 22-8A-4(a).

**DE:** Del. Code Ann. tit. 16, § 2503(b)(4).

**DC:** D.C. Code Ann. § 6-2422(d).

**GA:** Ga. Code Ann. § 31-32-3(a)(4).

**IL:** Ill. Ann. Stat. ch. 755, § 35/3(3)(e).

**IN:** Ind. Code Ann. § 16-36-4-8(c)(4).

**KS:** Kan. Stat. Ann. § 65-28, 103(a)(4).

**KY:** Ky. Rev. Stat. Ann. § 311.625(2)(e).

**ND:** N.D. Cent. Code § 23-06.4-03.1.d.

**SC:** S.C. Code Ann. § 44-77-40(2).

**UT:** Utah Code Ann. § 75-2-1104(3)(d).

**WV:** W. Va. Code § 16-30-3(b)(4).

**WI:** Wis. Stat. Ann. § 154.03(1)(c).

**WY:** Wyo. Stat. § 35-22-102(a).

[31] **CT:** Conn. Gen. Stat. Ann. § 19a-576.

**NJ:** N.J. Stat. Ann. § 26:2H-56.

See **Ch. 12.**

[32] Neb. Rev. Stat. § 20-404(1).

or effect if the declarant is a patient in a skilled nursing facility or a long-term health care facility unless one of the witnesses to the declaration is a patient advocate or ombudsman designated by the State Department of Aging.[33] Other statutes provide either that one of the witnesses be designated by a state agency[34] or that, in addition to the required witnesses, the medical director of the nursing home must verify the declaration.[35]

## § 11.7   Notarization

Some states require that a directive be notarized.[36] Other statutes, although not mentioning a requirement of notarization in the substantive portion of the statute, contain such a requirement in the sample form directive.[37]

## § 11.8   Recitals

Many of the living will statutes that contain form directives[38] require an attestation by the declarant that at the time of execution he is of sound

---

[33] Cal. Health & Safety Code § 7187.

[34] **DE:** Del. Code Ann. tit. 16, § 2506(c).

   **DC:** D.C. Code Ann. § 6-2423.

   **ND:** N.D. Cent. Code § 23-06.4-03.2.

   **SC:** S.C. Code Ann. § 44-77-40(3).

[35] **GA:** Ga. Code Ann. § 31-32-4 (medical director or staff physician or other person on hospital staff not participating in declarant's care must verify declaration).

   **OH:** *But see* Ohio Rev. Code Ann. § 2133.02(B)(1) (prohibiting administrator of nursing home in which declarant is receiving care from being witness).

[36] **AZ:** Ariz. Rev. Stat. Ann. § 36-3221(A)(3).

   **HI:** Haw. Rev. Stat. § 327D-3(b)(5).

   **IA:** Iowa Code Ann. § 144A.3(2).

   **KY:** Ky. Rev. Stat. Ann. § 311.625(2).

   **NH:** N.H. Rev. Stat. Ann. § 137-H:3.

   **NC:** N.C. Gen. Stat. § 90-321(c)(4).

   **OH:** Ohio Rev. Code Ann. § 2133-02(A)(1).

   **SC:** S.C. Code Ann. § 44-77-40(4).

   **WV:** W. Va. Code § 16-30-3(a).

[37] **CO:** Colo. Rev. Stat. § 15-18-104(3).

   **TN:** Tenn. Code Ann. § 32-11-105.

[38] See § **10.10.**

mind and that he acts freely,[39] and others require such an attestation by the witnesses.[40]

---

[39] **AL:** Ala. Code § 22-8A-4.

**CO:** Colo. Rev. Stat. § 15-18-104(3).

**CT:** Conn. Gen. Stat. Ann. § 19a-575.

**DC:** D.C. Code Ann. § 6-2422(c).

**FL:** Fla. Stat. Ann. § 765.303.

**GA:** Ga. Code Ann. § 31-32-3(b).

**HI:** Haw. Rev. Stat. § 327D-4(A).

**ID:** Idaho Code § 39-4504.

**IL:** Ill. Ann. Stat. ch. 755, § 35/3.

**IN:** Ind. Code Ann. § 16-36-4-10.

**KS:** Kan. Stat. Ann. § 65-28, 103(c).

**KY:** Ky. Rev. Stat. Ann. § 311.625(1).

**LA:** La. Rev. Stat. Ann. § 40:1299.58.3.C(1).

**MD:** Md. Code Ann., Health-Gen. § 5-603(I)(C).

**MN:** Minn. Stat. Ann. § 145B.04.

**MS:** Miss. Code Ann. § 41-41-107(1).

**NH:** N.H. Rev. Stat. Ann. § 137-H:3.

**NC:** N.C. Gen. Stat. § 90-321.

**ND:** N.D. Cent. Code § 23-06.4-03.3.a.

**OK:** Okla. Stat. Ann. tit. 63, § 3101.4(B).

**OR:** Or. Rev. Stat. § 127.610(1).

**PA:** Pa. Cons. Stat. Ann. tit. 20, § 5404(b).

**RI:** R.I. Gen. Laws § 23-4.11-3(d).

**SC:** S.C. Code Ann. § 44-77-50.

**TN:** Tenn. Code Ann. § 32-11-105.

**TX:** Tex. Health & Safety Code Ann. § 672.004.

**UT:** Utah Code Ann. § 75-2-1104(4).

**VT:** Vt. Stat. Ann. tit. 18, § 5253.

**VA:** Va. Code Ann. § 54.1-2984.

**WA:** Wash. Rev. Code Ann. § 70.122.030(1) (must aver possession of *capacity* to make health care decisions).

**WV:** W. Va. Code § 16-30-3(d).

**WI:** Wis. Stat. Ann. § 154.03(2).

**WY:** Wyo. Stat. § 35-22-102(d).

[40] **AL:** Ala. Code § 22-8A-4.

**AK:** Alaska Stat. § 18.12.010(c).

**AZ:** Ariz. Rev. Stat. Ann. § 36-3221(A)(3).

# REQUIREMENTS FOR IMPLEMENTATION

## § 11.9 Incompetence; Terminal Illness or Permanent Unconsciousness

In drafting living will statutes, legislatures have had to confront one of the same fundamental problems faced by courts in right-to-die cases:[41] defining the scope

---

**AR:** Ark. Stat. Ann. § 20-17-202(c).

**CA:** Cal. Health & Safety Code § 7186.5(b).

**CO:** Colo. Rev. Stat. § 15-18-104(3).

**CT:** Conn. Gen. Stat. Ann. § 19a-570.

**DC:** D.C. Code Ann. § 6-2422(c).

**GA:** Ga. Code Ann. § 31-32-3(b).

**HI:** Haw. Rev. Stat. § 327D-4(A).

**ID:** Idaho Code § 39-4504.

**IL:** Ill. Ann. Stat. ch. 755, § 35/3.

**IN:** Ind. Code Ann. § 16-36-4-10.

**KS:** Kan. Stat. Ann. § 65-28,103(c).

**KY:** Ky. Rev. Stat. Ann. § 311.625(1).

**LA:** La. Rev. Stat. Ann. § 40:1299.58.3.C(1).

**ME:** Me. Rev. Stat. Ann. tit. 18-A, § 5-702(b).

**MD:** Md. Code Ann., Health-Gen. § 5-603(I)(C).

**MN:** Minn. Stat. Ann. § 145B.03(2).

**MS:** Miss. Code Ann. § 41-41-107(1).

**MO:** Mo. Ann. Stat. § 459.015(3).

**MT:** Mont. Code Ann. § 50-9-103(1).

**NE:** Neb. Rev. Stat. § 20-404(2).

**NV:** Nev. Rev. Stat. Ann. § 449.610.

**NH:** N.H. Rev. Stat. Ann. § 137-H:3.

**NJ:** N.J. Stat. Ann. § 26:2H-56.

**NC:** N.C. Gen. Stat. Ann. § 90-321(d).

**ND:** N.D. Cent. Code § 23-06.4-03.3.a.

**OH:** Ohio Rev. Code Ann. § 2133.02(B)(1).

**OR:** Or. Rev. Stat. § 127.610(1).

**PA:** Pa. Cons. Stat. Ann. tit. 20, § 5404(b).

**RI:** R.I. Gen. Laws § 23-4.11-3(d).

**SC:** S.C. Code Ann. § 44-77-50.

**TN:** Tenn. Code Ann. § 32-11-105.

**UT:** Utah Code Ann. § 75-2-1104(4).

**WA:** Wash. Rev. Code Ann. § 70.122.030(1).

**WI:** Wis. Stat. Ann. § 154.03(2).

**WY:** Wyo. Stat. § 35-22-102(d).

[41] See **Ch. 8.**

of and limits on the right. The statutes are not intended to permit everyone who has executed a living will to forgo medical care under all circumstances. Rather, most statutes use one or more of several terms—*terminal condition, permanent unconsciousness, qualified patient,* and *life-sustaining procedure*—to describe the category of persons whose living wills are effective and the circumstances under which they are enforceable.[42] That is, under most statutes a living will becomes effective only if the patient is terminally ill or permanently unconscious; some statutes use the phrase *qualified patient* to refer to such a person.[43]

---

[42] **AL:** Ala. Code § 22-8A-3(5).

**AK:** Alaska Stat. § 18.12.100(6).

**AR:** Ark. Code Ann. § 20-17-201(7).

**CA:** Cal. Health & Safety Code § 7186(h).

**CO:** Colo. Rev. Stat. § 15-18-103(9).

**DC:** D.C. Code Ann. § 6-2421(5).

**IL:** Ill. Ann. Stat. ch. 755, § 35/2(g).

**IN:** Ind. Code Ann. § 16-36-4-4.

**IA:** Iowa Code Ann. § 144A.2(7).

**KS:** Kan. Stat. Ann. § 65-28,102(e).

**KY:** Ky. Rev. Stat. Ann. § 311.621.

**LA:** La. Rev. Stat. Ann. § 40:1299.58.2(7).

**ME:** Me. Rev. Stat. Ann. tit. 18-A, § 5-701(b)(1).

**MT:** Mont. Code Ann. § 50-9-102(11).

**NE:** Neb. Rev. Stat. § 20-403(9).

**NV:** Nev. Rev. Stat. Ann. § 449.585.

**NH:** N.H. Rev. Stat. Ann. § 137-H:2(V).

**ND:** N.D. Cent. Code § 23-06.4-04.

**OH:** Ohio Rev. Code Ann. § 2133.01(Z).

**OK:** Okla. Stat. Ann. tit. 63, § 3101.3(10).

**OR:** Or. Rev. Stat. § 127.605(5).

**PA:** Pa. Cons. Stat. Ann. tit. 20, § 5403.

**TX:** Tex. Health & Safety Code Ann. § 672.002(8).

**VA:** Va. Code Ann. § 54.1-2982.

**WA:** Wash. Rev. Code Ann. § 70.122.020(8).

**WV:** W. Va. Code § 16-30-2(5).

**WI:** Wis. Stat. Ann. § 154.01(6).

**WY:** Wyo. Stat. § 35-22-101(a)(viii).

Uniform Rights of the Terminally Ill Act, § 1(7), 9B U.L.A. 127, 129 (West Supp. 1994) [hereinafter 1989 URTIA]; Uniform Rights of the Terminally Ill Act, § 1(7), 9B U.L.A. 609, 611 (1985) [hereinafter 1985 URTIA]. *But see* UHCDA (contains no requirement of terminal illness or permanent unconsciousness).

[43] **AL:** Ala. Code § 22-8A-3(5) ("afflicted with a terminal condition").

**AR:** Ark. Code Ann. § 20-17-201(7).

**CA:** Cal. Health & Safety Code § 7186(h).

**ID:** *But see* Idaho Code § 39-4503(2) (does not require terminal illness; defines qualified patient as one who is of sound mind and 18 years of age).

Further, even if a patient fits this description, only a *life-sustaining procedure* may be withheld or withdrawn. Finally, the purpose of living wills is to provide instructions about the patient's medical treatment when the patient is no longer able to do so contemporaneously. Thus, a living will ordinarily does not become effective until the declarant has lost decisionmaking capacity.[44] Not all living wills clearly provide that this is the case,[45] though it should be inferred to be so from the purpose of living wills.

**Terminal Condition.**    A patient is in a *terminal condition* if the medical condition is incurable and irreversible; that is, without administering life-sustaining treatment the condition will, in the opinion of the attending physician, result in death in a relatively short time.[46] A number of states define *terminal condition*

---

**LA:** La. Rev. Stat. Ann. § 40:1299.58.2(7).

**RI:** R.I. Gen. Laws § 23-4.11-2(g).

1989 URTIA § 1(7), (9).

[44] **CA:** *See, e.g.,* Cal. Health & Safety Code § 7187.5 (declaration becomes operative when declarant determined "no longer able to make decisions regarding administration of life-sustaining treatment").

UHCDA §§ 2(c), (d), 5(a), 11(a).

[45] **AL:** *See, e.g.,* Ala. Code § 22-8A-7 (wishes of patient who has executed living will "supersede the effect of the declaration")

[46] **AL:** Ala. Code § 22-8A-3(6).

**AK:** Alaska Stat. § 18.12.100(7).

**AR:** Ark. Code Ann. § 20-17-201(9).

**CA:** Cal. Health & Safety Code § 7186(j).

**CO:** Colo. Rev. Stat. § 15-18-103(10).

**CT:** Conn. Gen. Stat. Ann. § 19a-570(3).

**DE:** Del. Code Ann. tit. 16, § 2501(e).

**DC:** D.C. Code Ann. § 6-2421(6).

**FL:** Fla. Stat. Ann. § 765.101(17).

**GA:** Ga. Code Ann. § 31-32-2(13).

**HI:** Haw. Rev. Stat. § 327D-2.

**IL:** Ill. Ann. Stat. ch. 755, § 35/2(h).

**IN:** Ind. Code Ann. § 16-36-4-5.

**IA:** Iowa Code Ann. § 144A.2(8).

**KY:** Ky. Rev. Stat. Ann. § 311.621(16).

**LA:** La. Rev. Stat. Ann. § 40:1299.58.2(9).

**ME:** Me. Rev. Stat. Ann. tit. 18-A, § 5-701(b)(9).

**MD:** Md. Code Ann., Health-Gen. § 5-601(q).

**MN:** Minn. Stat. Ann. § 145B.02(8).

**MS:** Miss. Code Ann. § 41-41-113.

**MO:** Mo. Ann. Stat. § 459.010(6).

**MT:** Mont. Code Ann. § 50-9-102(14).

**NE:** Neb. Rev. Stat. § 20-403(11).

to include permanent or persistent vegetative state and/or irreversible coma.[47] Other statutes reach the same result by defining *qualified patient* as one who is in a terminal condition or a persistent vegetative state.[48] The amended Hawaii

---

**NV:** Nev. Rev. Stat. Ann. § 449.590.

**NH:** N.H. Rev. Stat. Ann. § 137-H:2(VI).

**NJ:** N.J. Stat. Ann. § 26:2H-55 ("A determination of a specific life expectancy is not required as a precondition for a diagnosis of a 'terminal condition,' but a prognosis of a life expectancy of six months or less, with or without the provision of life-sustaining treatment based upon reasonable medical certainty, shall be deemed to constitute a terminal condition.").

**NM:** N.M. Stat. Ann. § 24-7-2(f).

**ND:** N.D. Cent. Code § 23-06.4-02.7.

**OH:** Ohio Rev. Code Ann. § 2133.01(AA).

**OK:** Okla. Stat. Ann. tit. 63, § 3101.3(12).

**OR:** Or. Rev. Stat. § 127.605(6).

**PA:** Pa. Cons. Stat. Ann. tit. 20, § 5403.

**RI:** R.I. Gen. Laws § 23-4.11-2(h).

**SC:** S.C. Code Ann. § 44-77-20(4).

**TN:** Tenn. Code Ann. § 32-11-103 (9).

**TX:** Tex. Health & Safety Code Ann. § 672.003(9).

**UT:** Utah Code Ann. § 75-2-1103(10).

**VT:** Vt. Stat. Ann. tit. 18, § 5252(5).

**VA:** Va. Code Ann. § 54.1-2982.

**WA:** Wash. Rev. Code Ann. § 70.122.020(9).

**WV:** W. Va. Code § 16-30-2(6).

**WI:** Wis. Stat. Ann. § 154.01(8).

**WY:** Wyo. Stat. § 35-22-101(a)(ix).

*See also* 1989 URTIA § 1(9).

[47] **FL:** Fla. Stat. Ann. § 765.101(17)(b).

**HI:** Haw. Rev. Stat. § 327D-2.

**IA:** Iowa Code Ann. § 144A.2(8).

**LA:** La. Rev. Stat. Ann. § 40:1299.58.2(7).

**NE:** Neb. Rev. Stat. § 20-403(11).

**NV:** Nev. Rev. Stat. Ann. § 449.590.

**OH:** Ohio Rev. Code Ann. § 2133.01(U).

**RI:** R.I. Gen. Laws § 23-4.11-2(h).

**TN:** Tenn. Code Ann. § 32-11-103(9).

**VA:** Va. Code Ann. § 54.1-2982.

[48] **AR:** Ark. Code Ann. § 20-17-201(7).

**CA:** Cal. Health & Safety Code § 7186(h).

**CO:** Colo. Rev. Stat. § 15-18-103(9).

**IA:** Iowa Code Ann. § 144A.2(7).

**ME:** Me. Rev. Stat. Ann. tit. 18-A, § 5-701(b)(7).

**NE:** Neb. Rev. Stat. § 20-403(9).

**NV:** Nev. Rev. Stat. Ann. § 449.585.

statute, however, achieves this result by deleting the definition of "qualified patient" and adding a definition of "permanent loss of the ability to communicate concerning medical treatment decisions," which includes being in a persistent vegetative state or a deep coma or having a permanent loss of the capacity to participate in medical treatment decisions.[49] Still other statutes reach the same result by including a separate definition of *persistent vegetative state* or *permanent unconsciousness*.[50] The Uniform Health-Care Decisions Act drops these requirements and allows individuals to specify their own triggering conditions, if any.[51]

Many living will statutes define these terms in an interdependent and tautological fashion. The two versions of the Uniform Rights of the Terminally Ill Act (URTIA) attempt, with some success, to overcome these problems. The 1989 URTIA makes *incurable and irreversible* conjunctive requirements in contrast with the 1985 version that made these requirements disjunctive. Therefore,

---

**NH:** N.H. Rev. Stat. Ann. § 137-H:2(V).

**OH:** Ohio Rev. Code Ann. § 2133.01(Z).

**OK:** Okla. Stat. Ann. tit. 63, § 3101.3(10).

**OR:** Or. Rev. Stat. § 127.605(5).

**PA:** Pa. Cons. Stat. Ann. tit. 20, § 5403.

**TX:** Tex. Health & Safety Code Ann. § 672.002(8).

**WA:** Wash. Rev. Code Ann. § 70.122.020(8).

**WI:** Wis. Stat. Ann. § 154.01(6).

**WY:** Wyo. Stat. § 35-22-101(a)(viii).

[49] **HI:** Haw. Rev. Stat. § 327D-2.

[50] **AR:** Ark. Code Ann. § 20-17-201(11).

**CA:** Cal. Health & Safety Code § 7186(h).

**CT:** Conn. Gen. Stat. Ann. § 19a-570(4).

**GA:** Ga. Code Ann. § 31-32-2(9).

**KY:** Ky. Rev. Stat. Ann. § 311.621(12).

**ME:** Me. Rev. Stat. Ann. tit. 18-A, § 5-701(b)(10).

**MD:** Md. Code Ann., Health-Gen. § 5-601(o).

**NE:** Neb. Rev. Stat. § 20-403(6).

**NH:** N.H. Rev. Stat. Ann. § 137-H:2(VII).

**NJ:** N.J. Stat. Ann. § 26:2H-55.

**OK:** Okla. Stat. Ann. tit. 63, § 3101.3(7).

**PA:** Pa. Cons. Stat. Ann. tit. 20, § 5403.

**SC:** S.C. Code Ann. § 44-77-20(7).

**UT:** Utah Code Ann. § 75-2-1103(8).

**VA:** Va. Code Ann. § 54.1-2982.

**WA:** Wash. Rev. Code Ann. § 70.122.020(6).

**WI:** Wis. Stat. Ann. § 154.01(5m).

**WY:** Wyo. Stat. § 35-22-101(a)(V) ("irreversible coma").

[51] UHCDA §§ 2(a), 4.

under the 1989 URTIA, "[a] condition which is reversible but incurable is not a terminal condition,"[52] and treatment may not be forgone for a patient in such a condition. This is a more restrictive formulation. For example, it would not permit the forgoing of life-sustaining treatment pursuant to a statutory living will for "certain types of disorders, such as kidney disease requiring dialysis, and diabetes requiring continued use of insulin."[53]

Several other things should be noted about the URTIA definition of terminal condition. Perhaps most important is that it allows for the forgoing of treatment when the patient is in a persistent vegetative state because such a condition is both incurable and irreversible and because such patients would die in a relatively short time without the treatment.[54] This has been a controversial and problematic situation in states in which living will legislation is drafted differently, and especially when the treatment in question is tube-feeding.[55]

Another important feature of the URTIA definition of terminal condition is that it requires that death occur "in a relatively short time," rather than using a more restrictive term such as "imminent," and rather than using a fixed period of time as some living will statutes do.[56] As the commentary explains, this terminology better permits the exercise of medical judgment by "avoid[ing] both the unduly constricting meaning of 'imminent' and the artificiality of . . . fixed time periods."[57] This allows physicians to consider "the strength of the diagnosis, the type of disorder . . . in the judgment that death will result within a relatively short time . . . [judgments which] physicians must and do make."[58]

**Life-Sustaining Treatment.**    A *life-sustaining treatment* is one that will serve only to prolong the process of dying.[59]

---

[52] 1989 URTIA § 1(9) cmt.

[53] *Id. See also* Ariz. Rev. Stat. Ann. § 36-3201(6) (disjunctive).

[54] *See, e.g.,* McConnell v. Beverly Enters.-Conn., Inc., 553 A.2d 596 (Conn. 1989) (patient in a persistent vegetative state is terminally ill).

[55] *See, e.g.,* Cruzan v. Harmon, 760 S.W.2d 408 (Mo. 1988) (patient in a persistent vegetative state is not terminally ill).

[56] 1989 URTIA § 1(9) cmt.

[57] *Id.*

[58] *Id.*

[59] **AL:** Ala. Code § 22-8A-3(3) (1990).

   **AK:** Alaska Stat. § 18.12.100(4) (1986).

   **AR:** Ark. Code Ann. § 20-17-201(4).

   **CA:** Cal. Health & Safety Code § 7186(d).

   **CO:** Colo. Rev. Stat. § 15-18-103(7).

   **CT:** Conn. Gen. Stat. Ann. § 19a-570(1) ("life support system").

   **DE:** Del. Code Ann. tit. 16, § 2501(d).

   **DC:** D.C. Code Ann. § 6-2421(3).

   **FL:** Fla. Stat. Ann. § 765.101(11).

   **GA:** Ga. Code Ann. § 31-32-2(6).

Combining these definitions leads to a somewhat circular description of the class of persons for whom a statutory living will may be implemented. When each of the relevant definitions is inserted in the other, something like the following results: Treatment may be forgone if the patient is incurably or irreversibly ill, such that without the administration of treatment (which will

---

**HI:** Haw. Rev. Stat. § 327D-2.

**ID:** Idaho Code § 39-4503(3).

**IL:** Ill. Ann. Stat. ch. 755, § 35/2(d).

**IN:** Ind. Code Ann. § 16-36-4-1.

**IA:** Iowa Code Ann. § 144A.2(5).

**KS:** Kan. Stat. Ann. § 65-28,102(c).

**KY:** Ky. Rev. Stat. Ann. § 311.621(11)(b).

**LA:** La. Rev. Stat. Ann. § 40:1299.58.2(4).

**ME:** Me. Rev. Stat. Ann. tit. 18-A, § 5-701(b)(4).

**MD:** Md. Code Ann., Health-Gen. § 5-601(m)(ii).

**MS:** Miss. Code Ann. § 41-41-103(b).

**MO:** Mo. Ann. Stat. § 459.010(3).

**MT:** Mont. Code Ann. § 50-9-102(7).

**NE:** Neb. Rev. Stat. § 20-403(5).

**NV:** Nev. Rev. Stat. Ann.§ 449.570.

**NH:** N.H. Rev. Stat. Ann. § 137-H:2.

**NJ:** *Cf.* N.J. Stat. Ann. § 26:2H-55 ("'Life-sustaining treatment' means the use of any medical device or procedure ... that uses mechanical or other artificial means to sustain, restore or supplant a vital bodily function, and thereby increase the expected life span of a patient.").

**NM:** N.M. Stat. Ann. § 24-7-2(c).

**NC:** N.C. Gen. Stat. § 90-321(2).

**ND:** N.D. Cent. Code § 23-06.4-02.4.

**OH:** Ohio Rev. Code Ann. § 2133.01(Q).

**OK:** Okla. Stat. Ann. tit. 63, § 3101.3(6).

**OR:** Or. Rev. Stat. § 127.605(3).

**PA:** Pa. Cons. Stat. Ann. tit. 20, § 5403.

**RI:** R.I. Gen. Laws § 23-4.11-2(d).

**SC:** S.C. Code Ann. § 44-77-20(2).

**TX:** Tex. Health & Safety Code Ann. § 672.002(6).

**UT:** Utah Code Ann. § 75-2-1103(7)(i).

**VT:** Vt. Stat. Ann. tit. 18, § 5252(2).

**VA:** Va. Code Ann. § 54.1-2982.

**WA:** Wash. Rev. Code Ann. § 70.122.020(5).

**WV:** W. Va. Code § 16-30-2(3).

**WI:** Wis. Stat. Ann. § 154.01(5).

**WY:** Wyo. Stat. § 35-22-101(a).

1989 URTIA § 1(4).

serve only to prolong the process of dying), death will, in the opinion of the attending physician, result in a relatively short time.

Although intended to overcome the highly tautological nature of the definitional provisions of many living will statutes, the definitional provisions of the URTIA[60] are still somewhat tautological. Further, it is not clear from the URTIA's definition whether, if a patient is a qualified patient, all forms of treatment or only those treatments that themselves prolong the process of dying may be forgone.

Because most living will statutes state that they are not intended to preempt common-law rights,[61] the failure of a particular patient to fit these definitions does not necessarily mean that life-sustaining treatment may not be forgone, but only that it may not be forgone pursuant to the living will statute. Careful drafting of advance directives might avoid these statutory limitations.[62]

## § 11.10  Waiting Period

In addition to requiring that a patient be terminally ill or permanently unconscious for a directive to be implemented, a few statutes require a waiting period between the time the patient is diagnosed as terminally ill or permanently unconscious (and in some, certified as being incompetent) and the time when the declaration may be implemented.[63]

## § 11.11  Pregnancy

Many states do not permit the implementation of an otherwise valid directive if it would result in the forgoing of life-sustaining treatment and the patient is

---

[60] 1989 URTIA § 1(4) cmt., (7) cmt., (9) cmt.; 1985 URTIA § 1(4) cmt., (7) cmt., (9) cmt.

[61] See §§ 10.10–10.14.

[62] CT: McConnell v. Beverly Enters.-Conn., Inc., 553 A.2d 596 (Conn. 1989) (permitting termination of tube feeding pursuant to oral directive).

FL: Browning v. Herbert, 568 So. 2d 4 (Fla. 1990) (permitting termination of tube feeding pursuant to written directive not in compliance with living will statute).

See §§ 10.10–10.14 and Ch. 13.

[63] CO: Colo. Rev. Stat. § 15-18-104(3) (waiting period of seven consecutive days).

OH: Ohio Rev. Code Ann. § 2133.09(B)(2) (12-month waiting period before artificial nutrition and hydration can be removed from permanently unconscious patient), *held inapplicable to nondeclarant in In re* Myers, 610 N.E.2d 663, 668 (P. Ct. Summit County, Ohio 1993) ("Since Carla's diagnosis and non-recovery are unquestioned, an additional nine-month wait serves no purpose. Carla's diagnosis will not change in nine months. Such a requirement, under the circumstances of this case, has no rationale to support it, and appears to be an arbitrary time requirement. The requirement is unreasonable.").

OK: Okla. Stat. Ann. tit. 63, § 3107(B), (C).

SC: S.C. Code Ann. § 44-77-30 (six hours' administration of active treatment).

pregnant at the time.[64] Such provisions raise serious constitutional questions.[65] Some statutes render a directive invalid for a pregnant declarant only if the fetus is viable.[66] The latter approach is more likely to withstand constitutional

---

[64] **AL:** Ala. Code § 22-8A-4(a).

**CA:** Cal. Health & Safety Code § 7189.5(c).

**CT:** Conn. Gen. Stat. Ann. § 19a-574.

**DE:** Del. Code Ann. tit. 16, § 2503(d).

**FL:** Fla. Stat. Ann. § 765.113(2) (unless principal expressly delegates such authority in writing or surrogate has sought and received court approval).

**GA:** Ga. Code Ann. § 31-32-3(b) (unless fetus is not viable and declarant has indicated in document that she wants living will carried out if she is pregnant).

**HI:** Haw. Rev. Stat. § 327D-6.

**IL:** Ill. Ann. Stat. ch. 755, § 35/3(c).

**IN:** Ind. Code Ann. § 16-36-4-8(d).

**KS:** Kan. Stat. Ann. § 65-28,103(a).

**KY:** Ky. Rev. Stat. Ann. § 311.625(1).

**MD:** *But see* Md. Code Ann., Health-Gen. § 5-603 ("If I am pregnant my agent shall follow these specific instructions.").

**MN:** Minn. Stat. Ann. § 145B.13(3).

**MS:** Miss. Code Ann. § 41-41-107 (form).

**MO:** Mo. Ann. Stat. § 459.025.

**NH:** N.H. Rev. Stat. Ann. § 137-H:14(l).

**ND:** N.D. Cent. Code § 23-06.4-08.4.

**OK:** Okla. Stat. Ann. tit. 63, § 3101.8(C).

**PA:** Pa. Cons. Stat. Ann. tit. 20, § 5414(a).

**SC:** S.C. Code Ann. § 44-77-70.

**TX:** Tex. Health & Safety Code Ann. § 672.019.

**UT:** Utah Code Ann. § 75-2-1109.

**WA:** Wash. Rev. Code Ann. § 70.122.030 (form).

**WI:** Wis. Stat. Ann. § 154.07(2).

**WY:** Wyo. Stat. § 35-22-102(b).

[65] **WA:** *Cf.* DiNino v. State *ex rel.* Gorton, 684 P.2d 1297 (Wash. 1984) (in action by woman challenging pregnancy provision who was neither pregnant nor terminally ill, state conceded that provision in living will statute's optional sample living will could be deleted and living will would still be valid, but that a directive requiring termination of a pregnancy prior to removal of life support from mother would be invalid because it ignores state's potential interest in life of fetus). See § **9.55.**

[66] **AK:** Alaska Stat. § 18.12.040(c).

**AZ:** Ariz. Rev. Stat. Ann. § 36-3262 (sample form).

**AR:** Ark. Code Ann. § 20-17-206(c) (if fetus could develop to viability with life-sustaining treatment continued).

**CO:** Colo. Rev. Stat. § 15-18-104(2).

**GA:** Ga. Code Ann. § 31-32-3(b) (document must also specifically indicate that declarant wants living will carried out if she is pregnant).

challenge, as is the approach of the 1985 URTIA, which prohibits a pregnant patient's directive from being given effect only if the declarant so provides.[67]

## § 11.12 Nutrition and Hydration

As the case law has become more accepting of the notion that artificial nutrition and hydration should be treated no differently from any other form of life-sustaining medical treatment,[68] living will statutes have been revised to reflect this development. The controversy over permitting the forgoing of artificial nutrition and hydration manifested itself in the significant number of statutes that originally prohibited or limited the implementation of a directive that would result in the withholding or withdrawing of tube-feeding. At one time, a sizeable number of living will statutes prohibited the forgoing of artificial nutrition and hydration pursuant to a statutory living will. Today, however, only one state contains an outright prohibition.[69] Most statutes that address this issue require that nutrition and hydration be provided only if they are necessary for the patient's comfort.[70] The URTIA provides that "comfort care" may be

---

**IA:** Iowa Code Ann. § 144A.6.2.

**MT:** Mont. Code Ann. § 50-9-202(3).

**NE:** Neb. Rev. Stat. § 20-408(3).

**NV:** Nev. Rev. Stat. Ann. § 449.624(4).

**OH:** Ohio Rev. Code Ann. § 2133.06(B).

**RI:** R.I. Gen. Laws § 23-4.11-6(c).

1989 URTIA §§ 6(c), 7(f).

[67] *See* 1985 URTIA § 6(c). *Compare* 1989 URTIA § 6(c) ("Life-sustaining treatment must not be withheld or withdrawn pursuant to a declaration from an individual known to the attending physician to be pregnant so long as it is probable that the fetus will develop to the point of live birth with continued application of life-sustaining treatment.") *with id.* § 6 cmt. ("Nevertheless, in states that wish to accommodate the declaration of a pregnant woman, the wording from the prior version of the Act may be used. Differences from the Uniform Act in this specific application would not undermine the interest in uniformity served by the act."). *See, e.g.,* N.J. Stat. Ann. § 26:2H-56.

[68] See **§ 9.39.**

[69] **MO:** Mo. Ann. Stat. § 459.010(3).

[70] **AZ:** Ariz. Rev. Stat. Ann. § 36-3262 (sample form).

**AR:** Ark. Code Ann. § 20-17-206(b).

**CA:** Cal. Health & Safety Code § 7186.5(b).

**CO:** Colo. Rev. Stat. § 15-18-104(2.6).

**GA:** Ga. Code Ann. § 31-32-2(6).

**IL:** Ill. Ann. Stat. ch. 755, § 35/2(2)(d).

**IA:** Iowa Code Ann. § 144A.2(5).

**ME:** Me. Rev. Stat. Ann. tit. 18-A, § 5-702(b).

**MT:** Mont. Code Ann. § 50-9-202(2).

administered to patients "notwithstanding a declaration instructing withdrawal or withholding of life-sustaining treatment,"[71] and includes artificial nutrition and hydration as a type of "comfort care"[72] along with analgesia. These developments are consistent with the case law on forgoing artificial nutrition and hydration[73] and the provision of comfort care.[74]

Some statutes now expressly permit the forgoing of artificial nutrition and hydration pursuant to a directive, though there is no reason to believe that such express statutory authority is necessary.[75] They accomplish this in a number of ways: (1) by specifically stating that they may be forgone,[76] and/or (2) by including artificial nutrition and hydration in the definition of the kinds of treatments that may be forgone pursuant to a living will,[77] and/or (3) by

---

**NE:** Neb. Rev. Stat. § 20-408(2).

**NV:** Nev. Rev. Stat. Ann. § 449.624(3).

**NH:** N.H. Rev. Stat. Ann. § 137-H:2.

**NJ:** N.J. Stat. Ann. § 26:2H-67.b.

**ND:** N.D. Cent. Code § 23-06.4-02.4.

**OH:** Ohio Rev. Code Ann. § 2133.02(A)(3)(a).

**OK:** Okla. Stat. Ann. tit. 63, § 3101.3(6).

**OR:** Or. Rev. Stat. § 127.605(3).

**PA:** Pa. Cons. Stat. Ann. tit. 20, § 5404(b).

**SC:** S.C. Code Ann. § 44-77-20(2).

**UT:** Utah Code Ann. § 75-2-1103(7)(b).

**VA:** Va. Code Ann. § 54.1-2982.

**WA:** Wash. Rev. Code Ann. § 70.122.020(5).

**WI:** Wis. Stat. Ann. § 154.03(1).

**WY:** Wyo. Stat. § 35-22-101(a)(vi).

[71] 1989 URTIA § 6(b) cmt.

[72] 1989 URTIA § 6(b); 1985 URTIA § 6(b).

[73] See § **9.39.**

[74] See § **9.2.**

[75] **MO:** *But see* Mo. Ann. Stat. § 459.010(3).

[76] **ND:** N.D. Cent. Code § 23-06.4-3.1.

**NV:** Nev. Rev. Stat. Ann. § 449.624(3).

**OH:** Ohio Rev. Code Ann. § 2133.09.

**WI:** Wis. Stat. Ann. § 154.03(1) (introduction) ("declarant may not authorize the withholding or withdrawal of nutrition or hydration that is administered or otherwise received by the declarant through means other than a feeding tube unless declarant's physician advises that . . . the administration is medically contraindicated").

See § **9.39.**

[77] **AZ:** Ariz. Rev. Stat. Ann. § 36-3201(2) (defines *artificially administrated* as "providing food or fluids through a medically invasive procedure").

**CO:** Colo. Rev. Stat. § 15-18-103(1.5), (7).

**CT:** Conn. Gen. Stat. Ann. § 19a-570(1).

**GA:** Ga. Code Ann. § 31-32-2(6).

including them in the checklist of treatments in the statutory living will form that the declarant may check as treatments to be forgone,[78] and/or (4) through a

---

**HI:** Haw. Rev. Stat. § 327D-2.

**IL:** Ill. Ann. Stat. ch. 755, § 35/2(d) (definition of death-delaying procedure includes intravenous feeding or medication but also states that "nutrition and hydration shall not be withdrawn or withheld . . . if [it] would result in death solely from dehydration or starvation rather than from the existing terminal condition").

**IA:** Iowa Code Ann. § 144A.2(5).

**KY:** Ky. Rev. Stat. Ann. § 311.623(1)(b).

**LA:** La. Rev. Stat. Ann. § 40:1299.58.2(5).

**ME:** Me. Rev. Stat. Ann. tit. 18-A, § 5-701(4).

**MD:** Md. Code Ann., Health-Gen. § 5-601(m)(2).

**NH:** N.H. Rev. Stat. Ann. § 137-H:2(VIII).

**NJ:** N.J. Stat. Ann. § 26:2H-55.

**OK:** Okla. Stat. Ann. tit. 63, § 3101.3(6).

**PA:** Pa. Cons. Stat. Ann. tit. 20, § 5403.

**UT:** Utah Code Ann. § 75-2-1104(4).

**VA:** Va. Code Ann. § 54.1-2982.

**WA:** Wash. Rev. Code Ann. § 70.122.020(5).

**WY:** Wyo. Stat. § 35-22-101(vi).

[78] **AK:** Alaska Stat. § 18.12.010(c).

**AZ:** Ariz. Rev. Stat. Ann. § 36-3262.

**CA:** Cal. Health & Safety Code § 7186.5(b).

**CO:** Colo. Rev. Stat. § 15-18-104(3).

**CT:** Conn. Gen. Stat. Ann. § 19a-575.

**GA:** Ga. Code Ann. § 31-32-3(b).

**HI:** Haw. Rev. Stat. § 327D-4.

**ID:** Idaho Code § 39-4504.

**KY:** Ky. Rev. Stat. Ann. § 311.625(1).

**ME:** Me. Rev. Stat. Ann. tit. 18-A, § 5-702(b).

**MD:** Md. Code Ann., Health-Gen. § 5-603.

**MN:** Minn. Stat. Ann. § 145B.04.

**NV:** Nev. Rev. Stat. Ann. § 449.610.

**NH:** N.H. Rev. Stat. Ann. § 137-H:3.

**ND:** N.D. Cent. Code § 23-6.4-3.3.

**OK:** Okla. Stat. Ann. tit. 63, § 3101.4(B).

**PA:** Pa. Cons. Stat. Ann. tit. 20, § 5404(b).

**RI:** R.I. Gen. Laws § 23-4.11-3(d).

**SC:** S.C. Code Ann. § 44-77-50.

**SD:** S.D. Codified Laws Ann. § 34-12D-3.

**TN:** Tenn. Code Ann. § 32-11-105.

**VA:** Va. Code Ann. § 54.1-2984.

**WA:** Wash. Rev. Code Ann. § 70.122.030(1).

UHCDA § 4.

provision permitting declarants specifically to request that artificial nutrition and hydration be or not be administered.[79] Other statutes distinguish between "artificial technology to assist nutrition and hydration" and "normal nutritional aids such as a spoon or a straw."[80]

To the extent that a living will statute is not considered to preempt common-law or state constitutional rights,[81] a provision prohibiting the forgoing of artificial nutrition and hydration should not apply to situations in which no

---

[79] **AZ:** Ariz. Rev. Stat. Ann. § 36-3262 (sample form).

**CO:** Colo. Rev. Stat. § 15-18-104(3) (sample form).

**GA:** Ga. Code Ann. § 31-32-3(b).

**IN:** Ind. Code Ann. § 16-36-4-10 (sample form).

**KY:** Ky. Rev. Stat. Ann. § 311.625(1) (sample form).

**ME:** Me. Rev. Stat. Ann. tit. 18-A, § 5-702(b).

**MD:** Md. Code Ann., Health-Gen. § 5-603 (sample form).

**NV:** Nev. Rev. Stat. Ann. § 449.624(3).

**NH:** N.H. Rev. Stat. Ann. § 137-H:3.

**ND:** N.D. Cent. Code § 23-06.4-3.3 (sample form).

**OH:** Ohio Rev. Code Ann. § 2133.02(A)(3)(a) (forgoing artificial nutrition and hydration conditioned upon explicit statement in capital letters in declaration that attending physician may withhold or withdraw nutrition and hydration if declarant is in permanently unconscious state and attending physician and one other physician who have examined declarant must determine to reasonable degree of medical certainty that nutrition or hydration will not serve to provide comfort to declarant).

**OK:** Okla. Stat. Ann. tit. 63, § 3101.4(B) (form declaration).

**PA:** Pa. Cons. Stat. Ann. tit. 20, § 5404(b).

**RI:** R.I. Gen. Laws § 23-4.11-3(d).

**SC:** S.C. Code Ann. § 44-77-50 (form declaration).

**TN:** Tenn. Code Ann. § 32-11-103(5) (permitted only if living will specifically authorizes it using statutorily approved language).

**WA:** Wash. Rev. Code Ann. § 70.122.030(1) (declarant must indicate by check mark on form that artificial nutrition or hydration is or is not to be provided).

**WI:** Wis. Stat. Ann. § 154.03(2) (form declaration) (if not specified in declaration, artificial nutrition and hydration will be administered).

[80] **CT:** McConnell v. Beverly Enters.-Conn., Inc., 553 A.2d 596, 602–03 (Conn. 1989).

**NH:** *Accord* N.H. Rev. Stat. Ann. § 137-H:2(VII), (IX) (definitions distinguish artificial nutrition and hydration from sustenance).

**OK:** *Accord* Okla. Stat. Ann. tit. 63, § 3080.2(5) ("'Nutrition' means sustenance administered by way of the gastrointestinal tract.").

**SD:** *Accord* S.D. Codified Laws Ann. § 34-12D-1(4) (definition of life-sustaining treatment excludes oral administration of food and water).

**WI:** *Accord* Wis. Stat. Ann. § 154.03(1) (introduction) ("declarant may not authorize the withholding or withdrawal of nutrition or hydration that is administered or otherwise received by the declarant through means other than a feeding tube unless declarant's physician advises that . . . the administration is medically contraindicated").

[81] See §§ **10.10–10.14.**

directive has been made pursuant to the statute. This was the Florida Supreme Court's holding in the *Browning* case. The patient's living will was not made pursuant to the statute and could not have been because it was made before the statute was enacted. The court held that the then-existing statutory prohibition on the forgoing of artificial nutrition and hydration was inapplicable because the Florida state constitutional right of privacy guaranteed the right to decline all forms of medical treatment.[82] Indeed, provisions prohibiting the forgoing of artificial nutrition and hydration could turn out to be unconstitutional on federal due process or equal protection grounds under an extension of the reasoning in *Cruzan v. Director*.[83]

## § 11.13  Duration of Directive

In most states, a directive remains effective until revoked by the declarant. Most statutes provide that a declaration can be revoked at any time and without regard to the declarant's mental state.[84] Under some early living will statutes, which are now amended, a directive expired after a fixed period of time from its execution. The intent of such provisions was to force declarants to review their living wills to determine if the wills still reflected their wishes.[85] Worthy though this goal may be, merely getting people to execute a living will the first time is difficult

---

[82] **FL:** Browning v. Herbert, 568 So. 2d 4 (Fla. 1990). *See also* Browning v. Herbert, 543 So. 2d 258, 264–65 (Fla. Dist. Ct. App. 1989) ("While we authorized the discontinuance of a naso-gastric tube in the *Corbett* decision, this court made that decision under the constitutional right rather than under the statutory right. . . . Following the *Corbett* decision, bills to overrule the *Corbett* interpretation were introduced in both the Florida Senate and the Florida House of Representatives. Fla. S.B. 898 (1987); Fla. H.B. 1387 (1987); Fla. H.B. 670 (1986). The proposed legislation was unsuccessful.") (citing Morgan, *Florida Law and Feeding Tubes— The Right of Removal,* 17 Stetson L. Rev. 109, 134 (1988)); Corbett v. D'Alessandro, 487 So. 2d 368, 370–71 (Fla. Dist. Ct. App. 1986) ("[A]lthough chapter 765 [Fla. Stat. Ann. §§ 765.01–765.15] . . . excludes the right to decline sustenance providing life-prolonging measures, that chapter does not affect the otherwise existing constitutional rights of persons in a permanent vegetative state with no reasonable prospect of regaining cognitive brain function to forego the use of artificial life sustaining measures.").

**ME:** *Compare In re* Gardner, 534 A.2d 947 (Me. 1987) *with id.* at 958 (Clifford, J., dissenting).

**MO:** *But see* Cruzan v. Harmon, 760 S.W.2d 408 (Mo. 1988), *aff'd,* Cruzan v. Director, 497 U.S. 261 (1990).

[83] 497 U.S. 261 (1990).

[84] *Cf.* UHCDA § 3(b) ("An individual may revoke all or part of an advance health-care directive . . . at any time.").

[85] **CA:** Cal. Health & Safety Code § 7189.5 (repealed).

**GA:** Ga. Code Ann. § 31-32-6(a), (b) (directive executed prior to March 28, 1986, has seven-year duration; directive executed thereafter is effective until revoked).

**ND:** N.D. Cent. Code § 23-06.4-14 (directive executed under prior law is valid for five years from July 10, 1989).

enough,[86] and getting them to update it periodically may mean that many lapse, thereby making living wills even less widespread and useful for decision-making. As a court observed about the original California living will statute, "the typically human characteristics of procrastination and reluctance to contemplate the need for such arrangements . . . makes [*sic*] this a tool which will all too often go unused by those who might desire it."[87] The Uniform Health-Care Decisions Act has resolved this issue by specifying that an advance directive is valid "if it complies with this [Act], regardless of when . . . it was executed."[88]

## § 11.14   Revocation

The general methods of revocation prescribed by living will statutes include physical destruction, cancellation (which is not defined), written revocation, and verbal revocation.[89] In some jurisdictions, a written living will may be orally revoked.[90] However, even where there is not express authority for oral revocation, the fact that the terms of a living will may be repudiated by a patient even of questionable competence constitutes a form of oral revocation.[91] In addition to these methods of revocation, the South Carolina statute includes a provision for the optional appointment of an agent who is authorized to revoke the declaration on behalf of the declarant.[92] Most written and verbal revocations

---

[86] See § 11.1.

[87] Barber v. Superior Court, 195 Cal. Rptr. 484, 489 (Ct. App. 1983).

[88] UHCDA § 2(h).

[89] *See* 1989 URTIA § 4(a); 1985 URTIA § 4(a).

[90] *See, e.g.,* Browning v. Herbert, 543 So. 2d 258, 272 (Fla. Dist. Ct. App. 1989).

[91] **AL:** Ala. Code § 22-8A-7.
   **AR:** Ark. Code Ann. § 20-17-206(a).
   **CA:** Cal. Health & Safety Code § 7189.5(a).
   **DC:** D.C. Code Ann. § 6-2426.
   **HI:** Haw. Rev. Stat. § 327D-7.
   **IL:** Ill. Ann. Stat. ch. 755, § 35/7.
   **KS:** Kan. Stat. Ann. § 65-28,106.
   **MN:** Minn. Stat. Ann. § 145B.05.
   **NE:** Neb. Rev. Stat. § 20-408(1).
   **NH:** N.H. Rev. Stat. Ann. § 137-H:3.
   **OK:** Okla. Stat. Ann. tit. 63, § 3101.8(A).
   **TX:** Tex. Health & Safety Code Ann. § 672.007.
   **WI:** Wis. Stat. Ann. § 154.07(2).
   **UT:** Utah Code Ann. § 75-2-1108.
   1989 URTIA § 6(a).

[92] *See* S.C. Code Ann. §§ 44-77-50, -80(4).

become effective when the physician is informed of such a revocation.[93] The Uniform Health-Care Decisions Act resolves this issue in the most sensible fashion by providing that "[a]n individual may revoke all or part of an advance health-care directive ... at any time and in any manner that communicates an intent to revoke."[94] It also provides that an earlier directive is revoked by a later one to the extent that they are in conflict.[95]

# MISCELLANEOUS PROVISIONS

## § 11.15  Notification to Attending Physician

Most living will statutes provide that it is the responsibility of the declarant (or, in some statutes, someone representing the declarant) to notify the attending physician of the existence of a directive.[96] In some jurisdictions, if the declarant

---

[93] **NJ:** *See, e.g.,* N.J. Stat. Ann. § 26:2H-57.b.1 (revocation effective if health care representative, physician, nurse, or other health care professional or "other reliable witness" is notified).

**KY:** *But see* Ky. Rev. Stat. Ann. § 311.627(3) ("Any revocation ... shall become effective immediately. An attending physician or health care facility shall not be required to administer treatment in accordance with the revocation until the time notice of the revocation is received.").

1985 URTIA § 4(a)

[94] UHCDA § 3(b).

[95] UHCDA § 3(e).

[96] **AL:** Ala. Code § 22-8A-4(b).

**AK:** Alaska Stat. § 18.12.010(b).

**CO:** Colo. Rev. Stat. § 15-18-104(1).

**DC:** D.C. Code Ann. § 6-2422(b).

**FL:** Fla. Stat. Ann. § 765.302(2).

**HI:** Haw. Rev. Stat. § 327D-8.

**IL:** Ill. Ann. Stat. ch. 755, § 35/3(d).

**IN:** Ind. Code Ann. § 16-36-4-8(e).

**IA:** Iowa Code Ann. § 144A.3(3).

**KS:** Kan. Stat. Ann. § 65-28,103(b).

**KY:** Ky. Rev. Stat. Ann. § 311.633(1).

**LA:** La. Rev. Stat. Ann. § 40:1299.58.3B(1).

**MD:** Md. Code Ann., Health-Gen. § 5-602(f)(1).

**MO:** Mo. Ann. Stat. § 459.015.2.

**MT:** Mont. Code Ann. § 50-9-103(2).

**ND:** N.D. Cent. Code § 23-06.4-04.

**TN:** Tenn. Code Ann. § 32-11-104(b).

**TX:** Tex. Health & Safety Code Ann. § 672.003(e).

**UT:** Utah Code Ann. § 75-2-1110.

is comatose or incompetent, "any other person may notify the physician of the existence of the declaration,"[97] but as a practical matter, even in the absence of such a provision, notification will often be made by a family member rather than the declarant. Mississippi requires declarations to be filed with the bureau of vital statistics of the state board of health, but there is no mention of notifying the attending physician or making the directive a part of the patient's record.[98] Other statutes require that any person having possession of a directive deliver it to the attending physician, or if they have knowledge of its existence but not possession to so inform the attending physician.[99]

## § 11.16   Filing in Declarant's Medical Record

The directive should be made part of the patient's medical record, as should any revocation.[100] Most statutes specifically place this responsibility on the patient's attending physician.[101]

---

**VA:** Va. Code Ann. § 54.1-2983.

**WV:** W. Va. Code § 16-30-3(c).

**WI:** Wis. Stat. Ann. § 154.03(1).

**WY:** Wyo. Stat. § 35-22-102(c).

1989 URTIA § 3 ("A declaration becomes operative when . . . it is communicated to the attending physician.").

[97] **FL:** Fla. Stat. Ann. § 765.302(2).

**LA:** La. Rev. Stat. Ann. § 40:1299.58.3.B(2).

**KY:** Ky. Rev. Stat. Ann. § 311.633(1).

**MD:** Md. Code Ann., Health-Gen. § 5-602(f)(1).

**TX:** Tex. Health & Safety Code Ann. § 672.003(e).

**VA:** Va. Code Ann. § 54.1-2983.

[98] Miss. Code Ann. § 41-41-115(1).

[99] **HI:** Haw. Rev. Stat. § 327D-9.

**VT:** Vt. Stat. Ann. tit. 18, § 5258.

**WV:** W. Va. Code § 16-30-3(c).

**WY:** Wyo. Stat. § 35-22-102(c).

[100] 1989 URTIA § 4(b); 1985 URTIA § 4(b).

[101] **AL:** Ala. Code § 22-8A-4(b).

**AK:** Alaska Stat. § 18.12.010(b).

**AR:** Ark. Code Ann. § 20-17-205.

**CA:** Cal. Health & Safety Code § 7186.5(c).

**CO:** Colo. Rev. Stat. § 15-18-104(1).

**CT:** Conn. Gen. Stat. Ann. § 19a-578(b).

**DC:** D.C. Code Ann. § 6-2422(b).

**FL:** Fla. Stat. Ann. § 765.302(2).

**HI:** Haw. Rev. Stat. § 327D-8.

**IL:** Ill. Ann. Stat. ch. 755, § 35/3(d).

## § 11.17 Immunity

Every living will statute confers some form of immunity from legal liability on health care professionals who comply with a living will executed in accordance with the statute. As might be expected, they do not confer wholesale immunity; rather, most confer qualified immunity conditioned on the physician's having acted in good faith and pursuant to reasonable medical standards.[102] For the

---

**IN:** Ind. Code Ann. § 16-36-4-8(e).

**IA:** Iowa Code Ann. § 144A.4(2).

**KS:** Kan. Stat. Ann. § 65-28,103(b).

**KY:** Ky. Rev. Stat. Ann. § 311.633(1).

**LA:** La. Rev. Stat. Ann. §§ 40:1299.58.1–.10.

**MD:** Md. Code Ann., Health-Gen. § 5-602(f)(2).

**MN:** Minn. Stat. Ann. § 145B.06(1).

**MO:** Mo. Ann. Stat. § 459.015.2.

**MT:** Mont. Code Ann. § 50-9-103(5).

**NE:** Neb. Rev. Stat. § 20-404(3).

**NV:** Nev. Rev. Stat. Ann. § 449.600(2).

**NH:** N.H. Rev. Stat. Ann. § 137-H:5.

**NJ:** N.J. Stat. Ann. § 26:2H-62.a.

**ND:** N.D. Cent. Code § 23-06.4-07.

**OH:** Ohio Rev. Code Ann. § 2133.02(C).

**OK:** Okla. Stat. Ann. tit. 63, § 3101.4(C).

**OR:** Or. Rev. Stat. § 127.625(2)(a).

**PA:** Pa. Cons. Stat. Ann. tit. 20, § 5404(d).

**RI:** R.I. Gen. Laws § 23-4.11-3(b).

**TN:** Tenn. Code Ann. § 32-11-104(b).

**TX:** Tex. Health & Safety Code Ann. § 672.003(e).

**UT:** Utah Code Ann. § 75-2-1110.

**VA:** Va. Code Ann. § 54.1-2987.

**WV:** W. Va. Code § 16-30-3(c).

**WI:** Wis. Stat. Ann. § 154.03(1).

**WY:** Wyo. Stat. § 35-22-102(c).

1989 URTIA § 4(b).

[102] **AL:** Ala. Code § 22-8A-7.

**AR:** Ark. Code Ann. § 20-17-208(b) ("in accord with reasonable medical standards").

**CA:** Cal. Health & Safety Code § 7190.5(b).

**DC:** D.C. Code Ann. § 6-2427(a).

**KY:** Ky. Rev. Stat. Ann. § 311.635(3) ("in good faith").

**MD:** Md. Code Ann., Health-Gen. § 5-609(c) (unless did not act in good faith).

**OK:** Okla. Stat. Ann. tit. 63, § 3101.10(B).

**RI:** R.I. Gen. Laws § 23-4.11-8(b).

**SC:** S.C. Code Ann. § 44-77-90.

UHCDA § 9; 1989 URTIA § 9; 1985 URTIA § 8(b).

immunity provision to apply, the patient from whom treatment is withheld must fit the statutory requirements for making a directive. This is possibly the only advantage to drafting a living will in accordance with the statute.[103]

## § 11.18  Obligation to Comply or Transfer

The attending physician of a patient who has executed a statutorily based living will, assuming that the appropriate conditions for the invocation and application of the directive exist, is in almost all states required to make reasonable efforts either to comply with it or to transfer the patient.[104] Transfer

---

[103] See §§ **10.15** and **17.24.**

[104] **AL:** Ala. Code § 22-8A-8(a).

**AK:** Alaska Stat. § 18.12.050.

**AZ:** Ariz. Rev. Stat. Ann. § 36-3205(C)(1).

**AR:** Ark. Code Ann. § 20-17-207.

**CA:** Cal. Health & Safety Code § 7190.

**CO:** Colo. Rev. Stat. § 15-18-113(5).

**CT:** Conn. Gen. Stat. Ann. § 19a-580a.

**FL:** Fla. Stat. Ann. § 765.308.

**GA:** Ga. Code Ann. § 31-32-8(b)(1).

**HI:** Haw. Rev. Stat. § 327D-11.

**IL:** Ill. Ann. Stat. ch. 755, § 35/6(6)(c).

**IN:** Ind. Code Ann. § 16-36-4-13(e) (unless physician has reason to believe directive is invalid or that declarant no longer intends directive to be in force, and declarant is unable to reaffirm directive).

**IA:** Iowa Code Ann. § 144A.8(1).

**KS:** Kan. Stat. Ann. § 65-28,107(a).

**KY:** *But see* Ky. Rev. Stat. Ann. § 311.633(2) (no duty to transfer, just not to impede a request to transfer).

**LA:** La. Rev. Stat. Ann. § 40:1299.58.7.B.

**ME:** Me. Rev. Stat. Ann. tit. 18-A, § 5-708.

**MD:** Md. Code Ann., Health-Gen. § 5-613(a).

**MN:** *But see* Minn. Stat. Ann. § 145B.06(l) (no duty to transfer competent patient after physician gives notice of noncompliance).

**MS:** Miss. Code Ann. § 41-41-115(2).

**MO:** Mo. Ann. Stat. § 459.030(1).

**MT:** Mont. Code Ann. § 50-9-203.

**NE:** Neb. Rev. Stat. § 20-409.

**NV:** Nev. Rev. Stat. Ann. § 449.628.

**NH:** N.H. Rev. Stat. Ann. § 137-H:6.

**NJ:** N.J. Stat. Ann. § 26:2H-62.b.

**NM:** N.M. Stat. Ann. § 24-7-5(b).

**ND:** N.D. Cent. Code § 23-06.4-09.

of a patient, especially when there is contention about treatment, is not always possible.[105]

# § 11.19  Penalties

## Noncompliance with Directive

Some states provide a criminal penalty for willful or bad-faith failure to comply with a directive or transfer the patient,[106] while in others[107] the penalty is merely

---

**OH:** Ohio Rev. Code Ann. § 2133.10(A).

**OK:** Okla. Stat. Ann. tit. 63, § 3101.9.

**OR:** Or. Rev. Stat. § 127.625(3).

**PA:** Pa. Cons. Stat. Ann. tit. 20, § 5409(a).

**RI:** R.I. Gen. Laws § 23-4.11-7.

**SC:** S.C. Code Ann. § 44-77-100.

**TN:** Tenn. Code Ann. § 32-11-108.

**TX:** Tex. Health & Safety Code Ann. § 672.016(c).

**UT:** Utah Code Ann. § 75-2-1112(2).

**VT:** Vt. Stat. Ann. tit. 18, § 5256.

**VA:** Va. Code Ann. § 54.1-2987.

**WA:** *But see* Wash. Rev. Code Ann. § 70.122.060(2) (physician required to inform patient or patient's representative of existence of any policy or practice that would preclude honoring patient's directive if patient chooses to remain at facility; physician or facility, with patient, must prepare written plan, to be filed with patient's directive, that specifies physician's or facility's intended action should directive become operative; physician or facility then has no obligation to honor patient's directive).

**WV:** W. Va. Code § 16-30-7(b).

**WI:** Wis. Stat. Ann. § 154.07(l)(c).

**WY:** Wyo. Stat. § 35-22-104(b).

1989 URTIA § 8.

[105] See § **17.23.**

[106] **AR:** Ark. Code Ann. § 20-17-209(a) (misdemeanor).

**CA:** Cal. Health & Safety Code § 7191 (misdemeanor).

**ME:** Me. Rev. Stat. Ann. tit. 18-A, § 5-710(a).

**MT:** Mont. Code Ann. § 50-9-206(1) (misdemeanor).

**NE:** Neb. Rev. Stat. § 20-411(1) (class I misdemeanor).

**NV:** Nev. Rev. Stat. Ann. § 449.660(1) (gross misdemeanor).

1989 URTIA § 10(a), (b) (penalty for willfully failing to record determination of terminal condition or terms of declaration).

[107] **DC:** D.C. Code Ann. § 6-2427(b).

**HI:** Haw. Rev. Stat. § 327D-11(c).

**MO:** Mo. Ann. Stat. § 459.045(1) (failure to comply with act is unprofessional conduct).

**NJ:** N.J. Stat. Ann. § 26:2H-78 (intentional failure to act in accordance with statute is grounds for discipline or professional misconduct).

to classify the failure as unprofessional conduct, thereby allowing state licensing authorities to decide whether to impose a penalty. In some states, the living will statute also expressly provides the basis for a civil cause of action.[108] The Uniform Health-Care Decisions Act provides for "statutory damages" for certain violations of the Act[109] but does not impose criminal penalties.

## Forgery, Alteration, or Concealment

Most statutes prescribe criminal penalties for forging, altering, or concealing the existence of a statutory living will. When such conduct results in the *continuation* of treatment in disregard of the declarant's will, the penalty is ordinarily less serious than if the conduct results in the *termination* of treatment against the declarant's will. Thus, the concealment, alteration, or forgery of a declaration or of a revocation resulting in continuation of treatment is usually (but not always) a misdemeanor,[110] although it may also form the basis for civil

---

**OK:** Okla. Stat. Ann. tit. 63, § 3101.11.

**RI:** R.I. Gen. Laws § 23-4.11-9(a).

**SC:** S.C. Code Ann. § 44-77-100.

**TN:** Tenn. Code Ann. § 32-11-108.

**UT:** Utah Code Ann. § 75-2-1112(3).

**WI:** Wis. Stat. Ann. § 154.07(l)(c).

[108] **AK:** Alaska Stat. § 18.12.070.

**NE:** Neb. Rev. Stat. § 20-402(1).

**RI:** R.I. Gen. Laws § 23-4.11-9(e).

**TN:** Tenn. Code Ann. § 32-11-108(a).

[109] UHCDA § 10.

[110] **AL:** Ala. Code § 22-8A-8(b).

**AK:** Alaska Stat. § 18.12.070.

**AR:** Ark. Code Ann. § 20-17-209(c).

**CA:** Cal. Health & Safety Code § 7191(c).

**CO:** Colo. Rev. Stat. § 15-18-113(1), (2) (class 1 misdemeanor or class 4 felony).

**DC:** D.C. Code Ann. § 6-2427(c) (fine of $5,000 or 3 years' imprisonment).

**FL:** Fla. Stat. Ann. § 765.310(1) (felony of third degree).

**GA:** Ga. Code Ann. § 31-32-10.

**HI:** Haw. Rev. Stat. § 327D-17(b).

**IN:** Ind. Code Ann. § 16-36-4-15 (class D felony).

**KS:** Kan. Stat. Ann. § 65-28,107(b).

**ME:** Me. Rev. Stat. Ann. tit. 18-A, § 5-710(c).

**MD:** Md. Code Ann., Health-Gen. § 5-610(a).

**MN:** Minn. Stat. Ann. § 145B.10(l).

**MO:** Mo. Ann. Stat. § 459.045(3).

**NE:** Neb. Rev. Stat. § 20-411(3) (class I misdemeanor).

**NV:** Nev. Rev. Stat. Ann. § 449.660(3).

liability.[111] One who forges a living will or withholds or conceals a revocation, so that treatment is withheld, is ordinarily subject to a more serious penalty.[112]

---

**NM:** N.M. Stat. Ann. § 24-7-10(b) (third-degree felony, $5,000 fine or 2 to 10 years' imprisonment).

**ND:** N.D. Cent. Code § 23-06.4-11.1 (class A misdemeanor).

**OR:** Or. Rev. Stat. § 127.650(2).

**PA:** Pa. Cons. Stat. Ann. tit. 20, § 5415 (felony of third degree).

**RI:** R.I. Gen. Laws § 23-4.11-9(c) (imprisoned for no less than six months but for no more than one year or fined not less than $2,000 but no more than $5,000).

**TX:** Tex. Health & Safety Code Ann. § 672.018(a).

**UT:** Utah Code Ann. § 75-2-1115(1) (class B misdemeanor).

**VA:** Va. Code Ann. § 54.1-2989 (class 6 felony).

**WA:** Wash. Rev. Code Ann. § 70.122.090.

**WI:** Wis. Stat. Ann. § 154.15(1) (fine or 30 days' imprisonment).

**WY:** Wyo. Stat. § 35-22-107(a).

1989 URTIA § 10(c).

[111] **AK:** Alaska Stat. § 18.12.070.

**IL:** Ill. Ann. Stat. ch. 755, § 35/8(8).

**LA:** La. Rev. Stat. Ann. § 40:1299.58.9(a).

**SC:** S.C. Code Ann. § 44-77-160(c).

[112] **AL:** Ala. Code § 22-8A-8(c) (class C felony).

**AR:** Ark. Code Ann. § 20-17-209(d) (class D felony).

**CA:** Cal. Health & Safety Code § 7191(d) (unlawful homicide).

**CO:** Colo. Rev. Stat. § 15-18-113(3), (4) (declaration is class 2 felony; revocation, misdemeanor).

**DC:** D.C. Code Ann. § 6-2427(d) (unlawful homicide).

**FL:** Fla. Stat. Ann. § 765.310(2) (felony of second degree).

**GA:** Ga. Code Ann. § 31-32-10 (criminal homicide).

**IL:** Ill. Ann. Stat. ch. 755, § 35/8(8)(b) (involuntary manslaughter).

**IN:** Ind. Code Ann. § 16-36-4-16 (class C felony).

**KS:** Kan. Stat. Ann. § 65-28,107(c) (class e felony).

**LA:** La. Rev. Stat. Ann. § 40:1299.58.9.B (subject to prosecution).

**ME:** Me. Rev. Stat. Ann. tit. 18-A, § 5-710(d).

**MN:** Minn. Stat. Ann. § 145B.10(2) (aggravated forgery).

**MS:** Miss. Code Ann. § 41-41-121 (felony: 20 years' imprisonment).

**MO:** Mo. Ann. Stat. § 459.045(4) (class B felony).

**NV:** Nev. Rev. Stat. Ann. § 449.660(4) (murder).

**NJ:** N.J. Stat. Ann. § 26:2H-78.4.d (crime of fourth degree).

**NM:** N.M. Stat. Ann. § 24-7-10(a) (second-degree felony: $10,000 fine or 10 to 50 years' imprisonment).

**ND:** N.D. Cent. Code § 23-06.4-11.2 (class C felony).

**OR:** Or. Rev. Stat. § 127.650(1).

**PA:** Pa. Cons. Stat. Ann. tit. 20, § 5415 (criminal homicide).

**RI:** R.I. Gen. Laws § 23-4.11-9(d) (imprisoned for no less than one year but no more than five years or fined not less than $5,000 but no more than $10,000).

In some jurisdictions the penalty is the same regardless of whether the misconduct results in the continuation or the forgoing of treatment.[113] However, in Delaware, the statute treats wrongful administration of treatment as a felony and wrongful termination as a misdemeanor.[114]

## § 11.20   Execution as Condition of Medical Care or Insurance

Most living will statutes contain a provision stating that one who has executed a declaration shall not be adversely affected in the purchase of life insurance[115] or that the execution of a declaration may not be made a condition for the issuance of health insurance or the provision of health care services.[116] A number of statutes also provide that the forgoing of life-sustaining treatment pursuant to a

---

**SC:** S.C. Code Ann. § 44-77-160 (subject to prosecution in accordance with criminal laws).

**TX:** Tex. Health & Safety Code Ann. § 672.018(b) (criminal homicide).

**UT:** Utah Code Ann. § 75-2-1115(2) (criminal homicide).

**VA:** Va. Code Ann. § 54.1-2989 (class 2 felony).

**WA:** Wash. Rev. Code Ann. § 70.122.090 (first-degree murder).

**WV:** W. Va. Code § 16-30-7(d) (felony: 1 to 5 years' imprisonment).

**WI:** Wis. Stat. Ann. § 154.15(2) ($10,000 fine or 10 years' imprisonment).

**WY:** Wyo. Stat. § 35-22-107(b) (felony).

1989 URTIA § 10(d)–(f).

[113] **HI:** Haw. Rev. Stat. § 327D-17(b) (misdemeanor).

**IA:** Iowa Code Ann. § 144A.10 ("serious misdemeanor").

**MD:** Md. Code Ann., Health-Gen. § 5-610(B) (misdemeanor: $10,000 and/or one year of imprisonment).

**MT:** Mont. Code Ann. § 50-9-206(3), (4) (misdemeanor: $500 fine or one year of imprisonment).

**NE:** Neb. Rev. Stat. § 20-411(3) (class I misdemeanor).

**NH:** N.H. Rev. Stat. Ann. § 137-H:15 (class b felony).

**OK:** Okla. Stat. Ann. tit. 63, § 3101.11(C), (D) (felony).

**TN:** Tenn. Code Ann. § 32-11-109.

**VT:** Vt. Stat. Ann. tit. 13, § 1801 (criminal provisions).

1989 URTIA § 10(d)–(f).

[114] Del. Code Ann. tit. 16, § 2508(a), (b).

[115] **OH:** *See, e.g.,* Ohio Rev. Code Ann. § 2133.12(B)(1)(a).

1989 URTIA § 11(b); 1985 URTIA § 10(b).

[116] **AL:** Ala. Code § 22-8A-9(c).

**AK:** Alaska Stat. § 18.12.080(c).

**AR:** Ark. Code Ann. § 20-17-210(c).

**AZ:** Ariz. Rev. Stat. Ann. § 36-3207(A).

**CA:** Cal. Health & Safety Code § 7191.5(c).

**CO:** Colo. Rev. Stat. § 15-18-111.

living will does not constitute suicide and therefore does not invalidate life insurance policies.[117]

---

**CT:** Conn. Gen. Stat. Ann. § 19a-580b.

**DE:** Del. Code Ann. tit. 16, § 2507(c).

**DC:** D.C. Code Ann. § 6-2428(c).

**FL:** Fla. Stat. Ann. § 765.108.

**GA:** Ga. Code Ann. § 31-32-9(c).

**HI:** Haw. Rev. Stat. § 327D-16.

**ID:** Idaho Code § 39-4509(3).

**IL:** Ill. Ann. Stat. ch. 755, § 35/9(c).

**IN:** Ind. Code Ann. § 16-36-4-17(d).

**IA:** Iowa Code Ann. § 144A.11(3).

**KS:** Kan. Stat. Ann. § 65-28,108(c).

**KY:** Ky. Rev. Stat. Ann. § 311.637(2).

**LA:** La. Rev. Stat. Ann. § 40:1299.58.10(4).

**MD:** Md. Code Ann., Health-Gen. § 5-614(c).

**ME:** Me. Rev. Stat. Ann. tit. 18-A, § 5-711(c).

**MS:** Miss. Code Ann. § 41-41-119(4).

**MO:** Mo. Ann. Stat. § 459.055(5).

**MT:** Mont. Code Ann. § 50-9-205(3).

**NE:** Neb. Rev. Stat. § 20-412(3).

**NV:** Nev. Rev. Stat. Ann. § 449.650(3).

**NH:** N.H. Rev. Stat. Ann. § 137-H:11(I).

**NJ:** N.J. Stat. Ann. § 26:2H-75.

**NM:** N.M. Stat. Ann. § 24-7-8(C).

**NC:** N.C. Gen. Stat. § 90-321(g).

**ND:** N.D. Cent. Code § 23-06.4-11(3).

**OH:** Ohio Rev. Code Ann. § 2133.12(B)(3), (4).

**OK:** Okla. Stat. Ann. tit. 63, § 3101.12.

1989 URTIA § 11(c) ("A person may not prohibit or require the execution of a declaration as a condition for being insured for, or receiving, health-care services."); 1985 URTIA § 11(c).

[117] **AL:** Ala. Code § 22-8A-9(a).

**AK:** Alaska Stat. § 18.12.080(a).

**AZ:** Ariz. Rev. Stat. Ann. § 36-3210.

**AR:** Ark. Code Ann. § 20-17-210(a).

**CA:** Cal. Health & Safety Code § 7191.5(a).

**CO:** Colo. Rev. Stat. § 15-18-111.

**DE:** Del. Code Ann. tit. 16, § 2507(a).

**DC:** D.C. Code Ann. § 6-2428(a).

**FL:** Fla. Stat. Ann. § 765.309(2).

**GA:** Ga. Code Ann. § 31-32-9(a).

**HI:** Haw. Rev. Stat. § 327D-14.

**IL:** Ill. Ann. Stat. ch. 755, § 35/9(a).

## § 11.21 Portability

One of the potential limitations of living wills drafted pursuant to living will statutes is their possible invalidity in a jurisdiction other than the one in which they are executed. Several statutes address the potentially serious problems arising from the need to enforce in one jurisdiction a living will executed in another. They either provide that a living will is valid if it is in compliance with

---

**IN:** Ind. Code Ann. § 16-36-4-17(a).

**IA:** Iowa Code Ann. § 144A.11(l).

**KS:** Kan. Stat. Ann. § 65-28,108(a).

**KY:** Ky. Rev. Stat. Ann. § 311.638(1).

**LA:** La. Rev. Stat. Ann. § 40:1299.58.10(B)(1).

**ME:** Me. Rev. Stat. Ann. tit. 18-A, § 5-711(a).

**MD:** Md. Code Ann., Health-Gen. § 5-614(a).

**MN:** Minn. Stat. Ann. § 145B.14.

**MS:** Miss. Code Ann. § 41-41-119(1).

**MO:** Mo. Ann. Stat. § 459.055(5) (by implication).

**MT:** Mont. Code Ann. § 50-9-205(1).

**NE:** Neb. Rev. Stat. § 20-412(7).

**NV:** Nev. Rev. Stat. Ann. § 449.650(1).

**NH:** N.H. Rev. Stat. Ann. § 137-H:10(1).

**NJ:** N.J. Stat. Ann. § 26:2H-77(a).

**NM:** N.M. Stat. Ann. § 24-7-8(A).

**NC:** N.C. Gen. Stat. § 90-320(b) (by implication).

**ND:** N.D. Cent. Code § 23-06.4-11(1).

**OH:** Ohio Rev. Code Ann. § 2133.12(A).

**OK:** Okla. Stat. Ann. tit. 63, § 3101.12.

**OR:** Or. Rev. Stat. § 127.645(3).

**PA:** Pa. Cons. Stat. Ann. tit. 20, § 5410(a).

**RI:** R.I. Gen. Laws § 23-4.11-10(a).

**SC:** S.C. Code Ann. § 44-77-110.

**SD:** S.D. Codified Laws Ann. § 34-12D-20.

**TN:** Tenn. Code Ann. § 32-11-110(a).

**TX:** Tex. Health & Safety Code Ann. § 672.017.

**UT:** Utah Code Ann. § 75-2-1116.

**VT:** Vt. Stat. Ann. tit. 18, § 5260.

**VA:** Va. Code Ann. § 54.1-2991.

**WA:** Wash. Rev. Code Ann. § 70.122.070(1).

**WV:** W. Va. Code § 16-30-8(a).

**WI:** Wis. Stat. Ann. § 154.11(1).

**WY:** Wyo. Stat. § 35-22-109 (by implication).

UHCDA § 13(b).

the law of the state where it was executed[118] or where it is to be enforced[119] or both.[120] Provisions such as these make a relatively simple problem very difficult for they require that individuals—who, in the first instance, will be health care professionals—in one state know or be able to ascertain and interpret the law of another state. One simple solution to this problem is that employed in the Utah living will statute, which creates a presumption that a directive executed in another state complies with the provisions of the Utah living will statute and is therefore enforceable unless otherwise indicated in the instrument.[121] While such a provision is desirable, it is probably not necessary. Under the case law of all jurisdictions that have considered the issue—and probably under all that will do so—a written instrument provides the kind of evidence necessary to satisfy the very highest standard for decisionmaking for incompetent patients and should presumptively govern.[122] The Uniform Health-Care Decisions Act has resolved this issue by specifying that an advance directive is valid "if it complies with this [Act], regardless of . . . where it was executed."[123]

---

[118] **AK:** Alaska Stat. § 18.12.090.

**AZ:** Ariz. Rev. Stat. Ann. § 36-3208 (if it does not conflict with criminal laws of Arizona).

**LA:** La. Rev. Stat. Ann. § 40:1299.58.10(D).

**SC:** S.C. Code Ann. § 44-77-40.

[119] **HI:** Haw. Rev. Stat. § 327D-25.

**MN:** Minn. Stat. Ann. § 145B.16.

[120] **AR:** Ark. Code Ann. § 20-17-212.

**CA:** Cal. Health & Safety Code § 7192.5.

**FL:** Fla. Stat. Ann. § 765.112.

**IA:** Iowa Code Ann. § 144A.3(4).

**ME:** Me. Rev. Stat. Ann. tit. 18-A, § 5-713.

**MD:** Md. Code Ann., Health-Gen. § 5-617.

**MT:** Mont. Code Ann. § 50-9-111.

**NE:** Neb. Rev. Stat. § 20-414.

**NV:** Nev. Rev. Stat. Ann. § 449.690(1).

**NH:** N.H. Rev. Stat. Ann. § 137-H:14-a.

**NJ:** N.J. Stat. Ann. § 26:2H-76.

**ND:** N.D. Cent. Code § 23-06.4-13.

**OH:** Ohio Rev. Code Ann. § 2133.14.

**OK:** Okla. Stat. Ann. tit. 63, § 3101.14.

**RI:** R.I. Gen. Laws § 23-4.11-12.

**SC:** S.C. Code Ann. § 44-77-30.

**TN:** Tenn. Code Ann. § 32-11-111.

**VA:** Va. Code Ann. § 54.1-2993.

1989 URTIA § 13.

[121] Utah Code Ann. § 75-2-1119.

[122] See §§ **7.4–7.9.**

[123] UHCDA § 2(h).

## § 11.22  Table of Living Will Statutes

### Table 11–1

### Living Will Statutes

**AL:**  Ala. Code §§ 22-8A-1 to -10
**AK:**  Alaska Stat. §§ 18.12.010–.100
**AZ:**  Ariz. Rev. Stat. Ann. §§ 36-3201 to -3262
**AR:**  Ark. Code Ann. §§ 20-17-201 to -218
**CA:**  Cal. Health & Safety Code §§ 7185–7194.5
**CO:**  Colo. Rev. Stat. §§ 15-18-101 to -113
**CT:**  Conn. Gen. Stat. Ann. §§ 19a-570 to -580c
**DE:**  Del. Code Ann. tit. 16, §§ 2501–2509
**DC:**  D.C. Code Ann. §§ 6-2421 to -2430
**FL:**  Fla. Stat. Ann. §§ 765.101–.401
**GA:**  Ga. Code Ann. §§ 31-32-1 to -12
**HI:**  Haw. Rev. Stat. §§ 327D-1 to -27
**ID:**  Idaho Code §§ 39-4501 to -4509
**IL:**  Ill. Ann. Stat. ch. 755, §§ 35/1–10
**IN:**  Ind. Code Ann. §§ 16-36-4-1 to -21
**IA:**  Iowa Code Ann. §§ 144A.1–.12
**KS:**  Kan. Stat. Ann. §§ 65-28,101 to -28,109
**KY:**  Ky. Rev. Stat. Ann. §§ 311.621–.643
**LA:**  La. Rev. Stat. Ann. §§ 40:1299.58.1–.10
**ME:**  Me. Rev. Stat. Ann. tit. 18-A, §§ 5-701 to -714
**MD:**  Md. Code Ann., Health-Gen. §§ 5-601 to -618
**MN:**  Minn. Stat. Ann. §§ 145B.01–.17
**MS:**  Miss. Code Ann. §§ 41-41-101 to -121
**MO:**  Mo. Ann. Stat. §§ 459.010–.055
**MT:**  Mont. Code Ann. §§ 50-9-101 to -111, -201 to -206
**NE:**  Neb. Rev. Stat. §§ 20-401 to -416
**NV:**  Nev. Rev. Stat. Ann. §§ 449.535–.690
**NH:**  N.H. Rev. Stat. Ann. §§ 137-H:1–:15
**NJ:**  N.J. Stat. Ann. §§ 26:2H-53 to -78
**NM:**  N.M. Stat. Ann. §§ 24-7-1 to -11
**NC:**  N.C. Gen. Stat. §§ 90-320 to -323
**ND:**  N.D. Cent. Code §§ 23-06.4-01 to -14
**OH:**  Ohio Rev. Code Ann. §§ 2133.01–.15
**OK:**  Okla. Stat. Ann. tit. 63, §§ 3101.1–.16
**OR:**  Or. Rev. Stat. §§ 127.505–.660, .995
**PA:**  Pa. Cons. Stat. Ann. tit. 20, §§ 5401–5416
**RI:**  R.I. Gen. Laws §§ 23-4.11-1 to -14
**SC:**  S.C. Code Ann. §§ 44-77-10 to -160
**SD:**  S.D. Codified Laws Ann. §§ 34-12D-1 to -22
**TN:**  Tenn. Code Ann. §§ 32-11-101 to -112
**TX:**  Tex. Health & Safety Code Ann. §§ 672.001–.021
**UT:**  Utah Code Ann. §§ 75-2-1101 to -1119
**VT:**  Vt. Stat. Ann. tit. 18, §§ 5251–5262; Vt. Stat. Ann. tit. 13, § 1801
**VA:**  Va. Code Ann. §§ 54.1-2981 to -2993
**WA:**  Wash. Rev. Code Ann. §§ 70.122.010–.920
**WV:**  W. Va. Code §§ 16-30-1 to -13
**WI:**  Wis. Stat. Ann. §§ 154.01–.15
**WY:**  Wyo. Stat. §§ 35-22-101 to -109

# Bibliography

## General

Benton, E. "The Constitutionality of Pregnancy Clauses in Living Will Statutes." *Vanderbilt Law Review* 43 (1990): 1821.

Chapman, M. "The Uniform Rights of the Terminally Ill Act: Too Little, Too Late?" *Arkansas Law Review* 42 (1989): 319.

Dyke, M. Note. "A Matter of Life and Death: Pregnancy Clauses in Living Will Statutes." *Boston University Law Review* 70 (1990): 867.

English, D. "The Health-Care Decisions Act Represents a Major Advance." *Trusts and Estates* 133 (1994): 32.

English, D., and A. Meisel. "The Uniform Health-Care Decisions Act." *Estate Planning* 21 (1994): 355.

Gould, L. "Right to Die Legislation: The Effect on Physicians' Liability." *Mercer Law Review* 39 (1988): 517.

Lerner, M. "State Natural Death Acts: Illusory Protection of Individuals' Life-Sustaining Treatment Decisions." *Harvard Journal on Legislation* 29 (1992): 175.

Lobe, S. "The Will to Die: A Survey of State Living Will Legislation and Case Law." *Probate Law Journal* 9 (1989): 47.

MacAvoy-Snitzer, J. Note. "Pregnancy Clauses in Living Will Statutes." *Columbia Law Review* 87 (1987): 1280.

Orentlicher, D. "The Limits of Legislation." *Maryland Law Review* 53 (1994): 1255.

Steinle, S. "Living Wills in the United States and Canada: A Comparative Analysis." *Case Western Reserve Journal of International Law* 24 (1992): 435.

## Specific States

**AZ:**   Morgan, S. Comment. "Selecting Medical Treatment: Does Arizona's Living Will Statute Help Enforce Decisions?" *Arizona State Law Journal,* 1986, no. 2: 275.

**AR:** Chapman, M. "The Uniform Rights of the Terminally Ill Act: Too Little, Too Late?" *Arkansas Law Review* 42 (1989): 319.

Leflar, R. "Liberty and Death: Advance Health Care Directives and the Law of Arkansas." *Arkansas Law Review* 39 (1986): 375.

**CO:** Marsh, L. "Living Will Legislation in Colorado: An Analysis of the Colorado Medical Treatment Decision Act in Relation to Similar Developments in Other Jurisdictions." *Denver University Law Review* 64 (1987): 5.

**CT:** Lieberson, A. "A Comprehensive Look at Connecticut's Living Will Statute." *Connecticut Probate Law Journal* 7 (1992): 49.

**FL:** Calder, M. "Chapter 765 Revisited: Florida's New Advance Directives Law." *Florida State University Law Review* 20 (1992): 292.

**IL:** Burkey, A. Comment. "Natural Death Legislation in Illinois—the Illinois Living Will Act." *Southern Illinois University Law Journal,* 1984, no. 3: 465.

Collins, B. Comment. "The Right to Die in Illinois: A Comprehensive Scheme." *Northern Illinois University Law Review* 8 (1988): 427.

**IN:** Mooney, C. "Indiana's Living Wills and Life-Prolonging Procedures Act: A Reform Proposal." *Indiana Law Review* 20 (1987): 539.

**LA:** Vitiello, M. "Louisiana's Natural Death Act and Dilemmas in Medical Ethics." *Louisiana Law Review* 46 (1985): 259.

**ME:** Merlan, E. Comment. "Maine's Living Will Act and the Termination of Life-Sustaining Medical Procedures." *Maine Law Review* 39 (1987): 83.

**MI:** Lankfer, M. "Living Wills and Durable Powers Authorizing Medical Treatment Decisions." *Michigan Bar Journal* 64 (1985): 684.

**MS:** Vitiello, M. "Death with Dignity in Mississippi? An Analysis of Mississippi's Natural Death Act." *Mississippi Law Journal* 54 (1984): 459.

**MO:** Johnson, S. "The Death-Prolonging Procedures Act and Refusal of Treatment in Missouri." *St. Louis University Law Journal* 30 (1986): 805.

Thieman, S. Comment. "Missouri's Living Will Statute: All Dressed Up with No Place to Go?" *UMKC Law Review* 57 (1989): 531.

**MT:** Schimke, T. "The Natural Death Act: Protection for the Right to Die." *Montana Law Review* 47 (1986): 379.

**NH:** Raiche, M., et al. "Is Living Will the Best Revenge? New Hampshire's Living Will Statute." *New Hampshire Bar Journal* 28 (1986): 45.

**NJ:** Armstrong, P., and R. Olick. "Innovative Legislative Initiatives: The New Jersey Declaration of Death and Advance Directives for Health Care Acts." *Seton Hall Legislation Journal* 16 (1992): 177.

Cantor, N. "Advance Directives and the Pursuit of Death with Dignity: New Jersey's New Legislation." *Rutgers Law Review* 44 (1992): 335.

**NY:** Vile, S. "Living Wills in New York: Are They Valid?" *Syracuse Law Review* 38 (1987): 1369.

**ND:** Oliver, L. Note. "The Right to Die in North Dakota: The North Dakota Living Will Act." *North Dakota Law Review* 66 (1990): 495.

**OH:** Mitrovich, P. "Analysis of Ohio's Living Will Statute and Beyond." *Ohio Northern University Law Review* 18 (1992): 759.

**PA:** Wentworth, P. Comment. "Termination of Life-Prolonging Medical Treatment: An Analysis of Pennsylvania's Proposed Medical Treatment Decision Act." *Dickinson Law Review* 92 (1988): 839.

**TX:** Garlo, D. "The Texas Natural Death Act: Interpretation, Application and Fine-Tuning." *Texas Bar Journal* 53 (1990): 10.

Greenfield, R. Comment. "The Recent Amendments to the Texas Natural Death Act: Implications for Health Care Providers." *St. Mary's Law Journal* 17 (1986): 1003.

**TN:** Fockler, J. "Living Wills, Organ Donation, and Durable Powers of Attorney." *Tennessee Bar Journal* 23 (1987): 23.

**WV:** Keeley, I. "Advance Medical Directives in West Virginia." *West Virginia Law Review* 94 (1992): 875.

**WI:** Willms, A. "The Appointment of an Agent for Medical Treatment Decisions." *Wisconsin Bar Bulletin* 61 (1988): 16.

# CHAPTER 12

# HEALTH CARE POWERS OF ATTORNEY (PROXY DIRECTIVES)

## § 12.1 Nature and Purpose of Proxy Directives

Although living wills are better known and have a longer heritage than proxy directives, more states—all but one—now have a legislative basis for the issuance of a proxy directive than for living wills. The statutes that form the legal basis for the designation of a health care proxy are usually referred to as *health care proxy* or *health care power of attorney* statutes.

It is now generally recognized that proxy directives are an important alternative or supplement to—and might even be preferable to—living wills in end-of-life decisionmaking for incompetent patients. Indeed, if one had to make a choice between a proxy directive alone or living will alone, the former is probably far more useful. Fortunately, however, there is no reason why a choice must be made between the two; a directive that combines appointing an agent for health care decisionmaking and giving instructions to that agent is also feasible, and some advance directive statutes specifically provide for this.

The purpose of proxy directives, as stated or reflected in legislation, is to permit individuals to exercise their right to make decisions about medical treatment—usually decisions to decline treatment, but also decisions to consent to it—after they lose the contemporaneous ability to do so.[1] Unlike living wills, which are often either so vague as to be of little assistance or so specific that they might not apply to the particular decision to be made, proxy directives avoid these dual dilemmas through their flexibility. Proxy directives help health care professionals by providing assurance that a particular person has authority to act

---

[1] **CO:** Colo. Rev. Stat. § 15-14-504(1).

**DC:** D.C. Code Ann. § 21-2201.

**DE:** Del. Code Ann. tit. 16, § 2502.

**FL:** Fla. Stat. Ann. § 765.102.

**GA:** Ga. Code Ann. § 31-36-2(a).

**HI:** Haw. Rev. Stat. § 551D-2.

**IL:** Ill. Ann. Stat. ch. 755, § 45/4-1.

**IA:** Iowa Code Ann. § 144A.1 (historical note).

**MD:** Md. Code Ann., Health-Gen. § 5-602(a).

**MN:** Minn. Stat. Ann. § 145C.02.

**NE:** Neb. Rev. Stat. § 30-3401(1).

**NJ:** N.J. Stat. Ann. § 26:2H-54.

**NY:** N.Y. Pub. Health Law (legislative note).

**ND:** N.D. Cent. Code § 23-06.5-01.

**OK:** Okla. Stat. Ann. tit. 63, § 3101.2(A).

**PA:** Pa. Cons. Stat. Ann. tit. 20, § 5402(a).

**VT:** Vt. Stat. Ann. tit. 14, § 3451.

**WV:** W. Va. Code § 16-30A-2(b)(5).

Uniform Health-Care Decisions Act, 9B U.L.A. 93 (introductory note) [hereinafter UHCDA].

on behalf of a patient who lacks decisionmaking capacity.[2] Proxy directives, like living wills, also help to avoid the need for judicial involvement in end-of-life decisionmaking for incompetent patients.[3]

Proxy directives can be made more useful both to health care professionals and to the proxy if they also contain instructions about the kind of health care that the declarant does and does not want or incorporate by reference the declarant's living will.[4] At least in theory, the health care professional then has a greater degree of assurance that the proxy, when making decisions about the declarant's medical care, is implementing to the greatest extent possible the patient's wishes.[5] Furthermore, to the extent that a jurisdiction requires the application of a subjective standard or a substituted judgment standard in decisionmaking for incompetent patients,[6] a proxy directive without instructions might not satisfy either of these standards.[7]

---

[2] *See* Ill. Ann. Stat. ch. 755, § 45/4-1 ("[T]he General Assembly recognizes . . . that particular rules and forms are necessary for health care agencies to insure their validity and efficacy and to protect health care providers so that they will honor the authority of the agent at all times.").

[3] *See* W. Va. Code § 16-30A-2(b)(5) ("It is the intent of the Legislature . . . that the courts should not be the usual venue for making such decisions.").

[4] **AK:** *See, e.g.,* Alaska Stat. § 13.26.335 (presumably to reduce possible confusion, statutory form for durable power of attorney, which must be substantially followed, contains checkoff box whereby principal indicates that he has separately executed living will).

**ID:** *See, e.g.,* Idaho Code § 39-4505 (stated purpose of durable power of attorney statute is effectuation of directives already given in living will: "[i]n order to implement the general desires of a person as expressed in the 'living will,' a competent person may appoint any adult person to exercise a durable power of attorney for health care").

**WV:** *See, e.g.,* W. Va. Code § 16-30A-2(b)(4).

[5] *See* Cohen-Mansfield et al., *The Decision to Execute a Durable Power of Attorney for Health Care and Preferences Regarding the Utilization of Life-Sustaining Treatments in Nursing Home Residents,* 151 Archives Internal Med. 289 (1991) (two-thirds of 93 nursing home patients had not discussed their preferences about medical care with anyone despite fact that 90% would choose close relative to make their health care decisions if they lost decision-making capacity); Tomlinson et al., *An Empirical Study of Proxy Consent for Elderly Persons,* 30 Gerontologist 54, 59 (1990) (in experimental situation, surrogates selected by patient "did not increase the likelihood that [the surrogate] would make decisions that the [patient] would prefer" over those made by close family members or patient's physician).

[6] See §§ **7.4–7.10.**

[7] **US:** *But see* Cruzan v. Director, 497 U.S. 261, 290 (1990) (O'Connor, J., concurring) (failure to honor patient's intent could be avoided if states were to consider "the patient's appointment of a proxy to make health care decisions on her behalf" . . . "an equally probative source of evidence" as living will).

**MD:** *But see* Mack v. Mack, 618 A.2d 744, 757–58 (Md. 1993) (health care power of attorney meets subjective standard or substituted judgment standard) (by implication).

**NY:** *But see In re* Westchester County Medical Ctr. (O'Connor), 531 N.E.2d 607, 612 (N.Y. 1988) (same).

## § 12.2  Terminology

Proxy directives are sometimes referred to as *health care powers of attorney* because a durable power of attorney was frequently the instrument used to designate a proxy before the widespread enactment of statutes expressly providing for the appointment of a health care proxy.[8] The term *health care power of attorney* should be confined to the *instrument* used to appoint someone to make health care decisions for another, and the term *proxy* or *health care proxy* should be used to refer to the person so designated. Some statutes refer to the proxy as an *agent,* the *holder of the power,* or as *attorney in fact,* the latter two borrowing from conventional power-of-attorney terminology. (In order to serve as an attorney in fact, the individual so appointed need not be a lawyer, that is, an attorney at law.) However, not all statutes follow this logic in their terminology.[9] This chapter uses the terms *proxy* and *agent* and uses them interchangeably.

Some statutes refer to the proxy as a surrogate,[10] and a proxy *is* a kind of surrogate, but the two terms are not coterminous. A proxy is a particular kind of surrogate, namely, one who is appointed by the patient. Similarly, a guardian is a surrogate appointed by a court. The distinction is not always important, but when it is, the overlapping terminology can lead to some confusion. Thus, it is probably best to confine the use of the term *surrogate* to a person who makes decisions on behalf of another when that person acquires his authority to act by operation of law, be it common law[11] or a surrogate decisionmaking statute.[12]

A *proxy directive* is a statement—usually contained in a written instrument but possibly an oral statement[13]—by which one individual designates another to make health care decisions for him.[14] Health care proxy statutes usually refer to the person appointing a proxy as a *declarant,* but this person may also be referred to as a *principal, grantor, settlor,* or *creator.* In this chapter, the terms *principal, declarant,* and *patient* will be used interchangeably to refer to an individual who has appointed a health care proxy.

---

[8] *See, e.g., In re* Peter, 529 A.2d 419 (N.J. 1987).

[9] *See, e.g.,* Mass. Gen. Laws. Ann. ch. 201D, § 1 (referring to document as "health care proxy").

[10] **FL:** Fla. Stat. Ann. § 765.101(16).

[11] See §§ **5.9–5.14.**

[12] See **Ch. 14.**

[13] See §§ **10.16, 12.3,** and **12.4.**

[14] *See, e.g.,* Or. Rev. Stat. § 127.505(10) (durable power of attorney for health care is "a power of attorney that authorizes an agent to make health care decisions for the principal when the principal is incapable").

## § 12.3 —Proxy Directives and Standards for Surrogate Decisionmaking

Advance directives have acquired added importance in light of the Supreme Court's decision in *Cruzan v. Director.*[15] If, as *Cruzan* holds, a state may constitutionally require that the subjective standard (or the substituted judgment standard) be met in order to limit or terminate treatment of an incompetent patient, proof of the patient's wishes becomes crucial. Although oral proof can, in principle, meet either the subjective standard or the substituted judgment standard, much unnecessary complication (including litigation) can be avoided if there is an adequate written advance directive expressing the patient's wishes.

The limitations on human foresight mean that even when a person has gone to the effort of providing instructions in a written living will, its terms may prove inapplicable to the decision that in fact needs to be made. It is for this reason that attorneys who draft advance directives and physicians who implement them are increasingly concluding that proxy directives are superior to instruction directives. However, it is not yet certain that proxy directives—or at least those that merely designate a proxy decisionmaker but do not contain expressions of the patient's intent—will be found to satisfy the subjective standard or substituted judgment standard.

A power of attorney that merely empowers a proxy to make health care decisions for the principal[16] might be found not to meet this standard. Even a power of attorney specifically authorizing the agent to make decisions about forgoing life-sustaining treatment might be found not to suffice if the requirement is that the patient have authorized the forgoing of the specific treatment being administered.[17] In *Cruzan,* Justice Brennan (in dissent) felt that a state is entitled to place certain restrictions on the choice of a surrogate to ensure that the surrogate "is the one whom the patient himself would have selected to make that choice for him" and to ensure that the surrogate is not improperly motivated.[18] For Justice Brennan, a power of attorney would suffice in protecting these state interests because "a State generally must . . . repose the choice with the person whom the patient himself would most likely have chosen as proxy."[19] Justice O'Connor, in a concurring opinion, agreed, stating that it "may well be constitutionally required [for a state to give effect to the decisions of a

---

[15] 497 U.S. 261 (1990).

[16] *See, e.g., In re* Peter, 529 A.2d 419 (N.J. 1987).

[17] *See* Cruzan v. Director, 497 U.S. 261, 323 (1990) (Brennan, J., dissenting) ("The [Missouri] court did not specifically define what kind of evidence it would consider clear and convincing, but its general discussion suggests that only a living will or equivalently formal directive from the patient when competent would meet this standard. *See* [Cruzan v. Harmon,] 760 S.W.2d, at 424–425.").

[18] *Id.* at 328.

[19] *Id.*

surrogate decisionmaker] to protect the patient's liberty interest in refusing medical treatment."[20]

This question was taken up at some length by the Florida Supreme Court shortly after *Cruzan* was handed down. This court's very sensible resolution in *Browning v. Herbert*[21] was that when a patient designates a proxy to make health care decisions, those decisions are valid and enforceable if they meet the requisite standard for decisionmaking for incompetent patients, which in Florida is the substituted judgment standard.[22] However, a judicial challenge may be brought to any decision made by a surrogate, whether patient-designated or otherwise, on the ground that the decision being made is not the one the patient would have made. If such a challenge is brought, a *written* designation of a proxy "establishes a rebuttable presumption that constitutes clear and convincing evidence of the patient's wishes."[23] Further, for an oral designation to be effective, there must be written instructions (that is, a living will) for the proxy to follow.[24] It is preferable, though not mandatory, that the appointment of a health care proxy be in writing in all jurisdictions, and that the appointment be accompanied by some instructions about the patient's wishes.[25]

There is some judicial authority in support of the proposition that a health care power of attorney meets the subjective or substituted judgment standard even if specific instructions are not provided. In discussing the subjective standard for decisionmaking for incompetent patients, the New Jersey Supreme Court in *Conroy* mentioned durable powers of attorney as one way in which a patient's intent might be made known.[26] Subsequently, in the *Peter* case, that court was

---

[20] **US:** Cruzan v. Director, 497 U.S. at 289 (O'Connor, J., concurring).

**MI:** *But see* Werth v. Taylor, 475 N.W.2d 426 (Mich. Ct. App. 1991) (patient's own prior competent refusal of treatment need not be respected because it did not specifically anticipate that refused treatment might be necessary to save patient's life).

**NJ:** *But see In re* Hughes, 611 A.2d 1148 (N.J. Super. Ct. App. Div. 1992) (same).

**OH:** *But see* University of Cincinnati Hosp. v. Edmond, 506 N.E.2d 299 (C.P. Hamilton County, Ohio 1986) (same).

**PA:** *But see In re* Estate of Dorone, 534 A.2d 452 (Pa. 1987) (same).

[21] 568 So. 2d 4 (Fla. 1990).

[22] *Id.* at 13.

[23] *Id.* at 16.

[24] *Id.* at 15.

[25] **FL:** Browning v. Herbert, 568 So. 2d at 16.

**MI:** *See also* Werth v. Taylor, 475 N.W.2d 426, 430 (Mich. Ct. App. 1991) (implying that implicit oral designation of husband to make decisions while patient was recovering from surgery was not valid).

**NJ:** *In re* Jobes, 529 A.2d 434 (N.J. 1987).

[26] **NJ:** *In re* Conroy, 486 A.2d 1209, 1229–30 (N.J. 1985). *See also In re* Clark, 510 A.2d 136, 142 (N.J. Super. Ct. Ch. Div. 1986).

**PA:** *See also* Pocono Medical Ctr. v. Harley, 11 Fiduc. Rep. 2d 128 (C.P. Monroe County, Pa. 1990).

actually faced with a durable power of attorney, drafted specifically for medical decisionmaking, authorizing a friend of the patient to make " 'all medical decisions' " for her and " 'to be given full and complete authority to manage and direct her medical care.' "[27] The court held that, although New Jersey's durable power of attorney statute "does not specifically authorize conveyance of durable authority to make medical decisions, it should be interpreted that way."[28]

Similarly, though in dictum, the New York Court of Appeals stated in *O'Connor* that since the legislative enactment of the springing durable power of attorney, there is "no longer any reason in principle why those wishing to appoint another to express their specific or general desires with respect to medical treatment, in the event they become incompetent, may not do so formally through a power of attorney."[29] This is especially noteworthy in light of the tenacious adherence by the New York Court of Appeals to the subjective standard. Although this is not the holding of *O'Connor,* it is certainly a strong inference that in New York the subjective standard may be satisfied by a properly executed health care power of attorney as well as by an instruction directive.

There may, however, be some practical problems. First, there is the question of whether, in fact, the proxy knows the patient's wishes or values from which those wishes could be inferred. Justice Handler of the New Jersey Supreme Court, concurring both in *Jobes* and *Peter,* clearly articulated and explained this concern:

> [I]t is not the mere signing over of authority that makes the resulting decision an expression of the patient's right of self-determination. It is important that the durable power of attorney was given by the patient to someone who knows her well. Hilda Peter's giving of a durable power of attorney to her close friend Eberhard Johanning was itself an assertion. Through her action, Ms. Peter showed that she thought Mr. Johanning knew her well enough to make the treatment decision for her that she would have wanted made. Obviously there will be cases involving durable powers of attorney in which confidence in the holder may not be so strong.[30]

Second, it is preferable that the patient specifically provide that the proxy has authority to terminate life-sustaining treatment. In *Peter,* this deficiency was

---

[27] *In re* Peter, 529 A.2d 419, 426 n.7 (N.J. 1987).

[28] *Id.* at 426. See § **12.25.**

[29] **NY:** *In re* Westchester County Medical Ctr. (O'Connor), 531 N.E.2d 607, 612 (N.Y. 1988) (construing N.Y. Gen. Oblig. Law § 5-1601).

 **MD:** *Accord* Mack v. Mack, 618 A.2d 744, 757–58 (Md. 1993) (health care power of attorney meets subjective standard or substituted judgment standard) (by implication).

[30] *In re* Jobes, 529 A.2d 434, 457 n.10 (N.J. 1987) (Handler, J., concurring). *Accord In re* Peter, 529 A.2d at 430 (Handler, J., concurring).

cured by the proxy's explanation that the patient orally directed him to refuse life-sustaining treatment on her behalf in a situation like this, together with nine "reliable hearsay accounts of her disinclination for the kind of treatment" that the proxy was seeking to discontinue.[31]

## § 12.4   Legal Basis for Proxy Directives

The firmest legal basis for proxy directives are statutes specifically authorizing their creation. All jurisdictions except Alabama now have either a freestanding health care power of attorney statute, a combined living will and health care power of attorney statute, or a provision in a living will statute authorizing the designation of a health care proxy. See **Table 12–1 in § 12.52.**

In the absence of such a statute—or more likely in the instance of a failure to comply with statutory formalities—there is still reasonable ground for concluding that a state's general durable power of attorney may serve as the basis for designation of a health care proxy. Although in theory there is no reason why the oral designation of a proxy should not be effective, in practice there is just enough uncertainty about its legitimacy that, when combined with additional uncertainties (however justified or unjustified they may be) about the nature of the decision that the proxy is to make, physicians, health care administrators, and their legal counsel may be reluctant to rely on an oral designation unless they have witnessed it themselves. This is especially so if the person claiming to act under an oral appointment is not a close family member of the patient. This is not to say that health care providers should never regard such a person as a valid surrogate but only that there is a higher degree of comfort regarding someone who is to serve as surrogate if he is a close family member than if he is one who purports to have been orally designated by the patient to speak for the patient.

It is preferable that the writing used to appoint a proxy for health care decisionmaking be based either on a health care power of attorney statute or on a general durable power of attorney statute. However, there is no precedent for concluding that a writing not conforming to either kind of statute is per se invalid,[32] and in principle the appointment may be oral.[33]

---

[31] **NJ:** *In re* Peter, 529 A.2d at 426.

  **MI:** *But see* Werth v. Taylor, 475 N.W.2d 426, 430 (Mich. Ct. App. 1991) (implying that implicit oral designation of husband to make decisions while patient was recovering from surgery was not valid).

[32] See §§ **10.10–10.12.**

[33] *See* Browning v. Herbert, 568 So. 2d 4, 15 (Fla. 1990). See § **10.16.**

## § 12.5 —Types of Health Care Power of Attorney Statutes

Health care power of attorney statutes provide the firmest basis for the designation of a health care proxy. There are a few slightly different types of health care power of attorney statutes:

1. Those specifically designed for the purpose of authorizing the appointment of a proxy for health care decisionmaking

2. General durable power of attorney statutes containing a provision expressly permitting the designation of a proxy for health care decisionmaking

3. Provisions of living will or surrogate decisionmaking statutes permitting the appointment of a proxy for health care decisionmaking

4. General durable power of attorney statutes that, although not mentioning health care decisionmaking, have been judicially construed to permit the appointment of a proxy for health care decisionmaking or that may be used to appoint a proxy for that purpose because another statute (such as a living will statute or surrogate decisionmaking statute) specifically authorizes such use.

Because these different kinds of statutes achieve essentially the same purpose, they will be discussed in this chapter without distinguishing among them.

In addition to these statutes, a few related statutes, not discussed in this chapter, focus on more specific issues. Do-not-resuscitate statutes sometimes permit the appointment of a proxy to make decisions about do-not-resuscitate orders.[34] There are other, more general statutes, such as Minnesota's "patient's rights" statute, which authorizes the selection of a representative to participate in a patient's treatment plan.[35]

## § 12.6 —Powers of Attorney and Durable Powers of Attorney

A *power of attorney* is an instrument for granting legal authority to another person (the attorney in fact, agent, or proxy) to act on behalf of the grantor (the principal). Usually this power is limited in that it authorizes the agent to act only in those matters specified in the instrument.

### Common-Law Powers of Attorney

Common-law powers of attorney suffer from a serious limitation, especially for health care decisionmaking, because the agent's authority to act for the principal

---

[34] See **§ 9.9.**

[35] *See* Minn. Stat. Ann. § 144.651(10).

lapses when the principal becomes incompetent.[36] Thus, it is not possible for individuals interested in planning for the possibility that they may lose decision-making capacity, either temporarily or permanently, to designate the manner in which or the person by whom their affairs will be handled should this contingency arise. Rather, they are forced to rely on the more paternalistic and cumbersome process of guardianship, which is especially so if the individual's incompetence is only temporary, as, for example, during recuperation from an elective surgical operation. In addition, guardianship proceedings do not ordinarily permit the incompetent to designate the guardian, whereas a power of attorney permits the principal to choose the agent.

### Durable Powers of Attorney

The limitations on common-law powers of attorney are responsible for the enactment in all jurisdictions of statutes authorizing the execution of durable powers of attorney,[37] many modeled on the Uniform Durable Power of Attorney Act.[38] A *durable* power of attorney is a written instrument by which the principal designates another as his agent and which becomes or remains effective even when the principal becomes incapacitated.[39]

There is no reason based on durable power of attorney statutes themselves, or on the case law construing them, why a general durable power of attorney cannot be used to designate a proxy for medical decisionmaking in addition to or instead of financial transactions. A number of courts have approved their use.[40] In fact, durable powers of attorney are ideally suited to health care

---

[36] Restatement (Second) of Agency §§ 120, 122 (1957) (loss of capacity by principal terminates authority of agent without notice to latter).

**PA:** Pocono Medical Ctr. v. Harley, 11 Fiduc. Rep. 2d 128, 133 (C.P. Monroe County, Pa. 1990) (for power of attorney to be effective, it must recite that "this power of attorney shall become effective upon my disability or incapacity").

[37] **US:** Cruzan v. Director, 497 U.S. 261, 292 n.3 (1990) (O'Connor, J., concurring) (collecting statutes).

**NY:** Saunders v. State, 492 N.Y.S.2d 510, 516 (Sup. Ct. Nassau County 1985).

[38] 8A U.L.A. 275 (1994). *See also* Uniform Probate Code, 8 U.L.A. 431 (1983) (identical to Uniform Durable Power of Attorney Act).

[39] Uniform Durable Power of Attorney Act § 1, 8A U.L.A. 99, 99 (1994).

[40] **US:** Cruzan v. Director, 497 U.S. at 290 (O'Connor, J., concurring) ("Some state courts have suggested that an agent appointed pursuant to a general durable power of attorney statute would also be empowered to make health care decisions on behalf of the patient.") (citing *In re* Peter, 529 A.2d 419 (N.J. 1987); 73 Md. Op. Att'y Gen. 253 (Op. No. 88-046, Oct. 17, 1988) (interpreting Md. Code Ann., Est. & Trusts §§ 13-601 to -602 (1974), as authorizing delegates to make health care decisions)).

**FL:** Browning v. Herbert, 543 So. 2d 258, 266 (Fla. Dist. Ct. App. 1989), *aff'd,* 568 So. 2d 4 (Fla. 1990) ("A durable power of attorney can be created in Florida if the person designated to act is a family member. § 709.08, Fla. Stat. The statute authorizing a durable power of attorney does not expressly refer to medical treatment decisions. By combining the written declaration suggested in section 765.05, Florida Statutes (1987), with a durable family power of attorney

decisionmaking: it is precisely for the possible future inability to make one's own decisions that individuals need and wish to plan. Under a common-law power of attorney, the agent's authority terminates when an individual loses decisionmaking capacity, which for purposes of health care decisionmaking is precisely when an agent's authority should *commence*. By contrast, a *durable* power of attorney can be drafted so that the agent's authority will commence when the individual loses capacity to make health care decisions (a so-called *springing* power of attorney).[41]

The use of a durable power of attorney to appoint a proxy to make health care decisions does nothing more than use an existing legal instrument to fashion a proxy directive. A durable power of attorney can also be used to incorporate instructions to the named agent, thereby providing a recognized legal vehicle for the promulgation of a living will as well.

## REQUIREMENTS FOR EXECUTION AND IMPLEMENTATION

### § 12.7   Who May Execute Health Care Power of Attorney

Health care power of attorney statutes contain a variety of provisions that place limitations on the kinds of persons who may appoint a health care proxy.

---

under section 709.08, Florida Statutes, it is possible that a surrogate decisionmaker could be established who had detailed information concerning the desires of the patient.").

**LA:** *But see* La. Civ. Code Ann. art. 2997(A)(7) (power of attorney statute requires express conferral of authority to make health care decisions; health care decisions defined as "other than declarations of life-sustaining procedures").

**NJ:** *In re* Conroy, 486 A.2d 1209, 1229 (N.J. 1985) (patient's intent about life-sustaining treatment might be evidenced in durable power of attorney).

**NY:** *In re* Westchester County Medical Ctr. (O'Connor), 531 N.E.2d 607, 612 n.2 (N.Y. 1988). *But cf.* Saunders v. State, 492 N.Y.S.2d 510, 516 (Sup. Ct. Nassau County 1985) (expressing "concerns about the use of a power of attorney . . . because 'the application of the durable power to making health care decisions on behalf of principals has not been widely used and is not completely certain'").

**OK:** *But see* Okla. Op. Att'y Gen. No. 91-2 (May 6, 1991) (ruling that living will statute "provide[s] the exclusive method by which individuals may request that they be denied life-sustaining treatment").

[41] **NY:** *See In re* Westchester County Medical Ctr. (O'Connor), 531 N.E.2d at 612 n.2 (citing N.Y. Gen. Oblig. Law. § 5-1602).

Uniform Rights of the Terminally Ill Act, § 2(c), 9B U.L.A. 96, 101 [hereinafter 1989 URTIA]. UHCDA § 2(c). See § **13.22.**

## § 12.8  —Age

Some statutes specifically limit the execution of a health care power of attorney to persons over 18 years.[42] Other statutes require that one be an adult to execute a health care power of attorney, but do not statutorily define "adult."[43] Other

---

[42] **AR:** Ark. Code Ann. § 20-17-202 (living will statute permitting proxy appointment).

**CO:** Colo. Rev. Stat. § 15-14-504(1)(a) ("adult" defined as 18 years or older).

**CT:** Conn. Gen. Stat. Ann. § 19a-576(a).

**IA:** Iowa Code Ann. § 144B.1.5; Iowa Code Ann. § 144A.2(l) (allows proxy decisionmaking in absence of living will).

**KY:** Ky. Rev. Stat. Ann. § 311.621(1).

**ME:** Me. Rev. Stat. Ann. tit. 18-A, § 5-702(a).

**MD:** Md. Code Ann., Health-Gen. § 5-601(f) (at least 18 or with the same capacity as adult to consent).

**MI:** Mich. Comp. Laws § 700.496(1), *construed in* Rosebush v. Oakland County Prosecutor, 491 N.W.2d 633, 636 n.4 (Mich. Ct. App. 1992) ("The advance directive of a mature minor, stating the desire that life-sustaining treatment be refused, should be taken into consideration or enforced when deciding whether to terminate the minor's life support treatment or refuse medical treatment.").

**MN:** Minn. Stat. Ann. § 145C.01(8).

**MT:** Mont. Code Ann. § 50-9-103(1).

**NE:** Neb. Rev. Stat. § 30-3402(1) (19 years of age or is or has been married).

**NV:** Nev. Rev. Stat. Ann. § 449.600.1.

**NH:** N.H. Rev. Stat. Ann. § 137-J:1(IX).

**NJ:** N.J. Stat. Ann. § 26:2H-55.

**NY:** N.Y. Pub. Health Law § 2980(1) (must be 18 or parent of child or has married).

**NC:** N.C. Gen. Stat. § 32A-17.

**ND:** N.D. Cent. Code § 23-06.5-17.

**OH:** Ohio Rev. Code Ann. § 1337.11(A).

**OK:** Okla. Stat. Ann. tit. 63, § 3101.4(A).

**OR:** Or. Rev. Stat. § 127.505(11) (must be 18 and "not incapable").

**PA:** Pa. Cons. Stat. Ann. tit. 20, § 5404(a) (must be 18 years of age or older or have graduated from high school or have married).

**RI:** R.I. Gen. Laws § 23-4.10-2.

**SC:** S.C. Code Ann. § 62-5-504(A)(9).

**UT:** Utah Code Ann. § 75-2-1106(1).

**WV:** W. Va. Code § 16-30A-6(a).

**WI:** Wis. Stat. Ann. § 155.05.

[43] **AZ:** Ariz. Rev. Stat. Ann. § 36-3221(A).

**DE:** Del. Code Ann. tit. 16, § 2502(a).

**FL:** Fla. Stat. Ann. § 765.101(16).

**LA:** La. Rev. Stat. Ann. § 40:1299.58.3.

**MA:** Mass. Gen. Laws Ann. ch. 201D, § 2.

statutes, however, allow "a person"[44] to designate a proxy, suggesting that persons under the age of majority may execute a health care power of attorney. It is likely, however, that when there is no statutory limitation, only "mature" minors[45] would be authorized to execute a health care power of attorney. For example, the Indiana statute[46] authorizes one who may consent to his own health care[47] to either appoint a representative or serve as another's proxy. The statute includes as one capable of consenting to his own health care an emancipated minor of at least 14 years of age who is financially independent from his parents and living apart, who is or has been married, or who is in the military service.[48]

## § 12.9　—Capacity

Many statutes contain the express requirement that the principal not be incompetent at the time of execution of a health care power of attorney.[49] No jurisdiction

---

**MN:** Minn. Stat. Ann. § 145B.03(1).

**NV:** Nev. Rev. Stat. Ann. § 449.810.

**NY:** N.Y. Pub. Health Law § 2980(1).

**VA:** Va. Code Ann. § 54.1-2983.

**VT:** Vt. Stat. Ann. tit. 14, § 3452(8).

**WY:** Wyo. Stat. § 35-22-102(a).

[44] **AK:** Alaska Stat. § 13.26.332.

**CA:** Cal. Civ. Code §§ 2430–2445, 2500.

**CT:** Conn. Gen. Stat. Ann. § 19a-576(a).

**GA:** Ga. Code Ann. § 31-36-5(a).

**HI:** Haw. Rev. Stat. § 551D-2.5(a) (person who has attained age of majority).

**ID:** Idaho Code § 39-4505 ("a competent person").

**IL:** Ill. Ann. Stat. ch. 755, § 45/4-1 ("individual").

**ME:** Me. Rev. Stat. Ann. tit. 18-A, § 5-501.

**MS:** Miss. Code Ann. § 41-41-155(g).

**MO:** Mo. Ann. Stat. § 404.705.1.

**NM:** N.M. Stat. Ann. § 45-5-501(A).

**PA:** Pa. Cons. Stat. Ann. tit. 20, § 5604(a).

**TN:** Tenn. Code Ann. § 34-6-203(a)(3).

**WA:** Wash. Rev. Code Ann. § 11.94.010.

[45] See § **15.3.**

[46] Ind. Code Ann. § 16-36-1-7(a).

[47] *Id.* § 16-36-1-3.

[48] **IN:** Ind. Code Ann. § 16-36-1-3(2).

**TX:** *Accord* Tex. Civ. Prac. & Rem. Code Ann. § 135.001(1) (person executing instrument must be "a person 18 years of age or older or a person under 18 years of age who has had the disabilities of minority removed").

UHCDA § 2(a) (adult or emancipated minor may give instruction).

[49] **AR:** Ark. Code Ann. § 20-17-202(a).

**CT:** Conn. Gen. Stat. Ann. § 19a-577(a).

expressly permits the execution of a health care power of attorney by or for an incompetent person, which, however, is permitted by at least one living will statute.[50] Most durable power of attorney statutes do not explicitly require that the principal himself attest that he is of sound mind and acting freely when executing the instrument. However, prudence dictates that this be done anyway. In addition, in those jurisdictions requiring the use of—or substantially following— a sample form, the forms frequently contain language indicating that the principal is "fully informed as to all the contents of this form and understand[s] the full import of this grant of powers."[51]

---

**DC:** D.C. Code Ann. § 21-2205(a).

**FL:** Fla. Stat. Ann. § 765.101(14).

**HI:** Haw. Rev. Stat. § 551D-2.5(a).

**ID:** Idaho Code § 39-4505.

**KY:** Ky. Rev. Stat. Ann. § 311.629(1).

**MD:** Md. Code Ann., Health-Gen. § 5-602(a).

**MN:** Minn. Stat. Ann. § 145B.03(1).

**MT:** Mont. Code Ann. § 50-9-103(1).

**NE:** Neb. Rev. Stat. § 30-3402(11).

**NY:** N.Y. Pub. Health Law § 2980(1).

**NC:** N.C. Gen. Stat. § 32A-17.

**OH:** Ohio Rev. Code Ann. § 1337.12(A)(1).

**OK:** Okla. Stat. Ann. tit. 63, § 3101.4(A).

**OR:** Or. Rev. Stat. § 127.505(11).

**PA:** Pa. Cons. Stat. Ann. tit. 20, § 5404(a).

**SC:** S.C. Code Ann. § 62-5-504(A)(9).

**VA:** Va. Code Ann. § 54.1-2983.

**WV:** W. Va. Code § 16-30A-6.

**WI:** Wis. Stat. Ann. § 155.05.

**WY:** Wyo. Stat. § 3-5-213.

[50] **AR:** Ark. Code Ann. § 20-17-214. See §§ **11.4–11.5.**

[51] **CA:** Cal. Civ. Code § 2500.

**CT:** *Accord* Conn. Gen. Stat. Ann. § 19a-577(a).

**DC:** *Accord* D.C. Code Ann. § 21-2207 (form need not be substantially followed).

**FL:** *Accord* Fla. Stat. Ann. § 765.203.

**GA:** *Accord* Ga. Code Ann. § 31-36-10(a)(7).

**HI:** *Accord* Haw. Rev. Stat. § 551D-2.6.

**IL:** *Accord* Ill. Ann. Stat. ch. 755., § 45/4-10.

**LA:** *Accord* La. Rev. Stat. Ann. § 40:1299.58.3(C)(1).

**MD:** *Accord* Md. Code Ann., Health-Gen. § 5-603(i)(c).

**NE:** *Accord* Neb. Rev. Stat. § 30-3408(1).

**NH:** *Accord* N.H. Rev. Stat. Ann. § 137-J:15.

**NC:** *Accord* N.C. Gen. Stat. § 32A-25(8).

**ND:** *Accord* N.D. Cent. Code § 23-06.5-17.

**OK:** *Accord* Okla. Stat. Ann. tit. 63, § 3101.4(b).

## § 12.10   Disclosure Statement

Some statutes require that a health care power of attorney contain a disclosure statement, which is a warning directed to the principal notifying the principal of the legal effect of a health care power of attorney and of the agent's authority to make decisions about the principal's medical treatment. It must also notify the principal of his ability to limit the duration of the power of attorney and of the agent's powers and must describe the mechanisms the principal may use to revoke the power of attorney.[52] The use of a statutorily prescribed form for a health care power of attorney triggers different warning requirements in some jurisdictions.[53]

---

**PA:** *Accord* Pa. Cons. Stat. Ann. tit. 20, § 5404(b) (may but need not be in the following form).

**SC:** *Accord* S.C. Code Ann. § 62-5-504(D).

**TN:** *Accord* Tenn. Code Ann. § 34-6-295.

**TX:** *Accord* Tex. Civ. Prac. & Rem. Code Ann. § 135.016.

**VT:** *Accord* Vt. Stat. Ann. tit. 14, § 3466.

**VA:** *Accord* Va. Code Ann. § 54.1-2984 (suggested form).

**WI:** *Accord* Wis. Stat. Ann. § 155.05.

**WY:** *Accord* Wyo. Stat. § 3-5-202(a)(iii)(A) (no sample form; language in statute); Wyo. Stat. § 35-22-102(d).

[52] **CA:** Cal. Civ. Code §§ 2433(a), (b), 2500, 2501(a).

**DC:** D.C. Code Ann. § 21-2203 (optional disclosure requirement).

**IL:** Ill. Ann. Stat. ch. 755, § 45/4-10(a).

**MS:** Miss. Code Ann. § 41-41-163.

**NE:** Neb. Rev. Stat. § 30-3408.

**NV:** Nev. Rev. Stat. Ann. § 449.830.

**NH:** N.H. Rev. Stat. Ann. § 137-J:3(I).

**NC:** N.C. Gen. Stat. § 32A-25 (warning included in declaration form).

**ND:** N.D. Cent. Code § 23-06.5-17.

**OH:** Ohio Rev. Code Ann. § 1337.17 (disclosure requirement for form sold or distributed in Ohio for use by adults who wish to execute health care power of attorney but who are not advised by attorney).

**OR:** Or. Rev. Stat. § 127.530.

**RI:** R.I. Gen. Laws § 23-4.10-2.

**SC:** S.C. Code Ann. § 62-5-504(D).

**TN:** Tenn. Code Ann. § 34-6-205.

**TX:** Tex. Civ. Prac. & Rem. Code Ann. § 135.015.

**VT:** Vt. Stat. Ann. tit. 14, § 3454(a).

**WI:** Wis. Stat. Ann. § 155.30 (notice included in form).

UHCDA § 4.

[53] See § **12.11.**

## § 12.11  Statutorily Prescribed Form

Health care power of attorney statutes frequently include a sample power of attorney form, but in most jurisdictions use of the form is optional.[54] However, in others the sample form must be used.[55]

---

[54] **AK:** Alaska Stat. § 13.26.332.

**AZ:** Ariz. Rev. Stat. Ann. § 36-3224.

**AR:** Ark. Code Ann. § 20-17-202.

**CA:** Cal. Civ. Code § 2507.

**CT:** Conn. Gen. Stat. Ann. § 19a-577(a).

**DC:** D.C. Code Ann. § 21-2207.

**FL:** Fla. Stat. Ann. § 765.203.

**GA:** Ga. Code Ann. § 31-36-10.

**HI:** Haw. Rev. Stat. § 551D-2.6.

**ID:** Idaho Code § 39-4505.

**IA:** Iowa Code Ann. § 144B.5.1.

**KS:** Kan. Stat. Ann. § 58-632.

**KY:** Ky. Rev. Stat. Ann. § 311.625.

**ME:** Me. Rev. Stat. Ann. tit. 18-A, § 5-702(c).

**MD:** Md. Code Ann., Health-Gen. § 5-603.

**MN:** Minn. Stat. Ann. § 145B.04; Minn. Stat. Ann. § 145C.05.

**MS:** Miss. Code. Ann. § 41-41-163.

**MT:** Mont. Code Ann. § 50-9-103(3).

**NE:** Neb. Rev. Stat. § 30-3408(1).

**NV:** Nev. Rev. Stat. Ann. § 449.830.

**NH:** N.H. Rev. Stat. Ann. § 137-J:15.

**NM:** N.M. Stat. Ann. § 45-5-501.B.

**NY:** N.Y. Pub. Health Law § 2981(5)(D).

**NC:** N.C. Gen. Stat. § 32A-25.

**ND:** N.D. Cent. Code § 23-06.5-16.

**OH:** Ohio Rev. Code Ann. § 1337.13(a)(1).

**OK:** Okla. Stat. Ann. tit. 63, § 3101.4(B).

**PA:** Pa. Cons. Stat. Ann. tit. 20, § 5404(b).

**SC:** S.C. Code Ann. § 62-5-504(D) (must be substantially in the following form).

**TX:** Tex. Civ. Prac. & Rem. Code Ann. § 135.016.

**UT:** Utah Code Ann. § 75-2-1106(1).

**VT:** Vt. Stat. Ann. tit. 14, § 3454(b).

**VA:** Va. Code Ann. § 54.1-2984.

**WV:** W. Va. Code § 16-30A-18 (must "substantially compl[y] with the requirements set forth herein").

**WI:** Wis. Stat. Ann. § 155.30.

The California durable power of attorney statute contemplates the use of a printed form that is sold or otherwise distributed in the state. If used without advice of legal counsel, it must limit the authority it confers to health care decisions and must contain a warning that the instrument gives the proxy the power to make health care decisions, including consent to withholding or withdrawing life-sustaining treatment, if the principal does not object at the time the treatment is withheld or withdrawn, or if the power is not limited in the instrument. The form must notify the principal of methods of revocation, and it must notify the principal of his ability to place limitations on the proxy's authority concerning any matter, such as types of treatment the proxy may refuse and the duration of effectiveness of the power of attorney. The form must also state that it becomes effective only when the principal loses decisionmaking capacity.[56] If an individually prepared health care power of attorney is used, it must either include the same set of warnings as are required for forms, or a certificate must be attached to the instrument, signed by the principal's attorney, stating that the principal was advised of the consequences of signing a health care power of attorney.[57]

In addition to the durable power of attorney statute, California has a separate statutory form durable power of attorney for health care.[58] While the two statutes are basically consistent, the durable power of attorney for health care statute permits acknowledgment before a notary as a witnessing option.[59] The use of the statutory form is optional.[60] One study concludes that the short-form health care power of attorney is not helpful to physicians in communicating patients' wishes about specific procedures because the general instructions are often inconsistent with the specific preferences held by still-competent patients at the time a decision actually needed to be made.[61]

The Ohio statute contains a similar, though more restrictive, provision for the use of a health care power of attorney form without the advice of counsel. For

---

**WY:** *Compare* Wyo. Stat. § 35-22-102(d) (living will statute contains optional form for designation of agent) *with* Wyo. Stat. §§ 3-5-201 to -213 (health care power of attorney statute contains no form).

UHCDA § 4.

[55] **OR:** Or. Rev. Stat. § 127.530.

**RI:** R.I. Gen. Laws § 23-4.10-2.

[56] **CA:** Cal. Civ. Code §§ 2433(a), 2500, 2501(a).

**FL:** *Cf. In re* Dubreuil, 603 So. 2d 538 (Fla. Dist. Ct. App. 1992) (patient's spouse is not patient's surrogate decisionmaker if patient possesses decisionmaking capacity).

[57] Cal. Civ. Code §§ 2433(c), 2501(b).

[58] *Id.* §§ 2500–2508.

[59] *Id.* § 2432(3).

[60] *Id.* § 2500.

[61] Schneiderman et al., *Relationship of General Advance Directive Instructions to Specific Life-Sustaining Treatment Preferences in Patients with Serious Illness,* 152 Archives Internal Med. 2114 (1992).

example, a proxy appointed by such a form "never will be authorized to" terminate a list of treatments.[62]

## § 12.12   Witnesses and Authentication

Most statutes prescribe a procedure for verification of the power of attorney's authenticity. Some require the instrument to be acknowledged before witnesses (usually two) who personally know the principal and either witness the signing of the document or verify it through an acknowledgment of the signature.[63] Others provide the option of two witnesses or acknowledgment before a notary.[64] Some states require only one witness.[65]

---

[62] Ohio Rev. Code Ann. § 1337.17.

[63] **AR:** Ark. Code Ann. § 20-17-202(a).

**CA:** Cal. Civ. Code § 2502.

**CT:** Conn. Gen. Stat. Ann. § 19a-576(a).

**FL:** Fla. Stat. Ann. § 765.202(1).

**GA:** Ga. Code Ann. § 31-36-5(a).

**LA:** La. Rev. Stat. Ann. § 40:1299.58.3(A)(2).

**ME:** Me. Rev. Stat. Ann. tit. 18-A, § 5-702(c). *But cf.* Me. Rev. Stat. Ann. tit. 18-A, § 5-501 (requiring power of attorney containing authority to consent to medical or other professional care to be notarized).

**MS:** Miss. Code Ann. § 41-41-159(1)(i).

**MT:** Mont. Code Ann. § 50-9-103(1).

**NE:** Neb. Rev. Stat. § 30-3404(5).

**NH:** N.H. Rev. Stat. Ann. § 137-J:5.

**ND:** N.D. Cent. Code § 23-06.5-05.

**OK:** Okla. Stat. Ann. tit. 63, § 3101.4(A).

**OR:** Or. Rev. Stat. § 127-515.

**PA:** Pa. Cons. Stat. Ann. tit. 20, § 5404(a).

**RI:** R.I. Gen. Laws § 23-4.10-2.9.

**SC:** S.C. Code Ann. § 62-5-504(C)(1)(c).

**TN:** Tenn. Code Ann. § 34-6-203(a)(3).

**TX:** Tex. Civ. Prac. & Rem. Code Ann. § 135.004(a).

**VA:** Va. Code Ann. § 54.1-2983.

**WV:** W. Va. Code § 16-30A-6(a).

**WI:** Wis. Stat. Ann. § 155.10(1)(c).

*But see* UHCDA § 4 (witnesses recommended but not required).

[64] **AZ:** Ariz. Rev. Stat. Ann. § 36-3221(A)(3) (notarized or witnessed by at least one adult).

**CA:** Cal. Civ. Code § 2432(a)(3).

**DE:** Del. Code Ann. tit. 16, § 2503(a)(4).

**HI:** Haw. Rev. Stat. §§ 55D-2.5(b)(4), (5) (shall be signed in presence of two or more witnesses and have all signatures notarized at same time.

Many states require that at least one of the witnesses be a person who is not related to the principal by blood, marriage, or adoption[66] and not be entitled to any portion of the principal's estate upon the principal's death.[67] The witnessing

---

**ID:** Idaho Code § 39-4505.8.

**IA:** Iowa Code Ann. § 144B.3.1.b.

**KS:** Kan. Stat. Ann. § 58-629(e).

**KY:** Ky. Rev. Stat. Ann. § 311.625.

**MD:** Md. Code Ann., Health-Gen. § 5-602(C)(1).

**MN:** Minn. Stat. Ann. § 145B.03(2); Minn. Stat. Ann. § 145C.03(1).

**MS:** Miss. Code Ann. § 41-41-159(1)(b).

**NE:** Neb. Rev. Stat. § 30-34-3404(5).

**NV:** Nev. Rev. Stat. Ann. § 449.840.1.

**NJ:** N.J. Stat. Ann. § 26:2H-56.

**NC:** N.C. Gen. Stat. § 32A-16 (two witnesses and notary).

**OH:** Ohio Rev. Code Ann. § 1337.12(A)(1)(b).

**TN:** Tenn. Code Ann. § 34-6-203(3)(a)(3). (two witnesses and notary).

**UT:** Utah Code Ann. § 75-2-1106(1) (only notary public required).

**WV:** W. Va. Code § 16-30A-6(a)(4), (5) (requires both signature of two witnesses and acknowledgment before notary).

**WY:** Wyo. Stat. § 3-5-202(a)(iii).

[65] **IL:** Ill. Ann. Stat. ch. 755, § 45/4-10(a)(7).

**IN:** Ind. Code Ann. § 16-8-12-6(b)(3).

[66] **AZ:** Ariz. Rev. Stat. Ann. § 36-3221(D).

**CA:** Cal. Civ. Code §§ 2432(e)(1), 2500.

**DC:** D.C. Code Ann. § 21-2205(d).

**FL:** Fla. Stat. Ann. § 765.202(2).

**ID:** Idaho Code § 39-4505.8.

**IA:** Iowa Code Ann. § 144B.3.3.

**MS:** Miss. Code Ann. § 41-41-159(2).

**NV:** Nev. Rev. Stat. Ann. § 449.840.3(a).

**OR:** Or. Rev. Stat. § 127.515(2)(a)(A).

**RI:** R.I. Gen. Laws § 23-4.10-2.

**TN:** Tenn. Code Ann. § 34-6-203(e)(1).

**WY:** Wyo. Stat. § 3-5-202(d)(i).

[67] **AZ:** Ariz. Rev. Stat. Ann. § 36-3221(D).

**CA:** Cal. Civ. Code §§ 2432(e)(2), 2500.

**DC:** D.C. Code Ann. § 21-2205(d).

**ID:** Idaho Code § 39-4505.8.

**MD:** Md. Code Ann., Health-Gen. § 5-602(c)(2)(ii).

**MS:** Miss. Code Ann. § 41-41-159(2).

**NV:** Nev. Rev. Stat. Ann. § 449.840.3(b).

**OK:** Okla. Stat. Ann. tit. 63, § 3101.4(A).

requirements of several statutes are even more stringent, requiring that neither of the witnesses be related to the principal by blood, marriage, or adoption or entitled to any portion of the principal's estate.[68]

Most statutes that require witnesses or allow witnesses (rather than a notary) to authenticate a power of attorney also require that the witnesses attest to the circumstances surrounding the execution of the power of attorney. The most commonly used attestations that witnesses must make are

1. the principal is personally known to the witness; and/or
2. the principal signed or acknowledged his signature in the presence of the witness; and/or
3. the principal appeared to be of sound mind and under no duress, fraud, or undue influence at the time of execution.[69]

---

**OR:** Or. Rev. Stat. § 127.515(2)(a)(B).

**RI:** R.I. Gen. Laws § 23-4.10-2.

**TN:** Tenn. Code Ann. § 34-6-203(e)(2).

**WY:** Wyo. Stat. § 3-5-202(d)(ii).

[68] **CT:** Conn. Gen. Stat. Ann. § 19a-576(b), (c).

**DE:** Del. Code Ann. tit. 16, § 2503(b).

**III:** Haw. Rev. Stat. § 551D-2.5(b)(4)(B).

**KS:** Kan. Stat. Ann. § 58-629(e)(1) (also disqualified if "directly financially responsible for the principal's health care").

**MI:** Mich. Comp. Laws § 700.496(3).

**MN:** Minn. Stat. Ann. § 145B.03(d) (neither witness entitled to portion of estate).

**NE:** Neb. Rev. Stat. § 30-3405(1).

**NH:** N.H. Rev. Stat. Ann. § 137-J:5.

**NC:** N.C. Gen. Stat. § 32A-16(6)(i), (ii).

**ND:** N.D. Cent. Code § 23-06.5-05.

**OH:** Ohio Rev. Code Ann. § 1337.12(B).

**SC:** S.C. Code Ann. § 62-5-504(C)(1)(c).

**TX:** Tex. Civ. Prac. & Rem. Code Ann. § 135.004(b)(3), (4).

**VT:** Vt. Stat. Ann. tit. 14, § 3456.

**VA:** Va. Code Ann. § 54.1-2982.

**WV:** W. Va. Code § 16-30A-6(b).

**WI:** Wis. Stat. Ann. § 155.10(2)(a), (b).

**WY:** Wyo. Stat. § 35-22-102(a).

[69] **AZ:** Ariz. Rev. Stat. Ann. § 36-3221(A)(3).

**CA:** Cal. Civ. Code §§ 2432(a)(3)(A), 2500.

**CT:** Conn. Gen. Stat. Ann. § 19a-577(a).

**DC:** D.C. Code Ann. § 21-2205(c).

**HI:** Haw. Rev. Stat. § 551D-2.6.

**ID:** Idaho Code § 39-4505.8 (only one of witnesses need so attest).

Some statutes create a presumption that the principal was "of sound mind" when the power of attorney was executed.[70]

## § 12.13 —Execution of Advance Directive in a Health Care Facility

When an advance directive is executed in a health care facility, there is reason to be concerned that a patient's decisionmaking capacity and/or voluntariness may be more questionable than when the patient is outside such a facility. Consequently, some jurisdictions require that additional precautions be taken.

Chief among them is the requirement that those who serve as witnesses be "qualified" witnesses. Although the qualifications and disqualifications vary, the statutes exhibit a disinclination to allow those associated with the provision

---

**KY:** Ky. Rev. Stat. Ann. § 311.625.

**ME:** Me. Rev. Stat. Ann. tit. 18-A, § 5-702(c).

**MD:** Md. Code Ann., Health-Gen. § 5-603(i)(c) (attestation that will signed in presence of witness and that declarant appears to be competent).

**MS:** Miss. Code Ann. § 41-41-159(2).

**MT:** Mont. Code Ann. § 50-9-103(3) (attestation that declarant voluntarily signed document while in presence of witnesses).

**NE:** Neb. Rev. Stat. § 30-3408(1).

**NV:** Nev. Rev. Stat. Ann. § 449.830(8).

**NH:** N.H. Rev. Stat. Ann. § 137-J:5.

**NJ:** N.J. Stat. Ann. § 26:2H-56.

**NY:** N.Y. Pub. Health Law § 2981(2).

**NC:** N.C. Gen. Stat. § 32A-16(6).

**ND:** N.D. Cent. Code § 23-06.5-05.

**OH:** Ohio Rev. Code Ann. § 1337.12(B).

**OK:** Okla. Stat. Ann. tit. 63, § 3101.4(B).

**OR:** Or. Rev. Stat. § 127.515(2).

**PA:** Pa. Cons. Stat. Ann. tit. 20, § 5404(b).

**RI:** R.I. Gen. Laws § 23-4.10-2.

**SC:** S.C. Code Ann. § 62-5-504(C)(1)(c).

**TN:** Tenn. Code Ann. § 34-6-203(a)(3) (attestation as to principal's state of mind and relation of agent to principal and principal's estate).

**TX:** Tex. Civ. Prac. & Rem. Code Ann. § 135.004(c).

**VT:** Vt. Stat. Ann. tit. 14, § 3456 (must attest that principal was of sound mind, free of duress, and signed instrument voluntarily and while aware of its nature).

**WI:** Wis. Stat. Ann. § 155.30.

**WY:** Wyo. Stat. § 3-5-202(a)(iii)(A).

[70] **MD:** Md. Code Ann., Health-Gen. § 5-602(c)(2)(ii).

**WV:** W. Va. Code § 16-30A-8.

of health care to serve as a witness because of a real or perceived conflict of interest. Thus, in many states, a health care provider,[71] an employee of a health care provider,[72] an operator of a health care facility,[73] an employee of a health

---

[71] **AZ:** Ariz. Rev. Stat. Ann. § 36-3221(C)(2).

**CA:** Cal. Civ. Code § 2500.

**ID:** Idaho Code § 39-4505.8.

**IA:** Iowa Code Ann. § 144B.3.2.a.

**MD:** Md. Code Ann., Health-Gen. § 5-602(c)(1).

**MI:** Mich. Comp. Laws § 700.496(3).

**MN:** Minn. Stat. Ann. § 145C.03(3) (at least one witness must not be principal's health care provider).

**MS:** Miss. Code Ann. § 41-41-159(2).

**NE:** Neb. Rev. Stat. § 30-3404(5).

**NV:** Nev. Rev. Stat Ann. § 449.840(2)(a).

**NH:** N.H. Rev. Stat. Ann. § 137-J:5 (no more than one witness can be principal's health care provider).

**ND:** N.D. Cent. Code § 23-06.5-05.

**RI:** R.I. Gen. Laws § 23-4.10-2.

**TN:** Tenn. Code Ann. § 34-6-203(d)(1).

**TX:** Tex. Civ. Prac. & Rem. Code Ann. § 135.004(b)(2).

**WI:** Wis. Stat. Ann. § 155.10(2)(d).

**WY:** Wyo. Stat. § 3-5-202(c)(i).

[72] **AZ:** Ariz. Rev. Stat. Ann. § 36-3221(C)(2) (if directly involved with provision of health care to principal).

**CA:** Cal. Civ. Code §§ 2432(d)(2), 2500 (employee of principal's health care provider).

**DE:** Del. Code Ann. tit. 16, § 2503(b)(5).

**DC:** D.C. Code Ann. § 21-2205(c).

**HI:** Haw. Rev. Stat. § 551D-2.5(b)(4)(C).

**ID:** Idaho Code § 39-4505.8.

**IA:** Iowa Code Ann. § 144B.3.2.b.

**MI:** Mich. Comp. Laws § 700.496(3).

**MN:** Minn. Stat. Ann. § 145C.03(3) (at least one witness must not be an employee of principal's health care provider).

**MS:** Miss. Code Ann. § 41-41-159(2).

**NE:** Neb. Rev. Stat. § 30-3405(1) (no more than one witness may be employee of health care provider).

**NV:** Nev. Rev. Stat. Ann. § 449.840.2(b).

**NH:** N.H. Rev. Stat. Ann. § 137-J:5 (no more than one witness shall be principal's health care provider's employee).

**NC:** N.C. Gen. Stat. § 32A-16(6)(iii).

**ND:** N.D. Cent. Code § 23-06.5-05.

**RI:** R.I. Gen. Laws § 23-4.10-2.

**SC:** S.C. Code Ann. § 62-5-504(C)(1)(c).

care facility,[74] the principal's attending physician,[75] and the proxy[76] are disqualified from serving as witnesses, as is a person who signs the declaration on behalf of and at the direction of the declarant.[77]

---

**TN:** Tenn. Code Ann. § 34-6-203(d)(2).

**TX:** Tex. Civ. Prac. & Rem. Code Ann. § 135.004(b)(2).

**VA:** *But see* Va. Code Ann. § 54.1-2982 ("Employees of . . . physician's offices who act in good faith, shall be permitted to serve as witnesses.").

**WY:** Wyo. Stat. § 3-5-202(c)(ii).

[73] **CA:** Cal. Civ. Code §§ 2432(d)(4), 2500.

**ID:** Idaho Code § 39-4505-5.8.

**KY:** Ky. Rev. Stat. Ann. § 311.625.

**NE:** Neb. Rev. Stat. § 30-3405-1 (no more than one witness may be administrator of health care provider).

**NV:** Nev. Rev. Stat. Ann. § 449.840.2(c).

**OH:** Ohio Rev. Code Ann. § 1337.12(B) (administrator of nursing home in which principal is receiving care).

**RI:** R.I. Gen. Laws § 23-4.10-2.

**TN:** Tenn. Code Ann. § 34-6-203(d)(4).

**WY:** Wyo. Stat. § 3-5-202(c)(iv), (vi).

[74] **AZ:** Ariz. Rev. Stat. Ann. § 36-3221(C)(2) (if directly involved with provision of health care to principal).

**CA:** Cal. Civ. Code §§ 2432(d)(5), 2500.

**DE:** Del. Code Ann. tit. 16, § 2503(b)(5).

**DC:** D.C. Code Ann. § 21-2205(c).

**HI:** Haw. Rev. Stat. § 551D-2.5(b)(4)(C).

**ID:** Idaho Code § 39-4505.8.

**KY:** Ky. Rev. Stat. Ann. § 311.625.

**MI:** Mich. Comp. Laws § 700.496(3).

**MN:** Minn. Stat. Ann. § 145C.03(3) (at least one witness must not be principal's health care provider).

**MS:** Miss. Code Ann. § 41-41-159(2).

**NV:** Nev. Rev. Stat. Ann. § 449.840.2(d).

**NC:** N.C. Gen. Stat. § 32A-16(6)(iii).

**RI:** R.I. Gen. Laws § 23-4.10-2.

**SC:** S.C. Code Ann. § 62-5-504(C)(1)(c) (no more than one witness).

**TN:** Tenn. Code Ann. § 34-6-203(d)(5).

**VA:** *But see* Va. Code Ann. § 54.1-2982 ("Employees of health care facilities . . . who act in good faith, shall be permitted to serve as witnesses.").

**WY:** Wyo. Stat. § 3-5-202(c)(v), (vii).

[75] **AZ:** Ariz. Rev. Stat. Ann. § 36-3221(C)(2).

**CA:** Cal. Civ. Code § 2432(d)(1).

**DC:** D.C. Code Ann. § 21-2205(c) (or employee).

**HI:** Haw. Rev. Stat. § 551D-2.5(b)(4)(C).

**MI:** Mich. Comp. Laws § 700.496(3).

**MN:** Minn. Stat. Ann. § 145C.03(3) (at least one witness must not be an employee of principal's health care provider).

**NE:** Neb. Rev. Stat. § 30-3405(1).

**NC:** N.C. Gen. Stat. § 32A-16(6)(iii).

**OH:** Ohio Rev. Code Ann. § 1337.12(B).

**OR:** Or. Rev. Stat. § 127.515(2)(b)(B).

**SC:** S.C. Code Ann. § 62-5-504(C)(1)(c).

**VT:** Vt. Stat. Ann. tit. 14, § 3456 (or employee).

**WV:** W. Va. Code § 16-30A-6(b).

**WY:** Wyo. Stat. § 3-5-202(c)(i).

[76] **AZ:** Ariz. Rev. Stat. Ann. § 36-3221(C)(1).

**CA:** Cal. Civ. Code §§ 2432(d)(3), 2500.

**CT:** Conn. Gen. Stat. Ann. § 19a-576(a).

**FL:** Fla. Stat. Ann. § 765.202(2).

**ID:** Idaho Code § 39-4505.8.

**IN:** Ind. Code Ann. § 16-8-12-6(C)(3).

**IA:** Iowa Code Ann. § 144B.3.2.c.

**KS:** Kan. Stat. Ann. § 58-629(e)(1).

**KY:** Ky. Rev. Stat. Ann. § 311.625.

**MD:** Md. Code Ann., Health-Gen. § 5-602(c)(2)(ii).

**MA:** Mass. Gen. Laws Ann. ch. 201D, § 2.

**MI:** Mich. Comp. Laws § 700.496(3).

**MN:** Minn. Stat. Ann. § 145B.03(2)(d); Minn. Stat. Ann. § 145C.03(3).

**MS:** Miss. Code Ann. § 41-41-159(2).

**NE:** Neb. Rev. Stat. § 30-3401(1).

**NV:** Nev. Rev. Stat. Ann. § 449.840.2(e).

**NH:** N.H. Rev. Stat. Ann. § 137-J:5.

**NJ:** N.J. Stat. Ann. § 26:2H-56.

**NY:** N.Y. Pub. Health Law § 2981(2)(a).

**ND:** N.D. Cent. Code § 23-06.5-05.

**OH:** Ohio Rev. Code Ann. § 1337.12(B).

**OR:** Or. Rev. Stat. § 127.515(2)(b)(B).

**RI:** R.I. Gen. Laws § 23-4.10-2.

**SC:** S.C. Code Ann. § 62-5-504(C)(1)(c).

**TN:** Tenn. Code Ann. § 34-6-203(d)(3).

**TX:** Tex. Civ. Prac. & Rem. Code Ann. § 135.004(b)(1).

**VT:** Vt. Stat. Ann. tit. 14, § 3456.

**WV:** W. Va. Code § 16-30A-6(b).

**WI:** Wis. Stat. Ann. § 155.10(2)(e).

**WY:** Wyo. Stat. § 3-5-202(c)(iii).

[77] **PA:** Pa. Cons. Stat. Ann. tit. 20, § 5404(a).

Although many statutes disqualify the attending physician from serving as a witness because of a potential conflict of interest, the Georgia statute requires that a health care power of attorney be witnessed by the attending physician if executed in a hospital or nursing facility.[78] A few statutes provide that if the principal is a patient in a facility for the care of mentally ill or mentally retarded persons, one witness must be either a physician or a mental health professional.[79] California requires that one of the witnesses be a patient's advocate or ombudsman if the principal is in a skilled nursing facility when the power of attorney is executed.[80] In Vermont, an ombudsman must attest that he "has explained the nature and effect of the durable power of attorney for health care to the principal" when the principal is a patient in a skilled nursing facility.[81] In North Dakota, unless the principal reads, and acknowledges in writing, a statement explaining the nature and effect of the health care power of attorney, a member of the clergy, an attorney, or a person designated by the Department of Human Services or the county court must sign a statement affirming that he has explained the nature and effect of the health care power of attorney to the principal at the time of execution if the principal is a resident of a long-term care facility,[82] and in the case of a hospital, by a person designated by the hospital.[83]

## § 12.14  Notarization

Only a few health care power of attorney statutes expressly require notarization,[84] although others include space for a notary's signature and seal in their sample forms.[85]

---

[78] **GA:** Ga. Code Ann. § 31-36-10(a)(7).

[79] **CT:** Conn. Gen. Stat. Ann. § 19a-576(b), (c) (providing that if principal resides in facilities operated or licensed by Department of Mental Health or Mental Retardation, at least one witness must be unaffiliated with facility and at least one witness must be physician or clinical psychologist with specialized training in mental illness or developmental disabilities).

**MD:** Md. Code Ann., Health-Gen. § 5-602(c)(2)(ii).

**MN:** Minn. Stat. Ann. § 145C.03(3).

**NY:** N.Y. Pub. Health Law § 2981(2).

[80] Cal. Civ. Code §§ 2432(f), 2500.

[81] Vt. Stat. Ann. tit. 14, § 3460(b).

[82] N.D. Cent. Code § 23-06.5-10.2.

[83] *Id.* § 23-06.5-10.3.

[84] **HI:** Haw. Rev. Stat. § 551D-2.5(b)(5).

**ME:** Me. Rev. Stat. Ann. tit. 18-A, § 5-501.

**NC:** N.C. Gen. Stat. § 32A-16(3).

**TN:** Tenn. Code Ann. § 34-6-203(a)(3).

**UT:** Utah Code Ann. § 75-2-1106(1).

**WV:** W. Va. Code § 16-30A-6(a).

[85] **AK:** Alaska Stat. § 13.26.332.

**CT:** Conn. Gen. Stat. Ann. § 19a-577(a).

## § 12.15  Commencement of Proxy's Powers

There are several different ways in which a proxy's authority to make medical decisions can be triggered. As the next two sections explain, the main condition for transferring decisionmaking authority is the principal's loss of decision-making capacity. However, this is not universally so, and in addition, under some statutes, that is not a sufficient condition.

## § 12.16  —Loss of Decisionmaking Capacity

A general durable power of attorney can be drafted so as to take effect upon execution or on the happening of some condition, generally the "incapacity" (or similar language) of the principal. The latter form of durable power of attorney is referred to as a *springing* durable power of attorney.[86] The disadvantage of the former is that the agent is empowered to act for the principal immediately even though the principal might have no need or wish to delegate authority at present, a situation which could lead to conflict between the principal and agent about what health care should be administered and what forgone. In practice, however, should the agent seek to assert authority when the principal is competent and does not wish the agent to act, the principal may revoke the power of attorney.[87] However, if it has been relied on by a third party, the revocation will probably not be effective as to actions involving that party.[88]

In health care decisionmaking generally and end-of-life decisionmaking in particular, principals will ordinarily wish to transfer decisional authority to their proxies only when they lose decisionmaking capacity, and therefore the spring-ing power of attorney is what will ordinarily be used and is what is contemplated by most statutes. The disadvantage of the *springing* power of attorney, however, is that it requires a determination of the principal's incapacity. Although in some instances there may be no doubt that the principal lacks capacity (such as when the principal is unconscious), there is a range of situations in which a principal's

---

**KY:** Ky. Rev. Stat. Ann. § 311.625.

**MD:** Md. Code Ann., Health-Gen. § 5-603 (attestation that will signed in presence of witness and that declarant appears to be competent).

**NH:** N.H. Rev. Stat. Ann. § 137-J:15.

**NM:** N.M. Stat. Ann. § 45-5-501.B (space provided for notarization but no space for wit-nesses' signatures in sample form).

[86] **NY:** *See In re* Westchester County Medical Ctr. (O'Connor), 531 N.E.2d 607, 612 n.2 (N.Y. 1988) (citing N.Y. Gen. Oblig. Law § 5-1602).

Uniform Durable Power of Attorney Act, § 1, 8A U.L.A. 99, 99 (1994). UHCDA § 2(c).

[87] Uniform Durable Power of Attorney Act § 5, 8A U.L.A. 275, 284 (1994).

[88] **CT:** Conn. Gen. Stat. Ann. § 19a-576(b), (c).

Uniform Durable Power of Attorney Act § 4(a), 8A U.L.A. 275 (1994) (death of principal "does not revoke or terminate the agency as to the attorney in fact or other person, who, without actual knowledge of the death of the principal, acts in good faith under the power").

capacity may be questionable (such as intoxication or dementia) and in which the principal is at least able to express a view or contest the agent's assertion of authority.[89] Although some health care power of attorney statutes define lack of capacity (or incompetence),[90] application of the definition can be problematic. In disputed cases, it may still be necessary to obtain a judicial determination of incompetence for the power of attorney to become operative, which is precisely what one is seeking to avoid by executing a health care power of attorney.

Some health care power of attorney statutes explicitly permit the principal to choose whether the power is to become effective upon execution or whether the power is to take effect at the time of the principal's disability.[91] Because only a few states require a determination that the principal is disabled or incompetent

---

[89] See §§ 7.45–7.46.

[90] **CO:** Colo. Rev. Stat. § 15-14-505(4) (defines "decisional capacity").

**CT:** Conn. Gen. Stat. Ann. § 19a-570(6).

**FL:** Fla. Stat. Ann. § 765.101(9).

**GA:** Ga. Code Ann. § 31-36-7(1).

**ID:** Idaho Code § 39-4505.

**KS:** Kan. Stat. Ann. § 58-629(b).

**MD:** Md. Code Ann., Health-Gen. § 2-601(l) (defines "incapable of making an informed decision").

**NE:** Neb. Rev. Stat. § 30-3402(7) (defines "incapable").

**NH:** N.H. Rev. Stat. Ann. § 137-J:1(IV) (defines "capacity to make health care decisions").

**NJ:** N.J. Stat. Ann. § 26:2H-55 (defining decisionmaking capacity).

**NY:** N.Y. Pub. Health Law § 2980(3).

**ND:** N.D. Cent. Code § 23-06.5-02.3 (defining "capacity to make health decisions").

**OH:** Ohio Rev. Code Ann. § 1337.11(N) (cross-reference to statutory provision outside of health care power of attorney).

**OR:** Or. Rev. Stat. § 127.505(8).

**PA:** Pa. Cons. Stat. Ann. tit. 20, § 5403.

**TX:** Tex. Civ. Prac. & Rem. Code Ann. § 135.001(4).

**VT:** Vt. Stat. Ann. tit. 14, § 3452(3).

**VA:** Va. Code Ann. § 54.1-2982 (defines "incapable of making an informed decision").

**WV:** W. Va. Code § 16-30A-3.

**WI:** Wis. Stat. Ann. § 155.01(8) ("incapacity").

**WY:** Wyo. Stat. § 3-5-201(a)(vii) ("incompetent person").

UHCDA § 1 ("capacity").

[91] **AK:** Alaska Stat. § 13.26.332.

**IL:** Ill. Ann. Stat. ch. 755, § 45/4-10(a)(3).

**MD:** Md. Code Ann., Health-Gen. § 2-603(II)(A)(4).

**NM:** N.M. Stat. Ann. § 45-5-501.B.

before the agent's power to make decisions becomes effective,[92] it is advisable for a principal to state the conditions for determining when he has lost decision-making capacity and thus when the proxy is to assume decisionmaking authority. The common statutory approach is to specify that one or two physicians must certify that the patient has lost decisionmaking capacity.[93] A few statutes allow

---

[92] **AZ:** Ariz. Rev. Stat. Ann. § 36-3223(A).

**CO:** Colo. Rev. Stat. § 15-14-506(3).

**CT:** Conn. Gen. Stat. Ann. § 19a-579.

**FL:** Fla. Stat. Ann. § 765.204(3).

**HI:** Haw. Rev. Stat. § 551D-2.5(d).

**ID:** Idaho Code § 39-4505 (agent's power effective only when principal "is unable to communicate rationally").

**ME:** Me. Rev. Stat. Ann. tit. 18-A, § 5-703.

**MN:** Minn. Stat. Ann. § 145C.06 (agent's authority effective when principal is unable to make or communicate health care decisions as determined by principal's attending physician).

**MT:** Mont. Code Ann. § 50-9-105(1)(b).

**NE:** Neb. Rev. Stat. § 30-3417(2).

**NH:** N.H. Rev. Stat. Ann. § 137-J:2(III).

**NJ:** N.J. Stat. Ann. § 26:2H-59(a).

**NC:** N.C. Gen. Stat. § 32A-20(a).

**ND:** N.D. Cent. Code § 23-06.5-03.3 (agent's authority in effect only when principal lacks capacity to make health care decisions as certified by principal's attending physician and filed in medical record).

**OH:** Ohio Rev. Code Ann. § 1337.12(A)(1).

**OK:** Okla. Stat. Ann. tit. 63, § 3101.5(A)(2) (declarant no longer able to make decisions regarding administration of life-sustaining treatment).

**PA:** Pa. Cons. Stat. Ann. tit. 20, § 5405.

**SC:** S.C. Code Ann. § 62-5-504(D).

**SD:** S.D. Codified Laws Ann. § 59-7-2.6.

**WV:** W. Va. Code § 16-30A-3 (agent's power effective only when principal is unable to "communicate . . . in an unambiguous manner").

**WI:** Wis. Stat. Ann. § 155.05(2) (unless otherwise specified in the instrument).

**WY:** Wyo. Stat. § 3-5-201(a) (attorney in fact does not have authority to make particular health care decision if principal is able to give informed consent with respect to that decision).

UHCDA § 2(c) (agent's authority only effective upon determination that principal lacks capacity, unless otherwise specified in directive).

[93] **AK:** Alaska Stat. § 13.26.353(a).

**CT:** Conn. Gen. Stat. Ann. § 19a-570(6); Conn. Gen. Stat. Ann. § 19a-579.

**DC:** D.C. Code Ann. § 21-2204(a), (b).

**FL:** Fla. Stat. Ann. § 765.204(2) (two physicians must determine incapacity, one must be attending physician).

a principal who, because of religious reasons or moral beliefs, has no attending physician to designate a person to determine when the principal has lost the capacity to make decisions. This person cannot be the proxy or the principal's spouse or heir and must certify in writing before a notary or a justice of the peace that the principal has lost decisionmaking capacity.[94]

---

**IA:** Iowa Code Ann. § 144B.6.1.

**KS:** Kan. Stat. Ann. § 58-29(3)(b).

**KY:** Ky. Rev. Stat. Ann. § 311.629.

**ME:** Me. Rev. Stat. Ann. tit. 18-A, § 5-703.

**MD:** Md. Code Ann., Health-Gen. § 5-601(l) (defines "incapable of making an informed decision"); Md. Code Ann., Health-Gen. § 5-606(A).

**MA:** Mass. Gen. Laws Ann. ch. 201D, § 6.

**MI:** Mich. Comp. Laws § 700.496(8).

**MO:** Mo. Ann. Stat. § 404.825.

**MT:** Mont. Code Ann. § 50-9-105(l)(b).

**NE:** Neb. Rev. Stat. § 30-3412(1).

**NV:** Nev. Rev. Stat. Ann. § 449.617.

**NH:** N.H. Rev. Stat. Ann. § 137-J:2(III).

**NJ:** N.J. Stat. Ann. § 26:2H-60(a).

**NY:** N.Y. Pub. Health Law § 2983(1) (attending physician must determine to reasonable degree of medical certainty).

**NC:** N.C. Gen. Stat. § 32A-20(a).

**ND:** N.D. Cent. Code § 23-06.5-03.3.

**OH:** Ohio Rev. Code Ann. § 1337.12(A)(1) (attending physician of principal).

**OK:** Okla. Stat. Ann. tit. 63, § 3101.4(B).

**PA:** Pa. Cons. Stat. Ann. tit. 20, §§ 5405, 5408.

**SC:** S.C. Code Ann. § 62-5-504(B)(4).

**SD:** S.D. Codified Laws Ann. § 59-7-2.6 (by implication).

**TX:** Tex. Civ. Prac. & Rem. Code Ann. § 135.002(b).

**VT:** Vt. Stat. Ann. tit. 14, § 3453(c).

**VA:** Va. Code Ann. § 54.1-2983.

**WV:** W. Va. Code § 16-30A-3.

**WI:** Wis. Stat. Ann. § 155.05(2) (two physicians or physician and licensed psychologist).

**WY:** Wyo. Stat. § 3-5-209(c).

UHCDA § 2(d) (primary physician, unless otherwise specified).

[94] **MD:** Md. Code Ann., Health-Gen. § 2-603 (II)(A)(4).

**NH:** N.H. Rev. Stat. Ann. § 137-J:2(III).

**OK:** Okla. Stat. Ann. tit. 63, § 3101.4(E) (designated individual must be specified and included as part of advance directive).

## § 12.17 —Terminal Condition or Permanent Unconsciousness

Many living will statutes condition the operation of the instructions in the living will on the patient's medical condition.[95] Some, but a fewer number of, health care power of attorney statutes allow the proxy to make decisions only if the patient is in a certain type of medical condition, such as terminal illness or permanent unconsciousness.[96]

---

[95] See § 11.9.

[96] **AR:** Ark. Code Ann. §§ 20-17-201(7), -202(e).

**CT:** *Cf.* Conn. Gen. Stat. Ann. § 19a-571(a) (if attending physician does not judge patient to be in a terminal condition or permanently unconscious, "beneficial medical treatment including nutrition and hydration must be provided").

**KY:** Ky. Rev. Stat. Ann. § 311.629 (prohibiting forgoing of artificial nutrition and hydration unless patient is terminally ill or other conditions are met).

**LA:** La. Rev. Stat. Ann. § 40:1299.58.3(C)(1).

**ME:** Me. Rev. Stat. Ann. tit. 18-A, § 5-703.

**MN:** *Compare* Minn. Stat. Ann. § 145B.04 (proxy directive authorized by living will statute to be followed if declarant is in terminal condition and unable to participate in health care decisions) *with* Minn. Stat. Ann. § 145C.06 (proxy's authority effective when principal is unable to make or communicate health care decisions as determined by principal's attending physician).

**MT:** Mont. Code Ann. § 50-9-105(1)(b) (declaration becomes operative when declarant is determined by attending physician to be in a terminal condition).

**NE:** Neb. Rev. Stat. § 30-3418(2) (attorney in fact does not have authority to consent to withholding or withdrawal of life-sustaining procedure unless principal is suffering from terminal condition or is in persistent vegetative state and power of attorney for health care explicitly grants such authority to attorney in fact or intent of principal to have life-sustaining treatment withheld or withdrawn can be established by clear and convincing evidence).

**NV:** Nev. Rev. Stat. Ann. § 449.613(1) (form declaration conditions proxy's authority on existence of "incurable and irreversible condition that, without the administration of life-sustaining treatment, will . . . cause my death within a relatively short time").

**NC:** N.C. Gen. Stat. § 32A-25(3)(E) (in form directive, agent can authorize withholding or withdrawal of life-sustaining procedures only if principal is terminally ill, is permanently in a coma, suffers severe dementia, or is in persistent vegetative state).

**OH:** Ohio Rev. Code Ann. § 1337.13(B) (principal must be in terminal condition or permanently unconscious state for agent to refuse or withdraw life-sustaining treatment).

**OR:** Or. Rev. Stat. § 127.540(6)(a), (b) (agent can withhold or withdraw life-sustaining procedures, not including artificial nutrition and hydration, if principal has specifically directed, if principal is comatose and there is no reasonable possibility of return to cognitive sapient state, or if principal has terminal condition, and committee of physicians concurs with attending physician in principal's condition; statute unclear as to whether last requirement applies to prior one or prior two conditions).

## § 12.18  Recordkeeping and
## Notification Requirements

For the principal's wishes to be effectuated, the attending physician must be aware of the existence of a health care power of attorney. A few statutes expressly require the principal, or someone acting on the principal's behalf, to notify the attending physician that a health care power of attorney has been executed.[97] As a practical matter, if the principal has not provided the physician with a copy of the power of attorney or mentioned its existence before losing decisionmaking capacity, the responsibility for doing so necessarily falls to the proxy or some other party who knows of its existence. In Illinois, the principal or agent is required to notify health care providers of any amendment to or revocation of a health care power of attorney.[98] In Iowa, only notice of revocation must be given to the attending physician, but not notice of the existence of the power of attorney,[99] which makes no sense in practice.

Some statutes require that a copy of a health care power of attorney be made a part of the principal's medical record.[100] It is unclear, however, whether these

---

**PA:** Pa. Cons. Stat. Ann. tit. 20, § 5404(b) (must be in terminal condition or permanent state of unconsciousness).

**SD:** S.D. Codified Laws Ann. § 59-7-2.7 (one circumstance under which attorney in fact or agent can authorize withholding or withdrawal of artificial nutrition or hydration is if not needed for comfort care and attending physician "reasonably believes that the principal's death will occur within approximately one week").

**TN:** Tenn. Code Ann. § 34-6-204(d) ("attorney in fact . . . may make health care decisions for the principal who has a condition from which the attending physician has determined that there can be no recovery and death is imminent").

**WV:** W. Va. Code § 16-30A-18 (in form directive, agent can authorize withholding or withdrawal of life-prolonging intervention only after two physicians examine the declarant and determine that such intervention offers no medical hope or benefit).

**WY:** Wyo. Stat. § 35-22-102(d) (living will form directive conditions proxy's powers on existence of "incurable injury, disease or other illness certified to be a terminal condition").

[97] **CT:** Conn. Gen. Stat. Ann. § 19a-579 (appointment of health care agent operative upon furnishing instrument/writing to attending physician).

**FL:** Fla. Stat. Ann. § 765.302(2) (if proxy provision is in living will).

**GA:** Ga. Code Ann. § 31-36-7(1).

**IL:** Ill. Ann. Stat. ch. 755, § 45/4-7(a).

**MD:** Md. Code Ann., Health-Gen. § 5-602(F)(1); Md. Health-Gen. Code Ann. § 5-606(A).

**NJ:** N.J. Stat. Ann. § 26:2H-59(a) (by implication).

**ND:** N.D. Cent. Code § 23-06.5-17.

**VA:** Va. Code Ann. § 54.1-2983.

UHCDA § 4 (sample form addresses declarant: "Give a copy of the . . . form to your physician.").

[98] Ill. Ann. Stat. ch. 755, § 45/4-7(a).

[99] Iowa Code Ann. § 144A.4.

[100] **CT:** Conn. Gen. Stat. Ann. § 19a-578(b).

**DE:** Del. Code Ann. tit. 16, § 2506(b).

**GA:** Ga. Code Ann. § 31-36-7(1).

provisions apply only to individuals who are already patients in a health care facility or whether they also apply to individuals who are not in a health care facility but who have executed health care powers of attorney and given them to their physicians.

## § 12.19  Designation of Successor or Concurrent Proxies

Some statutes expressly allow the designation in the power of attorney of a successor proxy to assume the duties of the first-named proxy if the latter is unable or unwilling to serve.[101] Some also expressly provide that the successor proxy's powers are the same as those of the original proxy.[102]

---

**IL:** Ill. Ann. Stat. ch. 755, § 45/4-7(a) (any amendment or revocation must also be made part of record).

**KY:** Ky. Rev. Stat. Ann. § 311.633.

**ME:** Me. Rev. Stat. Ann. tit. 18-A, § 5-702(c).

**MD:** Md. Code Ann., Health-Gen. § 5-602(F)(2)(I).

**MI:** Mich. Comp. Laws § 700.496(2).

**MN:** Minn. Stat. Ann. § 145B.06(1)(a).

**MT:** Mont. Code Ann. § 50-9-103(5).

**NE:** Neb. Rev. Stat. § 30-3409.

**NV:** Nev. Rev. Stat. Ann. § 449.600.2.

**NY:** N.Y. Pub. Health Law § 2984(1).

**OK:** Okla. Stat. Ann. tit. 63, § 3101.4(C).

**OR:** Or. Rev. Stat. § 127.510(3) (withdrawal of agent must be made part of principal's medical records).

**PA:** Pa. Cons. Stat. Ann. tit. 20, § 5404(d).

**VA:** Va. Code Ann. § 54.1-2983.

**WV:** W. Va. Code § 16-30A-11.

**WI:** Wis. Stat. Ann. § 155.60(3).

UHCDA § 7(b) (health care provider who knows of declaration).

[101] **AK:** Alaska Stat. § 13.26.335(2).

**AZ:** Ariz. Rev. Stat. Ann. § 36-3224 (sample form).

**CA:** Cal. Civ. Code § 2500(9).

**DC:** D.C. Code Ann. § 21-2207.

**FL:** Fla. Stat. Ann. § 765.202(3) ("alternate surrogate").

**GA:** Ga. Code Ann. § 31-36-10(a).

**ID:** Idaho Code § 39-4505.

**IL:** Ill. Ann. Stat. ch. 755, § 45/4-10(a)(5).

**KY:** Ky. Rev. Stat. Ann. § 311.633.

**ME:** Me. Rev. Stat. Ann. tit. 18-A, § 5-702(c).

**MD:** Md. Code Ann., Health-Gen. § 5-603(II)(A)(1).

**MA:** Mass. Gen. Laws Ann. ch. 201D, § 2.

**MN:** Minn. Stat. Ann. § 145B.04; Minn. Stat. Ann. § 145C.05(2)(1).

**MO:** Mo. Ann. Stat. § 404.723.2.

**MT:** Mont. Code Ann. § 50-9-103(3).

**NE:** Neb. Rev. Stat. § 30-3403(1).

**NV:** Nev. Rev. Stat. Ann. §§ 449.613.1, .860.1.

**NH:** N.H. Rev. Stat. Ann. § 137-J:14.

**NM:** N.M. Stat. Ann. § 45-5-501.B.

**NY:** N.Y. Pub. Health Law § 2981(5)(D).

**NC:** N.C. Gen. Stat. § 32A-25(1).

**ND:** N.D. Cent. Code § 23-06.5-17.

**OK:** Okla. Stat. Ann. tit. 63, § 3101.4(B).

**OR:** Or. Rev. Stat. § 127.510(1).

**PA:** Pa. Cons. Stat. Ann. tit. 20, § 5404(b) ("substitute surrogate"); Pa. Cons. Stat. Ann. tit. 20, § 5602(b)(2).

**RI:** R.I. Gen. Laws § 23-4.10-2.

**SC:** S.C. Code Ann. § 62-5-504(K).

**TX:** Tex. Civ. Prac. & Rem. Code Ann. § 135.016.

**VT:** Vt. Stat. Ann. tit. 14, § 3456.

**VA:** Va. Code Ann. § 54.1-2984.

**WV:** W. Va. Code § 16-30A-5(b) (If both the primary agent and the named successor are "unable, unwilling or disqualified to serve, then the medical power of attorney shall lapse. However, such lapse shall not prevent any advance directives, statement of personal values or specific instructions therein from serving as guidelines for the medical or health care of the principal.").

**WI:** Wis. Stat. Ann. § 155.05(5).

UHCDA § 4.

[102] **AK:** Alaska Stat. § 13.26.335(2).

**CA:** Cal. Civ. Code § 2500(9).

**ID:** Idaho Code § 39-4505.7.

**ME:** Me. Rev. Stat. Ann. tit. 18-A, § 5-702(c).

**MT:** Mont. Code Ann. § 50-9-103(3).

**NV:** Nev. Rev. Stat. Ann. § 449.830.7.

**NH:** N.H. Rev. Stat. Ann. § 137-J:14.

**NC:** N.C. Gen. Stat. § 32A-25(1).

**ND:** N.D. Cent. Code § 23-06.5-17.

**OK:** Okla. Stat. Ann. tit. 63, § 3101.4(B).

**RI:** R.I. Gen. Laws § 23-4.10-2.8.

**SC:** S.C. Code Ann. § 62-5-504(K)(1).

**TX:** Tex. Civ. Prac. & Rem. Code Ann. § 135.016.

**VA:** Va. Code Ann. § 54.1-2984.

**WV:** W. Va. Code § 16-30A-5(a).

**WI:** Wis. Stat. Ann. § 155.30.

A few statutes permit the designation of more than one proxy, and the principal may specify whether each proxy may act "separately, without the consent of any other agent,"[103] or whether agreement among the agents is required.[104] If the principal fails to specify whether proxies must act jointly or may act separately, some statutes provide that the proxies must act jointly.[105] General power of attorney statutes often provide that, if there are co-agents, they must act jointly unless the instrument specifically provides that they are permitted to act severally.[106] Several states provide for an "alternate agent" to serve when the primary agent is unable, unwilling, or unavailable to do so. Once the primary agent becomes available or competent, decisionmaking authority returns to him, thus creating a shifting of power between the primary agent and the alternate agent.[107] Although desirable in theory, this kind of provision could lead to the same kind of conflict between proxies as can occur between a principal and a proxy when the former's decisionmaking capacity is questionable but not clearly absent.[108]

---

[103] **AK:** Alaska Stat. § 13.26.332.

**CT:** *Accord* Conn. Gen. Stat. Ann. § 19a-578(b).

**KY:** *Accord* Ky. Rev. Stat. Ann. § 311.625.

**MO:** *Accord* Mo. Ann. Stat. § 404.707(1).

**NM:** *Accord* N.M. Stat. Ann. § 45-5-501.B.

**PA:** *Accord* Pa. Cons. Stat. Ann. tit. 20, § 5602(b)(1).

[104] **AK:** Alaska Stat. § 13.26.332.

**KY:** Ky. Rev. Stat. Ann. § 311.625.

**MN:** Minn. Stat. Ann. § 145C.05(2)(1).

**NM:** N.M. Stat. Ann. § 45-5-501.B.

**PA:** Pa. Cons. Stat. Ann. tit. 20, § 5602(b)(1).

[105] **AK:** Alaska Stat. § 13.26.341.

**KY:** Ky. Rev. Stat. Ann. § 311.625.

**NM:** N.M. Stat. Ann. § 45-5-501.B.

**PA:** Pa. Cons. Stat. Ann. tit. 20, § 5602(b)(1).

[106] **MN:** *See, e.g.,* Minn. Stat. Ann. § 523.23.1.

**NY:** *See, e.g.,* N.Y. Gen. Oblig. Law § 5-1601(a).

[107] **CT:** Conn. Gen. Stat. Ann. § 19a-577(a).

**MA:** Mass. Gen. Laws Ann. ch. 201D, § 2.

**NE:** Neb. Rev. Stat. § 30-3403(1) (authority of successor attorney in fact ceases when original attorney in fact becomes available, able, and willing to serve).

**NJ:** N.J. Stat. Ann. § 26:2H-58(a)(3).

**NY:** N.Y. Pub. Health Law § 2981(6).

UHCDA § 4.

[108] See §§ **7.45–7.46** and **12.15.**

In addition to providing for the appointment of a successor proxy, some statutory forms allow the declarant to direct the attending physician to withhold or withdraw treatment that only prolongs the process of dying and is not necessary for the declarant's comfort if the appointed proxy is not available or is unwilling to serve.[109]

## § 12.20   Persons Disqualified from Acting as Proxy

In general, the same classes of persons disqualified from serving as witnesses to a health care power of attorney[110] are also disqualified from serving as proxies, although many statutes are somewhat less restrictive in their requirements for serving as a proxy than for serving as a witness. As with the qualifications for witnessing the instrument, statutes also vary in the specific qualifications for one to serve as a proxy. Some of the more prevalent and important disqualifications are

- the treating health care provider[111]
- an employee of the treating health care provider[112] or an employee of the treating health care provider who is not a relative of the principal[113]

---

[109] **MT:** Mont. Code Ann. § 50-9-103(3).

**SC:** S.C. Code Ann. § 62-5-504(C)(1)(d).

**WI:** Wis. Stat. Ann. § 155.05(3).

[110] See **§ 12.12.**

[111] **CA:** Cal. Civ. Code §§ 2432(b)(1), 2500.

**CT:** Conn. Gen. Stat. Ann. § 19a-576(e) (attending physician).

**GA:** Ga. Code Ann. § 31-36-5(b) (if directly or indirectly involved in health care rendered to patient).

**HI:** Haw. Rev. Stat. § 551D-2.5(e).

**ID:** Idaho Code § 39-4505.1.

**IL:** Ill. Ann. Stat. ch. § 755, § 45/4-5 (attending physician and any other health care provider may not act as agent).

**IA:** Iowa Code Ann. § 144B.4.1.

**KS:** Kan. Stat. Ann. § 58-629(d) (unless related to principal or both are members of same religious community and are "bound by vows to a religious life").

**MA:** Mass. Gen. Laws Ann. ch. 201D, § 3.

**MN:** Minn. Stat. Ann. § 145C.03(2)(1).

**MS:** Miss. Code Ann. § 41-41-161(a).

**MO:** Mo. Ann. Stat. § 404.815 (unless related to principal or both are members of same religious community "bound by vows to a religious life").

**NE:** Neb. Rev. Stat. § 30-3406(1).

**NV:** Nev. Rev. Stat. Ann. § 449.820.1(a).

**NJ:** N.J. Stat. Ann. § 26:2H-58(a)(2) (physician may not simultaneously serve as agent and attending physician).

**NH:** N.H. Rev. Stat. Ann. § 137-J:4(I).

**NY:** N.Y. Pub. Health Law § 2981(3).

**NC:** N.C. Gen. Stat. § 32A-18 ("person who is not engaged in providing health care to the principal for remuneration").

**ND:** N.D. Cent. Code § 23-06.5-04.1.

**OH:** Ohio Rev. Code Ann. § 1337.12(A)(2).

**OR:** Or. Rev. Stat. § 127.520(1) (principal's attending physician).

**RI:** R.I. Gen. Laws § 23-4.10-2.

**SC:** S.C. Code Ann. § 62-5-504(C)(1)(d).

**TN:** Tenn. Code Ann. § 34-6-203(b)(1).

**TX:** Tex. Civ. Prac. & Rem. Code Ann. § 135.003(1).

**VT:** Vt. Stat. Ann. tit. 14, § 3455(1).

**WV:** W. Va. Code § 16-30A-6(c).

**WI:** Wis. Stat. Ann. § 155.05(3).

**WY:** Wyo. Stat. § 3-5-202(b)(i).

[112] **CT:** Conn. Gen. Stat. Ann. § 19a-577(a).

**KS:** Kan. Stat. Ann. § 58-629(d) (unless related to principal or both are members of same religious community and are "bound by vows to a religious life").

**MN:** Minn. Stat. Ann. § 145C.03(2)(2).

**MS:** Miss. Code Ann. § 41-41-161(b).

**NC:** N.C. Gen. Stat. § 32A-18 ("person who is not engaged in providing health care to the principal for remuneration").

[113] **CA:** Cal. Civ. Code §§ 2432.5(a), 2500 (allows employee who "is a relative of the principal by blood, marriage, or adoption" to serve).

**ID:** Idaho Code § 39-4505.1 (disqualifies only "nonrelative" employees).

**MD:** Md. Code Ann., Health-Gen. § 5-602(B)(2).

**MA:** Mass. Gen. Laws Ann. ch. 201D, § 3.

**MO:** Mo. Ann. Stat. § 404.815.

**NE:** Neb. Rev. Stat. § 30-3406(2).

**NV:** Nev. Rev. Stat. Ann. § 449.820.2.

**NH:** N.H. Rev. Stat. Ann. § 137-J:4(II).

**NY:** N.Y. Pub. Health Law § 2981(3).

**ND:** N.D. Cent. Code § 23-06.5-04.2.

**OH:** Ohio Rev. Code Ann. § 1337.12(A)(2).

**OR:** Or. Rev. Stat. § 127.520(1) (disqualifies employee of principal's attending physician only when unrelated by blood, marriage, or adoption).

**RI:** R.I. Gen. Laws § 23-4.10-2.

**SC:** S.C. Code Ann. § 62-5-504(C)(1)(d).

**TN:** Tenn. Code Ann. § 34-6-203(f)(1).

**TX:** Tex. Civ. Prac. & Rem. Code Ann. § 135.003(2).

**VT:** Vt. Stat. Ann. tit. 14, § 3455(2).

**WV:** W. Va. Code § 16-30A-6(c).

**WI:** Wis. Stat. Ann. § 155.05(3).

**WY:** Wyo. Stat. § 3-5-203(a)(i).

- an owner or operator of a health care facility[114]
- an employee of a health care facility[115] or an employee of a health care facility who is not a relative of the principal.[116]

---

[114] **CA:** Cal. Civ. Code §§ 2432(b)(1), 2500.

**CT:** Conn. Gen. Stat. Ann. § 19a-576(d) (restriction inapplicable if operator is related to patient by blood, marriage, or adoption).

**ID:** Idaho Code § 39-4505.1.

**KS:** Kan. Stat. Ann. § 58-629(d) (unless related to principal or both are members of same religious community and are "bound by vows to a religious life").

**KY:** Ky. Rev. Stat. Ann. § 311.625 (where principal is resident or patient, unless owner or operator is related to principal).

**MN:** Minn. Stat. Ann. § 145C.03(2)(1).

**NE:** Neb. Rev. Stat § 30-3406(3) (if unrelated to principal).

**NV:** Nev. Rev. Stat. Ann. § 449.820.1(c) (unless operator of health care facility is spouse, legal guardian, or next-of-kin of principal).

**NH:** N.H. Rev. Stat. Ann. § 137-J:4(III).

**NY:** N.Y. Pub. Health Law § 2981(3).

**ND:** N.D. Cent. Code § 23-06.5-04.3.

**OH:** Ohio Rev. Code Ann. § 1337.12(A)(2) (administrator of nursing home in which principal is receiving care).

**OR:** Or. Rev. Stat. § 127.520(2) (in which principal is patient or resident).

**RI:** R.I. Gen. Laws § 23-4.10-2.

**TN:** Tenn. Code Ann. § 34-6-203(b)(1).

**TX:** Tex. Civ. Prac. & Rem. Code Ann. § 135.003(3) (disqualifies principal's "residential care provider").

**VT:** Vt. Stat. Ann. tit. 14, § 3455(3) (disqualifies principal's "residential care provider").

**WV:** W. Va. Code § 16-30A-6(c) (where principal is patient).

**WY:** Wyo. Stat. § 3-5-202(b)(i).

UHCDA § 2(b) (employee of residential long-term health care institution).

[115] **KS:** Kan. Stat. Ann. § 58-629(d) (unless related to principal or both are members of same religious community and are "bound by vows to a religious life").

**MN:** Minn. Stat. Ann. § 145C.03 subd. 2(2).

**NC:** N.C. Gen. Stat. § 32A-18 ("person who is not engaged in providing health care to the principal for remuneration").

[116] **CA:** Cal. Civ. Code §§ 2432.5, 2500 (allows employee who "is a relative of the principal by blood, marriage, or adoption" to serve).

**CT:** Conn. Gen. Stat. Ann. § 19a-576(d).

**ID:** Idaho Code § 39-4505.1(a) (disqualifies only "nonrelative" employees).

**IA:** Iowa Code Ann. § 144B.4.2.

**KY:** Ky. Rev. Stat. Ann. § 311.625 (where principal is resident or patient of facility).

**MD:** Md. Code Ann., Health-Gen. § 5-602(B)(2).

**MO:** Mo. Ann. Stat. § 404.815.

## § 12.21 Nomination of Guardian or Conservator

Some health care power of attorney statutes permit the principal to nominate a person to serve as guardian or conservator should a judicial proceeding be commenced to appoint one.[117] The West Virginia statute provides that if a guardian becomes necessary, the agent named in the power of attorney shall be appointed guardian "absent good cause shown against such designation."[118]

---

**NE:** Neb. Rev. Stat. § 30-3406(3).

**NV:** Nev. Rev. Stat. Ann. § 449.820.2.

**NH:** N.H. Rev. Stat. Ann. § 137-J:4(IV).

**NJ:** N.J. Stat. Ann. § 26:2H-58(a)(2).

**NY:** N.Y. Pub. Health Law § 2981(3).

**ND:** N.D. Cent. Code § 23-06.5-04.4.

**OH:** Ohio Rev. Code Ann. § 1337.12(A)(2).

**OR:** Or. Rev. Stat. § 127.520(2) (disqualifies employee only when unrelated by blood, marriage, or adoption and only when principal is patient or resident of that facility).

**RI:** R.I. Gen. Laws § 23-4.10-2.

**SC:** S.C. Code Ann. § 62-5-504(C)(1)(d).

**TN:** Tenn. Code Ann. § 34-6-203(f)(1).

**TX:** Tex. Civ. Prac. & Rem. Code Ann. § 135.003(4) (disqualifies unrelated employees of principal's "residential care provider").

**VT:** Vt. Stat. Ann. tit. 14, § 3455(4) (disqualifies unrelated employees of principal's "residential care provider").

**WV:** W. Va. Code § 16-30A-6(c).

**WI:** Wis. Stat. Ann. § 155.05(3).

**WY:** Wyo. Stat. § 3-5-203(a)(i).

UHCDA § 2(b) (employee of residential long-term health care institution).

[117] **AK:** Alaska Stat. § 13.26.335.

**CA:** Cal. Civ. Code §§ 2402(b), 2500.

**CT:** Conn. Gen. Stat. Ann. § 19a-576(d).

**GA:** Ga. Code Ann. § 31-36-10(a)(6).

**IL:** Ill. Ann. Stat. ch. 755, § 45/4-10(a)(6).

**KS:** Kan. Stat. Ann. § 58-629(b).

**MN:** Minn. Stat. Ann. § 145B.03.3; Minn. Stat. Ann. § 145C.07(2).

**NC:** N.C. Gen. Stat. § 32A-22(b).

**PA:** Pa. Cons. Stat. Ann. tit. 20, § 5604(c)(2). *Cf. In re* Sylvester, 598 A.2d 76 (Pa. Super. Ct. 1991) (person given power of attorney of principal's estate should not be replaced with judicially appointed guardian unless principal's interests are not being served).

**WA:** Wash. Rev. Code Ann. § 11.94.010.1(1).

**WV:** W. Va. Code § 16-30A-7.

UHCDA § 2(g).

[118] W. Va. Code § 16-30A-4(e).

## POWERS AND DUTIES OF THE PROXY

### § 12.22   Scope of Proxy's Authority to Make Health Care Decisions

A proxy's authority is generally subject to a duty to act in accordance with the principal's wishes and in the principal's best interests.[119] In some jurisdictions,

---

[119] **AZ:** Ariz. Rev. Stat. Ann. § 36-3203(C).

**CA:** Cal. Civ. Code §§ 2434(b), 2500 (duty to act consistent with desires of principal or, if principal's desires unknown, to act in best interests of principal).

**CO:** Colo. Rev. Stat. § 15-14-506(2).

**DE:** Del. Code Ann. tit. 16, § 2502 (agent must act with due regard for benefit and interests or appointer).

**DC:** D.C. Code Ann. § 21-2206(c).

**FL:** Fla. Stat. Ann. § 765.205(1)(a), (b).

**GA:** Ga. Code Ann. § 31-36-10(b).

**IL:** Ill. Ann. Stat. ch. 755, § 45/4-10(b).

**IN:** Ind. Code Ann. § 16-8-12-6(h).

**IA:** Iowa Code Ann. § 144B.6.2.

**KS:** Kan. Stat. Ann. § 58-629(c) (agent has duty to act consistently with expressed desires of principal).

**KY:** Ky. Rev. Stat. Ann. § 311.629.

**MD:** Md. Code Ann., Health-Gen. § 5-605(C)(2).

**MA:** Mass. Gen. Laws Ann. ch. 201D, § 5.

**MI:** Mich. Comp. Laws § 700.496(9) (construed in Martin v. Martin, 504 N.W.2d 917, 923 (Mich. Ct. App. 1993)).

**MN:** Minn. Stat. Ann. § 145C.07(3); Minn. Stat. Ann. § 145B.06(2).

**MS:** Miss. Code Ann. § 41-41-165(3).

**MO:** Mo. Ann. Stat. § 404.710.5.

**NE:** Neb. Rev. Stat. § 30-3418(1).

**NV:** Nev. Rev. Stat. Ann. § 449.830.

**NH:** N.H. Rev. Stat. Ann. § 137-J:2(II).

**NJ:** N.J. Stat. Ann. § 26:2H-61(f).

**NY:** N.Y. Pub. Health Law § 2982(2).

**ND:** N.D. Cent. Code § 23-06.5-03.2.

**OH:** Ohio Rev. Code Ann. § 1337.13(A)(1).

**OR:** Or. Rev. Stat. § 127.535(4).

**RI:** R.I. Gen. Laws § 23-4.10-2.

**SC:** S.C. Code Ann. § 62-5-504(I).

**SD:** S.D. Codified Laws Ann. § 59-7-2.5.

**VT:** Vt. Stat. Ann. tit. 14, § 3453(b).

**VA:** Va. Code Ann. § 54.1-2984.

when the proxy's health care decision relates to the use or nonuse of life-sustaining treatment, those decisions must be consistent with the known wishes of the principal; otherwise, the proxy is not permitted to make decisions regarding the withholding or withdrawal of life support.[120]

Some statutes confer broad powers on agents appointed under health care power of attorney statutes.[121] By contrast, Pennsylvania's original health care

---

**WV:** W. Va. Code § 16-30A-4(b).

**WI:** Wis. Stat. Ann. § 155.20(5).

**WY:** Wyo. Stat. § 3-5-204(c).

UHCDA § 2(e).

[120] **CT:** Conn. Gen. Stat. Ann. § 19a-577(a).

**HI:** Haw. Rev. Stat. § 551D-2.5(c).

**ID:** Idaho Code § 39-4505.4.

**MI:** Mich. Comp. Laws § 700.496(9)(e).

**NE:** Neb. Rev. Stat. § 30-3418(c).

**NV:** Nev. Rev. Stat. Ann. § 449.850.2.

**OH:** Ohio Rev. Code Ann. § 1337.13(E)(2).

**OK:** Okla. Stat. Ann. tit. 63, § 3101.4(B).

**RI:** R.I. Gen. Laws § 23-4.10-2.

**WI:** Wis. Stat. Ann. § 155.20(4) (may consent to withholding or withdrawal of nonorally ingested nutrition or hydration if authorized to do so by instrument).

[121] **AR:** Ark. Code Ann. § 20-17-201(10).

**CA:** Cal. Civ. Code § 2500(3).

**CO:** Colo. Rev. Stat. § 15-14-506(1).

**DC:** D.C. Code Ann. § 21-2206(a)(1).

**FL:** Fla. Stat. Ann. § 765.205(l)(a) (all health care decisions unless expressly limited by principal).

**GA:** Ga. Code Ann. § 31-36-4.

**HI:** Haw. Rev. Stat. § 551D-2.5(a) (any lawful health care decision).

**IA:** Iowa Code Ann. § 144B.6.1.

**KS:** Kan. Stat. Ann. § 58-629(a)(1).

**LA:** La. Rev. Stat. Ann. § 40:1299.58.3(C)(1).

**ME:** Me. Rev. Stat. Ann. tit. 18-A, § 5-501.

**MD:** Md. Code Ann., Health-Gen. § 5-602(B)(1) (health care decisions).

**MN:** Minn. Stat. Ann. § 145B.03(l); Minn. Stat. Ann. § 145C.07(2) ("except as otherwise provided in the durable power of attorney for health care, appointment of the agent in a durable power of attorney for health care is considered a nomination of a guardian or conservator of the person").

**MT:** Mont. Code Ann. § 50-9-103(1).

**NV:** Nev. Rev. Stat. Ann. § 449.810 (decisions concerning health care).

**NH:** N.H. Rev. Stat. Ann. § 137-J:2(I).

**NJ:** N.J. Stat. Ann. § 26:2H-61(a).

**NC:** N.C. Gen. Stat. § 32A-19.

power of attorney statute was phrased so as to permit a proxy only to consent to treatment but not to refuse it.[122] However, courts that have considered a similar issue—whether a guardian who is statutorily empowered to consent to treatment is also empowered to refuse—have generally held that the power to consent implies the power to refuse treatment.[123] Some statutes explicitly define "health

---

**ND:** N.D. Cent. Code § 23-06.5-03.1.

**OH:** Ohio Rev. Code Ann. § 1337.12(A)(1) (subject to further restrictions on decisions terminating life support).

**PA:** Pa. Cons. Stat. Ann. tit. 20, § 5404(b) (medical treatment decisions).

**RI:** R.I. Gen. Laws § 23-4.10-2.

**SC:** S.C. Code Ann. § 62-5-504(D).

**SD:** S.D. Codified Laws Ann. § 59-7-2.5 (any health care decision).

**TN:** Tenn. Code Ann. § 34-6-204(b), (d).

**TX:** Tex. Civ. Prac. & Rem. Code Ann. § 135.002(a).

**UT:** Utah Code Ann. § 75-2-1106(1).

**VA:** Va. Code Ann. § 54.1-2984.

**WV:** W. Va. Code 16-30A-4(d)(6) (subject to further restrictions where decision affects life support).

**WY:** Wyo. Stat. § 3-5-204(a) (all matters of health care decisions).

UHCDA § 4 (agent may make all health care decisions unless specifically limited by declaration).

[122] Pa. Stat. Ann. tit. 20, § 5603(h)(2) (Purdon Supp. 1990) (repealed). *Cf.* Pa. Cons. Stat. Ann. tit. 20, § 5404(b) (referring to "medical treatment decisions").

[123] **AZ:** Rasmussen v. Fleming, 741 P.2d 674, 688 (Ariz. 1987) ("[T]he right to consent to or approve the delivery of medical care must necessarily include the right to consent to or approve the delivery of no medical care. To hold otherwise would . . . ignore the fact that oftentimes a patient's interests are best served when medical treatment is withheld or withdrawn. To hold otherwise would also reduce the guardian's control over medical treatment to little more than a mechanistic rubberstamp for the wishes of the medical treatment team. . . . [T]he Public Fiduciary as Rasmussen's guardian had the implied, if not express statutory authority to exercise Rasmussen's right to refuse medical treatment.").

**CA:** Drabick v. Drabick, 245 Cal. Rptr. 840, 850 (Ct. App. 1988) ("[A] common sense point about statutory interpretation [is that] a statute that requires a person to make a decision contemplates a decision either way.").

**IL:** *In re* Estate of Greenspan, 558 N.E.2d 1194 (Ill. 1990); Estate of Longeway v. Community Convalescent Ctr., 549 N.E.2d 292, 298 (Ill. 1989) ("[T]he Probate Act impliedly authorizes a guardian to exercise the right to refuse artificial sustenance on her ward's behalf. Section 11a-17 . . . specifically permits a guardian to make provisions for her ward's 'support, care, comfort, health, education and maintenance.' . . . Moreover, if the patient previously executed a power of attorney under the Powers of Attorney for Health Care Law (Ill. Rev. Stat. 1987, ch. 110-1/2, para. 804-1 *et seq.*), that act permits her to authorize her agent to terminate the food and water that sustain her (Ill. Rev. Stat. 1987, ch. 110-1/2, para. 804-10).").

**IN:** *In re* Lawrance, 579 N.E.2d 32, 39 (Ind. 1991) (statutorily authorized family member's "right to consent to the patient's course of treatment necessarily includes the right to refuse a course of treatment").

care decision" to mean "consent, refusal of consent, or withdrawal of consent to health care."[124] Other statutes reach the same result by authorizing the proxy to make decisions to the same extent that the principal could if the principal possessed decisionmaking capacity.[125]

---

**MD:** *In re* Riddlemoser, 564 A.2d 812, 816 n.4 (Md. 1989) (power "'to give necessary consent or approval for medical or other professional care, counsel, treatment, or service'" necessarily implies "power to withhold or withdraw consent to medical treatment") (quoting Md. Code Ann., Est. & Trusts § 13-708(b)(8) and citing with approval 73 Md. Op. Att'y Gen. 253 (Op. No. 88-046, Oct. 17, 1988)).

**MO:** *In re* Warren, 858 S.W.2d 263, 265 (Mo. Ct. App. 1993) ("The right [of a guardian] to consent to medical treatment necessarily includes the right to withhold consent."). *But see* Cruzan v. Harmon, 760 S.W.2d 408, 424 (Mo. 1988) (statute that "places an express, affirmative duty on guardians to assure that the ward receives medical care and provides the guardian with the power to give consent for that purpose" does not provide basis for contending that "guardian possesses authority, as a guardian, to order the *termination* of medical treatment") (emphasis added).

[124] **CA:** Cal. Civ. Code § 2430(c). *Accord* Cal. Civ. Code § 2500(1).

**DE:** Del. Code Ann. tit. 16, § 2502(b).

**FL:** Fla. Stat. Ann. § 765.101(6).

**GA:** Ga. Code Ann. § 31-36-4.

**ID:** Idaho Code § 39-4505.3.

**IA:** Iowa Code Ann. § 144B.1.4.

**MD:** Md. Code Ann., Health-Gen. § 5-602(B)(1) (health care decisions).

**MN:** Minn. Stat. Ann. § 145B.02(4); Minn. Stat. Ann. § 145C.01(5).

**MS:** Miss. Code Ann. § 41-41-155(d).

**NE:** Neb. Rev. Stat. § 30-3402(5).

**NH:** N.H. Rev. Stat. Ann. § 137-J:1(VI).

**NJ:** N.J. Stat. Ann. § 26:2H-55.

**NY:** N.Y. Pub. Health Law § 2980(6).

**ND:** N.D. Cent. Code § 23-06.5-02.5.

**OH:** Ohio Rev. Code Ann. § 1337.11(G).

**OR:** Or. Rev. Stat. § 127.505(5).

**RI:** R.I. Gen. Laws § 23-4.10-2.

**TN:** Tenn. Code Ann. § 34-6-201(3).

**TX:** Tex. Civ. Prac. & Rem. Code Ann. § 135.001(6).

**VT:** Vt. Stat. Ann. tit. 14, § 3452(5) ("any" health care).

**WY:** Wyo. Stat. § 3-5-201(a)(v).

UHCDA § 1(6) ("health care decision" includes directions to provide, withhold, or withdraw treatment).

[125] **AK:** Alaska Stat. § 13.26.332.

**AZ:** Ariz. Rev. Stat. Ann. § 36-3221.

**CO:** Colo. Rev. Stat. § 15-14-506(3).

**CA:** Cal. Civ. Code §§ 2434(b), 2500(3).

## § 12.23  Statutory Restrictions on Proxy's Powers

Although statutory restrictions on a proxy's powers vary from state to state, some commonalities exist. **Sections 12.24** through **12.29** discuss some of the more frequent restrictions.

## § 12.24  —Conflict Between Principal and Proxy

There are a number of ways in which a principal's and a proxy's preferences can conflict. First, prior to losing decisionmaking capacity, the principal may have expressed views, governing the decision to be made, to the proxy, to a third party, or through an instruction directive such as a living will. If there is clear and convincing evidence (or whatever other standard of proof might prevail[126]) that the principal's wishes expressed while competent are inconsistent with the

---

**DC:** D.C. Code Ann. § 21-2206(a) (subject to express limitations within durable power of attorney and in federal or District law).

**FL:** Fla. Stat. Ann. § 765.205(1)(b).

**GA:** Ga. Code Ann. § 31-36-10(b).

**HI:** Haw. Rev. Stat. § 551D-2.5(a).

**ID:** Idaho Code § 39-4505.3.

**IL:** Ill. Ann. Stat. ch. 755, § 45/4-1.

**KY:** Ky. Rev. Stat. Ann. § 311.629 (decision must be within accepted medical practice and is subject to limitations in instrument and enabling statute).

**MI:** Mich. Comp. Laws § 700.496(9)(c).

**MN:** Minn. Stat. Ann. § 145B.06(2); Minn. Stat. Ann. § 145C.07(1).

**MS:** Miss. Code Ann. § 41-41-165(2).

**NH:** N.H. Rev. Stat. Ann. § 137-J:2(I).

**NJ:** N.J. Stat. Ann. § 26:2H-61(f).

**NM:** N.M. Stat. Ann. § 45-5-501.B.

**NY:** N.Y. Pub. Health Law § 2982(1).

**NC:** N.C. Gen. Stat. § 32A-19(a).

**ND:** N.D. Cent. Code § 23-06.5-03.1.

**OH:** Ohio Rev. Code Ann. § 1337.13(A)(1).

**OK:** Okla. Stat. Ann. tit. 63, § 3101.4(B).

**RI:** R.I. Gen. Laws § 23-4.10-2.

**SC:** S.C. Code Ann. § 62-5-504(D).

**SD:** S.D. Codified Laws Ann. § 59-7-2.5 (decisions must comply with accepted medical practice).

**TN:** Tenn. Code Ann. § 34-6-204(b).

**VT:** Vt. Stat. Ann. tit. 14, § 3453(a) (subject to statutory limitations).

**WY:** Wyo. Stat. § 3-5-204(b).

[126] See § **5.61.**

proxy's decisions, the latter should not be honored. In Ohio, a proxy has no authority to withdraw the principal's informed consent to health care, given prior to losing decisionmaking capacity, unless there has either been a change in the principal's physical condition that substantially decreases the benefit of the health care, or the health care "is not, or is no longer, significantly effective in achieving the purposes for which the principal consented to its use."[127] Some statutes prohibit a proxy from revoking or invalidating any previously existing directive in the principal's living will.[128] In others, if the principal objects to the health care or to the withholding or withdrawal of health care authorized by a proxy, the matter is governed by the law that would apply if no health care power of attorney had been executed.[129] Other statutes do not limit the proxy's authority to make health care decisions unless that power was expressly negated or limited within the power of attorney instrument itself.[130]

A second situation of conflict between principal and agent can arise when the principal, though lacking decisionmaking capacity, still possesses the power to communicate[131] and voices a preference about decisionmaking different from that of the proxy. A number of statutes address this situation by specifying that the principal's wishes are to be honored over the proxy's directions whether or not the principal has the capacity to make a health care decision.[132] This results,

---

[127] Ohio Rev. Code Ann. § 1337.13(F).

[128] **KS:** Kan. Stat. Ann. § 58-629(b).

**MN:** Minn. Stat. Ann. § 145C.01(5).

[129] **MN:** Minn. Stat. Ann. § 145C.07(1).

**WY:** Wyo. Stat. § 3-5-210.

[130] **AK:** Alaska Stat. § 13.26.338.

**FL:** Fla. Stat. Ann. § 765.205(l)(a).

**NV:** Nev. Rev. Stat. Ann. § 449.830.

**NM:** *But cf.* N.M. Stat. Ann. § 45-5-501.B (health care decisions authorized only when expressly given within instrument).

**SC:** S.C. Code Ann. § 62-5-504(D).

**TN:** *But cf.* Tenn. Code Ann. § 34-6-204(b).

UHCDA § 4 (agent may make all health care decisions unless specifically limited by declaration).

[131] See §§ **7.45–7.46.**

[132] **CA:** Cal. Civ. Code §§ 2440, 2500.

**CO:** Colo. Rev. Stat. § 15-14-506(4)(a).

**IA:** Iowa Code Ann. § 144B.6.1.

**MI:** Mich. Comp. Laws § 700.496(13).

**MS:** Miss. Code Ann. § 41-41-179.

**NE:** Neb. Rev. Stat. § 30-3417(5) (principal's decision shall prevail unless principal is determined by county court to be incapable of making health care decisions).

**NH:** N.H. Rev. Stat. Ann. § 137-J:2(IV).

**NJ:** N.J. Stat. Ann. § 26:2H-63(b).

**OR:** Or. Rev. Stat. § 127.535(5).

in effect, in a revocation of the health care proxy, at least as to this particular decision.[133]

A closely related situation arises when the conditions for effectuation of the health care power of attorney have been met, but subsequently the principal regains decisionmaking capacity, either permanently or transiently. Many statutes limit the proxy's authority to make decisions to those occasions when the principal is unable to make a particular decision personally. In effect, such provisions reflect the fact that the loss of decisionmaking capacity may be a transitory phenomenon and recognize a kind of shifting authority between principal and proxy, with the principal making decisions when in possession of decisionmaking capacity, and the proxy, at all other times.[134]

---

**RI:** R.I. Gen. Laws § 23-4.10-2.

**TN:** Tenn. Code Ann. § 34-6-210.

**TX:** Tex. Civ. Prac. & Rem. Code Ann. § 135.002(c).

**VT:** Vt. Stat. Ann. tit. 14, § 3453(d).

[133] See § **12.38.**

[134] **AZ:** Ariz. Rev. Stat. Ann. § 36-3223(A).

**CA:** Cal. Civ. Code § 2434(a) ("the attorney in fact does not have authority to make a particular health care decision if the principal is able to give informed consent with respect to that decision"); Cal. Civ. Code § 2500.

**CO:** Colo. Rev. Stat. § 15-14-506(3).

**DC:** D.C. Code Ann. § 21-2206(b)(2).

**FL:** Fla. Stat. Ann. § 765.204(3).

**GA:** Ga. Code Ann. § 31-36-5(c) (agent does not have authority to make health care decision contrary to principal's if principal is able to understand general nature of procedure being consented to or refused).

**HI:** Haw. Rev. Stat. § 551D-2.5(d).

**IN:** Ind. Code Ann. § 16-8-12-6(f).

**KY:** Ky. Rev. Stat. Ann. § 311.629.

**MA:** Mass. Gen. Laws Ann. ch. 201D, § 6.

**MI:** Mich. Comp. Laws § 700.496(10).

**NE:** Neb. Rev. Stat. § 30-3419(2).

**NH:** N.H. Rev. Stat. Ann. § 137-J:2(IV).

**NJ:** N.J. Stat. Ann. § 26:2H-63(b).

**NY:** N.Y. Pub. Health Law § 2983(7).

**OH:** Ohio Rev. Code Ann. § 1337.13(A)(1).

**OR:** Or. Rev. Stat. § 127.535(1).

**PA:** Pa. Cons. Stat. Ann. tit. 20, § 5404(b) (surrogate has authority when principal is incompetent and in terminal condition or state of permanent unconsciousness).

**RI:** R.I. Gen. Laws § 23-4.10-2.

**SC:** S.C. Code Ann. § 62-5-504(D).

**SD:** S.D. Codified Laws Ann. § 59-7-2.6.

**TX:** Tex. Civ. Prac. & Rem. Code Ann. § 135.002(b).

**VT:** Vt. Stat. Ann. tit. 14, § 3453(c).

## § 12.25 —Life-Sustaining Treatment

Most health care power of attorney statutes specifically permit the withholding or withdrawal of treatment necessary to keep the patient alive.[135] Although this

---

**VA:** Va. Code Ann. § 54.1-2984.

**WI:** Wis. Stat. Ann. § 155.05(4) (desires of principal who does not have incapacity supersede effect of power of attorney for health care at all times).

UHCDA § 2(c) (agent's authority only effective upon determination that principal lacks capacity, unless otherwise specified in directive).

[135] **AZ:** Ariz. Rev. Stat. Ann. § 36-3223(B).

**AR:** Ark. Code Ann. § 20-17-202(b).

**CA:** Cal. Civ. Code §§ 2431, 2500.

**CO:** Colo. Rev. Stat. § 15-14-506(1).

**CT:** Conn. Gen. Stat. Ann. § 19a-577(a).

**DE:** Del. Code Ann. tit. 16, § 2502(c).

**DC:** D.C. Code Ann. § 21-2206(a).

**FL:** Fla. Stat. Ann. § 765.204(5).

**GA:** Ga. Code Ann. § 31-36-10(b)(1).

**HI:** Haw. Rev. Stat. § 551D-2.6.

**ID:** Idaho Code §§ 39-4505 to -4509.

**IA:** Iowa Code Ann. § 144B.3.1; Iowa Code Ann. § 144A.7.1.a.

**IL:** Ill. Ann. Stat. ch. 755, § 45/4-3.

**KY:** Ky. Rev. Stat. Ann. § 311.629.

**LA:** La. Rev. Stat. Ann. § 40:1299.58.3(C)(1).

**ME:** Me. Rev. Stat. Ann. tit. 18-A, § 5-702(1).

**MD:** Md. Code Ann., Health-Gen. § 5-606(B) (only if patient is in a terminal condition or a persistent vegetative state).

**MA:** Mass. Gen. Laws Ann. ch. 201D, § 5.

**MI:** Mich. Comp. Laws § 700.496(9)(e).

**MN:** Minn. Stat. Ann. § 145B.03(2)(b)(2); Minn. Stat. Ann. § 145C.04(1).

**MS:** Miss. Code Ann. § 41-41-163.

**MO:** Mo. Ann. Stat. § 404.820.1.

**MT:** Mont. Code Ann. § 50-9-103(1); Mont. Code Ann. § 50-9-103(4) (designation of proxy to be treated like declaration pursuant to living will statute if proxy is given written authorization to make decisions regarding withholding or withdrawal of life-sustaining treatment).

**NV:** Nev. Rev. Stat. Ann. §§ 449.830.6, .850.2.

**NH:** N.H. Rev. Stat. Ann. § 137-J:15.

**NJ:** N.J. Stat. Ann. § 26:2H-58(b).

**NM:** N.M. Stat. Ann. §§ 45-5-501 to -502.

**NY:** N.Y. Pub. Health Law § 2989(2).

**NC:** N.C. Gen. Stat. § 32A-19(a).

**ND:** N.D. Cent. Code § 23-06.5-17.

**OH:** Ohio Rev. Code Ann. § 1337.13(B) (only if patient is in terminal condition or permanently unconscious state).

is the primary purpose for which health care power of attorney statutes have been enacted and thus the specific conferral of authority for this purpose is redundant, that statutes explicitly do so eliminates any lingering uncertainty about the proxy's authority to forgo life-sustaining treatment.

Other statutes have been judicially[136] or administratively[137] construed as permitting proxies to make decisions about life-sustaining treatment. Some must be read in conjunction with living will statutes in order to infer such authority. For instance, a few living will statutes[138] authorize an agent appointed under a general durable power of attorney statute to make health care decisions. Other statutes refer to health care decisions but do not expressly mention decisions about life-sustaining treatment.[139] On the other hand, some statutes specifically

---

**OR:** Or. Rev. Stat. § 127.540(6), (7).

**PA:** Pa. Cons. Stat. Ann. tit. 20, § 5404(a).

**RI:** R.I. Gen. Laws § 23-4.10-2.

**SC:** S.C. Code Ann. § 62-5-504(D).

**SD:** S.D. Codified Laws Ann. §§ 59-7-2.1 to -2.8.

**TN:** Tenn. Code Ann. § 34-6-204(d).

**TX:** Tex. Civ. Prac. & Rem. Code Ann. § 135.015.

**UT:** Utah Code Ann. § 75-2-1106(1).

**VT:** Vt. Stat. Ann. tit. 14, § 3466(b).

**VA:** Va. Code Ann. § 54.1-2984.

**WV:** W. Va. Code §§ 16-30A-1 to -20.

**WY:** Wyo. Stat. § 3-5-204(a); Wyo. Stat. § 35-22-102(d).

UHCDA § 4 (end-of-life decisions).

[136] **AZ:** Rasmussen v. Fleming, 741 P.2d 674, 689 n.21 (Ariz. 1987) (authorizes use of general durable power of attorney statute, Ariz. Rev. Stat. Ann. § 14-5501 (1975), for health care decisionmaking).

**HI:** *In re* Crabtree, No. 86-0031 (Haw. Fam. Ct. 1st Cir. Apr. 26, 1990) (construing living will statute, Haw. Rev. Stat. § 327D-26 (Supp. 1988), to permit designation of proxy).

**NJ:** *In re* Peter, 529 A.2d 419 (N.J. 1987).

**NY:** *In re* Westchester County Medical Ctr. (O'Connor), 531 N.E.2d 607 (N.Y. 1988).

[137] **MD:** 73 Md. Op. Att'y Gen. 253, 276 (Op. No. 88-046, Oct. 17, 1988) ("A person (the principal) may use a durable power of attorney to direct an agent (the attorney in fact) to carry out the principal's specific directive concerning medical treatment, including the withholding or withdrawing of artificially administered sustenance under specified circumstances.") (cited with approval in Mack v. Mack, 618 A.2d 744, 757–58 (Md. 1993)).

[138] **CT:** Conn. Gen. Stat. Ann. § 19a-577(a).

**IA:** Iowa Code Ann. § 144A.71.

**MD:** Md. Code Ann., Health-Gen. § 5-606(B) (only if patient is in a terminal condition or a persistent vegetative state).

**MN:** Minn. Stat. Ann. § 145C.04(1).

[139] **IN:** Ind. Code Ann. § 16-8-12-6(g).

**KS:** Kan. Stat. Ann. § 58-629.

**KY:** Ky. Rev. Stat. Ann. § 311.629 (any health care decision).

*prohibit* a proxy from withholding or withdrawing life-sustaining treatment under certain conditions.[140] Some statutes permit the principal to limit the proxy's authority to make decisions about life-sustaining treatment,[141] and some statutory forms specifically provide for this option.[142] The Louisiana power of attorney statute requires that there be an express conferral of authority to make health care decisions, but health care decisions are defined as "other than declarations of life-sustaining procedures pursuant to" the living will act.[143]

---

**PA:** Pa. Cons. Stat. Ann. tit. 20, §§ 5601–5606.

**WA:** Wash. Rev. Code Ann. § 11.94.010.

**WI:** Wis. Stat. Ann. § 155.30.

[140] **AK:** Alaska Stat. § 13.26.344(1), (2) (specifically prohibits agent from authorizing termination of life-sustaining procedures; however, § 13.26.344(3) authorizes agent to enforce properly executed living will).

**TN:** Tenn. Code Ann. § 34-6-210 (nothing authorizes attorney in fact to consent to withholding or withdrawal of health care to keep principal alive if principal objects to withholding or withdrawal of health care).

**WV:** W. Va. Code § 16-30A-4(d) (agent may not terminate life-prolonging treatment unless "such life-prolonging intervention offers no medical hope of benefit").

See § **17.17.**

[141] **GA:** Ga. Code Ann. § 31-36-10(b)(1).

**IL:** Ill. Ann. Stat. ch. 755, § 45/4-10(a).

**NV:** Nev. Rev. Stat. Ann. § 449.600.1.

**NJ:** N.J. Stat. Ann. § 26:2H-58(b).

**NY:** N.Y. Pub. Health Law § 2981(5)(B).

**OR:** Or. Rev. Stat. § 127.530.

**VA:** Va. Code Ann. § 54.1-2983.

**WV:** W. Va. Code § 16-30A-4(d).

[142] **CA:** Cal. Civ. Code § 2500(4)(a).

**DC:** D.C. Code Ann. § 21-2207.

**GA:** Ga. Code Ann. § 31-36-10(a).

**ID:** Idaho Code § 39-4505.4.

**MD:** Md. Code Ann., Health-Gen. § 5-603(II)(A)(2)(D).

**MN:** Minn. Stat. Ann. § 145C.04(1).

**NE:** Neb. Rev. Stat. § 30-3408(1).

**NH:** N.H. Rev. Stat. Ann. § 137-J:15.

**NY:** N.Y. Pub. Health Law § 2981(5)(D).

**ND:** N.D. Cent. Code § 23-06.5-17.

**OK:** Okla. Stat. Ann. tit. 63, § 3101.4(B).

**RI:** R.I. Gen. Laws § 23-4.10-2.

**VT:** Vt. Stat. Ann. tit. 14, § 3466(a).

**VA:** Va. Code Ann. § 54.1-2984.

**WV:** W. Va. Code § 16-30A-18.

[143] La. Rev. Civ. Code Ann. art. 2997(A)(7).

Thus, it appears that only the living will statute's provision for the appointment of a proxy[144] may be used to confer authority to make decisions about life-sustaining treatment.

When the treatment in question is one that is likely to restore the patient's health rather than prolong the process of dying, it is not clear that a patient-designated proxy may be used to confer authority to make decisions about life-sustaining treatment.[145]

## § 12.26 —Artificial Nutrition and Hydration

The controversy over the propriety of forgoing artificial nutrition and hydration[146] is reflected in the large number of health care power of attorney statutes that have provisions dealing with this matter. Although most statutes are silent on the subject, a significant number prohibit the withholding or withdrawal of artificial nutrition and hydration under certain conditions.[147] The Ohio statute is

---

[144] La. Rev. Stat. Ann. § 40:1299.58.3(C)(1).

[145] **MI:** *See, e.g.,* Werth v. Taylor, 475 N.W.2d 426, 430 (Mich. Ct. App. 1991) (neither patient's prior competent refusal of treatment nor her husband's contemporaneous refusal of treatment on her behalf were binding in a medical emergency).

**PA:** *Cf. In re* Estate of Dorone, 534 A.2d 452 (Pa. 1987) (parental refusal of lifesaving blood transfusion not binding).

[146] See §§ **9.39–9.40.**

[147] **CO:** Colo. Rev. Stat. § 15-14-506(1).

**CT:** Conn. Gen. Stat. Ann. § 19a-571(a) (must be provided unless patient is in terminal condition or permanently unconscious).

**HI:** Haw. Rev. Stat. § 551D-2.5(c) (if such authority is explicitly stated in health care power of attorney).

**KY:** Ky. Rev. Stat. Ann. § 311.629.

**ME:** Me. Rev. Stat. Ann. tit. 18-A, § 5-702(c) (may be withheld or withdrawn unless optional provision regarding principal's desire to receive artificial nutrition and hydration is signed).

**MD:** Md. Code Ann., Health-Gen. § 5-603(II)(A)(2)(D).

**MN:** Minn. Stat. Ann. § 145C.04(1), Minn. Stat. Ann. § 145B.03(2)(b)(2) (if declaration states declarant's preferences regarding artificial administration of nutrition and hydration).

**MO:** Mo. Ann. Stat. § 404.820.1 (to withhold artificial nutrition and hydration there must be specific instructions; however, "[t]his limitation shall not be construed to require that artificially supplied nutrition and hydration be continued when, in the medical judgment of the attending physician, the patient cannot tolerate it"); Mo. Ann. Stat. § 404.847 ("In the absence of a specific writing, decisions regarding nutrition and hydration must be made in accordance with state and federal law.").

**NE:** Neb. Rev. Stat. § 30-3418(2).

**NV:** Nev. Rev. Stat. Ann. § 449.830.6 (if principal has expressly requested attending physician not to withhold or withdraw in power of attorney document).

**NH:** N.H. Rev. Stat. Ann. § 137-J:3(III).

**NY:** N.Y. Pub. Health Law § 2982(2)(B).

perhaps the most restrictive. A proxy does not have authority to withhold or withdraw nutrition or hydration unless the principal is in a terminal condition or in a permanently unconscious state and the principal's attending physician and one other physician have determined that nutrition or hydration will no longer serve to provide comfort to the principal. If the principal is in a permanently unconscious state, the principal must have explicitly authorized the proxy to withhold or withdraw nutrition or hydration.[148] In addition, if a "priority individual"[149] believes that comfort care is not being provided as required by statute, that individual may commence an action in probate court for an order mandating the provision of comfort care.[150]

In some states, a proxy is permitted to authorize the withholding or withdrawing of artificial nutrition and hydration only if the principal has specifically refused it,[151] or the principal's wishes regarding it are reasonably known or can

---

**OH:** Ohio Rev. Code Ann. § 1337.13(C), (E).

**OK:** Okla. Stat. Ann. tit. 63, § 3101.4(B) (under "Hydration and Nutrition for Incompetent Patients Act," Okla. Stat. Ann. tit. 63 §§ 3080.1–.5, nutrition and hydration may be withheld or withdrawn if specifically authorized by living will or health care power of attorney executed pursuant to statute).

**OR:** Or. Rev. Stat. § 127.540(6), (7).

**PA:** Pa. Cons. Stat. Ann. tit. 20, § 5414(a) (nutrition and hydration must be provided to pregnant woman who is incompetent and has terminal condition or is permanently unconscious).

**SD:** S.D. Codified Laws Ann. § 59-7-2.7 (may not be withheld or withdrawn if needed for comfort care or relief of pain, or if it can be physically assimilated by principal, or if benefits of providing artificial nutrition and hydration outweigh its burdens, or if there is no clear and convincing evidence that artificial nutrition and hydration was refused by principal prior to loss of decisional capacity).

**UT:** Utah Code Ann. § 75-2-1106.

**WV:** W. Va. Code § 16-30A-4(d)(6).

**WI:** Wis. Stat. Ann. § 155.20(4) (may consent to withholding or withdrawal of nonorally ingested nutrition or hydration if authorized to do so by instrument).

[148] Ohio Rev. Code Ann. § 1337.13(E).

[149] *Id.* § 1337.16(D)(1)(b) (defined as principal's guardian, spouse, adult children, parents, siblings).

[150] *Id.* § 1337.16(E).

[151] **MN:** Minn. Stat. Ann. §§ 145B.03(2)(b), 145B.13(2) (declarant must either state preference regarding artificial nutrition and hydration or expressly grant authority to proxy to make decisions about artificial nutrition and hydration; otherwise artificial nutrition and hydration must be administered if patient can accept it orally "except for clearly documented medical reasons").

**NE:** Neb. Rev. Stat. § 30-3418(2) (attorney in fact does not have authority to consent to withholding or withdrawal of life-sustaining procedure unless principal is suffering from terminal condition or is in persistent vegetative state and power of attorney for health care explicitly grants such authority to attorney in fact or intent of principal to have life-sustaining treatment withheld or withdrawn can be established by clear and convincing evidence).

**PA:** Pa. Cons. Stat. Ann. tit. 20, § 5404(b) (form directive).

**OK:** Okla. Stat. Ann. tit. 63, § 3101.4(B) (if provision regarding withholding or withdrawal of artificially administered nutrition and hydration is not signed by declarant, artificial nutrition and hydration will be provided); Okla. Stat. Ann. tit. 63, § 3080.4(A)(1).

with reasonable diligence be ascertained.[152] Some statutes prohibit the forgoing of "normal feeding procedures"—defined as the "[d]elivery of food and water directly to the digestive tract by cup, spoon, baby bottle or drinking straw"—by excluding them from the definition of artificial nutrition and hydration.[153] Other statutes require the provision of nutrition and hydration unless (1) death is imminent and expected within a few days, or (2) artificial nutrition and hydration cannot be assimilated by the principal, or (3) the provision of artificial nutrition and hydration will impose burdens disproportionate to the benefits.[154] However, even in these instances, artificial nutrition and hydration must be provided if necessary for the patient's comfort.[155] By contrast, other statutes specifically permit the proxy to authorize forgoing of artificial nutrition and hydration if he believes such a decision is consistent with the principal's desires.[156]

---

**OR:** Or. Rev. Stat. § 127.580(1)(a).

**SC:** S.C. Code Ann. § 62-5-504(D) (power of attorney must indicate whether declarant wishes to receive artificial nutrition and hydration; otherwise, agent will not have authority to direct that artificial nutrition and hydration necessary for comfort care or alleviation of pain be withdrawn).

**WI:** Wis. Stat. Ann. § 155.30 (unless principal indicates "yes" or "no" regarding use of artificial nutrition and hydration on instrument, artificial nutrition and hydration may not be withheld or withdrawn).

[152] **NY:** N.Y. Pub. Health Law § 2982(2)(B).

[153] **OR:** Or. Rev. Stat. § 127.580(2).

**IA:** *Accord* Iowa Code Ann. § 144B.6.3 (prohibits forgoing of simple nutrition and hydration— "nutrition or hydration except when they are required to be provided parenterally or through intubation"—by excluding it from definition of "health care").

**ME:** *Accord* Me. Rev. Stat. Ann. tit. 18-A, § 5-701(b)(4) (defines life-sustaining treatment as including artificial nutrition and hydration, which is the provision of nutrients and liquids through the use of tubes, intravenous procedures, or similar interventions").

**MA:** *Accord* Mass. Gen. Laws Ann. ch. 201D, § 13 ("non-artificial oral feeding").

**MN:** *Accord* Minn. Stat. Ann. §§ 145B.03(2)(b), .13(2) (declarant must either state preference regarding artificial nutrition and hydration or expressly grant authority to proxy to make decisions about artificial nutrition and hydration; otherwise, artificial nutrition and hydration must be administered if patient can accept it orally "except for clearly documented medical reasons").

**MO:** *Accord* Mo. Ann. Stat. § 404.820.2 (ingestion through "natural means").

**NE:** *Accord* Neb. Rev. Stat. § 30-3402(14).

**NH:** *Accord* N.H. Rev. Stat. Ann. § 137-J:1(II) ("natural ingestion of food or fluids by eating and drinking").

[154] **KY:** Ky. Rev. Stat. Ann. § 311.629.

**SD:** S.D. Codified Laws Ann. § 59-7-2.7(4).

[155] **KY:** Ky. Rev. Stat. Ann. § 311.629.

**SD:** S.D. Codified Laws Ann. § 59-7-2.7(4).

[156] **IL:** Ill. Ann. Stat. ch. 755, § 45/4-10(a), *construed in In re* Estate of Greenspan, 558 N.E.2d 1194, 1203 (Ill. 1990) (agent has authority to withhold or withdraw artificial nutrition and hydration even if patient had living will, which under living will statute cannot be used to

## § 12.27 —Pregnancy

Although there is very little case law dealing with the issue of forgoing life-sustaining treatment when the patient is pregnant[157] and despite the fact that the frequency with which this issue arises but is not litigated is probably extremely small, a substantial number of statutes address it. Some statutes contain restrictions on the proxy's authority to make decisions about the treatment of a pregnant patient if that decision would have the effect of terminating the pregnancy.[158] Most of these are blanket prohibitions on forgoing life-sustaining

---

forgo artificial nutrition and hydration, "so long as the agent under the power is available to act"; *and in* Estate of Longeway v. Community Convalescent Ctr., 549 N.E.2d 292 (Ill. 1989)).

**MD:** Md. Code Ann., Health-Gen. § 5-605(B).

**MN:** Minn. Stat. Ann. § 145C.01.

**MO:** Mo. Ann. Stat. § 404.820.4 (before withdrawing artificial nutrition and hydration, agent must either attempt to explain to principal the intention and consequences of withdrawal in order to give patient opportunity to refuse its removal or "[i]nsert in the patient's file a certification that the patient is comatose or consistently in a condition which makes it impossible for the patient to understand the intention to withdraw nutrition and hydration and the consequences to the patient").

**NV:** Nev. Rev. Stat. Ann. § 449.850.2.

**VA:** Va. Code Ann. § 54.1-2984.

UHCDA § 4 (artificial nutrition and hydration treated like any other health care unless specified in directive).

[157] See § **9.55.**

[158] **AR:** Ark. Code Ann. § 20-17-206(c).

**DE:** Del. Code Ann. tit. 16, § 2503(d).

**FL:** Fla. Stat. Ann. § 765.113(2) (unless principal expressly delegates such authority to surrogate in writing or surrogate has sought and received court approval).

**IA:** Iowa Code Ann. § 144A.7.3.

**KY:** Ky. Rev. Stat. Ann. § 311.629.

**MI:** Mich. Comp. Laws § 700.496(17).

**MN:** Minn. Stat. Ann. § 145B.13(3).

**MT:** Mont. Code Ann. § 50-9-106(6).

**NE:** Neb. Rev. Stat. § 30-3417(1)(b).

**NH:** N.H. Rev. Stat. Ann. § 137-J:2(V)(c).

**OH:** Ohio Rev. Code Ann. § 1337.13(D).

**OK:** Okla. Stat. Ann. tit. 63, § 3101.8(C).

**PA:** Pa. Cons. Stat. Ann. tit. 20, § 5414(a).

**RI:** R.I. Gen. Laws § 23-4.10-5(c).

**SC:** S.C. Code Ann. § 62-5-504(G).

**SD:** S.D. Codified Laws Ann. § 59-7-2.8.

**UT:** Utah Code Ann. § 75-2-1106(1).

**WI:** Wis. Stat. Ann. § 155.20(6) (may not make health care decisions for principal who is pregnant unless specifically authorized to do so in power of attorney).

**WY:** Wyo. Stat. § 35-22-102(b).

treatment when the patient is pregnant. However, under a few statutes, forgoing treatment is permissible if the continuation of the pregnancy or the treatment to be administered would pose a substantial risk to the mother's life or the fetus would not be born alive even if treatment were administered.[159] The New Jersey statute expressly provides for the principal to state the limitations, if any, to be placed on the proxy's authority if the principal is pregnant.[160] Under some statutes, if a pregnant woman's advance directive is overridden, the state is required to pay the woman's medical expenses and may obtain subrogation from her health insurer but not from her estate.[161]

## § 12.28  —Active Euthanasia

Many statutes expressly prohibit construing a health care power of attorney to permit active euthanasia or mercy killing.[162] Because such a prohibition merely

---

[159] **KY:** Ky. Rev. Stat. Ann. § 311.629 (also allows refusal of life-sustaining treatment if severe and intractable pain to mother).

**NH:** N.H. Rev. Stat. Ann. § 137-J:2(V)(c).

**OH:** Ohio Rev. Code Ann. § 1337.13(D).

**PA:** Pa. Cons. Stat. Ann. tit. 20, § 5414(a) (life-sustaining treatment, including nutrition and hydration, must be provided unless it will not maintain pregnant woman to permit continuing development and live birth of unborn child, will be physically harmful to pregnant woman, or will cause pain that cannot be alleviated with medication).

**RI:** R.I. Gen. Laws § 23-4.10-5(c) (durable power of attorney shall be given no force or effect as long as it is probable that fetus could develop to point of live birth with continued application of life-sustaining procedures).

**SD:** S.D. Codified Laws Ann. § 59-7-2.8.

[160] N.J. Stat. Ann. § 26:2H-58(a)(5).

[161] **MD:** Md. Code Ann., Health-Gen. § 5-605(B).

**MN:** Minn. Stat. Ann. § 145C.01.

**PA:** Pa. Cons. Stat. Ann. tit. 20, § 5414(c).

UHCDA § 13(c).

[162] **AR:** Ark. Code Ann. § 20-17-210(a).

**CA:** Cal. Civ. Code § 2443.

**CO:** Colo. Rev. Stat. § 15-14-504(4).

**DC:** D.C. Code Ann. § 21-2212.

**FL:** Fla. Stat. Ann. § 765.309(1).

**GA:** Ga. Code Ann. § 31-36-1(b).

**IN:** Ind. Code Ann. § 16-8-12-12.

**IA:** Iowa Code Ann. § 144B.12.2.

**LA:** La. Rev. Stat. Ann. § 40:1299.58.10(A).

**ME:** Me. Rev. Stat. Ann. tit. 18-A, § 5-711(g).

**MD:** Md. Code Ann., Health-Gen. § 5-611(C).

**MA:** Mass. Gen. Laws Ann. ch. 201D, § 12.

restates the construction ordinarily given to homicide statutes,[163] there is no reason to believe that the absence of such a provision would permit a proxy to validly authorize mercy killing.

## § 12.29   —Non-Life-Sustaining Treatments

In some jurisdictions, a proxy is statutorily barred from authorizing certain enumerated non-life-sustaining treatments, even when otherwise given broad powers to consent to treatment. These treatments include commitment to a mental health facility,[164] electroconvulsive therapy,[165] psychosurgery,[166] sterilization,[167] and abortion.[168]

---

**MN:** Minn. Stat. Ann. § 145B.14.

**MO:** Mo. Ann. Stat. § 404.847.

**MT:** Mont. Code Ann. § 50-9-205(7).

**NJ:** N.J. Stat. Ann. § 26:2H-77(a).

**NY:** N.Y. Pub. Health Law § 2989(3).

**ND:** N.D. Cent. Code § 23-06.5-01.

**OK:** Okla. Stat. Ann. tit. 63, § 3101.12(G).

**OR:** Or. Rev. Stat. § 127.570.

**PA:** Pa. Cons. Stat. Ann. tit. 20, § 5402(b).

**RI:** R.I. Gen. Laws § 23-4.10-9(f).

**SC:** S.C. Code Ann. § 62-5-504(0).

**UT:** Utah Code Ann. § 75-2-1116.

**VA:** Va. Code Ann. § 54.1-2990.

**WV:** W. Va. Code § 16-30A-16.

**WI:** Wis. Stat. Ann. § 155.70(7).

**WY:** Wyo. Stat. § 3-5-211.

[163] See **Ch. 18.**

[164] **CA:** Cal. Civ. Code § 2435(a).

**FL:** Fla. Stat. Ann. § 765.113(1) (unless principal expressly delegates such authority to surrogate in writing or surrogate has sought and received court approval).

**GA:** Ga. Code Ann. § 31-36-10(b)(1).

**MN:** Minn. Stat. Ann. § 145C.07(1).

**NV:** Nev. Rev. Stat. Ann. § 449.850.1(a).

**NH:** N.H. Rev. Stat. Ann. § 137-J:2(V)(a).

**ND:** N.D. Cent. Code § 23-06.5-03.5.

**OR:** Or. Rev. Stat. § 127.540(1).

**TX:** Tex. Civ. Prac. & Rem. Code Ann. § 135.002(f)(1).

**VT:** Vt. Stat. Ann. tit. 14, § 3453(3).

**VA:** Va. Code Ann. § 54.1-2986(C).

**WI:** Wis. Stat. Ann. § 155.20(2)(a)(1).

**WY:** Wyo. Stat. § 3-5-205(a)(i).

UHCDA § 13(e) (unless directive expressly provides).

[165] **CA:** Cal. Civ. Code § 2435(b).

**DC:** D.C. Code Ann. § 21-2211(b).

**FL:** Fla. Stat. Ann. § 765.113(1) (unless principal expressly delegates such authority to surrogate in writing or surrogate has sought and received court approval).

**NV:** Nev. Rev. Stat. Ann. § 449.850.1(b).

**OR:** Or. Rev. Stat. § 127.540(2).

**TX:** Tex. Civ. Prac. & Rem. Code Ann. § 135.002(f)(2).

**WI:** Wis. Stat. Ann. § 155.20(3).

**WY:** Wyo. Stat. § 3-5-205(a)(ii).

[166] **CA:** Cal. Civ. Code § 2435(c).

**DC:** D.C. Code Ann. § 21-2211(a).

**FL:** Fla. Stat. Ann. § 765.113(1) (unless principal expressly delegates such authority to surrogate in writing or surrogate has sought and received court approval).

**GA:** Ga. Code Ann. § 36-31-10(b)(1).

**NV:** Nev. Rev. Stat. Ann. § 449.850.1(c).

**ND:** N.D. Cent. Code § 23-06.5-03.5.

**OR:** Or. Rev. Stat. § 127.540(3).

**TX:** Tex. Civ. Prac. & Rem. Code Ann. § 135.002(f)(3).

**VA:** Va. Code Ann. § 54.1-2986(C).

**WI:** Wis. Stat. Ann. § 155.20(3).

**WY:** Wyo. Stat. § 3-5-205(iii).

[167] **CA:** Cal. Civ. Code § 2435(d).

**DC:** D.C. Code Ann. § 21-2211(a).

**FL:** Fla. Stat. Ann. § 765.113(1) (unless principal expressly delegates such authority to surrogate in writing or surrogate has sought and received court approval).

**GA:** Ga. Code Ann. § 31-36-10(b)(1).

**MD:** Md. Code Ann., Health-Gen. § 5-605(D); Md. Code Ann., Health-Gen. § 5-611(C); Md. Code Ann., Health-Gen. § 20-107(f)(1).

**NV:** Nev. Rev. Stat. Ann. § 449.850.1(d).

**NH:** N.H. Rev. Stat. Ann. § 137-J:2(V)(b).

**ND:** N.D. Cent. Code § 23-06.5-03.5.

**OR:** Or. Rev. Stat. § 127.540(4).

**VT:** Vt. Stat. Ann. tit. 14, § 3453(3).

**VA:** Va. Code Ann. § 54.1-2986(C) (nontherapeutic sterilization).

[168] **CA:** Cal. Civ. Code § 2435(e).

**DC:** D.C. Code Ann. § 21-2211(a).

**FL:** Fla. Stat. Ann. § 765.113(1) (unless principal expressly delegates such authority to surrogate in writing or surrogate has sought and received court approval).

**MD:** Md. Code Ann., Health-Gen. § 20-107(f)(1).

**MN:** Minn. Stat. Ann. § 145C.07(1).

**NV:** Nev. Rev. Stat. Ann. § 449-850.1(e).

**ND:** N.D. Cent. Code § 23-06.5-03.5.

**OR:** Or. Rev. Stat. § 127.540(5).

**TX:** Tex. Civ. Prac. & Rem. Code Ann. § 135.002(f)(4).

**VA:** Va. Code Ann. § 54.1-2986(C).

## § 12.30  Proxy's Authority Supersedes That of Other Decisionmakers

Unless a particular health care power of attorney instrument provides otherwise, some statutes provide that the power of attorney supersedes any preexisting instruction directive, any previously executed health care power of attorney, and any authority a guardian or conservator may have to make health care decisions.[169] In Minnesota, the designation of a health care proxy is equivalent to the appointment of a guardian or conservator unless otherwise provided.[170]

The relationship between the authority of a proxy appointed pursuant to a health care power of attorney and the instructions given in a living will are of particular importance, but few living will and health care power of attorney statutes address this point. Some specifically provide that the later-executed document governs in the event of a conflict between the two.[171] Some statutes

---

[169] **AK:** Alaska Stat. § 13.26.332.

**AZ:** Ariz. Rev. Stat. Ann. § 36-3209 (if conflicts among provisions of valid health care directives, most recent directive is deemed to represent wishes of patient).

**CA:** Cal. Civ. Code § 2437(d).

**DC:** D.C. Code Ann. § 21-2206(b)(1).

**FL:** Fla. Stat. Ann. § 765.205(3) (if court appoints guardian after designation of surrogate, surrogate shall continue to make health care decisions for principal).

**GA:** Ga. Code Ann. § 31-36-11.

**HI:** Haw. Rev. Stat. § 551D-2.6 (sample form includes provision stating "this durable power of attorney shall control in all circumstances").

**IA:** Iowa Code Ann. § 144B.6.1.

**MD:** Md. Code Ann., Health-Gen. § 5-603(II)(A)(2)(B).

**MA:** Mass. Gen. Laws Ann. ch. 201D, § 5.

**NE:** Neb. Rev. Stat. § 30-3420(5).

**NH:** N.H. Rev. Stat. Ann. § 137-J:12(II).

**NJ:** N.J. Stat. Ann. § 26:2H-61(b).

**NY:** N.Y. Pub. Health Law § 2982(4).

**ND:** N.D. Cent. Code § 23-06.5-13.1.

**OR:** Or. Rev. Stat. § 127.545(4).

**TN:** Tenn. Code Ann. § 34-6-204(a)(1).

**WI:** Wis. Stat. Ann. § 155.20(1). *But see* Wis. Stat. Ann. § 155.60(2) (if court determines that principal is incompetent and appoints guardian for principal, power of attorney for health care is revoked and invalid unless court finds that instrument should remain in effect).

**WY:** Wyo. Stat. § 3-5-204(a).

UHCDA § 6(b) (agent's health care decision takes precedence over that of guardian).

[170] **MN:** Minn. Stat. Ann. § 145B.03.3; Minn. Stat. Ann. § 145C.07(2).

[171] **ND:** N.D. Cent. Code § 23-06.5-13.2.

**TX:** Tex. Civ. Prac. & Rem. Code Ann. § 135.012.

**VT:** Vt. Stat. Ann. tit. 14, § 3463(b).

**WV:** W. Va. Code § 16-30A-4(d)(8).

provide that if there is a conflict between the proxy's decision and the living will, the living will takes precedence.[172] In Kansas, a proxy is specifically prohibited from revoking a statutorily based living will.[173] The Wisconsin statute provides that a valid durable health care power of attorney supersedes a valid living will when there is a direct conflict between provisions of the two.[174]

The most desirable approach is for the proxy to attempt to follow the patient's wishes as embodied in an instruction directive. However, a few statutes categorically give preference to the instructions given to a properly designated proxy over those contained in a living will.[175] By contrast, the Alaska statute authorizes a proxy to make decisions about life-sustaining treatment only if the patient has also executed a living will.[176]

## § 12.31   Withdrawal of the Proxy

A few statutes expressly recognize the proxy's right to withdraw from the performance of duties by giving notice to the principal or to the principal's attending physician if the principal is incompetent.[177] Other statutes provide for the de facto withdrawal of the proxy by directing the attending physician to

---

[172] **NC:** N.C. Gen. Stat. § 32A-15(c) (in event of conflict between living will and health care power of attorney, living will controls).

    **OK:** Okla. Stat. Ann. tit. 63, § 3101.4(B) (statutory form; living will takes precedence unless otherwise indicated in the directive by the declarant).

[173] Kan. Stat. Ann. § 58-629(b).

[174] **WI:** Wis. Stat. Ann. § 155.70(3).

    **MN:** *See also* Minn. Stat. Ann. § 145C.07(4)(most recent designation takes precedence).

[175] **GA:** Ga. Code Ann. § 31-36-11.

    **IL:** Ill. Ann. Stat. ch. 755, § 45/4-11 ("the living will shall not be operative so long as an agent is available who is authorized by a health care agency to deal with the subject of life-sustaining or death-delaying procedures for and on behalf of the principal").

    **NH:** N.H. Rev. Stat. Ann. § 137-J:12(II).

    **TN:** Tenn. Code Ann. § 34-6-207(g).

[176] **AK:** Alaska Stat. § 13.26.344(1)–(3).

[177] **KY:** Ky. Rev. Stat. Ann. § 311.629 (notice must also be given to any successor agent and to any health care facility awaiting agent's health care decision).

    **MI:** Mich. Comp. Laws § 700.496(7)(h) (principal may revoke at any time and in any manner sufficient to communicate intent to revoke).

    **MO:** Mo. Ann. Stat. § 404.705.4.

    **NE:** Neb. Rev. Stat. § 30-3407.

    **NJ:** N.J. Stat. Ann. § 26:2H-61(d).

    **ND:** N.D. Cent. Code § 23-06.5-06.

    **OR:** Or. Rev. Stat. § 127.525.

proceed as if there were no health care power of attorney if the proxy is unavailable or refuses to make a health care decision.[178]

## § 12.32  Powers Suspended in Emergency

If an emergency exists and a valid health care power of attorney is in effect, some statutes provide that the power of attorney's existence is to be disregarded.[179] This same result should obtain even in the absence of such a provision.[180]

## § 12.33  Miscellaneous Powers

Health care power of attorney statutes contain a number of miscellaneous provisions conferring authority on proxies to undertake acts necessary for the provision of medical and health care to the principal. These are discussed in §§ 12.34 through 12.36.

## § 12.34  —Medical Records

Because access to the principal's medical records may be necessary for the proxy to make an informed decision about the principal's health care, most health care power of attorney statutes expressly authorize the proxy's access to medical records.[181] The absence of such a provision, however, should not preclude access to medical records by proxies.

---

[178] **KY:** Ky. Rev. Stat. Ann. § 311.629.

**ME:** Me. Rev. Stat. Ann. tit. 18-A, § 5-702(c) (optional provision in form directing attending physician to withhold or withdraw life-sustaining treatment not necessary for comfort care if no individual who was appointed to serve as proxy is reasonably available or willing to serve).

**NY:** N.Y. Pub. Health Law § 2981(6).

**SD:** S.D. Codified Laws Ann. § 59-7-2.6.

[179] **CA:** Cal. Civ. Code § 2439(b).

**IA:** Iowa Code Ann. § 144B.10.

**MD:** Md. Code Ann., Health-Gen. § 5-607.

**NJ:** N.J. Stat. Ann. § 26:2H-70(b).

**OH:** Ohio Rev. Code Ann. § 1337.16(C).

**TN:** Tenn. Code Ann. § 34-6-209.

**WY:** Wyo. Stat. § 3-5-209(d).

[180] See §§ 3.23 and 10.23.

[181] **AK:** Alaska Stat. § 13.26.334(l)(1).

**CA:** Cal. Civ. Code §§ 2436, 2500(5).

## § 12.35 —Selection of Health Care Professionals

A few statutes expressly give the proxy authority to hire and discharge health care professionals.[182] Although it might be implicit in a statutory provision

---

**CO:** Colo. Rev. Stat. § 15-14-506(3).

**DC:** D.C. Code Ann. § 21-2206(a)(2), (a)(3).

**FL:** Fla. Stat. Ann. § 765.205(1)(d).

**GA:** Ga. Code Ann. § 31-36-11(4).

**ID:** Idaho Code § 39-4505.5(a).

**IL:** Ill. Ann. Stat. ch. 755, § 45/4-7(c), 4-10(b)(4).

**IN:** Ind. Code Ann. § 16-8-12-10 (Burns 1990).

**IA:** Iowa Code Ann. § 144B.7.

**KS:** Kan. Stat. Ann. § 58-629(a)(3).

**MA:** Mass. Gen. Laws Ann. ch. 201D, § 5.

**MD:** Md. Code Ann., Health-Gen. § 5-603(II)(A)(2)(A).

**MN:** Minn. Stat. Ann. § 145C.08; Minn. Stat. Ann. § 145B.08.

**MS:** Miss. Code Ann. § 41-41-167.

**MO:** Mo. Ann. Stat. § 404.840.2.

**NE:** Neb. Rev. Stat. § 30-3417(4).

**NV:** Nev. Rev. Stat. Ann. § 449.830.

**NH:** N.H. Rev. Stat. Ann. § 137-J:7(I).

**NY:** N.Y. Pub. Health Law § 2982(3).

**NC:** N.C. Gen. Stat. § 32A-25(3)(A).

**ND:** N.D. Cent. Code § 23-06.5-08.1.

**OH:** Ohio Rev. Code Ann. § 1337.13(A)(3).

**OR:** Or. Rev. Stat. § 127.535(3).

**RI:** R.I. Gen. Laws § 23-4.10-2.

**SC:** S.C. Code Ann. § 62-5-504(E)(1).

**TN:** Tenn. Code Ann. § 34-6-206.

**TX:** Tex. Civ. Prac. & Rem. Code Ann. § 135.007(1).

**VT:** Vt. Stat. Ann. tit. 14, § 3453(1).

**VA:** Va. Code Ann. § 54.1-2984.

**WV:** W. Va. Code § 16-30A-12.

**WI:** Wis. Stat. Ann. § 155.30(3).

**WY:** Wyo. Stat. § 3-5-206.

UHCDA § 8.

[182] **CA:** Cal. Civ. Code § 2504 (if statutory form is followed).

**DC:** D.C. Code Ann. § 21-2206(a)(4).

**KS:** Kan. Stat. Ann. § 58-629(a)(2).

**MD:** Md. Code Ann., Health-Gen. § 5-603(II)(A)(2)(B).

**NC:** N.C. Gen. Stat. § 32A-25(3)(B).

**SC:** S.C. Code Ann. § 62-5-504(E)(3).

empowering the proxy to select health care professionals, a few statutes expressly provide that a proxy is not prohibited from authorizing treatment by spiritual means in lieu of medical care when this is in accordance with the principal's religious beliefs.[183] Similarly, in a few states a proxy is not permitted to authorize care or medical treatments to which the principal objects on religious grounds.[184]

## § 12.36  —Releases of Liability

Under some statutes, the proxy, unless limited by the principal in the power of attorney, may grant a release of liability to a hospital or physician.[185]

## TERMINATION OF PROXY'S AUTHORITY

## § 12.37  Termination in General

Termination of the powers granted by a health care power of attorney can be accomplished through a variety of mechanisms. Most require a direct act of revocation by the principal, but a power of attorney may also terminate by operation of law or by judicial order.

---

**VA:** Va. Code Ann. § 54.1-2984.

**WV:** W. Va. Code § 16-30A-4(d)(4).

[183] **KS:** Kan. Stat. Ann. § 58-629(b).

**MD:** Md. Code Ann., Health-Gen. § 5-605(D).

**MN:** Minn. Stat. Ann. § 145B.17 ("[n]othing ... prohibits lawful treatment by spiritual means through prayer in lieu of medical treatment when treatment by spiritual means has been authorized by the declarant").

[184] **MI:** Mich. Comp. Laws § 700.496(22).

**NH:** N.H. Rev. Stat. Ann. § 137-J:14 ("If for moral or religious reasons you do not wish to be treated by a doctor or examined by a doctor for the certification that you lack capacity, you must say so in the document and name a person to be able to certify your lack of capacity.").

[185] **AK:** Alaska Stat. § 13.26.344(l)(6).

**CA:** Cal. Civ. Code §§ 2500(6)(b), 2504.

**ID:** Idaho Code § 39-4505.6(b).

**MD:** Md. Code Ann., Health-Gen. § 5-603(II)(A)(2)(A).

**MN:** Minn. Stat. Ann. § 145C.08.

**RI:** R.I. Gen. Laws § 23-4.10-2.

**SC:** S.C. Code Ann. § 62-5-504(D).

**VA:** Va. Code Ann. § 54.1-2984.

**WI:** Wis. Stat. Ann. § 155.30(3).

## § 12.38 Revocation by the Principal

Some statutes expressly allow the principal to designate an expiration date of a power of attorney.[186] Some permit the principal to revoke a health care power of attorney at any time, regardless of the principal's mental or physical condition. These statutes, therefore, impose no requirement that the principal, who must generally have been of "sound mind" to execute the instrument, also be of sound mind to revoke the instrument.[187] Other statutes require the principal to possess

---

[186] **AK:** Alaska Stat. § 13.26.332.

**CA:** Cal. Civ. Code § 2436.5 (health care power of attorney executed after January 1, 1984, but before January 1, 1992, expires seven years after date of execution; power of attorney executed on or after January 1, 1992, exists for indefinite period unless principal expressly limits duration); Cal. Civ. Code § 2500(8) (powers given by health care power of attorney exist for indefinite period unless principal expressly limits duration).

**FL:** Fla. Stat. Ann. § 765.202(5) (unless document states time of termination, designation remains in effect until revoked by principal).

**GA:** Ga. Code Ann. § 31-36-10(a).

**IL:** Ill. Ann. Stat. ch. 755, § 45/4-10(4).

**MO:** Mo. Ann. Stat. § 404.717.1(1).

**NV:** Nev. Rev. Stat. Ann. §§ 449.830.5, .860.4(a).

**NY:** N.Y. Pub. Health Law § 2981(5)(c).

**ND:** N.D. Cent. Code § 23-06.5-17.

**OH:** Ohio Rev. Code Ann. § 1337.12(a)(3).

**RI:** R.I. Gen. Laws § 23-4.10-2.

**TX:** Tex. Civ. Prac. & Rem. Code Ann. § 135.002(g).

UHCDA § 3(b).

[187] **AK:** Alaska Stat. § 13.26.332.

**CO:** Colo. Rev. Stat. § 15-14-505(4)(a).

**CT:** Conn. Gen. Stat. Ann. § 19a-579a(a).

**FL:** Fla. Stat. Ann. § 765.104(1).

**GA:** Ga. Code Ann. § 31-36-6(a).

**ID:** Idaho Code § 39-4506(1).

**IL:** Ill. Ann. Stat. ch. 755, § 45/4-6(a).

**IA:** Iowa Code Ann. § 144B.8.1.

**ME:** Me. Rev. Stat. Ann. tit. 18-A, § 5-704(a).

**MD:** Md. Code Ann., Health-Gen. § 5-604.

**MI:** Mich. Comp. Laws § 700.496(11)(d).

**MN:** Minn. Stat. Ann. § 145B.09(1); Minn. Stat. Ann. § 145C.09(1).

**MT:** Mont. Code Ann. § 50-9-104(1).

**NJ:** N.J. Stat. Ann. § 26:2H-57(d).

**OH:** Ohio Rev. Code Ann. § 1337.14(A).

**OK:** Okla. Stat. Ann. tit. 63, § 3101.6(A).

**OR:** Or. Rev. Stat. § 127.545(1).

the same capacity for revocation as for execution.[188] Neither approach is as desirable as what has evolved in the case law, in which the preferences of a patient who lacks decisionmaking capacity are not determinative but are given at least some, and possibly great, weight.[189] In some states, the principal is presumed to have the capacity to revoke a health care power of attorney, with the burden of rebutting the presumption falling on the individual who challenges the revocation.[190]

Most statutes provide for particular methods of revocation either in very broad, all-inclusive terms,[191] or through specific methods of revocation. Moreover, an

---

**PA:** Pa. Cons. Stat. Ann. tit. 20, § 5406(a).

**RI:** R.I. Gen. Laws § 23-4.10-3(a).

**TX:** Tex. Civ. Prac. & Rem. Code Ann. § 135.005(a)(1).

**VA:** Va. Code Ann. § 54.1-2985.

**WV:** W. Va. Code § 16-30A-13.

**WI:** Wis. Stat. Ann. § 155.40(1).

[188] **CA:** Cal. Civ. Code § 2437(a).

**DC:** D.C. Code Ann. § 21-2208(a).

**IN:** Ind. Code Ann. § 16-8-12-6(j) (Burns 1990).

**KY:** Ky. Rev. Stat. Ann. § 311.627.

**MS:** Miss. Code Ann. § 41-41-171(1).

**NE:** Neb. Rev. Stat. § 30-3420(1) (principal must be competent).

**NY:** N.Y. Pub. Health Law § 2985(1)(a).

**NC:** N.C. Gen. Stat. § 32A-20(b).

**WY:** Wyo. Stat. § 3-5-207(a).

[189] See §§ **7.45–7.46.**

[190] **CA:** Cal. Civ. Code § 2437(c).

**DC:** D.C. Code Ann. § 21-2208(c).

**IA:** Iowa Code Ann. § 144B.8.2.

**MD:** Md. Code Ann., Health-Gen. § 5-607.

**MA:** Mass. Gen. Laws Ann. ch. 201D, § 7.

**MS:** Miss. Code Ann. § 41-41-171(3).

**NY:** N.Y. Pub. Health Law § 2985(1)(b).

**TN:** Tenn. Code Ann. § 34-6-207(c).

**WY:** Wyo. Stat. § 3-5-207(c).

[191] **AZ:** Ariz. Rev. Stat. Ann. § 36-3202(A)(4) (any act that demonstrates specific intent to revoke or disqualify surrogate).

**AR:** Ark. Code Ann. § 20-17-204(a) (at any time and in any manner without regard to declarant's mental or physical condition).

**CT:** Conn. Gen. Stat. Ann. § 19a-579a(a).

**IL:** Ill. Ann. Stat. ch. 755, § 45/4-2(5) ("any manner communicated to the agent or to any other person related to the subject matter of the agency").

**IA:** Iowa Code Ann. § 144B.8.1.

**ME:** Me. Rev. Stat. Ann. tit. 18-A, § 5-704(a).

implied revocation occurs under those statutes providing that a patient's preferences are to be honored over the proxy's when the patient is of questionable
competency but is still able to express a preference that is in conflict with the
proxy's.[192]

## § 12.39 —Revocation by Written or Oral Statement

Most statutes permit a principal to revoke a health care power of attorney by
written or oral notification to the agent. Some require notice to be given to the
principal's attending physician or health care provider.[193] When revocation is
permitted by notice to the attending physician or health care provider rather than

---

**MA:** Mass. Gen. Laws Ann. ch. 201D, § 7.

**MI:** Mich. Comp. Laws § 700.496(7)(g).

**MN:** Minn. Stat. Ann. § 145B.09(1).

**MO:** Mo. Ann. Stat. § 404.850.1.

**MT:** Mont. Code Ann. § 50-9-104(1).

**NE:** Neb. Rev. Stat. § 30-3420(1).

**NH:** N.H. Rev. Stat. Ann. § 137-J:6(I).

**NJ:** N.J. Stat. Ann. § 26:2H-57(b)(1) ("oral or written notification . . . or by any other act evidencing intent to revoke").

**NY:** N.Y. Pub. Health Law § 2985(1)(a).

**NC:** N.C. Gen. Stat. § 32A-20(b).

**ND:** N.D. Cent. Code § 23-06.5-07.1(a).

**OH:** Ohio Rev. Code Ann. § 1337.14(A).

**OK:** Okla. Stat. Ann. tit. 63, § 3101.6(A).

**PA:** Pa. Cons. Stat. Ann. tit. 20, § 5406(a).

**RI:** R.I. Gen. Laws § 23-4.10-3(a).

**TX:** Tex. Civ. Prac. & Rem. Code Ann. § 135.005(a)(1) ("by any . . . act evidencing a specific intent to revoke the power").

**VT:** Vt. Stat. Ann. tit. 14, § 3457(a)(1).

**WI:** Wis. Stat. Ann. § 155.40(1).

[192] See **§ 12.24.**

[193] **AR:** Ark. Code Ann. § 20-17-204(a) (effective upon communication to attending physician or health care provider).

**CA:** Cal. Civ. Code § 2437(a)(2) (revocation of agent's authority to make health care decisions made by notifying health care provider).

**DC:** D.C. Code Ann. § 21-2208(a)(2) (revocation of agent's authority to make health care decisions made by notifying health care provider).

**IA:** Iowa Code Ann. § 144B.8.1 (revocation only effective as to a health care provider upon its communication to the provider).

**LA:** La. Rev. Stat. Ann. § 40:1299.58.4(3)(b) (revocation effective upon communication to attending physician).

**ME:** Me. Rev. Stat. Ann. tit. 18-A, § 5-704(a) (revocation effective upon communication to attending physician or other health care provider).

to the proxy, the attending physician or health care provider is required to note the revocation in the principal's medical record.[194] Some statutes require an attending physician or health care provider who receives notice of revocation to

---

**MD:** Md. Code Ann., Health-Gen. § 5-604 (oral revocation must be to health care provider).

**MA:** Mass. Gen. Laws Ann. ch. 201D, § 7 (agent or nursing staff, if informed of revocation, must notify attending physician).

**MN:** Minn. Stat. Ann. § 145B.09(1) (revocation effective when declarant communicates it to attending physician or other health care provider).

**MS:** Miss. Code Ann. § 41-41-171(1)(b) (written notification to health care provider revokes the agent's authority to make health care decisions for the principal).

**MT:** Mont. Code Ann. § 50-9-104(1) (revocation effective upon communication to attending physician).

**NE:** Neb. Rev. Stat. § 30-3420(a) (revocation effective upon communication to attending physician or to health care provider or attorney in fact, who must promptly inform attending physician of revocation).

**NV:** Nev. Rev. Stat. Ann. § 449.620 (effective upon communication to attending physician or other provider of health care) (health care proxy provision of living will).

**NY:** N.Y. Pub. Health Law § 2985(2)(b) (if staff member is informed of revocation, shall immediately notify physician).

**NC:** N.C. Gen. Stat. § 32A-20(b) (effective only upon communication to health care agent and to attending physician).

**OH:** Ohio Rev. Code Ann. § 1337.14(A) (if attending physician is aware of the durable power of attorney, then revocation effective upon its communication to attending physician or other health care personnel).

**OK:** Okla. Stat. Ann. tit. 63, § 3101.6(A).

**OR:** Or. Rev. Stat. § 127.545(2).

**PA:** Pa. Cons. Stat. Ann. tit. 20, § 5406(a) (effective upon communication to attending physician or health care provider).

**RI:** R.I. Gen. Laws § 23-4.10-3(a).

**SC:** S.C. Code Ann. § 62-5-504(L)(2) (health care provider informed of the revocation must notify attending physician and other providers); S.C. Code Ann. § 44-77-80 (effective upon communication to attending physician).

**TX:** Tex. Civ. Prac. & Rem. Code § 135.005(b) (health care provider informed of the revocation shall notify other providers).

**UT:** Utah Code Ann. § 75-2-1111(2) (oral revocation not otherwise known to attending physician is only effective upon receipt by attending physician and other providers of a written revocation).

**VT:** Vt. Stat. Ann. tit. 14, § 3457(b) (health care provider informed of the revocation must notify attending physician and other providers).

**VA:** Va. Code Ann. § 54.1-2985 (effective upon communication to attending physician).

**WV:** W. Va. Code § 16-30A-13 (written or verbal revocation effective only upon communication to attending physician).

**WY:** Wyo. Stat. § 3-5-207(a)(ii) (written notification to health care provider revokes the agent's authority to make health care decisions for the principal).

UHCDA § 3(c).

[194] **AR:** Ark. Code Ann. § 20-17-204(b).

**CA:** Cal. Civ. Code § 2437(a)(2)(b).

make a reasonable attempt to notify the proxy of the revocation.[195] A few states impose a duty on any person who knows of a revocation to make a reasonable

---

**DC:** D.C. Code Ann. § 21-2208(b).

**IA:** Iowa Code Ann. § 144B.8.1.

**KY:** Ky. Rev. Stat. Ann. § 311.627 (if revocation occurs while principal is inpatient, revocation must be entered in medical record).

**LA:** La. Rev. Stat. Ann. § 40:1299.58.4(2)(b).

**ME:** Me. Rev. Stat. Ann. tit. 18-A, § 5-704(b).

**MA:** Mass. Gen. Laws Ann. ch. 201D, § 7.

**MN:** Minn. Stat. Ann. § 145B.09(1).

**MS:** Miss. Code Ann. § 41-41-171(2).

**MO:** Mo. Ann. Stat. § 404.850.2.

**MT:** Mont. Code Ann. § 50-9-104(2).

**NE:** Neb. Rev. Stat. § 30-3420(3).

**NH:** N.H. Rev. Stat. Ann. § 137-J:6(II).

**NY:** N.Y. Pub. Health Law § 2985(2)(a)(i).

**ND:** N.D. Cent. Code § 23-06.5-07.2.

**OH:** Ohio Rev. Code Ann. § 1337.14(B).

**OK:** Okla. Stat. Ann. tit. 63, § 3101.6(B).

**OR:** Or. Rev. Stat. § 127.545(2).

**PA:** Pa. Cons. Stat. Ann. tit. 20, § 5406(b).

**RI:** R.I. Gen. Laws § 23-4.10-3(b). *But cf.* R.I. Gen. Laws § 23-4.10-2 (no requirement of entry into principal's medical record).

**SC:** S.C. Code Ann. § 62-5-504(L)(2).

**TN:** Tenn. Code Ann. § 34-6-207(b).

**TX:** Tex. Civ. Prac. & Rem. Code Ann. § 135.005(b).

**UT:** Utah Code Ann. § 75-2-1111(2).

**VT:** Vt. Stat. Ann. tit. 14, § 3457(b).

**WV:** W. Va. Code § 16-30A-13.

**WI:** Wis. Stat. Ann. § 155.40(4).

**WY:** Wyo. Stat. § 3-5-207(b); Wyo. Stat. § 35-22-103(a)(iii).

[195] **CA:** Cal. Civ. Code § 2437(a)(2)(b).

**DC:** D.C. Code Ann. § 21-2208(b).

**IL:** Ill. Ann. Stat. ch. 755, § 45/4-6(c).

**MA:** Mass. Gen. Laws Ann. ch. 201D, § 7.

**NY:** N.Y. Pub. Health Law § 2985(2)(a)(ii).

**SC:** S.C. Code Ann. § 62-5-504(L)(2).

**TN:** Tenn. Code Ann. § 34-6-207(b).

**TX:** Tex. Civ. Prac. & Rem. Code Ann. § 135.005(b).

**VT:** Vt. Stat. Ann. tit. 14, § 3457(b).

**WV:** *But see* W. Va. Code § 16-30A-13 (requiring attending physician to make record of revocation but not requiring notification of agent).

effort to notify the proxy,[196] and the principal or the proxy must also notify the health care provider of the revocation.[197] Other statutes require that notice be given but do not specify to whom it must be communicated.[198] Nevada's revocation provisions do not expressly provide for revocation by any method other than execution of a subsequent health care power of attorney or divorce, although written and oral revocation are implicitly permissible.[199] However, the statutory form power of attorney includes a warning to the principal that provides for revocation by oral or written notification of the proxy, treating physician, hospital, or other health care provider.[200] In North Carolina, a revocation becomes effective only upon communication by the principal to the principal's attending physician and to each health care proxy named in the revoked health care power of attorney.[201]

## § 12.40  —Revocation by Subsequent Power of Attorney

Many statutes provide for revocation by the valid execution of a subsequent health care power of attorney. Revocation by this method requires no separate notice of intent to revoke the previous power of attorney.[202]

---

[196] **CT:** Conn. Gen. Stat. Ann. § 19a-579a(a).

**GA:** Ga. Code Ann. § 31-36-6(e).

**IL:** Ill. Ann. Stat. ch. 755, § 45/4-6(c) ("Any person, other than the agent, to whom a revocation or amendment is communicated or delivered shall make all reasonable efforts to inform the agent of that fact as promptly as possible.").

[197] **CT:** Conn. Gen. Stat. Ann. § 19a-579a(b).

**GA:** Ga. Code Ann. § 31-36-7(1).

**IL:** Ill. Ann. Stat. ch. 755, § 45/4-7(a).

[198] **ID:** Idaho Code § 39-4506(1)(b), (c).

**IL:** Ill. Ann. Stat. ch. 755, § 45/4-6(a)(2), (3).

**KY:** Ky. Rev. Stat. Ann. § 311.627.

[199] Nev. Rev. Stat. Ann. §§ 449.860.2, .3.

[200] *Id.* § 449.830.

[201] N.C. Gen. Stat. § 32A-20(b).

[202] **AK:** Alaska Stat. § 13.26.332.

**AZ:** Ariz. Rev. Stat. Ann. § 36-3202(3).

**CA:** Cal. Civ. Code §§ 2437(d), 2500.

**DE:** Del. Code Ann. tit. 16, § 2504(a)(3).

**DC:** D.C. Code Ann. § 21-2208(d).

**FL:** Fla. Stat. Ann. § 765.104(1)(d) (if materially different from a previously executed advance directive).

**IA:** Iowa Code Ann. § 144B.8.3.

**KS:** Kan. Stat. Ann. § 58-632.

## § 12.41 —Revocation by Destruction

An expressly authorized means of revocation under a number of statutes is the destruction of the health care power of attorney by "being obliterated, burned, torn, or otherwise destroyed or defaced in a manner indicating an intention to revoke."[203]

---

**MD:** Md. Code Ann., Health-Gen. § 5-603.

**MI:** Mich. Comp. Laws § 700.496(11) (f).

**MN:** Minn. Stat. Ann. § 145C.09(1)(4).

**MS:** Miss. Code Ann. § 41-41-171(4).

**MO:** Mo. Ann. Stat. § 404.850.3.

**NE:** Neb. Rev. Stat. § 30-3420(4).

**NV:** Nev. Rev. Stat. Ann. § 449.860.3.

**NH:** N.H. Rev. Stat. Ann. § 137-J:6(I)(b).

**NJ:** N.J. Stat. Ann. § 26:2H-57(b)(2).

**NY:** N.Y. Pub. Health Law § 2985(1)(c).

**NC:** N.C. Gen. Stat. § 32A-20(b).

**ND:** N.D. Cent. Code § 23-06.5-07.1(b).

**OH:** Ohio Rev. Code Ann. § 1337.14(C).

**OR:** Or. Rev. Stat. § 127.545(3).

**RI:** R.I. Gen. Laws § 23-4.10-2.

**SC:** S.C. Code Ann. § 62-5-504(L)(1)(b).

**TN:** Tenn. Code Ann. § 34-6-207(d).

**TX:** Tex. Civ. Prac. & Rem. Code Ann. § 135.005(a)(2).

**VT:** Vt. Stat. Ann. tit. 14, § 3457(a)(2).

**WI:** Wis. Stat. Ann. § 155.40(1)(d).

**WY:** Wyo. Stat. § 3-5-207(d).

UHCDA § 3(e) (if subsequent directive conflicts with earlier directive, earlier directive revoked to the extent of the conflict).

[203] **GA:** Ga. Code Ann. § 31-36-6(a)(1).

**DE:** *Accord* Del. Code Ann. tit. 16, § 2504(a)(1).

**FL:** *Accord* Fla. Stat. Ann. § 765.104(1)(b).

**ID:** *Accord* Idaho Code § 39-4506(1)(a).

**IL:** *Accord* Ill. Ann. Stat. ch. 755, § 45/4-6(a)(1).

**KY:** *Accord* Ky. Rev. Stat. Ann. § 311.629.

**LA:** *Accord* La. Rev. Stat. Ann. § 40:1299.58.4(1).

**MD:** *Accord* Md. Code Ann., Health-Gen. § 5-603.

**MN:** *Accord* Minn. Stat. Ann. § 145C.09 subd. 1 (1).

**UT:** *Accord* Utah Code Ann. § 75-2-1111(1)(a).

**VA:** *Accord* Va. Code Ann. § 54.1-2985.

**WV:** *Accord* W. Va. Code § 16-30A-13(a).

**WI:** *Accord* Wis. Stat. Ann. § 155.40(1)(a).

**WY:** *Accord* Wyo. Stat. 35-22-103(a)(i).

## § 12.42  —Partial Revocation by Amendment

A few statutes expressly provide for the partial revocation by amendment of a health care power of attorney, for example, by changing the proxy or modifying the proxy's powers.[204]

## § 12.43  Termination by Operation of Law

Health care power of attorney statutes contain various provisions by which an instrument will terminate by operation of law.

### Fixed Duration

Only a California statute limits the duration of a health care power of attorney to a fixed period of time from the date of execution unless revoked prior to the expiration of that time period,[205] though the principal may select a shorter duration.[206] However, if the principal loses decisionmaking capacity before expiration of the period specified by statute or by the principal, the proxy's authority continues at least until the principal regains decisionmaking capacity.[207]

---

[204] **AK:** Alaska Stat. § 13.26.332 (one or more granted powers may be revoked "by completing a special power of attorney that includes the specific power in this document that you want to revoke").

**GA:** Ga. Code Ann. § 31-36-6(d).

**IL:** Ill. Ann. Stat. ch. 755, § 45/4-6(b) (durable power of attorney for health care "may be amended at any time by a written amendment").

**KY:** Ky. Rev. Stat. Ann. § 311.627.

**NY:** N.Y. Pub. Health Law § 2985(1)(d).

[205] Cal. Civ. Code § 2436.5 (applies only to health care power of attorney executed after January 1, 1984, but before January 1, 1992, or to one executed on or after January 1, 1992, containing statement expressly limiting duration).

[206] **CA:** Cal. Civ. Code § 2436.5 (applies only to health care power of attorney executed after January 1, 1984, but before January 1, 1992, or one executed on or after January 1, 1992, containing statement expressly limiting duration).

**MN:** *Accord* Minn. Stat. Ann. § 145C.05 subd. 2(4).

**NV:** *Accord* Nev. Rev. Stat. Ann. § 449.830(4).

**OH:** *Accord* Ohio Rev. Code Ann. § 1337.12(A)(3).

**OR:** *Accord* Or. Rev. Stat. § 127.510(3).

[207] **CA:** Cal. Civ. Code § 2436.5.

**MN:** *Accord* Minn. Stat. Ann. § 145C.09(1)(1).

**NV:** *Accord* Nev. Rev. Stat. Ann. § 449.860(4).

**OH:** *Accord* Ohio Rev. Code Ann. § 1337.12(A)(3).

**OR:** *Accord* Or. Rev. Stat. § 127.510(3).

**TX:** *Accord* Tex. Civ. Prac. & Rem. Code Ann. § 135.002(g).

**WA:** *Accord* Wash. Rev. Code Ann. § 11.94.010.2.

In other states, unless the power of attorney is revoked or a termination date is included in it by the principal, the proxy's authority continues until the principal dies or regains decisionmaking capacity.[208]

## Divorce

In many jurisdictions, when the principal and proxy are married to each other, their divorce acts automatically to revoke the power of attorney,[209] but when

---

[208] **ID:** Idaho Code § 39-4507.

**IL:** Ill. Ann. Stat. ch. 755, § 45/4-10(a).

**MS:** Miss. Code Ann. § 41-41-165(2).

**NV:** Nev. Rev. Stat. Ann. § 449.860.4.

**NY:** N.Y. Pub. Health Law § 2981(4)(c).

**NC:** N.C. Gen. Stat. § 32A-20(b).

**RI:** R.I. Gen. Laws § 23-4.10-2.

**TX:** Tex. Civ. Prac. & Rem. Code Ann. § 135.002(g).

**VA:** Va. Code Ann. § 54.1-2984.

**WA:** Wash. Rev. Code Ann. § 11.94.010.2.

[209] **CA:** Cal. Civ. Code § 2437(e).

**CO:** Colo. Rev. Stat. § 15-14-506(5)(c).

**CT:** Conn. Gen. Stat. Ann. § 19a-579b.

**DC:** D.C. Code Ann. § 21-2208(e).

**FL:** Fla. Stat. Ann. § 765.104(2) (unless otherwise provided in advance directive or in order of dissolution or annulment of marriage).

**GA:** Ga. Code Ann. § 31-36-6(b).

**ID:** Idaho Code § 39-4505.7.

**IL:** Ill. Ann. Stat. ch. 755, § 45/4-2(6).

**IA:** Iowa Code Ann. § 144B.12.3.

**MI:** Mich. Comp. Laws § 700.496(11)(g).

**MN:** Minn. Stat. Ann. § 145B.09(2); Minn. Stat. Ann. § 145C.09(2).

**MO:** Mo. Ann. Stat. § 404.717.6.

**NE:** Neb. Rev. Stat. § 30-3420(6) (unless divorce decree otherwise specifies).

**NV:** Nev. Rev. Stat. Ann. § 449.860.2.

**NH:** N.H. Rev. Stat. Ann. § 137-J:6(I)(c).

**NJ:** N.J. Stat. Ann. § 26:2H-57(c).

**NY:** N.Y. Pub. Health Law § 2985(1)(e).

**NC:** N.C. Gen. Stat. § 32A-20(c).

**ND:** N.D. Cent. Code § 23-06.5-07.1(c), .3.

**RI:** R.I. Gen. Laws § 23-4.10-2.

**TN:** Tenn. Code Ann. § 34-6-207(e).

**TX:** Tex. Civ. Prac. & Rem. Code Ann. § 135.005(a)(3).

**VT:** Vt. Stat. Ann. tit. 14, § 3457(a)(3).

**WV:** W. Va. Code § 16-30A-13(d).

**WI:** Wis. Stat. Ann. § 155.40(2).

divorce is the sole means of revocation, the spouse's designation as proxy is reinstated by the principal's remarriage to the former spouse.[210]

## § 12.44 Termination by Judicial Order

In some jurisdictions the proxy's authority is terminable by judicial order. The grounds for so doing are that the principal was not of sound mind or was under duress, fraud, or undue influence at the time of execution of the power of attorney,[211] or that the proxy authorized illegal acts or acts contrary to the principal's known desires or best interests.[212] In some jurisdictions, if a guardian is appointed subsequent to the execution of a health care power of attorney, the court may also terminate the health care power of attorney and vest the powers granted therein in the guardian.[213]

## § 12.45 Termination by Guardian or Conservator

Some statutes empower a guardian or conservator to revoke a health care power of attorney.[214] In others, a conservator or guardian may not revoke a health

---

WY: Wyo. Stat. § 3-5-207(e).

UHCDA § 3(d).

[210] CA: Cal. Civ. Code § 2437(e).

DC: D.C. Code Ann. § 21-2208(e).

WY: Wyo. Stat. § 3-5-207(e).

[211] TX: Tex. Civ. Prac. & Rem. Code Ann. § 135.017(a).

VT: Vt. Stat. Ann. tit. 14, § 3467.

[212] CA: Cal. Civ. Code § 2500.

IL: Ill. Ann. Stat. ch. 755, § 45/4-10(a) ("if it finds the agent is not acting properly").

IA: Iowa Code Ann. § 144B.6.1.

MA: Mass. Gen. Laws Ann. ch. 201D, § 17.

MI: Mich. Comp. Laws § 700.496(16).

NE: Neb. Rev. Stat. § 30-3421(1)(d).

NY: N.Y. Pub. Health Law § 2992(3).

OR: Or. Rev. Stat. § 127.550(1)(b).

RI: R.I. Gen. Laws § 23-4.10-2.

[213] CT: Conn. Gen. Stat. Ann. § 19a-579b.

IL: Ill. Ann. Stat. ch. 755, § 45/4-10.

MN: Minn. Stat. Ann. § 145C.09(2).

ND: N.D. Cent. Code § 23-06.5-07.3.

WI: Wis. Stat. Ann. § 155.60(2).

[214] IA: Iowa Code Ann. § 633.705.

KS: Kan. Stat. Ann. § 58-627(a).

NM: N.M. Stat. Ann. § 45-5-501.A.

care power of attorney directly but must petition a court for termination or suspension.[215]

# MISCELLANEOUS PROVISIONS

## § 12.46   Immunity of Health Care Providers

Like most living will statutes, health care power of attorney statutes confer immunity from criminal and civil liability, and from professional disciplinary action, on health care professionals who in good faith follow the instructions of a proxy acting in accordance with the principal's expressed wishes or in the principal's best interests.[216]

---

**WA:** Wash. Rev. Code Ann. § 11.94.010.1(1).

**WY:** Wyo. Stat. § 3-5-207(g).

**SC:** *Cf.* S.C. Code Ann. §§ 44-77-50, -80(4), -85 (proxy has authority to revoke principal's living will if empowered to do so in living will).

[215] **FL:** Fla. Stat. Ann. § 765.105 (patient's family, health care facility, attending physician, or any interested person may seek judicial review of surrogate's decision).

**ME:** Me. Rev. Stat. Ann. tit. 18-A, § 5-501.

**NE:** Neb. Rev. Stat. § 30-3422(5), (6).

**NH:** N.H. Rev. Stat. Ann. § 137-J:16.

**NY:** N.Y. Pub. Health Law § 2992.

**TX:** Tex. Civ. Prac. & Rem. Code Ann. § 135.006(a).

**VT:** Vt. Stat. Ann. tit. 14, § 3463(a).

[216] **AK:** Alaska Stat. § 13.26.353(b) (reasonable reliance on health care agent's directions).

**AZ:** Ariz. Rev. Stat. Ann. § 36-3205(A).

**AR:** Ark. Code Ann. § 20-17-208(b) ("in accord with reasonable medical standards").

**CA:** Cal. Civ. Code § 2438(a).

**CO:** Colo. Rev. Stat. § 15-14-508(2).

**CT:** Conn. Gen. Stat. Ann. § 19a-571(a).

**FL:** Fla. Stat. Ann. § 765.109(1).

**GA:** Ga. Code Ann. § 31-36-8.

**ID:** Idaho Code § 39-4508.

**IL:** Ill. Ann. Stat. ch. 755, § 45/4-4(8).

**IN:** Ind. Code Ann. § 16-8-12-9(a).

**IA:** Iowa Code Ann. § 144B.9.1; Iowa Code Ann. § 144A.9.

**KY:** Ky. Rev. Stat. Ann. § 311.635(1).

**ME:** Me. Rev. Stat. Ann. tit. 18-A, § 5-709(c).

**MD:** Md. Code Ann., Health-Gen. § 5-609(A).

**MA:** Mass. Gen. Laws Ann. ch. 201D, § 8.

**MI:** Mich. Comp. Laws § 700.496(14).

When a physician refuses to carry out the proxy's directions for reasons of conscience,[217] the statutes make the health care provider's immunity contingent on notification of the proxy,[218] transfer of the patient to a health care provider willing to follow the proxy's instructions,[219] or both notification and transfer.[220]

---

**MN:** Minn. Stat. Ann. § 145C.11(2).

**MS:** Miss. Code Ann. 41-41-173.

**MO:** Mo. Ann. Stat. § 404.855.

**MT:** Mont. Code Ann. § 50-9-204(1).

**NE:** Neb. Rev. Stat. § 30-3423(2).

**NH:** N.H. Rev. Stat. Ann. § 137-J:11(II).

**NJ:** N.J. Stat. Ann. § 26:2H-73(b).

**NY:** N.Y. Pub. Health Law § 2986(1).

**NC:** N.C. Gen. Stat. § 32A-24(b).

**ND:** N.D. Cent. Code § 23-06.5-12.2.

**OH:** Ohio Rev. Code Ann. § 1337.15(A).

**OK:** Okla. Stat. Ann. tit. 63, § 3101.10(B).

**OR:** Or. Rev. Stat. § 127.555(3).

**PA:** Pa. Cons. Stat. Ann. tit. 20, § 5407(a).

**RI:** R.I. Gen. Laws § 23-4.10-7(b).

**SC:** S.C. Code Ann. § 62-5-504(J)(2).

**SD:** S.D. Codified Laws Ann. § 59-7-2.8.

**TN:** Tenn. Code Ann. § 34-6-208(a), (b).

**TX:** Tex. Civ. Prac. & Rem. Code Ann. § 135.010(b).

**VA:** Va. Code Ann. § 54.1-2988.

**WI:** Wis. Stat. Ann. § 155.50(1).

**WY:** Wyo. Stat. § 3-5-208(a).

1989 URTIA, § 9, 9B U.L.A. 127, 141. UHCDA § 9(a).

[217] See **§ 17.23.**

[218] **OR:** Or. Rev. Stat. § 127.555(5).

**TX:** Tex. Civ. Prac. & Rem. Code Ann. § 135.008(c).

[219] **AR:** Ark. Code Ann. § 20-17-207.

**CT:** Conn. Gen. Stat. Ann. § 19a-580a.

**FL:** Fla. Stat. Ann. § 765.308(2) (must transfer to another health care provider within seven days or carry out wishes of patient or patient's surrogate).

**ID:** Idaho Code § 39-4508 (good-faith effort to assist patient in obtaining services of another physician).

**LA:** La. Rev. Stat. Ann. § 40:1299.58.7(B).

**ME:** Me. Rev. Stat. Ann. tit. 18-A, § 5-708.

**MA:** Mass. Gen. Laws Ann. ch. 201D, § 14 (either physician or agent must transfer).

**MN:** Minn. Stat. Ann. § 145B.07.

**MO:** Mo. Ann. Stat. § 404.830.1(3) (physician "shall not impede the attorney-in-fact from transferring the patient").

A few statutes grant immunity to a health care professional who fails to withdraw health care necessary to keep the patient alive when the proxy has requested that it be withdrawn.[221] A provision such as this is fundamentally inconsistent with the theory of surrogate decisionmaking. Physicians ought to be

---

**MT:** Mont. Code Ann. § 50-9-203 (requiring attending physician not willing to comply with agent's decisions to take all reasonable steps to transfer, but conditioning immunity on transfer).

**NH:** N.H. Rev. Stat. Ann. § 137-J:8(II).

**NY:** N.Y. Pub. Health Law § 2984(3)(b) (the physician, if unable or unwilling to follow the instructions of the agent, must help to arrange for transfer to a physician willing to honor the agent's decision; "[i]f the physician or the agent is unable to arrange such a transfer, the physician shall seek judicial relief or honor the agent's decision.").

**OH:** Ohio Rev. Code Ann. § 1337.16(B)(2)(a) (health care provider must not prevent transfer of patient).

**OK:** Okla. Stat. Ann. tit. 63, § 3101.9.

**RI:** R.I. Gen. Laws § 23-4.10-6.

**SC:** S.C. Code Ann. § 62-5-504(R).

**TN:** Tenn. Code Ann. § 34-6-214.

**UT:** Utah Code Ann. § 75-2-1112(2).

**VA:** Va. Code Ann. § 54.1-2987.

**WI:** Wis. Stat. Ann. § 155.50(1)(b).

[220] **AZ:** Ariz. Rev. Stat. Ann. § 36-3205(C)(1).

**CO:** Colo. Rev. Stat. § 15-14-507(1), (2).

**GA:** Ga. Code Ann. § 31-36-8(2) (provider responsible for transfer of patient if agent fails to do so).

**IL:** Ill. Ann. Stat. ch. 755, § 45/4-8(b).

**KY:** Ky. Rev. Stat. Ann. § 311.633.

**NE:** Neb. Rev. Stat. § 30-3428(2).

**NJ:** N.J. Stat. Ann. § 26:2H-62(b).

**NY:** N.Y. Pub. Health Law § 2984(3) (provider must transfer patient if agent fails to do so).

**ND:** N.D. Cent. Code § 23-06.5-09.2.

**PA:** Pa. Cons. Stat. Ann. tit. 20, § 5409(a).

**VT:** Vt. Stat. Ann. tit. 14, § 3459(b) (notify and actively assist in transfer).

**WV:** W. Va. Code § 16-30A-10(b) (transfer in conjunction with representative).

[221] **CA:** Cal. Civ. Code § 2438(c).

**CT:** Conn. Gen. Stat. Ann. § 19a-571(a).

**IA:** Iowa Code Ann. § 144B.2.

**MD:** Md. Code Ann., Health-Gen. § 5-609(A).

**MN:** Minn. Stat. Ann. § 145C.11(2).

**MS:** Miss. Code Ann. § 41-41-173(2).

**OH:** Ohio Rev. Code Ann. § 1337.15(B).

**PA:** 20 Pa. Cons. Stat. Ann. § 5409(c).

**TN:** Tenn. Code Ann. § 34-6-208(c).

**WY:** Wyo. Stat. § 3-5-208(b).

allowed to ignore the instructions of a proxy to terminate life-sustaining treatment only when those instructions are, in good faith, thought to be in conflict with the patient's known or presumed wishes or clearly in violation of the patient's best interests[222] or possibly when they conflict with the physician's conscientiously held objections to forgoing treatment.[223] With the exception of Alaska, which establishes specific civil penalties and damages for a health care provider's failure to comply with a proxy's good-faith decisions,[224] most statutes are silent and by implication leave patients to rely on common-law remedies such as actions for abandonment, lack of informed consent, and negligence to remedy a health care professional's failure to follow the proxy's directions.[225]

## § 12.47  Immunity of Proxies

Some statutes explicitly confer immunity from liability on a proxy for actions taken in good faith.[226] Some statutes expressly immunize the proxy from liability for costs of the principal's health care arising from exercise of the proxy's

---

[222] See **Ch. 7.**

[223] See § **17.23.**

[224] Alaska Stat. § 13.26.353(b).

[225] See **Ch. 17.**

[226] **AZ:** Ariz. Rev. Stat. Ann. § 36-3203(D).

**CO:** Colo. Rev. Stat. § 15-14-508(1).

**FL:** Fla. Stat. Ann. § 765.109.

**GA:** Ga. Code Ann. § 31-36-8(4).

**ID:** Idaho Code § 39-4508.

**IL:** Ill. Ann. Stat. ch. 755, § 45/4-8(d).

**IA:** Iowa Code Ann. § 144B.9.3.

**KY:** Ky. Rev. Stat. Ann. § 311.635.

**ME:** Me. Rev. Stat. Ann. tit. 18-A, § 5-709(d).

**MD:** Md. Code Ann., Health-Gen. § 5-609(B).

**MA:** Mass. Gen. Laws Ann. ch. 201D, § 8.

**MI:** Mich. Comp. Laws § 700.496(12) (even if revoked, immunity exists if agent has in good faith relied on his or her authority to make decisions).

**MN:** Minn. Stat. Ann. § 145C.11(1).

**MS:** Miss. Code Ann. § 41-41-175.

**MT:** Mont. Code Ann. § 50-9-204(4).

**NE:** Neb. Rev. Stat. § 30-3423(1).

**NH:** N.H. Rev. Stat. Ann. § 137-J:11(I).

**NJ:** N.J. Stat. Ann. § 26:2H-73(a).

**NY:** N.Y. Pub. Health Law § 2986(2).

**ND:** N.D. Cent. Code § 23-06.5-12.1.

powers.[227] In the absence of actual knowledge on the part of the proxy of the termination of a health care power of attorney, the proxy is absolved from liability arising from the exercise of his powers.[228]

---

**OH:** Ohio Rev. Code Ann. § 1337.15(G).

**OK:** Okla. Stat. Ann. tit. 63, § 3101.10(C).

**OR:** Or. Rev. Stat. § 127.555(2).

**SC:** S.C. Code Ann. § 62-5-504(J)(3).

**TX:** Tex. Civ. Prac. & Rem. Code Ann. § 135.010(a).

**VA:** Va. Code Ann. § 54.1-2988.

**WV:** W. Va. Code § 16-30A-14(a).

**WI:** Wis. Stat. Ann. § 155.50(3).

[227] **AZ:** Ariz. Rev. Stat. Ann. § 36-3203(4).

**GA:** Ga. Code Ann. § 31-36-10(b)(4) (health care at principal's expense).

**IL:** Ill. Ann. Stat. ch. 755, § 45/4-10(b)(3).

**KY:** Ky. Rev. Stat. Ann. § 311.635.

**MD:** Md. Code Ann., Health-Gen. § 5-609(B)(2).

**MA:** Mass. Gen. Laws Ann. ch. 201D, § 9.

**NE:** Neb. Rev. Stat. § 30-3417(3).

**NH:** N.H. Rev. Stat. Ann. § 137-J:13.

**NJ:** N.J. Stat. Ann. § 26:2H-61(c).

**NY:** N.Y. Pub. Health Law § 2987.

**ND:** N.D. Cent. Code § 23-06.5-14.

**SC:** S.C. Code Ann. § 62-5-504(F)(2).

**TX:** Tex. Civ. Prac. & Rem. Code Ann. § 135.011.

**VT:** Vt. Stat. Ann. tit. 14, § 3464.

**VA:** Va. Code Ann. § 54.1-2984.

**WI:** Wis. Stat. Ann. § 155.50(3) (unless agent is spouse of principal).

[228] **CA:** Cal. Civ. Code § 2437(f).

**FL:** Fla. Stat. Ann. § 765.104(3).

**GA:** Ga. Code Ann. § 31-36-8(3).

**ID:** Idaho Code § 39-4508.

**IL:** Ill. Ann. Stat. ch. 755, § 45/4-2(7).

**IA:** Iowa Code Ann. § 144B.9.6.

**ME:** Me. Rev. Stat. Ann. tit. 18-A, § 5-709(a).

**MI:** Mich. Comp. Laws § 700.496(12).

**MN:** Minn. Stat. Ann. § 145C.11(1).

**MS:** Miss. Code Ann. § 41-41-171(5).

**OR:** Or. Rev. Stat. § 127.555(2).

**TX:** Tex. Civ. Prac. & Rem. Code Ann. § 135.010(a).

## § 12.48 Penalties

### Forgery or Alteration

Some statutes impose penalties for willful forgery or unauthorized alteration of a health care power of attorney, and the severity of the penalties is usually proportionate to the potential consequences to the principal. Thus, the offense is treated as a felony when forgery or alteration is intended to and does cause withholding or withdrawal of life support.[229] When there is no intent to hasten

---

**VT:** Vt. Stat. Ann. tit. 14, § 3462(a).

**WV:** W. Va. Code § 16-30A-9.

**WY:** Wyo. Stat. § 3-5-207(f).

[229] **AR:** Ark. Code Ann. § 20-17-209(d) (class D felony).

**CA:** Cal. Civ. Code § 2442 ("unlawful homicide").

**CO:** Colo. Rev. Stat. § 15-18-113(3), (4) (declaration is class 2 felony; revocation is misdemeanor).

**DE:** Cf. Del. Code Ann. tit. 16, § 2508(b) ("Class C felony" "to create the false impression that another person has directed that maintenance medical treatment be utilized for the prolongation of his life" as opposed to intending to shorten life).

**FL:** Fla. Stat. Ann. § 765.310(2) (felony of second degree).

**GA:** Ga. Code Ann. § 31-36-9(2) (criminal homicide).

**IL:** Ill. Ann. Stat. ch. 755, § 45/4-9(b) (involuntary manslaughter).

**LA:** La. Rev. Stat. Ann. § 40:1299.58.9(B) ("subject to prosecution").

**ME:** Me. Rev. Stat. Ann. tit. 18-A, § 5-710(c) (class E felony).

**MD:** Md. Code Ann., Health-Gen. § 5-613(A) (health care provider not willing to comply shall notify person giving instruction and make every effort to assist with transfer).

**MN:** Minn. Stat. Ann. § 145C.13(2) (felony); Minn. Stat. Ann. § 145B.105(2) (felony).

**NE:** Neb. Rev. Stat. § 30-3432(1) (class II felony).

**NV:** Nev. Rev. Stat. Ann. § 449.660(4) (murder).

**NJ:** N.J. Stat. Ann. § 26:2H-78(c)(2) (crime of fourth degree).

**ND:** N.D. Cent. Code § 23-06.5-18.1 (class C felony).

**OR:** Or. Rev. Stat. § 127.585(1) (class A felony).

**PA:** Pa. Cons. Stat. Ann. tit. 20, § 5414 (criminal homicide).

**RI:** R.I. Gen. Laws § 23-4.10-8(d) (imprisonment for no less than one year but no more than five years or fine of no less than $5,000 but no more than $10,000).

**SC:** S.C. Code Ann. § 62-5-504(Q)(1) (if principal dies, person is subject to prosecution in accordance with criminal laws of South Carolina).

**UT:** Utah Code Ann. § 75-2-1115(2) (criminal homicide).

**VA:** Va. Code Ann. § 54.1-2989 (class 2 felony).

**WY:** Wyo. Stat. § 35-22-107(b) (felony with imprisonment not exceeding 20 years).

1989 URTIA § 10(d)–(f), 9B U.L.A. 127, 142.

death, or when the effect of withholding or withdrawal of life-sustaining treatment is not to hasten death, willful forgery or alteration of a health care power of attorney is not treated as seriously.[230] In some states, however, all such offenses, regardless of the potential consequences to the principal, are treated the same.[231]

## Concealment of Revocation

Different levels of penalties, also depending on the potential or actual consequence to the principal, are imposed for the willful concealment or destruction of the *revocation* of a health care power of attorney. The concealment of revocation that is intended to cause forgoing of life-sustaining treatment contrary to the wishes of the principal and that hastens the principal's death, is

---

[230] **AR:** Ark. Code Ann. § 20-17-209(c).

**CA:** Cal. Civ. Code § 2442 (no penalty unless forgery or alteration hastens principal's death).

**CO:** Colo. Rev. Stat. § 15-18-113(1), (2) (class 1 misdemeanor or class 4 felony).

**HI:** Haw. Rev. Stat. § 327D-17(b).

**IL:** Ill. Ann. Stat. ch. 755, § 45/4-9(a).

**MD:** Md. Code Ann., Health-Gen. § 5-609(B).

**MN:** Minn. Stat. Ann. § 145B.105(1) (gross misdemeanor if no bodily harm results); Minn. Stat. Ann. § 145C.13(1) (gross misdemeanor if no bodily harm results).

**NE:** Neb. Rev. Stat. § 30-3432(2) (class I misdemeanor).

**NV:** Nev. Rev. Stat. Ann. § 449.660(3).

**OR:** Or. Rev. Stat. § 127.585(2) (class A misdemeanor).

**PA:** Pa. Cons. Stat. Ann. tit. 20, § 5415 (felony of third degree).

**RI:** R.I. Gen. Laws § 23-4.10-8(c) (imprisonment for no less than six months but no more than one year or fine of no less than $2,000 but no more than $5,000).

**SC:** S.C. Code Ann. § 62-5-504(Q)(3) (person is responsible for payment of expenses or other damages incurred as result of wrongful act).

**UT:** Utah Code Ann. § 75-2-1115(1) (class B misdemeanor).

**VA:** Va. Code Ann. § 54.1-2989 (causing life-prolonging procedures to be utilized in contravention of previously expressed intent of patient is class 6 felony).

1989 URTIA § 10(c), 9B U.L.A. 127, 142.

[231] **HI:** Haw. Rev. Stat. § 327D-17(b) (misdemeanor).

**IA:** Iowa Code Ann. § 144A.10 ("serious misdemeanor").

**MD:** Md. Code Ann., Health-Gen. § 5-610(B) (misdemeanor punishable by fine not exceeding $10,000 or imprisonment not exceeding one year or both).

**MT:** Mont. Code Ann. § 50-9-206(3), (4) (misdemeanor punishable by fine not to exceed $500 or imprisonment for term not to exceed one year or both).

**OK:** Okla. Stat. Ann. tit. 63, § 3101.11(C), (D) (felony).

1989 URTIA § 10(d)–(f), 9B U.L.A. 127, 142. UHCDA § 10(b) (damages of $2,500 or actual damages, whichever is greater, plus attorneys' fees).

treated as a serious offense.[232] When there is no intent to cause withdrawal or withholding of life-sustaining treatment, or that result does not occur, concealment of revocation of a directive is a less serious offense.[233] In some states,

---

[232] **AR:** Ark. Code Ann. § 20-17-209(d) (class D felony).

**CA:** Cal. Civ. Code § 2442 ("unlawful homicide").

**CO:** Colo. Rev. Stat. § 15-18-113(3), (4) (declaration: class 2 felony).

**FL:** Fla. Stat. Ann. § 765.310(2) (felony of second degree).

**GA:** Ga. Code Ann. § 31-36-9(2) (criminal homicide).

**IL:** Ill. Ann. Stat. ch. 755, § 45/4-9(b) ("involuntary manslaughter").

**ME:** Me. Rev. Stat. Ann. tit. 18-A, § 5-710(d) (class B crime).

**MN:** Minn. Stat. Ann. § 145B.105(2) (felony); Minn. Stat. Ann. § 145C.13(2) (felony).

**NE:** Neb. Rev. Stat. § 30-3432(1) (class II felony).

**NV:** Nev. Rev. Stat. Ann. § 449.660(4) (murder).

**NJ:** N.J. Stat. Ann. § 26:2H-78(c)(1) (crime of fourth degree).

**ND:** N.D. Cent. Code § 23-06.5-18.1 (class C felony).

**OR:** Or. Rev. Stat. § 127.585(1) ("Class A felony").

**PA:** Pa. Cons. Stat. Ann. tit. 20, § 5415 (criminal homicide).

**RI:** R.I. Gen. Laws § 23-4.10-8(d) (imprisonment for no less than six months but no more than one year or fine of no less than $2,000 but no more than $5,000).

**SC:** S.C. Code Ann. § 62-5-504(Q)(1) (if principal dies, person is subject to prosecution in accordance with criminal laws of South Carolina).

**UT:** Utah Code Ann. § 75-2-1115(2) (criminal homicide).

**VA:** Va. Code Ann. § 54.1-2989 (class 2 felony).

[233] **AR:** Ark. Code Ann. § 20-17-209(c) (class A misdemeanor).

**CO:** Colo. Rev. Stat. § 15-18-113(1), (2) (class 1 misdemeanor or class 4 felony).

**HI:** Haw. Rev. Stat. § 327D-17(b).

**IL:** Ill. Ann. Stat. ch. 755, § 45/4-9(a) ("civilly liable").

**LA:** La. Rev. Stat. Ann. § 40:1299.58.9(A) (civilly liable).

**MN:** Minn. Stat. Ann. § 145B.105(1) (gross misdemeanor); Minn. Stat. Ann. § 145C.13(1) (gross misdemeanor).

**NE:** Neb. Rev. Stat. § 30-3432(2) (class I misdemeanor).

**NV:** Nev. Rev. Stat. Ann. § 449.660(3).

**ND:** N.D. Cent. Code § 23-06.5-18.2 (class A misdemeanor).

**OR:** Or. Rev. Stat. § 127.585(2) (class A misdemeanor).

**PA:** Pa. Cons. Stat. Ann. tit. 20, § 5415 (felony of third degree).

**RI:** R.I. Gen. Laws § 23-4.10-8(c) (imprisonment for no less than six months but no more than one year or fine of no less than $2,000 but no more than $5,000).

**SC:** S.C. Code Ann. § 62-5-504(Q)(3) (person is responsible for payment of expenses or other damages incurred as result of wrongful act).

**UT:** Utah Code Ann. § 75-2-1115(1) (class A misdemeanor).

**VA:** Va. Code Ann. § 54.1-2989 (class 6 felony).

**WI:** Wis. Stat. Ann. § 155.80(4) (fine of not more than $500 or imprisonment of not more than 30 days).

punishment for concealment of a revocation does not depend on the potential consequences to the principal.[234]

### Requiring Execution of Health Care Power of Attorney

Although most statutes prohibit a health care provider from requiring execution of a health care power of attorney as a condition for the receipt of health care services,[235] only few impose a penalty for doing so.[236]

## § 12.49 Execution as Condition for Receipt of Services and Insurance

A number of statutes prohibit requiring the execution of a health care power of attorney as a condition for admission to a health care facility,[237] receipt of

---

**WY:** Wyo. Stat. § 35-22-107(a) (misdemeanor).

1989 URTIA § 10(c), 9B U.L.A. 127, 142.

[234] **HI:** Haw. Rev. Stat. § 327D-17(b) (misdemeanor).

**IA:** Iowa Code Ann. § 144A.10 ("serious misdemeanor").

**MD:** Md. Code Ann., Health-Gen. § 5-610 (misdemeanor punishable by fine not exceeding $10,000 or imprisonment not exceeding one year or both).

**MT:** Mont. Code Ann. § 50-9-206(4).

**OK:** Okla. Stat. Ann. tit. 63, § 3101.11(D) (felony).

1989 URTIA § 10(d)–(f), 9B U.L.A. 127, 142. UHCDA § 10(b).

[235] See **§ 12.49.**

[236] **FL:** Fla. Stat. Ann. § 765.110(2) (subject to professional discipline, revocation of license or certification, and fine of not more than $500 per incident).

**IL:** Ill. Ann. Stat. ch. 755, § 45/4-9(c) ("Any person who requires or prevents execution of a health care agency as a condition . . . shall be civilly liable and guilty of a Class A misdemeanor.").

**GA:** Ga. Code Ann. § 31-36.9(3) (misdemeanor).

**ME:** Me. Rev. Stat. Ann. tit. 18-A, § 5-710(e) (class B crime).

**MD:** Md. Code Ann., Health-Gen. § 5-610(B) (misdemeanor punishable by fine not exceeding $10,000 or imprisonment not exceeding one year or both).

**MN:** Minn. Stat. Ann. § 145B.10(4).

**MT:** Mont. Code Ann. § 50-9-206(5) (misdemeanor punishable by fine not to exceed $500 or imprisonment for term not to exceed one year or both).

**NJ:** N.J. Stat. Ann. § 26:2H-78(c)(4) (crime of fourth degree).

**OK:** Okla. Stat. Ann. tit. 63, § 3101.11(E) (felony).

[237] **DC:** D.C. Code Ann. § 21-2209(a).

**FL:** Fla. Stat. Ann. § 765.110(2).

**IA:** Iowa Code Ann. § 144B.11.1.

**KY:** Ky. Rev. Stat. Ann. § 311.635.

**MI:** Mich. Comp. Laws § 700.496(18).

**MN:** Minn. Stat. Ann. §§ 145C.12(1), .13; Minn. Stat. Ann. § 145B.105.

treatment or health care services,[238] enrollment in a health insurance plan or receipt of health insurance benefits,[239] or life insurance underwriting.[240]

---

**NH:** N.H. Rev. Stat. Ann. § 137-J:9.

**ND:** N.D. Cent. Code § 23-06.5-10.1.

**OH:** Ohio Rev. Code Ann. § 1337.16(A).

**SC:** S.C. Code Ann. § 62-5-504(N).

**TN:** Tenn. Code Ann. § 34-6-211.

**TX:** Tex. Civ. Prac. & Rem. Code Ann. § 135.009(2)(A).

**WV:** W. Va. Code § 16-30A-16(b).

**WI:** Wis. Stat. Ann. § 155.70(2).

**WY:** Wyo. Stat. § 3-5-212.

[238] **AZ:** Ariz. Rev. Stat. Ann. § 36-3207(A).

**AR:** Ark. Code Ann. § 20-17-210(c).

**CT:** Conn. Gen. Stat. Ann. § 19a-580b.

**FL:** Fla. Stat. Ann. § 765.108.

**GA:** Ga. Code Ann. § 31-36-9(3).

**IA:** Iowa Code Ann. § 144B.11.1.

**KY:** Ky. Rev. Stat. Ann. § 311.635.

**ME:** Me. Rev. Stat. Ann. tit. 18-A, § 5-711(c).

**MD:** Md. Code Ann., Health-Gen. § 5-614(C).

**MI:** Mich. Comp. Laws § 700.496(18).

**MN:** Minn. Stat. Ann. § 145C.13(1); Minn. Stat. Ann. § 145B.105.

**MO:** Mo. Ann. Stat. § 404.835.1.

**MT:** Mont. Code Ann. § 50-9-205(3).

**NE:** Neb. Rev. Stat. § 30-3429(1).

**NH:** N.H. Rev. Stat. Ann. § 137-J:9.

**NJ:** N.J. Stat. Ann. § 26:2H-75.

**ND:** N.D. Cent. Code § 23-06.5-10.1.

**OH:** Ohio Rev. Code Ann. § 1337.16(A).

**OK:** Okla. Stat. Ann. tit. 63, § 3101.12(C).

**OR:** Or. Rev. Stat. § 127.565(2).

**PA:** Pa. Cons. Stat. Ann. tit. 20, § 5411(1).

**RI:** R.I. Gen. Laws § 23-4.10-9(c).

**SC:** S.C. Code Ann. § 62-5-504(N).

**TN:** Tenn. Code Ann. § 34-6-211.

**TX:** Tex. Civ. Prac. & Rem. Code Ann. § 135.009(2)(c).

**UT:** Utah Code Ann. § 75-2-1117.

**VT:** Vt. Stat. Ann. tit. 14, § 3460(a).

**VA:** Va. Code Ann. § 54.1-2991.

**WI:** Wis. Stat. Ann. § 155.70(2).

**WY:** Wyo. Stat. § 3-5-212; Wyo. Stat. § 35-22-108(c).

[239] **AZ:** Ariz. Rev. Stat. Ann. § 36-3207(A).

**AR:** Ark. Code Ann. § 20-17-210(c).

**CA:** Cal. Civ. Code § 2441.

**CO:** Colo. Rev. Stat. § 15-14-508(4).

**CT:** Conn. Gen. Stat. Ann. § 19a-580b.

**DE:** Del. Code Ann. tit. 16, § 2507(c).

**DC:** D.C. Code Ann. § 21-2209(a).

**FL:** Fla. Stat. Ann. § 765.108.

**GA:** Ga. Code Ann. § 31-36-9(3).

**ID:** Idaho Code § 39-4509(3).

**IL:** Ill. Ann. Stat. ch. 755, § 45/4-9(c).

**IA:** Iowa Code Ann. § 144B.11.1; Iowa Code Ann. § 144A.11.3.

**KY:** Ky. Rev. Stat. Ann. § 311.635 (by implication).

**LA:** La. Rev. Stat. Ann. § 40:1299.58.10(B)(4).

**ME:** Me. Rev. Stat. Ann. tit. 18-A, § 5-711(c).

**MA:** Mass. Gen. Laws Ann. ch. 201D, § 10.

**MD:** Md. Code Ann., Health-Gen. § 5-610 (misdemeanor punishable by fine not exceeding $10,000 or imprisonment not exceeding one year or both).

**MI:** Mich. Comp. Laws. § 700.496(19).

**MN:** Minn. Stat. Ann. § 145C.13(1); Minn. Stat. Ann. § 145B.105.

**MS:** Miss. Code Ann. § 41-41-181.

**MO:** Mo. Ann. Stat. § 404.835.2.

**MT:** Mont. Code Ann. § 50-9-205(3).

**NE:** Neb. Rev. Stat. § 30-3429(1).

**NH:** N.H. Rev. Stat. Ann. § 137-J:9.

**NJ:** N.J. Stat. Ann. § 26:2H-75.

**NY:** N.Y. Pub. Health Law § 2988.

**ND:** N.D. Cent. Code § 23-06.5-10.1.

**OH:** Ohio Rev. Code Ann. § 1337.16(A).

**OK:** Okla. Stat. Ann. tit. 63, § 3101.12(C).

**OR:** Or. Rev. Stat. § 127.565(2).

**PA:** Pa. Cons. Stat. Ann. tit. 20, § 5411(1).

**RI:** R.I. Gen. Laws § 23-4.10-9(c).

**SC:** S.C. Code Ann. § 62-5-504(N).

**TN:** Tenn. Code Ann. § 34-6-211.

**TX:** Tex. Civ. Prac. & Rem. Code Ann. § 135.009(2)(B).

**UT:** Utah Code Ann. § 75-2-1117.

**VT:** Vt. Stat. Ann. tit. 14, § 3460(a).

**VA:** Va. Code Ann. § 54.1-2991.

**WI:** Wis. Stat. Ann. § 155.70(5).

**WY:** Wyo. Stat. § 3-5-212; Wyo. Stat. § 35-22-108(c).

[240] **AR:** Ark. Code Ann. § 20-17-210(b).

**CO:** Colo. Rev. Stat. § 15-14-508(4).

**DE:** Del. Code Ann. tit. 16, § 2507(c).

**FL:** Fla. Stat. Ann. § 765.108.

These prohibitions are consistent with the federal Patient Self-Determination Act, which prohibits conditioning the provision of care "or otherwise discriminat[ing] against an individual based on whether or not the individual has executed an advance directive."[241] Some statutes prohibit health care providers, facilities, and insurers from discriminating in setting premiums for insurance solely because of the existence or nonexistence of a health care power of attorney.[242] In a few states, although a health care provider may not require the

---

**GA:** Ga. Code Ann. § 31-36-8(6).

**ID:** Idaho Code § 39-4509(2).

**IL:** Ill. Ann. Stat. ch. 755, § 45/4-8(e).

**IA:** Iowa Code Ann. § 144B.11.2; Iowa Code Ann. § 144A.11.2.

**KY:** Ky. Rev. Stat. Ann. § 311.635.

**LA:** La. Rev. Stat. Ann. § 40:1299.58.10(B)(2).

**ME:** Me. Rev. Stat. Ann. tit. 18-A, § 5-711(b).

**MA:** Mass. Gen. Laws Ann. ch. 201D, § 10.

**MI:** Mich. Comp. Laws. § 700.496(19).

**MN:** Minn. Stat. Ann. § 145B.11; Minn. Stat. Ann. § 145C.12(1).

**MS:** Miss. Code Ann. § 41-41-181.

**MT:** Mont. Code Ann. § 50-9-205(2).

**NE:** Neb. Rev. Stat. § 30-3429(2).

**NJ:** N.J. Stat. Ann. § 26:2H-75.

**NY:** N.Y. Pub. Health Law § 2988.

**OH:** Ohio Rev. Code Ann. § 1337.16(A).

**OK:** Okla. Stat. Ann. tit. 63, § 3101.12(B).

**OR:** Or. Rev. Stat. § 127.565(2).

**PA:** Pa. Cons. Stat. Ann. tit. 20, § 5410(b).

**RI:** R.I. Gen. Laws § 23-4.10-9(b).

**TN:** Tenn. Code Ann. § 34-6-213.

**UT:** Utah Code Ann. § 75-2-1117.

**VA:** Va. Code Ann. § 54.1-2991.

**WV:** W. Va. Code § 16-30A-14(b).

**WY:** Wyo. Stat. § 35-22-108(b).

[241] 42 U.S.C.A. § 1395cc(f)(1)(C) (West Supp. 1994); OBRA § 4751(a)(2), 42 U.S.C.A. § 1396a(w)(1)(C) (West Supp. 1994). See **§ 10.21.**

[242] **CO:** Colo. Rev. Stat. § 15-14-508(4).

**MN:** Minn. Stat. Ann. § 145C.12(1).

**NE:** Neb. Rev. Stat. § 30-3429(2).

**NH:** N.H. Rev. Stat. Ann. § 137-J:9.

**ND:** N.D. Cent. Code § 23-06.5-10.1.

**PA:** Pa. Cons. Stat. Ann. tit. 20, § 5410(b).

**TX:** Tex. Civ. Prac. & Rem. Code Ann. § 135.009(1).

**VT:** Vt. Stat. Ann. tit. 14, § 3460(a).

execution of a health care power of attorney,[243] once a patient has been in a health care facility for at least 48 hours, it is permissible to request patients to execute health care powers of attorney.[244] The basis for these provisions is the legislative concern that persons executing a health care power of attorney should do so freely, rather than doing so in order to obtain medical services or insurance.

Many statutes also provide that the forgoing of life-sustaining treatment pursuant to a health care power of attorney does not constitute suicide, so as not to invalidate life insurance policies.[245]

---

[243] **CT:** Conn. Gen. Stat. Ann. § 19a-580b.

**DC:** D.C. Code Ann. § 21-2209(a).

**MD:** Md. Code Ann., Health-Gen. § 5-614(C).

**MN:** Minn. Stat. Ann. § 145C.12(1).

[244] **CT:** Conn. Gen. Stat. Ann. § 19a-580b.

**DC:** D.C. Code Ann. § 21-2209(b).

**MN:** Minn. Stat. Ann. § 145C.12(1) (may not condition admission to health care facility).

[245] **AZ:** Ariz. Rev. Stat. Ann. § 36-3207(C).

**AR:** Ark. Code Ann. § 20-17-210(a).

**CA:** Cal. Civ. Code § 2443.

**DE:** Del. Code Ann. tit. 16, § 2507(a).

**FL:** Fla. Stat. Ann. § 765.309(2).

**GA:** Ga. Code Ann. § 31-36-8(6).

**IA:** Iowa Code Ann. § 144B.12.2; Iowa Code Ann. § 144A.11.1.

**LA:** La. Rev. Stat. Ann. § 40:1299.58.10(B)(1).

**ME:** Me. Rev. Stat. Ann. tit. 18-A, § 5-711(a).

**MD:** Md. Code Ann., Health-Gen. § 5-614(A).

**MA:** Mass. Gen. Laws Ann. ch. 201D, § 12.

**MI:** Mich. Comp. Laws § 700.496(20).

**MN:** Minn. Stat. Ann. § 145B.14.

**MO:** Mo. Ann. Stat. § 404.845.2.

**MT:** Mont. Code Ann. § 50-9-205(1).

**NE:** Neb. Rev. Stat. § 30-3429(2)(e).

**NJ:** N.J. Stat. Ann. § 26:2H-77(a).

**OK:** Okla. Stat. Ann. tit. 63, § 3101.12(A).

**OR:** Or. Rev. Stat. § 127.570.

**PA:** Pa. Cons. Stat. Ann. tit. 20, § 5410(a).

**RI:** R.I. Gen. Laws § 23-4.10-9(a).

**SC:** S.C. Code Ann. § 62-5-504(M).

**TN:** Tenn. Code Ann. § 34-6-213.

**UT:** Utah Code Ann. § 75-2-1116.

## § 12.50 Enforcement in Other Jurisdictions ("Portability")

Several statutes address the potentially serious problems arising from the need to enforce in one jurisdiction a health care power of attorney executed in another, referred to as *portability*. Most of these statutes provide that a health care power of attorney is valid if it is in compliance with the law of the state where it was executed,[246] where it is to be enforced,[247] or both.[248] An unreported

---

**VA:** Va. Code Ann. § 54.1-2991.

**WV:** W. Va. Code § 16-30A-14(a).

**WI:** Wis. Stat. Ann. § 155.70(1)(a).

**WY:** Wyo. Stat. § 3-5-211.

UHCDA § 13(b).

[246] **AZ:** Ariz. Rev. Stat. Ann. § 36-3208 (if it does not conflict with criminal laws of Arizona).

**CO:** Colo. Rev. Stat. § 15-14-509(2).

**MA:** Mass. Gen. Laws Ann. ch. 201D, § 11.

**NE:** Neb. Rev. Stat. § 30-3408(4).

**NY:** N.Y. Pub. Health Law § 2990.

**ND:** N.D. Cent. Code § 23-06.5-11.

**RI:** R.I. Gen. Laws § 23-4.10-11.

**TX:** Tex. Civ. Prac. & Rem. Code Ann. § 135.013.

**VT:** Vt. Stat. Ann. tit. 14, § 3461.

[247] **MN:** Minn. Stat. Ann. § 145B.16.

[248] **AR:** Ark. Code Ann. § 20-17-212.

**CA:** Cal. Civ. Code § 2445.

**FL:** Fla. Stat. Ann. § 765.112.

**KS:** Kan. Stat. Ann. § 58-630.

**ME:** Me. Rev. Stat. Ann. tit. 18-A, § 5-713.

**MD:** Md. Code Ann., Health-Gen. § 5-614(A); Md. Code Ann., Health-Gen. § 5-617.

**MN:** Minn. Stat. Ann. § 145C.04.

**MT:** Mont. Code Ann. § 50-9-111.

**NH:** N.H. Rev. Stat. Ann. § 137-J:10.

**NJ:** N.J. Stat. Ann. § 26:2H-76.

**OK:** Okla. Stat. Ann. tit. 63, § 3101.14.

**SC:** S.C. Code Ann. § 62-5-501(E).

**TN:** Tenn. Code Ann. § 34-6-215.

**VA:** Va. Code Ann. § 54.1-2993.

**WV:** W. Va. Code § 16-30A-17.

UHCDA § 2(h) (directive valid if it complies with the UHCDA "regardless of when or where executed").

Florida trial court case[249] recognized the authority of a proxy to act in Florida under a durable power of attorney executed in Massachusetts.

## § 12.51  Role of the Courts

Most statutes are silent on the role, if any, courts are to play in the implementation of a health care power of attorney. There is no reason, absent statutory direction to the contrary, that judicial involvement ought to be sought except in situations in which it would be sought in the absence of a health care power of attorney.[250] In this regard, the Michigan Court of Appeals has stated that the legislative intent underlying its health care power of attorney statute "is to respect the roles played by the patient, family, physicians, and spiritual advisors in the making of decisions regarding medical treatment, as well as the policy that courts need not delve into that decision-making process unless necessary to protect the patient's interests."[251] As a result, even in the absence of a health care power of attorney—indeed, in a situation in which the patient is a minor and could not have executed a health care power of attorney—there is no need for recourse to the courts unless an impasse is reached in decision-making.[252]

A small number of statutes contain provisions bearing on this issue but not requiring judicial review. The Connecticut statute provides that the probate court for the district in which the person is domiciled or is located has jurisdiction over any dispute concerning the meaning or application of a health care power of attorney.[253] Similarly, the Arizona statute includes provisions that allow an interested person to file a petition to determine the validity or effect of a health care directive or the decision of a surrogate.[254] Only Ohio has a requirement for judicial review but only if certain specified persons object to the forgoing of life-sustaining treatment.[255]

---

[249] *In re* Stone, No. 90-5867 (Fla. Cir. Ct. 17th Dist. Broward County June 24, 1991).

[250] See **Ch. 5.**

[251] Rosebush v. Oakland County Prosecutor, 491 N.W.2d 633, 638–39 (Mich. Ct. App. 1992).

[252] **MI:** Rosebush v. Oakland County Prosecutor, 491 N.W.2d at 637, 639.

   **MD:** *See also* Md. Code Ann., Health-Gen. § 5-612 (judicial remedies available if health care provider or family does not agree with suggested course of treatment).

   UHCDA § 14 (agent, patient, guardian, surrogate, healthcare provider, or institution may petition court to enjoin or direct a health care decision).

[253] Conn. Gen. Stat. Ann. § 19a-580c.

[254] Ariz. Rev. Stat. Ann. § 36-3206.

[255] Ohio Rev. Code Ann. § 1337.16(D).

## § 12.52   Table of Health Care Power of Attorney Statutes

### Table 12–1

### Health Care Power of Attorney Statutes

| | |
|---|---|
| **AK:** | Alaska Stat. §§ 13.26.332–.356 |
| **AZ:** | Ariz. Rev. Stat. Ann. §§ 36-3221 to -3224 |
| | Ariz. Rev. Stat. Ann. § 14-5501[1] |
| **AR:** | Ark. Code Ann. § 20-17-202[+] |
| **CA:** | Cal. Civ. Code §§ 2430–2445, 2500–2510 |
| **CO:** | Colo. Rev. Stat. §§ 15-14-501 to -509 |
| | Colo. Rev. Stat. §§ 15-18.5-101 to -103[+] |
| **CT:** | Conn. Gen. Stat. Ann. §§ 19a-570 to -580c[+] |
| | Conn. Gen. Stat. Ann. §§ 1-42 to -56[*] |
| **DE:** | Del. Code Ann. tit. 16, § 2502(b)[+] |
| **DC:** | D.C. Code Ann. §§ 21-2201 to -2213 |
| **FL:** | Fla. Stat. Ann. §§ 765.101–.401 |
| | Fla. Stat. Ann. § 709.08[*] |
| **GA:** | Ga. Code Ann. §§ 31-36-1 to -13 |
| **HI:** | Haw. Rev. Stat. §§ 551D-1 to -7[+,2] |
| **ID:** | Idaho Code §§ 39-4502 to -4509 |
| **IL:** | Ill. Ann. Stat. ch. 755, §§ 45/4-1 to -12[3] |
| **IN:** | Ind. Code Ann. § 16-36-1-7 |
| | Ind. Code Ann. §§ 30-5-1-1 to -10-4[*] |
| **IA:** | Iowa Code Ann. §§ 144B.1–.12[4] |
| | Iowa Code Ann. § 633.705[*] |
| | Iowa Code Ann. § 144A.7(1)[+] |
| **KS:** | Kan. Stat. Ann. §§ 58-625 to -632 |
| **KY:** | Ky. Rev. Stat. Ann. §§ 311.621 to .641[+] |
| **LA:** | La. Rev. Stat. Ann. § 40:1299.58.3(C)(1)[+] |
| | La. Civ. Code Ann. art. 2997(A)(7) |
| **ME:** | Me. Rev. Stat. Ann. tit. 18-A, §§ 5-701 to -714 |
| | Me. Rev. Stat. Ann. tit. 18-A, §§ 5-501 to -506[*] |
| **MD:** | Md. Code Ann., Health-Gen. §§ 5-601 to -618[1] |
| | Md. Code Ann., Est. & Trusts §§ 13-601 to -602[5] |
| **MA:** | Mass. Gen. Laws Ann. ch. 201D, §§ 1–17 |
| **MI:** | Mich. Comp. Laws § 700.496 |
| **MN:** | Minn. Stat. Ann. §§ 145C.01–.15 |
| | Minn. Stat. Ann. §§ 145B.01–.17[+] |
| **MS:** | Miss. Code Ann. §§ 41-41-151 to -183 |
| **MO:** | Mo. Ann. Stat. §§ 404.800–.870[6] |
| **MT:** | Mont. Code Ann. §§ 50-9-101 to -111, -201 to -206[+] |
| | Mont. Code Ann. §§ 72-5-501 to -502[7] |
| **NE:** | Neb. Rev. Stat. §§ 30-3401 to -3432 |
| **NV:** | Nev. Rev. Stat. Ann. §§ 449.800–.860 |
| | Nev. Rev. Stat. Ann. §§ 449.535–.690[+] |
| **NH:** | N.H. Rev. Stat. Ann. §§ 137-J:1–:16[*] |
| **NJ:** | N.J. Stat. Ann. §§ 26:2H-53 to -78 |
| | N.J. Stat. Ann. § 46:2B-8[8] |
| **NM:** | N.M. Stat. Ann. §§ 45-5-501 to -502[*] |
| **NY:** | N.Y. Pub. Health Law §§ 2980–2994 |
| **NC:** | N.C. Gen. Stat. §§ 32A-15 to -26 |

**ND:**   N.D. Cent. Code §§ 23-06.5-01 to -18
**OH:**   Ohio Rev. Code Ann. §§ 1337.11–.17
**OK:**   Okla. Stat. Ann. tit. 63, §§ 3101.1–.16[+]
**OR:**   Or. Rev. Stat. §§ 127.005–.737
**PA:**   Pa. Cons. Stat. Ann. tit. 20 §§ 5401–5416
         Pa. Cons. Stat. Ann. tit. 20 §§ 5601-5607[*]
**RI:**   R.I. Gen. Laws §§ 23-4.10-1 to -12
**SC:**   S.C. Code Ann. §§ 62-5-501 to -504
         S.C. Code Ann. § 44-77-50[+]
**SD:**   S.D. Codified Laws Ann. §§ 59-7-2.1 to -2.8[*]
         S.D. Codified Laws Ann. §§ 34-12C-1 to -8[+]
**TN:**   Tenn. Code Ann. §§ 34-6-201 to -215
**TX:**   Tex. Civ. Prac. & Rem. Code Ann. §§ 135.001–.018
**UT:**   Utah Code Ann. §§ 75-2-1101 to -1118[+]
**VT:**   Vt. Stat. Ann. tit. 14, §§ 3451–3467
**VA:**   Va. Code Ann. §§ 54.1-2981 to -2993[+]
**WA:**   Wash. Rev. Code Ann. §§ 11.94.010–.040[*]
**WV:**   W. Va. Code §§ 16-30A-1 to -20
**WI:**   Wis. Stat. Ann. §§ 155.01–.80
**WY:**   Wyo. Stat. §§ 3-5-201 to -213
         Wyo. Stat. § 35-22-102(d)[+]

---

[+] Proxy provision in living will statute.

[*] General durable power of attorney statute with health care decision-making provision.

[1] Rasmussen v. Fleming, 741 P.2d 674, 689 n.21 (Ariz. 1987) (dictum), appears to authorize the use of the general durable power of attorney statute, Ariz. Rev. Stat. Ann. § 14-5501 (1975), for health care decisionmaking.

[2] As construed by In re Crabtree, No. 86-0031 (Haw. Fam. Ct. 1st Cir. Apr. 26, 1990).

[3] See also Ill. Ann. Stat. ch. 755, §§ 40/4-1 to -11 (Michie Supp. 1994) (general durable power of attorney statute authorizing appointment of agent to make health care decisions but not specifically mentioning life-sustaining treatment).

[4] Iowa Code Ann. §§ 144B.1–.12 is a health care power of attorney statute. In addition, the living will statute, Iowa Code Ann. § 144A.71, authorizes an agent appointed under the durable power of attorney statute, Iowa Code Ann. § 633.705, to make health care decisions.

[5] General durable power of attorney statute not expressly authorizing agent to make health care decisions. However, 73 Md. Op. Att'y Gen. 253 (Op. No. 88-046, Oct. 17, 1988) concludes that "although [this provision] does not expressly authorize the delegation of health care decisionmaking, nothing in the statute or other law prevents it." Id. at 275. Therefore, "[a] person (the principal) may use a durable power of attorney to direct an agent (the attorney in fact) to carry out the principal's specific directive concerning medical treatment, including the withholding or withdrawing of artificially administered sustenance under specified circumstances." Id. at 276. Furthermore, the surrogate decisionmaking statute implies that the general durable power of attorney statute may be used for health care decisionmaking. See Md. Code Ann., Health-Gen. § 20-107(d) ("in the absence of a durable power of attorney that relates to medical care . . . any of the following individuals may give a substituted consent").

[6] This statute incorporates the procedures and requirements of an enumerated list of provisions from Missouri's durable power of attorney statute, Mo. Ann. Stat. §§ 404.705, .707.1, .707.2, .710, .714, .717, .723.1, .723.2, .727, .731.

[7] The living will statute, Mont. Code Ann. §§ 50-9-101 to -206, permits the use of either the living will statute or the general durable power of attorney statute, Mont. Code Ann. §§ 72-5-501 to -502, to appoint a health care proxy.

[8] General durable power of attorney, as construed by *In re* Peter, 529 A.2d 419 (N.J. 1987).

## Bibliography

### General

Collin, F. "Planning and Drafting Durable Powers of Attorney for Health Care." *Institute on Estate Planning* 22 (1988): 5.1.

Collin, F., et al. *Durable Powers of Attorney and Health Care Directives.* Colorado Springs: Shepard's/McGraw-Hill, 1994.

English, D. "The Health-Care Decisions Act Represents a Major Advance." *Trusts and Estates* 133 (1994): 32.

English, D. "The UPC and the New Durable Powers." *Real Property, Probate and Trusts Journal* 27 (1992): 333.

English, D., and A. Meisel. "The Uniform Health-Care Decisions Act." *Estate Planning* 21 (1994): 355.

Moore, D. "The Durable Power of Attorney as an Alternative to the Improper Use of Conservatorship for Health-Care Decisionmaking." *St. John's Law Review* 60 (1986): 631.

Orentlicher, D. "The Limits of Legislation." *Maryland Law Review* 53 (1994): 1255.

Swidler, R. "The Health Care Agent: Protecting the Choices and Interests of Patients Who Lack Capacity." *New York Law School Journal of Human Rights* 6 (1988): 1.

### Specific States

**CT:**   Garraty, C. "Durable Power of Attorney for Health Care: A Better Choice." *Connecticut Probate Law Journal* 7 (1992): 115.

**FL:**   Calder, M. "Chapter 765 Revisited: Florida's New Advance Directives Law." *Florida State University Law Review* 20 (1992): 292.

Krawitz, S. "Florida's Dynamic Health Care Directives Laws." *Florida Bar Journal* 66 (1992): 26.

**MI:**   Guilliat, S. "Michigan's Durable Power of Attorney for Health Care: Will It Live or Die?" *Detroit College of Law Review,* 1992, no. 2: 847.

Lankfer, M. "Living Wills and Durable Powers Authorizing Medical Treatment Decisions." *Michigan Bar Journal* 64 (1985): 684.

**MO:**  Patterson, J. "The Proxy Puzzle & the Durable Power of Attorney for Health Care Act." *Missouri Law Review* 57 (1992): 935.

Sheafor, C. "Missouri Health Care Durable Power of Attorney." *Washington University Law Quarterly* 70 (1992): 937.

**NJ:**  Armstrong P., and R. Olick. "Innovative Legislative Initiatives: The New Jersey Declaration of Death and Advance Directives for Health Care Acts." *Seton Hall Legislative Journal* 16 (1992): 177.

Cantor, N. "Advance Directives and the Pursuit of Death with Dignity: New Jersey's New Legislation." *Rutgers Law Review* 44 (1992): 335.

**NY:**  Hollander, J. "Health Care Proxies: New York's Attempt to Resolve the Right to Die Dilemma." *Brooklyn Law Review* 57 (1991): 145.

**TX:**  Premack, P. "Durable Power of Attorney for Health Care—Texas' New Legislation." *Texas Bar Journal* 53 (1990): 860.

**WI:**  Willms, A. "The Appointment of an Agent for Medical Treatment Decisions." *Wisconsin Bar Bulletin* 61 (1988): 16.

# CHAPTER 13

# DRAFTING AND ADMINISTRATION OF ADVANCE DIRECTIVES

# § 13.1  Introduction: Nonstatutory Advance Directives

The sometimes restrictive provisions of advance directive statutes can create serious obstacles for people who wish to plan for their future medical care in ways different from those prescribed by state legislatures. Many advance directive statutes restrict the applicability of advance directives to those who are terminally ill or permanently unconscious;[1] many also prohibit their enforcement for pregnant patients;[2] many others prohibit the forgoing of artificial nutrition and hydration if necessary to provide comfort.[3] In addition, individuals in the small number of jurisdictions without a living will or health care power of attorney statute might also wish to have one of those instruments available.

---

[1] See §§ **11.9** and **12.17.**

[2] See §§ **11.11** and **12.27.**

[3] See §§ **11.12** and **12.26.**

To avoid these barriers to advance health care planning, individuals can draft their own advance directives, rather than relying on a statutory basis for doing so and/or using statutory forms. The term *nonstatutory advance directive* will be used to refer to any advance directive not drafted in accordance with the statutory requirements of either a living will or health care power of attorney statute. It is not entirely certain that such advance directives are valid and enforceable, though there is substantial reason to believe that they are.[4] Because of the uncertain legal status of nonstatutory directives, it is important that declarants make efforts to enhance the validity and enforceability of such directives through careful attention to certain procedural and substantive considerations.

This chapter discusses the steps that declarants and health care institutions can take to help ensure the validity and enforceability of nonstatutory advance directives.

## § 13.2  Responsibilities of Declarants and Health Care Providers

The primary responsibility for initiating the drafting and execution of an advance directive, whether statutory or nonstatutory, is the declarant's, although health care institutions may choose to play some role in this process.[5] It is also the declarant's responsibility to ensure that health care professionals who implement directives are made aware of their existence and content. Another purpose of this chapter—discussed in §§ 13.33 to 13.38—is to explain the policies and procedures that health care providers can take to ensure an orderly decision-making process when a patient or potential patient has or wishes to have an advance directive.

## GENERAL DRAFTING CONSIDERATIONS

### § 13.3  Drafting the Nonstatutory Advance Directive

Because the validity and enforceability of nonstatutory advance directives are open to some question, such directives should be drafted with as much care and forethought as possible. At the least, this means complying with whatever procedural formalities may exist for drafting a statutory directive. However, advance directive statutes should be viewed merely as guides, not as binding when drafting a nonstatutory advance directive. When both statutory and common-law requirements exist, the more stringent should be adopted for the nonstatutory directive.

---

[4] See §§ 10.11–10.12.

[5] See §§ 13.33–13.38.

Compliance with the formalities of similar, but more familiar and better-accepted, legal instruments such as wills, trusts, and powers of attorney is also worth considering. When the requirements for some or all of these instruments are in conflict, the most stringent requirements should be followed. Thus, for example, if a health care power of attorney requires two witnesses and a living will only one, two witnesses are preferable for a nonstatutory directive; if a living will requires an oath from the witnesses that the declarant is of sound mind, but a health care power of attorney does not, it is advisable to include such a statement in a nonstatutory directive.[6]

## § 13.4   Contents of and Format for Nonstatutory Directives

A nonstatutory directive may be used to appoint a proxy, give instructions about one's wishes concerning medical treatment, or both. If a jurisdiction has a statutory basis for a health care power of attorney but not for a living will, instructions either to the proxy or to the physician may be added to the power of attorney or a separate nonstatutory living will can be drafted. Similarly, if a jurisdiction has a statutory basis for a living will but not for a health care power of attorney, the declarant might add a provision appointing a proxy or might draft a separate health care power of attorney using the state's general durable power of attorney as a guide. Indeed, as a general rule, the validity of an instrument for which there is no statutory basis might be enhanced by incorporating it into the statutorily recognized instrument.

The same is probably true if a declarant wishes to avoid using a statutorily based directive in a jurisdiction having an applicable advance directive statute. One way to do this is to use the format prescribed for a general durable power of attorney. Another is to use the statutory form advance directive but to modify it as wished. If, however, these modifications result in a conflict between the declarant's wishes and what is permitted by the statute, it is probably essential that the declarant expressly disavow in the document any reliance on or attempt to conform to the statute, possibly citing the statute as well. For instance, one might add a clause to the advance directive that says, "This advance directive is based on the common law and/or constitutional law of this jurisdiction and not the living will and/or health care power of attorney statute."

## § 13.5   —Designating a Proxy

If the declarant wishes to designate an agent for health care decisionmaking in a jurisdiction lacking a health care power of attorney statute, there are a few ways

---

[6] *See* Hastings Ctr., Guidelines on the Termination of Life-Sustaining Treatment and the Care of the Dying 78–79 (1987) (Part Three, I) [hereinafter Hastings Center Guidelines].

in which this can be done. First, the appointment of a proxy can be added to the instructions in a living will. Second, if the declarant does not wish to give instructions, it is probably preferable to make the appointment of a proxy through a conventional durable power of attorney. Third, the declarant may use a generic advance directive form or devise his own.

Regardless of what format is used, the directive should also name a contingent proxy or proxies in the event that the primary proxy is unable or unwilling to assume responsibility.[7] Alternatively, the declarant might wish expressly to empower the proxy to subdelegate authority if unable or unwilling to act.[8]

A declarant might also consider naming a group (such as some family members and/or friends) to act collectively as proxy, although the size of the group should be kept very small, probably no more than three people, so as not to make decisionmaking unduly cumbersome. If this approach is used, the declarant must specify whether, if one person is unable or unwilling to serve, the remaining group members are empowered to act as proxy or to name a contingent proxy to serve in the place of the unavailable or unwilling designee. The declarant should also specify how decisions are to be made if the group is unable to reach a consensus.

## § 13.6 —Scope of Decisionmaking Authority

A health care power of attorney can be used to appoint a proxy to make decisions not only about life-sustaining treatment but also about other kinds of health care. When a declarant wishes to empower a proxy to make decisions about life-sustaining treatment, it is highly advisable that the durable power of attorney specifically so state.[9] Furthermore, if the declarant wishes to confer authority to make decisions when the declarant is not terminally ill or permanently unconscious, that too should be stated because this is contrary to so many advance directive statutes.

## § 13.7 —Preference for Guardian

Although *intended* in large part to forestall the initiation of judicial proceedings when patients lose the ability to make decisions about their care, the existence of an advance directive cannot *guarantee* that such proceedings will not be

---

[7] *See, e.g.,* Nev. Rev. Stat. Ann. § 449.800 (Michie 1986). *See also* Hastings Center Guidelines 83, 84 (Part Three, IV(3)).

[8] *See* Uniform Model Health-Care Consent Act § 5 (proxy may subdelegate decisionmaking authority; Act not applicable to decisionmaking about life-sustaining treatment).

[9] **NJ:** *In re* Peter, 529 A.2d 419, 426 (N.J. 1987) ("It would have been better if Ms. Peter had specifically provided in her power of attorney that Mr. Johanning had authority to terminate life-sustaining treatment.").

instituted. Health care professionals might refuse to abide by the directive. Even when health care professionals do not doubt the legal validity and enforceability of advance directives in general, possible objections of either a legal or ethical nature to the contents of a particular directive may thwart its implementation.

Short of giving careful attention to the nature of the instructions contained in the directive and the formalities of execution,[10] there is very little that can be done in drafting an advance directive to prevent questioning of its validity and enforceability, especially when the directive lacks a statutory basis or is in conflict with statutory requirements. Consequently, it is naive to draft a non-statutory directive without taking into account the distinct possibility that it will not forestall the judicial proceedings that it was intended to avoid.

Two things should be done in anticipation of such a possibility. First, a declarant should provide that, if judicial proceedings are instituted for an adjudication of incompetence and appointment of a guardian, it is the declarant's preference that a particular individual be named guardian.[11] In effect, this permits the declarant to continue to express a preference for a particular surrogate decisionmaker in much the same way that the naming of a proxy in the advance directive itself does.

Second, if judicial proceedings for determining incompetence and appointing a guardian are avoided, questions might still be raised about following the decisions of a surrogate, whether designated by a proxy directive or otherwise. In anticipation of possible judicial or even nonjudicial review of a surrogate's decisions, a declarant should also expressly state that he wishes to have a court enforce the instructions given in the advance directive should judicial proceedings occur.

Although these suggestions can have no more than a hortatory effect on a court, that effect alone may prove of substantial value in convincing the court of the declarant's subjective intent and of the wisdom of following the advance directive, even if the health care professionals involved were not so moved. Thus, even if an advance directive does not forestall the initiation of judicial proceedings it may at least help to ensure the effectuation of the declarant's will through such proceedings.

## § 13.8  —Treatment Instructions

Although intended by most declarants to prevent overtreatment or treatment they would not wish to have, advance directives can also be used to prevent under-treatment, by giving instructions that certain treatments be administered that might otherwise be forgone if the declarant were in a particular condition. To prevent what would be, from the declarant's perspective, either undertreatment

---

[10] See §§ 12.11–12.18.

[11] See § 12.21.

or overtreatment, declarants should specify either in general or specific terms any treatments they wish to have forgone or administered and the circumstances under which they are to be forgone or administered.

This can be done in a number of ways, each having certain problems associated with it. First, a declarant can provide general characterizations of the kinds of treatment to be forgone. The difficulty with this approach is that the directions may be too vague to serve as useful guidance.[12] The solution to this problem would seem to be that the declarant instead give specific directions that certain treatments should be foregone or administered.

This approach, however, also has problems. Although an advance directive that is specific may provide excellent guidance to the attending physician and surrogate decisionmaker if the conditions for its invocation materialize,[13] if those conditions do not materialize, the advance directive will be of little or no use because it will provide no guidance (or at best, indirect and analogical guidance) with respect to the conditions that in fact exist.[14] To avoid this kind of situation, the declarant should specify these circumstances—such as terminal illness, permanent unconsciousness, inability of the treatment to do anything other than postpone the death, or phrases of that sort. Thus, it is advisable to combine general characterizations and specific directions by both giving specific instructions and including a catchall clause directing that other forms of extraordinary treatment not enumerated should also be forgone. The declarant should further state that the enumerated treatments that he wishes to have forgone are merely examples and are not intended to be inclusive.

## § 13.9    ——Generality versus Specificity

**General Characterizations.**   A declarant can describe treatments to be forgone in general terms, such as by specifying the forgoing of any treatment that would merely prolong the process of dying, or would not lead to recovery, or without which death will occur regardless of whether such treatment is administered. Another general way to refer to such treatments is by using such classic terms as "no heroic treatment," "no extraordinary measures," or "no artificial means."[15] Treatments to be forgone (or administered) can also be generally

---

[12] *See, e.g., In re* Westchester County Medical Ctr. (O'Connor), 531 N.E.2d 607 (N.Y. 1988). *See also* Hastings Center Guidelines 82 (Part Three, III(1)(b)).

[13] See §§ **13.21–13.27.**

[14] **NY:** *In re* Westchester County Medical Ctr. (O'Connor), 531 N.E.2d at 625 (Simons, J., dissenting) ("Inasmuch as it is now no longer sufficient to provide that 'all' life support systems be withdrawn, the patient must anticipate these distinctions and resolve them. If he or she fails to do so, the instructions will not be recognized."). *See also* Hastings Center Guidelines 82 (Part Three, III(1)(c)).

[15] *See, e.g.,* Ariz. Rev. Stat. Ann. §§ 36-3201 to -3210 art. 1 (note on legislative findings).

referred to as treatments the administration of which would be painful, expensive, or futile in terms of promoting recovery, health, or relief of pain.

The difficulty with these terms is that their imprecision can lead to confusion and misinterpretation, thereby effectively thwarting the declarant's intent.[16] They function no better in an advance directive than they do as standards to aid decisionmakers in the absence of an advance directive.[17] An advance directive that is too general in its instructions will provide little, or at least less useful, guidance to the declarant's attending physician and surrogate decisionmaker. To the extent that it fails to provide such guidance, it will fail to accomplish the dual purposes of an advance directive: implementing the wishes of the declarant and avoiding judicial proceedings. Furthermore, if judicial proceedings do occur and the advance directive becomes the subject of adjudication, its lack of specificity may affect its probative value. The more general a patient's statements, the less weight will usually be accorded them.[18] The validity and enforceability of an advance directive can be substantially enhanced by ensuring that it is as specific in substantive terms as possible by designating (1) the conditions under which the terms of the directive are to become operative (triggering events[19]) and (2) which treatments or kinds of treatments are to be forgone and which are to be administered.

**Specific Treatments.**    Declarants can identify, either alone or in combination with general characterizations of treatments to be forgone or administered, specific treatments that they do or do not wish to have administered. These might include cardiopulmonary resuscitation, a mechanical ventilator, or artificial nutrition and hydration, to cite only a few examples of treatments that some people find particularly objectionable, painful, or futile, and the forgoing of which has tended to generate litigation. Most declarants will probably focus on treatments they wish to have forgone, rather than ones to be administered. It is probably wise for declarants to state that they wish to have analgesic or "painkilling" medications administered, especially if other treatments are being

---

[16] **FL:** John F. Kennedy Memorial Hosp. v. Bludworth, 452 So. 2d 921, 922 (Fla. 1984).

**NJ:** *In re* Conroy, 486 A.2d 1209, 1231 n.7 (N.J. 1985) ("[A] general statement . . . in which someone may have said . . . in writing merely that he would not want to be 'artificially sustained' by 'heroic measures' if his condition was 'hopeless,' or that he would not want to have doctors applying life-sustaining procedures 'that would serve only to artificially prolong the dying process' if he were 'terminally ill' . . . might not in itself provide clear guidance to a surrogate decision-maker in all situations.").

**NY:** *In re* Westchester County Medical Ctr. (O'Connor), 531 N.E.2d 607, 625 (N.Y. 1988) (Simons, J., dissenting) ("physicians do not even agree on what is 'extraordinary' or 'ordinary' care").

See § **10.31.**

[17] See § **8.8.**

[18] See § **10.31.**

[19] See §§ **13.21–13.27.**

forgone pursuant to a directive or otherwise.[20] A declarant who wants adequate analgesia even if it risks causing his death should also so state because of the hesitance of many physicians to provide adequate pain relief precisely because of their concern that it will hasten death.[21] Declarants should also pay special attention to whether they would wish to have artificial nutrition and hydration administered or withheld because of the sometimes controversial nature of this issue.[22]

One form of advance directive that has received a great deal of publicity in medical and lay publications is the so-called medical directive.[23] This directive has a table of specific treatments and the conditions under which they could be administered. The declarant completes the form by checking a box in a row and column indicating which treatments he does or does not want under which circumstances. The difficulty with the use of such a document, however, as critics have charged, is that "American medicine is [already] awash in forms, [and a]ttempts to make the living will less ambiguous by developing comprehensive checklists with alternative scenarios may be too confusing and abstract."[24] Also, a checklist "may divert attention inappropriately away from treatment goals . . . and may provide a false sense of certainty."[25]

Careful drafting should attempt to strike a balance between generality and overspecificity, but it probably cannot eliminate them. Because advance directives attempt to anticipate circumstances that are essentially unknowable (and which may never materialize) and attempt to give directions about a process that is extremely subtle and complex, the dangers inherent in advance directives can never be fully eliminated. Thus, advance directives are a two-edged sword: if well drafted, they are the best means for implementing the declarant's will and possibly for avoiding judicial proceedings; but if not well drafted, they can create serious consequences for the declarant, including unwanted death.

## § 13.10   Drafting by an Attorney

Given the uncertain legal status of nonstatutory advance directives, it is prudent for them to be drafted, or at least reviewed, by an attorney who can be sure that they comply with the necessary formalities,[26] contain the appropriate kinds of

---

[20] *See* Hastings Center Guidelines 82 (Part Three, III(1)(d)).

[21] See § **9.38.**

[22] See §§ **9.39–9.40.**

[23] *See* Emanuel & Emanuel, *The Medical Directive: A New Comprehensive Advance Care Document,* 261 JAMA 3288 (1989).

[24] Annas, *The Health Care Proxy and the Living Will,* 324 New Eng. J. Med. 1210, 1210, 1211 (1991).

[25] Brett, *Limitations of Listing Specific Medical Interventions in Advance Directives,* 266 JAMA 825, 827–28 (1991).

[26] *See* Hastings Center Guidelines 78–79 (Part Three, I). See §§ **13.11–13.18.**

substantive terms,[27] and provide for proper notification.[28] Also, the mere fact of having a document drafted by a lawyer may be an indication of the seriousness of the declarant's intent, and thus may enhance the willingness of health care professionals (and possibly courts) to abide by the directive. This does not mean, however, that declarants should play no role in drafting their advance directives. In fact, in most cases (or at least when declarants are reasonably articulate about their wishes), it is helpful for the declarant to write the directive and then for an attorney to review it with an eye toward phrasing it in such a way as to enhance the likelihood of its being valid and enforceable.

**Legal versus Lay Terminology.**    The excessive caution that an attorney can bring to bear in drafting may prove of great value if litigation results. However, one of the primary reasons for executing advance directives is to avoid litigation, and this is probably better done through the avoidance of legal jargon. It is better that the directive be written in terminology comprehensible to laypersons (that is, potential surrogates), because they are the ones who must apply it, and to health care professionals, because, at least in the first instance, they determine whether to apply it. In fact, drafting the advance directive in consultation with one's physician may be as important or more important than seeking legal counsel.

The most important consideration in drafting a directive is to ensure that health care professionals apply it in the clinical context without the need for recourse to the judicial process. To achieve this result, it is important that the directive not intimidate or threaten the health care professionals who will either apply it or refuse to do so and who have the power to force recourse to the courts.

Overemphasis on legal terminology can make it difficult for health care professionals and surrogates to understand what it is the declarant wanted. Perhaps more significantly, legal terminology may cause a defensive reaction on the part of health care professionals, who may become anxious and uncertain about the validity of the directive simply because of its form, rather than its content. A physician or a health care administrator who is uncertain about the validity of the directive is more likely to balk at enforcing it, thereby frustrating the very purpose the declarant sought to achieve and creating results—delay, uncertainty, and possibly litigation—that the declarant wished to avoid.

However, a balance must be struck between these considerations and impressing health care professionals (and if unsuccessful, a court) that the declarant executed the advance directive with the appropriate degree of solemnity. Technical legal terms and forms can help in achieving this.

---

[27] See §§ 13.21–13.27.

[28] See §§ 13.28–13.32.

# FORMALITIES OF EXECUTION

## § 13.11   How Formalities Enhance Enforceability

The enforceability of advance directives can be enhanced by means other than careful attention to drafting. The formalities of execution, such as those associated with a testamentary disposition or even the lesser ones associated with the execution of a durable power of attorney, can serve to impress those to whom the document is addressed with the seriousness of purpose with which the maker of the instrument acts. The declarant who goes to the effort to obtain witnesses, to have the signatures notarized, and to engage in other like formalities impresses the attending physician (and a court, should the advance directive be subjected to adjudication) of his seriousness of purpose. This result is also true of a directive with carefully and precisely drafted substantive provisions, rather than one that merely speaks in general terms of wishing to avoid "extraordinary treatment" or "heroic measures." However, as noted previously, an overly formal directive also risks alienating health care professionals. Thus, with each of the formalities of execution discussed below, care must be taken to achieve a balance between the goals of impressing health care professionals (and possibly a court) with the seriousness with which the declarant made the advance directive and obtaining the attending physician's compliance with the directive's terms without resort to litigation.

## § 13.12   —Signature

Advance directives should be signed by the declarant whenever possible. If the declarant is illiterate or is so physically incapacitated as to be unable to sign, the directive should contain a statement to that effect. There should also be attestation to this fact by any witnesses.

## § 13.13   —Typed or Holographic Directives

An advance directive may be either holographic (handwritten) or produced by a word processor. A word-processed directive might impress those who are requested to act on it with the declarant's seriousness of purpose. Other than that and legibility, there is no particularly compelling reason for preferring a word-processed directive. If the declarant is physically incapable of writing, the directive may be dictated by the declarant and handwritten or word processed by another.

## § 13.14 —Date

If questions ever arise as to the competence of the declarant at the time of execution,[29] it will be necessary to know when the directive was executed before such questions can be resolved, and thus an advance directive should be dated with the date of its original execution. It will also be necessary to know the date of execution if the enforceability of the directive is questioned on the ground of staleness.

## § 13.15 —Witnesses

The signing of an advance directive by the declarant should be witnessed. More than anything else, this can give assurance that the declarant is competent and acting voluntarily. In general, it is probably best to abide by the witnessing requirements of the advance directive statute of the jurisdiction in which a nonstatutory directive is executed.[30] Such requirements, however, are sometimes quite rigid and may make the execution of an advance directive more cumbersome than it would be to adhere to the witnessing requirements for a durable power of attorney or will.

**Number.**   For safety's sake, the number of persons who witness the signing of the directive should be the greater of that required by a testamentary disposition, a durable power of attorney, or the advance directive statute in the jurisdiction in which a nonstatutory directive is executed. Further, it is not unreasonable to meet the witnessing requirements for jurisdictions with more exacting requirements in anticipation of the possibility that the directive will need to be applied in a jurisdiction other than the one in which it is executed.[31]

**Qualifications and Disqualifications.**   Witnesses to nonstatutory advance directives should be adults (that is, over the legal age of majority) who are themselves of sound mind. One need not have any special qualifications to act as a witness; however, there are a number of characteristics that should be avoided when choosing witnesses.

Even the mere appearance of a conflict of interest should be avoided in the selection of witnesses to the declarant's execution of the directive. Thus, the selection of any witness who might appear to stand to benefit from the declarant's death should be avoided in order to escape the inference later that he may have improperly induced the declarant to execute the directive. There are certain relationships between the declarant and other parties that militate

---

[29] See § **13.18.**

[30] See §§ **11.6** and **12.12.**

[31] See § **13.19.**

against their use as witnesses. Although there is no case or statutory law specifically disqualifying the following individuals, the prudent course is to exclude as witnesses, as many advance directive statutes do, any individuals likely to benefit from a health care decision made by virtue of the terms of an advance directive. It is probably best not to use as a witness an individual who would be disqualified from serving under the jurisdiction's advance directive statute.

(1) *Testamentary Beneficiaries and Heirs.* Many advance directive statutes do not permit anyone to be a witness who is a beneficiary of the declarant's estate either under the declarant's will or by the laws of intestate succession.[32] Thus, when executing a nonstatutory advance directive in a jurisdiction with an advance directive statute having such a requirement, it is preferable that the witnesses be neither beneficiaries under a will nor statutory heirs.

(2) *Family and Close Friends.* Forgoing of treatment may financially benefit third parties by ending the financial obligations associated with the declarant's medical care. In addition, if a trust exists that pays any of the declarant's health care costs, other beneficiaries of the trust stand to gain financially from his death. Consequently, some advance directive statutes disqualify persons responsible for the declarant's health care costs from serving as witnesses.[33] Although this limitation runs contrary to the clear trend in the courts of strongly approving the practice of having close family members make decisions to forgo life-sustaining treatment for incompetent patients without any judicial review,[34] when a jurisdiction's advance directive statute disqualifies such persons as witnesses it is prudent to abide by this principle in a nonstatutory directive as well.

In addition to terminating financial obligations, the death of a patient may also lift emotional burdens from his family and friends. Those who are responsible for caring for the patient at home are especially likely to be affected, but even when the patient is being cared for in a hospital, nursing home, or hospice, a protracted illness can take a serious emotional toll on family and friends. Although the patient's death may leave them grief stricken, it may also relieve them of this significant emotional burden.

None of the advance directive statutes categorically proscribes individuals who will benefit from the patient's death from serving as witnesses. However, most prohibit family members and health care personnel from so serving.[35] It is similarly prudent to avoid any appearance of impropriety that might arise from having such individuals witness nonstatutory directives.

---

[32] See §§ **11.6** and **12.12.**

[33] See §§ **11.6** and **12.12.**

[34] See §§ **5.12–5.14.**

[35] See §§ **11.6** and **12.12.**

(3) *Health Care Personnel.* Many advance directive statutes prohibit the declarant's physician, anyone in the employ of the physician, or any employee of a health care facility in which the declarant is currently a patient from serving as a witness to an advance directive,[36] probably on the assumption that there may be or appear to be a conflict between the interests of such individuals and the declarant. As to the declarant's attending physician, this assumption is inconsistent with the fiduciary nature of the doctor-patient relationship. Nonetheless, because of these statutory provisions and because of the possible inferences that these individuals may have improperly influenced the declarant to execute a directive or improperly influenced the content of the directive for their own personal benefit or the benefit of the health care institution that employs them, it is best that they be avoided as witnesses for nonstatutory directives too.

## § 13.16   —Notarization

Declarants must decide whether an advance directive should be notarized. Those who use a form directive containing an optional space for notarization will especially need to confront the question. There is no ironclad requirement that a nonstatutory advance directive be notarized, but notarization might help to impress those who are faced with implementing the directive with the declarant's seriousness of purpose. However, some potential declarants will be deterred from executing a directive if there are practical barriers to doing so, and notarization is one such barrier. The fact that the advance directive statutes of only a few jurisdictions require notarization[37] suggests that it can be eliminated from nonstatutory advance directives without unduly jeopardizing their validity and enforceability. This should not be a concern, however, when the declarant has sought legal counsel in preparing the directive, and attorneys generally should have the advance directives that they draft notarized.

When a directive is notarized, it should state that the directive was properly made before a duly authorized officer (usually but not always a notary), followed by the date, signature, and title of the officer, and it should otherwise be in conformance with the jurisdiction in which it is executed and/or the jurisdiction in which it is likely to be implemented if they differ and if the latter is known.

## § 13.17   —Updating

An old directive might command less respect than a more recent directive containing precisely the same provisions because a number of factors existing at

---

[36] See §§ **11.6** and **12.12.**

[37] See §§ **11.7** and **12.14.**

the time of implementation may be different from those the declarant contemplated at the time of declaration. That is, a person's will expressed today might not be his will tomorrow, and the greater the time between the advance directive and its implementation, the greater the uncertainty that the earlier will and the current one are the same.[38]

Furthermore, if the directive names a proxy, there is the possibility that with the passage of time the designated person will not remain the declarant's choice. As individuals marry, divorce, have children, and experience deaths of family and friends, and as their values change, so might their preference for a proxy. Indeed, the proxy might have predeceased the declarant.

Although the courts have had little occasion to address this issue, prudence suggests that advance directives should be periodically reviewed and updated to reflect changes in the declarant's health, values, and personal and family situations, or changes in medical technology.[39] Even if no changes are made in the directive, at the least the declarant should ratify it in some way that gives evidence that it reflects his *current* will. Although any time period for updating is arbitrary, five years appears to be neither so short as to create hardships for the declarant nor so long as to make the directive stale.

This can be done most simply by merely re-signing and dating the directive. Declarants might add a statement that they have reviewed the advance directive and that it reflects their currently held views. Finally, rewitnessing could also be undertaken, attesting to the declarant's soundness of mind and freedom of action at the time of reexecution.[40] Whether any of these renewed formalities are necessary is impossible to say. For those who do not update nonstatutory advance directives, some comfort may be taken from the fact that no advance directive statute places a durational limit on the effectiveness of a statutory directive.

Although updating should not prove burdensome, it is very easy for declarants to forget, and attorneys should maintain a system for notifying clients for whom they have drafted advance directives of the need to update, as they would for wills and trusts when they become aware of significant changes in the testator's or settlor's circumstances or in the laws affecting such instruments.

## § 13.18   —Recitals

Advance directives should include a statement in which the declarant attests that at the time of execution he is of sound mind and that he acts freely. The precise

---

[38] **NY:** *Cf. In re* Westchester County Medical Ctr. (O'Connor), 531 N.E.2d 607, 613 (N.Y. 1988) ("As a threshold matter, the trier of fact must be convinced, as far as is humanly possible, that the strength of the individual's beliefs and the durability of the individual's commitment to those beliefs . . . make a recent change of heart unlikely.").

[39] *See* Hastings Center Guidelines 81 (Part Three, II(5)).

[40] See § **13.18.**

wording can vary but ought to attest to the declarant's competence and voluntariness. In addition, it is advisable that witnesses attest to the fact that the signatory of the directive is whom he purports to be, and that the declarant is competent and signing voluntarily.[41] Many advance directive statutes that contain form directives require such an attestation by the declarant and/or by the witnesses.[42]

Also, if a nonstatutory advance directive is executed in a jurisdiction having an advance directive statute (or more than one), it is advisable that the directive recite that it is not intended to be governed by the statute(s). Although most advance directive statutes provide that they do not supersede common-law rights and the few courts to have considered the issue have so held,[43] it might be preferable to draft two directives of identical substance, one complying with the act and one not. Each should state that the nonstatutory advance directive is intended to govern in preference to the statutory directive. This is especially important in jurisdictions in which there are restrictions in the advance directive statute on the authority of the declarant to authorize certain kinds of actions such as the forgoing of artificial nutrition and hydration, the implementation of a directive during pregnancy, or the implementation of the directive when the declarant is not in a terminal condition or permanently unconscious.

## § 13.19   Validity in Other Jurisdictions (Portability)

Even if an advance directive is valid and enforceable in the jurisdiction in which it is executed, there is no guarantee that the declarant will reside in that jurisdiction when the directive is needed. Some advance directive statutes provide for the enforcement of "foreign" advance directives (referred to as "portability"),[44] and therefore, some efforts should be taken to enhance the prospects for validity and enforceability of nonstatutory advance directives in other jurisdictions.

One simple precaution is that when one moves to another jurisdiction permanently, or temporarily for a significant period of time (especially persons with residences in more than one place), a directive should be reexecuted to comply with the necessary formalities of the new jurisdiction of residence. Short of redrafting a directive each time the declarant sets foot in another jurisdiction (which, in addition to being impractical, might not even be foolproof), there are

---

[41] **FL:** *Cf.* John F. Kennedy Memorial Hosp. v. Bludworth, 432 So. 2d 611, 620 (Fla. Dist. Ct. App. 1983) (advance directive should be "duly proved by the testimony or recent affidavit of at least one of two disinterested witnesses as to the due execution of the document and the mental capacity of the patient at the time of execution"), *rev'd on other grounds,* 452 So. 2d 921 (Fla. 1984).

[42] See § **11.8.**

[43] See §§ **10.10–10.12.**

[44] See §§ **10.24, 11.21,** and **12.50.**

two things that should be done to enhance validity and enforceability in other jurisdictions. First, the declarant should include a provision in the directive stating that the declaration is intended to be enforceable in all jurisdictions and not solely the one in which it is executed. Second, and more important though more difficult, the declarant should attempt to comply with the most stringent formalities of execution for advance directives across all American jurisdictions.

## § 13.20   Severability Clause

The validity and enforceability of an advance directive can be enhanced by the inclusion of a severability clause, stating that if any portion of the directive is determined to be unenforceable, it is the intent of the declarant that the validity and enforceability of the remainder should still be enforceable. For example, if a declarant executes a nonstatutory advance directive in an attempt to evade a restriction on forgoing life-sustaining treatment if pregnant, and that restriction is held to be unenforceable, the declarant might still wish for the declaration to be enforced after childbirth.

Although it is most likely that a severability clause would become operative if the directive were subjected to judicial review, it is possible that it might prove useful even in the clinical setting. A physician who might be reluctant to abide by an advance directive because of one unacceptable provision might nonetheless abide by the remainder if there were some clause so directing, preferably written in lay language.

In some situations the deletion of a particular provision of an advance directive might render the remainder useless. However, in other situations, major provisions of the directive might remain intact and relevant to the declarant's current situation. Even if the directive were to be rendered worthless qua directive, it would nonetheless still provide evidence of the declarant's desires that would be useful in either a clinical or a judicial setting in implementing the substituted judgment or subjective standard.

## TRIGGERING EVENTS

## § 13.21   When the Directive Becomes Effective

Possibly the single most important aspect of any advance directive is the circumstances under which it is to become operative. There are actually two separate but related issues. The first concerns when the proxy (if one is appointed) assumes decisionmaking authority. The second involves the circumstances under which treatment is to be forgone or administered.

Advance directive statutes ordinarily contain a provision describing the class of patients for whom an advance directive may be implemented.[45] In addition, statutory form directives frequently state the conditions under which the directive goes into effect.[46] Special attention should be paid to this issue when the reason for the declarant's executing a nonstatutory directive is an attempt to avoid the restrictions in many advance directive statutes that permit a directive to be implemented only if the patient is terminally ill or permanently unconscious. Declarants should clearly state the conditions under which they wish for instructions to become effective or for a proxy to be empowered to forgo life-sustaining treatment.

## § 13.22    Triggering Operation of Directive: Incompetence

By definition, an advance directive is a document executed by a person possessing decisionmaking capacity, to become effective when and if the declarant loses decisionmaking capacity. If a nonstatutory directive is embodied in a durable power of attorney, there must be language in it to the effect that it "become[s] effective upon the disability or incapacity of the principal."[47] A durable power of attorney may be drafted so that it becomes effective upon *execution* and remains in force if the principal becomes incapacitated. When such a power of attorney is executed for health care decisionmaking, it is not solely an advance directive but also a contemporaneous transfer of decisionmaking authority, which might or might not be what a particular declarant wishes. However, a durable power of attorney may be drafted so that it becomes effective only if and when the principal becomes incapacitated. The latter form of durable power of attorney is referred to as a "springing" durable power of attorney.[48] Both kinds of powers of attorney have their advantages and disadvantages.

For health care decisionmaking, a declarant ordinarily will not wish to transfer decisionmaking authority to a proxy while the declarant remains competent, and therefore a springing power of attorney is preferable. However, one difficulty that a springing power of attorney presents is that there must be some mechanism for triggering the transfer of decisionmaking authority from the declarant to the proxy. The concept that is usually used in advance directive statutes to demarcate the point at which the proxy's decisionmaking authority commences, and should ordinarily be employed in nonstatutory directives as well, is decisionmaking incompetence or incapacity.

---

[45] See §§ **11.9** and **12.17.**

[46] See §§ **11.3** and **12.11.**

[47] Uniform Durable Power of Attorney Act § 1.

[48] *See* Uniform Durable Power of Attorney Act § 1; Uniform Rights of the Terminally Ill Act § 2(c) (1989 draft) [hereinafter 1989 URTIA]. *See also In re* Westchester County Medical Ctr. (O'Connor), 531 N.E.2d 607, 612 n.2 (N.Y. 1988) (citing N.Y. Gen. Oblig. Law § 5-1602).

The declarant should spell out some way in which incompetence is to be determined. One way is to follow the general method in advance directive statutes of vesting this authority in the declarant's attending physician and/or one or more other physicians, but in practice it can be very difficult to specify in advance who these people are to be.[49] Otherwise, a judicial determination of incompetence might be necessary, which would undercut the goal of avoiding judicial proceedings. Further, once proceedings commence for determining incompetence, it is possible that the court will appoint a guardian who might not be the proxy named in the advance directive, thereby further undermining the declarant's wishes. Indeed, it is probably best to make the operation of the advance directive depend on the declarant's loss of decisionmaking capacity rather than "incompetence," because the latter could be construed to denote the need for a judicial proceeding.[50]

An advance directive should definitely state that it becomes operative if the declarant is unconscious. But that is unlikely to be sufficient because the declarant might become incapacitated without being unconscious. This possibility could be addressed, for example, by a statement that "this directive becomes effective when I am incapable of making decisions as determined by my attending physician, or by my attending physician with the concurrence of [number] other physicians chosen by my attending physician [or by my spouse]." Alternatively, a declarant might wish for an advance directive to go into effect only under the most extreme type of incompetence, such as unconsciousness. The danger with this approach is that it might fail to provide a means for decisionmaking in a range of situations in which it is needed.

One way of attempting to walk a middle course between specificity and generality is for a declarant to provide broad discretion for others to determine when the advance directive is to become operative but to reserve for himself the authority to overrule or countermand the directive even if he lacks decisionmaking capacity but is still able to communicate.[51] Many statutes permit declarants to revoke statutory advance directives regardless of their decisionmaking capacity.[52]

## § 13.23  Triggering Forgoing of Treatment

If an advance directive is purely a proxy directive, specifying that it becomes operative when the declarant loses decisionmaking capacity gives the proxy decisionmaking authority when that condition is met. However, if the directive

---

[49] 1989 URTIA § 3; Uniform Rights of the Terminally Ill Act § 3 (1985 draft) ("A declaration becomes operative when . . . the declarant is determined by the attending physician to be in a terminal condition and no longer able to make decisions regarding administration of life-sustaining treatment.") [hereinafter 1985 URTIA].

[50] See § 4.2.

[51] See §§ 7.45–7.46.

[52] See §§ 11.14 and 12.38.

is an instruction or a combined instruction and proxy directive, in addition to a provision for triggering the operation of the directive, there should also be provisions for triggering forgoing (or administering) of treatment. Advance directives should be as specific as possible in directions they give both about the level of the declarant's impairment needed to trigger the directive and the forms of treatment that the declarant wishes to avoid or to have.[53]

Because of the dual dangers inherent in instruction directives—that they will be either so specific that they will not apply to the circumstances of the declarant's medical condition or that they will be so general that they offer little guidance to surrogate decisionmakers (or, worse, lead to the forgoing of treatment in circumstances not envisioned or desired by the declarant)—it is critical when specifying treatments to be forgone that the conditions under which they are to be forgone are also made clear. Take, for example, a declarant who wishes to avoid cardiopulmonary resuscitation in the context of an incurable illness such as Alzheimer's disease. If that declarant simply states that he does not want cardiopulmonary resuscitation, and if he were hospitalized for routine elective surgery and experienced a cardiac arrest from some postoperative condition from which he could be returned to his healthy preoperative condition, he might not be resuscitated because of the directive despite the fact that this is not what he contemplated when he executed the directive.

## § 13.24  —Medical Condition

An instruction or a combined proxy and instruction directive might specify that it becomes effective when the declarant's medical condition assumes some particular quality, such as when the declarant becomes terminally, incurably, or hopelessly ill. Because these terms do not necessarily mean the same things,[54] it is important that they be used disjunctively, otherwise the directive will not become effective until all are met. Also, because of their vague and uncertain meaning, it is best for a declarant either to avoid their use or to use them but to describe them with reference to examples of acceptable and unacceptable levels of cognitive and/or physical functioning.

A state's advance directive statute can provide some guidance both in choosing and giving meaning to such terms. In fact, when drafting an instruction or combined directive in a jurisdiction in which there is an advance directive statute, it is probably prudent to use the conditions for triggering the operation of statutory directives, unless they are plainly more restrictive than the declarant

---

[53] **NJ:** *In re* Conroy, 486 A.2d 1209, 1230–31 (N.J. 1985) ("[A]ny details about the level of impaired functioning and the forms of medical treatment that one would find tolerable should be incorporated into advance directives to enhance their later usefulness as evidence."). *Cf. In re* Peter, 529 A.2d 419, 426 (N.J. 1987) (living will should specifically explain patient's preferences about life-sustaining treatment).

**NY:** Saunders v. State, 492 N.Y.S.2d 510 (Sup. Ct. Nassau County 1985).

[54] See §§ **8.10–8.12.**

wishes. All advance directive statutes contain such triggering conditions.[55] Indeed, it is the restrictive nature of these conditions that will often create the basis for a declarant to seek to draft a nonstatutory advance directive. However, it is logical to assume that a declarant who wishes to have life-sustaining medical treatment withheld or withdrawn when he is hopelessly ill or incurably ill will also wish to avoid it when he meets the usual statutory conditions, so that it is not avoidance of the statutory conditions that one wishes as much as broadening of those conditions.

## § 13.25  —Manner of Determination

When the implementation of an advance directive is made contingent upon the existence of a particular medical condition, the directive should state how and by whom that condition is to be determined. Again, it is advisable to follow any advance directive statutory or common-law requirements when drafting this aspect of a nonstatutory directive.

The simplest requirement to administer is that the declarant's *attending physician* must find that the medical condition that is necessary for the directive to become operative does exist.[56] It might be desirable for the declarant to name that person in the directive but, because it is possible that some other physician will have the responsibility for caring for the declarant, it is necessary to state alternatively that "any other physician who has responsibility for my care may make such determination in the absence of" the named physician.

Unfortunately, the simplest solution may not be the best. For the same reason that the case law often requires that physicians other than, or in addition to, the attending physician certify that the declarant is terminally ill or permanently unconscious or whatever is necessary to forgo life-sustaining treatment, it is probably best for a directive to require that at least one other physician in addition to the attending physician certify that the triggering condition is met. This serves not only to enhance the validity and enforceability of the directive but to provide a measure of protection for the declarant against hasty or otherwise ill-advised decisionmaking. The directive should also state who should select the additional physician or physicians, with the most likely choice being the declarant's attending physician, the proxy if one is named, or members (named or unnamed) of the declarant's family.

To cover the probably rare situation in which a declarant is at home and has no attending physician when a decision about life-sustaining treatment is

---

[55] See §§ 11.9 and 12.17.

[56] *See, e.g.,* 1989 URTIA § 3 ("A declaration becomes operative when (i) it is communicated to the attending physician and (ii) the declarant is determined by the attending physician to be in a terminal condition and no longer able to make decisions regarding the administration of life-sustaining treatment."); 1985 URTIA § 3 ("A declaration becomes operative when . . . the declarant is determined by the attending physician to be in a terminal condition and no longer able to make decisions regarding administration of life-sustaining treatment.").

thought to arise—a situation most likely to involve not starting (as opposed to stopping) a treatment—a provision should also be added directing the declarant's caretakers to consult with some physician or with a particular physician to determine whether a triggering condition specified by the declarant in fact exists.

## § 13.26 —Administration of Particular Treatment

Rather than making a directive become operative on the existence of a particular medical condition, it can instead be made operative contingent on the need for administering a particular kind of treatment or a general category of treatment. Thus, a directive could specify that it becomes operative if, for example, the use of a mechanical ventilator, artificial nutrition and hydration, or cardiopulmonary resuscitation were to become medically indicated. If the directive is exclusively a proxy directive, it then becomes the proxy's responsibility and prerogative to make decisions for the declarant; if it is exclusively an instruction directive, the attending physician should then follow the directive's instructions.

Alternatively, a declarant might describe the trigger in more general terms, specifying that the directive becomes operative if there are medical indications for administering any treatment that would "merely prolong the process of dying," or "not lead to recovery," or be "extraordinary" or "heroic." However, there is no reason to believe that such terms function any better in an advance directive to guide decisionmaking than they do in the absence of one. Their imprecision can lead to confusion and misinterpretation, thereby effectively thwarting the declarant's intent.

## § 13.27 —Pregnancy

Women who execute a directive while still able to bear children need to consider whether they wish to include a provision stating that the directive is to be operative or inoperative if they are pregnant when the triggering condition exists. Many advance directive statutes suspend the operation of a directive executed thereunder if the declarant is pregnant.[57] The case law[58] has not authoritatively addressed the effectiveness of advance directives during pregnancy, and the constitutionality of the provisions in some advance directive statutes suspending their effectiveness during pregnancy is suspect, especially if the prohibition on forgoing treatment were to be imposed before viability.[59]

---

[57] See §§ 11.11 and 12.27.

[58] See § 9.55.

[59] See §§ 9.55, 11.11, and 12.27.

## NOTIFICATION

### § 13.28  Necessity for Notification

An advance directive is of no use if it is not brought to the attention of those responsible for the declarant's health care and to the attention of a proxy (if one is named) or surrogate (if the directive is exclusively an instruction directive).[60] Thus, there are a number of people who should be given a copy of an advance directive to increase the likelihood that it will be available when needed. Advance directive statutes ordinarily make it the legal responsibility of declarants to inform attending physicians of the existence of the directive, and then place responsibility on the attending physician to see that the directive is implemented.[61] Although the Patient Self-Determination Act[62] requires that institutional health care providers ask patients at the time of admission if they have an advance directive,[63] such a request will be ineffective if the declarant lacks decisionmaking capacity at the time of admission. Thus, declarants of any directive (statutory or nonstatutory) should take measures to make the existence and content of the directive known to those who will be called upon to implement them.

Because the need for using a directive may occur at times and in places distant from those of execution, it is unwise for a declarant to rely on notification to one person. It is essential that the declarant's personal physician be advised of the existence of a directive. However, there is no way to be sure that one's personal physician will be the attending physician when the directive is needed or will even be aware that the declarant is ill if, for example, he becomes ill when he is away from home. Therefore, others, such as family members, also need to know of the existence and location of a directive. Similarly, even if the declarant becomes ill at home, it is possible that his personal physician may be absent and that care will be administered by others.

### § 13.29  —To Declarant's Physician

The most sensible course is for a declarant to provide a copy of the directive to his personal physician, as one would ordinarily leave a copy of a will with one's

---

[60] **NJ:** *Cf.* McVey v. Englewood Hosp. Ass'n, 524 A.2d 450 (N.J. Super. Ct. App. Div.), *cert. denied,* 528 A.2d 12 (N.J. 1987) (hospital not liable for refusing to honor purported oral statement of presently incompetent patient).

[61] See § **11.15.**

[62] Pub. L. No. 101-508, §§ 4206, 4751 (OBRA), 104 Stat. 1388-115 to -117, 1388-204 to -206 (codified at 42 U.S.C.A. § 1395cc(f)(1) & *id.* § 1396a(a) (West Supp. 1994)). See § **10.21.**

[63] 42 U.S.C.A. § 1395cc(f)(1)(a)(i), (ii); OBRA § 4751(a)(2), 42 U.S.C.A. § 1396a(w)(1)(A).

attorney. It is important that the physician not merely be informed of the existence of the directive but also be provided with a copy, review it with the declarant, and file it prominently in the declarant's medical record. This is especially important if the declarant is a member of a health maintenance organization or has a personal physician who is a member of a group practice so that, if some other physician is treating the declarant, the directive will not be overlooked. Review with one's attending physician also provides the declarant with an opportunity to attempt to ascertain whether the physician understands the directive and is willing to apply it in the appropriate circumstances. A declarant whose physician is unsympathetic to the directive can then decide whether to obtain a different physician.

A declarant currently undergoing treatment for a serious illness or a declarant who is hospitalized should remind the attending physician of the existence of the directive and possibly provide another copy if the original notice to the physician was not recent. This will remind the physician of the existence and content of the directive and provide the declarant and physician with an opportunity to discuss the directive in the context of a concrete medical condition, which may help to sharpen the physician's understanding of the declarant's wishes. If the declarant is already in a health care institution, it is essential to determine if the contents of the directive comply with or offend the attending physician's (or the institution's) policies or code of professional or personal ethics, and thus whether there will be any difficulty applying it should the necessity arise.[64] If such difficulty is foreseeable, the declarant might, while still competent, wish to change physicians, change health care institutions, or modify the directive.

## § 13.30 —To Health Care Institution

The issue of forgoing life-sustaining treatment is most likely to occur when the declarant is a patient in a hospital, hospice, or nursing home. Because such institutions should have policies regarding the use of advance directives[65] and because even in the absence of such policies they have substantial influence over the manner in which medicine is practiced by physicians on their staff, it is also desirable to inform an appropriate employee of the institution of the existence and content of a directive.

It is important that all members of the health care team know of the existence and content of the directive and have an opportunity to determine whether it complies with or offends their own personal or professional code of ethics, and thus whether they will have any difficulty applying it should the necessity arise. In the case of a statutory directive, it is usually required for them to inform the

---

[64] See § **17.23.**

[65] See § **10.21.**

attending physician so that appropriate arrangements can be made either to transfer the care of the patient to others or, at a minimum, to inform the patient or family members or friends to arrange for other care for the patient.[66] In the case of a nonstatutory directive, there is strong support in the case law for a parallel obligation.[67]

## § 13.31   —By Noninstitutionalized Declarants

Declarants who are not in a health care institution will ordinarily find it difficult, if not impossible, to predict where they might someday receive health care and thus to inform such health care institutions about the existence and content of their advance directives. This difficulty will be greatest for individuals who are young and healthy when they execute a directive. The task may be considerably simpler for those who are chronically ill and have already been in and out of health care institutions and therefore have a better idea of where they are likely to receive future treatment. The chances of notifying the correct health care institution might be enhanced (though it might not be a simple matter to do so) by providing a copy of an advance directive to all hospitals in which one's personal physician has staff privileges, especially if the institutions already have a medical record for the declarant and/or if they have a central registry of advance directives.[68]

Even if it is impossible to notify a health care institution of the existence and content of a directive, declarants should attempt to learn about the policies toward advance directives of those health care institutions with which their personal physicians are affiliated. If they are able to identify some that are more favorably inclined toward advance directives than others, they should inform their physician and family that they wish to be treated there should the need arise. Indeed, it is probably wise to include a provision in the directive to that effect.

## § 13.32   —To Proxy or Surrogate; Family and Friends

A notarized copy of an advance directive should be given to any person named in the directive as a proxy or alternate proxy. In addition to enhancing the likelihood that the directive will be available when needed, this also reminds the declarant to ask a potential proxy whether he wishes to serve as a proxy. Furthermore, it gives the potential proxy an opportunity to discuss the

---

[66] See §§ 11.18 and 12.46.

[67] See § 17.23.

[68] See § 13.37.

instructions, if any, in the directive or, more generally, the declarant's wishes whether expressed in the directive or not, and thereby enhances the likelihood that the directive will be implemented.[69] Such a discussion will assist the proxy in carrying out the declarant's will, or alternatively convince him that he should not accept the appointment because he is unable to carry out, or has reservations about carrying out, the declarant's wishes.

It is essential that a declarant inform those persons most likely to serve as surrogates (usually close family members and/or friends) of the existence and content of an advance directive and even provide them with a copy, preferably, a notarized one. This should be done even if the directive does not appoint a proxy. In terms of making sure that the directive is available and ready to be used when circumstances require, this is certainly as important as and possibly even more important than notifying the declarant's personal physician.

## ADMINISTRATION OF ADVANCE DIRECTIVES BY HEALTH CARE INSTITUTIONS

### § 13.33 Development of Institutional Policy

For a number of reasons, it is important if not essential that health care institutions (hospitals, nursing homes, hospices, home health care agencies, and medical transport services) develop policies governing the administration of advance directives. The failure to have a policy can lead to uncertainty, confusion, and inconsistency when a patient (or the patient's proxy, family, or friend) presents an advance directive to his physician. Uncertainty, confusion, and inconsistency can themselves become prime ingredients in creating grounds for a lawsuit against the health care institution and/or the attending physician. Furthermore, the Patient Self-Determination Act requires institutional health care providers participating in the Medicare or Medicaid programs to have "written policies and procedures."[70] Some state statutes[71] have similar requirements, and JCAHO accreditation standards parallel the requirements of the Patient Self-Determination Act.[72]

---

[69] **NJ:** *See In re* Peter, 529 A.2d 419, 426 (N.J. 1987) ("It would have been better if Ms. Peter had specifically provided in her power of attorney that Mr. Johanning had authority to terminate life-sustaining treatment.").

[70] 42 U.S.C.A. § 1395cc(f)(1) (West Supp. 1994); *id.* § 1396a(w)(1) (applicable to "all adult individuals receiving medical care" concerning "an individual's rights under State law ... to make decisions concerning [their] medical care, including the right to accept or refuse [treatment,] ... the right to formulate advance directives[, and] the written policies of the provider or organization respecting the implementation of such rights"). See § **10.21.**

[71] *See, e.g.,* N.J. Stat. Ann. § 26:2H-65(1), (2).

[72] *See* Joint Comm'n on Accreditation of Healthcare Orgs., Accreditation Manual for Hospitals (1992) (standard R1.1.1.3.2).

## § 13.34   Limitations on Institutional Policy

Although institutions are relatively free to determine the content of their policies for administering advance directives, some limitations are established by advance directive statutes and by case law.[73] At one extreme, a hospital policy providing that all directions in advance directives must be complied with surely is too broad, for it could commit the hospital to performing clearly illegal acts, such as active euthanasia, if a patient's advance directive so requested. At the other extreme, a hospital policy categorically refusing to consider the contents of a patient's advance directive could result in unauthorized treatment, thereby leading to civil liability to the patient or his estate.

Any institutional policy on advance directives must also take into account any case law on advance directives that exists in that jurisdiction, especially as regards nonstatutory advance directives. However, at this time such case law in any particular state may be sparse or nonexistent. If that is so, health care institutions are well-advised to follow the trends developing nationally as long as they do not conflict with any specific case-law or statutory requirements to the contrary in the jurisdiction in which the health care institution is located.

In jurisdictions with advance directive statutes, care must be taken to ensure that institutional policies do not conflict with the requirements of that legislation, certainly as regards statutory directives. In policies governing the administration of advance directives, health care institutions should accord nonstatutory advance directives at least as much respect as they must accord statutory directives. Indeed, because of the fact that most advance directive statutes are not intended to preempt the common law,[74] it is arguable that even greater leeway ought to be permitted in the administration of nonstatutory directives.

In addition to case law and statutory law regarding advance directives, at least equal attention must be paid to the developing common law concerning the right to forgo life-sustaining treatment apart from advance directives. The spirit of this body of law will establish limitations on what a health care institution may and must do in developing a policy for the administration of advance directives.

## § 13.35   Notice to Health Care Personnel

It is imperative that health care institutions make the existence and content of their policy governing the administration of advance directives known to all physicians with staff privileges and to all other professional health care personnel employed by the institution. (This is arguably required by the provision of the Patient Self-Determination Act mandating that institutional health care

---

[73] *See, e.g.,* Browning v. Herbert, 568 So. 2d 4 (Fla. 1990) (promulgating rules for giving effect to written living wills, oral living wills, written appointment of a proxy, and oral appointment of a proxy).

[74] See §§ 10.10–10.11.

providers conduct education for their staff and for the community about advance directives.[75]) Failure to do so causes uncertainty, confusion, and inconsistency in the administration of advance directives. In addition, knowledge of the policy will assist physicians to whom patients or their families have previously given advance directives in knowing what to say to them about their validity and enforceability and what actually to do with the directive.[76] Also, it might generally sensitize health care personnel to what advance directives are and to how to deal both with the patients who have them and with the patients' proxies and families. Knowledge of the policy will also put individual health care professionals on notice that their personal or professional ethics may be inconsistent with institutional policy,[77] thus allowing such differences to be dealt with outside the context of caring for a particular patient, which is likely to be advantageous to the institution, to the health care professional, and to the patient.

## § 13.36   Notice to Patients and Families

It is equally important, if not more so, that patients and their families be informed of a health care institution's advance directive policy. This is now required by the Patient Self-Determination Act.[78] Knowledge of the policy's existence can help in educating patients and families about what advance directives are and what they can and cannot accomplish. This, in turn, may encourage patients to execute a directive. Second, knowledge of the policy's content may alleviate some of the anxieties of patients and families about whether patients' wishes will be honored. Alternatively, a patient or family member who does not take comfort in the content of the institution's policy might seek care in another institution in order to avoid potential conflict. It is better that this occur in a calm and reflective atmosphere than when a crisis develops over implementing the patient's instructions. The ill will generated toward the institution and the attending physician will be less, the strain on the patient and family will not be as great, and it will be simpler to transfer to another health care institution a patient who is in better physical and mental condition than a patient who is incompetent and/or near death. It certainly will be simpler if the patient is admitted at the outset to a health care institution whose policies are consistent with his wishes than to attempt to transfer the patient later if a conflict develops.

The manner in which notice of the existence and content of the institution's policy is to be given is a delicate matter. There are two general ways in which

---

[75] *See* 42 U.S.C.A. §§ 1395cc(f)(1)(E), 1396a(w)(1)(E) (West Supp. 1994). See § **10.21.**

[76] See § **13.37.**

[77] See § **17.23.**

[78] 42 U.S.C.A. § 1395cc(f)(1)(a)(i), (ii) (West Supp. 1994); *id.* § 1396a(w)(1)(A). See § **10.21.**

this can be accomplished: universal notification to all patients, and selective notification to patients thought to be most likely to become incompetent, such as critically or terminally ill patients. The Patient Self-Determination Act requires that notice of institutional policies be given at the time of admission to a hospital as an inpatient or at the time of admission to a skilled nursing home as a resident.[79] This requirement is also reflected in some state statutes[80] and in JCAHO accreditation requirements.[81] In some (and perhaps many) cases, notification at the time of admission is pro forma. Patients will be told about the policy, but they might not fully understand it because, at the time of admission, information about advance directives can easily get lost in the shuffle of a seemingly endless quantity of forms that must be signed and other information that is provided and because the individuals who process admissions to hospitals and nursing homes are not necessarily likely to be skilled in communicating with patients about such issues.

It is also possible that universal notification, especially at the time of admission, will have an undesirable impact on patients. The message that patients might take away from being told about advance directives is that they are expected to become critically ill, to die, or to lose decisionmaking capacity. This could frighten many patients with little or no benefit to most. Thus, from the standpoint of concern for the normal anxiety that patients experience on admission to a health care institution and from the institution's public relations standpoint, universal notification might be ill-advised. This is especially so in acute care hospitals where most patients will never need an advance directive. It might be a less significant concern in long term care facilities where a large proportion of the patients will lose decisionmaking capacity and die. Such institutions should work closely with medical transport services to coordinate policies so that patients' advance directives are not overlooked by the latter out of ignorance of their existence.[82] It should be of no concern in hospice care where patients are usually consciously aware of their impending death and have chosen hospice care because of its special expertise in dealing with dying patients.

On balance, it is probably best (and it is legally required) that, at the time of admission, pro forma compliance with the Patient Self-Determination Act be practiced. Nothing precludes the provision of additional information subsequent to the actual time of admission, and that is what should occur. Repetitive provision of information is more likely to ensure that it gets to precisely those patients and families who need it or who are most likely to need it. During the

---

[79] 42 U.S.C.A. §§ 1395cc(f), 1396a(a)(57) & (58), 1396a(w). See § **10.21.**

[80] *See, e.g.,* N.J. Stat. Ann. § 26:2H-65(1), (2).

[81] *See* Joint Comm'n on Accreditation of Healthcare Orgs., Accreditation Manual for Hospitals (standard R1.1.1.3.2).

[82] *See* Miles & Crimmins, *Orders to Limit Emergency Treatment for an Ambulance Service in a Large Metropolitan Area,* 254 JAMA 525 (1985).

initial nursing evaluation, nurses can provide the same or additional information as that provided at admission. Written information can be left at nursing stations and at patient and family lounges. Nurses and social workers can be instructed to offer to answer questions about advance directives. And, perhaps most important, information can be given to patients' families who in some cases will be in a better position than the patient to know whether the patient has already executed an advance directive and to produce it if he has or to discuss with the patient the possibility of executing an advance directive.

## § 13.37   Maintenance of Registry

A central provision of an institutional policy should be the maintenance of a registry for advance directives. A registry is a system by which the health care institution receives and accepts advance directives from patients and potential patients, files them, and makes them available to a patient's attending physician and other health care personnel who need to know about them.[83] In the case of declarants for whom a medical record already exists (both those who are currently inpatients and those who are only potentially so), this involves filing them conspicuously in the patient's medical record, preferably in a section exclusively for that purpose so that they will not be overlooked. In the case of a declarant for whom no medical record currently exists, the health care institution needs to devise a system for ensuring that advance directives are filed in the medical record when it is created.

Prior to the enactment of the Patient Self-Determination Act, making a registry available to potential patients might have alleviated some of the difficulty that declarants have in ensuring that their directives come to the attention of those who may someday render them care and need to know of the existence and content of the directives. The Patient Self-Determination Act should resolve that problem, but it will not resolve the problem of the patient who is incompetent at the time of admission and thus cannot provide his advance directive at that time and whose family does not know of the existence or of the location of the advance directive. For this reason, a hospital-based registry of advance directives for potential patients might still prove useful.

Beyond the basic provision of maintaining a registry, health care institutions should consider establishing a mechanism for learning of the existence of advance directives from their patients on admission, perhaps in combination with a universal notification procedure. A statewide repository for advance directives is also a possible aid in making sure that advance directives are available when they are needed.[84]

---

[83] *Cf.* Kleinman & Lowy, *Ethical Considerations in Living Organ Donation and a New Approach— An Advance-Directive Organ Registry,* 152 Archives Internal Med. 1484 (1992).

[84] **CA:** 1994 Cal. Legis. Serv. ch. 1280 (S. 1857) (effective Jan. 1, 1995) (requiring Secretary of State to establish registry for health care powers of attorney.

**ND:** N.D. S. Res. 4013, 53d Leg. (1993) (enacted) (directing state legislative council to "study the feasibility of establishing a central repository for" advance directives).

## § 13.38 Assisting Patients in Drafting Advance Directives

Health care institutions wishing to pursue a more aggressive policy toward the use of advance directives should consider incorporating provisions in their policies to encourage patients to execute advance directives. Such provisions might be purely informational, such as a pamphlet to inform patients what advance directives are, what they can accomplish, and what their limitations are. The information might include organizations that can be contacted for further information about advance directives.

Health care providers might wish to take an even more active stance toward promoting the execution of advance directives. The Patient Self-Determination Act[85] does not require health care institutions to give patients forms for advance directives or to provide any other kind of assistance to patients in executing advance directives. Health care providers should realize that if they do make form directives (either statutory or nonstatutory) available, they should be prepared to deal with patients seeking assistance in executing a directive. At least some patients who are told that they are entitled to have an advance directive will want to execute one and will request assistance in doing so. As a practical matter, it is difficult to see how health care institutions will be able to avoid providing assistance. They will be placed in the awkward position of either having just informed patients that they are entitled to have an advance directive and then denying them assistance in preparing one or providing such assistance. At least one state statute requires such assistance to be provided.[86] When a health care institution does provide assistance to patients in drafting and executing advance directives, it must avoid even the appearance of pressuring patients into executing an advance directive and must not serve in any prohibited witnessing capacity.[87] The Patient Self-Determination Act prohibits health care institutions from conditioning the provision of care "or otherwise discriminat[ing] against an individual based on whether or not the individual has executed an advance directive."[88]

---

[85] See § 10.21.

[86] NJ: *See* N.J. Stat. Ann. § 26:2H-65(2).

[87] See §§ 11.6, 12.12, and 13.15.

[88] 42 U.S.C.A. § 1395cc(f)(1)(C) (West Supp. 1994); *id.* § 1396a(w)(1)(C).

## Bibliography

Alexander, G. *Writing a Living Will: Using a Durable Power-of-Attorney.* New York: Praeger, 1988.

Buckley, W. "Videotaping Living Wills: Dying Declarations Brought to Life." *Valparaiso University Law Review* 22 (1987): 39.

Colen, B. *The Essential Guide to a Living Will.* New York: Prentice Hall, 1991.

Collin, F. "Planning and Drafting Durable Powers of Attorney for Health Care." *Institute on Estate Planning* 22 (1988): 5.1.

Collin, F., et al. *Durable Powers of Attorney and Health Care Directives.* Colorado Springs: Shepard's/McGraw-Hill, 1994.

Collins, E. *The Complete Guide to Living Wills: How to Safeguard Your Treatment Choices.* New York: Bantam Books, 1991.

Commission on Legal Problems of the Elderly. American Bar Association. *Health Care Powers of Attorney: An Introduction and Sample Form.* Washington: American Bar Association, Commission on Legal Problems of the Elderly, 1990.

McCuaig, V., and J. Albert. "Health Care Proxies: How Do We Inform Our Clients?" *New York State Bar Journal* 63 (1991): 24.

Outerbridge, D., and A. Hersh. *Easing the Passage: A Guide for Prearranging and Ensuring a Pain-Free and Tranquil Death Via a Living Will, Personal Medical Mandate, and Other Medical, Legal, and Ethical Resources.* New York: Harper Collins Publishers, 1991.

Schlesinger, E. "Dealing with the Dying Client." *Institute on Estate Planning* 9 (1975): 2.1.

Williams, P. *The Living Will and the Durable Power of Attorney for Health Care Book: With Forms.* Oak Park, Ill.: Gaines, 1991.

# CHAPTER 14

# SURROGATE (FAMILY) DECISIONMAKING STATUTES

## § 14.1   Introduction

A gradually increasing number of states have enacted legislation designating who possesses the legal authority to make medical decisions on behalf of patients who are unable to do so for themselves and who have not themselves designated another to do so (through a health care power of attorney or otherwise). These pieces of legislation are usually referred to as "surrogate decisionmaking" statutes, but sometimes as "family decisionmaking" statutes. The Uniform Model Health-Care Consent Act[1] and the Uniform Health-Care Decisions Act[2] contain such provisions.

The primary purpose of these statutes is to make clear what is at least implicit in the case law: that the customary medical professional practice of using family

---

[1] Uniform Model Health-Care Consent Act § 4, 9 U.L.A. 453, 461 (West 1988 & Supp. 1994).

[2] Uniform Health-Care Decisions Act, 9 U.L.A. pt. I at 93 (West Supp. 1994).

members to make decisions for patients who lack decisionmaking capacity and who lack an advance directive is legally valid, and that ordinarily judicial proceedings need not be initiated for the appointment of a guardian.[3] Another purpose of these statutes is to provide a means, short of cumbersome and possibly expensive guardianship proceedings, for designating a surrogate decisionmaker when the patient has no close family members to act as surrogate.

Although some statutory surrogate decisionmaking provisions deal exclusively with surrogate decisionmaking, most are part of larger enactments dealing with related topics such as living wills, health care powers of attorney, combined advance directives, and/or informed consent. See **Table 14–1** in **§ 14.10.** The reach of some of these statutes is extremely narrow. For example, the Georgia[4] and New York[5] surrogate decisionmaking provisions are part of statutes dealing only with decisionmaking about cardiopulmonary resuscitation.[6] The California statute applies only to decisionmaking for residents of skilled nursing or intermediate care facilities.[7]

The statutes leave a variety of issues unclear. The silence of the statutes on many issues is unfortunate because it is likely to lead to conflict within the families of incompetent patients and confusion among health care personnel, thereby generating the litigation the statutes were intended to avoid.

### § 14.2    Coordination with Advance Directives

Most surrogate decisionmaking statutes specifically provide that they must be implemented with regard to an advance directive, if one has been executed. Most importantly, a surrogate designated by a patient through a health care power of attorney has priority over a statutory surrogate,[8] and a patient's living

---

[3] See §§ 5.12–5.14.

[4] **GA:** Ga. Code Ann. §§ 31-39-1 to -9.

[5] **NY:** N.Y. Pub. Health Law § 2965.

[6] See §§ 9.7–9.30.

[7] **CA:** Cal. Civ. Code § 1418.8 (automatically repealed as of Jan. 1, 1995, unless reenacted before that date).

    **WV:** *See also* W. Va. Code § 16-5B-8a (applies to consent to health care services in extended care facilities operated in connection with hospitals).

[8] **CO:** Colo. Rev. Stat. § 15-18.5-103(1) (if no guardian with medical decisionmaking authority, no health care agent, or other known person with legal authority to provide such consent or refusal on patient's behalf).

    **DC:** D.C. Code Ann. § 21-2210(a).

    **IN:** Ind. Code Ann. § 16-8-12-4(a).

    **MD:** Md. Code Ann., Health-Gen. § 20-107(d) (absence of durable power of attorney for health care or judicially appointed guardian).

    **NY:** N.Y. Pub. Health Law § 2965(2)(a) (when health care agent or designated surrogate are not available or competent to make decision).

will[9] is to be honored in preference to a statutory surrogate's decisions if there is no patient-designated surrogate (proxy).[10] Finally, some statutes provide that a statutory surrogate has authority to act only if the patient has neither a living will nor a health care power of attorney, or one cannot be readily located.[11]

---

**SD:** S.D. Codified Laws Ann. § 34-12C-3 (absence of durable power of attorney for health care or appointed guardian).

**WV:** W. Va. Code § 16-5C-5a(b) (when no guardian or applicable durable power of attorney); W. Va. Code § 16-5B-8a (when no guardian or applicable durable power of attorney); W. Va. Code § 16-30B-7(a).

**WY:** Wyo. Stat. § 3-5-209(b).

[9] **CT:** Conn. Gen. Stat. Ann. § 19a-571(a) (gives decisionmaking preference to patient's health care agent second only to patient's physician if treatment preferences are known to physician).

**HI:** Haw. Rev. Stat. § 327D-21(a).

**IA:** Iowa Code Ann. § 144A.7 (gives health care decisionmaking preference to patient's attorney in fact).

**LA:** La. Rev. Stat. Ann. § 40:1299.58.5(A)(2) (permits surrogate decisionmaker to execute declaration regarding withholding or withdrawal of life-sustaining procedures when individual has not previously done so).

**MD:** Md. Code Ann., Health-Gen. § 5-608(A).

**NM:** N.M. Stat. Ann. § 24-7-8.1(A).

**NC:** N.C. Gen. Stat. § 90-322(b).

**OR:** Or. Rev. Stat. § 127.635(2).

**TX:** Tex. Health & Safety Code Ann. § 672.007 (if no living will and no legal guardian).

**WY:** Wyo. Stat. § 35-22-105(b).

[10] **FL:** Browning v. Herbert, 568 So. 2d 4, 13 (Fla. 1990) ("We emphasize and caution that when the patient has left instructions regarding life-sustaining treatment, the surrogate must make the medical choice that the patient, if competent, would have made, and not one that the surrogate might make for himself or herself, or that the surrogate might think is in the patient's best interests. . . . 'The surrogate decisionmaker must be confident that he or she can and is voicing the patient's decision.'").

[11] **AZ:** Ariz. Rev. Stat. Ann. § 36-3231(A).

**AR:** Ark. Code Ann. § 20-17-214 (permits surrogate decisionmaker to execute declaration regarding use of life-sustaining treatment on behalf of incompetent).

**FL:** Fla. Stat. Ann. § 765.401(1).

**IL:** Ill. Ann. Stat. ch. 755, § 40/15 (specifically states that act does not apply to instances in which patient has an operative, unrevoked living will or an authorized agent under a durable power of attorney for health care); Ill. Ann. Stat. ch. 755, § 40/20 (provides that in the event that an unrevoked advance directive [living will or durable power of attorney for health care] is no longer valid because of technical deficiency or inapplicability to patient's condition, document may be used as evidence of patient's wishes).

**KY:** Ky. Rev. Stat. Ann. § 311.631(1) (if adult has not executed an advance directive or "to the extent the advance directive does not address a decision that must be made").

**ME:** Me. Rev. Stat. Ann. tit. 18-A, § 5-707(a).

**MT:** Mont. Code Ann. § 50-9-106.

**NV:** Nev. Rev. Stat. Ann. § 449.626.

**OH:** Ohio Rev. Code Ann. § 2133.08(A)(1)(b).

In some, statutes, however, there is no apparent attempt to coordinate surrogate decisionmaking provisions with advance directives.[12] However, even in the absence of an express provision that a patient-designated surrogate or a living will should presumptively take priority over a statutory surrogate, that ought to be the result because of the high value accorded to self-determination in medical decisionmaking. A patient-designated surrogate and a living will, in theory at least, better honor self-determination because they are manifestations of the patient's own will.

## § 14.3  When Statute Becomes Operative

Most statutes contain a set of conditions, which when satisfied trigger the statute's operation. Generally, these conditions include the inability of a patient to make or communicate informed health care decisions,[13] or a determination by

---

UT: Utah Code Ann. § 75-2-1107(1).

VA: Va. Code Ann. § 54.1-2986.

Uniform Rights of the Terminally Ill Act § 7(a), 9B U.L.A. 96, 109 (Supp. 1992) (if terminal condition and no longer able to make decisions regarding administration of life-sustaining treatment) [hereinafter 1989 URTIA].

[12] GA: Ga. Code Ann. §§ 31-9-1 to -7; Ga. Code Ann. §§ 31-39-1 to -9 (CPR statute).

ID: Idaho Code §§ 39-4301 to -4306.

IN: Ind. Code Ann. § 16-8-11-14 (provision in living will that provides list of persons that physician may consult with to attempt to ascertain patient's intentions and validity of declaration regarding withholding or withdrawal of life-sustaining procedures).

LA: La. Rev. Stat. Ann. § 40:1299.53.

MS: Miss. Code Ann. § 41-41-3.

MO: Mo. Ann. Stat. § 431.061 (consent statute).

SC: S.C. Code Ann. §§ 44-66-10 to -80.

TX: Tex. Health & Safety Code Ann. §§ 313.001–.007 (consent statute). *But cf.* Tex. Health & Safety Code Ann. § 313.004(a) (patient's spouse, adult children, and parents have higher priority than "the individual clearly identified to act for the patient by the patient before the patient became incapacitated").

UT: Utah Code Ann. § 78-14-5.

WA: Wash. Rev. Code Ann. § 7.70.065.

[13] AZ: Ariz. Rev. Stat. Ann. § 36-3231(A).

AR: Ark. Code Ann. § 20-17-214.

CO: Colo. Rev. Stat. § 15-18.5-103.

DC: D.C. Code Ann. § 21-2204.

GA: Ga. Code Ann. § 31-9-2.

IN: Ind. Code Ann. § 16-8-12-4(a).

KY: Ky. Rev. Stat. Ann. § 311.631(1).

MD: Md. Code Ann., Health-Gen. § 20-107(a)(2).

the attending physician that the person is in a terminal condition or irreversible coma or is permanently unconscious.[14] Some statutes, however, provide that the individual must be both (1) unable to make or communicate health care decisions, and (2) in a terminal condition, irreversible coma, or state of permanent unconsciousness.[15]

## § 14.4  Priority of Persons Who May Serve as Surrogates

The purpose of surrogate decisionmaking statutes is to clarify who has authority to make decisions for a patient lacking in decisionmaking capacity when that patient has failed to appoint a surrogate. Thus, most surrogate decisionmaking statutes include as their centerpiece a list, in order of priority, of persons who

---

**NY:** N.Y. Pub. Health Law § 2964(2)(3).

**SC:** S.C. Code Ann. § 44-66-30(A).

**TX:** Tex. Health & Safety Code Ann. § 313.004(a) (comatose, incapacitated, or otherwise mentally or physically incapable of communication).

**VA:** Va. Code Ann. § 54.1-2986(A); Va. Code Ann. § 16-5B-8a(b) (informed consent for health care services of extended care facility operated in connection with hospital); Va. Code Ann. § 16-5C-5a(b) (informed consent for nursing home or personal care home health care services).

[14] **CT:** Conn. Gen. Stat. Ann. § 19a-571(a).

**GA:** Ga. Code Ann. § 31-39-2(4) (based on determination by attending physician with concurrence of another physician, adult candidate for nonresuscitation defined as patient who has medical condition that can reasonably be expected to result in imminent death, is in noncognitive state with no reasonable possibility of regaining cognitive functions, or is person for whom CPR would be medically futile).

**IL:** Ill. Ann. Stat. ch. 755, § 40/10, *construed in In re Austin,* 615 N.E.2d 411, 418 (Ill. App. Ct. 1993).

**IN:** Ind. Code Ann. § 16-8-11-14(a).

**IA:** Iowa Code Ann. § 144A.7(1).

**LA:** La. Rev. Stat. Ann. § 40:1299.58.2(7).

**NC:** N.C. Gen. Stat. § 90-322(a).

**OR:** Or. Rev. Stat. § 127.635(1).

**TX:** Tex. Health & Safety Code Ann. § 672.002(8).

[15] **ME:** Me. Rev. Stat. Ann. tit. 18-A, § 5-707(a).

**MT:** Mont. Code Ann. § 50-9-106(1).

**NV:** Nev. Rev. Stat. Ann. § 449.626(1).

**NM:** N.M. Stat. Ann. § 24-7-8.1(A).

**OH:** Ohio Rev. Code Ann. § 2133.08(A)(1)(a).

**UT:** Utah Code Ann. § 75-2-1107(1).

**WY:** Wyo. Stat. § 35-22-105(b); Wyo. Stat. § 3-5-209(b).

1989 URTIA § 7(a).

may act as surrogate decisionmakers.[16] The person usually heading the list is the patient's spouse. Also high on the lists are the patient's adult offspring, parents, and adult siblings. Beyond that the statutes vary widely, listing (in descending order of frequency) a guardian of the person, nearest living relative or competent relative, grandchild, grandparent, friend, and attending physician. Some also include a guardian of the patient's estate, heirs at law, clergy, domestic partner, religious superior if a member of a religious order, and/or other person to whom one's wishes were made known. Because there is considerable variation among states, each state's list must be specifically consulted.

---

[16] **AZ:** Ariz. Rev. Stat. Ann. § 36-3231(A).

**AR:** Ark. Code Ann. § 20-17-214.

**CO:** Colo. Rev. Stat. § 15-18.5-103(3).

**CT:** Conn. Gen. Stat. Ann. § 19a-571(a).

**DC:** D.C. Code Ann. § 21-2210(a).

**FL:** Fla. Stat. Ann. § 765.401(1).

**GA:** Ga. Code Ann. § 31-39-2(b) (CPR statute); Ga. Code Ann. § 31-39-2(3) (consent statute).

**ID:** Idaho Code § 39-4303.

**IL:** Ill. Ann. Stat. ch. 755, § 40/25(a).

**IN:** Ind. Code Ann. § 16-8-12-4 (health care consent); Ind. Code Ann. § 16-8-11-14(g) (living will statute).

**IA:** Iowa Code Ann. § 144A.7(1).

**KY:** Ky. Rev. Stat. Ann. § 311.631(1).

**LA:** La. Rev. Stat. Ann. § 40:1299.58.5(2) (living will statute); La. Rev. Stat. Ann. § 40:1299.53(A) (medical consent).

**ME:** Me. Rev. Stat. Ann. tit. 18-A, § 5-707(b).

**MD:** Md. Code Ann., Health-Gen. § 5-605(A)(2); Md. Code Ann., Health-Gen. § 20-107(d).

**MS:** Miss. Code Ann. § 41-41-3.

**MT:** Mont. Code Ann. § 50-9-106(2).

**NV:** Nev. Rev. Stat. Ann. § 449.626(2).

**NY:** N.Y. Pub. Health Law § 2965(2).

**NC:** N.C. Gen. Stat. § 90-322(b).

**ND:** N.D. Cent. Code § 23-12-13(1).

**OH:** Ohio Rev. Code Ann. § 2133.08(B).

**OR:** Or. Rev. Stat. § 127.635(2).

**SC:** S.C. Code Ann. § 44-66-30(A).

**SD:** S.D. Codified Laws Ann. § 34-12C-3.

**TX:** Tex. Health & Safety Code Ann. § 313.004(a); Tex. Health & Safety Code Ann. § 672.009(b).

**UT:** Utah Code Ann. § 78-14-5(4); Utah Code Ann. § 75-2-1107(2)(b).

**VA:** Va. Code Ann. § 54.1-2986.

**WA:** Wash. Rev. Code Ann. § 7.70.065(1).

**WV:** W. Va. Code § 16-5C-5a(b); W. Va. Code § 16-5B-8a(b); W. Va. Code § 16-30B-7(a). 1989 URTIA § 7(b).

Although the intent of such priority lists is a good one—to eliminate possible confusion about who has the legal authority to make decisions for incompetent patients—the result of surrogate-designation pursuant to statute is not only mechanical but can be contrary or even inimical to the patient's wishes or best interests.[17] This would occur, for example, if the patient were estranged from his spouse or parents. However, it is not clear that the result would be much different in the absence of a statute because the ordinary custom of physicians, sanctioned by judicial decision,[18] is to look to incompetent patients' close family members to make decisions for them. In the absence of a statute, the physician might ignore a spouse known to be estranged from the patient in favor of another close family member as surrogate, but because there is nothing in most statutes to permit a physician to ignore the statutory order of priority, the result could be worse under a statute than in its absence.

It is not always clear whether statutes that list parents among surrogate decisionmakers intend to allow a parent of a minor child to serve as surrogate for that child, though that is clearly the common-law rule.[19] Some surrogate decision-making statutes specifically provide that a parent may be a surrogate deci-sionmaker for a minor child.[20] However, most specifically apply to surrogate decisionmaking for persons who are over the age of 18 years.[21] In some of these

---

[17] *See, e.g.,* Loewy, *Advance Directives and Surrogate Laws: Ethical Instruments or Moral Cop-out?,* 152 Archives Internal Med. 1973, 1973 (1992) (surrogate decisionmaking statutes "motivated less by a genuine respect for actual informed patient choice than by the feeling that physicians and hospitals now need not trouble themselves in making truly critical and some-times agonizing decisions").

[18] See §§ **5.10–5.14.**

[19] *See, e.g.,* Mo. Ann. Stat. § 431.061(1), (2). See §§ **15.2–15.4.**

[20] **AR:** Ark. Code Ann. § 20-17-214; Ark. Code Ann. § 20-9-602(2) (parent empowered to consent to treatment of "minor child or . . . adult child of unsound mind").

**GA:** Ga. Code Ann. § 31-9-2(a)(2); Ga. Code Ann. § 31-39-4(d) (CPR).

**ID:** Idaho Code § 39-4303(a).

**IL:** Ill. Ann. Stat. ch. 755, § 40/20(b)(1), *construed in* C.A. v. Morgan, 603 N.E.2d 1171, 1178 n.1 (Ill. App. Ct. 1992).

**IN:** Ind. Code Ann. § 16-8-12-4(b).

**LA:** La. Rev. Stat. Ann. § 40:1299.53(A)(6).

**MS:** Miss. Code Ann. § 41-41-3(b).

**UT:** Utah Code Ann. § 78-14-5(4)(a).

[21] **AZ:** Ariz. Rev. Stat. Ann. § 36-3231 (adult).

**CO:** Colo. Rev. Stat. § 15-18.5-103(3) (adult).

**DC:** D.C. Code Ann. § 21-2210 (adult).

**FL:** Fla. Stat. Ann. § 765.401 (adult).

**HI:** Haw. Rev. Stat. § 327D-21 (age of majority).

**IN:** Ind. Code Ann. § 16-8-11-14.

**IA:** Iowa Code Ann. § 144A.7 (adult).

**KY:** Ky. Rev. Stat. Ann. § 311.631(1) (adult).

statutes, though, there are separate provisions dealing with decisionmaking for minors.[22]

## § 14.5  Unavailability of Potential Surrogates

When an individual or class of individuals entitled to make decisions for a patient declines to serve or is not available within a reasonable time for consultation, statutes generally provide that the next priority individual or class of individuals is authorized to make decisions.[23] In addition, some statutes

---

**LA:** La. Rev. Stat. Ann. § 40:1299.58.5 (adult) (parent authorized to consent for minor child).

**ME:** Me. Rev. Stat. Ann. tit. 18-A, § 5-707(b).

**MD:** Md. Code Ann., Health-Gen. § 5-601(F) (competent individual).

**MT:** Mont. Code Ann. § 50-9-102(11).

**NV:** Nev. Rev. Stat. Ann. § 449.585.

**NY:** N.Y. Pub. Health Law § 2965(1).

**OH:** Ohio Rev. Code Ann. § 2133.08, *construed in In re* Myers, 610 N.E.2d 663, 668 (P. Ct. Summit County, Ohio 1993) (statute inapplicable to decisionmaking for minor).

**OR:** Or. Rev. Stat. § 127.635.

**SC:** S.C. Code Ann. § 44-66-20(6) (statute does not affect delivery of health care to minors unless they are married or have been judicially determined to be emancipated).

**SD:** S.D. Codified Laws Ann. § 34-12C-3 (adult).

**TX:** Tex. Health & Safety Code Ann. § 672.009 (adult); Tex. Health & Safety Code Ann. § 313.00(2)(1) (adult or person who has had disabilities of minority removed).

**UT:** Utah Code Ann. § 75-2-1107(1).

**VA:** Va. Code Ann. § 54.1-2986 (adult).

**WV:** W. Va. Code § 16-30B-3(a).

**WY:** Wyo. Stat. § 35-22-105(b) (adult).

1989 URTIA.

[22] **IN:** Ind. Code Ann. § 16-8-12-4(b).

**LA:** La. Rev. Stat. Ann. § 40:1299.53(A)(6).

**MD:** Md. Code Ann., Health-Gen. § 5-602(E)(1).

**UT:** Utah Code Ann. § 78-14-5(4)(a).

**WV:** W. Va. Code § 16-30B-3(j).

[23] **DC:** D.C. Code Ann. § 21-2210(d).

**KY:** Ky. Rev. Stat. Ann. § 311.631(1).

**ME:** Me. Rev. Stat. Ann. tit. 18-A, § 5-707(c).

**MD:** Md. Code Ann., Health-Gen. § 5-605(A)(2).

**MT:** Mont. Code Ann. § 50-9-106(3).

**NV:** Nev. Rev. Stat. Ann. § 449.626(3).

**ND:** N.D. Cent. Code § 23-12-13(1).

**OH:** Ohio Rev. Code Ann. § 2133.08(C).

provide that if no designated surrogate decisionmaker is available for consultation, the patient's attending physician may make the necessary decisions.[24]

It is not clear, if a lower priority individual serves as surrogate because of the unavailability of a higher priority individual, whether the former thereby acquires the authority to act as surrogate permanently or only until the latter becomes available. In some situations it will not matter because a decision will be made to forgo life-sustaining treatment and the patient will die, but in others—perhaps most—there will be a series of decisions that need to be made.

## § 14.6 Resolution of Disputes Among Potential Surrogates

Most statutes do not specifically anticipate that there may be disagreement among the persons in a particular class of individuals who are designated to serve as surrogate (for example, the patient's adult offspring or the patient's siblings), or that there may be disagreement between the person who is authorized to act as a surrogate by virtue of a high priority on the list (for example, the patient's spouse) and someone lower on the priority list (for example, a sibling of the patient) who would be authorized to act as surrogate if a higher priority

---

**SC:** S.C. Code Ann. § 44-66-20(8) (if attending physician or health care provider determines that delay presents substantial risk of disfigurement, loss or impairment of body part, or serious threat to health of patient).

**TX:** Tex. Health & Safety Code Ann. § 313.004(a) (available after a reasonably diligent inquiry).

**WA:** Wash. Rev. Code Ann. § 7.70.065(2).

**WV:** W. Va. Code § 16-5C-5a (nursing home must document good-faith efforts to contact permitted representatives of all members of class before next class is contacted); W. Va. Code § 16-5B-8a (extended care facility operated in connection with hospital must document good-faith efforts to contact permitted representatives of all members of class before next class is contacted); W. Va. Code § 16-30B-7(b).

1989 URTIA § 7(c).

[24] **AZ:** Ariz. Rev. Stat. Ann. § 36-3231(B) (physician may make health care decisions after consulting with and obtaining recommendations of institutional ethics committee or after consulting with second physician who concurs with decision).

**GA:** Ga. Code Ann. § 31-39-4(e) (attending physician may issue do-not-resuscitate order if ethics committee or similar panel concurs).

**ID:** Idaho Code § 39-4303(c) (if medical emergency or substantial likelihood of endangerment to health of individual, attending physician or dentist may authorize and/or provide necessary health care treatment or procedures).

**NY:** N.Y. Pub. Health Law § 2966(1) (attending physician may issue do-not-resuscitate order).

**NC:** N.C. Gen. Stat. § 90-322(b) (attending physician may withhold or discontinue extraordinary means to prolong life).

**OR:** Or. Rev. Stat. § 127.635(3) (attending physician may withdraw life-sustaining procedures).

individual were not available. In practice, disagreements of these kinds may not be at all infrequent, and therefore the failure of most statutes to address them could easily lead to precisely the kind of uncertainty (and potentially to litigation) that surrogate decisionmaking statutes were enacted to avoid. Although some statutes do recognize that there may be disagreement, the manner in which this disagreement is to be resolved varies considerably.

Even more fundamentally, the statutory provisions addressing disagreements between potential surrogates seem to have been drafted without any awareness that the proper role of the surrogate is not to make a decision per se but to make a decision on the basis of a particular substantive standard, and that the standard dictates the kind of evidence that is to be taken into account. The statutory provisions that do address the resolution of conflicts among members of a class of surrogates are unduly concerned with procedure at the expense of substance. The role of surrogates—or of all members of a class of surrogates if there is more than one—should be to discern and articulate the wishes of the *patient*,[25] not their own wishes; and if the patient's actual or probable wishes are unknown, in some jurisdictions it is their role to determine the *interests* of the patient, not their own wishes or interests.[26] Any decision made by a surrogate that is not based on some conception of the *patient's* wishes or interests is almost certain to be an illegitimate decision.

If the focus is on the patient's actual or probable treatment preferences—or if unknown, the patient's interests—it might be less likely for there to be conflicts between members of a class of surrogates than if the focus is, wrongly, on the wishes or interests of the surrogates. If members of the health care team can get the disputants to focus on the patient's wishes and interests rather than on the disputants' own wishes and interests, it might prove easier to avoid or resolve disputes while remaining faithful to the statutory and common-law standards for decisionmaking by surrogates. This is an extremely important point, not only as a matter of law but also as a matter of clinical practice. When members of a class of surrogates are warring with each other over what decision is to be made about a relative's medical treatment, it may prove helpful for physicians (and lawyers, if they are involved at this stage) to remind the warring parties of their proper role.

None of the surrogate decisionmaking statutes have such a focus. However, some have provisions for disqualifying individuals from serving as a surrogate, presumably on the basis that they do not know the patient's wishes or are unable to carry them out. For instance, the South Carolina statute provides that if a physician or health care provider has knowledge that before becoming unable to consent, the patient did not want the person in question to act as surrogate, the physician or health care provider may not give priority or authority to decide to that person.[27] In Maine and South Dakota, a patient may anticipatorily disqualify

---

[25] See §§ 7.4–7.9.

[26] See §§ 7.11–7.25.

[27] S.C. Code Ann. § 44-66-40(B).

others from consenting to withholding or withdrawing life-sustaining treatment by any writing signed by the patient that designates an individual as disqualified.[28] Such provisions may, however, be of little practical use. Any individual who has the foresight to address matters of surrogate decisionmaking is possibly more likely to have designated a surrogate through a health care power of attorney, thereby avoiding the effect of surrogate decisionmaking statutes, than to disqualify one or more individuals from acting under the statute.

The Illinois statute anticipates what is possibly a more likely situation: an objection by a patient to either the surrogate decisionmaker or to a decision made by the surrogate. If that occurs, the provisions of the statute do not apply.[29] If the patient is competent when objecting, the patient should be viewed as the decisionmaker wholly apart from the statute,[30] but if the patient is not competent when objecting, the statute does not address how decisionmaking should proceed.[31]

In the statutes that do contain a formula for resolving disputes, they are of the following types:

1.  *Equal Division of Opinion in Class.* Most statutes are silent as to what is to occur if there is an equal division of opinion among members of the same class of potential surrogates. The Ohio statute expressly provides that if equal division of a priority class of individuals occurs, no consent to withhold or withdraw life-sustaining treatment may be given.[32] Though the statute does not so state, presumably treatment must be continued, at least until one of the individuals changes his mind and the tie is broken or until judicial resolution is sought. Similarly, the Washington statute provides that if a person of higher priority refuses to give authorization, or if there are two or more individuals in the same class and the decision is not unanimous among all available class members, no person may validly authorize the administration of health care,[33] and presumably the judicial appointment of a guardian must be obtained. Others at least provide direction as to how *not* to proceed in such a situation, namely, that the next class of individuals is not authorized to make decisions.[34]

---

[28] **ME:** Me. Rev. Stat. Ann. tit. 18-A, § 5-707(g).

   **SD:** S.D. Codified Laws Ann. § 34-12C-3.

[29] Ill. Ann. Stat. ch. 755, § 40/20(c).

[30] See §§ **3.3** and **10.14.**

[31] See §§ **7.45–7.46.**

[32] Ohio Rev. Code Ann. § 2133.08(C).

[33] Wash. Rev. Code Ann. § 7.70.065(2)(a), (b).

[34] **ME:** Me. Rev. Stat. Ann. tit. 18-A, § 5-707(c).

   **MT:** Mont. Code Ann. § 50-9-106(3).

   **NV:** Nev. Rev. Stat. Ann. § 449.626(3).

   **OH:** Ohio Rev. Code Ann. § 2133.08(C).

   **WA:** Wash. Rev. Code Ann. § 7.70.065(2)(b).

   1989 URTIA § 7(c).

2. *Majority Governs.* Some statutes provide that the decision of the majority of a class of surrogates governs. For example, in Illinois[35] and Virginia,[36] when two or more surrogate decisionmakers at the same priority level disagree about the health care matter at issue, the majority of available persons in that category controls the decision.

3. *Petitioning for Guardianship.* One remedy for resolving serious disagreement or a deadlock is for any member of the group to seek judicial guidance by petitioning for guardianship. Some statutes specifically provide for this remedy,[37] but even when they do not, recourse to the courts is appropriate under general common-law principles.[38] Other statutes provide that any individual in a priority category may seek guardianship of the patient.[39] In Virginia, however, the statute permits *any* person to petition a court to enjoin the withholding, withdrawal, or provision of life-sustaining treatment.[40]

4. *Consensus.* A less drastic approach than initiating judicial proceedings, and one that ought to be tried first regardless of what the statutes prescribe, is for the disputants, with the assistance of members of the health care team, to attempt to reach a consensus among themselves. Only a few statutes state that it is the responsibility of the group of individuals at the same priority level to make reasonable efforts to reach a consensus among themselves regarding the decision for the patient.[41]

---

[35] Ill. Ann. Stat. ch. 755, § 40/25(a).

[36] Va. Code Ann. § 54.1-2986(A).

[37] **IL:** Ill. Ann. Stat. ch. 755, § 40/25(a).

[38] See **§ 5.31.**

[39] **CO:** Colo. Rev. Stat. § 15-18.5-103(4)(a).

**DC:** D.C. Code Ann. § 21-2210 (may challenge decision made by person of higher priority).

**IL:** Ill. Ann. Stat. ch. 755, § 40/25(d).

**ME:** Me. Rev. Stat. Ann. tit. 18-A, § 5-707(f) (person with significant relationship with incapacitated individual may challenge decision).

**NY:** N.Y. Pub. Health Law § 2965(4)(d) (if attending physician has notice of opposition to a surrogate's consent to do-not-resuscitate order, physician shall submit matter to dispute mediation system).

**OH:** Ohio Rev. Code Ann. § 2133.08(E) (provides extensive guidelines regarding procedure to challenge decision of surrogate decisionmaker).

**SC:** S.C. Code Ann. § 44-66-30(B) (petition for guardianship or order determining what care is to be provided).

**WV:** W. Va. Code § 16-30B-7(d) (individual on priority list may challenge decision).

[40] Va. Code Ann. § 54.1-2986(E).

[41] **CO:** Colo. Rev. Stat. § 15-18.5-103(4)(a).

**IL:** Ill. Ann. Stat. ch. 755, § 40/25(a).

**LA:** La. Rev. Stat. Ann. § 40:1299.58.5(A)(3); La. Rev. Stat. Ann. § 40:1299.53(B).

5. *Other Approaches.* In cases of conflict between decisionmakers, the Maryland statute allows the health care provider to consult with the institution's statutorily mandated patient care advisory committee. The physician can then either act in accordance with the committee's recommendation or transfer the patient.[42] The Missouri statute allows consent by one authorized surrogate to be sufficient even if another authorized surrogate disagrees or even protests possible treatment,[43] thereby potentially exacerbating rather than resolving disagreement among next of kin.

## § 14.7  Scope of Decisionmaking Authority

Although many of the surrogate decisionmaking statutes give surrogate decisionmakers broad discretion to make health care or medical treatment decisions,[44] some are limited to decisions regarding the withholding or withdrawal of life-sustaining procedures, or even more narrowly to decisions not to resuscitate, that do not involve a substantial risk to life, or only to patients in particular kinds of facilities. See **Table 14–1.** In addition, some specifically prohibit decisions regarding certain procedures such as abortion or sterilization,[45] and some contain specific guidelines for surrogates to follow in making

---

[42] Md. Code Ann., Health-Gen. § 5-605(B)(1).

[43] Mo. Ann. Stat. § 431.061(4).

[44] **AZ:** Ariz. Rev. Stat. Ann. § 36-3231.

**CO:** Colo. Rev. Stat. §§ 15-18.5-101 to -103.

**DC:** D.C. Code Ann. §§ 21-2210, -2211.

**FL:** Fla. Stat. Ann. § 765.401.

**GA:** Ga. Code Ann. §§ 31-39-1 to -9.

**ID:** Idaho Code § 39-4303.

**IN:** Ind. Code Ann. § 16-8-12-4.

**LA:** La. Rev. Stat. Ann. § 40:1299.53(A).

**MD:** Md. Code Ann., Health-Gen. § 5-602(A).

**MS:** Miss. Code Ann. § 41-41-3.

**MO:** Mo. Ann. Stat. § 431.061(1).

**SC:** S.C. Code Ann. §§ 44-66-10 to -80.

**SD:** S.D. Codified Laws Ann. § 34-12C-3.

**TX:** Tex. Health & Safety Code Ann. § 672.009.

**UT:** Utah Code Ann. § 78-14-5(4).

**WA:** Wash. Rev. Code Ann. § 7.70.065.

[45] **DC:** D.C. Code Ann. §§ 21-2210, -2211.

**GA:** Ga. Code Ann. § 31-9-5.

**LA:** La. Rev. Stat. Ann. § 40:1299.51.

**MD:** Md. Code Ann., Health-Gen. § 20-107(f)(1).

**ND:** N.D. Cent. Code § 23-12-13(4).

**VA:** Va. Code Ann. § 54.1-2986(C).

decisions for pregnant patients[46] or when the decision involves the withholding or withdrawal of artificial nutrition and hydration.[47] Other restrictions upon decisionmaking may apply as well when the decision involves a patient who is a potential organ donor[48] or a neonate,[49] requires treatment for mental illness of certain kinds,[50] or is considered to be only temporarily unable to make a health care decision.[51]

---

[46] **IA:** Iowa Code Ann. § 144A.7(3) (procedure of appointing surrogate decisionmaker shall not be in effect for patient who is known to attending physician to be pregnant with a fetus that could develop to the point of live birth with continued application of life-sustaining procedures).

**MS:** Miss. Code Ann. § 41-41-3 (statute may not "be construed to abridge any right of an adult . . . who is not pregnant . . . to refuse such consent as to [her] own person").

**MT:** Mont. Code Ann. § 50-9-106 (surrogate may not authorize forgoing of life-sustaining treatment for patient known to attending physician to be pregnant if probable that fetus will develop to point of live birth with continued application of life-sustaining treatment).

**NV:** Nev. Rev. Stat. Ann. § 449.626(b) (same).

**OH:** Ohio Rev. Code Ann. § 2133.08(G) (life-sustaining treatment may not be foregone in case of pregnant patient without declaration if forgoing of treatment would terminate pregnancy, unless attending physician and one other physician determine that fetus would not be born alive).

1989 URTIA § 7(f).

[47] **AZ:** Ariz. Rev. Stat. Ann. § 36-3231(D).

**CO:** Colo. Rev. Stat. § 15-18.5-103(6) (surrogate may not forgo nutrition and hydration unless physicians certify that it is merely prolonging dying and is unlikely to result in restoration of patient to independent neurological functioning).

**CT:** Conn. Gen. Stat. Ann. § 19a-571(a) (surrogate may not forgo nutrition and hydration unless patient is in terminal condition or permanently unconscious).

**KY:** Ky. Rev. Stat. Ann. § 311.631(4) (may only authorize forgoing artificial nutrition and hydration if death is expected within a few days, patient is permanently unconscious, or artificial nutrition and hydration cannot be assimilated, or when burden of providing it outweighs benefit).

[48] **HI:** Haw. Rev. Stat. § 327D-20 (no physician participating in decision to withdraw or withhold life-sustaining procedures for declarant may participate in transplanting vital organs of declarant to another).

[49] **IL:** Ill. Ann. Stat. ch. 755, § 40/40 (nothing in this statute supersedes provision of 45 C.F.R. § 1340.15 concerning provision of "appropriate" nutrition, hydration, and medication to neonates).

[50] **DC:** D.C. Code Ann. §§ 21-2210, -2211 (psychosurgery, convulsive therapy, or behavior modification involving adverse stimuli).

**LA:** La. Rev. Stat. Ann. § 40:1299.52 (except as provided in living will statute, provisions of medical consent law shall not apply to care and treatment of mentally ill).

**MD:** Md. Code Ann., Health-Gen. § 20-107(f)(1) (treatment or hospitalization of patient with mental illness).

**TX:** Tex. Health & Safety Code Ann. § 313.004 (voluntary inpatient mental health services).

**VA:** Va. Code Ann. § 54.1-2986(C) (psychotherapy or admission to mental retardation facility or psychiatric hospital).

[51] **SC:** S.C. Code Ann. § 44-66-30(E) (surrogate not authorized to make health care decisions on behalf of patient who is unable to consent if patient's inability to consent is temporary and delay occasioned by postponing treatment until patient regains ability to consent will not result in significant detriment to patient's health).

## § 14.8  Substantive Standards for Decisionmaking

Most surrogate decisionmaking statutes provide at least limited guidance concerning the standard that the surrogate is to apply in making a decision for the patient, although some statutes (Arkansas, Louisiana, Mississippi, Missouri, North Carolina, and Oregon) do not contain any standard. In the long run, this could turn out to be the most important aspect of surrogate decisionmaking statutes. Although statutory clarification that family members have the legal authority to make decisions for incompetent patients without judicial appointment as guardian is helpful, the customary medical practice of doing so is so well established that if that is all the statutes accomplished, they would be of marginal value.

What is far less certain in jurisdictions without any precedential case law is the standard to which the surrogate must adhere in order to make a legally valid decision about forgoing or administering life-sustaining treatment. This is a central issue in all appellate cases of first impression. Although it is true that virtually all appellate cases that have addressed the issue have adopted the substituted judgment standard,[52] that does not mean that every court that considers this issue anew will necessarily do so. And if there is inadequate evidence to meet the substituted judgment standard, the legitimacy of applying the best interests standard—the standard which is often applied if the substituted judgment standard cannot be satisfied but which is not nearly as widely accepted[53]— is open to even greater uncertainty.

With only minor exceptions, the statutory standards are consistent with the common-law standards for surrogate decisionmaking. Most statutes expressly or impliedly require that a subjective or substituted judgment standard be applied.[54] In most of the statutes, it is sometimes explicit but sometimes only

---

[52] See §§ 7.7–7.10.

[53] See §§ 7.11–7.25.

[54] **CO:** Colo. Rev. Stat. §§ 15-18.5-101 to -103 (implicit substituted judgment standard; person selected as proxy decisionmaker should be person who has close relationship with patient and who is most likely to be currently informed of patient's wishes regarding medical treatment decisions).

**DC:** D.C. Code Ann. § 21-2210(b) (substituted judgment or best interests standard; decision shall be based on known wishes of patient or, if wishes are not known and cannot be ascertained, on good-faith belief regarding best interests of patient).

**FL:** Fla. Stat. Ann. § 765.401(2) (substituted judgment standard; proxy's decision to withhold or withdraw life-prolonging procedures must be supported by clear and convincing evidence that decision would have been one that patient would have chosen had he been competent).

**GA:** Ga. Code Ann. § 31-9-2(b) (substituted judgment standard; person authorized to consent shall act in good faith to consent to surgical or medical treatment or procedures that patient would have wanted had patient understood circumstances under which such treatment or procedures are provided); Ga. Code Ann. § 31-39-4(c) (substituted judgment standard; consent to order not to resuscitate must be based in good faith upon what surrogate determines patient would have wanted had patient understood circumstances under which order was being considered).

**IL:** Ill. Ann. Stat. ch. 755, § 40/20(b)(1) (mixed substituted judgment/best interests standard; surrogate decisionmaker shall make decisions for adult patient conforming as close as possible to what patient would have done or intended under circumstances, taking into account evidence that includes, but is not limited to, patient's personal, philosophical, religious, and moral beliefs and ethical values relative to purposes of life, sickness, medical procedures, suffering, and death; where possible, surrogate shall determine how patient would have weighed burdens and benefits of initiating or continuing life-sustaining treatment against burdens and benefits of that treatment), *construed in* C.A. v. Morgan, 603 N.E.2d 1171, 1183 (Ill. App. Ct. 1992) ("[T]he Act adopts the substituted judgment test to be used when the patient had expressed views on the subject before becoming incompetent.").

**IA:** Iowa Code Ann. § 144A.7(1) (subjective or substituted judgment standard; individual shall be guided by express or implied intentions of patient).

**KY:** Ky. Rev. Stat. Ann. § 311.631(3) (priority individual shall act "in accordance with any advance directive executed by the individual").

**ME:** Me. Rev. Stat. Ann. tit. 18-A, § 5-707(d) (best interests standard; decision must be made in best interests of individual consistent with individual's desires, if known, and in good faith).

**MD:** Md. Code Ann., Health-Gen. § 5-605(C) (substituted judgment standard; decisions based on patient's wishes).

**NM:** N.M. Stat. Ann. § 24-7-8.1(A) (substituted judgment standard; decision to remove maintenance medical treatment may be made by physician when all family members who can be contacted through reasonable diligence agree in good faith that patient, if competent, would choose to forgo treatment).

**NY:** N.Y. Pub. Health Law § 2965(3)(a) (substituted judgment or best interests standard; surrogate shall make decision regarding CPR on basis of adult patient's wishes, including a consideration of patient's religious and moral beliefs, or, if patient's wishes are unknown and cannot be ascertained, on basis of patient's best interests).

**ND:** N.D. Cent. Code § 23-12-13(3) (substituted judgment standard; must determine patient would consent if not incapacitated).

**TX:** Tex. Health & Safety Code Ann. § 672.009(c); Tex. Health & Safety Code Ann. § 313.005(c) (substituted judgment standard; treatment decision must be based on knowledge of what patient would desire, if known).

**VA:** Va. Code Ann. § 54.1-2986(A) (substituted judgment/best interests standard; any person authorized to consent must base decision on patient's religious beliefs and basic values and any preferences previously expressed by patient regarding such treatment to extent they are known, and if unknown or unclear, on patient's best interests).

**WA:** Wash. Rev. Code Ann. § 7.70.065(3) (substituted judgment/best interests standard; person authorized to consent must first determine in good faith that patient, if competent, would consent to proposed health care; if such determination cannot be made, decision to consent to proposed health care may be made only after determining that proposed health care is in patient's best interests).

**WV:** W. Va. Code § 16-30B-8(a) (surrogate shall make health care decisions "[i]n accordance with the person's wishes including religious and moral beliefs").

**WY:** Wyo. Stat. § 35-22-105(b) (substituted judgment standard; physician may remove maintenance medical treatment when all family members who can be contacted through reasonable diligence agree in good faith that patient, if competent, would choose to forgo that treatment); Wyo. Stat. § 3-5-209(b) (same).

implicit that the subjective standard is the preferable standard and that the substituted judgment standard should be applied only if the subjective standard cannot be met. Only the Ohio statute expressly requires application of a subjective standard unless it cannot be met, in which case the substituted judgment standard is to be applied.[55] Some statutes specifically provide that it is impermissible for the surrogate's decision to conflict with the patient's expressed wishes.[56] Oddly, the South Dakota statute seems to require application of a subjective standard, but if it cannot be met, the best interests standard may be applied without first attempting to apply a substituted judgment standard.[57]

In those jurisdictions requiring the application of a subjective and/or substituted judgment standard, the statute sometimes provides that a best interests standard may be applied if one of the other standards cannot be met.[58] In other

---

[55] Ohio Rev. Code Ann. § 2133.08(D) (decision shall be valid only if it is consistent with any previously expressed intent of patient; if no previously expressed intent by patient, consent shall be valid only if it is consistent with type of informed consent decision that patient would have made, as inferred from lifestyle and character of patient and any other evidence of desires of patient prior to his becoming no longer able to make informed decisions regarding administration of life-sustaining treatment).

[56] **ME:** Me. Rev. Stat. Ann. tit. 18-A, § 5-707(d) (decision must be made in best interests of individual consistent with individual's desires, if known, and in good faith; consent is not valid if it conflicts with expressed intention of individual).

**MD:** Md. Code Ann., Health-Gen. § 20-107(f)(2) (substituted consent may not be given if health care provider is aware that person for whom health care is proposed has expressed disagreement with decision to provide health care).

**MT:** Mont. Code Ann. § 50-9-106(4) (decision to grant or withhold consent must be made in good faith; consent is not valid if it conflicts with expressed intention of individual).

**NV:** Nev. Rev. Stat. Ann. § 449.626(4) (decision to grant or withhold consent must be made in good faith; consent is not valid if it conflicts with expressed intention of individual).

1989 URTIA § 7(d).

[57] S.D. Codified Laws Ann. § 34-12C-3 (person authorized to make health care decision for incapacitated person shall be guided by express wishes of incapacitated person, if known, and shall otherwise act in good faith, in incapacitated person's best interests, and may not arbitrarily refuse consent; person making health care decision for incapacitated person shall consider recommendation of attending physician, decision incapacitated person would have made if he had decisional capacity, if known, and decision that would be in best interests of incapacitated person).

[58] **DC:** D.C. Code Ann. § 21-2210(b) (decision shall be based on known wishes of patient or, if wishes are not known and cannot be ascertained, on good-faith belief regarding best interests of patient).

**IL:** Ill. Ann. Stat. ch. 755, § 40/20(b)(1) (surrogate should weigh burdens and benefits of initiating or continuing life-sustaining treatment against burdens and benefits of that treatment), *construed in* C.A. v. Morgan, 603 N.E.2d 1171, 1183 (Ill. App. Ct. 1992) ("The Health Care Surrogate Act expressly recognizes that the best interests standard, rather than substituted judgment, applies in the case of incompetents, including minors, whose consent or desire cannot be discerned.").

jurisdictions, it is possible to infer that the statute intends for a best interests standard to be used,[59] but in the remaining statutes it is unclear whether treatment must be continued when the subjective or substituted judgment standard cannot be met. This approach is also consistent with the common law, which varies considerably about the permissibility of using the best interests standard.[60] Other statutes require the surrogate decisionmaker to act in good faith.[61] Only

---

**KY:** Ky. Rev. Stat. Ann. § 311.631(3) (priority individual shall act "in the best interest of the individual who does not have decisional capacity").

**ME:** Me. Rev. Stat. Ann. tit. 18-A, § 5-707(d) (decision must be made in best interests of individual consistent with individual's desires, if known, and in good faith).

**MD:** Md. Code Ann., Health-Gen. § 5-605(C).

**NY:** N.Y. Pub. Health Law § 2965(3)(a) (surrogate shall make decision regarding CPR on basis of adult patient's wishes, including a consideration of patient's religious and moral beliefs, or, if patient's wishes are unknown and cannot be ascertained, on basis of patient's best interests).

**ND:** N.D. Cent. Code § 23-12-13(3).

**SD:** S.D. Codified Laws Ann. § 34-12C-3 (person authorized to make health care decision for incapacitated person shall be guided by express wishes of incapacitated person, if known, and shall otherwise act in good faith, in incapacitated person's best interests, and may not arbitrarily refuse consent; person making health care decision for incapacitated person shall consider recommendation of attending physician, decision incapacitated person would have made if he had decisional capacity, if known, and decision that would be in best interests of incapacitated person).

**VA:** Va. Code Ann. § 54.1-2986(A) (any person authorized to consent must base decision on patient's religious beliefs and basic values and any preferences previously expressed by patient regarding such treatment to extent they are known, and if unknown or unclear, on patient's best interests).

**WA:** Wash. Rev. Code Ann. § 7.70.065(3) (person authorized to consent must first determine in good faith that patient, if competent, would consent to proposed health care; if such determination cannot be made, decision to consent to proposed health care may be made only after determining that proposed health care is in patient's best interests).

**WV:** W. Va. Code § 16-30B-8(a)(2).

**WY:** Wyo. Stat. § 35-22-105(b) (physician may remove maintenance medical treatment when all family members who can be contacted through reasonable diligence agree in good faith that patient, if competent, would choose to forgo that treatment); Wyo. Stat. § 3-5-209(b) (same).

[59] **IL:** Ill. Ann. Stat. ch. 755, § 40/20(b)(1) (where possible, surrogate shall determine how patient would have weighed burdens and benefits of initiating or continuing life-sustaining treatment against burdens and benefits of that treatment).

**TX:** Tex. Health & Safety Code Ann. § 672.009(c) (treatment decision must be based on what patient would desire, if known).

[60] See §§ 7.11–7.25.

[61] **CT:** Conn. Gen. Stat. Ann. § 19a-571(a) (all persons acting on behalf of patient shall act in good faith; physician to use best medical judgment).

**KY:** Ky. Rev. Stat. Ann. § 311.631(3) (surrogate shall act in good faith, in accordance with patient's advance directives, and in best interest of patient).

**MT:** Mont. Code Ann. § 50-9-106(4) (decision to grant or withhold consent must be made in good faith; consent is not valid if it conflicts with expressed intention of individual).

Indiana purports to apply a best interests standard without first requiring an attempt to apply a subjective or substituted judgment standard.[62] However, if express or implied evidence of the patient's wishes were known and conflicted with the decision of a surrogate pursuant to a best interests standard, the more subjective standards should govern.[63]

## § 14.9   Immunity

Those surrogate decisionmaking provisions that are part of living will, health care power of attorney, combined advance directive, or DNR legislation partake of the statutory immunity provided by those statutes.[64] Some of the free standing surrogate decisionmaking statutes confer on physicians and other health care providers immunity from civil and criminal liability and from professional discipline if they act in conformity with the surrogate decisionmaking statute.[65] Some also confer immunity on surrogates.[66] The scope of and standards for applying these provisions are variable.

---

**NV:** Nev. Rev. Stat. Ann. § 449.626(4) (decision to grant or withhold consent must be made in good faith; consent is not valid if it conflicts with expressed intention of individual).

**ND:** N.D. Cent. Code § 23-12-13(3) (determination of patient's interests must be in good faith).

1989 URTIA § 7(d) (decision to grant or withhold consent must be made in good faith; consent not valid if it conflicts with expressed intention of individual).

[62] Ind. Code Ann. § 16-8-12-4(d) (individual authorized to consent shall act in good faith and in best interests of individual incapable of consenting), *construed in In re* Lawrance, 579 N.E.2d 32 (Ind. 1991).

[63] **CA:** *But see* Drabick v. Drabick, 245 Cal. Rptr. 840 (Ct. App. 1988) (holding that best interests standard takes precedence, at least as to patient in persistent vegetative state). See § **7.2.**

[64] See §§ **11.17** and **12.46.** See also § **17.24.**

[65] **CO:** Colo. Rev. Stat. § 15-18.5-101.

**IL:** Ill. Ann. Stat. ch. 755, § 40/30.

**IN:** Ind. Code Ann. § 16-36-1-10.

**SC:** S.C. Code Ann. § 44-66-70.

**WV:** W. Va. Code § 16-30B-1.

[66] **IL:** Ill. Ann. Stat. ch. 755, § 40/30.

**IN:** Ind. Code Ann. § 16-36-1-10.

**SC:** S.C. Code Ann. § 44-66-70.

**TX:** Tex. Health & Safety Code Ann. § 313.007(a) (if acting in good faith).

## § 14.10   Table of Surrogate Decisionmaking Statutes

### Table 14–1

### Surrogate Decisionmaking Statutes

| | |
|---|---|
| **AZ:** | Ariz. Rev. Stat. Ann. § 36-3231[1] |
| **AR:** | Ark. Code Ann. § 20-17-214[2] |
| | Ark. Code Ann. § 20-9-602(2)[3,a] |
| **CA:** | Cal. Civ. Code § 1418.8[b] |
| **CO:** | Colo. Rev. Stat. §§ 15-18.5-101 to -103 |
| **CT:** | Conn. Gen. Stat. Ann. § 19a-571[1] |
| **DC:** | D.C. Code Ann. § 21-2210[4] |
| **FL:** | Fla. Stat. Ann. § 765.401[2] |
| **GA:** | Ga. Code Ann. §§ 31-9-1 to -7[3] |
| | Ga. Code Ann. §§ 31-39-1 to -9[5] |
| **HI:** | Haw. Rev. Stat. § 327D-21[c] |
| **ID:** | Idaho Code § 39-4303[3] |
| **IL:** | Ill. Ann. Stat. ch. 755, §§ 40/1–40/55 |
| **IN:** | Ind. Code Ann. §§ 16-36-1-1 to -14 |
| | Ind. Code Ann. § 16-36-4-13[2] |
| **IA:** | Iowa Code Ann. § 144A.7[2] |
| **KY:** | Ky. Rev. Stat. Ann. § 311.631 |
| **LA:** | La. Rev. Stat. Ann. § 40:1299.53(A)[3] |
| | La. Rev. Stat. Ann. § 40:1299.58.5[2] |
| **ME:** | Me. Rev. Stat. Ann. tit. 18-A, § 5-707(b)[3] |
| **MD:** | Md. Code Ann., Health-Gen. § 5-605(B)[1] |
| | Md. Code Ann., Health-Gen. § 20-107(f)(2) |
| **MS:** | Miss. Code Ann. § 41-41-3[3] |
| **MO:** | Mo. Ann. Stat. § 431.061[3] |
| **MT:** | Mont. Code Ann. §§ 50-9-101 to -106[2] |
| **NV:** | Nev. Rev. Stat. Ann. §§ 449.535–.690[2] |
| **NM:** | N.M. Stat. Ann § 24-7-8.1.(A)[2] |
| **NY:** | N.Y. Pub. Health Law § 2965(4)[5] |
| **NC:** | N.C. Gen. Stat. § 90-322[2] |
| | N.C. Gen. Stat. §§ 32A-28 to -34[d] |
| **ND:** | N.D. Cent. Code § 23-12-13[3] |
| **OH:** | Ohio Rev. Code Ann. § 2133.08[2] |
| **OR:** | Or. Rev. Stat. § 127.635(2)[1] |
| **SC:** | S.C. Code Ann. §§ 44-66-10 to -80 |
| **SD:** | S.D. Codified Laws Ann. § 34-12C-3[3] |
| **TX:** | Tex. Health & Safety Code Ann. §§ 313.001–.007 |
| | Tex. Health & Safety Code Ann. §§ 672.006, .009[2] |
| **UT:** | Utah Code Ann. § 78-14-5(4)(b), (d)[3] |
| | Utah Code Ann. §§ 75-2-1105, -1107[2] |
| **VA:** | Va. Code Ann. § 54.1-2986[1] |
| **WA:** | Wash. Rev. Code Ann. § 7.70.065[3] |
| **WV:** | W. Va. Code §§ 16-30B-1 to -16 |
| | W. Va. Code § 16-5B-81[e] |
| **WY:** | Wyo. Stat. § 35-22-105(b)[2] |
| | Wyo. Stat. § 3-5-209(b)[4] |

[a] Applies only to parent of minor adult child of unsound mind

[b] Applies only to residents in skilled nursing or intermediate care facilities

[c] As interpreted by *In re* Crabtree, No. 86-0031 (Haw. Fam. Ct. 1st Cir. Apr. 26, 1990)

[d] Authorizes parents of minor children to delegate decisions relating to child's health care

[e] Applies only to consent to health care services in extending care facilities operated in connection with hospitals

[1] combined living will and health care power of attorney advance directive statute

[2] living will statute

[3] medical consent or informed consent statute

[4] health care power of attorney statute

[5] applicable only to cardiopulmonary resuscitation

# Bibliography

Areen, J. "The Legal Status of Consent Obtained from Families of Adult Patients to Withhold or Withdraw Treatment." *JAMA* 258 (1987): 229.

English, D. "The Health-Care Decisions Act Represents a Major Advance." *Trusts and Estates* 133 (May 1994): 32.

English, D., and A. Meisel. "The Uniform Health-Care Decisions Act." *Estate Planning* 21 (1994): 355.

Hamann, A. "Family Surrogate Laws: A Necessary Supplement to Living Wills and Durable Powers of Attorney." *Villanova Law Review* 28 (1993): 103.

Loewy, E. "Advance Directives and Surrogate Laws: Ethical Instruments or Moral Cop-out?" *Archives of Internal Medicine* 152 (1992): 1973.

Orentlicher, D. "The Limits of Legislation." *Maryland Law Review* 53 (1994): 1255.

# PART V

# DECISIONMAKING FOR CHILDREN

# CHAPTER 15

# DECISIONMAKING FOR CHILDREN AND NEWBORNS: COMMON-LAW APPROACH

## GENERAL PRINCIPLES OF MEDICAL
## DECISIONMAKING FOR CHILDREN

### § 15.1   Introduction

This chapter discusses the legal principles of decisionmaking about the treatment of children and the special application of these principles in right-to-die cases. The number of right-to-die cases involving children is relatively small,[1] but the principles articulated in them are generally consistent with those evolving in the cases of adult incompetent patients. This is quite understandable because, for legal purposes, children are presumed to be incompetent. There are, however, some differences in principles that, although not illustrated by the right-to-die cases involving children, are made clear in other cases[2] and in legislation and regulations concerning medical decisionmaking for children.[3] To the extent that these basic principles are the same for children as for adults, they are not reiterated in detail in this chapter. Instead the appropriate general chapters on these subjects should be consulted.

### § 15.2   Presumptions of Children's Incompetence
### and Parents as Natural Guardians

Traditionally, the status of infancy has been equated with legal incompetence for purposes of medical decisionmaking.[4] Consequently, children are presumed to

---

[1] **AL:** *Cf.* Gallups v. Carter, 534 So. 2d 585 (Ala. 1988).

**CO:** Carothers v. Department of Insts., 845 P.2d 1179 (Colo. 1993).

**FL:** *In re* Barry, 445 So. 2d 365 (Fla. Dist. Ct. App. 1984).

**GA:** *In re* Doe, 418 S.E.2d 3 (Ga. 1992); *In re* L.H.R., 321 S.E.2d 716 (Ga. 1984).

**IL:** C.A. v. Morgan, 603 N.E.2d 1171 (Ill. App. Ct. 1992).

**LA:** *In re* P.V.W., 424 So. 2d 1015 (La. 1982).

**ME:** *In re* Swan, 569 A.2d 1202 (Me. 1990).

**MA:** *In re* Beth, 587 N.E.2d 1377 (Mass. 1992); Custody of a Minor, 434 N.E.2d 601 (Mass. 1982).

**MI:** Rosebush v. Oakland County Prosecutor, 491 N.W.2d 633 (Mich. Ct. App. 1992).

**NY:** Weber v. Stony Brook Hosp., 467 N.Y.S.2d 685 (App. Div.) (per curiam), *aff'd,* 456 N.E.2d 1186 (N.Y.), *cert. denied,* 464 U.S. 1026 (1983); *In re* Richardson, 581 N.Y.S.2d 708 (Sup. Ct. Monroe County 1992).

**OH:** *In re* Myers, 610 N.E.2d 663 (P. Ct. Summit County, Ohio 1993); *In re* Crum, 580 N.E.2d 876 (P. Ct. Franklin County, Ohio 1991).

**WA:** *In re* Grant, 747 P.2d 445 (Wash. 1987), *modified,* 757 P.2d 534 (Wash. 1988).

**WV:** Belcher v. Charleston Area Medical Ctr., 422 S.E.2d 827 (W. Va. 1992).

[2] See §§ **15.5–15.6.**

[3] See **Ch. 16.**

[4] Wilkins, *Children's Rights: Removing the Parental Consent Barrier to Medical Treatment of Minors,* 1975 Ariz. St. L.J. 31 ("Because medical decisions are so important, in most instances

lack the capacity to make decisions about their medical care. The correlative of this presumption is another presumption: that a child's parents are the "natural guardians"[5] who will act in the child's best interests,[6] and who thereby possess the authority to make medical decisions for the child without the necessity of being judicially appointed as guardians.[7] To say that parents are natural guardians is to recognize that a child is de jure incompetent and therefore need not be adjudicated incompetent. According to the Georgia Supreme Court, quoting the United States Supreme Court, the basis of this presumption

> is the importance of the family in our society. . . . "The law's concept of the family rests on a presumption that parents possess what a child lacks in maturity, experience, and capacity for judgment required for making life's difficult decisions. More importantly, historically it has recognized that natural bonds of affection lead parents to act in the best interests of their children." . . . The right of the parent to speak for the minor child is so imbedded in our tradition and common law that it

---

irreversible, and because some minors, especially the younger ones, are thought to be incapable of adequately assessing all pertinent factors, the legal capacity of all minors to make medical decisions has been removed."). *See generally* 42 Am. Jur. 2d *Infants* § 8 (1969).

[5] National Ctr. for State Courts, Guidelines for State Court Decision Making in Life-Sustaining Medical Treatment Cases 113 (2d ed. 1992) (standard 22(A)). 61 Am. Jur. 2d *Physicians and Surgeons* § 178 (Supp. 1987) ("Consent to health care for a minor not authorized to consent . . . may be given by a parent . . . if there is no guardian or other representative.").

[6] **CA:** *In re* Phillip B., 156 Cal. Rptr. 48 (Ct. App. 1979), *cert. denied,* 445 U.S. 949 (1980).

**MA:** Custody of a Minor, 379 N.E.2d 1053, 1065 (Mass. 1978).

**MI:** Rosebush v. Oakland County Prosecutor, 491 N.W.2d 633, 637 (Mich. Ct. App. 1992) ("It is well established that parents speak for their minor children in matters of medical treatment.") (citing first edition of this treatise).

**MO:** Morrison v. State, 252 S.W.2d 97 (Mo. Ct. App. 1952).

**NJ:** Roselle v. City of East Orange, 181 A.2d 751 (N.J. 1962).

**NY:** *In re* Brooklyn Hosp., 258 N.Y.S.2d 621 (Sup. Ct. 1965).

**OH:** *In re* Clark, 185 N.E.2d 128 (C.P. Ohio 1962).

[7] **CO:** Carothers v. Department of Insts., 845 P.2d 1179 (Colo. 1993) (guardianship proceeding necessary only when parents not acting in best interests of child) (dictum).

**DE:** Newmark v. Williams, 588 A.2d 1108, 1115 (Del. 1991) ("Parental authority to make fundamental decisions for minor children is also a recognized common law principle. A doctor commits the tort of battery if he or she performs an operation under normal circumstances without the informed consent of the patient.").

**GA:** *In re* Doe, 418 S.E.2d 3, 6 n.7 (Ga. 1992); *In re* L.H.R., 321 S.E.2d 716, 722 (Ga. 1984) ("[T]he beginning presumption is that the parent has the child's best interest at heart.").

**IL:** C.A. v. Morgan, 603 N.E.2d 1171, 1180 (Ill. App. Ct. 1992).

**MI:** Rosebush v. Oakland County Prosecutor, 491 N.W.2d 633, 636–37 (Mich. Ct. App. 1992).

**WV:** Belcher v. Charleston Area Medical Ctr., 422 S.E.2d 827, 838 (W. Va. 1992).

Uniform Model Health-Care Consent Act § 4(b)(2), 9 U.L.A. 453, 461 (1988) [hereinafter UMHCCA].

has been suggested that the constitution requires that the state respect the parent's decision in some areas.[8]

The presumption of parental decisionmaking has been described as "sacred."[9] Thus, it "can be invaded for only the most compelling reasons."[10] The strength of these presumptions is based on the fact that

> [t]he primacy of the familial unit is a bedrock principle of law. *See Stanley v. Illinois,* 405 U.S. 645, 651, 92 S. Ct. 1208, 1212 (1972). . . . Courts, therefore, give great deference to parental decisions involving minor children. In many circumstances the State simply is not an adequate surrogate for the judgment of a loving, nurturing parent. . . . As one commentator aptly recognized, the "law does not have the capacity to supervise the delicately complex interpersonal bonds between parent and child."[11]

## § 15.3 —Mature Minors: Rebuttability of Presumption of Incompetence

The presumptions of incapacity and parental authority are rebuttable if the child is emancipated or mature by common-law or statutory standards. Traditionally, a child who is emancipated possesses most of the legal rights of an adult,[12] including medical decisionmaking capacity.[13] More recently, the common law has come to recognize that, although not emancipated for all purposes, some children are mature enough to make their own medical decisions either in general or in particular circumstances.[14] (There has been less support for this

---

[8] **GA:** *In re* L.H.R., 321 S.E.2d at 722 (*quoting* Parham v. J.R., 442 U.S. 584, 602 (1979)).

**MA:** *Accord In re* McCauley, 565 N.E.2d 411, 413 (Mass. 1991) ("Courts have recognized that the relationship between parents and their children is constitutionally protected, and, therefore, that the private realm of family life must be protected from unwarranted State interference").

[9] Newmark v. Williams, 588 A.2d at 1115.

[10] *Id.*

[11] *Id.* (quoting Goldstein, *Medical Care for the Child at Risk: On State Supervention of Parental Autonomy,* 86 Yale L.J. 645, 650 (1977)).

[12] 67A C.J.S. *Parent and Child* § 6 (1978); Uniform Health-Care Decisions Act § 2(a), 9 U.L.A. pt. I at 93, 105 (West Supp. 1994); UMHCCA § 2(2)(i).

[13] *See* Holder, *Minors' Rights to Consent to Medical Care,* 257 JAMA 3400 (1987); Pilpel, *Minors' Rights to Medical Care,* 36 Alb. L. Rev. 462, 464–65 (1972); National Ctr. for State Courts, Guidelines for State Court Decision Making in Life-Sustaining Medical Treatment Cases 109 (2d ed. 1992) (standard 21).

[14] **CADC:** Kozup v. Georgetown Univ., 851 F.2d 437, 439 (D.C. Cir. 1988) (citing Bonner v. Moran, 126 F.2d 121 (D.C. Cir. 1941)).

**DGA:** Novak v. Cobb County-Kennestone Hosp. Auth., 849 F. Supp. 1559 (N.D. Ga. 1994) (refusing to recognize right of mature minor to refuse treatment).

**IL:** *In re* E.G., 549 N.E.2d 322 (Ill. 1989).

trend in legislation,[15] although the Uniform Health-Care Decisions Act acknowledges the legal authority of mature minors to make advance directives.[16]) This frequently occurs when their parents are not available to make medical decisions and the need for medical care is urgent, yet not so urgent that the emergency exception to informed consent may be invoked.[17] Increasingly, there is also legislative recognition of the need and desirability for older children, and sometimes all children, to be empowered to authorize their own medical care in certain kinds of circumstances.[18] Usually these are situations in which children

---

**KS:** Younts v. St. Francis Hosp. & Sch. of Nursing, Inc., 469 P.2d 330 (Kan. 1970).

**ME:** *Cf. In re* Swan, 569 A.2d 1202 (Me. 1990) (oral advance directive of 17-year-old enforced).

**MI:** Bakker v. Welsh, 108 N.W. 94 (Mich. 1906). *Cf.* Rosebush v. Oakland County Prosecutor, 491 N.W.2d 633, 636 n.4 (Mich. Ct. App. 1992) ("The advance directive of a mature minor, stating the desire that life-sustaining treatment be refused, should be taken into consideration or enforced when deciding whether to terminate the minor's life-support treatment or refuse medical treatment.") (dictum).

**MS:** Gulf & S.I.R.R. v. Sullivan, 119 So. 501 (Miss. 1928).

**NY:** *Cf. In re* Seiferth, 127 N.E.2d 820 (N.Y. 1955) (although not permitting 14-year-old boy to make decision to refuse treatment for surgical treatment of cleft palate, court heavily weighed his opposition along with his father's). *But cf. In re* Long Island Jewish Medical Ctr. (Malcolm), 557 N.Y.S.2d 239 (Sup. Ct. Queens County 1990) (while not rejecting mature minors doctrine, evidence was that minor was not mature).

**OH:** Lacey v. Laird, 139 N.E.2d 25 (Ohio 1956). *Cf. In re* Crum, 580 N.E.2d 876 (P. Ct. Franklin County, Ohio 1991) (oral advance directive of 12-year-old given weight).

**PA:** *In re* Green, 292 A.2d 387 (Pa. 1972).

**TN:** Cardwell v. Bechtol, 724 S.W.2d 739 (Tenn. 1987).

**WV:** Belcher v. Charleston Area Medical Ctr, 422 S.E.2d 827 (W. Va. 1992).

*See also* National Ctr. for State Courts, Guidelines for State Court Decision Making in Life-Sustaining Medical Treatment Cases 109 (2d ed. 1992) (standard 21); UMHCCA § 2(2)(ii)–(iv). *See generally* Pilpel, *Minors' Rights to Medical Care,* 36 Alb. L. Rev. 462, 466 (1972); Stern, *Medical Treatment and the Teenager: The Need for Parental Consent,* 7 Clearinghouse Rev. 1, 3 (1973); Comment, *Minors' Rights to Medical Care,* 14 J. Fam. L. 581, 592 (1975–1976). *But see* O.G. v. Baum, 790 S.W.2d 839 (Tex. Ct. App. 1990) (court did not abuse discretion in appointing temporary guardian of 16-year-old patient of Jehovah's Witness faith, because "state and federal law is unsettled" as to whether he had federal or state constitutional or state common-law right to refuse treatment as mature minor, and evidence was inadequate as to his competency and maturity); Restatement (Second) of Torts § 892A cmt. b (1977) ("If the person consenting is a child . . . the consent may still be effective . . . although the consent of a parent . . . is expressly refused.").

[15] See §§ **11.5** and **12.8.**

[16] Uniform Health-Care Decisions Act § 2(a), (b).

[17] *See* Holder, *Minors' Rights to Consent to Medical Care,* 257 JAMA 3400 (1987).

[18] Pilpel, *Minors' Rights to Medical Care,* 36 Alb. L. Rev. 462, 467 (1972); Wadlington, *Minors and Health Care: The Age of Consent,* 11 Osgoode Hall L.J. 115, 121 (1973); Wilkins, *Children's Rights: Removing the Parental Consent Barrier to Medical Treatment of Minors,* 1975 Ariz. St. L.J. 31, 37; Comment, *Minors' Consent to Medical Care,* 14 J. Fam. L. 581, 593 (1975–1976).

are assumed to be unwilling to seek and obtain treatment if they must obtain parental consent, such as treatment for drug and alcohol abuse, emotional or mental disturbance, contraception, venereal disease, and pregnancy.[19] Finally, the Supreme Court has given constitutional protection to the right of a mature minor, at least insofar as the termination of a pregnancy is concerned. Parental permission cannot be made a prerequisite for a mature minor to obtain an abortion. However, a state may require that there be a judicial determination that the minor is mature, and if that is not the case, for the court to make the decision in the minor's best interests, which may include consideration of parental wishes.[20] In fashioning this requirement, the Court stated that the "abortion decision differs in important ways from other decisions that may be made during minority" but made clear that the basis for the distinction is that abortion, unlike other important decisions such as marriage, cannot be postponed, or it will be made by default with far-reaching consequences.[21] The same can be said of decisions about lifesaving medical treatment, and it is likely that the mature minor rule in this context might also be found to have a constitutional, as well as common-law, basis.

Probably the leading opinion is that of the Illinois Supreme Court in *In re E.G.*[22] The patient was a 17-year-old member of the Jehovah's Witness faith, suffering from an acute nonlymphatic leukemia, the treatment of which would have been advanced by blood transfusions, and which she and her mother both refused. There was expert testimony that without blood transfusions, it was likely that E.G. would die within a month, and that chemotherapy accompanied by transfusions achieves remission in about 80 percent of patients. However, the long-term prognosis was not optimistic, the survival rate being 20 to 25 percent.

The court described the patient as "a minor, but one who was just months shy of her eighteenth birthday, and an individual that the record indicates was mature for her age."[23] The age of majority in Illinois, as in most states, is 18, and thus under a somewhat constrained reading of the precedents, the trial court had entered an order finding E.G. to be neglected and had appointed a guardian to consent to treatment, as her mother had also refused to authorize it. In upholding a reversal of the trial court, the supreme court observed that the age of majority "is not an impenetrable barrier that magically precludes a minor from possessing and exercising certain rights normally associated with adulthood," and that no "'bright line' age restriction of 18 is tenable in restricting the rights of mature minors, whether the rights be based on constitutional or other grounds."[24]

---

[19] UMHCCA § 2 cmt.

[20] Bellotti v. Baird, 443 U.S. 622, 642 (1979) (plurality opinion); *accord* Planned Parenthood of Southeastern Pa. v. Casey, 505 U.S. ____, 112 S. Ct. 2791 (1992) (plurality opinion).

[21] Bellotti v. Baird, 443 U.S. at 643.

[22] 549 N.E.2d 322 (1989).

[23] *Id.* at 325.

[24] *Id.* at 325–26.

Consequently, the court held that "mature minors may possess and exercise rights regarding medical care that are rooted in this State's common law."[25] However, when the treatment refused is for a "life-threatening health problem, . . . the State's *parens patriae* interest is greater than if the health care matter is less consequential."[26]

This much of the opinion seems uncontroversial and merely restates the developing law,[27] though with a greater degree of clarity and authority. However, the court added that in such a situation, if the minor's family—described as "parents . . . , adult siblings, and other relatives"—disagree with the mature minor's decision, "this opposition would weigh heavily against the minor's right to refuse."[28] This latter limitation seems untenable. Apart from the rather broad group of individuals whose objections may be taken into account, there seems to be no more valid ground for considering these objections in the case of a mature minor than in the case of an adult. And in the case of adults, the interests of third parties have been increasingly given short shrift.[29]

Another important case involving a mature minor, because it did not merely recognize the rule but also set forth tests for its application, is *Belcher v. Charleston Area Medical Center.* The case involved a patient of 17 years and 8 months for whom a DNR order was written with the consent of his parents and who died when CPR was withheld pursuant to that order. In a wrongful death action claiming that, because of his maturity, the decision not to resuscitate should have been made by the minor patient, the court adopted the mature minor rule. It also rejected the argument that any common-law mature minor rule that might exist was abrogated by legislation specifically providing for circumstances in which the consent of a minor must be obtained.[30] The court set forth a test for determining maturity. First, whether a minor is mature is a question of fact:

---

[25] *Id.* at 326.

[26] *Id.* at 327.

[27] **DGA:** *But see* Novak v. Cobb County-Kennestone Hosp. Auth., 849 F. Supp. 1559 (N.D. Ga. 1994) (refusing to recognize right of mature minor to refuse treatment).

**NY:** *But see In re* Long Island Jewish Medical Ctr. (Malcolm), 557 N.Y.S.2d 239 (Sup. Ct. Queens County 1990) (no reasons given for finding that patient, a few weeks short of his 18th birthday, who had refused on religious grounds a blood transfusion for the treatment of cancer in combination with chemotherapy and radiation, which would provide a probability of survival of between 20 and 25%, and who was certain to die without the transfusion, was not a mature minor).

**TX:** *But see* O.G. v. Baum, 790 S.W.2d 839 (Tex. Ct. App. 1990) (court did not abuse discretion in appointing temporary guardian of 16-year-old patient of Jehovah's Witness faith, because "state and federal law is unsettled" as to whether he had federal or state constitutional or state common-law right to refuse treatment as mature minor, and evidence was inadequate as to his competency and maturity).

[28] In re E.G., 549 N.E.2d at 328.

[29] See § **8.17.**

[30] **WV:** 422 S.E.2d 827, 837 (W. Va. 1992) (quoting Cardwell v. Bechtol, 724 S.W.2d 739 (Tenn. 1987)).

There is no "hard and fast" rule that would provide a particular age for determining a mature minor. . . . Whether the child has the capacity to consent depends upon the age, ability, experience, education, training, and degree of maturity or judgment obtained by the child, as well as upon the conduct and demeanor of the child at the time of the procedure or treatment . . . [and] whether the minor has the capacity to appreciate the nature, risks, and consequences of the medical procedure to be performed, or the treatment to be administered or withheld.[31]

The court also recognized two difficulties that this rule causes for the attending physician. First, the wishes of a mature minor and those of one or both of the parents might be in conflict. In such a case, "the physician's good faith assessment of the minor's maturity level would immunize him or her from liability for the failure to obtain parental consent."[32] Second, "this [rule] places the doctor in the difficult position of making the determination of whether the minor at issue is mature," a decision for which the doctor "will often be second-guessed."[33] "Consequently," the court recognized, "the doctor, as in every other decision with which he or she is faced, must exercise his or her best medical judgment."[34] The court further advised that "[t]his case is another of many illustrations of the need for good record-keeping in the medical profession. Needless to point out, once the doctor has determined that the minor is mature, this determination should be duly noted as part of the patient's records."[35] This does not seem like precaution enough. When there is conflict between the family and a putatively mature minor, a physician should obtain a second opinion about the child's competency, preferably from a child psychiatrist or psychologist. Any lingering doubt could be removed by a court order. These disputes might be less amenable to resolution in the clinical setting (and thus the need for a court order might prove to be more frequent) than in the case of conflicts among family members of adult incompetent patients. Parents of dying children might have more difficulty in accepting the hopelessness of their child's condition than in the case of adult patients.

The Maine Supreme Court and Michigan Court of Appeals have extended the mature minor rule in sanctioning oral advance directives by mature minors. In *Swan*, the Maine case, the patient was age 17⅓ years when an accident resulted in his lapsing into a persistent vegetative state.[36] The court observed that the

---

[31] **WV:** Belcher v. Charleston Area Medical Ctr., 422 S.E.2d at 837–38.

**NY:** *Accord In re* Long Island Jewish Medical Ctr. (Malcolm), 557 N.Y.S.2d 239.

[32] Belcher v. Charleston Area Medical Ctr., 422 S.E.2d at 838.

[33] *Id.* at 837.

[34] *Id.*

[35] *Id.* at 837 n.14.

[36] **ME:** *In re* Swan, 569 A.2d 1202 (Me. 1990).

**MI:** *Accord* Rosebush v. Oakland County Prosecutor, 491 N.W.2d 633, 636 n.4 (Mich. Ct. App. 1992) ("The advance directive of a mature minor, stating the desire that life-sustaining treatment be refused, should be taken into consideration or enforced when deciding whether to terminate the minor's life-support treatment or refuse medical treatment.").

patient's age "is at most a factor to be considered . . . in assessing the serious-ness and deliberativeness with which his declarations were made."[37] In the Michigan case, *Rosebush,* the court permitted the oral statements of a 16-year-old patient in a persistent vegetative state made when she was 10½ to be taken into account in making a decision about whether to forgo life-sustaining treatment under the substituted judgment standard.[38] An Ohio court followed the same tack when it applied a substituted judgment standard, though in conjunction with a best interests standard, in the case of a 17-year-old patient who had been in a persistent vegetative state since age 12. The evidence that the court found that supported the application of a substituted judgment stand-ard was that witnesses testified that the patient, Dawn, had "expressed her concern regarding a foster child brought into her home who suffered from spina bifida. The foster child, D.J., was confined to a wheel chair and was severely handicapped. Dawn advised her parents and friends that it was unfair for D.J. to have to live that type of existence and she would not want to do so."[39] The court observed that at the age of 12, "she did not have the experience nor the insight to make informed decisions as to her future health care. However, Dawn was exposed to a severely handicapped individual and expressed her opinion that she felt she would not want to live in a severely handicapped situation. From that evidence the court can conclude that Dawn, if she were aware of her present condition, would not want to remain in her current state."[40]

## § 15.4   —Rebuttability of Presumption of Parental Decisionmaking Authority

The presumption of parental decisionmaking authority is also rebuttable and may be supervened if the exercise of that authority constitutes neglect or abuse, or is not exercised in the child's best interests.[41] Parental decisional authority

---

[37] *In re* Swan, 569 A.2d at 1205.

[38] Rosebush v. Oakland County Prosecutor, 491 N.W.2d at 636 n.4.

[39] *In re* Crum, 580 N.E.2d 876, 882 (P. Ct. Franklin County, Ohio 1991).

[40] *Id. Cf. In re* Myers, 610 N.E.2d 663, 670 (P. Ct. Summit County, Ohio 1993) (although patient "is considered legally incompetent as a minor, her age and apparent maturity permit this court to give some weight to her prior statements on removal" of feeding tube).

[41] **CA:** *Cf.* Dority v. Superior Court, 193 Cal. Rptr. 288 (Ct. App. 1983).

**DE:** Newmark v. Williams, 588 A.2d 1108 (Del. 1991).

**GA:** *In re* Doe, 418 S.E.2d 3 (Ga. 1992); *In re* L.H.R., 321 S.E.2d 716, 722 (Ga. 1984) ("In a case of suspected neglect or abuse or when the parent assumes a stance which in any way endangers the child, the parent's right to speak for the child may be lost.").

**MA:** *In re* McCauley, 565 N.E.2d 411 (Mass. 1991).

**TN:** *In re* Hamilton, 657 S.W.2d 425 (Tenn. Ct. App. 1983).

should also be supervened when the parent lacks decisionmaking capacity.[42] As a practical matter, when there is only one parent and that parent lacks decision-making capacity, or when both parents lack decisionmaking capacity, the attending physician often looks to other close family members in much the same way as would be the case if the patient were an incompetent adult.[43] For instance, in the case of the treatment of a child whose parents are unmarried and who lives with his mother and the mother's parents, the attending physician might turn to the grandparents to act as surrogates for their grandchild.[44]

When there are no other family members available to act as surrogate, when the family members are at intractable odds with each other about what decision to make,[45] when the family member speaking for the patient is not the one authorized by a surrogate decisionmaking statute,[46] or when the decision at issue seems too important to rely on such an informal mechanism, the proper course is to seek the appointment of a guardian, either directly through the judicial process or indirectly through the appropriate child protective services agency.

## § 15.5   Parental Informed Consent and Exceptions

As their child's natural guardians, parents are empowered to make medical decisions on the child's behalf in the same manner and to the same extent as any surrogate decisionmaker. In the first instance, this means that decisions are to be made in accordance with the informed consent doctrine.[47] Parents must be provided with the same information as would be provided to the surrogate of an adult incompetent patient, which in turn is the same information that would be provided to the patient if he or she were competent.[48] However, although

---

[42] **MI:** Rosebush v. Oakland County Prosecutor, 491 N.W.2d 633, 637 (Mich. Ct. App. 1992) (citing first edition of this treatise).

President's Comm'n for the Study of Ethical Problems in Medicine & Biomedical & Behavioral Research, Deciding to Forego Life-Sustaining Treatment 216 (1983) ("health care provider should seek to have a court appoint a surrogate in place of the parents, on the grounds that the *parents are incapacitated to make the decision*") (emphasis added) [hereinafter President's Comm'n, Deciding to Forego Life-Sustaining Treatment]. See § **5.24.**

[43] See § **5.10.**

[44] *Cf.* President's Comm'n, Deciding to Forego Life-Sustaining Treatment 217.

[45] **GA:** *Cf. In re* Doe, 418 S.E.2d 3 (Ga. 1992).

**OH:** *See, e.g., In re* Myers, 610 N.E.2d 663 (P. Ct. Summit County, Ohio 1993).

See § **5.31.**

[46] See **Ch. 14.**

[47] **DE:** Newmark v. Williams, 588 A.2d 1108, 1115–16 (Del. 1991) (child cannot be treated without parents' informed consent). See § **3.3.**

[48] **FL:** *In re* Barry, 445 So. 2d 365, 371 (Fla. Dist. Ct. App. 1984) ("It is, we think, the right and obligation of the parents in such an instance to exercise their responsibility and prerogative . . . of making an informed determination as to whether these extraordinary measures should be continued.").

ordinarily patients and surrogates must be provided with information about alternative therapies, including the option of no treatment,[49] when no treatment is a legally unacceptable alternative for their child, parents need not necessarily be provided with information about that option.[50]

The exceptions to informed consent requirements apply very nearly as they do when competent adults make decisions for themselves or surrogates make decisions for incompetent adults. If there is a bona fide medical emergency, consent need not be obtained from the parents;[51] if the parents waive the right to be informed or the right to decide or both, information may be withheld or treatment rendered without consent;[52] and if the parents themselves lack decisionmaking capacity, the attending physician must look elsewhere for an appropriate surrogate decisionmaker.[53]

An important limitation on the exceptions to informed consent applies to the therapeutic privilege,[54] which ought to be even more circumscribed in its scope when used to withhold information from surrogate decisionmakers, including the parents of minor children, than it is when applied to competent adult patients. Indeed, it is even arguable that the therapeutic privilege has no place in decisionmaking for incompetent patients as a justification for withholding information from surrogates.[55]

## § 15.6  Parental Right to Refuse Treatment of Child

The authority of parents to make medical decisions for their children, including the right to decline recommended treatment, is a constitutionally protected

---

Council on Ethical & Judicial Affairs, American Medical Ass'n, Code of Medical Ethics § 2.215, at 52 (1994). See § **7.38.**

[49] See § **3.15.**

[50] **CA10:** *But see* Johnson v. Thompson, 971 F.2d 1487, 1499 (10th Cir. 1992) (implying but not holding that if parents of handicapped newborn infant failed to give informed consent to withholding of treatment because physician provided inadequate information, cause of action for lack of informed consent would lie if infant would have survived if treated).

**NJ:** Iafelice v. Zarafu, 534 A.2d 417 (N.J. Super. Ct. App. Div. 1987) (physicians and hospitals have no duty to inform parents of infant with life-threatening condition of option of withholding treatment and letting child die).

[51] See § **3.23.**

[52] See § **3.26.**

[53] **MI:** Rosebush v. Oakland County Prosecutor, 491 N.W.2d 633, 637 n.5 (Mich. Ct. App. 1992) ("where the parents of a minor child for some reason are themselves incompetent to act as surrogate decision makers, and other family members are unavailable or unwilling to act as surrogates, a guardian should be appointed to exercise the minor's rights on behalf of the minor") (dictum) (citing first edition of this treatise). See § **5.24.**

[54] See § **3.25.**

[55] **NY:** *Cf.* Darrah v. Kite, 301 N.Y.S.2d 286, 292 (App. Div. 1969) (Although there might be justification for not telling patients of the possible risks or dangers, there is no reason for not fully disclosing to a guardian or responsible third party.).

interest.[56] It derives from the constitutional right of privacy in familial matters[57] and includes the right to impose on a child treatment to which the child objects.[58] In addition to having a constitutional basis, "[p]arental authority to make fundamental decisions for minor children is also a recognized common law principle. A doctor commits the tort of battery if he or she performs an operation under normal circumstances without the informed consent of the patient."[59]

In exercising their right to make an informed decision about their child's treatment, parents might decide to forgo treatment altogether, or to forgo the treatment preferred by the child's physician. They might choose a treatment the physician believes to be inferior to the recommended one or even to be detrimental to the child's well-being. However, parental autonomy is not absolute. The state has an interest, enforceable through the exercise of the parens patriae power, to limit the exercise of parental autonomy when it threatens to cause serious harm to the child,[60] though "the state . . . has a serious burden of

---

[56] **US:** Parham v. J.R., 442 U.S. 584 (1979).

**CA:** *In re* Phillip B., 156 Cal. Rptr. 48, 50 (Ct. App. 1979) ("It is fundamental that parental autonomy is constitutionally protected.").

**MA:** *In re* McCauley, 565 N.E.2d 411, 413 (Mass. 1991) ("The right to the free exercise of religion, including the interests of parents in the religious upbringing of their children is, of course, a fundamental right protected by the Constitution. Wisconsin v. Yoder, 406 U.S. 205, 214, 92 S. Ct. 1526, 1532, 32 L. Ed. 2d 15 (1972)."); Custody of a Minor, 393 N.E.2d 836, 843 (Mass. 1979).

**MI:** Rosebush v. Oakland County Prosecutor, 491 N.W.2d 633, 636–37 (Mich. Ct. App. 1992) ("It is well established that parents speak for their minor children in matters of medical treatment. [Citations omitted.] Because medical treatment includes the decision to decline lifesaving intervention, . . . it follows that parents are empowered to make decisions regarding withdrawal or withholding of lifesaving or life-prolonging measures on behalf of their children.") (citing first edition of this treatise).

**NY:** *In re* Hofbauer, 393 N.E.2d 1009, 1013 (N.Y. 1979) ("[E]very parent has a fundamental right to rear its child.").

[57] **US:** Wisconsin v. Yoder, 406 U.S. 205 (1972); Pierce v. Society of Sisters, 268 U.S. 510 (1925); Meyer v. Nebraska, 262 U.S. 390 (1923).

**DE:** Newmark v. Williams, 588 A.2d 1108, 1115 (Del. 1991).

[58] Parham v. J.R., 442 U.S. 584 (1979).

[59] Newmark v. Williams, 588 A.2d at 1115.

[60] **CA:** *In re* Phillip B., 156 Cal. Rptr. 48, 51 (Ct. App. 1979).

**DE:** Newmark v. Williams, 588 A.2d at 1116.

**IL:** *In re* E.G., 549 N.E.2d 322, 328 (Ill. 1989).

**MA:** *In re* McCauley, 565 N.E.2d at 413 ("When a child's life is at issue, 'it is not the rights of the parents that are chiefly to be considered. The first and paramount duty is to consult the welfare of the child.'"); Custody of a Minor, 393 N.E.2d 836 (Mass. 1979) ("[F]amily autonomy . . . may be limited where . . . parental decisions will jeopardize the health or safety of a child.").

**NJ:** State v. Perricone, 181 A.2d 751, 756 (N.J. 1962) ("'neither rights of religion nor rights of parenthood are beyond limitation'").

justification before abridging parental autonomy by substituting its judgment for that of the parents."[61] However, the state's interest "fades . . . as the minor gets older and disappears upon her reaching adulthood."[62]

Reported cases involving the reach of parental decisional authority concerning the treatment of children did not appear until the latter part of the nineteenth century[63] and thereafter only a few can be found. However, it is likely that the volume of trial court cases is far greater, and press accounts of trial court proceedings testify to the tremendous controversy that such cases often engender.

There are a variety of different kinds of cases involving parental refusals of treatment. In many of the litigated cases, the impetus to refuse treatment is religiously motivated.[64] In fact

> [t]he case of a child who may bleed to death because of the parents' [religiously inspired] refusal to authorize a blood transfusion presents the classic example. . . . Even when the parents' decision to decline necessary treatment is based on . . . religious beliefs, it must yield to the State's interests, as *parens patriae,* in protecting the health and welfare of the child.[65]

---

**NY:** Fosmire v. Nicoleau, 551 N.E.2d 77 (N.Y. 1990); *In re* Storar, 420 N.E.2d 64, 73 (N.Y.), *cert. denied,* 454 U.S. 858 (1981).

**TN:** *In re* Hamilton, 657 S.W.2d 425 (Tenn. Ct. App. 1983).

*See generally* Annotation, *Power of Public Authorities to Order Medical Care for a Child over Objection of Parent or Guardian,* 30 A.L.R.2d 1138 (1953).

[61] **CA:** *In re* Phillip B., 156 Cal. Rptr. 48, 51 (Ct. App. 1979).

**DE:** *Accord* Newmark v. Williams, 588 A.2d at 1110 ("[T]he State has the burden of proving by clear and convincing evidence that intervening in the parent-child relationship is necessary to ensure the safety or health of the child, or to protect the public at large.").

**TN:** *In re* Hamilton, 657 S.W.2d 425.

[62] **IL:** *In re* E.G., 549 N.E.2d at 327.

[63] *See* Heinemann's Appeal, 96 Pa. 112 (1880) (court removed custody from father and placed children with grandmother on the basis that father had refused to call a physician when children were ill and instead substituted his own medical treatment).

[64] See §§ 2.9 and 9.3.

[65] *In re* Storar, 420 N.E.2d at 73 (citing Jehovah's Witnesses v. King County Hosp., 278 F. Supp. 448 (W.D. Wash. 1967)).

**CA:** *Accord* Eric B. v. Ted B., 235 Cal. Rptr. 22 (Ct. App. 1987).

**DE:** *But see* Newmark v. Williams, 588 A.2d 1108 (statutory "spiritual treatment exemptions" permit refusal of treatment of child when likelihood of cure is "only" 40% and when treatment entails "terrible temporary and potentially permanent side effects," including risk of death).

**MA:** *Accord In re* McCauley, 565 N.E.2d 411 (Mass. 1991). *Cf.* Twitchell v. Commonwealth, 617 N.E.2d 609 (Mass. 1993) (parents can be convicted of involuntary manslaughter for relying on spiritual healing of child when failure to obtain medical care leads to child's death).

**NY:** *Accord In re* Sampson, 278 N.E.2d 918 (N.Y. 1972).

**PA:** *Accord In re* Cabrera, 552 A.2d 1114 (Pa. Super. Ct. 1989).

**TN:** *Accord In re* Hamilton, 657 S.W.2d 425 (Tenn. Ct. App. 1983).

Many other reported cases (and probably the large proportion of cases that never result in litigation) are not based on religious objection but on a parent's view of what constitutes appropriate health care which differs substantially from the attending physician's recommendation and sometimes from what most parents would choose for their child.[66] For instance, some highly controversial cases have involved the treatment of cancer with unconventional and generally unaccepted therapies.[67]

Prior to about 1980, most of the reported cases raising the legitimacy of parental refusal of treatment involved children for whom there was a reasonable probability that the treatment could save their lives. Because the prognosis for the child's recovery in these cases was good if not excellent, the courts almost uniformly ordered treatment.[68] When parents decline treatment and that causes the child's death, criminal penalties may also be imposed.[69] However, when the treatment is merely likely to improve the child's physical or psychological well-being, and the child's condition is not life-threatening and thus the treatment is not lifesaving, the courts generally have been unwilling to override parental refusals of treatment.[70] When parents choose among reasonable alternatives,

---

*See generally* Rampino, Annotation, *Power of Court or Other Public Agency to Order Medical Treatment over Parental Religious Objections for Child Whose Life Is Not Immediately Endangered,* 52 A.L.R.3d 1118 (1973).

[66] *See* Williams, Annotation, *Power of Court or Other Public Agency to Order Medical Treatment for Child over Parental Objections Not Based on Religious Grounds,* 97 A.L.R.3d 421 (1980).

[67] **MA:** *E.g.,* Custody of a Minor, 393 N.E.2d 836 (Mass. 1979).

**NY:** *E.g., In re* Hofbauer, 393 N.E.2d 1009 (N.Y. 1979).

[68] **MA:** *E.g.,* Custody of a Minor, 393 N.E.2d 836.

**NY:** *E.g., In re* Storar, 420 N.E.2d at 73 ("A parent or guardian has a right to consent to medical treatment on behalf of an infant. . . . The parent, however, may not deprive a child of life saving treatment, however well intentioned.").

**PA:** *E.g., In re* Cabrera, 552 A.2d 1114 (blood transfusion ordered for child with sickle-cell anemia who had stroke, to prevent recurrence, where transfusion was only treatment available).

*See generally* Williams, Annotation, *Power of Court or Other Public Agency to Order Medical Treatment for Child over Parental Objections Not Based on Religious Grounds,* 97 A.L.R.3d 421 (1980).

[69] **CA:** *See, e.g.,* Walker v. Superior Court, 222 Cal. Rptr. 87 (Ct. App. 1986), *aff'd,* 763 P.2d 852 (Cal. 1988).

**MA:** *See, e.g.,* Twitchell v. Commonwealth, 617 N.E.2d 609 (Mass. 1993) (parents can be convicted of involuntary manslaughter for relying on spiritual healing of child when failure to obtain medical care leads to child's death; conviction reversed on ground that parents did not have fair warning of meaning of statute).

**PA:** *See, e.g.,* Commonwealth v. Barnhart, 497 A.2d 616 (Pa. 1985), *allocatur denied,* 538 A.2d 874 (Pa.), *cert. denied,* 488 U.S. 817 (1988).

[70] **NY:** *See, e.g., In re* Seiferth, 127 N.E.2d 820 (N.Y. 1955) (correction of cleft palate). *But see In re* Sampson, 279 N.E.2d 918 (N.Y. 1972) (ordering treatment of non-life-threatening condition for alleged psychological benefit of the child over religiously based objection of child's mother).

**PA:** *See, e.g., In re* Green, 292 A.2d 387 (Pa. 1972) (correction of curvature of spine).

even if the condition is life-threatening,[71] courts frequently honor the parental decision because "it is not for the courts to determine the most 'effective' treatment."[72] When the consequences are not life-threatening but are grave, parental refusals of treatment will often be respected, especially where the treatment itself may be dangerous.[73] However, parents may be subjected to prosecution for and conviction of criminal homicide for a child's death resulting from the rejection of medical treatment in favor of "spiritual healing" as opposed to a choice between reasonable medical alternatives.[74]

Some cases have been litigated over the propriety of forgoing life-sustaining treatment in children.[75] Many times, litigation results not because of genuine

---

[71] **DCO:** *See, e.g.,* Cheng v. Wheaton, 745 F. Supp. 819 (D. Conn. 1990).

**CA:** *Compare In re* Phillip B., 156 Cal. Rptr. 48 (Ct. App. 1979) (parental refusal of cardiac surgery is not a failure to provide necessities of life) *with In re* Phillip B., 188 Cal. Rptr. 781 (Ct. App. 1983) (terminating custodial rights of natural parents and permitting guardians to consent to cardiac catheterization).

**DE:** *See, e.g.,* Newmark v. Williams, 588 A.2d 1108 (Del. 1991).

**IN:** *See, e.g., In re* Infant Doe, No. GU8204-00 (Ind. Cir. Ct. Monroe County Apr. 12, 1982), *writ of mandamus dismissed sub nom.* State *ex rel.* Infant Doe v. Baker, No. 482 S 140 (Ind. May 27, 1982), *cert. denied,* 464 U.S. 961 (1983) (parental choice of no treatment resulting in death of handicapped newborn infant).

**MA:** *But see* Custody of a Minor, 393 N.E.2d 836 (Mass. 1979) (laetrile administered in Mexican clinic for treatment of cancer constitutes child neglect).

**NY:** Weber v. Stony Brook Hosp., 456 N.E.2d 1186 (N.Y. 1983) (parental choice of more conservative treatment of handicapped newborn infant); *In re* Hofbauer, 393 N.E.2d 1009 (N.Y. 1979) (administration of laetrile for treatment of cancer under supervision of licensed physician is legitimate exercise of parental decisional authority).

*See also* Gathman, *The Journey of a Child and His Heart: A Decade of Transformation in the Legal, Medical, and Ethical Care of a Child with Down Syndrome,* 3 Cambridge Q. Healthcare Ethics 173 (1994) (describing life of Phillip B.).

**TN:** *But see In re* Hamilton, 657 S.W.2d 425 (Tenn. Ct. App. 1983).

[72] **DE:** Newmark v. Williams, 588 A.2d 1108 (statutory provision permits Christian Science parents to choose spiritual healing in preference to chemotherapy for leukemia when chemotherapy is only 40% likely to effect cure).

**NY:** *Accord* Weber v. Stony Brook Hosp., 456 N.E.2d 1186 (parents of handicapped newborn infant are entitled to choose a conservative course of therapy). *Cf. In re* Storar, 420 N.E.2d 64, 73 (N.Y. 1981) (citing *In re* Hofbauer, 393 N.E.2d 1009 (N.Y. 1979).

**NJ:** *But see* Iafelice v. Zarafu, 534 A.2d 417 (N.J. Super. Ct. App. Div. 1987) (physicians not required to inform parents of handicapped newborn infant of alternative of withholding treatment and permitting child to die).

[73] **PA:** *See, e.g., In re* Tuttendario, 21 Pa. D. 516 (1912) (refusal of treatment for rickets because treatment may have been more dangerous than disease).

**WA:** *See, e.g., In re* Hudson, 126 P.2d 765 (Wash. 1942) (refusal of treatment for deformity of arm because treatment may have caused death).

[74] **MA:** *See* Twitchell v. Commonwealth, 617 N.E.2d 609 (Mass. 1993).

[75] See §§ **15.7–15.8.**

conflicts between parents and health care professionals but because of uncertainty among the latter concerning the scope of parental authority to forgo life-sustaining treatment for children. Far more controversial have been the cases, mostly unreported, involving the withholding of treatment from handicapped newborn infants.[76]

These different kinds of cases help to define a spectrum of decisionmaking about forgoing treatment for children. One end is clearly marked by the case of the child who is dead by brain-death standards but not by traditional standards, that is, whose respiration and circulation are being continued by life-support equipment. There is no doubt in such cases that life-support systems may[77] and, indeed, must[78] be terminated. The other end of the spectrum is characterized by cases of children with life-threatening conditions who, if treated, will clearly survive.[79] In between, proceeding from cases in which the forgoing of life-sustaining treatment is most likely to be legitimate, are those involving children who almost certainly will die of a life-threatening condition[80] or who have a low probability of recovery even if treatment is administered;[81] those involving children for whom there is virtually no chance for recovery (for example, children who are in a persistent vegetative state) but who are not likely to die from their condition as long as medical care is continued;[82] and those

---

[76] See **Ch. 16.**

[77] **AL:** *See, e.g.,* Gallups v. Carter, 534 So. 2d 585 (Ala. 1988) (upholding summary judgment in favor of physicians alleged to have terminated life support from brain-dead patient in absence of her family's consent).

**CA:** *See, e.g.,* Dority v. Superior Court, 193 Cal. Rptr. 288 (Ct. App. 1983).

[78] **NJ:** *See, e.g.,* Strachan v. John F. Kennedy Memorial Hosp., 538 A.2d 346 (N.J. 1988). *But see Brain-Dead Florida Girl Will Be Sent Home on Life Support,* N.Y. Times, Feb. 19, 1994, at 7 (nat'l ed.) (parents of 13-year-old girl whom doctors diagnosed as dead by brain-death criteria insisted that she was alive and that life-sustaining medical treatment be continued; hospital agreed to continue life support at its expense in parents' home because " 'the nursing staff is wrung out' "); *Hospital Fights Parents' Wish to Keep Life Support for a "Brain Dead" Child,* N.Y. Times, Feb. 12, 1994, at 6 (nat'l ed.); *Public Hospital to Finance Home Care of Brain-Dead Teenager,* 3 Health L. Rep. (BNA) 287 (1994). See § **9.48.**

[79] **PA:** *See, e.g., In re* Cabrera, 552 A.2d 1114 (Pa. Super. Ct. 1989).

[80] **MA:** *See, e.g.,* Custody of a Minor, 434 N.E.2d 601 (Mass. 1982).

[81] **DE:** *See, e.g.,* Newmark v. Williams, 588 A.2d 1108 (Del. 1991) (40% probability of survival with treatment).

**IL:** *In re* E.G., 549 N.E.2d 322 (Ill. 1989) (patient likely to die within a month without treatment may refuse treatment about 80% likely to achieve remission although long-term survival rate is only 20 to 25%.).

**NY:** *In re* Long Island Jewish Medical Ctr. (Malcolm), 557 N.Y.S.2d 239 (Sup. Ct. Queens County 1990) (20 to 25% probability of survival with treatment).

**TN:** *In re* Hamilton, 657 S.W.2d 425 (Tenn. Ct. App. 1983) (probability of long-term remission between 25 and 50%).

[82] **FL:** *See, e.g., In re* Barry, 445 So. 2d 365 (Fla. Dist. Ct. App. 1984).

**GA:** *See, e.g., In re* Doe, 418 S.E.2d 3 (Ga. 1992); *In re* L.H.R., 321 S.E.2d 716 (Ga. 1984).

involving children, usually handicapped newborn infants, who are faced with life-threatening conditions that in varying degrees are susceptible to correction but who suffer from one or more other conditions that will seriously compromise the quality of their existence[83] or who will likely suffer serious side effects from the condition, previously life-threatening but now "corrected."[84]

Also near this end of the spectrum are cases involving children for whom treatment is of questionable benefit and cases in which the treatment itself might impose serious risk or at least discomfort. For example, in *Newmark v. Williams*,[85] the court refused to find that a child suffering from deadly Burkitt's lymphoma, an aggressive cancer, whose parents subscribed to Christian Science beliefs, was neglected because the parents refused chemotherapy; that treatment offered "only" a 40 percent likelihood of cure but also had "terrible temporary and potentially permanent side effects," including the risk of death.[86] A similar factual situation arose in *In re McCauley*,[87] in which the court ordered the administration of treatment, a blood transfusion. However, *McCauley* is distinguishable from *Newmark* because of "the substantial chance for a cure and a normal life for the child if she underwent the recommended treatment; and . . . the minimal risks to the child's health which would result from the treatment."[88]

The problem of determining standards for withholding treatment in these different kinds of cases is conceptually the same as that for adults. The only difference is that the application of subjective and substituted judgment standards is either difficult or impossible when children are involved, though courts have applied these standards to mature minors[89] and even to infants.[90]

---

LA: *See, e.g., In re* P.V.W., 424 So. 2d 1015 (La. 1982).

ME: *See, e.g., In re* Swan, 569 A.2d 1202 (Me. 1990).

MN: *See, e.g., In re* Welfare of Steinhaus (Redwood County Ct. Juv. Div. Minn. Sept. 11, 1986), *amended* (Oct. 13, 1987) (discussed in § **16.26**).

[83] IN: *See, e.g., In re* Infant Doe, No. GU8204-00 (Ind. Cir. Ct. Monroe County Apr. 12, 1982).

ME: Maine Medical Ctr. v. Houle, Civ. Action No. 74-145 (Super. Ct. Cumberland County, Me. Feb. 14, 1974).

NY: *In re* Cicero, 421 N.Y.S.2d 965 (Sup. Ct. Bronx County 1979). See § **16.18**.

[84] NY: *See, e.g.,* Weber v. Stony Brook Hosp., 467 N.Y.S.2d 685 (App. Div. 1983).

[85] DE: 588 A.2d 1108 (Del. 1991).

[86] *Id.* at 1118.

[87] MA: 565 N.E.2d 411 (Mass. 1991).

[88] *Id.* at 414.

[89] See § **15.3**.

[90] FL: *See, e.g., In re* Barry, 445 So. 2d 365 (Fla. Dist. Ct. App. 1984).

MA: *In re* Beth Israel Medical Ctr. (Weinstein), 519 N.Y.S.2d 511 (Sup. Ct. N.Y. County 1987); Custody of a Minor, 434 N.E.2d 601 (Mass. 1982).

WA: *In re* Grant, 747 P.2d 445 (Wash. 1987), *modified,* 757 P.2d 534 (Wash. 1988).

See § **15.9**.

# RIGHT-TO-DIE LITIGATION INVOLVING CHILDREN

## § 15.7  Background

Most of the litigation over the domain of parental decisional authority has concerned administering *lifesaving* treatments. In these cases, parents have not wanted harm or death to befall their children, though that has been the likely consequence if treatment were forgone. Rather, parents generally have been motivated in this litigation by what one court characterized as a "preference . . . [for] diverse lifestyles"[91] or "the right of parents to raise their children as they think best,"[92] sometimes but not always religiously motivated.

By contrast, there have not been nearly as many reported cases concerning the forgoing of *life-sustaining* treatment, that is, cases in which the parents contended that their children should be allowed to die because of their hopeless condition.[93] The number of cases involving children is much smaller than the number concerning adult patients, which is probably explained by the lesser uncertainty about the authority of parents to make such decisions for their minor children than about family members making them for adult relatives. The procedural and substantive principles that have developed in children's cases are virtually identical to those governing decisionmaking about life-sustaining

---

[91] **CA:** *In re* Phillip B., 156 Cal. Rptr. 48, 51 (Ct. App. 1979).

**DCT:** *Accord* Cheng v. Wheaton, 745 F. Supp. 819 (D. Conn. 1990) (mother of child with rheumatoid arthritis advocated use of homeopathy or traditional Chinese medicine as alternative to surgery).

**IL:** *Accord In re* E.G., 549 N.E.2d 322, 324 (Ill. 1989) (mature minor's "decision was not based on any wish to die, but instead was grounded in her religious convictions").

**MA:** *Accord* Twitchell v. Commonwealth, 617 N.E.2d 609 (Mass. 1993) (religious beliefs).

[92] *In re* Phillip B., 156 Cal. Rptr. at 51 (although case might be one in which parental motivation was otherwise).

[93] **AL:** *Cf.* Gallups v. Carter, 534 So. 2d 585 (Ala. 1988).

**CA:** *Cf.* Dority v. Superior Court, 193 Cal. Rptr. 288 (Ct. App. 1983).

**CO:** Carothers v. Department of Insts., 845 P.2d 1179 (Colo. 1993).

**FL:** *In re* Barry, 445 So. 2d 365 (Fla. Dist. Ct. App. 1984).

**GA:** *In re* Doe, 418 S.E.2d 3 (Ga. 1992); *In re* L.H.R., 321 S.E.2d 716 (Ga. 1984).

**IL:** C.A. v. Morgan, 603 N.E.2d 1171 (Ill. App. Ct. 1992).

**LA:** *In re* P.V.W., 424 So. 2d 1015 (La. 1982).

**ME:** *In re* Swan, 569 A.2d 1202 (Me. 1990).

**MA:** *In re* Beth, 587 N.E.2d 1377 (Mass. 1992); Custody of a Minor, 434 N.E.2d 601 (Mass. 1982).

**MI:** Rosebush v. Oakland County Prosecutor, 491 N.W.2d 633 (Mich. Ct. App. 1992).

treatment for adult incompetent patients. Further, the litigation that has arisen has been prompted largely by the same concerns that exist with adults—namely, the possibility of liability for withholding treatment that results in death.[94]

## § 15.8 Substantive Rights: Source and Scope

The sources and scope of the substantive right to forgo life-sustaining treatment on behalf of a child are similar to those for adult incompetent patients. "[T]his right is not lost," said the Georgia Supreme Court, "because of the incompetence or youth of the patient."[95] Courts have cited the common-law right of

---

**NJ:** *Cf.* Iafelice v. Zarafu, 534 A.2d 417 (N.J. Super. Ct. App. Div. 1987).

**NY:** Weber v. Stony Brook Hosp., 456 N.E.2d 1186 (N.Y. 1983); *In re* Cicero, 421 N.Y.S.2d 965 (Sup. Ct. Bronx County 1979).

**OH:** *In re* Myers, 610 N.E.2d 663 (P. Ct. Summit County, Ohio 1993); *In re* Crum, 580 N.E.2d 876 (P. Ct., Franklin County, Ohio 1991).

**WA:** *In re* Grant, 747 P.2d 445 (Wash. 1987), *modified,* 757 P.2d 534 (Wash. 1988).

**WV:** Belcher v. Charleston Area Medical Ctr., 422 S.E.2d 827 (W. Va. 1992).

[94] **DE:** *See, e.g.,* Newmark v. Williams, 588 A.2d 1108, 1110 (Del. 1991) (fear of criminal prosecution).

**FL:** *In re* Barry, 445 So. 2d at 371–72.

**LA:** *In re* P.V.W., 424 So. 2d at 1020.

**ME:** *In re* Swan, 569 A.2d at 1204–05.

**MI:** Rosebush v. Oakland County Prosecutor, 491 N.W.2d at 692 (fear of criminal liability for homicide).

**OH:** *Cf. In re* Myers, 610 N.E.2d 663 (judicial review sought because of disagreement among parents).

[95] **GA:** *In re* L.H.R., 321 S.E.2d 716, 722 (Ga. 1984).

**FL:** *Accord In re* Barry, 445 So. 2d 365, 370 (Fla. Dist. Ct. App. 1984) ("[T]he constitutional right of privacy would be an empty right if one who is incompetent were not granted the right of a competent counterpart to exercise his rights.").

**IL:** *Accord In re* E.G., 549 N.E.2d 322, 326 (Ill. 1989) ("We see no reason why this right of dominion over one's own person should not extend to mature minors. Furthermore, we find support for this conclusion in a decision of one of our sister States.").

**MI:** *Accord* Rosebush v. Oakland County Prosecutor, 491 N.W.2d 633, 681–82 (Mich. Ct. App. 1992).

**OH:** *Accord In re* Crum, 580 N.E.2d 876, 881–82 (P. Ct. Franklin County, Ohio 1991) ("[T]he legislature intended, in the enactment of the above statutes, to ensure that a minor ward shall not lose his right to consent or refuse to consent to medical treatment because of his incompetency, such right being encompassed in the individual's liberty interests.").

**WA:** *Accord In re* Grant, 747 P.2d 445, 449 (Wash. 1987), *modified,* 757 P.2d 534 (Wash. 1988) ("An incompetent individual does not lose the right to have life sustaining treatment withheld by virtue of his or her incompetency.").

self-determination or autonomy or privacy,[96] and federal[97] and state[98] constitutional rights of privacy.[99] However, there are some statutory bases applicable only to children.[100]

By and large, the courts seem to use a prognostic approach to define the boundaries of the right to die.[101] The state's interest in the child's life is not significant enough to warrant overriding parental authority if the child is terminally ill,[102] irreversibly ill,[103] or incurably ill,[104] or if there is no hope of

---

[96] **LA:** *See In re* P.V.W., 424 So. 2d 1015 (La. 1982) (citing *In re* Spring, 405 N.E.2d 115 (Mass. 1980); Eichner v. Dillon, 420 N.E.2d 64 (N.Y. 1981)).

[97] **IL:** *See In re* E.G., 549 N.E.2d 322.

**LA:** *See In re* P.V.W., 424 So. 2d 1015 (citing *In re* Quinlan, 355 A.2d 647 (N.J. 1976)).

**OH:** *See In re* Crum, 580 N.E.2d 876, 878 (P. Ct. Franklin County, Ohio 1991).

**WA:** *See In re* Grant, 747 P.2d 445, 449 (Wash. 1987), *modified,* 757 P.2d 534 (Wash. 1988).

[98] **FL:** *In re* Barry, 445 So. 2d at 370.

[99] **FL:** *In re* Barry, 445 So. 2d at 370.

**GA:** *In re* L.H.R., 321 S.E.2d at 722 (not stating whether source is state or federal constitution).

**OH:** *In re* Crum, 580 N.E.2d 876 (constitutionally protected liberty interest).

**WA:** *In re* Grant, 747 P.2d at 449 (federal and state constitutions).

[100] **AZ:** *See* Ariz. Rev. Stat. Ann. § 36-2281(c).

**DE:** *See* Newmark v. Williams, 588 A.2d 1108, 1112 (Del. 1991) (statutory spiritual treatment exemptions).

**LA:** *See In re* P.V.W., 424 So. 2d at 1020 (legislature recognized right of permanently comatose child to have parents and physicians discontinue artificially sustained life under certain conditions) (citing La. Rev. Stat. Ann. § 40:1299.36.3(c)).

**MN:** *See* Minn. Stat. Ann. § 260.105(10)(e)(1)–(3).

**RI:** *See* R.I. Gen. Laws § 40-11-3.

See § **16.27.**

[101] See §§ **8.9–8.13.**

[102] **FL:** *In re* Barry, 445 So. 2d at 371.

**GA:** *See In re* L.H.R., 321 S.E.2d at 722.

**LA:** *In re* P.V.W., 424 So. 2d 1015.

**MA:** Custody of a Minor, 434 N.E.2d 601 (Mass. 1982).

**MI:** Rosebush v. Oakland County Prosecutor, 491 N.W.2d 633, 684 (Mich. Ct. App. 1992).

**WA:** *In re* Grant, 747 P.2d at 449.

[103] **FL:** *In re* Barry, 445 So. 2d at 371.

**GA:** *In re* L.H.R., 321 S.E.2d at 441.

**LA:** *In re* P.V.W., 424 So. 2d 1015.

**MA:** Custody of a Minor, 434 N.E.2d at 609.

**MI:** Rosebush v. Oakland County Prosecutor, 491 N.W.2d at 684.

**WA:** *In re* Grant, 747 P.2d at 449.

[104] **FL:** *In re* Barry, 445 So. 2d at 371.

**GA:** *In re* L.H.R., 321 S.E.2d at 719.

**MA:** Custody of a Minor, 434 N.E.2d at 607.

**MI:** Rosebush v. Oakland County Prosecutor, 491 N.W.2d at 637.

**WA:** *In re* Grant, 747 P.2d at 451.

recovery.[105] For example, when a child is terminally ill, "the question is not of life or death but the manner of dying."[106] Although the state has a legitimate interest in the life of a child,

> [w]here . . . the parents' informed decision is backed by uncontroverted medical evidence that their young child is terminally ill and that his condition is incurable and irreversible, their decision . . . overrides any interest of the state in prolonging their child's life through extraordinary measures.[107]

However, even when a child is in a persistent vegetative state and thus not technically terminally ill, there is "no state interest great enough to compel the parents to continue to submit their child to a life support system. To do so would merely prolong . . . death."[108]

## § 15.9  —Standards for Decisionmaking by Surrogates

Surrogate decisionmakers for adult patients are bound by the subjective standard to implement the patient's own prior competent decision or by the substituted judgment standard to attempt to decide as the patient himself would if he were capable of doing so.[109] Only if those standards cannot be applied because of a lack of information about what the patient would have decided, is it permissible to make decisions pursuant to more objective standards,[110] if at all.[111]

---

[105] **GA:** *In re* Doe, 418 S.E.2d 3, 6 (Ga. 1992); *In re* L.H.R., 321 S.E.2d at 722.

**MI:** Rosebush v. Oakland County Prosecutor, 491 N.W.2d at 636 n.2 ("no medical probability of substantial recovery").

**OH:** *In re* Myers, 610 N.E.2d 663 (P. Ct. Summit County, Ohio 1993); *In re* Crum, 580 N.E.2d 876 (P. Ct. Franklin County, Ohio 1991).

[106] **MA:** Custody of a Minor, 434 N.E.2d at 609 (citing *In re* Dinnerstein, 380 N.E.2d 134 (Mass. App. Ct. 1978)).

[107] **FL:** *In re* Barry, 445 So. 2d at 371.

[108] **FL:** *In re* Barry, 445 So. 2d at 371.

**GA:** *Accord In re* L.H.R., 321 S.E.2d 716.

**LA:** *Accord In re* P.V.W., 424 So. 2d 1015.

**OH:** *Accord In re* Myers, 610 N.E.2d 663 (applying best interests standard for guardian to employ in decisionmaking); *In re* Crum, 580 N.E.2d 876.

[109] See §§ **7.4–7.10.**

[110] See §§ **7.11–7.25.**

[111] **ME:** *Cf. In re* Swan, 569 A.2d 1202 (Me. 1990) (court found that mature minor had met subjective standard without specifically deciding that only such a standard would suffice).

**MO:** *See* Cruzan v. Harmon, 760 S.W.2d 408 (Mo. 1988) (requiring continuation of treatment in absence of clear and convincing evidence that patient herself had authorized forgoing of feeding tube).

**NY:** *In re* Westchester County Medical Ctr. (O'Connor), 531 N.E.2d 607 (N.Y. 1988) (same).

By contrast, the predominant standard by which parental authority to make medical decisions for children is assessed has been the best interests standard.[112] The use of this standard in decisionmaking for children long antedates end-of-life decisionmaking cases. This standard is the only sensible one for very young children who may have little or no awareness of their condition, prognosis with and without treatment, treatment options, and other information relevant to decisionmaking. In such cases it is impossible for the parents or anyone else to know what the child would have wanted had he or she been competent to decide. These situations are like those involving never-competent adult patients.[113]

The application of subjective standards is plausible in the case of older children, who, if conscious, would almost certainly be considered mature minors.[114] Despite the difficulty, if not the utter implausibility, of applying subjective standards to infants and young children,[115] some courts have held the substituted judgment standard applicable to decisionmaking about life-sustaining treatment for even very young children.[116] In so doing, they open themselves up to the same charges of unequal treatment of never-competent patients as were lodged against the Massachusetts Supreme Judicial Court for applying the substituted judgment standard to a never-competent adult.[117] The statement of a Florida appellate court in *Barry* that "it is proper for the court to exercise its substituted judgment *even absent evidence of intention of the incompetent person*"[118] illustrates the contradiction. The substituted judgment standard explicitly calls for

---

[112] National Ctr. for State Courts, Guidelines for State Court Decision Making in Life-Sustaining Medical Treatment Cases 115 (2d ed. 1992) (standard 23).

[113] **MI:** Rosebush v. Oakland County Prosecutor, 491 N.W.2d 633, 639 (Mich. Ct. App. 1992) ("[A]s applied to immature minors and other never-competent patients, the substituted judgment standard is inappropriate because it cannot be ascertained what choice the patient would have made if competent.") (citing first edition of this treatise). See § **7.10.**

[114] *See, e.g., In re* Swan, 569 A.2d 1202 (Me. 1990). *See* National Ctr. for State Courts, Guidelines for State Court Decision Making in Life-Sustaining Medical Treatment Cases 115 (2d ed. 1992) (standard 23).

[115] **FL:** *See, e.g., In re* Barry, 445 So. 2d 365, 371 (Fla. Dist. Ct. App. 1984) ("The [substituted judgment] doctrine has been helpful in the case of adults, but it is difficult to apply to children or young adults.").

**IL:** *See, e.g.,* C.A. v. Morgan, 603 N.E.2d 1171 (Ill. App. Ct. 1992) (applying best interests standard to decisionmaking for infant because the "substituted judgment test . . . is of limited relevance in the case of immature minors").

[116] **FL:** *See In re* Barry, 445 So. 2d at 371 (infant).

**GA:** *Cf. In re* L.H.R., 321 S.E.2d 716, 718–19 (infant).

**MA:** *See In re* Beth, 587 N.E.2d 1377 (Mass. 1992) (16-year-old child was an infant when she became persistently vegetative); Custody of a Minor, 434 N.E.2d 601 (Mass. 1982) (infant). *Cf. In re* Hier, 464 N.E.2d 959, 965 (Mass. App. Ct. 1984) (substituted judgment approach has theoretical utility in case of a person who has never had capacity to express a meaningful view).

[117] See § **7.10.**

[118] *In re* Barry, 445 So. 2d at 371 (emphasis added).

the application of the incompetent's wishes; thus, it is impossible to apply when there is no evidence of those wishes, let alone when the person has never possessed any ability to formulate or to consciously express wishes. The court's further statement that "the court must be guided primarily by the judgment of the parents who are responsible for their child's well-being"[119] is a tacit admission that substituted judgment cannot work for an infant and thus underscores the absurdity of attempts to apply it.

The Massachusetts Supreme Judicial Court attempted to explain away this problem in *Custody of a Minor:*

> In a case like this one, involving a child who is incompetent by reason of his tender years, we think that the substituted judgment doctrine is consistent with the "best interests of the child" test. It is true that, when applying the "best interests" test, the inquiry is essentially objective in nature, and the decisions are made not by, but on behalf of, the child. . . . Nevertheless, the best interests analysis, like that of the substituted judgment doctrine, requires a court to focus on the various factors unique to the situation of the individual for whom it must act. . . . As a practical matter, the criteria to be examined and the basic applicable reasoning are the same.[120]

That court later seems to have realized the difficulty created by the application of a substituted judgment standard to a never-competent patient. In *McCauley,* the court reverted to earlier precedents and applied a test more akin to a best interests standard, in which it balanced "(1) the 'natural rights' of parents; (2) the interests of the child; and (3) the interests of the State,"[121] and cited an earlier Massachusetts case, also with the name *Custody of a Minor,*[122] in support. *Custody of a Minor* involved the authority of parents to treat with an unconventional therapy a child suffering from a cancer that might possibly have been cured. It, along with *McCauley,* is distinguishable from another case titled *Custody of a Minor,*[123] because the latter, which applied the substituted judgment standard, involved a do-not-resuscitate order for a child whose prognosis for recovery was virtually nonexistent. Whether this factual distinction justifies the application of a different decisionmaking standard, however, is highly questionable[124] and is an issue that was not addressed by the Massachusetts Supreme

---

[119] *Id.*

[120] 434 N.E.2d 601, 608 (Mass. 1982). *Accord In re* Beth, 587 N.E.2d at 1382 n.11.

[121] *In re* McCauley, 565 N.E.2d 411, 413 (Mass. 1991).

[122] **MA:** 379 N.E.2d 1053 (Mass. 1978).

> **DE:** *See also* Newmark v. Williams, 588 A.2d 1108, 1114 (Del. 1991) (adopting and describing test in *Custody of a Minor* as "tripartite balancing test").

[123] Custody of a Minor, 434 N.E.2d 601 (Mass. 1982).

[124] **IL:** *Cf.* Curran v. Bosze, 566 N.E.2d 1319 (Ill. 1990) (best interests standard, not substituted judgment standard, applicable to deciding whether 3½-year-old twins could be tested to determine compatibility for bone marrow donation to half-brother).

Judicial Court in *McCauley*, which did not discuss or cite the do-not-resuscitate case. This is especially so in light of the Massachusetts court's subsequent holding in *In re Beth*,[125] in which the court once again applied a substituted judgment standard to an infant.

Instead of engaging in such semantic acrobatics, courts are better advised to follow the lead of the New Jersey Supreme Court in *Conroy*[126] in attempting to fashion more precise guidelines for the application of the best interests standard for decisionmaking for infants and children.[127] Under the best interests standard,

> [s]everal relevant factors must be taken into consideration before a state insists upon medical treatment rejected by the parents. The state should examine the seriousness of the harm the child is suffering or the substantial likelihood that he will suffer serious harm; the evaluation for the treatment by the medical profession; the risks involved in medically treating the child; and the expressed preferences of the child.[128]

The Delaware Supreme Court did this in *Newmark v. Williams*.[129] This case involved a three-year-old child suffering from Burkitt's lymphoma, a non-Hodgkins lymphoma that would be fatal in from six to eight months if untreated but for which there was a 40 percent likelihood of cure if it were treated. The court applied a test for evaluating the legitimacy of the parents' religiously motivated refusal of treatment, which it referred to sometimes as a best interests test and sometimes as a balancing test. Under this approach, the decisionmaker must not only consider the child's best interest but must also balance that against various state interests, weighing the interests of the parents, the child, and the state in determining whether the child is neglected as a consequence of the parental refusal to authorize recommended treatment.[130] In determining what is in the child's best interests, the trial court should consider two factors:

> the effectiveness of the treatment and . . . the child's chances of survival with and without medical care . . . [and] the nature of the treatments and their effect on the

---

[125] 587 N.E.2d 1377 (Mass. 1992).

[126] *In re* Conroy, 486 A.2d 1209 (N.J. 1985). See §§ **7.16–7.20.**

[127] **IL:** *See, e.g.,* C.A. v. Morgan, 603 N.E.2d 1171 (Ill. App. Ct. 1992) (applying best interests standard to decisionmaking for infant because the "substituted judgment test . . . is of limited relevance in the case of immature minors").

**MI:** *See, e.g.,* Rosebush v. Oakland County Prosecutor, 491 N.W.2d 633 (Mich. Ct. App. 1992) (holding best interests standard applicable if substituted judgment standard could not be met in case of patient who was 10 years old when she entered persistent vegetative state).

**OH:** *See, e.g., In re* Crum, 580 N.E.2d 876 (P. Ct. Franklin County, Ohio 1991) (applying, in case of 17-year-old in persistent vegetative state since age 12, both a substituted judgment standard and a best interests standard).

[128] *In re* Phillip B., 156 Cal. Rptr. 48, 51 (Ct. App. 1979).

[129] 588 A.2d 1108 (Del. 1991).

[130] *Id.* at 1115.

child. . . . This analysis is consistent with the principle that State intervention in the parent-child relationship is only justifiable under compelling conditions [because t]he State's interest in forcing a minor to undergo medical care diminishes as the risks of treatment increase and its benefits decrease.[131]

Applying this test, the court held that the parental refusal could not be over-ridden because the "proposed medical treatment was highly invasive, painful, involved terrible temporary and potentially permanent side effects, posed an unacceptably low chance of success, and a high risk that the treatment itself would cause his death."[132] The fact that the basis for the parental objection was religious does not appear to have played any role in the court's decision. In a case that employed similar reasoning, the Massachusetts Supreme Judicial Court came to the opposite conclusion and ordered administration of a blood transfusion in connection with a bone marrow aspiration in order to obtain a more certain diagnosis of the nature of the child's cancer and thus whether it was treatable.[133]

As children become older and start to develop an awareness, and later an understanding, of the information material to decisionmaking about treatment, they are able to begin developing and expressing views about treatment. The application of subjective standards then begins to make sense. Thus, a few courts have applied a substituted judgment standard in the cases of older children, who might have been mature minors, but also held that if the standard could not be met, a best interests standard was to be applied.[134]

## § 15.10   Decisionmaking Procedures

The procedural questions in decisionmaking for children are essentially the same as those for adults[135]—namely, incompetence, surrogacy, and review of

---

[131] *Id.* at 1117.

[132] *Id.* at 1118.

[133] *In re* McCauley, 565 N.E.2d 411 (Mass. 1991).

[134] **CA:** *See In re* Phillip B., 156 Cal. Rptr. 48, 51 (Ct. App. 1979) (state should examine expressed preferences of mentally retarded child).

**MI:** *See* Rosebush v. Oakland County Prosecutor, 491 N.W.2d 633, 637 (Mich. Ct. App. 1992) ("in making decisions for minors or other incompetent patients, surrogate decision makers should make the best approximation of the patient's preference on the basis of available evidence; if such preference was never expressed or is otherwise unknown, the surrogate should make a decision based on the best interests of the patient"; permanently unconscious since age 10½).

**OH:** *See In re* Crum, 580 N.E.2d 876 (P. Ct. Franklin County, Ohio 1991) (patient permanently unconscious since age 12).

[135] *In re* L.H.R., 321 S.E.2d 716, 723 (Ga. 1984) ("[T]here is no legal difference between the situations of infant and the incompetent adult who has made no living will.").

decisions.[136] However, the resolution of some of these issues is usually far simpler when dealing with children than with adults.

## § 15.11 —Determination of Incompetence

The threshold issue in decisionmaking for adults of whether the patient is incompetent, and the closely related issue of who is to make this determination,[137] are ordinarily absent when the patient is a child because children are presumed to be incompetent by virtue of their age alone.[138] However, if the child is mature, and capable in fact of making the decision in question—that is, the child would not be adjudicated incompetent if he were an adult with the same qualities—the child should not be divested of decisionmaking authority based exclusively on age.[139]

## § 15.12 —Designation of a Surrogate

The questions of who is to select a surrogate decisionmaker and who is the appropriate person to act as surrogate are ordinarily also cut short when the patient is a child rather than an incompetent adult. The child's parents are presumed to be the appropriate surrogate decisionmakers.[140] This presumption operates in right-to-die cases[141] as well as in other cases involving health care decisionmaking for children. This means that there is ordinarily no need to have the parents judicially appointed as guardians.[142] Only if the parents themselves

---

[136] See **Ch. 5.**

[137] See **Ch. 4** and **§§ 5.8–5.11.**

[138] See **§§ 15.2–15.3.**

[139] See **§ 15.3.**

[140] **GA:** *In re* L.H.R., 321 S.E.2d 716, 722 (Ga. 1984) ("[T]he beginning presumption is that the parent has the child's best interest at heart."). See **§ 15.2.**

[141] **DE:** *Cf.* Newmark v. Williams, 588 A.2d 1108, 1115 (Del. 1991) ("Parental authority to make fundamental decisions for minor children is also a recognized common law principle.").

**FL:** *See In re* Barry, 445 So. 2d 365 (Fla. Dist. Ct. App. 1984).

**GA:** *See In re* Doe, 418 S.E.2d 3, 6 (Ga. 1992); *In re* L.H.R., 321 S.E.2d at 722.

**IL:** *See* C.A. v. Morgan, 603 N.E.2d 1171, 1180 (Ill. App. Ct. 1992) ("As primary caregivers, parents or other close family members ordinarily are the ones charged with making the difficult determination of what is in a terminally-ill child's best interests.").

**LA:** *See In re* P.V.W., 424 So. 2d 1015 (La. 1982).

[142] **FL:** *See In re* Barry, 445 So. 2d 365.

**GA:** *See In re* L.H.R., 321 S.E.2d at 723 ("Since the parents are the natural guardians of the infant, where there are parents no legal guardian and no guardian ad litem need be appointed.").

**LA:** *See In re* P.V.W., 424 So. 2d 1015.

lack decisionmaking capacity,[143] are suspected of neglect or abuse,[144] or are in conflict with each other[145] or with other participants in the decisionmaking process,[146] or if the decision the parents make endangers the child[147] should parental authority to act as surrogate decisionmakers be questioned.

Disagreement between a child's parents can seriously complicate the decision-making process, which can be further complicated when either or both of their views begin to shift. In *In re Doe*,[148] the father favored continuing all treatment and the mother completely disagreed; then the mother favored the administration of some treatments but not CPR; and eventually the mother began to waver even about withholding CPR. At the time of trial the parents were either in agreement or were so close that the court assumed that they were. The treatment that was the subject of litigation was cardiopulmonary resuscitation, the administration and withholding of which is governed by statute in Georgia.[149] In dictum, the court interpreted the statute to permit either parent to consent to the entry of a DNR order. But when the parents disagree, the statute also permits the other parent to revoke the DNR order. The net result is that when there is disagreement about the administration of CPR, the attending physician is bound to administer it if one parent wants it to be administered.[150]

If the child has no parents, or if the parents are unavailable to act as decisionmakers or lack decisionmaking capacity, surrogate selection is usually not possible without recourse to judicial or, at least, administrative proceedings.[151] In most jurisdictions, child protective services authorities should be contacted by those responsible for the child's medical care. They will sometimes act as surrogate decisionmakers or will seek the judicial appointment of a guardian.

---

[143] **MA:** *In re* Beth, 587 N.E.2d 1377, 1380 (Mass. 1992).

[144] **GA:** *In re* L.H.R., 321 S.E.2d at 722, 723.

[145] **CA4:** *See, e.g., In re* Baby "K," 16 F.3d 590 (4th Cir. 1994), *cert. denied,* 115 S. Ct. 91 (1994).

   **GA:** *See, e.g., In re* Doe, 418 S.E.2d 3.

   **OH:** *See, e.g., In re* Myers, 610 N.E.2d 663 (P. Ct. Summit County, Ohio 1993) (mother, father, and stepmother in disagreement, requiring judicial appointment of a guardian).

[146] **FL:** *See In re* Barry, 445 So. 2d at 372.

   **GA:** *See In re* L.H.R., 321 S.E.2d at 723.

[147] **FL:** *See In re* Barry, 445 So. 2d at 372.

   **GA:** *See In re* L.H.R., 321 S.E.2d at 722.

[148] 418 S.E.2d 3 (Ga. 1992).

[149] *See* Ga. Code Ann. §§ 31-39-1 to -9.

[150] *In re* Doe, 418 S.E.2d 3, 7 (Ga. 1992).

[151] **MA:** *See, e.g., In re* Doe, 583 N.E.2d 1263 (Mass. 1992); Custody of a Minor, 434 N.E.2d 601 (Mass. 1982).

   **TX:** O.G. v. Baum, 790 S.W.2d 839 (Tex. Ct. App. 1990).

## § 15.13  —Confirmation of Diagnosis

Decisionmaking about life-sustaining treatment for children is not necessarily the sole province of the surrogate and the attending physician. In the case of an adult patient, courts often require that there be some confirmation of the relevant medical facts, most notably the patient's prognosis, by physicians other than the attending physician.[152] This practice should also be observed when the patient is a child.[153]

## § 15.14  —Judicial Review

Once a decision has been made in the clinical setting based on the informed decision of the parents and without recourse to the courts for a judicial determination of incompetence or appointment of a guardian, "the decision whether to end the dying process is a personal decision for family members or those who bear a legal responsibility for the patient,"[154] and there is ordinarily no need to obtain judicial approval of that decision.[155] However, if health care professionals believe the parents' decision is substantively inappropriate, judicial review should be sought.[156] Review may also be necessary if someone other than the child's parent is acting as surrogate decisionmaker.[157] Guardianship statutes

---

[152] See § **5.59.**

[153] **FL:** *In re* Barry, 445 So. 2d 365, 372 (Fla. Dist. Ct. App. 1984) (diagnosis should always be confirmed by at least two physicians).

    **GA:** *In re* L.H.R., 321 S.E.2d 716, 722–23 (Ga. 1984).

    **MI:** *Cf.* Rosebush v. Oakland County Prosecutor, 491 N.W.2d 633, 638 (Mich. Ct. App. 1992) ("We agree with the principles set forth in *Barry* and *In re LHR*.").

[154] *In re* L.H.R., 321 S.E.2d 716, 723 (Ga. 1984).

[155] **FL:** *In re* Barry, 445 So. 2d 365 (Fla. Dist. Ct. App. 1984).

    **GA:** *In re* L.H.R., 321 S.E.2d 716.

    **LA:** *In re* P.V.W., 424 So. 2d 1015 (La. 1982).

    **MA:** *Cf. In re* Beth, 587 N.E.2d 1377, 1380 (Mass. 1992) (judicial oversight not required for do-not-resuscitate order in Massachusetts, following *In re* Dinnerstein, 380 N.E.2d 134 (Mass. App. Ct. 1978)).

    **MI:** Rosebush v. Oakland County Prosecutor, 491 N.W.2d 633, 637 (Mich. Ct. App. 1992).

[156] **FL:** *In re* Barry, 445 So. 2d 365.

    **GA:** *In re* Doe, 418 S.E.2d 3, 6 (Ga. 1992); *In re* L.H.R., 321 S.E.2d 716.

    **MI:** Rosebush v. Oakland County Prosecutor, 491 N.W.2d at 639 (judicial involvement needed "only when the parties directly concerned disagree about treatment, or other appropriate reasons are established for the court's involvement").

    **NY:** *Cf.* Weber v. Stony Brook Hosp., 456 N.E.2d 1186 (N.Y. 1983).

[157] **MA:** Custody of a Minor, 434 N.E.2d 601, 608 (Mass. 1982) (absent loving family with whom physicians may consult, issue is best resolved by requiring judicial determination).

    **NY:** *Cf. In re* Richardson, 581 N.Y.S.2d 708 (Sup. Ct. Monroe County 1992) (pursuant to statute, court may review DNR order for minor).

ordinarily give courts the authority to approve the decisions of guardians to forgo life-sustaining treatment for a minor ward if such approval is sought.[158]

Decisions about forgoing life-sustaining treatment are, perhaps, more routinely made without judicial participation or blessing when the patient is a child than when the patient is an adult. Nonetheless, cases involving children can raise substantial uncertainty about what are proper decisionmaking procedures and acceptable decisions, and they can give rise to significant fear of civil and criminal liability. Because of such concerns, the courts have held, as they have in the case of adults,[159] that even when judicial review is not required "the courts are always available to protect the rights of the individual."[160] Although judicial review is not routinely required, the requisites of such proceedings, such as "the appointment of an attorney . . . the appointment of an independent physician . . . the joinder of the attorney general and the local district attorney, and . . . procedural due process which requires proof of the underlying facts by at least clear and convincing evidence,"[161] can add important safeguards to the child's interests. In the only case to give explicit attention to this issue, the Illinois Supreme Court held that judicial review is required when the issue is refusal of lifesaving treatment by a mature minor[162] because of the high value placed by Illinois public policy on the "sanctity of life" and because of the parens patriae power of the state to protect persons incompetent to protect themselves,[163] although review is not necessarily routinely required in the case of an adult.[164]

When judicial review is sought, it is frequently on an emergency basis.[165] The medical situations involved are usually not emergencies in the strict sense but rather gradually become urgent because a resolution cannot be achieved in the clinical setting, or they are emergencies that could have been

---

[158] **OH:** *See, e.g., In re* Myers, 610 N.E.2d 663, 669 (P. Ct. Summit County, Ohio 1993) ("R.C. 2111.50(F) gives the probate court full parens patriae powers: 'When considering any question related [to], and issuing orders for, medical or surgical care or treatment of incompetents or minors subject to guardianship, the probate court has full parens patriae powers unless otherwise provided by a section of the Revised Code.'").

[159] See § **5.27.**

[160] **GA:** *In re* L.H.R., 321 S.E.2d 716, 723 (Ga. 1984). *Accord In re* Doe, 418 S.E.2d 3, 5 (Ga. 1992).

    **FL:** *Accord In re* Barry, 445 So. 2d 365, 372 (Fla. Dist. Ct. App. 1984).

    **LA:** *Accord In re* P.V.W., 424 So. 2d 1015, 1020 (La. 1982).

    **MI:** *Accord* Rosebush v. Oakland County Prosecutor, 491 N.W.2d 633, 638 (Mich. Ct. App. 1992).

[161] *In re* P.V.W., 424 So. 2d at 1020.

[162] See § **15.3.**

[163] *In re* E.G., 549 N.E.2d 322, 327–28 (Ill. 1989).

[164] *Cf. In re* Estate of Greenspan, 558 N.E.2d 1194 (Ill. 1990); Estate of Longeway v. Community Convalescent Ctr., 549 N.E.2d 292 (Ill. 1989). See §§ **5.26, 5.37,** and **5.41.**

[165] **DGA:** *See, e.g.,* Novak v. Cobb County-Kennestone Hosp. Auth., 849 F. Supp. 1559 (N.D. Ga. 1994).

    **TX:** *See, e.g.,* O.G. v. Baum, 790 S.W.2d 839 (Tex. Ct. App. 1990).

anticipated.[166] Consequently, courts are often faced with an urgent application by hospital counsel for an order authorizing the patient's attending physicians to administer treatment. And, given the actual or alleged exigency of the circumstances, this order is often granted at least to maintain the status quo. In *Fosmire v. Nicoleau*,[167] involving an application for authorization to provide blood transfusions in connection with a cesarean delivery, the New York Court of Appeals took a dim view of what has become conventional practice in most jurisdictions of obtaining an ex parte order.[168] The court held that "[a]pplications for court-ordered medical treatment affect important rights of the patients and should generally comply with due process requirements of notice and the right to be heard before the order is signed. [Citation omitted.]"[169] However, because due process is a "flexible concept," the court acknowledged that there might be some cases in which it is not feasible to accord prior notice and a right to be heard, but in such situations "the court should make some effort to communicate with the patient or responsible relatives if only to give prompt notice that the order has been signed."[170] However, these exceptional cases could often be avoided if physicians would raise these issues earlier and not turn what should be a decisionmaking process into a waiting game with patients or their families until an emergency develops.

## § 15.15 ——Standard of Proof

There is no reason why the standard of proof in judicial decisionmaking about life-sustaining medical treatment should be different for children from the standard when the patient is an adult. Thus, although few courts have considered the issue in the context of children,[171] the clear-and-convincing-evidence standard ought to be applied.[172]

---

[166] **CA9:** *See, e.g.,* Niebla v. County of San Diego, 967 F.2d 589 (Table), 1992 WL 140250 (9th Cir. 1992) (unpublished).

**MA:** *See, e.g., In re* McCauley, 565 N.E.2d 411 (Mass. 1991).

**PA:** *See, e.g., In re* Cabrera, 552 A.2d 1114 (Pa. Super. Ct. 1989).

[167] 551 N.E.2d 77 (N.Y. 1990).

[168] **CA9:** *See, e.g.,* Niebla v. County of San Diego, 967 F.2d 589, 1992 WL 140250.

**DGA:** *See, e.g.,* Novak v. Cobb County-Kennestone Hosp. Auth., 849 F. Supp. 1559.

**DFL:** *See, e.g.,* McKenzie v. Doctors' Hosp. of Hollywood, Inc., 765 F. Supp. 1504 (S.D. Fla. 1991).

[169] Fosmire v. Nicoleau, 551 N.E.2d at 80.

[170] *Id.*

[171] **DE:** *Cf.* Newmark v. Williams, 588 A.2d 1108, 1110 (Del. 1991) ("State has the burden of proving by clear and convincing evidence that intervening in the parent-child relationship is necessary.").

**IL:** C.A. v. Morgan, 603 N.E.2d 1171, 1181 (Ill. App. Ct. 1992) (where best interests standard applies, there must be "clear and convincing evidence" of patient's prognosis).

[172] See §§ 5.61–5.62.

## Bibliography

Bennett, R. "Allocation of Child Medical Care Decisionmaking Authority: A Suggested Interest Analysis." *Virginia Law Review* 62 (1976): 285.

Breen, S. "Is There a Juvenile Right to Die? The Capacity-Intent Dichotomy." *Journal of Juvenile Law* 12 (1991): 98.

Comment. "Minors' Rights to Medical Care." *Journal of Family Law* 14 (1975–1976): 581.

Clayton, E. "Screening and Treatment of Newborns." *Houston Law Review* 29 (1992): 85.

Deaver, B. "The Competency of Children." *Cooley Law Review* 4 (1987): 522.

Farrell, H. "Consent to Medical Care of Minors: Who Has Authority in Texas?" *Texas Bar Journal* 42 (1979): 25.

Goldstein, J. "Medical Care for the Child at Risk: On State Supervention of Parental Autonomy." *Yale Law Journal* 86 (1977): 645.

Holder, A. "Minors' Rights to Consent to Medical Care." *JAMA* 257 (1987): 3400.

Lebit, L. "Compelled Medical Procedures Involving Minors and Incompetents and Misapplication of the Substituted Judgment Doctrine." *Journal of Law and Health* 7 (1992–1993): 107.

Mark, L. "The Competent Child's Preferences in Critical Medical Decisions: A Proposal for Its Consideration." *Western State University Law Review* 11 (1983): 25.

Massie, A. "Withdrawal of Treatment for Minors in a Persistent Vegetative State: Parents Should Decide." *Arizona Law Review* 35 (1993): 173.

Pilpel, H. "Minors' Rights to Medical Care." *Albany Law Review* 36 (1972): 462.

Plastine, L. "'In God We Trust': When Parents Refuse Medical Treatment for Their Children Based upon Their Sincere Religious Beliefs." *Seton Hall Constitutional Law Journal* 3 (1993): 123.

Redding, R. "Children's Competence to Provide Informed Consent for Mental Health Treatment." *Washington & Lee Law Review* 50 (1993): 695.

Skegg, S. "Consent to Medical Procedures on Minors." *Modern Law Review* 6 (1973): 370.

Stern, J. "Medical Treatment and the Teenager: The Need for Parental Consent." *Clearinghouse Review* 7 (1973): 1.

Tomkins, B. "Health Care for Minors: The Right to Consent." *Saskatchewan Law Review* 40 (1974–1975): 41.

Wadlington, W. "Minors and Health Care: The Age of Consent." *Osgoode Hall Law Journal* 11 (1973): 115.

Wilkins, L. "Children's Rights: Removing the Parental Consent Barrier to Medical Treatment of Minors." *Arizona State Law Journal,* 1975, no. 1: 31.

# CHAPTER 16

# DECISIONMAKING FOR HANDICAPPED INFANTS

---

## § 16.1  Introduction

In recent years, in the view of some, the common-law principles governing medical decisionmaking for children have proved inadequate when dealing with a special class of children: handicapped newborn infants. As a consequence, legislation and regulations, primarily federal but also state,[1] have been adopted to address this issue. This chapter discusses the general problem of decisionmaking about life-sustaining treatment for handicapped newborn infants and focuses on legislative and regulatory developments.[2]

# SOCIAL AND HISTORICAL CONTEXT

## § 16.2  Historical Background

Infanticide—the practice of permitting certain newborn infants to die, usually from starvation, from exposure to the elements or to beasts of prey, or from some combination of these factors—is a well-documented practice in many cultures[3] and can be traced to ancient Greece and Rome[4] and earlier.[5] In some places at some times, such babies have been actively killed, rather than dying from neglect,[6] which under the circumstances might have been a kinder fate. In

---

[1] See § 16.27.

[2] *See generally* Mackler, Neonatal Intensive Care (National Reference Ctr. for Bioethics Literature, Kennedy Inst. of Ethics, Georgetown Univ. 1989) (scope note 11) (annotated bibliography on decisionmaking about life-sustaining treatment for handicapped newborn infants).

[3] *See* H. Kuhse & P. Singer, Should the Baby Live? 108 (1985) (ethnographic reports of 393 societies in 302 of which infanticide was said to be practiced "at least occasionally").

[4] *See id.* at 111–12.

[5] *See* R. Weir, Selective Nontreatment of Handicapped Newborns 6–7 (1984).

[6] *See* H. Kuhse & P. Singer, Should the Baby Live? 99–100, 102, 104, 106 (1985); R. Weir, Selective Nontreatment of Handicapped Newborns 6–20 (1984).

ancient Rome and in the Middle Ages, death from neglect evidently was not considered to be so serious:

> With infanticide as a punishable crime restricted to acts of direct killing, parents and their accomplices in numerous societies abandoned unwanted infants with no possibility of being criminally charged for the child's death. The result was that during the Middle Ages, exposure through abandonment "was practiced on a gigantic scale with absolute impunity, noticed by writers with most frigid indifference and, at least in the case of destitute parents, considered a very venial offense."[7]

An important, though not the exclusive, motivation for this practice was the elimination of physically or mentally handicapped, and thus assumedly burdensome and nonproductive, persons from the society. Even in the absence of any conscious wish to allow such babies to die, handicapped infants in ancient societies and in more modern times have also died because of ignorance as to how to correct their life-threatening conditions. Thus, whether by neglect, design, or lack of choice, many seriously handicapped newborns have suffered the fate of early death.

## § 16.3  Public Attitudes

Increasing medical knowledge and technology, especially in this century, have gradually made it possible to save the lives of some handicapped and premature newborns who previously would have died even had they been provided with life's basic necessities. With this increased capability has come a difficult moral and legal dilemma: when it is possible to save the lives of such babies through known medical means, is it obligatory to do so regardless of the quality of life that the infant can reasonably be expected to lead now and in the future?

This dilemma has long existed to some extent in all such cases, except perhaps those in which a newborn child literally could not be fed because of the nature of its defect. However, the continued existence of this dilemma in modern times, even after the discovery of incipient means for keeping some handicapped children alive, had been largely unknown to the general public or easily ignored as long as childbirth occurred predominantly in the home. As childbirth moved increasingly to hospitals, the dilemma raised by the practice of withholding treatment from handicapped newborns became far more difficult to avoid.

In the United States, it was not until 1973 that the general public became aware that the practice of infanticide still existed. The publication of two articles

---

[7] R. Weir, Selective Nontreatment of Handicapped Newborns 10 (1984) (quoting W.E.H. Lecky, A History of European Morals from Augustus to Charlemagne, as *quoted by* Silverman, *Mismatched Attitudes About Neonatal Death,* 11 Hastings Center Rep. 12 (Dec. 1981)).

in the same issue of the *New England Journal of Medicine*[8] helped to create increased, if not widespread, awareness in the health care professions as well as the larger public of what had long been a well-kept secret.[9] One of the articles reported that over a two-and-one-half-year period, 14 percent of the 43 deaths in a neonatal intensive care unit were related to the withholding of treatment from infants, most of whom suffered from multiple congenital anomalies.[10] Other studies suggested that withholding lifesaving treatment from handicapped newborn infants might have been even more widespread.[11] In addition, two other surveys in 1976 and 1977 found that most pediatricians would honor parental wishes not to treat correctable congenital anomalies in Down's syndrome infants.[12]

Since the mid-1970s, forgoing lifesaving treatment for handicapped newborns has created significant controversy in the popular press, in the professional literature, and among lawmaking institutions. The most likely explanation for this, in light of the relatively low incidence of such clinical cases, is twofold. First, these cases involve not merely children, or even infants, but newborn infants, which are the natural objects of an unparalleled level of tenderness and concern. The thought of inappropriately withholding treatment from any person stirs strong emotions, but even more so when the patients are newborn infants.

Closely related has been the concern that treatment is inappropriately withheld, that is, withheld because the lives of handicapped infants are devalued by health care professionals, by parents, and by society at large. The specific fear is that when a child is born with a correctable life-threatening condition, such as an esophageal atresia (an esophagus that does not connect to the stomach, and hence prevents the child from being fed), the condition will go uncorrected if the child also suffers from some other condition that is not life-threatening but that might socially devalue the child's life, such as Down's syndrome or some other condition that results in a serious physical or mental handicap. An alternative explanation, however, is not that health care professionals devalue the lives of handicapped newborn infants but that they merely follow the customary practice of "yield[ing] to parent wishes . . . as physicians have done for generations."[13]

---

[8] *See* Duff & Campbell, *Moral and Ethical Dilemmas in the Special-Care Nursery,* 289 New Eng. J. Med. 890 (1973); Shaw, *Dilemmas of "Informed Consent" in Children,* 289 New Eng. J. Med. 885 (1973).

[9] *See* Lantos, *Baby Doe Five Years Later: Implications for Child Health,* 317 New Eng. J. Med. 444, 444 (1987) ("Until the 1970s, passive euthanasia of imperiled newborns was a pseudo-secret. Doctors all knew about it, as evidenced by footnotes in the surgical literature, but there was a euphemistic language for it, so it never had to be acknowledged or dealt with explicitly. After a surgical technique to treat hydrocephalus became available in England in the late 1950s, the rate of 'stillbirths' among babies with myelomeningocele dropped dramatically—a development that occasioned ironic comment but no moral outrage.").

[10] Duff & Campbell, *Moral and Ethical Dilemmas in the Special-Care Nursery,* 289 New Eng. J. Med. 890 (1973).

[11] S. Rep. No. 246, 98th Cong., 2d Sess. 8 (1984), *reprinted in* 1984 U.S.C.C.A.N. 2918, 2925.

[12] *Id.* at 2926.

[13] Duff & Campbell, *Moral and Ethical Dilemmas in the Special-Care Nursery,* 289 New Eng. J. Med. 890, 891 (1973).

Such fears are not altogether unfounded.[14] There is a related concern, also not entirely unfounded, that infants with Down's syndrome (and perhaps with other socially devalued conditions) are sometimes allowed to die even when they have no life-threatening condition.[15] Some, and possibly many, decisions to withhold treatment from handicapped infants might be motivated not merely by estimates of the social value of the child's life but also by considerations of the "seemingly pointless, crushing burdens" of an emotional and financial nature that the child would impose on its family.[16]

## § 16.4   Attitudes in the Health Professions

The sometimes devaluing attitudes of families, health care professionals, and the public toward handicapped infants are compounded by several other factors. Ignorance in the health professions about the correctability of some birth defects sometimes limits the degree to which treatment is even offered to parents.[17] This is compounded by ignorance about the kinds of lives that developmentally disabled children and adults can live, so that even when physicians are aware of the medical options, they might not explain them because of their lack of understanding that the lives of many handicapped individuals can be rewarding to themselves and to others. In addition, the validity of prognostication for low-birth-weight babies and for some kinds of handicapping conditions is very poor, especially at the time of birth and in the period shortly thereafter.[18]

---

[14] **CA:** *See, e.g., In re* Phillip B., 188 Cal. Rptr. 781, 797 n.9 (Ct. App. 1983) (natural parents of teenage boy with Down's syndrome refused recommended cardiac surgery because "[t]hey felt that surgery would be merely life-prolonging rather than life-saving, presenting the possibility that they would be unable to care for Phillip during his later years").

**IN:** *In re* Infant Doe, No. GU8204-00 (Ind. Cir. Ct. Monroe County Apr. 12, 1982), *writ of mandamus dismissed,* No. 482 S 140 (Ind. May 27, 1982), *cert. denied,* 464 U.S. 961 (1983), discussed in § **16.6.**

**ME:** Maine Medical Ctr. v. Houle, Civ. Action No. 74-145, slip op. at 4 (Super. Ct. Cumberland County, Me. Feb. 14, 1974) (correction of tracheal-esophageal fistula not "heroic measures except for the doctor's opinion that probable brain damage has rendered life not worth preserving"), *discussed in Death Ruled Natural for Deformed Baby Denied Sustenance,* N.Y. Times, Jan. 18, 1974, at 27, *and in Judge Orders Care for Mongoloid Child,* N.Y. Times, Oct. 2, 1973, at 3.

[15] *See* H. Kuhse & P. Singer, Should the Baby Live? 8 & passim (1985) (expert evidence that common medical practice in England is to let Down's syndrome infants die).

[16] Duff & Campbell, *Moral and Ethical Dilemmas in the Special-Care Nursery,* 289 New Eng. J. Med. 890 (1973).

[17] President's Comm'n for the Study of Ethical Problems in Medicine & Biomedical & Behavioral Research, Deciding to Forego Life-Sustaining Treatment 223 (1983) (parents receive outdated or incomplete information from physicians) [hereinafter President's Comm'n, Deciding to Forego Life-Sustaining Treatment]; United States Comm'n on Civil Rights, Medical Discrimination Against Children with Disabilities 27 (1989).

[18] President's Comm'n, Deciding to Forego Life-Sustaining Treatment 220–23; Goldworth & Stevenson, *The Real Challenge of "Baby Doe": Considering the Sanctity and Quality of Life,* 28 Clinical Pediatrics 119, 120 (1989) ("Except for certain chromosomal and genetic abnormalities,

At least at the time of birth, parents of handicapped newborn infants are usually unaware that support programs exist.[19] This ignorance is quite understandable but needs to be corrected by health care professionals. However, physicians and other health care professionals might also be unaware of the range of support programs, both private and public, that is available, and often ignore the possibility of giving the baby up for adoption.[20]

## LEGAL BACKGROUND

### § 16.5 Early Cases

Beginning in the 1970s, at about the same time as the publication of the articles revealing the practice of withholding treatment from handicapped infants,[21] a trickle of cases began to be litigated over the legitimacy of this practice. Most were resolved at the trial court level, usually with an order that the child be treated.[22] An unreported 1974 case[23] in Maine gained some notoriety, but it was not until 1979 that there was a reported case involving withholding of treatment from handicapped newborn infants, and that too was a trial court decision.[24] The case arose when proceedings were instituted for the judicial appointment of a guardian to consent to surgery to repair a meningomyelocele in a newborn infant whose parents refused treatment, stating they would " 'let God decide' if the

---

the ability to predict the outcome for an individual infant is extremely limited."); Rhoden, *Treating Baby Doe*, 16 Hastings Center Rep. 34 (July 1986); Young & Stevenson, *Limiting Treatment for Extremely Premature Low-Birth-Weight Infants (500 to 750 g)*, 144 Am. J. of Diseases of Children 549 (1990).

[19] *See* S. Rep. No. 246, 98th Cong., 2d Sess. 10 (1984), *reprinted in* 1984 U.S.C.C.A.N. 2918, 2927. *See also* Baldwin, *Infant Death: Life and Death in Newborn Special Care Units, Bureau of Health System Regulation,* Connecticut State Dep't of Health Servs. mimeo. 5 (Mar. 1982), *cited in* President's Comm'n, Deciding to Forego Life-Sustaining Treatment 209.

[20] *See* S. Rep. No. 246, 98th Cong., 2d Sess. 11 (1984), *reprinted in* 1984 U.S.C.C.A.N. 2918, 2928 *et seq.* (discussing adoption opportunities). *Cf. id.* at 2935–37. *See also* Baldwin, *Infant Death: Life and Death in Newborn Special Care Units, Bureau of Health System Regulation,* Connecticut State Dep't of Health Servs. mimeo. 5 (Mar. 1982), *cited in* President's Comm'n, Deciding to Forego Life-Sustaining Treatment 209.

[21] See §§ 16.2–16.3.

[22] *See* J. Robertson, *Dilemma in Danville,* 11 Hastings Center Rep. 5 (Oct. 1981).

[23] Maine Medical Ctr. v. Houle, Civ. Action No. 74-145 (Super. Ct. Cumberland County, Me. Feb. 14, 1974) (guardian ad litem appointed to consent to repair of a tracheal esophageal fistula after parents had directed attending physician not to operate and to cease intravenous feeding of their severely handicapped newborn infant), *discussed in Deformed Infant Is Operated on by Court Order Despite Parents,* N.Y. Times, Feb. 17, 1974, at 52.

[24] **NY:** *In re* Cicero, 421 N.Y.S.2d 965 (Sup. Ct. Bronx County 1979).

child is to live or die."[25] The next reported case, which was also the first appellate case, did not arise until 1983.[26]

The trickle of cases, or at least public awareness of them, began to grow in the early 1980s. A court in Florida ordered surgery for spina bifida in a newborn who would be paralyzed from the knees down, incontinent, and possibly mentally retarded even if the surgery were performed.[27] In 1981, Siamese twins, born in Illinois to a father who was a physician and a mother who was a nurse, were left to die of starvation at the direction of the parents and concurrence of the attending physicians until an anonymous complaint led to the filing of a neglect petition and the temporary transfer of custody to the state.[28] In what might have been the first contemporary criminal prosecution for withholding treatment from a handicapped newborn infant, criminal charges for conspiracy to commit murder and endangering the life and health of children were filed against those parents and physicians.[29] As of a year later, the babies were alive and the heart condition of one of them, originally thought to be life-threatening, had improved, and the criminal charges had been dropped.[30]

This trickle of cases never became a flood or even a stream. The regulatory and legislative interventions that subsequently occurred[31] might have deterred some or even much litigation. Although the legislation and regulation seem to raise as many questions as they answer, in fact there has been no further reported litigation.[32] Possibly the private atmosphere in which such decisionmaking occurs explains the low incidence of litigation.[33] This kind of atmosphere both reflects and encourages a traditional system of decisionmaking in which, "with rare exceptions, these choices [to forgo therapy] have been made by parents and physicians without review by courts or any other body."[34] Indeed, the traditional standard of organized medicine, as reflected in an opinion of the Judicial Council of the American Medical Association, is that "the decision

---

[25] *Id.* at 966.

[26] **NY:** *See* Weber v. Stony Brook Hosp., 467 N.Y.S.2d 685 (App. Div. 1983), discussed in **§ 16.8.**

[27] *A Judge Sentences Baby Elin to Life,* Newsweek, July 6, 1981, at 24.

[28] *The Moral Dilemma of Siamese Twins,* Newsweek, June 22, 1981, at 40.

[29] *See* Robertson, *Dilemma in Danville,* 11 Hastings Center Rep. 5 (Oct. 1981).

[30] N.Y. Times, May 16, 1982, at A-49, col. 1.

[31] See §§ **16.7** and **16.9–16.20.**

[32] See § **16.23.**

[33] S. Rep. No. 246, 98th Cong., 2d Sess. 9 (1984), *reprinted in* 1984 U.S.C.C.A.N. 2918, 2926 ("[M]ost decisions in medicine involve confidentiality and, hence, secrecy. Even in semipublic places like a hospital, detailed deliberations are not open to scrutiny and, hence, the law has had little toward which to react.") (citing Duff & Campbell, *Moral and Ethical Dilemmas in the Special-Care Nursery,* 289 New Eng. J. Med. 890 (1973)).

[34] President's Comm'n, Deciding to Forego Life-Sustaining Treatment 207.

whether to exert maximal efforts to sustain life should be the choice of the parents."[35]

It is not clear, however, that the atmosphere in which decisionmaking for infants occurs differs in terms of privacy from that in which decisionmaking about life-sustaining treatment for adults occurs, and the volume of litigation in the latter context has been much greater. This explanation is further belied by the fact that "a significant number of care and protection petitions are initiated by hospitals or members of their staffs, since they are often the only persons outside the family in a position to detect signs of abuse, neglect, or abandonment."[36]

Another possible explanation is that the number of such cases in the clinical context is relatively small. However, although the incidence of denial of treatment to handicapped infants is difficult to document, one estimate is that 400 infants with spina bifida alone are subjected to some form of denial or delay of treatment each year.[37]

Not until 1982 did these cases begin to attract systematic legal analysis, first by administrative agencies, then by the courts and legislatures. However, a systematic body of case law like that engendered by the *Quinlan* case, and parallel to the right-to-die cases involving adults, has never really emerged.[38]

The problem for law is to establish standards for determining when it is appropriate to withhold treatment for handicapped infants, that is, when it is the proper practice of medicine and when it constitutes a crime.[39] A former Surgeon General expressed this point concisely in testimony before a congressional subcommittee:

> Let me stress here that some problems are simply not correctable. Some handicapped infants, unfortunately, face imminent death. For such infants it is very important to note that we do not seek to fruitlessly prolong the process of dying, rather, we seek to guarantee that infants who would live, given ordinary care, will not be denied the opportunity for life by those who would decide that their lives are not worth living.[40]

---

[35] American Medical Ass'n, Current Opinions of the Judicial Counsel § 2.14 (1984), *superseded by* Council on Ethical & Judicial Affairs, American Medical Ass'n, Code of Medical Ethics: Current Opinions with Annotations § 2.215, at 51 (1994).

[36] Custody of a Minor, 434 N.E.2d 601, 607 (Mass. 1982).

[37] S. Rep. No. 246, 98th Cong., 2d Sess. 9 (1984), *reprinted in* 1984 U.S.C.C.A.N. 2918, 2926. *See also* President's Comm'n, Deciding to Forego Life-Sustaining Treatment 207 ("decisions to forego therapy are part of everyday life in the neonatal intensive care unit").

[38] See §§ **16.23–16.27.**

[39] *See generally* Robertson, *Involuntary Euthanasia of Defective Newborns: A Legal Analysis,* 27 Stan. L. Rev. 213 (1975).

[40] S. Rep. No. 246, 98th Cong., 2d Sess. 9 (1984), *reprinted in* 1984 U.S.C.C.A.N. 2918, 2926. *See also In re* Cicero, 421 N.Y.S.2d 965, 967–68 (Sup. Ct. Bronx County 1979) ("This is not a case where the court is asked to preserve an existence which cannot be a life. What is asked is that a child born with handicaps be given a reasonable opportunity to live, to grow and hopefully to surmount those handicaps. . . . [W]here a child has a reasonable chance to live a useful, fulfilled life, the court will not permit parental inaction to deny that chance.").

## § 16.6  *Infant Doe* Case

In April 1982, what has come to be known as the *Infant Doe* case[41] made nationwide headlines when, in Bloomington, Indiana, the parents of a newborn infant with Down's syndrome and tracheal-esophageal fistula declined repair of the fistula. Down's syndrome (formerly known as mongolism) is characterized by an extra chromosome 21, which can cause varying degrees of mental retardation and congenital anomalies such as serious but repairable heart defects and repairable defects of the esophagus and/or gastrointestinal system. These latter defects prevent an infant from receiving any nutrition, and if not treated death from starvation ensues within a short time. Those afflicted with Down's syndrome who survive infancy usually reach adulthood.[42] The father of Infant Doe had been a public school teacher and had on occasion worked closely with children with Down's syndrome and other handicaps. The parents felt that "a minimally acceptable quality of life was never present for a child suffering from such a condition," and further that it was not in the best interests of the infant, their other two children, and the family entity as a whole for the infant to be treated.[43] The administration of the hospital in which the baby was born filed an emergency petition seeking to have the parents' refusal of surgery overridden.

The court heard testimony from the mother's obstetrician that he and other members of the obstetrical group believed that the infant should remain at the hospital where he was born, knowing that surgery was not possible there and that the child would soon die. This recommendation was based on the fact that "even if surgery were successful, the possibility of a minimally adequate quality of life was non-existent due to the child's severe and irreversible mental retardation."[44] The infant's pediatrician and a pediatric consultant, although agreeing with the obstetrician's prognosis, recommended in testimony that the infant be immediately transferred to another hospital where corrective surgery could be performed.

In a one sentence conclusion, the trial court determined that the parents, having been fully informed of the available alternative courses of treatment, "have the right to choose a medically recommended course of treatment for their child in the present circumstances."[45] However, it also appointed local child welfare authorities as the child's guardian ad litem to determine whether to appeal the case. They decided not to do so. The district attorney then petitioned the juvenile court to determine whether the infant was neglected under state law. This petition was denied, and a writ of mandamus in the Indiana Supreme Court was dismissed as moot because of the child's death.[46]

---

[41] *In re* Infant Doe, No. GU8204-00 (Ind. Cir. Ct. Monroe County Apr. 12, 1982).

[42] 1 Harrison's Principles of Internal Medicine 321 (R. Petersdorf et al. eds., 11th ed. 1987).

[43] *In re* Infant Doe, No. GU8204-00, slip op. at 2 (Ind. Cir. Ct. Monroe County Apr. 12, 1982).

[44] *Id.*

[45] *Id.* at 3.

[46] State *ex rel.* Infant Doe v. Baker, No. 482 S 140 (Ind. May 27, 1982), *cert. denied,* 464 U.S. 961 (1983).

The *Infant Doe* case created significant public controversy. Just why this was so is not clear because, based on the reports in the literature,[47] it is apparent that a very limited course of palliative therapy for seriously handicapped newborn infants was neither a novel nor an uncommon occurrence. Possibly it was the fact that the infant in question suffered from Down's syndrome, which is not a particularly serious handicapping condition, either mentally or physically, in the broad spectrum of congenital abnormalities. A markedly changed public attitude toward Down's syndrome might also have been responsible for the outcry caused by the *Infant Doe* case. In the decade or so between the publication of the articles revealing the practice of permitting handicapped newborns to die and *Infant Doe,* a great deal of progress had been made in deinstitutionalizing, educating and training, and otherwise normalizing the lives of mildly and moderately retarded persons.

## § 16.7   Rehabilitation Act (Section 504) Regulations

The *Infant Doe* case and the ensuing publicity were the impetus for a series of federal regulatory actions. Within a few weeks of the decision, the Director of the Office of Civil Rights of the United States Department of Health and Human Services (DHHS), in response to a directive from the President and citing " 'heightened public concern' " caused by the *Infant Doe* case,[48] issued a Notice to Health Care Providers on the subject of "Discriminating Against the Handicapped by Withholding Treatment or Nourishment."[49] This notice stated that conditions such as Down's syndrome are handicaps within the meaning of section 504 of the Rehabilitation Act of 1973[50] and the implementing rules,[51] and the DHHS threatened to terminate federal financial assistance to any hospital engaging in discriminatory conduct against handicapped newborns or "facilitating discriminatory conduct" by the parents of the children.

Within 10 months, the DHHS notice was superseded by an interim final rule announcing a "vigorous federal role."[52] Also issued pursuant to section 504 of the Rehabilitation Act, the rule required health care providers that were recipients of federal funds to post a notice "in a conspicuous place" in obstetric and pediatric wards stating that

---

[47] See §§ **16.3** and **16.5.**

[48] Bowen v. American Hosp. Ass'n, 476 U.S. 610, 617 (1986).

[49] Department of Health & Human Servs., *Health Care Financing Administration, Medicare Part A Intermediary Letter,* HCFA-Pub. 60A, Transmittal No. 82-11 (May 1982).

[50] 29 U.S.C.A. § 794 (West 1985 & Supp. 1994).

[51] 45 C.F.R. § 84.3(j) (1994).

[52] Department of Health & Human Servs., Nondiscrimination on the Basis of Handicap, 48 Fed. Reg. 9630, 9630 (Mar. 7, 1983).

## DISCRIMINATORY FAILURE TO FEED AND CARE FOR
## HANDICAPPED INFANTS IN THIS FACILITY IS
## PROHIBITED BY FEDERAL LAW

and directing that persons having notice of such violations telephone a toll-free Handicapped Infant Hotline.[53] Enforcement of this rule was promptly enjoined for failure to comply with the Administrative Procedure Act, and the court declined to rule on substantive challenges to its legality and constitutionality.[54]

To correct the procedural deficiency, the DHHS issued a proposed rule requiring the posting of the same notice, no smaller than 8½ by 11 inches, including the telephone hotline number, but with additional information about contacting state child protective services agencies.[55] One important difference between the interim final rule and the proposed rule was a requirement that federally assisted state child protective services agencies utilize their "full authority pursuant to State law to prevent instances of medical neglect of handicapped infants."[56] The commentary to the proposed rule allowed for the withholding of treatment when "an infant would not benefit medically from a particular treatment,"[57] because such a child would not be an "otherwise qualified handicapped individual" within the meaning of section 504 of the Rehabilitation Act. Further, the regulation contained a list of conditions, not intended to be exhaustive, for which treatment categorically could not be denied.[58]

On the basis of its analysis of responses to the proposed rule, the DHHS then issued a final rule.[59] Although not deviating substantially from the proposed rule, one important change was that the categorical conditions requiring treatment under the proposed rule were described as illustrative only in the final rule.[60] In addition, the final rule contained a provision recommending but not requiring that hospitals establish infant care review committees "to assist . . . in the development of standards, policies and procedures for providing treatment to handicapped infants and in making decisions concerning medically beneficial treatment in specific cases."[61] This rule was declared invalid, on the basis of litigation growing out of a case involving another handicapped newborn,[62] in

---

[53] *Id.* at 9631.

[54] American Academy of Pediatrics v. Heckler, 561 F. Supp. 395 (D.D.C. 1983).

[55] *See* 48 Fed. Reg. 30,846, 30,850, 30,851 (July 5, 1983) ("telephone complaint procedure" which "shall not be limited to normal business hours").

[56] *Id.* at 30,851.

[57] *Id.* at 30,846. *See also id.* at 30,851–52 app.

[58] *Id.*

[59] *See* 49 Fed. Reg. 1622 (Jan. 12, 1984).

[60] *Id.* at 1654 app. C(a)(5).

[61] *Id.* at 1651. See § **16.22.**

[62] See § **16.8.**

suits brought by the American Hospital Association, the American Medical Association, and others, on the ground that it was promulgated without statutory authority.[63]

## § 16.8  Judicial Invalidation of Section 504 Regulations

While the DHHS was in the process of promulgating and revising the administrative rules occasioned by the *Infant Doe* case,[64] a handicapped infant, known as Baby Jane Doe in the ensuing litigation, was born in New York with spina bifida, microcephaly, and hydrocephalus. After consultation with neurological experts, nurses, religious counselors, and a social worker, the parents chose a conservative course of treatment, which involved not performing surgery but otherwise providing necessary medical care and nourishment.[65] They did so because "corrective surgery that was likely to prolong the child's life . . . would not improve many of her handicapping conditions."[66]

Unlike the *Infant Doe* case in Indiana, no one from among the physicians providing care to the mother or infant, other members of the health care team, or the hospital administration disputed the propriety of the parents' course of action. However, a petition challenging the parental choice was filed, in a case that came to be known as *Weber v. Stony Brook Hospital,* by a person described by the New York Court of Appeals as a "resident of the State of Vermont, with no disclosed connection with Baby Jane Doe or her family"[67] and by the United States Supreme Court as "an unrelated attorney named Washburn."[68] The trial court appointed a guardian ad litem, determined that the baby was in need of immediate surgery to preserve her life, and authorized the guardian ad litem to consent to the procedures. However, the next day the appellate division reversed, observing that the two expert witnesses agreed that "the parents' choice of a course of conservative treatment, instead of surgery, was well within accepted medical standards" and would "not place the infant in imminent danger of death."[69]

---

[63] Bowen v. American Hosp. Ass'n, 476 U.S. 610 (1986). See § **16.8.**

[64] See § **16.7.**

[65] Weber v. Stony Brook Hosp., 467 N.Y.S.2d 685, 686 (App. Div.) (per curiam), *aff'd,* 456 N.E.2d 1186 (N.Y.), *cert. denied,* 464 U.S. 1026 (1983).

[66] Bowen v. American Hosp. Ass'n, 476 U.S. 610, 620 (1986).

[67] Weber v. Stony Brook Hosp., 456 N.E.2d at 1187.

[68] Bowen v. American Hosp. Ass'n, 476 U.S. at 620.

[69] Weber v. Stony Brook Hosp., 467 N.Y.S.2d at 685. *See also* Colen, *What Ever Happened to Baby Jane Doe?,* 24 Hastings Center Rep. 2 (May–June 1994) ("Now a ten-year-old . . . [who] is not only a self-aware little girl, who experiences and returns the love of her parents, she also attends a school for developmentally disabled children—once again proving that medicine is an art, not a science, and clinical decisionmaking is best left in the clinic, to those who will

The New York Court of Appeals affirmed but did not address one of the fundamental issues, the propriety of the parents' choice. Instead, it dealt with the other fundamental issue, namely, who has the authority to make such choices. In its opinion, the court chastised the petitioner, the guardian ad litem, and the trial court for failing to follow statutory procedures for determining when the state may intervene against the wishes of a parent on behalf of a child so that the child's needs are properly met. The failure to follow these procedures, the court observed, subjected the parents, already "[c]onfronted with the anguish of the birth of a child with severe physical disorders," to unauthorized and unprecedented litigation.[70]

After the initiation of the state court proceedings, the DHHS also "received a complaint from a 'private citizen' that Baby Jane Doe was being discriminatorily denied medically indicated treatment."[71] DHHS referred the complaint to the New York State Child Protective Service pursuant to the procedures described in the pending proposed rule on nontreatment of handicapped infants.[72] This investigation was concluded with a finding by the state authorities that there was no reason for state intervention.

The DHHS also began its own investigation to determine the hospital's compliance with section 504 of the Rehabilitation Act and sought to examine the hospital's records in the treatment of Baby Jane Doe. The hospital declined to make the records available, in part because of the parental refusal to consent to their release; DHHS then brought an action to compel production of the records.[73] The uncontradicted evidence established that the hospital stood ready to perform the surgical procedures and that it had not performed them only because the parents had refused to consent and not because the infant was handicapped.[74] The court denied the government's motion, finding that the hospital had clearly not violated section 504 of the Rehabilitation Act because it lacked the legal right to perform medical procedures on a child without parental consent, and that the parental decision, as confirmed by state judicial proceedings,[75] was a "reasonable choice among alternative medical treatments."[76] Without reaching the question of the familial right of privacy, the court nonetheless commented that it found this claim to be "extremely weak."[77]

---

have to live with the decisions being made."); *"Baby Jane Doe" Turns 9 This Year,* N.Y. Times, May 17, 1992, at 44 (late city ed.); United States Comm'n on Civil Rights, Medical Discrimination Against Children with Disabilities 40 (1989) ("As of 1987, Baby Jane . . . was talking, using a wheelchair, and going to school.").

[70] Weber v. Stony Brook Hosp., 456 N.E.2d at 1188.

[71] Bowen v. American Hosp. Ass'n, 476 U.S. at 621.

[72] 48 Fed. Reg. 30,846 (July 5, 1983). See **§ 16.7.**

[73] United States v. University Hosp., 575 F. Supp. 607 (E.D.N.Y. 1983), *aff'd on other grounds,* 729 F.2d 144 (2d Cir. 1984).

[74] United States v. University Hosp., 575 F. Supp. at 614.

[75] See **§ 16.8.**

[76] United States v. University Hosp., 575 F. Supp. at 615.

[77] *Id.*

The Court of Appeals for the Second Circuit affirmed the dismissal,[78] and the Supreme Court, in *Bowen v. American Hospital Ass'n*,[79] finally put an end to the point and counterpoint of regulation and litigation that had been going on for four years by holding that the final rule issued by the DHHS[80] was not authorized by section 504 of the Rehabilitation Act, thereby affirming the holdings of the lower courts.[81]

The Court rejected both of two possible bases for the final rule. The first was that "a hospital's refusal to furnish a handicapped infant with medically beneficial treatment 'solely by reason of his handicap' constitutes unlawful discrimination."[82] The Court found that withholding medical treatment from handicapped infants when the parents refuse such treatment does not violate section 504. In such a case, the infant is not "otherwise qualified" and has not been denied treatment "solely by reason of handicap,"[83] as the statute requires. "Indeed," the Court observed, "it would almost certainly be a tort as a matter of state law to operate on an infant without parental consent."[84] The failure of the DHHS when the rules were first promulgated to recognize that withholding of consent by parents is not discriminatory denial of treatment by *hospitals* was not cured by basing the final rule on reported instances in which parents had refused consent because, in those cases, treatment had been administered after investigation by state authorities.[85]

The second basis proffered by DHHS for the final rule was that a hospital's failure to report instances of suspected medical neglect to the appropriate state child protective services agency might also violate section 504 of the Rehabilitation Act. The Court acknowledged that "a hospital's selective refusal to report medical neglect of handicapped infants might violate section 504" but, in the absence of any specific evidence that this had occurred, there was no basis for the final rule.[86] Although DHHS had conducted 49 investigations, summarized in the preamble to the final rule, they did "not reveal *any* case in which a hospital either failed, or was accused of failing, to make an appropriate report to a state agency."[87] If the basis for federal intervention is perceived discrimination against handicapped infants in violation of section 504, the Court said, "deference cannot fill the lack of an evidentiary foundation on which the Final Rules must rest."[88]

---

[78] United States v. University Hosp., 729 F.2d 144, 156 (2d Cir. 1984).

[79] 476 U.S. 610 (1986) (plurality opinion).

[80] 49 Fed. Reg. 1622 (Jan. 12, 1984), discussed in § **16.7.**

[81] See § **17.21.**

[82] Bowen v. American Hosp. Ass'n, 476 U.S. at 628.

[83] *Id.* at 630.

[84] *Id.*

[85] *Id.* at 636.

[86] *Id.* at 637–38.

[87] *Id.*

[88] 476 U.S. at 643.

## CHILD ABUSE AMENDMENTS OF 1984

### § 16.9  Nature and Purpose of Child Abuse Amendments of 1984

While the litigation was proceeding in the Baby Jane Doe case, and in light of the ruling invalidating the DHHS rules based on the Rehabilitation Act,[89] Congress entered the arena that DHHS and the courts had occupied for two years. The result was the Child Abuse Amendments of 1984[90] to the Child Abuse Prevention and Treatment and Adoption Reform Act,[91] originally enacted in 1974 to combat child abuse and neglect, provide training and technical assistance to public and private organizations, provide funding for research and demonstration projects, and provide grants to the states to establish or strengthen existing programs for the prevention, detection, and treatment of child abuse and neglect.[92] By expanding the statutory definition of "child abuse" to include the "withholding of medically indicated treatment,"[93] Congress sought to establish a firmer footing for a federal regulatory presence in decisionmaking about the treatment of handicapped infants than that provided by the Rehabilitation Act of 1973.

Under the Child Abuse Amendments and the implementing rule, states receiving grants pursuant to the legislation "must establish programs and/or procedures within [their] protective service system to respond to reports of medical neglect, including reports of the withholding of medically indicated treatment for disabled infants with life-threatening conditions."[94] However, state child protective services agencies might be barred by their state constitutions from promulgating these rules.[95]

All states have a child protective services system, under which physicians and sometimes other health care personnel are required to report instances of actual or suspected child abuse or neglect. All state statutes confer immunity from civil and criminal liability for reports made in good faith and impose penalties for failure to make mandated reports.[96] However, the provisions of the Child Abuse Amendments and regulations apply only to those states accepting federal child

---

[89] See § **16.8.**

[90] Pub. L. No. 98-457, tit. 1, §§ 121–128, 98 Stat. 1749 (1984) (codified as amended in scattered sections of 42 U.S.C.A. (West 1992 & Supp. 1994)).

[91] Pub. L. No. 93-247, 88 Stat. 4 (1974).

[92] 50 Fed. Reg. 14,878, 14,878 commentary (Apr. 15, 1985).

[93] 42 U.S.C.A § 5102 (West 1992 & Supp. 1994).

[94] 50 Fed. Reg. at 14,878. The requirement is contained in a new clause K in § 4(b)(2) of the act, 50 Fed. Reg. at 14,878, and implemented through 45 C.F.R. § 1340.15(c) (1993). *See also* 42 U.S.C.A. § 5103(b)(2)(K).

[95] *See* Newman, *Baby Doe, Congress and the States: Challenging the Federal Treatment Standard for Impaired Infants,* 15 Am. J. Law & Med. 1 (1989).

[96] 49 Fed. Reg. 48,160, 48,162 (proposed Dec. 10, 1984).

abuse funds, and not all do.[97] Under the Rehabilitation Act's *Infant Doe* regulations,[98] only health care institutions accepting Medicare reimbursement were obligated to comply, so that in theory individual health care institutions could opt out of coverage. Under the Child Abuse Amendments, however, participation is on a state-by-state basis rather than on an individual institutional basis.

## § 16.10   DHHS Interpretative Guidelines to Child Abuse Amendments

The *Infant Doe* regulations had engendered a great deal of opposition and hostility from a number of respected and politically influential groups such as the American Medical Association, the American Hospital Association, and the American Pediatric Association.[99] On the other hand, the regulatory efforts had been supported by a number of other important interest groups, including an "uneasy alliance between right-to-life groups and several advocacy groups for the handicapped."[100] The Child Abuse Amendments were the result of a very careful and delicate political compromise reflecting a "consensus among many medical, professional, and advocacy organizations that action was needed to adopt protections for disabled infants with life-threatening conditions,"[101] achieved only after " 'painstaking negotiations' involving the diverse coalition" of groups.[102] Thus, "each word of the statutory definition 'was chosen with utmost care.' "[103]

Consequently, in drafting regulations to implement the Child Abuse Amendments, DHHS withdrew from the final rule a number of the proposed rule's definitions that went beyond the statutory definitions and, according to the principal sponsors, beyond the legislative intent. This was done to "allay concerns that the proposed rule could have been construed so as to distort the

---

[97] United States Comm'n on Civil Rights, Medical Discrimination Against Children with Disabilities 111–12 & n.4 (1989) (listing states); Barnet, *Baby Doe: Nothing to Fear but Fear Itself,* 10 J. Perinatology 307, 310 (1990); Clearinghouse on Child Abuse and Neglect Information State Grant Summaries, 1988 (Dec. 1988); Ellis & Luckasson, *Denying Treatment to Infants with Handicaps: A Comment on Bowen v. American Hospital Association,* 24 Mental Retardation 237, 239 (1986).

[98] *See* 49 Fed. Reg. 1622 (Jan. 12, 1984), discussed in § **16.7.**

[99] *See* American Academy of Pediatrics v. Heckler, 561 F. Supp. 395 (D.D.C. 1983); American Hosp. Ass'n v. Heckler, 585 F. Supp. 541 (S.D.N.Y. 1984).

[100] Lantos, *Baby Doe Five Years Later: Implications for Child Health,* 317 New Eng. J. Med. 444, 445 (1987) (citing Page & Karnofsky, *The Antiabortion Movement and Baby Jane Doe,* 11 J. Health Pol., Pol'y & L. 255 (1986)).

[101] 49 Fed. Reg. 48,160, 48,160 (1984) (proposed rule).

[102] 50 Fed. Reg. 14,878, 14,879 (1985) (quoting letter to DHHS from principal sponsors of the Child Abuse Amendments, Senators Hatch, Denton, Cranston, Nickles, Dodd, and Kassebaum criticizing the DHHS proposed rule). *See also* 49 Fed. Reg. 48,160 (proposed rule).

[103] 50 Fed. Reg. at 14,879 commentary.

Congressional compromise by establishing binding rules of law that might compound rather than resolve the myriad of real-life problems in intensive care nurseries."[104]

However, rather than entirely eliminating the regulatory definitions that had been a part of the proposed rule, DHHS changed them to "interpretative guidelines" and included them as an appendix to the final rule in order to "giv[e] all parties the benefits of very relevant interpretations of the statute by the agency charged with its implementation"[105] and "because the Department continues to believe that guidance relating to interpretations of key terms used in the statutory definition of 'withholding of medically indicated treatment' will aid in effective implementation of the statute."[106]

The DHHS further explained that

> the Department does not seek to establish these interpretative guidelines as binding rules of law, nor to prejudge the exercise of reasonable medical judgment in responding to specific circumstances. Rather, this guidance is intended to assist in interpreting the statutory definition so that it may be rationally and thoughtfully applied in specific contexts in a manner fully consistent with the legislative intent.[107]

The interpretative guidelines "avoid using examples of specific diagnoses to elaborate on meaning . . . [to] allay concerns that the proposed rule presented what some commenters referred to as a 'cookbook approach' to the practice of medicine."[108]

Despite the DHHS disavowal that the guidelines are "binding rules of law," they will be difficult to ignore. One unreported case discussed and applied the interpretative guidelines as if they were binding, although noting that they were not.[109]

## § 16.11 Nature of Regulatory Scheme

The joint explanatory statement by the principal sponsors of the Child Abuse Amendments characterizes them as "requir[ing] States which participate in the State grant program to have in place procedures and/or programs . . . for the purpose of responding to the reporting of medical neglect, including instances of withholding of medically indicated treatment from disabled infants with life-threatening conditions."[110] Thus, at least on their face, the Child Abuse

---

[104] *Id.* at 14,882.

[105] *Id.*

[106] *Id.* at 14,880.

[107] 45 C.F.R. pt. 1340 app. at 294 (1991).

[108] 50 Fed. Reg. at 14,880.

[109] *See In re* Welfare of Steinhaus, slip op. 8–9 & passim (Redwood County Ct. Juv. Div. Minn. Sept. 11, 1986), *amended* (Oct. 13, 1987), discussed in § **16.27.**

[110] Joint Explanatory Statement by Principal Sponsors of Compromise Amendment Regarding Services and Treatment for Disabled Infants, S. Rep. No. 246, 98th Cong., 2d Sess. 40 (1984), *reprinted in* 1984 U.S.C.C.A.N. 2969, 2969.

Amendments and final rule merely mandate mechanisms for responding to reports made by health care providers to state child protective services agencies of instances of "medical neglect."[111] In reality, however, both the statute and regulations, in a complex and intricate fashion, define what treatment is medically indicated[112] and what treatment is not,[113] instead of merely leaving such substantive matters to state law.

## § 16.12 —Medical Neglect

The term *medical neglect* is the keystone of the statutory scheme, and its definition is crucial to understanding the obligations of health care institutions, health care personnel, parents, and state child protective services agencies thereunder. In effect, treatment must be administered if failing to do so would constitute medical neglect. Medical neglect is itself defined by reference to a number of other terms used in the statute and/or regulations.[114]

The commentary to the final rule reaffirms the existing common law of health care decisionmaking by parents for children, namely, that "[t]he decision to provide or withhold medically indicated treatment . . . except in highly unusual circumstances, [should be] made by the parents or legal guardian."[115] Neither child protective services agencies[116] nor infant care review committees[117] are to make such treatment decisions.[118] The commentary also restates the presumption of parental authority to make decisions for their children in collaboration with the attending physicians.[119]

However, the commentary is vague in describing the limits of parental decisional authority, stating that "[t]he parents' role as decision maker must be respected and supported unless they choose a course of action inconsistent with applicable standards established by law."[120] Although not explaining whether "established by law" refers to case law or the Child Abuse Amendments themselves, the content of the final rule is such that it probably does change the

---

[111] 42 U.S.C.A. § 5103(b)(2)(K) (West Supp. 1994). *See also* 45 C.F.R. § 1340.15(c) (1994). Medical neglect is discussed in §§ **16.12–16.20.**

[112] See §§ **16.13** and **16.20.**

[113] See §§ **16.16–16.19.**

[114] See §§ **16.13–16.19.**

[115] 50 Fed. Reg. 14,878, 14,880 (1985).

[116] See §§ **16.11** and **16.21.**

[117] See § **16.22.**

[118] 50 Fed. Reg. at 14,880–81.

[119] *Id.* at 14,880 ("Parents are the decision makers concerning treatment for their disabled infant, based on the advice and reasonable medical judgment of their physician (or physicians)."). See § **15.2.**

[120] 50 Fed. Reg. at 14,880.

existing, or at least the developing, substantive case law.[121] Furthermore, in order to be eligible for federal child abuse funding, states must comply with "documentation" requirements[122] of a detailed nature that shape the substance of state law.[123]

Finally, the commentary underscores the separation of powers and roles between the regulatory scheme it creates and the already existing medical system by explaining that the legislation is not intended to require child protection workers to practice medicine or second-guess reasonable medical judgments. Rather, Congress intended that child protective services agencies respond to reports of suspected medical neglect under procedures designed to ascertain whether any decision to withhold treatment was based on reasonable medical judgment consistent with the definition of "withholding of medically indicated treatment."[124]

Given the history of federal regulatory efforts in these matters,[125] some skepticism about this remark is understandable. This skepticism is reinforced by the fact that, although the Child Abuse Amendments are facially a reporting scheme, what must be reported to child protective services authorities are situations that might not constitute child neglect under existing state common law.[126]

Nonetheless, the implicit conceptual underpinnings of the Child Abuse Amendments are consistent with the case-law development of the right to die. A core concept of both the statute and the case law is the patient's prognosis.[127] Basically, if the patient's prognosis, even with treatment, is hopeless, treatment need not be administered.[128] As prognosis improves, under both the Child Abuse Amendments and the case law, the surrogate's authority to decline lifesaving treatment diminishes. However, there are some very important differences between the Child Abuse Amendments and the common law.[129]

## § 16.13 Basic Requirement: Provision of Medically Indicated Treatment

Although in form the Child Abuse Amendments and their regulations are a reporting scheme, in effect they create an obligation to administer treatment

---

[121] See §§ 16.23–16.27.

[122] 45 C.F.R. § 1340.15(d) (1994).

[123] *Id.* § 1340.15(d)(2)(i)–(iii).

[124] 50 Fed. Reg. at 14,881.

[125] See §§ 16.7 and 16.10.

[126] See §§ 16.23–16.26.

[127] See §§ 8.9–8.13.

[128] See §§ 16.15–16.18.

[129] See §§ 16.22–16.26.

under certain circumstances. The central requirement is that health care institutions *report instances of medical neglect,* which the regulations define as "the failure to provide adequate medical care."[130] Medical neglect includes, but is not limited to, the "withholding of medically indicated treatment from a disabled infant with a life-threatening condition."[131] Thus, in substance, the basic duty is to provide medically indicated treatment. The failure to do so constitutes medical neglect. This standard is inconsistent with the prevailing standard in the medical profession,[132] which is also generally accepted by the courts,[133] that physicians are obligated only to provide children, including handicapped newborn infants, with treatment that is in their "best interests," a standard which takes into account the child's quality of life, a factor seemingly rejected by the Child Abuse Amendments and regulations.[134]

The meaning of medically indicated treatment depends on the meaning of several other terms that are defined in the final rule. Withholding of medically indicated treatment has two components. First, it consists of "the failure to respond to an infant's life-threatening conditions by providing treatment."[135] Second, treatment is defined to include all treatments that, according to the reasonable medical judgment of the attending physician, are most likely to be effective in ameliorating or correcting such life-threatening conditions.[136]

**Medical Evaluation.** The interpretative guidelines explain that it was the intent of Congress that treatment include medical evaluation as well as medical intervention.[137] Thus, failing to obtain evaluations or consultations in response to an infant's life-threatening conditions constitutes the withholding of medically indicated treatment. And if parents of a handicapped infant refuse to agree to evaluations or consultations that, in the reasonable medical judgment of the attending physician, are needed, "this would be a matter for appropriate action by the child protective services system."[138]

**Multiple Treatments.** Treatment, according to the interpretative guidelines, should not be viewed in isolation from the context of the series of treatments embodied in a treatment plan. Thus, "withholding of medically indicated treatment" would occur if parents refuse an intervention that is part of a total plan

---

[130] 45 C.F.R. § 1340.15(b) (1994). *See also* 50 Fed. Reg. 14,878, 14,887 (1985).

[131] 42 U.S.C.A. § 5103(b)(2)(K) (West Supp. 1994). *See also* 45 C.F.R. § 1340.15(b)(1).

[132] Council on Ethical & Judicial Affairs, American Medical Ass'n, Code of Medical Ethics § 2.215, at 51 (1994).

[133] See § **15.9.**

[134] 45 C.F.R. pt. 1340 app. at 219 (interpretative guideline no. 9). See § **16.25.**

[135] 42 U.S.C.A. § 5102(3). *See also* 45 C.F.R. § 1340.15(b)(2).

[136] 42 U.S.C.A. § 5102(3). *See also* 45 C.F.R. § 1340.15(b)(2).

[137] 50 Fed. Reg. at 14,890 app.

[138] *Id.*

involving multiple interventions over a period of time that is likely to be effective in ameliorating or correcting all life-threatening conditions.[139]

## § 16.14   —Life-Threatening Condition

*Life-threatening condition* is not defined in the statute, and its definition in the proposed regulations[140] engendered so much controversy that it was eliminated from the final rule. However, the discussion in the interpretative guidelines explains the view of the DHHS (in the same language used in the proposed regulation) that the term "include[s] a condition that, in the treating physician's or physicians' reasonable medical judgment, significantly increases the risk of the onset of complications that may threaten the life of the infant."[141] Also, "where a condition may not, strictly speaking, by itself be life-threatening, but where the condition significantly increases the risk of the onset of complications that may threaten the life of the infant," the condition is to be considered life-threatening and treatment is medically indicated if available.[142]

The illustration given in the proposed rule is of "an infant born with an open myelomeningocele (a protrusion of a portion of the spinal cord and its enclosing membranes through a bony defect in the vertebral column)." The commentary on this example states that

> [s]uch a condition may not, strictly speaking, by itself be life-threatening. However, the grave risk associated with an open myelomeningocele is the onset of an infection that may be life-threatening or might increase or add to the disability. Such cases are clearly within the scope of the circumstances to which Congress intended the analysis embodied in the definition of "withholding of medically indicated treatment" to apply.[143]

It was not the intent of DHHS to include within the meaning of life-threatening conditions irreversible conditions for which no corrective treatment is available.[144] The interpretative guidelines explain that

> [t]he Department's interpretation implies nothing about whether, or what, treatment should be provided. It simply makes clear that the [statutory] criteria . . . for evaluating whether, or what, treatment should be provided are applicable.[145]

---

[139] 45 C.F.R. pt. 1340 app. at 214.

[140] 49 Fed. Reg. 48,160, 48,166 (Dec. 10, 1984) ("The term 'life-threatening condition' means a condition that threatens the life of the infant or that significantly increases the risk of the onset of complications that may threaten the life of the infant.").

[141] 45 C.F.R. pt. 1340 app. at 215 (1994).

[142] *Id.*

[143] 49 Fed. Reg. 48,160, 48,163 (Dec. 10, 1984).

[144] 50 Fed. Reg. 14,878, 14,889 app (1985).

[145] *Id.*

Even if the condition is life-threatening, treatment is not necessarily medically indicated.[146] "That is just the start, not the end, of the analysis. The analysis then takes fully into account the reasonable medical judgment regarding potential effectiveness of possible treatments, and the like."[147]

## § 16.15   —Reasonable Medical Judgment

The concept of "reasonable medical judgment" is central to the entire regulatory scheme. This concept seeks to achieve a balance between "the ethical morass of either quality-of-life assessments or cost-effectiveness evaluations" on the one hand and a technological imperative to treat on the other.[148]

Whether a treatment is *medically indicated* "turns substantially on the 'reasonable medical judgment' of the treating physician or physicians."[149] The statute does not define the term, but the regulatory definition is the same as that of the conference committee report: "a medical judgment that would be made by a reasonably prudent physician, knowledgeable about the case and the treatment possibilities with respect to the medical conditions involved."[150]

## § 16.16   Exceptions to Basic Requirement: Treatment Not Medically Indicated

Both the statute and administrative rules list several types of situations in which treatment is not considered to be medically indicated and therefore need not be administered.[151] Each of these situations implements the more fundamental principle that prognosis is the determinative factor.

The statute and administrative rule provide that treatment is not medically indicated, and therefore need not be administered, if any one of the following conditions is met:

1. "The infant is chronically and irreversibly comatose"[152]
2. "The provision of such treatment would merely prolong dying"[153]

---

[146] See § **16.16.**

[147] 50 Fed. Reg. at 14,889 app.

[148] Lantos, *Baby Doe Five Years Later: Implications for Child Health,* 317 New Eng. J. Med. 444, 445 (1987).

[149] *Id.*

[150] 45 C.F.R. § 1340.15(b)(3)(ii) (1994).

[151] 42 U.S.C.A. § 5102(3) (West Supp. 1994). *See also* 45 C.F.R. § 1340.15(b)(2) (1994).

[152] 42 U.S.C.A. § 5102(3)(A). *See also* 45 C.F.R. § 1340.15(b)(2)(i).

[153] 42 U.S.C.A. § 5102(3)(B)(i). *See also* 45 C.F.R. § 1340.15(b)(2)(ii). See § **16.17.**

3.  Treatment would "not be effective in ameliorating or correcting all of the infant's life-threatening conditions"[154]

4.  Treatment would "otherwise be futile in terms of the survival of the infant"[155]

5.  "[T]reatment would be virtually futile in terms of the survival of the infant and the treatment itself would be inhumane."[156]

The meaning of the first of these—irreversible coma—depends wholly on reasonable medical judgment. The meaning of the others, however, requires additional explanation.

### § 16.17  —Treatment Not Medically Indicated If Merely Prolongs Dying

Treatment need not be administered if it would merely prolong dying. The refusal of parents to consent to its administration is not medical neglect, because such treatment is not medically indicated.[157] A conceptual difficulty is that, because everyone will eventually die, "it might be said that a treatment that will not totally eliminate a medical condition but will give a patient many years of life 'merely prolongs dying'."[158] This approach would effectively eliminate any duty to administer treatment even when death would probably occur many years hence and there is a reasonable probability that the patient could live a meaningful life between the time of treatment and death. The commentary to the proposed rule explains that

> [b]ecause Congress included "ameliorating" conditions in its test for analyzing medical effectiveness and because the term "merely prolong dying" is used in conjunction with "otherwise be futile in terms of the survival of the infant," it appears clear that Congress intended the term "merely prolong dying" to apply only where death is imminent and treatment will do no more than postpone the act of dying.[159]

---

[154] 42 U.S.C.A. § 5102(3)(B)(ii). *See also* 45 C.F.R. § 1340.15(b)(2)(ii). See § **16.18.**

[155] 42 U.S.C.A. § 5102(3)(B)(ii). *See also* 45 C.F.R. § 1340.15(b)(2)(ii). The term "futile" is not defined in the statute, final rule, or interpretative guidelines, although the term "virtually futile" is defined in the interpretative guidelines. See § **16.19.**

[156] 42 U.S.C.A. § 5102(3)(B)(iii). *See also* 45 C.F.R. § 1340.15(b)(2)(iii). See § **16.19.**

[157] 42 U.S.C.A. § 5102(3)(B)(i) (West Supp. 1994); 45 C.F.R. § 1340.15(b)(2)(ii) (1994).

[158] 49 Fed. Reg. 48,160, 48,164 (1984).

[159] *Id.*

However, "[m]any commenters on the proposed rule, as well as the principal sponsors of the Child Abuse Amendments, urged deletion of the word 'imminent' and its connotation of immediacy."[160] According to the interpretative guidelines, in the legislative negotiations leading up to the compromise that was embodied in the Child Abuse Amendments,[161] it developed that "reasonable medical judgments can and do result in nontreatment decisions regarding some conditions for which treatment will do no more than temporarily postpone a death that will occur in the near future, but not necessarily within days."[162] Consequently, the word "imminent" was deleted from the final rule, but DHHS

> interprets the term "merely prolong dying" as referring to situations where the prognosis is for death and, in the treating physician's (or physicians') reasonable medical judgment, further or alternative treatment would not alter the prognosis in an extension of time that would not render the treatment futile.

> [DHHS] continues to interpret Congressional intent as not permitting the "merely prolong dying" provision to apply where many years of life will result from the provision of treatment, or where the prognosis is not for death in the near future, but rather the more distant future. . . . In addition . . . the Department's interpretation is that reasonable medical judgments will be formed on the basis of knowledge about the condition(s) involved, the degree of inevitability of death, the probable effect of any potential treatments, the projected time period within which death will probably occur, and other pertinent factors.[163]

### § 16.18    —Treatment Not Medically Indicated If Ineffective in Ameliorating All Life-Threatening Conditions

Treatment is not medically indicated and therefore need not be administered if it would not be effective in ameliorating or correcting all of the infant's life-threatening conditions.[164] This means that if a handicapped newborn infant suffers from more than one life-threatening condition, for at least one of which (in the reasonable medical judgment of the attending physician) there is no corrective treatment, treatment need not be administered for any of the conditions, correctable or not.[165] The only exception is that "appropriate nutrition, hydration, and medication" must still be provided.[166]

---

[160] 45 C.F.R. pt. 1340 app. at 217 (interpretative guideline no. 5).

[161] See § 16.10.

[162] 45 C.F.R. pt. 1340 app. at 217 (interpretative guideline no. 5).

[163] *Id. See* C.A. v. Morgan, 603 N.E.2d 1171 (Ill. App. Ct. 1992) (to enter do-not-resuscitate order for infant, death need not be imminent if condition is incurable and fatal).

[164] 42 U.S.C.A. § 5102(3)(B)(ii) (West Supp. 1994); 45 C.F.R. § 1340.15(b)(ii) (1994).

[165] *See* Joint Explanatory Statement by Principal Sponsors of Compromise Amendment Regarding Services and Treatment for Disabled Infants, S. Rep. No. 246, 98th Cong., 2d Sess. 41 (1984), *reprinted in* 1984 U.S.C.C.A.N. 2969, 2970.

[166] See § 16.20.

Treatment can be ineffective in the context of future life-threatening conditions or in the context of palliative treatment.

### Future Life-Threatening Conditions

> The interpretative guidelines explain that if a disabled infant suffers from more than one life-threatening condition and, in the treating physician's or physicians' reasonable medical judgment, there is no effective treatment for one of these conditions *that threatens the life of the infant in the near future,* then the infant is not covered by the terms of the amendment (except with respect to appropriate nutrition, hydration, and medication) concerning the withholding of medically indicated treatment; *but if the nontreatable condition will not become life-threatening until the more distant future, the infant is covered by the terms of the amendment.*[167]

This interpretative guideline is based on the same Congressional intent as that underlying the interpretative guideline addressing the permissibility of withholding treatment when its administration would merely prolong dying. That is, if a condition will not become life-threatening until the more distant future, it should not be the basis for withholding treatment.[168]

The commentary to the proposed regulation gives some helpful illustrations. An example of a situation in which a correctable condition need not be treated is an "infant born with anencephaly (congenital absence of the brain) and omphalocele (congenital protrusion of abdominal organs into the umbilical cord)."[169] Because the anencephaly is not correctable, no corrective efforts need be undertaken for the correctable omphalocele, even though the omphalocele is a life-threatening condition.

The commentary also provides an example to illustrate the existence of a situation in which a life-threatening condition must be corrected:

> An example would be a infant with duodenal atresia (a closure or lack of a normal opening in the duodenum), an imminently life-threatening condition that is surgically correctable, and a second condition, such as Down's syndrome (which is associated with a shortened life expectancy). . . . Congress did not intend that the presence of a noncorrectable condition [Down's syndrome] which although not imminently life-threatening would become life-threatening in the future, would be the basis for a decision to withhold treatment for the correctable condition [duodenal atresia].[170]

### Palliative Treatment

When an infant has more than one life-threatening condition, at least one of which is not treatable and will cause death in the near future, a palliative

---

[167] 45 C.F.R. pt. 1340 app. at 217 (interpretative guideline no. 6).

[168] *Id.* at 218.

[169] 49 Fed. Reg. 48,160, 48,164 (1984).

[170] *Id.*

treatment that will, in the physician's reasonable medical judgment, ameliorate the infant's overall condition even though it will not ameliorate or correct each condition, does not fall within the exception to the withholding of treatment, and thus palliative treatment must be administered.[171]

> The example given in the proposed rule is of an infant with a noncorrectable, life-threatening congenital heart defect and an imperforate anus. Although no treatment is available to correct the heart defect or prevent death of the infant, treatment is available, in this example a colostomy, to ameliorate the infant's overall condition by relieving the severe pain associated with the intestinal obstruction caused by the imperforate anus. . . . Congress did not intend to exclude humane treatment that will ameliorate the infant's overall condition, taking *all* conditions into account, even if the treatment would not correct or ameliorate *each* condition. [Thus], such treatment is not excluded from the statutory definition.[172]

### § 16.19 —Treatment Not Medically Indicated If Futile, or Virtually Futile and Inhumane

Treatment is not medically indicated and therefore need not be provided if it would be futile in terms of the infant's survival.[173] No statutory or regulatory definition of *futile* is provided, but according to the interpretative guidelines, a treatment is virtually futile if it is "highly unlikely to prevent death in the near future"[174] and reasonable medical judgment determines whether a treatment is virtually futile.[175] Thus, absolute certitude is not required in determining that a treatment is futile; rather, the attending physician must believe that treatment is futile on the basis of reasonable medical judgment.[176]

In addition, treatment is not medically indicated and need not be provided if it would be virtually futile in terms of the survival of the infant and the treatment itself would be inhumane.[177] According to the interpretative guidelines, a treatment is inhumane if "the treatment *itself* involves significant medical contraindications and/or significant pain and suffering for the infant that clearly outweigh the very slight potential benefit of the treatment for an infant highly unlikely to survive."[178]

---

[171] 45 C.F.R. pt. 1340 app. at 218 (interpretative guideline no. 7).

[172] 49 Fed. Reg. 48,160, 48,164 (Dec. 10, 1984).

[173] 42 U.S.C.A. § 5102(3)(B)(ii) (West Supp. 1994); 45 C.F.R. § 1340.15(b)(2)(ii) (1994).

[174] 45 C.F.R. pt. 1340 app. at 219 (interpretative guideline no. 8). *See generally* Lantos et al., *Survival After Cardiopulmonary Resuscitation in Babies of Very Low Birthweight: Is CPR Futile Therapy?*, 318 New Eng. J. Med. 91 (1988).

[175] 45 C.F.R. pt. 1340 app. at 219 (interpretative guideline no. 8).

[176] See § **16.15.**

[177] 42 U.S.C.A. § 5102(3)(B)(iii); 45 C.F.R. § 1340.15(b)(2)(iii).

[178] 45 C.F.R. pt. 1340 app. at 219 (interpretative guideline no. 9) (emphasis added).

The term "itself" requires that only the burdens imposed by the treatment, and not by the infant's medical condition, be taken into account. Thus, any consideration of the infant's quality of life, according to the DHHS, is inconsistent with the legislative intent.[179] The interpretative guidelines explain that "[t]he balance is clearly to be between the very slight chance that treatment will allow the infant to survive and the negative factors relating to the process of the treatment."[180] The Conference Committee Report adds that "[t]he use of the term 'inhumane' is not intended to suggest that consideration of the humaneness of a particular treatment is not legitimate in any other context; rather, it is recognized that it is appropriate for a physician, in the exercise of reasonable medical judgment, to consider that factor in selecting among effective treatments."[181]

## § 16.20  Duty to Provide Nutrition, Hydration, and Medication

The statute and final rule specifically define medically indicated treatment so as to prohibit the withholding of "appropriate nutrition, hydration, and medication."[182] This requirement appears to be a categorical imperative, except for the fact that it is modified by the word "appropriate." (If categorical, it is at odds with the developing right to die in the case law, especially with respect to the provision of food and water.[183]) Neither the statute nor the final rule explains what "appropriate" means. However, the interpretative guidelines offer an oblique explanation in noting that some commenters on the proposed rule made the point that,

> for example . . . very potent pharmacologic agents, like other methods of medical intervention, can produce results [that accomplish] no more than . . . merely prolong[ing] dying, or [are] futile in terms of the survival of the infant. . . . [T]herefore, the Department should clarify that the provision regarding "appropriate nutrition, hydration or medication" should not be construed entirely independently of the circumstances under which other treatment need not be provided.[184]

However, the DHHS rejected the suggestion that "appropriate nutrition, hydration, and medication" be thus clarified, but the explanation given is not helpful in understanding what "appropriate" does mean:

---

[179] *Id.* See § **16.25.**

[180] *Id.*

[181] Joint Explanatory Statement by Principal Sponsors of Compromise Amendment Regarding Services and Treatment for Disabled Infants, S. Rep. No. 246, 98th Cong., 2d Sess. 41 (1984), *reprinted in* 1984 U.S.C.C.A.N. 2969, 2970.

[182] 42 U.S.C.A. § 5102(3) (West Supp. 1994); 45 C.F.R. § 1340.15(b)(2) (1994).

[183] See § **16.26.**

[184] 45 C.F.R. pt. 1340 app. at 220 (interpretative guideline no. 10).

As noted . . . in the discussion of palliative treatment [in interpretative guideline no. 7], the Department recognizes that there is no absolutely clear line between medication and [other treatment] that would justify excluding the latter from the scope of palliative treatment that reasonable medical judgment would find medically indicated, notwithstanding a very poor prognosis.

Similarly, the Department recognizes that in some circumstances, certain pharmacologic agents, not medically indicated for palliative purposes, might, in the exercise of reasonable medical judgment, also not be indicated for the purpose of correcting or ameliorating any particular condition because they will, for example, merely prolong dying. However, the Department believes the word "appropriate" in this proviso of the statutory definition is adequate to permit the exercise of reasonable medical judgment in the scenario referred to by these commenters.[185]

This is reinforced by the concluding remark of the interpretative guideline, stating that "it should be clearly recognized that the statute is completely unequivocal in requiring that all infants receive 'appropriate nutrition, hydration, and medication' regardless of their condition or prognosis."[186]

The most plausible interpretation of the meaning of the term "appropriate" is that it is intended to require the administration of nutrition, hydration, and medication in accordance with reasonable medical judgment. However, if this is the intended meaning, it is redundant because the provision of medical treatment is already required to be measured by the standard of reasonable medical judgment.[187]

Another interpretation is that the term is intended to permit the withholding of nutrition, hydration, and medication in instances in any of the five exceptions to the basic requirement of providing medically indicated treatment to handicapped newborn infants.[188] The difficulty posed by this interpretation is that it is also redundant. If nutrition, hydration, and medication could be withheld in such cases under the general exception that treatment need not be provided, there would be no need to imply it by the use of the word "appropriate" because the statute explicitly permits the forgoing of all other treatments under such circumstances. Furthermore, this interpretation is inconsistent with the syntax of the statute which states that "the term [withholding of medically indicated treatment] does not include the failure to provide treatment (other than appropriate nutrition, hydration, or medication)."[189]

An alternative construction is that the term "appropriate" is intended to import legal rather than medical standards in determining whether and what kind of nutrition, hydration, and medication are to be administered. That is, these terms could be used by courts to add a judicial gloss to the statutory prohibition. It is

---

[185] *Id.*

[186] *Id.*

[187] *See* 45 C.F.R. § 1340.15(b)(3)(ii). See § **16.14.**

[188] See §§ **16.16–16.19.**

[189] 42 U.S.C.A. § 5102(3).

possible that the statutory prohibition was intended only to refer to withholding those interventions that could be withheld under case-law standards. This particular construction seems unlikely in light of the legislative history of the Child Abuse Amendments, which seem to have been intended to supersede the existing and developing case law rather than to incorporate it into the statute and regulations or permit its further development.[190]

Perhaps the most sensible interpretation of this requirement, though one that is not necessarily supported by its language or legislative history, is that "appropriate" nutrition, hydration, and medication is that which is necessary to keep the infant comfortable.[191]

## § 16.21 Enforcement

States that receive child abuse assistance grants are to establish a means (described in the administrative rule as "programs, procedures, or both"[192]) within their child protective services system for reporting and investigating instances of medical neglect, including the withholding of medically indicated treatment.[193] The Child Abuse Amendments and final rule establish basic standards but not detailed procedures. They do not prescribe any particular process or investigative steps that must be followed by state child protective services agencies in every case, and they build upon existing state agencies, rather than create a new system and a new bureaucracy[194] or rely on federal enforcement as was the case under the invalidated Rehabilitation Act regulations.[195] However, the final rule does require state child protective services agencies "to pursue any legal remedies including the authority to initiate legal proceedings in a court of competent jurisdiction, as may be necessary to prevent the withholding of medically indicated treatment from disabled infants with life threatening conditions."[196]

Although these requirements do not operate directly on hospitals,[197] states must involve health care facilities in the enforcement process,[198] and there is an

---

[190] See §§ **16.6, 16.7,** and **16.10.**

[191] *See* Council on Ethical & Judicial Affairs, American Medical Ass'n, Code of Medical Ethics § 2.215, at 52 (1994) ("When life-sustaining treatment is withheld or withdrawn, comfort care must not be discontinued.").

[192] *See* 45 C.F.R. § 1340.15(b), (c)(2)–(4) (1994) (further explaining these terms).

[193] 42 U.S.C.A. § 5103 (West Supp. 1994). *See also* 45 C.F.R. § 1340.15(c)(1).

[194] 50 Fed. Reg. 14,878, 14,881 (1985).

[195] See § **16.7.**

[196] 45 C.F.R. § 1340.15(c)(2)(iii).

[197] 50 Fed. Reg. at 14,883 ("[M]atters relating to the internal affairs of hospitals are beyond the scope of this regulation.").

[198] 45 C.F.R. § 1340.15(c)(2). *See also* 50 Fed. Reg. at 14,881 ("[I]n responding to such reports, CPS agencies are to coordinate and consult with individuals designated by and within the hospital in order to avoid unnecessary disruption of ongoing hospital activities.").

indirect federal regulatory effect because the states are required to engage in certain procedures that require hospital cooperation. For instance, the regulation does not directly require health care facilities to designate a contact person, but in effect they must do so because states are required to "contact each health care facility to obtain the name, title, and telephone number of the individual(s) designated by such facility for the purpose of the coordination, consultation, and notification activities" required by the regulation.[199] Further, the commentary to the rule states that DHHS "strongly encourage[s] hospitals to make this information known within the facility as a way of assuring the protection of infants."[200] States are also required to develop a "coordination and communications system whose purpose is to assure that reports of suspected medical neglect are made at optimum speed."[201]

**Reporting Withholding of Medically Indicated Treatment.**    All state child neglect and abuse statutes require physicians to report known or suspected child abuse. Some also require that other persons—such as other health care professionals and especially school nurses, teachers, and others in frequent professional contact with children—make such reports. (Reporting by others is encouraged by state statutory provisions conferring immunity for good-faith reports.[202]) Thus, because the Child Abuse Amendments and regulations require states accepting federal child abuse grants to deem the withholding of medically indicated treatment as child abuse, reporting the withholding of medically indicated treatment is, in effect, required by federal laws in those states.

**Access to Medical Records.**    Investigation and enforcement of state statutory prohibitions on child abuse, including the withholding of medically indicated treatment, often require access to certain medical information, independent medical examinations of the infant, and appropriate court orders to enforce the statutory and regulatory requirements. To ensure appropriate investigation and enforcement, state child protective services agencies are required to adopt procedures for obtaining "[a]ccess to medical records and/or other pertinent information when such access is necessary to assure an appropriate investigation of a report of medical neglect."[203] State child protective services agencies are also required to adopt procedures for obtaining an independent medical

---

[199] 45 C.F.R. § 1340.15(c)(3).

[200] 50 Fed. Reg. at 14,883.

[201] 45 C.F.R. § 1340.15(c)(3). *See also* 50 Fed. Reg. at 14,883 (explaining that "[t]his communications system should operate whether the reports are made by the designated individual(s) or by any other person, and whether they are reports requesting CPS agency intervention and legal protection of an infant or reports requesting an initial CPS agency investigation").

[202] 49 Fed. Reg. 48,160, 48,162 (proposed Dec. 10, 1984). *See also* 50 Fed. Reg. at 14,881 ("anyone at any time may report").

[203] 45 C.F.R. § 1340.15(b), (c)(4)(i).

examination of the infant, by judicial order or otherwise "when necessary to assure an appropriate resolution of a report of medical neglect."[204]

## § 16.22  Infant Care Review Committees

The Child Abuse Amendments require the DHHS to develop and publish model guidelines for "infant care review committees"[205] to be established within health care institutions for "educating hospital personnel and families of disabled infants with life-threatening conditions, recommending institutional policies and guidelines concerning the withholding of medically indicated treatment . . . , and offering counsel and review in cases involving disabled infants with life-threatening conditions."[206] This aspect of the legislation reflects a recommendation of the President's Commission that hospitals caring for seriously ill newborns "should provide for internal review [within the hospital] whenever parents and the attending physician decide that life-sustaining therapy should be forgone."[207] It was not the congressional intent for an infant care review committee—a kind of ethics committee—to replace parents as decisionmakers. "The parents' role as decision maker must be respected and supported unless they choose a course of action inconsistent with applicable standards established by law."[208]

The subsequently invalidated regulations promulgated pursuant to the Rehabilitation Act of 1973 encouraged but did not require hospitals to establish infant care review committees.[209] The Child Abuse Act Model Guidelines are also voluntary ("purely advisory"[210]), and if a hospital does establish an internal review committee or other mechanism, it need not follow the model guidelines,[211] which cover such topics as membership and administration of an infant care review committee[212] and the functions of the committee, described as educational,[213] policy development,[214] and case-specific counsel and review.[215]

---

[204] *Id.* § 1340.15(b), (c)(4)(ii).

[205] Child Abuse Amendments of 1984, Pub. L. No. 98-457, § 124(b), 98 Stat. 1749, 1754 (codified as amended at 42 U.S.C.A. § 5103 notes (Historical and Statutory Procedures and Programs for Responding to Reports of Medical Neglect).

[206] Department of Health & Human Servs., Services and Treatment for Disabled Infants; Model Guidelines for Health Care Providers to Establish Infant Care Review Committees, 50 Fed. Reg. 14,893 (Apr. 15, 1985).

[207] President's Comm'n, Deciding to Forego Life-Sustaining Treatment 227. *See also* Council on Ethical & Judicial Affairs, American Medical Ass'n, Code of Medical Ethics § 2.215 (1994).

[208] 50 Fed. Reg. 14,878 14,880–81 (1985).

[209] 49 Fed. Reg. 1622, 1651 (Jan. 12, 1984). See **§ 16.7.**

[210] 50 Fed. Reg. at 14,893.

[211] *Id.*

[212] *Id.* guideline III.

[213] *Id.* at 14,894 guideline IV.

[214] *Id.* guideline V.

[215] *Id.* at 14,895 guideline VI.

## § 16.23   Relationship of Child Abuse Amendments
## to State Case Law

The relationship between the Child Abuse Amendments and the case law of medical decisionmaking for children is difficult to discern. It will take some time before it becomes clear what effect each will have on the other, and indeed whether the statutory approach might cut short the development of the case law.

There are several reasons for this. First, there are many ambiguities in the meaning of some of the key terms employed in the statute and regulations,[216] which will be clarified, if at all, either through further litigation or revisions of the statutes and/or regulations. Second, the political contexts in which both were drafted[217] might color the manner in which they are interpreted by courts, state child protective services agencies, and the DHHS. Finally, there is very thin judicial precedent directly on point by which to determine just what the case law of medical decisionmaking for handicapped infants is. Therefore, principles have to be extrapolated from two other areas of the case law: the common law of medical decisionmaking for children (about both ordinary and lifesaving treatment)[218] and the general body of case law about life-sustaining treatment that is developing in cases involving incompetent adult patients.

There are at least three areas in which the Child Abuse Amendments and the state case law of medical decisionmaking about life-sustaining treatment diverge: age limits, quality of life, and the provision of nutrition, hydration, and medication.

## § 16.24   —Age Limits

The Child Abuse Amendments are generally applicable only to medical decisionmaking for children less than one year old.[219] Substantive principles of state law regarding the forgoing of life-sustaining treatment apply equally to all patients regardless of age, unless the child is a mature minor, which handicapped newborn infants clearly are not.[220] The only exceptions are that the regulatory standards also apply to the evaluation of medical neglect involving a child older than one year "who has been continuously hospitalized since birth, who was

---

[216] See §§ **16.12–16.19.**

[217] See § **16.10.**

[218] See **Ch. 15.**

[219] 45 C.F.R. § 1340.15(b)(3)(i) (1994) (however, regulations are not to "be construed to imply that treatment should be changed or discontinued when an infant reaches one year of age, or to affect or limit any existing protections available under State laws regarding medical neglect of children over one year of age").

[220] See § **15.3.**

born extremely prematurely, or who has a long-term disability."[221] These terms are not defined in the statute or regulations.

## § 16.25   —Quality of Life

Perhaps one of the most significant changes that the Child Abuse Amendments potentially work concerns quality-of-life considerations in decisionmaking. Although neither the statute nor the regulations expressly mention quality of life, the commentary to the final rule explains that the definitional sections "make clear that [they do] not sanction decisions based on subjective opinions about the future 'quality of life' of a retarded or disabled person."[222] Rather, the focus is "on the potential effectiveness of treatment in ameliorating or correcting life-threatening conditions."[223] The clear intent of DHHS is to prohibit quality-of-life considerations from being taken into account in the decisionmaking process. Whether in fact this will occur is unclear because the term "quality of life" is not defined in the statute or regulations and has two different meanings (quality-to-self and social utility) in the case law.[224]

The earlier cases involving life-sustaining treatment of adults almost uniformly eschewed use of "quality of life," or when mentioning it did so by rejecting it as a valid consideration in decisionmaking about forgoing life-sustaining treatment. Since 1982, however, courts gradually have expressly recognized what had been implicit all along, namely, that a patient's quality of life is a highly relevant consideration.[225] Only by clearly specifying what is meant by quality of life and by distinguishing between the two meanings of the term has this development been able to occur. The more recent case law distinguishes between the quality of a patient's life to himself and the quality of that life to others. In decisionmaking about life-sustaining treatment, when an incompetent patient's subjective preferences about treatment are unknown, the surrogate is not only free to take into account the quality of the patient's life to the patient himself but is also increasingly enjoined to do so.[226] However,

---

[221] 45 C.F.R. § 1340.15(b)(3)(i). *See* C.A. v. Morgan, 603 N.E.2d 1171, 1192 (Ill. App. Ct. 1992) (McMorrow, J., dissenting) (criticizing majority for ignoring Child Abuse Amendments in its decision to authorize entry of DNR order for an infant).

[222] 50 Fed. Reg. 14,878, 14,889 app. (1985).

[223] *Id.*

[224] See §§ **9.31–9.33.**

[225] *See, e.g.,* Barber v. Superior Court, 195 Cal. Rptr. 484, 493 (Ct. App. 1983) (quality of life may be considered). *See also* Council on Ethical & Judicial Affairs, American Medical Ass'n, Code of Medical Ethics: Current Opinions with Annotations § 2.17, at 33 (1994) ("In the making of decisions for the treatment of seriously disabled newborns . . . [q]uality of life is a factor to be considered in determining what is best for the individual.").

[226] Council on Ethical & Judicial Affairs, American Medical Ass'n, Code of Medical Ethics § 2.215, at 51 (1994) ("Care must be taken to evaluate the newborn's expected quality of life from the child's perspective."). See §§ **7.7–7.9.**

surrogates are prohibited from taking into account factors that measure the value of the patient's life to others, such as the patient's economic unproductiveness; his consumption of resources that might produce greater results if devoted to another (for example, a scarce intensive care unit bed); the emotional costs imposed on the patient's family, friends, and professional caretakers; and the demoralization that might occur from the continual caring for hopelessly ill people.[227]

Equally important is the consideration, in the case of mentally retarded patients, that such persons are often devalued by society even when not hopelessly ill.[228] Courts have been insistent that the fact that the patient is mentally retarded or otherwise handicapped—that is, that society might not value and respect his life as much as that of others—is an irrelevant consideration.[229] Although the judicial implementation of this view has not always equalled the intensity with which it has been expressed,[230] the basic proposition is fundamentally sound. Similarly, the President's Commission recommended a standard for the treatment of handicapped infants that "excludes consideration of the

---

[227] *See* Council on Ethical & Judicial Affairs, American Medical Ass'n, Code of Medical Ethics: Current Opinions with Annotations § 2.17, at 33 (1994). *But see* Barber v. Superior Court, 195 Cal. Rptr. at 493 ("[S]ince most people are concerned about the well-being of their loved ones, the surrogate may take into account the impact of the decision on those people closest to the patient."). See § **7.24.**

[228] See §§ **16.2–16.3.**

[229] **ME:** Maine Medical Ctr. v. Houle, Civ. Action No. 74-145 (Super. Ct. Cumberland County, Me. Feb. 14, 1974) ("[H]eroic measures" would not be required if a handicapped newborn infant's life could not be saved, but such measures may not be forgone based on doctor's qualitative evaluation of the value of the life to be preserved and in such case are not heroic.).

**MA:** *See, e.g., In re* Doe, 583 N.E.2d 1263 (Mass. 1992); Superintendent of Belchertown State Sch. v. Saikewicz, 370 N.E.2d 417 (Mass. 1977).

**NJ:** *Cf.* Iafelice v. Zarafu, 534 A.2d 417 (N.J. Super. Ct. App. Div. 1987) (physicians not required to inform parents of handicapped newborn infant of alternative of withholding treatment and permitting child to die).

**NY:** *See, e.g., In re* Storar, 420 N.E.2d 64 (N.Y. 1981); *In re* Cicero, 421 N.Y.S.2d 965 (Sup. Ct. Bronx County 1979) (where handicapped newborn infant has a reasonable chance to live a useful, fulfilled life, court is not being asked to preserve an existence that cannot be a life and therefore treatment must be administered). *But see* Weber v. Stony Brook Hosp., 456 N.E.2d 1186 (N.Y. 1983) (parents of handicapped newborn infant are entitled to choose a conservative course of therapy).

**WA:** *In re* Hamlin, 689 P.2d 1372 (Wash. 1984) (recognizing need for closer scrutiny in right-to-die cases involving mentally retarded persons but permitting the forgoing of treatment).

[230] **CA:** *See, e.g., In re* Phillip B., 156 Cal. Rptr. 48 (Ct. App. 1979), *cert. denied,* 445 U.S. 949 (1980), *overruled by implication, In re* Phillip B., 188 Cal. Rptr. 781 (Ct. App. 1983), discussed in § **16.5.** *See also* Gathman, *The Journey of a Child and His Heart: A Decade of Transformation in the Legal, Medical, and Ethical Care of a Child with Down Syndrome,* 3 Cambridge Q. Healthcare Ethics 173 (1994) (describing life of Phillip B.).

**MA:** *See, e.g., In re* Doe, 583 N.E.2d 1263; Superintendent of Belchertown State Sch. v. Saikewicz, 370 N.E.2d 417; *In re* R.H., 622 N.E.2d 1071 (Mass. App. Ct. 1993).

negative effects of an impaired child's life on other persons, including parents, siblings, and society."[231]

The basic principle of the Child Abuse Amendments is that "medical treatment decisions are not to be made on the basis of subjective opinions about the future 'quality of life' of a retarded or disabled person."[232] Neither the regulations nor the commentary, however, explain whether considering quality of life of the patient to himself is prohibited along with assessments of quality of life to others. The commentary states only that DHHS interpreted "the law" as not permitting "life and death treatment decisions to be made on the basis of subjective opinions regarding the future 'quality of life' of a retarded or disabled person."[233] It is not clear whether the phrase "the law" refers to the Child Abuse Amendments or to the preexisting case law; if the latter, it would not be consistent with the case law allowing considerations of one's quality of life to oneself.

Situations involving adults might be distinguished from those involving newborns, older infants, or even young children on two grounds. First, quality of life to oneself might be more predicable for adults than for children. Second, the quality of an individual's life, even to himself, is both a relative and an absolute matter. In the case of adults, there is a baseline against which to measure impaired quality, which is lacking in the case of younger children.[234]

## § 16.26  —Nutrition, Hydration, and Medication

The clearest point of departure between the Child Abuse Amendments and final rule on the one hand and the case law on the other concerns the provision of nutrition and hydration. The language of both the statute and the regulations categorically prohibits the withholding of nutrition, hydration, and medication, even in cases in which all other treatments might be forgone. By contrast, virtually every case to consider the issue has concluded that nutrition and hydration, at least when administered other than orally, is to be considered a medical procedure like any other and may be forgone on the same grounds as other treatments.[235] Rather than categorically prohibiting the withholding of

---

[231] President's Comm'n, Deciding to Forego Life-Sustaining Treatment 219.

[232] 50 Fed. Reg. 14,878, 14,879 (1985).

[233] *Id.*

[234] **FL:** *But see In re* Barry, 445 So. 2d 365, 371 (Fla. Dist. Ct. App. 1984) (applying substituted judgment standard to infant).

 **GA:** *Cf. In re* L.H.R., 321 S.E.2d 716, 718–19 (Ga. 1984) (infant).

 **MA:** *In re* Beth, 587 N.E.2d 1377 (Mass. 1992) (applying substituted judgment standard to infant); Custody of a Minor, 434 N.E.2d 601 (Mass. 1982) (same).

 See § **15.9.**

[235] See § **9.39.**

artificial nutrition and hydration, the case law has attempted to articulate a principle for deciding when the forgoing of artificial nutrition and hydration is appropriate. The difference between the two can best be accounted for as the "politicization of withholding food and water from infants [because] [t]he government has not entered, in such a detailed way, into the control of many other medical practices."[236] The only possible legal reconciliation between the statutory and case law positions is the fact that the Child Abuse Amendments and final rule modify the prohibition on the withholding of nutrition and hydration by the term "appropriate," which is susceptible to a variety of interpretations that might be consistent with the judicial trend.[237]

The prohibition on the withholding of appropriate medication is even more difficult to understand. Apart from the meaning of the term "appropriate," there has been no controversy whatever in the case law about the withholding of medications in circumstances under which it would be otherwise permissible to forgo life-sustaining treatment. It is possible that, with respect to medication, the term "appropriate" is intended to refer to palliative medications; that is, medications intended for the comfort of a handicapped newborn infant may not be withheld even if all other treatment is, which is hardly controversial.[238]

Both the prohibition on withholding nutrition and hydration and the prohibition on withholding medications raise serious constitutional problems. These prohibitions create distinctions both between classes of persons and forms of treatment that are at least prima facie denials of equal protection. The Child Abuse Amendments and regulations treat infants less than one year old differently from older children and from adults. Unless there is at least a rational basis for this distinction, it is unconstitutional. Similarly, they treat nutrition, hydration, and medication differently from other forms of medical interventions, a distinction for which, again, there must be at least a rational basis.

Perhaps the most graphic illustration of the differential treatment accorded children versus adults is the unreported Baby Lance case in Minnesota.[239] Although it involved the withdrawal of a mechanical ventilator rather than nutrition, hydration, or medication, it demonstrates the different results that can occur under the Child Abuse Amendments in contrast with judicial precedents. In its first ruling, the trial court held that the ventilator could not be disconnected because the infant was in a persistent vegetative state that, on the basis of medical testimony, it concluded was different from the chronically comatose exception to the provision of medically indicated treatment in the Child Abuse

---

[236] Frader, *Forgoing Life-Sustaining Food and Water: Newborns, in* By No Extraordinary Means 181 (J. Lynn ed., 1986).

[237] See § **16.20.**

[238] See § **9.2.**

[239] *In re* Welfare of Steinhaus (Redwood County Ct. Juv. Div. Minn. Sept. 11, 1986), *amended* (Oct. 13, 1987).

Amendments[240] (and in the Minnesota statutes that had incorporated the federal standards into state law[241]).

Had the patient been an adult, the case would have been governed by Minnesota case law under which the Minnesota Supreme Court had held that it was permissible for a ventilator to be disconnected from an adult incompetent patient in a persistent vegetative state, a patient whose wishes were also unknown.[242] How such a different result can be justified is difficult to discern, and in a subsequent ruling, the trial court in Baby Lance revised its holding on the basis that the testimony of the attending physician actually did establish that the infant was "chronically and irreversibly comatose."[243]

## § 16.27   Relationship of Child Abuse Amendments to State Statutes

In addition to federal regulatory and legislative responses, some states have enacted legislation to protect the interests of handicapped newborn infants.[244] The state statutes resemble the federal Child Abuse Amendments in several ways. First, in a general way they too are intended to protect handicapped newborn infants from the inappropriate withholding of treatment, which includes nutrition and hydration. Like the federal statute, they rely on the concept of reasonable medical judgment to determine what treatment should be administered. They also reject quality-of-life considerations in determining whether treatment is to be administered or forgone. One important difference, however, is that the state statutes impose criminal penalties for noncompliance.

## § 16.28   Effect of Child Abuse Amendments and Regulations

It is very difficult to assess what impact, if any, the Child Abuse Amendments and regulations have had on decisionmaking about treating, not treating, or

---

[240] See § 16.16.

[241] Minn. Stat. § 260.015 (2a)(5).

[242] See In re Torres, 357 N.W.2d 332 (Minn. 1984).

[243] In re Welfare of Steinhaus (Redwood County Ct. Juv. Div. Minn. Sept. 11, 1986), amended (Oct. 13, 1987) (finding of fact no. 5). See also Cranford, The Persistent Vegetative State: The Medical Reality (Getting the Facts Straight), 18 Hastings Center Rep. 27 (Feb.–Mar. 1988).

[244] See Feldman & Murray, State Legislation and the Handicapped Newborn: A Moral and Political Dilemma, 12 Law, Med. & Health Care 156 (Sept. 1984).

AZ: Ariz. Rev. Stat. Ann. § 36-2281.

IN: Ind. Code Ann. § 31-6-4-3(f).

LA: La. Rev. Stat. Ann. § 40:1299.36.1(A)(1)(a).

limiting treatment of handicapped newborn infants. There has not been any reported litigation under the Child Abuse Amendments—in no small part because they probably do not create a private right of action—although ironically there are cases alleging discriminatory failures to treat handicapped newborn infants under section 504 of the Rehabilitation Act.[245] There is some evidence that the new laws have affected clinical practice and other evidence that they have not. The truth is probably that some physicians' practices have been changed by the law and that some have not, just as it was true before their enactment that there was variation in clinical practice.

The Kopelman study[246] is one of the more informative. One important finding is that in the context of specific cases, there is significant disagreement among physicians about what the federal regulations require. In one case, 61 percent thought the federal regulations required the performance of a diagnostic procedure, 22 percent did not, and 17 percent were uncertain; in a second case, 30 percent thought the regulations required treatment, 52 percent did not, and 18 percent were uncertain; in a third case, 47 percent thought treatment was required, 39 percent did not, and 14 percent were uncertain. The survey also studied whether the regulations had affected physicians' conduct. Again the findings were variable, but it is clear that many physicians believe that the regulations require them to provide treatment that is contrary to what their own judgment, or their judgment informed by the parents' judgment, would have dictated. Another study comes to similar conclusions.[247]

There is anecdotal evidence suggesting that the net effect of the Child Abuse Amendments and implementing regulations has been to encourage physicians to err on the side of providing treatment,[248] an inclination to which many neonatologists may already be predisposed.[249]

---

MN: Minn. Stat. Ann. § 260.105(10)(e)(3).

RI: R.I. Gen. Laws § 40-11-3.

[245] **CA10:** *See, e.g.,* Johnson v. Thompson, 971 F.2d 1487 (10th Cir. 1992) (based on events occurring prior to enactment of Child Abuse Amendments).

**DVA:** *See, e.g., In re* Baby "K," 832 F. Supp. 1022 (E.D. Va. 1993), *aff'd on other grounds,* 16 F.3d 590 (4th Cir.), *cert. denied,* 115 S. Ct. 91 (1994).

[246] Kopelman et al., *Neonatologists Judge the "Baby Doe" Regulations,* 318 New Eng. J. Med. 677 (1988).

[247] *See* Carter, *Neonatologists and Bioethics After Baby Doe,* 13 J. Perinatology 146 (1993).

[248] *See, e.g.,* Eckholm, *Costs and Hope Battle in Intensive Care Units,* N.Y. Times, Dec. 22, 1991, at 1 (nat'l ed.); Felsenthal, *Who Has Right to Decide Fate of Preemies?,* Wall St. J., Nov. 2, 1994, at B1 ("[M]edical advances have encouraged doctors to become ever more tenacious in treating the thousands of premature babies born each year. . . . Insurers and hospitals rarely balk at the huge cost of these cases, in part because of ethical concerns about cutting off an infant's care."); Kolata, *Smallest Survivors: Dilemmas of Prematurity,* N.Y. Times, Sept. 30, 1991, at A-1 (late ed.) (in 1988 survey, doctors "more inclined to treat babies with problematic prognoses" and "paying less heed to parents' wishes than they did when they were surveyed in 1977"). *See also* Rosenthal, *As More Tiny Infants Live, Choices and Burdens Grow,* N.Y. Times, Sep. 29, 1991, § 1, at 1 (late ed.); Brody, *For Babies, An Ounce Can Alter Quality of Life,* N.Y. Times, Oct. 1, 1991, at A1 (late ed.).

[249] Lantos, *Baby Doe Five Years Later: Implications for Child Health,* 317 New Eng. J. Med. 444, 446 (1987) (crisis intervention tends to eclipse prevention among neonatologists).

The most extensive—though by no means definitive—study of the effect of the Child Abuse Amendments and regulations is a report of the United States Commission on Civil Rights.[250] Based on others' surveys,[251] the Commission concluded that "a significant proportion of [physicians] would participate in denial of treatment in certain circumstances . . . [and that] denial of treatment is not infrequent."[252] However, as the Commission acknowledged, "surveys of attitudes toward denial of treatment do not provide direct evidence of the number of actual cases" of treatment denial.[253] Furthermore, it is a matter of dispute as to whether treatment is required to be provided in the hypothetical cases from which the survey data were derived. Another Commission finding is that some state child protective services agencies charged with the implementation of the Child Abuse Amendments delegate this responsibility to hospital infant care review committees[254] or "to the same organized elements of the medical profession who have strongly objected to the Child Abuse Amendments."[255] On balance, the report concludes that there are still incidents in which handicapped newborn infants are not treated but does not provide convincing evidence that these incidents violate federal law.

While most of the attention to the effects of the Child Abuse Amendments has been accorded to handicapped newborn infants, another important group covered by the statute and regulations are low-birth-weight infants. There is evidence that very low-birth-weight infants (those under 750 grams) are at high risk for mental retardation, cerebral palsy, visual disability, and poor school performance.[256]

---

[250] United States Comm'n on Civil Rights, Medical Discrimination Against Children with Disabilities (1989), *summarized in* Boyd & Thompson, Comment, *United States Commission on Civil Rights—Medical Discrimination Against Children with Disabilities: An Abstract*, 6 J. Contemp. Health L. & Pol'y 379 (1990).

[251] Berseth et al., *Longitudinal Development in Pediatric Residents of Attitudes Toward Neonatal Resuscitation*, 140 Am. J. Diseases Children 766 (1986); Kopelman et al., *Neonatologists Judge the "Baby Doe" Regulations*, 318 New Eng. J. Med. 677 (1988); Siperstein et al., *Medical Decisions and Prognostications of Pediatricians for Infants with Meningomyelocele*, 113 J. Pediatrics 835 (1988).

[252] United States Comm'n on Civil Rights, Medical Discrimination Against Children with Disabilities 104 (1989).

[253] *Id.*

[254] *Id.* at 111–13.

[255] *Id.* at 113.

[256] Hack et al., *School-Age Outcomes in Children with Birth Weights Under 750g*, 331 New Eng. J. Med. 753 (1994).

## Bibliography

Bowes, W. "The Disabled Newborn—Diagnosis, Prognosis, and Outcome: The Fetal View." *Issues in Law and Medicine* 2 (1987): 435.

Carter, B. "Neonatalogists and Bioethics After Baby Doe." *Journal of Perinatology* 13 (1993): 146.

Charlesworth, M. "Disabled Newborn Infants and the Quality of Life." *Journal of Contemporary Health Law and Policy* 9 (1993): 129.

Developments in the Law. "Medical Technology and the Law." *Harvard Law Review* 103 (1990): 1519.

Dickens, B. "Medicine and the Law—Withholding Paediatric Medical Care." *Canada Bar Review* 62 (1984): 196.

Fost, N. "Baby Doe: Problems and Solutions." *Arizona State Law Journal,* 1984, no. 4: 637.

Goldstein, J. "Not for the Law to Approve or Disapprove—A Comment on Professor Mnookin's Paper." *Arizona State Law Journal,* 1984, no. 4: 685.

Gostin, L. "A Moment in Human Development: Legal Protection, Ethical Standards and Social Policy on the Selective Non-Treatment of Handicapped Neonates." *American Journal of Law and Medicine* 11 (1985): 31.

Gottesman, M. "Civil Liability for Failing to Provide "Medically Indicated Treatment" to a Disabled Infant." *Family Law Quarterly* 20 (1986): 61.

Kuhse, H., and P. Singer. "Severely Handicapped Newborns: For Sometimes Letting—and Helping—Die." *Law, Medicine and Health Care* 14 (1986): 149.

Horan, D. "Euthanasia, Medical Treatment and the Mongoloid Child; Death as a Treatment of Choice." *Baylor Law Review* 27 (1975): 76.

Jonsen, A. "Traditional Distinctions for Making Ethical Judgments." *Arizona State Law Journal,* 1984, no. 4: 661.

Lantos, J. "Baby Doe Five Years Later: Implications for Child Health." *New England Journal of Medicine* 317 (1987): 444.

Lipman, Z. "The Criminal Liability of Medical Practitioners for Withholding Treatment from Severely Defective Newborn Infants." *Australia Law Journal* 60 (1986): 286.

McLone, D. "The Diagnosis, Prognosis, and Outcome for the Handicapped Newborn: A Neonatal View." *Issues in Law and Medicine* 2 (1986): 15.

Minow, M. "Beyond State Intervention in the Family: For Baby Jane Doe." *University of Michigan Journal of Law Reform* 18 (1985): 933.

Mnookin, R. "Two Puzzles." *Arizona State Law Journal,* 1984, no. 4: 667.

Moseley, K. "The History of Infanticide in Western Society." *Issues in Law and Medicine* 1 (1986): 345.

Paris, J., and J. Fletcher. "Infant Doe Regulations and the Absolute Requirement to Use Nourishment and Fluids for the Dying Infant." *Law, Medicine and Health Care* 11, no. 5 (1983): 210.

Rhoden, N. "Treatment Dilemmas for Imperiled Newborns: Why Quality of Life Counts." *Southern California Law Review* 58 (1985): 1283.

Robertson, J. "Involuntary Euthanasia of Defective Newborns: A Legal Analysis." *Stanford Law Review* 27 (1975): 213.

Schneider, C. "Rights Discourse and Neonatal Euthanasia." *California Law Review* 76 (1988): 151.

Shapiro, R., and R. Barthel. "Infant Care Review Committees: An Effective Approach to the Baby Doe Dilemma?" *Hastings Law Journal* 37 (1986): 827.

Turnbull, H. "Incidence of Infanticide in America: Public and Professional Attitudes." *Issues in Law and Medicine* 1 (1986): 363.

Vitiello, M. "Baby Jane Doe: Stating a Cause of Action Against the Officious Intermeddler." *Hastings Law Journal* 37 (1986): 863.

Vitiello, M. "On Letting Seriously Ill Minors Die: A Review of Louisiana's Natural Death Act." *Loyola Law Review* 31 (1985): 67.

Weir, R. *Selective Nontreatment of Handicapped Newborns: Moral Dilemmas in Neonatal Medicine.* New York: Oxford University Press, 1984.

# PART VI

# LIABILITY

# CHAPTER 17

# CIVIL LIABILITY

# § 17.1  Introduction

Most litigation concerning end-of-life decisionmaking has been initiated as a result of the inability of a patient (or surrogate) and the patient's attending physician (and/or health care administrators) to agree on whether or not treatment may be terminated or withheld. Originally, such suits were instituted either by competent patients or by the surrogates of incompetent patients to compel physicians to refrain from administering unwanted treatment. In recent years, however, a small number of actions have been initiated by health care providers seeking a declaration that it is permissible to withhold or withdraw treatment that the patient (or more likely, the family of an incompetent patient) wants to have administered but that the provider not does not wish to administer. Regardless of who has initiated the litigation, the actions have been almost uniformly for equitable relief in the form of an injunction, a declaratory judgment, or both.

In a few instances, lawsuits have been filed seeking damages, usually for the administration of unwanted treatment, though occasionally for the *failure* to administer treatment. This chapter is concerned principally, though not exclusively, with lawsuits for damages arising from the administration of unwanted treatment. Unauthorized treatment encompasses several related but distinct tort theories: assault and battery, intentional infliction of emotional distress, and invasion of privacy. Depending on what is meant by the term *unauthorized treatment,* there may also be a basis for recovery in negligence. Although liability for not administering treatment is touched on in this chapter, the law in this area is far more underdeveloped. Most of the discussion of this problem is to be found in **Chapter 19,** dealing with "futile" medical treatment.

Despite the fact that the principles of law on which actions for damages are based are well established, there have not been a large number of them arising from a physician's refusal to withhold or withdraw life-sustaining medical treatment. This is especially noteworthy in light of the fact that most of the reported right-to-die cases have arisen as a result of a physician's or health care institution's unwillingness to honor the wishes of a competent patient or the surrogate of an incompetent patient[1] to forgo life-sustaining medical treatment.

---

[1] **MI:** Young v. Oakland Gen. Hosp., 437 N.W.2d 321, 326 (Mich. Ct. App. 1989) ("duty is breached when the patient does not consent to the treatment or, if the patient is incompetent, the patient's surrogate decisionmaker does not consent to the treatment").

Virtually all right-to-die cases have sought exclusively declaratory and/or injunctive relief; few have involved a concurrent[2] or subsequent[3] claim for damages for unauthorized treatment despite the fact that there was, in fact, unauthorized treatment. By far, the greatest number of claims for damages—though relatively small in number—have been filed after treatment was eventually terminated, either without a court order or with a court order but in an unreported case.[4]

Although some commentators have suggested that there is a far greater potential for civil liability for *not* honoring a request to terminate treatment than there is for honoring such a request,[5] the actual litigation does not—or does not

---

[2] *See, e.g.,* Bartling v. Superior Court, 209 Cal. Rptr. 220 (Ct. App. 1984). *See also* Bartling v. Glendale Adventist Medical Ctr., 229 Cal. Rptr. 360 (Ct. App. 1986).

[3] **MA:** *Cf.* Spring v. Geriatric Auth., 475 N.E.2d 727 (Mass. 1985) (suit for damages for publicity given to forgoing life-sustaining treatment); *In re* Spring, 405 N.E.2d 115 (Mass. 1980) (action to terminate life-sustaining treatment).

**NY:** Fosmire v. Nicoleau, 551 N.E.2d 77 (N.Y. 1990) (action for damages for nonconsensual blood transfusion); Nicoleau v. Brookhaven Memorial Hosp. Ctr., 581 N.Y.S.2d 382 (App. Div. 1992) (action for injunctive relief to prevent administration of blood transfusion). *Cf.* Grace Plaza of Great Neck, Inc. v. Elbaum, 623 N.E.2d 513 (N.Y. 1993) (suit against husband of deceased patient for refusal to pay for unwanted treatment); Elbaum v. Grace Plaza of Great Neck, Inc., 544 N.Y.S.2d 840 (App. Div. 1989) (action to terminate life-sustaining treatment).

**OH:** *See, e.g.,* Estate of Leach v. Shapiro, 469 N.E.2d 1047 (Ohio Ct. App. 1984) (suit for damages for unauthorized treatment); Leach v. Akron Gen. Medical Ctr., 426 N.E.2d 809 (C.P. P. Div. Summit County, Ohio 1980) (action to terminate life-sustaining treatment).

[4] **CA3:** *See, e.g.,* Kranson v. Valley Crest Nursing Home, 755 F.2d 46 (3d Cir. 1985).

**CA11:** *See, e.g.,* Bendiburg v. Dempsey, 909 F.2d 463 (11th Cir. 1990).

**DCO:** *See, e.g.,* Ross v. Hilltop Rehabilitation Hosp., 676 F. Supp. 1528 (D. Colo. 1987).

**AL:** *See, e.g.,* Camp v. White, 510 So. 2d 166 (Ala. 1987).

**CA:** *See, e.g.,* Westhart v. Mule, 261 Cal. Rptr. 640 (Ct. App. 1989) (ordered not published).

**GA:** *See, e.g.,* Kirby v. Spivey, 307 S.E.2d 538 (Ga. Ct. App. 1983).

**IL:** *See, e.g.,* Corlett v. Caserta, 562 N.E.2d 257 (Ill. App. Ct. 1990).

**IN:** *See, e.g.,* Payne v. Marion Gen. Hosp., 549 N.E.2d 1043 (Ind. Ct. App. 1990).

**IA:** *See, e.g.,* Morgan v. Olds, 417 N.W.2d 232 (Iowa Ct. App. 1987).

**MI:** *See, e.g.,* Werth v. Taylor, 475 N.W.2d 426 (Mich. Ct. App. 1991); Young v. Oakland Gen. Hosp., 437 N.W.2d 321 (Mich. Ct. App. 1989).

**NJ:** *See, e.g.,* Strachan v. John F. Kennedy Memorial Hosp., 538 A.2d 346 (N.J. 1988); McVey v. Englewood Hosp. Ass'n, 524 A.2d 450 (N.J. Super. Ct. App. Div. 1987).

**OH:** *See, e.g.,* Anderson v. St. Francis-St. George Hosp., 614 N.E.2d 841 (Ohio Ct. App. 1992).

**WA:** *See, e.g.,* Shorter v. Drury, 695 P.2d 116 (Wash. 1985); Benoy v. Simons, 831 P.2d 167 (Wash. Ct. App. 1992); Strickland v. Deaconess Hosp., 735 P.2d 74 (Wash. Ct. App. 1987).

**WV:** *See, e.g.,* Belcher v. Charleston Area Medical Ctr., 422 S.E.2d 827 (W. Va. 1992).

[5] Cohen, *Refusing and Forgoing Treatment, in* 3 Treatise on Health Care Law (Macdonald et al. eds., 1993); Cohen, *Civil Liability for Providing Unwanted Life Support, in* 2 BioLaw 499 (1987); Miller, *Right-to-Die Damage Actions: Developments in the Law,* 65 Denv. U. L. Rev. 181, 184 (1988) ("If health care providers face any real danger it is that continuation of unwanted treatment may itself result in liability.").

yet—bear this out. It seems true that there is a greater risk of *litigation* from providing unwanted treatment than from not providing wanted treatment, but the reported cases do not support the claim that there is a greater risk of *liability*. With the exception of one case, which is not a conventional right-to-die case, seeking as it did damages for the failure to remove life support from a patient who had been pronounced dead,[6] there are no *reported*[7] instances of the imposition of liability for the provision of unwanted life-sustaining medical treatment (although there are some jury verdicts or settlements awarding damages for unwanted life-sustaining medical treatment[8]). However, there have been several awards of attorneys' fees, if not damages, in cases involving the provision of unwanted life-sustaining medical treatment.[9]

One of the stated reasons that litigation to recover damages for unauthorized life-sustaining medical treatment has generally not been successful is the feeling on the part of the courts that the law was not yet—at the time of litigation—well enough established to impose liability on a physician for not terminating life-sustaining medical treatment and, in effect, letting the patient die.[10] As the law becomes better established, it is less likely that the courts will continue to find this to be a compelling reason to avoid the imposition of liability. However, when that occurs, plaintiffs will encounter two other serious obstacles to liability. The first is the fact that the damages available under existing tort law remedies are likely to be extremely small if the patient is already extremely ill. The other is the fact that under state law, some causes of action and/or some types of damages (namely, pain and suffering or mental anguish) are barred by survival statutes.[11]

Despite the infrequency of litigation seeking damages arising from end-of-life decisionmaking, it is important to emphasize that most of the litigation has resulted from the provision of unwanted treatment rather than from the withholding of desired treatment. Thus, the so-called conservative advice not infrequently given by attorneys to health care institutions and physicians that it

---

[6] **NJ:** *See* Strachan v. John F. Kennedy Memorial Hosp., 538 A.2d 346 (N.J. 1988). See § **17.6.**

[7] *See* Miller, *Right-to-Die Damage Actions: Developments in the Law,* 65 Denv. U. L. Rev. 181, 189, 197 (1988) (discussing settlements of damages actions in two cases, Estate of Leach v. Shapiro, 469 N.E.2d 1047 (Ohio Ct. App. 1984), and Galvin v. University Hosp. of Cleveland, No. 115873 (C.P. Cuyahoga County, Ohio filed Sept. 8, 1986)).

[8] Gasner, *Financial Penalties for Failing to Honor Patient Wishes to Refuse Treatment,* 11 St. Louis U. Pub. L. Rev. 499 (1992).

[9] See § **17.26.**

[10] **CA:** *See, e.g.,* Bartling v. Glendale Adventist Medical Ctr., 229 Cal. Rptr. 360, 364 (Ct. App. 1986).

**NY:** *See, e.g.,* Grace Plaza of Great Neck, Inc. v. Elbaum, 623 N.E.2d 513 (N.Y. 1993) (husband of patient obligated to pay nursing home bill incurred between time he sought to have treatment terminated and the time a court order was issued).

**WA:** *See, e.g.,* Benoy v. Simons, 831 P.2d 167, 171 (Wash. Ct. App. 1992) (intentional infliction of emotional distress).

[11] See § **17.25.**

is best when in doubt to "play it safe" and administer treatment rather than to permit a patient to die from withholding or withdrawing treatment does not rest on a solid foundation.[12]

# STATE LAW REMEDIES

## § 17.2 Battery

The provision of treatment to a patient without valid consent constitutes a battery. This is so well accepted that it barely warrants citation. The Supreme Court in *Cruzan* summarized it this way:

> At common law, even the touching of one person by another without consent and without legal justification was a battery. [Citation omitted.] Before the turn of the century, this Court observed that "[n]o right is held more sacred, or is more carefully guarded, by the common law, than the right of every individual to the possession and control of his own person, free from all restraint or interference of others, unless by clear and unquestionable authority of law." *Union Pacific R. Co. v. Botsford,* 141 U.S. 250, 251, 11 S.Ct. 1000, 1001, 35 L.Ed. 734 (1891). This notion of bodily integrity has been embodied in the requirement that informed consent is generally required for medical treatment.[13]

Its application in the context of end-of-life decisionmaking, while of more recent vintage, can hardly be disputed.[14]

The core of the cause of action for battery is the touching of another person without valid consent—that is, consent either of the person, or, if the person is incapable of giving consent, of one authorized to consent for him. In the medical context, the rendition of treatment to a patient—at least when that treatment involves a touching of the patient—constitutes a battery unless there is valid consent.[15] In other words, what legitimates treatment is consent.[16] However, the mere act of touching another person, even without consent, is not a battery.

---

[12] *See, e.g.,* Rodriguez v. Pino, 634 So. 2d 681 (Fla. Dist. Ct. App. 1994) (holding that physician who abided by decision of competent patient to forgo life-sustaining treatment is not liable in damages for failing to override the patient's refusal).

[13] Cruzan v. Director, 497 U.S. 261, 269 (1990).

[14] **IA:** *See, e.g.,* Morgan v. Olds, 417 N.W.2d 232, 236 (Iowa Ct. App. 1987) ("When a doctor implements a course of treatment without obtaining the patient's consent, he breaches his duty and is liable to the patient for any resultant damages.").

**OH:** *See, e.g.,* Anderson v. St. Francis-St. George Hosp., 614 N.E.2d 841 (Ohio Ct. App. 1992); Estate of Leach v. Shapiro, 469 N.E.2d 1047 (Ohio Ct. App. 1984).

[15] *See, e.g.,* Anderson v. St. Francis-St. George Hosp., 614 N.E.2d at 844 ("[W]hen a physician treats a person without consent, the doctor has committed a battery.").

[16] *Id.* ("[A] physician's acts are lawful when the patient expressly consents prior to medical treatment.").

There must also be an intent to bring about harmful or offensive contact with that person.[17] Instances of actual intent in the doctor-patient relationship are rare; one would have to prove that in providing treatment, the physician's *purpose* was to cause harmful or offensive contact with the patient.[18] On the other hand, the fact that the physician is acting with best of motives is irrelevant. Indeed, even beneficial treatment constitutes a battery if it is nonconsensual[19] because contact with the plaintiff need not be harmful to constitute the grounds for liability. Contact that is offensive is also grounds for liability,[20] and contact is considered to be offensive if it is unwanted.[21]

Intent can also be established even if it was not the defendant's *purpose* to cause harmful or offensive contact. "Constructive intent" will suffice. If it can be established that even though the physician's purpose was not to cause harmful or offensive contact with the patient, he knew that harmful or offensive contact was substantially certain to occur, "intent" is established.[22] Again, in the doctor-patient relationship, it is likely to be very rare that a physician will know with substantial certainty that the provision of treatment will cause *harmful* contact with the patient. However, when a patient (or surrogate) has put the physician on notice that he does not want a particular treatment, then the subsequent rendition of that treatment to the patient is offensive, and the doctor knows with substantial certainty that the treatment will be *offensive,* because it is unwanted.

In sum, it is the absence of valid consent to treatment—that is, absence of consent of a competent patient or of consent of the surrogate of an incompetent patient—that renders the subsequent treatment actionable as a battery.

Although unauthorized treatment usually consists of the wrongful *initiation* of treatment, it may also arise from the wrongful *continuation* of treatment that has been lawfully (that is, consensually) begun.[23] There are a large number of

---

[17] Restatement (Second) of Torts § 13(a) (1965).

[18] *Id.* § 8A cmt. b ("Intent is not . . . limited to consequences which are desired. If the actor knows that the consequences are certain, or substantially certain, to result from his act, and still goes ahead, he is treated by the law as if he had in fact desired to produce the result.").

[19] *See, e.g.,* Estate of Leach v. Shapiro, 469 N.E.2d 1047, 1051 (Ohio Ct. App. 1984) ("A physician who treats a patient without consent commits a battery, even though the procedure is harmless or beneficial. [Citation omitted.]").

[20] *See, e.g.,* Lounsbury v. Capel, 836 P.2d 188, 192–93 (Utah 1992) ("Common law battery does not require that the nonconsensual contact be injurious. Rather, proof of an unauthorized invasion of the plaintiff's person, even if harmless, entitles him to at least nominal damages. W. Keeton, et al., Prosser and Keeton on the Law of Torts § 9, at 40 (5th ed. 1984).)". *See also* Restatement (Second) of Torts § 18.

[21] Restatement (Second) of Torts § 18 cmt. c.

[22] *Id.* § 8A cmt. b ("Intent is not . . . limited to consequences which are desired. If the actor knows that the consequences are certain, or substantially certain, to result from his act, and still goes ahead, he is treated by the law as if he had in fact desired to produce the result.").

[23] **OH:** Estate of Leach v. Shapiro, 469 N.E.2d 1047 (Ohio Ct. App. 1984). See § **8.6.**

such cases dating back to the end of the nineteenth century, though largely outside the context of life-sustaining treatment.[24]

## § 17.3 —Refusal of Treatment; Absence of Consent

Unauthorized treatment may take either of two general forms: treatment in the face of an express refusal or treatment in the absence of legally valid consent. The first is relatively simple, although it can become complicated in the case of an incompetent patient when there are questions about whether or not a surrogate has legally valid decisionmaking authority.[25]

Absence of consent is less straightforward. It, too, can be complicated by the question of who has the authority to make decisions for an incompetent patient, but for present purposes the more serious problem arises from the multiplicity of ways in which the term *consent* is used. However, as a general proposition, it is safe to say that absence of consent (or the absence of one of the recognized exceptions to consent[26]) is also grounds for liability.

Absence of consent may take a number of forms. The simplest occurs when the attending physician either fails to seek consent or seeks it but does not obtain it. The latter may occur either because the person authorized to give consent refuses to consent (which then puts it in the category of explicit refusal) or because that person has, as yet, issued no decision. Another possibility is that the patient or surrogate gives the physician permission to administer treatment, but that permission does not rise to the level of legally valid consent. That may occur for a number of reasons. The first is that the physician has not provided the decisionmaker adequate information as required by the doctrine of informed consent. This is more likely to be successfully litigated as negligence for failure to obtain informed consent (that is, inadequate disclosure[27]) than as a battery. The second possibility is that the person who gives or withholds permission for treatment does not have the legal authority to do so. If the patient is competent, but the physician relies on the authorization of someone else to treat or withhold

---

[24] *See* Annotation, *Consent As Condition of Right to Perform Surgical Operation,* 76 A.L.R. 562 (1932); Annotation, *Consent As Condition of Right to Perform Surgical Operation,* 139 A.L.R. 1370 (1942); Annotation, *Liability of Physician or Surgeon for Extending Operation or Treatment Beyond That Expressly Authorized,* 56 A.L.R.2d 695 (1957); Annotation, *Power of Courts or Other Public Agencies, in the Absence of Statutory Authority, to Order Compulsory Medical Care for Adult,* 9 A.L.R.3d 1391 (1966). *Cf.* Annotation, *Mental Competency of Patient to Consent to Surgical Operation or Medical Treatment,* 25 A.L.R.3d 1439 (1969); Sarno, Annotation, *Civil Liability for Physical Measures Undertaken in Connection with Treatment of Mentally Disordered Patient,* 8 A.L.R.4th 464 (1981).

[25] See **Chs. 8** and **14.**

[26] See **§§ 3.23** and **3.25–3.26.**

[27] See **§§ 17.11–17.12.**

treatment,[28] this should ordinarily be actionable as battery because of the absence of legally valid consent.[29] Finally, it is also a battery if the physician relies on the patient's own permission, but the patient lacks decisionmaking capacity. However, it might also be actionable as negligence if the physician fails to use reasonable care in determining whether or not the patient possesses or lacks decisionmaking capacity. Another possible way of viewing this, depending on the meaning of decisionmaking capacity,[30] is that the physician provides enough information but that the patient (or surrogate[31]) does not sufficiently understand it.[32] This ordinarily should be treated as battery, though arguably it is negligence if the physician did not use reasonable care in ascertaining whether or not the patient understood the information.[33]

## § 17.4  —Application to Right-to-Die Cases

Battery ought to be one of the easiest causes of action in which to recover for unwanted administration of life-sustaining treatment. Perhaps the leading battery case in the end-of-life decisionmaking context is the *Leach* case. Mrs. Leach, who was suffering from amyotrophic lateral sclerosis, was admitted to the hospital because of difficulty breathing. Thereafter, she suffered a cardiac arrest, was resuscitated, and was placed on a ventilator and nasogastric tube. After four months of unconsciousness in what was probably a persistent vegetative state,[34] her husband requested that she be removed from the ventilator. The attending physician refused to do so without a court order, despite his acknowledging "her condition to be 'hopeless' and 'her ultimate demise is only a matter of time.' "[35] A court order was eventually obtained.

Thereafter, her family brought suit claiming damages for battery and intentional infliction of emotional distress. The trial court dismissed the claims, but the appeals court reinstated them. In so doing, it recognized that the failure to

---

[28] **IN:** *See, e.g.,* Payne v. Marion General Hosp., 549 N.E.2d 1043 (Ind. Ct. App. 1990).

   **WV:** *See, e.g.,* Belcher v. Charleston Area Medical Ctr., 422 S.E.2d 827 (W. Va. 1992).

[29] **WV:** *But see* Belcher v. Charleston Area Medical Ctr., 422 S.E.2d 827 (obtaining authorization to treat mature minor from parents rather than minor constitutes lack of informed consent).

[30] See **Ch. 4.**

[31] *See, e.g., In re* Department of Veteran's Affairs Medical Ctr., 749 F. Supp. 495 (S.D.N.Y.), *aff'd,* 914 F.2d 239 (2d Cir. 1990).

[32] *See, e.g.,* Estate of Leach v. Shapiro, 469 N.E.2d 1047, 1052 (Ohio Ct. App. 1984) ("There is no legal defense to battery based on consent if a patient's consent to touching is given without sufficient knowledge and understanding of the nature of the touching."). See **§ 3.17.**

[33] See **§ 3.20.**

[34] Estate of Leach v. Shapiro, 469 N.E.2d 1047, 1052 (Ohio Ct. App. 1984) ("chronic vegetative condition").

[35] Leach v. Akron Gen. Medical Ctr., 426 N.E.2d 809, 811 (C.P. P. Div. Summit County, Ohio 1980).

terminate life-sustaining medical treatment could constitute a battery if there were not legally valid consent to its administration or if consent to its continuation were withdrawn.

The court also recognized that the emergency exception to the requirement of consent (and informed consent) has the potential for seriously undermining the right of self-determination because "a physician could circumvent the express wishes of a terminal patient by waiting to act until the patient was comatose and critical."[36] The emergency exception, based on the notion of implied consent, cannot overcome an express agreement between a physician and patient not to treat. Therefore, if the patient (or her lawful surrogate) had expressly informed the physician before the emergency arose that in the event of a subsequent emergency she did not want to be treated, the emergency would not legitimate administration of treatment, and the physician would be liable for battery. However, the court seriously weakened this holding by requiring that the patient's anticipatory refusal of treatment must be as informed as it would be in the case of contemporaneous informed consent.[37]

Another case in which the court seemed receptive to not merely recognizing rights but enforcing them through the award of damages for their violation is also an Ohio case, *Anderson v. St. Francis-St. George Hospital.*[38] The patient in *Anderson* was admitted to the defendant hospital suffering from chest pain. As a result of a discussion with his physician, a do-not-resuscitate order was entered. Nevertheless, he was resuscitated by hospital employees when he suffered a ventricular fibrillation. The administrator of the patient's estate brought an action alleging, among other things, battery based on the nonconsensual resuscitation.

The appellate court reversed the dismissal of the battery claim, stating that "i[f] decedent's instructions specifically precluded the treatment given, [defendant] committed a battery."[39] On remand, the plaintiff would be required to prove that the patient in fact consented to the do-not-resuscitate order, the patient suffered harm, and the harm resulted from the resuscitation.[40] The court also recognized what many courts seem to be willing to overlook in battery cases, namely, that battery may be established even if the treatment is medically beneficial, though the damages in such an event are nominal.[41]

The *Bartling* case would seem to be equally as clear a case of battery as *Leach* and *Anderson,* and although the case denied recovery, it appears to establish a precedent for recovery in future cases. Mr. Bartling was hospitalized for the "treatment of severe chronic depression. At the time of his admission, [he] was

---

[36] Estate of Leach v. Shapiro, 469 N.E.2d at 1053.

[37] See §§ **10.7, 10.22,** and **17.11–17.12.**

[38] 614 N.E.2d 841 (Ohio Ct. App. 1992), *opinion after remand,* 1995 WL 109128 (Ohio Ct. App. Mar. 15, 1995).

[39] *Id.* at 844.

[40] *Id.* at 845.

[41] *Id.* at 846 (citing Lacey v. Laird, 139 N.E.2d 25 (Ohio 1956)).

suffering from pulmonary emphysema, atherosclerotic cardiovascular disease, coronary arteriosclerosis, an abdominal aneurysm and lung cancer."[42] A lung biopsy caused a collapsed lung, which necessitated that he be put on a ventilator.

After several weeks on the ventilator, he requested that he be taken off, and when met with the refusal of his physician to do so, he petitioned and ultimately obtained judicial relief. There was no question that Mr. Bartling was competent, so that even if his initially being placed on a ventilator did not constitute a battery because justified by the emergency exception,[43] the subsequent refusal to take him off the ventilator most surely did. Recovery was denied on the battery and other claims because, according to the court, "respondents could not reasonably have foreseen that their effort to preserve life was legally tantamount to a 'conscious disregard' of appellants' rights"[44] given the uncertain state of California law.

This is a rather weak excuse for the denial of recovery in one of the clearest cases of battery. It had been established in California law for almost a half century[45] that treatment without consent, let alone over a competent patient's refusal, is actionable as a battery. Furthermore, a similar state of the law in Ohio had not prevented the recognition of the same cause of action in the *Leach* case. Indeed, the legal backdrop in Ohio was, if anything, weaker than in California for there had been no prior appellate judicial declaration in Ohio of the right to forgo life-sustaining treatment, as there had been in California.[46] And in *Leach,* the patient was incompetent, further weakening the claim because of the less certain status of a surrogate's authority to withdraw or withhold consent than that of a competent patient such as Mr. Bartling.

Thus, *Bartling* illustrates better than any other case the extreme reluctance of courts to penalize health care providers for providing treatment to patients even if the patient did not want it. Courts may be willing to issue orders to doctors to stop treatment, thus recognizing that treatment is not always an unalloyed good, yet they are unwilling to provide the best deterrent to unwanted treatment, the award of damages. For some courts, treatment, it seems, *is* an unalloyed good when the alternative is to impose liability on health care providers.

The *Elbaum* case[47] in New York rested on reasoning similar to, but slightly different from, that employed in *Bartling.* In New York the law governing the

---

[42] Bartling v. Glendale Adventist Medical Ctr., 229 Cal. Rptr. 360, 361 (Ct. App. 1986).

[43] See §§ **3.23** and **10.22.**

[44] **CA:** Bartling v. Glendale Adventist Medical Ctr., 229 Cal. Rptr. at 364.

**NY:** *Accord* Grace Plaza of Great Neck, Inc. v. Elbaum, 623 N.E.2d 513 (N.Y. 1993) (husband of patient obligated to pay nursing home bill incurred between time he sought to have treatment terminated and the time a court order was issued).

**WA:** *Accord* Benoy v. Simons, 831 P.2d 167, 171 (Wash. Ct. App. 1992) (intentional infliction of emotional distress).

[45] *See* Valdez v. Percy, 96 P.2d 142 (Cal. Ct. App. 1939) (cited in Thor v. Superior Court, 855 P.2d 375 (Cal. 1993)).

[46] *See* Barber v. Superior Court, 195 Cal. Rptr. 484 (Ct. App. 1983).

[47] Grace Plaza of Great Neck, Inc. v. Elbaum, 623 N.E.2d 513 (N.Y. 1993).

termination of life-sustaining treatment to an incompetent patient is, and was at the time that the underlying controversy in *Elbaum* arose, very clear, namely, that there must be clear and convincing evidence that the *patient* made a decision for treatment to be terminated prior to losing decisionmaking capacity. In other words, in New York, life-sustaining treatment of an incompetent patient may be forgone only on the basis of a subjective standard, and not a substituted judgment or best interests standard.[48] What was unclear, if anything was, was the application of the law to the facts.

The litigation began in May 1988 and ended three appellate opinions and more than five years later.[49] The patient around whom the litigation centered was transferred from a hospital, following treatment for a stroke, to Grace Plaza nursing home in September 1986. At the time of admission to the nursing home, she was in a persistent vegetative state and was being fed by a gastrostomy tube.[50] Slightly more than a year later, her husband, the defendant in the instant action, wrote a letter advising the nursing home administration "that it was his wife's wish that she be allowed to die naturally should she fall into an 'irreversible vegetative state,' and he instructed the nursing home to remove Mrs. Elbaum's feeding tube."[51] Mr. Elbaum had previously written the nursing home requesting that CPR not be administered in the event of a cardiopulmonary arrest and "that no heroic measures were to be taken to sustain her life . . . [and in] the event Mrs. Elbaum developed an infection, no antibiotics or drug treatments were to be administered, and that no mechanical or other artificial respiratory means were to be used to sustain her life."[52] Mr. Elbaum also advised Mrs. Elbaum's attending physician "that his wife had expressly stated that she would not want the use of feeding tubes if she were in an irreversible vegetative state."[53]

Because the nursing home would not comply with Mr. Elbaum's request to terminate artificial nutrition and hydration, he brought an action to compel it to abide by his instructions. In *Elbaum I,* the appellate division held that there was adequate evidence to meet New York's exacting standard for terminating life-sustaining medical treatment from an incompetent patient—namely, that the patient herself, prior to losing decisionmaking capacity, expressed the intent not to be treated under such circumstances.[54] The court granted an injunction

---

[48] See § **7.5.**

[49] *See* Elbaum v. Grace Plaza of Great Neck, Inc., 544 N.Y.S.2d 840 (App. Div. 1989) (holding patient's artificial nutrition and hydration could be terminated) [hereinafter Elbaum I]; Grace Plaza of Great Neck, Inc. v. Elbaum, 588 N.Y.S.2d 853 (App. Div. 1992) (holding nursing home entitled to collect monies owed it by Mr. Elbaum for Mrs. Elbaum's care) [hereinafter Elbaum II], *aff'd,* Grace Plaza of Great Neck, Inc. v. Elbaum, 623 N.E.2d 513 (N.Y. 1993) [hereinafter Elbaum III].

[50] Elbaum III, 623 N.E.2d at 514.

[51] *Id.*

[52] Elbaum I, 544 N.Y.S.2d at 843.

[53] *Id.*

[54] *See In re* Westchester County Medical Ctr. (O'Connor), 531 N.E.2d 607 (N.Y. 1988); *In re* Storar, 420 N.E.2d 64 (N.Y. 1981). See § **7.5.**

requiring the nursing home either to transfer Mrs. Elbaum to another facility in which the artificial nutrition and hydration would be terminated, or to assist in the termination, or to permit a physician of the family's choosing to do so. Thereafter, the tube-feeding was discontinued and Mrs. Elbaum died.[55]

When Mrs. Elbaum was first admitted to the nursing home, Mr. Elbaum signed an agreement accepting financial responsibility for his wife's care. However, when the nursing home refused to remove the feeding tube, he ceased to pay.[56] Thereafter, the nursing home brought an action for breach of contract for the sums it claimed were owed to it by Mr. Elbaum, and he counterclaimed for damages for assault and battery. The trial court granted summary judgment for Mr. Elbaum on the nursing home's claim and dismissed the counterclaim, but the appellate division reversed the dismissal of the nursing home's claim for payment.[57]

Mr. Elbaum's argument was that he was not liable for the cost of care and treatment because the nursing home breached the terms of the admission agreement that he had signed. More specifically, the defense to the claim for payment was proffered asserting that "continued treatment in contravention of [Mrs. Elbaum's] wishes violated the contract and excused any obligation to pay"[58] "because it denied [Mrs. Elbaum] her legal right to determine the course of her own treatment."[59]

The nursing home responded that Mr. Elbaum "did not present any documentary evidence indicating his wife's intentions and that [under New York law as established in *In re O'Connor* and *In re Storar,*] he could not make the decision to discontinue life support systems for her."[60] Absent such evidence, no obligation arose to discontinue treatment until a court declared what Mrs. Elbaum's wishes were, and when in fact this occurred, the nursing home did honor them. Indeed, the nursing home argued, had it acquiesced in Mr. Elbaum's request, it might have incurred criminal liability for doing so. Consequently, it did not violate Mrs. Elbaum's rights.

Although acknowledging that there is no obligation to pay for nonconsensual treatment,[61] the New York Court of Appeals adopted the nursing home's argument and concluded that this was not nonconsensual treatment because the nursing home acted in good faith in its determination that it lacked the kind of evidence required by New York law to determine that Mrs. Elbaum had objected to the treatment. The court firmly disavowed any requirement that a *court* must always pass on the adequacy of such evidence. However, given the stringent "specific subjective intent" standard that must be met in New York for the

---

[55] Elbaum III, 623 N.E.2d at 514 n.*.

[56] *Id.* at 514.

[57] Elbaum II.

[58] Elbaum III at 514.

[59] *Id.* at 515.

[60] *Id.* at 514.

[61] *Id.* at 515 (citing Shapira v. United Medical Serv., Inc., 205 N.E.2d 293 (N.Y. 1965)).

termination of life support,[62] "[i]f a provider harbors some uncertainty on the matter, it acts within the dictates of *O'Connor* if it refuses to discontinue treatment until the issue is legally determined."[63]

Finally, the court affirmed the dismissal of Mr. Elbaum's counterclaim for assault and battery and punitive damages because "the continued treatment of Mrs. Elbaum was required for much of the period at issue here because plaintiff was subject to a [court] order directing it to continue treatment" and because there was a good-faith dispute over what the patient wanted.[64]

As difficult as it is for courts to award damages for unauthorized treatment in the case of *hopelessly* ill patients, it is even more difficult when there is an excellent chance that, through the administration of the very treatment that the patient has refused, the patient can be restored to, or very nearly to, the status quo ante. There are a number of cases exemplifying this phenomenon, all involving members of the Jehovah's Witness faith who have refused, and then nevertheless been administered, blood transfusions.[65] *Werth v. Taylor*[66] is typical. Several weeks before the expected date of delivery of twins, the plaintiff went to the hospital where she would deliver them to "preregister," which involved filling out several forms, including a "Refusal to Permit Blood Transfusion" form. At the time of admission, her husband signed another "Refusal to Permit Blood Transfusion" form. The delivery went smoothly, but a few hours afterward she was observed to be bleeding. A surgeon discussed surgery (dilation and curettage) with the plaintiff and her husband and their prior refusals of blood transfusions. Surgery was then performed, but the bleeding continued. The anesthesiologist ordered a transfusion, but before it was given, the surgeon informed him that the plaintiff was a Jehovah's Witness. According to the surgeon, the anesthesiologist "responded by saying something like 'that may be, but she needs the blood.'"[67]

The plaintiffs sued for malpractice and battery. The trial court granted summary judgment for the defendants, and the court of appeals affirmed. On appeal, the court acknowledged that competent patients have a right to refuse treatment, but because "the trial court determined that [plaintiff's] refusals were made

---

[62] See § 7.5.

[63] Elbaum III at 515 (citing *In re* Westchester County Medical Ctr. (O'Connor), 531 N.E.2d 607 (N.Y. 1988)).

[64] *Id.*

[65] **CA9:** *See, e.g.,* Niebla v. County of San Diego, 967 F.2d 589, 1992 WL 140250 (9th Cir. 1992) (unpublished).

**DFL:** *See, e.g.,* McKenzie v. Doctors' Hosp. of Hollywood, Inc., 765 F. Supp. 1504 (S.D. Fla. 1991), *aff'd without opinion,* 974 F.2d 1347 (11th Cir. 1992).

**DGA:** *See, e.g.,* Novak v. Cobb County-Kennestone Hosp. Auth., 849 F. Supp. 1559 (N.D. Ga. 1994).

**NY:** *See, e.g.,* Nicoleau v. Brookhaven Memorial Hosp. Ctr., 581 N.Y.S.2d 382 (App. Div. 1992).

[66] 475 N.W.2d 426 (Mich. Ct. App. 1991).

[67] *Id.* at 427.

when she was contemplating merely routine elective surgery and not when life-threatening circumstances were present,"[68] the plaintiff's refusal of treatment was not a "fully informed, contemporaneous decision," and hence was not binding.[69] "Her prior refusals had not been made when her life was hanging in the balance or when it appeared that death might be a possibility if a transfusion were not given. Clearly, her refusals were, therefore, not contemporaneous or informed."[70]

This reasoning is not easily reconciled with that in the *Anderson* case.[71] In both *Anderson* and *Werth,* the patients made anticipatory rather than contemporaneous decisions. Indeed, the circumstances in both cases dictated that they could only make anticipatory decisions. In both cases, at the time the treatment in question was being rendered, an emergency existed and they could not contemporaneously consent; the patient in *Anderson* was suffering a cardiac arrest and the patient in *Werth* was anesthetized. In *Anderson* the court, in effect, enforced an advance directive; in *Werth* the court refused to do so. The only real difference between the two cases was that in *Werth,* there was a very high likelihood that with treatment that was being refused (blood transfusion), the patient would probably be restored to health, whereas in *Anderson,* either the treatment (CPR) might not accomplish its intended goal (resuscitation), or it would revive the patient but in a severely compromised state, or the patient would inevitably suffer another cardiac arrest. In *Werth* the patient was the picture of health but for this easily treatable condition; in *Anderson* the patient was inevitably dying regardless of what treatment was administered.

In cases in which Jehovah's Witnesses have sought equitable relief to prevent the administration of a blood transfusion, the courts have been far more receptive to their claims than in damages actions brought after transfusions have been administered. The reason for this distinction is simple. In all the equitable relief cases, the patients have already been administered the transfusion and are appealing a factually moot matter either to vindicate their rights or to establish a precedent for themselves or for other members of the Jehovah's Witness faith. It is a comparatively simple matter for the courts to grant the relief because the patient is alive and will not die as a result of the court's decision.

By contrast, the trial courts in these same cases and the trial and appellate courts in suits for damages face a very different matter. They are being asked, respectively, either to issue a decree that will possibly lead to the death of a

---

[68] *Id.* at 429.

[69] **MI:** Werth v. Taylor, 475 N.W.2d 426, 430 (Mich. Ct. App. 1991).

**NJ:** *Accord In re* Hughes, 611 A.2d 1148 (N.J. Super. Ct. App. Div. 1992).

**OH:** *Cf.* University of Cincinnati Hosp. v. Edmond, 506 N.E.2d 299 (C.P. Hamilton County, Ohio 1986); Estate of Leach v. Shapiro, 469 N.E.2d 1047 (Ohio Ct. App. 1984).

See §§ **17.11–17.12.**

[70] Werth v. Taylor, 475 N.W.2d at 430.

[71] Anderson v. St. Francis-St. George Hosp., 614 N.E.2d 841 (Ohio Ct. App. 1992).

person whose live can be saved or to award damages to a patient whose life has been saved, to be paid by the physician who saved the life. Taken together, these cases demonstrate the willingness of courts to vindicate retrospectively the right to refuse treatment—when doing so may have little practical consequence, or at least little practical consequence to any currently identifiable person—but not to do so when it will lead to the loss of life or the imposition of damages.

## § 17.5   Intentional Infliction of Emotional Distress

An action for intentional infliction of emotional distress—sometimes referred to as the tort of "outrage"[72]—is another possible theory of recovery for unauthorized treatment. (It is also a possible theory of recovery for the failure to provide desired treatment.[73]) It has two advantages over battery. First, even though a battery action will lie if the patient is not physically harmed (or is even medically benefited) by the treatment as long as the treatment is nonconsensual, only nominal damages may be recovered. More substantial damages may be obtained for intentional infliction of emotional distress even if there is no physical harm to the patient. Second, intentional infliction of emotional distress may provide a form of recovery for damages for harm to third parties as well as to the patient.[74]

In general, the cause of action for intentional infliction of emotional distress requires proof of

> (1) outrageous conduct by the defendant, (2) intent to cause or reckless disregard of the probability of causing emotional distress, (3) severe emotional suffering and (4) actual and proximate causation of emotional distress.[75]

Damages may be recovered for any resultant bodily harm as well as for the severe emotional distress.[76]

---

[72] **AL:** *See, e.g.,* Gallups v. Cotter, 534 So. 2d 585 (Ala. 1988).

**NJ:** *See, e.g.,* Strachan v. John F. Kennedy Memorial Hosp., 538 A.2d 346 (N.J. 1988).

**WA:** *See, e.g.,* Benoy v. Simons, 831 P.2d 167 (Wash. Ct. App. 1992); Strickland v. Deaconess Hosp., 735 P.2d 74 (Wash. Ct. App. 1987).

[73] *See, e.g.,* Morgan v. Olds, 417 N.W.2d 232 (Iowa Ct. App. 1987).

[74] See § **17.7.**

[75] **CA:** Bartling v. Glendale Adventist Medical Ctr., 229 Cal. Rptr. 360, 364 (Ct. App. 1986). *Accord* Westhart v. Mule, 261 Cal. Rptr. 640 (Ct. App. 1989) (ordered not published).

**IA:** *Accord* Morgan v. Olds, 417 N.W.2d 232.

**WA:** *Accord* Benoy v. Simons, 831 P.2d 167; Strickland v. Deaconess Hosp., 735 P.2d 74.

*See also* Restatement (Second) of Torts § 46.

[76] Restatement (Second) of Torts § 46(1) (1965).

**Mental Element: Intent or Recklessness.** As is the case with other intentional torts,[77] intent may be established by proof of actual intent (that is, by showing that the defendant's *purpose* was to cause infliction of severe emotional distress) or by proof of constructive intent (that is, by showing that the defendant knew with substantial certainty that severe emotional distress would result).[78] Unlike other intentional torts, the mental element of intentional infliction of emotional distress may be established in a third way by showing *recklessness* rather than intent.[79] That is, if the physician acted with reckless disregard for whether or not his conduct would inflict severe emotional distress, the cause of action is established even if he did not actually or constructively intend this result.[80]

**Outrageous Conduct.** What constitutes outrageous conduct either in the context of decisionmaking about life-sustaining treatment or otherwise is not susceptible to precise specification. The test that the courts generally put forth is whether the facts would lead an average member of the community to exclaim that the conduct was outrageous.[81] Thus, when physicians inserted a feeding tube over the objection of the wife of an incompetent patient, the court held that this conduct was

> simply not the type which reasonable persons would regard as so extreme as to exceed all bounds usually tolerated in a civilized society. . . . [The doctors] did what any other physicians similarly situated would have done—no more, no less. In light of [the wife's] inaction [—she made no effort to have the feeding tube removed, nor, assuming she did but the doctors refused, did she seek court intervention—], this is hardly a case in which 'the recitation of the facts to an average member of the community would arouse his [or her] resentment against the actor, and lead him [or her] to exclaim, "Outrageous!"[82]

Another court, in denying damages to the wife of a man in a vegetative state, who died after being weaned from a ventilator, defined outrageous conduct as "'conduct exceeding all bounds usually tolerated by decent society.'"[83] The

---

[77] See §§ **17.2–17.4.**

[78] Restatement (Second) of Torts § 8A.

[79] *Id.* § 46(1).

    **IA:** *See, e.g.,* Morgan v. Olds, 417 N.W.2d 232 (Iowa Ct. App. 1987).

    **WA:** *See, e.g.,* Benoy v. Simons, 831 P.2d 167, 171.

[80] Morgan v. Olds, 417 N.W.2d at 237 ("The actor's conduct is in reckless disregard of the safety of another if he does an act or intentionally fails to do an act which it is his duty to the other to do, knowing or having reason to know of facts which would lead a reasonable man to realize, not only that his conduct creates an unreasonable risk of physical harm to another, but also that such risk is substantially greater than that which is necessary to make his conduct negligent.").

[81] Restatement (Second) of Torts § 46 cmt. d. *See, e.g.,* Benoy v. Simons, 831 P.2d at 171.

[82] Westhart v. Mule, 261 Cal. Rptr. 640, 645 (Ct. App. 1989) (ordered not published) (quoting Restatement (Second) of Torts § 46 cmt. d).

[83] Morgan v. Olds, 417 N.W.2d at 237.

court refused to find that the physician's decision not to put the patient back on a ventilator when it became clear that he could not survive without it was outrageous. At worst, there was a misunderstanding by the wife about what the physician intended to do or a misunderstanding by the physician about the wife's agreement with the plan not to put the patient back on the ventilator from which he was weaned if he could not breathe on his own.

It is for the court to make a threshold determination of whether the defendant's conduct is "so extreme and outrageous as to permit recovery."[84] The court may find as a matter of law that it is or is not,[85] or that it is a question about which reasonable people may disagree, thereby leaving it to a jury for ultimate determination.[86]

## § 17.6 —Application to Right-to-Die Cases

Despite decisions holding open the possibility of a claim for intentional infliction of emotional distress for the unauthorized administration of life-sustaining treatment, establishing such a claim has proved to be extremely difficult. Only one claim has succeeded[87] (and it is not even clear that the theory on which recovery was predicated was intentional infliction of emotional distress), and several have failed. What is clear is that a physician's unauthorized administration per se of life-sustaining treatment might constitute battery, but it does not constitute the intentional infliction of emotional distress.[88]

The likelihood of recovery for intentional infliction of emotional distress is complicated by the fact that it is a relatively new and still-developing area of tort law. This is even truer when it is applied in the context of life-sustaining medical treatment. In addition, the requirement of outrageous conduct is likely to pose an especially serious obstacle to recovery. Even though it cannot be formally incorporated into law, as members of society judges and jurors know that the medical profession's commitment is to maintaining life in most circumstances, and the presumption is that a patient desires life, and therefore desires treatment to be maintained. Thus, it may prove difficult for a trier of fact to view initiation or continuation of treatment as outrageous conduct even in the face of a request to terminate it.

---

[84] Restatement (Second) of Torts § 46 cmt. h. *See, e.g.,* Westhart v. Mule, 261 Cal. Rptr. at 645.

[85] *See, e.g.,* Westhart v. Mule, 261 Cal. Rptr. at 645 (holding as a matter of law that doctors' insertion of feeding tube in incompetent patient over objection of patient's wife is not outrageous conduct).

[86] Restatement (Second) of Torts § 46 cmt. h. *See, e.g.,* Westhart v. Mule, 261 Cal. Rptr. at 645.

[87] **NJ:** *See* Strachan v. John F. Kennedy Memorial Hosp., 538 A.2d 346 (N.J. 1988).

[88] *See, e.g.,* Westhart v. Mule, 261 Cal. Rptr. 640, 643 n.6 (Ct. App. 1989) (ordered not published) (denying recovery for intentional infliction of emotional distress but noting that "'some of this sounds like a claim of battery or something other than an intentional infliction of emotional distress'").

The first reported case seeking recovery for intentional infliction of emotional distress for unauthorized life-sustaining medical treatment is *Bartling v. Glendale Adventist Medical Center.*[89] The claim ultimately failed for the same reason that the battery claim in this case failed,[90] namely, that "respondents could not reasonably have foreseen that their effort to preserve life was legally tantamount to a 'conscious disregard' of appellants' rights."[91] But even had the underlying law concerning the patient's right to refuse treatment been more clearly established, the claim would have failed because the court found other fatal barriers to recovery.

The first was proof of intent. The court found the requisite intent to be lacking because the facts did not "show a malevolent or reckless disregard for [the patient's] painful struggle for medical self-determination."[92] This conclusion is justified only if what the court had in mind was a theory based on actual intent or recklessness. However, it overlooks the possibility of establishing intent on the basis of constructive intent. In order to establish intent, the plaintiff did not need to show that the defendant *wanted* to inflict severe emotional distress on the plaintiff; instead, constructive intent—in the form of a showing that the defendant *knew* that severe emotional distress was substantially certain to result—should have sufficed.[93] Proof of constructive intent would have been far simpler given the facts of *Bartling* because the patient, while in the hospital, executed a living will and brought a judicial action to enforce it. A jury could have readily inferred from the living will that the attending physician and other health care professionals knew with substantial certainty that the patient would suffer severe emotional distress if treated. The living will stated that

> I find intolerable the living conditions forced upon me by my deteriorating lungs, heart and blood vessel systems and find intolerable my being continuously being connected to this ventilator, which sustains my every breath and my life for the past six and one-half (6½) weeks . . . [and] is contrary to my every wish, and constitutes a battery upon my person.[94]

Furthermore, the plaintiff did not even need to establish actual or constructive intent; a showing that the physicians acted with reckless disregard of whether or not their conduct would inflict severe emotional distress on the plaintiff would

---

[89] 229 Cal. Rptr. 360 (Ct. App. 1986).

[90] See § 7.4.

[91] Bartling v. Glendale Adventist Medical Ctr., 229 Cal. Rptr. at 364.

[92] *Id.*

[93] Restatement (Second) of Torts § 8A cmt. b (1965). *See also id.* § 46 cmt. i ("The rule stated . . . applies where the actor desires to inflict severe emotional distress, and also where he knows that such distress is certain, or substantially certain, to result from his conduct.").

[94] Bartling v. Glendale Adventist Medical Ctr., 229 Cal. Rptr. at 361.

have been sufficient.[95] The court found that recklessness was absent, but the facts of the case strongly support the contrary finding.

The second stumbling block concerned proof of outrageous conduct. The court concluded that outrageous conduct was not shown despite "obviously acute [suffering], [because] the facts . . . do not rise to the level of . . . atrocious and indecent behavior on the part of [the defendants]."[96] The court justified this conclusion by stressing that the defendant physician and hospital "acted on what they believed to be prevailing community medical and legal standards and did not use their superior position to intentionally harass or intimidate the Bartlings."[97]

*Bartling* is one of the clearest cases of intentional infliction of emotional distress in the context of unauthorized administration of life-sustaining medical treatment. Thus, if recovery was unsuccessful in that case, there is a strong temptation to conclude that recovery for unauthorized administration of life-sustaining treatment will never be viable under this theory. Yet, that conclusion is probably not warranted because situations such as those in *Bartling* may be decided differently as the law concerning a patient's right to refuse life-sustaining treatment becomes better established.

Three years after *Bartling,* another division of the California Court of Appeal held in *Westhart v. Mule*[98] that the administration of life-sustaining treatment did not constitute intentional infliction of emotional distress. However, it did not employ the same reasoning as the court did in *Bartling,* thus suggesting that in that short intervening period of time the law regarding the forgoing of life-sustaining treatment had become far better established and that the reason put forth in *Bartling* for denying recovery would no longer suffice.

At the time of admission to the hospital, the patient in *Westhart* was extremely ill—"suffering from congestive heart failure, pneumonia, chronic organic brain syndrome secondary to previous multiple strokes, and dehydration"—and had been for eight years. He "'was unable to walk, speak, make decisions for himself regarding his health care, and unable to communicate his wishes, desires, and consent regarding the course and scope of his medical treatment,'" and as a result, his wife had assumed decisionmaking authority for him. She informed the defendant-physicians that no "'extraordinary or heroic measures [were to be] taken to prolong [her husband's] deteriorating condition.'" More

---

[95] Restatement (Second) of Torts § 46 cmt. i (The rule of intentional infliction of emotional distress "applies also where [the defendant] acts recklessly . . . in deliberate disregard of a high probability that the emotional distress will follow."). *See also* Restatement (Second) of Torts § 500 cmt. f ("It is enough that [the actor] realizes or, from facts which he knows, should realize that there is a strong probability that harm may result even though he hopes or even expects that his conduct will prove harmless.").

[96] Bartling v. Glendale Adventist Medical Ctr., 229 Cal. Rptr. at 365.

[97] *Id.*

[98] 261 Cal. Rptr. 640 (Ct. App. 1989) (ordered not published).

specifically, she told them she did not want him put on a ventilator or for cardiopulmonary resuscitation to be administered or for " 'any heroic measures' [to be] taken because her husband was basically a 'vegetable.' "[99]

Nonetheless, the physicians surgically implanted a feeding tube in Mr. Westhart. The complaint alleged that

> [t]wo hospital nurses, acting on defendants' behalf, spoke with [Mrs.] Westhart by telephone and attempted to obtain her consent. During the conversation, according to the complaint, Westhart "was crying hysterically and under the emotional duress of living with the stress and strain of her husband's condition for the previous eight years." One of the two nurses claimed Westhart "did give permission for the surgery, but the other nurse claimed she did not feel it was voluntary and would therefore not sign the consent form."[100]

The trial court dismissed the complaint on the ground that the defendants exercised professional judgment in administering the treatment.

The appeals court affirmed, but on an additional ground. It felt that Mrs. Westhart's failure to make any effort to have the feeding tube removed, either by asking the doctors or by seeking a judicial order, "essentially forecloses her claim she suffered severe emotional distress as a result of the doctors' extreme and outrageous conduct."[101] This inaction, taken together with the fact that the defendants "did what any other physicians similarly situated would have done— no more, no less,"[102] would not constitute outrageous conduct in the eyes of the average member of the community.

*Westhart* is somewhat less tolerant of customary medical practice than is *Bartling,* resting its holding on the plaintiff's inaction as well as on the doctors' conduct. However, it too displays an inordinate and unwarranted deference to customary practice—unwarranted because it is essentially at odds with the fundamental right of an incompetent patient to have life-sustaining treatment forgone by his lawful surrogate. An alternative reading of *Westhart,* as well as some of the other intentional infliction of emotional distress cases denying recovery, is that a physician's administration of unauthorized treatment *is* a legally compensable wrong; the wrong, however, is not intentional infliction of emotional distress but battery.[103]

Another case that failed for reasons similar to *Bartling,* though the facts appear much weaker, is *Benoy v. Simons.*[104] In *Benoy,* the parents and grandparents of a

---

[99] *Id.* at 641.

[100] *Id.*

[101] *Id.* at 645.

[102] *Id.*

[103] *Id.* at 643 n.6 ("At the hearing on the demurrer to Westhart's first amended complaint, the court aptly noted 'some of this sounds like a claim of battery or something other than an intentional infliction of emotional distress.' ").

[104] 831 P.2d 167 (Wash. Ct. App. 1992).

low-birth-weight baby, who was treated by defendants (physician and hospital), brought suit on a number of theories, including intentional infliction of emotional distress. The emotional distress claim was not only for unauthorized treatment but for a variety of other acts the physician was alleged to have committed, including pressuring the grandparents to become the child's guardians (because the mother was a teenager and thought to be incapable of caring for the child), misleading them into believing the child was improving when his condition was deteriorating, telling his mother to take his body home on the bus from the hospital where he died, and billing for needless care.[105]

The dismissal of the complaint was affirmed for three reasons. First, the plaintiffs could not prove intent or recklessness.[106] Second, according to the appeals court, the evidence did not permit the defendants' conduct to be characterized as "outrageous":

> Even assuming the events occurred as described by the Benoys, Dr. Simon's conduct did not fall within the perimeters of that which may be categorized as outrageous. The meetings between and among the health care providers, Dr. Simon, Saundra and her parents were good faith attempts to appoint a guardian for Dustin. Neither Saundra nor her parents would consent; they cannot now characterize the attempt as outrageous conduct. The other allegations are similarly not accurately characterized.[107]

This is hard to understand if the plaintiffs' allegations are taken as true, as they must be for the purpose of ruling on a motion to dismiss. Finally, citing *Bartling,* the court concluded that the plaintiffs failed to show that the physician "acted other than in conformance with his professional obligation to preserve the life of his patient."[108]

When a claim of intentional infliction of emotional distress is based on an allegation that treatment was administered in violation of a patient's purported *oral* advance directive, as was the case in *McVey v. Englewood Hospital Ass'n,*[109] proof of outrageous conduct may be even more difficult than in a case such as *Bartling* in which the patient is competent and personally issues the directions not to treat. The patient in *McVey* suffered a severe stroke at the age of 91 and was hospitalized. She was in a deep coma and suffering from respiratory failure, so she was placed on a ventilator. On the evening of admission to the hospital, the neurologist told her two daughters that her brain activity was minimal and that she would probably die if taken off the ventilator. The daughters "requested, indeed demanded," that the ventilatory support be

---

[105] *Id.* at 170.

[106] *Id.* at 171 ("They have not shown Dr. Simon intended to cause them emotional distress or acted recklessly.").

[107] *Id.*

[108] *Id.*

[109] 524 A.2d 450 (N.J. Super. Ct. App. Div. 1987).

discontinued because she "had orally expressed the wish not to be artificially maintained if a situation such as this were to arise."[110] The health care providers refused to terminate life support because the patient was not brain dead. Eventually a guardianship proceeding was commenced, the daughters were appointed co-guardians, they authorized the termination of ventilatory support, and the patient died.

After her death, the daughters sued the hospital and doctors, but it is not entirely clear from the reported case what causes of action were pleaded. The only clue is that they sought compensatory and punitive damages for the "emotional suffering alleged to have arisen from the failure of the defendants to honor [the patient's] wishes."[111] The appellate court upheld the grant of summary judgment for the defendants. Its basis for so doing was that "[m]edical professionals are not now, and should not be, charged with the non-medical duty to determine the existence, veracity and effect of an incompetent's orally expressed wishes."[112] The court implied that a judicial proceeding needed to be held to establish the patient's wishes, and only then could the physicians be compelled to terminate treatment, if at all. In fact, a guardianship proceeding was held and the patient's daughters were appointed co-guardians, but there is no indication whether an inquiry was held concerning what the patient's wishes were.

The court rejected the argument that because physicians are immune from civil and criminal liability if they rely on the "presumed or actual wish of the incompetent respecting termination of life support,"[113] they are *required* to terminate treatment when requested to do so by family members reporting the very same "presumed or actual wish" of the patient.[114] This was arguably a correct statement of New Jersey law at the time of the decision of the case in April 1987.[115] However, less than three months later, the New Jersey Supreme Court handed down two decisions making it clear that there is no need for routine guardianship proceedings in end-of-life decisionmaking cases and that family members are ordinarily authorized to make such decisions in the absence of judicial proceedings.[116]

The holding in *McVey* rests in part on the assumption that "[m]edical professionals are not now, and should not be, charged with the nonmedical duty to

---

[110] McVey v. Englewood Hosp. Ass'n, 524 A.2d at 451.

[111] *Id.* at 452.

[112] *Id.*

[113] *Id.* (citing John F. Kennedy Memorial Hosp. v. Bludworth, 452 So. 2d 921 (Fla. 1984); Barber v. Superior Court, 195 Cal. Rptr. 484 (Ct. App. 1983)).

[114] *Id.* ("It is a very different thing . . . to assert that failure to comply with such undocumented requests, and absent the appointment of a guardian, constitutes an actionable breach of a duty owed to the patient and family.").

[115] *See In re* Conroy, 486 A.2d 1209 (N.J. 1985) (seemingly requiring a guardianship proceeding before termination of life support). See §§ 5.11 and 5.14.

[116] *See In re* Jobes, 529 A.2d 434 (N.J. 1987); *In re* Peter, 529 A.2d 419 (N.J. 1987). See § 5.14.

determine the existence, veracity and effect of an incompetent's orally expressed wishes."[117] While that might have been true at the time of the decision, it is a more dubious assumption today. That is especially so for health care institutions in light of the enactment of the federal Patient Self-Determination Act, which imposes a number of duties on health care institutions concerning the determination of a patient's wishes about life-sustaining medical treatment, including "ensur[ing] compliance with requirements of State law . . . respecting advance directives."[118]

The only case in which damages have been awarded for intentional infliction of emotional distress in the context of decisionmaking about life-sustaining treatment, *Strachan v. John F. Kennedy Memorial Hospital,*[119] further illustrates, because of the extreme facts of the case, how difficult it is to establish liability under this theory. The patient was taken to the defendant-hospital as a result of a self-inflicted gunshot wound. On arrival, he was placed on a ventilator but was determined to be dead, by brain-death standards, a determination that was subsequently confirmed by other physicians. A physician explained to the patient's parents that he was "brain dead" and asked them to consider donating the patient's organs for transplantation. They were uncertain about what to do and agreed to return the following day to decide. In the meantime, the patient was maintained on a ventilator in order to preserve the organs for transplantation. The parents returned to the hospital as scheduled and informed the doctor then on duty that they had decided not to make a donation, and requested that their son be removed from the ventilator. The doctor asked them to "'think it over some more,'"[120] and when the patient's father asked a nurse when the ventilator would be turned off, he was told that it could not be without an order from the hospital administrator. The hospital administrator, in consultation with the hospital attorney, ordered that additional tests be conducted to confirm that the patient was dead. These tests did confirm the original diagnosis of death. Approximately three days after the patient arrived at the hospital and was first "declared" dead, the ventilator was turned off, and his body was turned over to his parents for burial.

Thereafter, the family brought suit against the hospital and its administrator seeking recovery for emotional distress, based on the theory that the hospital should have had procedures for determining death in accordance with brain-death standards and that they delayed in turning over the body for burial. The court refused to impose a duty on hospitals "to have in place procedures for the removal of a dead body from a life-support mechanism."[121] Its reasoning in this regard is not strong:

---

[117] McVey v. Englewood Hosp. Ass'n, 524 A.2d 450, 452 (N.J. Super. Ct. App. Div. 1987).

[118] 42 U.S.C.A. § 1395cc(f)(1)(D) (West 1992 & Supp. 1994); *id.* § 1396a(w)(1)(D). See § **10.21.**

[119] 538 A.2d 346 (N.J. 1988).

[120] *Id.* at 347.

[121] *Id.* at 349.

The imposition of a paperwork duty does little to advance either the mission of health-care providers or the needs of society. If "procedures" are to be viewed as more than mere "paperwork" and considered indispensable in this area—in the nature of a standard that governs the medical community—then those procedures should be designed and imposed by those most directly involved, the physicians and hospitals themselves. That is the business of the medical community itself, not of this Court.[122]

This reasoning exhibits an undue deference to health care professionals, a deference not warranted by the facts of the case.

However, the court did uphold the plaintiff's claim that the hospital was liable for delay in releasing the patient's body. The theory under which it did so is somewhat unclear. The court analyzed the right to recovery as if it were a claim for intentional infliction of emotional distress, yet it seems to have based recovery at least in part on the hospital's negligence in not having a policy and procedures for removing brain-dead patients from a ventilator.[123]

The facts constituting the basis for liability are that the hospital personnel believed the patient to be dead on arrival as underscored by the fact that they would have harvested his organs at that time had his parents consented. Yet they delayed three days in actually terminating the ventilatory support. What appears to be central to the holding are the combination of the initial belief that the patient was dead, the delay in removing him from the ventilator, and the efforts to obtain consent from his parents to donate his organs. What is indisputable, however, is the length to which health care professionals must go in order to be held liable for intentional infliction of emotional distress.

Finally, the court made clear that the nature of the cause of action was a breach of duty owed the parents directly. Because the son was dead, he suffered no legal wrong from defendants' conduct: "Plaintiffs' distress, therefore, was not the result of witnessing another's injury, but rather the result of a breach of duty owed directly to plaintiffs."[124] The court declined to consider whether, in such a case, there must be physical injury to recover for an emotional distress claim because of "the long-recognized exception for negligent handling of a corpse."[125] Further, the court appeared to have no doubt that the plaintiffs suffered emotional distress, as gleaned from its recitation that

---

[122] *Id. But see In re* Jobes, 529 A.2d 434 (N.J. 1987) (nursing home could not enforce unwritten policy).

[123] *Id.* at 349–50 ("That is not to say, however, that the absence of such procedures may not be relevant on the issue of whether these defendants fulfilled the obligation that surely they had: to act reasonably in the face of plaintiffs' request to turn over the body. . . . We take the expert's testimony to mean that if a hospital is going to insist on forms and procedures, then it should have them available and in place, or at the least improvise them on the spot, in order to fulfill its underlying obligation to take reasonable steps to release the body to the next of kin.").

[124] *Id.* at 352. See § **17.7.**

[125] *Id.*

[t]he record in this case reveals particularly compelling evidence of distress. Although plaintiffs were told that their son was brain dead and nothing further could be done for him, for three days after requesting that their son be disconnected from the respirator plaintiffs continued to see him lying in bed, with tubes in his body, his eyes taped shut, and foam in his mouth. His body remained warm to the touch. Had Jeffrey's body been removed from the respirator when his parents requested, a scene fraught with grief and heartache would have been avoided, and plaintiffs would have been spared additional suffering.[126]

Yet another barrier to recovery for intentional infliction of emotional distress in end-of-life decisionmaking cases is that in most jurisdictions the cause of action dies with the person who was harmed.[127] It is also possible that a third party's cause of action[128] also dies with the patient.[129]

In addition to the possibility of providing a remedy for unauthorized treatment, intentional infliction of emotional distress also provides a potential theory for recovery for damages arising from other kinds of harmful conduct in the end-of-life decisionmaking process. For example, the unauthorized *forgoing* of treatment might also give rise to a cause of action for intentional infliction of emotional distress.[130] In one particularly unusual case in which the health care professionals participating in decisionmaking about life-sustaining treatment allegedly released information to the news media about the case, a cause of action for intentional infliction of emotional distress was dismissed, but only because the defendant was protected by statutory immunity as a "public employer."[131]

## § 17.7 —Recovery by Third Parties

The cause of action for intentional infliction of emotional distress might also provide a basis for recovery for third parties—especially the patient's family,

---

[126] *Id.* at 351.

[127] **CA:** *See, e.g.,* Bartling v. Glendale Adventist Medical Ctr., 229 Cal. Rptr. 360, 364 (Ct. App. 1986) ("decedent's cause of action for pain and suffering dies with him").

**NJ:** *Cf.* Strachan v. John F. Kennedy Memorial Hosp., 538 A.2d 346, 352 (N.J. 1988) ("Because Jeffrey was no longer alive, defendants breached no duty owed him by their failure to turn off the respirator.").

**WA:** *See, e.g.,* Strickland v. Deaconess Hosp., 735 P.2d 74 (Wash. Ct. App. 1987).

*See generally* Miller, *Right-to-Die Damage Actions: Developments in the Law,* 65 Denv. U. L. Rev. 181, 210–12 (1988).

[128] See § **17.25.**

[129] Strachan v. John F. Kennedy Memorial Hosp., 538 A.2d 346 (N.J. 1988) (but not clear whether this refers to intentional or negligent infliction of emotional distress).

[130] **AL:** *See, e.g.,* Gallups v. Carter, 534 So. 2d 585 (Ala. 1988) (affirmance of summary judgment for defendants in action against physicians for removing brain-dead patient from life-support system).

**IA:** *See, e.g.,* Morgan v. Olds, 417 N.W.2d 232 (Iowa Ct. App. 1987).

[131] **MA:** *See* Spring v. Geriatric Auth., 475 N.E.2d 727 (Mass. 1985).

but possibly other individuals close to the patient—who suffer emotional distress when a health care professional administers treatment without valid consent or in the face of an express refusal.[132] It might also provide a theory for recovery for the nonconsensual withholding or withdrawal of life-sustaining treatment.[133]

There are actually two distinct situations in which third parties might recover for the intentional infliction of emotional distress in the context of end-of-life decisionmaking. First, if the health care provider engages in outrageous conduct *to the patient* that intentionally or recklessly causes severe emotional distress to the third party, the third party might recover. Section 46 of the *Restatement (Second) of Torts,* from which most courts take their cue in actions seeking damages for intentional infliction of emotional distress, expressly provides for recovery by a third person.[134] This is the kind of claim ordinarily pleaded in the context of end-of-life decisionmaking.

A third party might also recover if the health care provider engages in outrageous conduct *to the third party* that intentionally or recklessly causes severe emotional distress to that person. In this kind of situation, the cause of action should proceed under a standard intentional infliction of emotional distress theory because the intent to cause harm is directed at the same person who suffers the harm.[135]

## Outrageous Conduct to the *Patient* Resulting in Harm to Third Party

The elements of the cause of action are slightly different when the plaintiff is a third party rather than the patient. First, the medical decision to initiate or continue treatment, despite the lack of authorization to do so, must be shown to have been made with intent to cause severe emotional distress to the third party rather than to the patient. As is the case with other intentional torts, there need not be proof of actual intent—that it was the physician's *purpose* to cause severe emotional distress to the plaintiff. Intent may be established by showing that the defendant *knew* that the administration of treatment without authorization was substantially certain to cause serious emotional distress to the third party

---

[132] **IA:** *But see* Morgan v. Olds, 417 N.W.2d 232, 237 (Iowa Ct. App. 1987) (termination of treatment, allegedly without the survivors' permission, was held to be conduct not "rising to the level of outrageousness necessary to recover" for intentional infliction of emotional distress).

**MA:** *Cf.* Spring v. Geriatric Auth., 475 N.E.2d 727 (Mass. 1985).

**OH:** *See* Estate of Leach v. Shapiro, 469 N.E.2d 1047 (Ohio Ct. App. 1984).

[133] *See, e.g.,* Morgan v. Olds, 417 N.W.2d 232.

[134] Restatement (Second) of Torts § 46(2) ("[w]here such conduct is directed at a third party").

[135] *Id.* § 46(1).

(constructive intent), or the defendant acted in *reckless disregard* of causing serious emotional distress to that person.[136]

Second, the plaintiff must be present at the time of the defendant's outrageous conduct.[137] There are no decided medical decisionmaking cases dealing with this issue, and the single comment to the *Restatement* touching on this requirement is not particularly helpful.[138] Most cases are strict in requiring the physical presence of the plaintiff at the time of the outrageous conduct toward the third party.[139] In the context of unauthorized treatment, this probably means that the family member must be present when unauthorized treatment is initiated or at some point in the course of its administration—presumably to enhance the reliability that the plaintiff actually did suffer severe emotional distress.[140]

As is the case with actions for intentional infliction of emotional distress brought by the patient, the conduct must be outrageous. This will probably prove to be a serious barrier to liability just as it is in patient-plaintiff cases. For example, in *Morgan v. Olds*,[141] the wife of a patient, who died after he was weaned from a ventilator by his physicians and not put back on when he was unable to breathe on his own, brought an action against the physicians. The court affirmed the trial court's refusal to submit the case to the jury on a theory of intentional infliction of emotional distress, commenting that "[w]hile the situation was a tragic one, we feel the most plaintiff's evidence shows is possibly a misunderstanding and not conduct rising to the level of outrageousness necessary to recover under plaintiff's theory."[142]

**Immediate Family Member.**  The *Restatement* requires that the third party be an "immediate family member" unless the emotional distress is accompanied by physical injury. A comment to the *Restatement* suggests that these should be "near relatives, or at least close associates."[143] For purposes of recovering for intentional infliction of emotional distress, the Washington Court of Appeals has defined an "immediate family member" in the context of end-of-life decision-making as "those who are permitted to bring wrongful death actions." Under

---

[136] *Id.* § 8A.

[137] *Id.* § 46(2)(a), (b).

**WA:** Benoy v. Simons, 831 P.2d 167, 171 (Wash. Ct. App. 1992).

[138] Restatement (Second) of Torts § 46 cmt. l ("The cases thus far decided . . . have limited such liability to plaintiffs who were present at the time, as distinguished from those who discover later what has occurred.").

[139] **WY:** *But see* R.D. v. W.H., 875 P.2d 26 (Wyo. 1988) (where plaintiff was present in immediate aftermath of suicide resulting from defendant's outrageous conduct, court held facts placed case within caveat to cmt. l of § 46 holding presence requirement unnecessary).

[140] *See* Restatement (Second) of Torts § 46 cmt. k ("Normally, severe emotional distress is accompanied or followed by shock, illness, or other bodily harm, which in itself affords evidence that the distress is genuine and severe.").

[141] 417 N.W.2d 232 (Iowa Ct. App. 1987).

[142] *Id.* at 237.

[143] Restatement (Second) of Torts § 46 cmt. l.

Washington statutes, this includes "spouses, children, stepchildren, parents, and siblings,"[144] and therefore the court denied recovery to the sons (and their wives) of a patient's former wife (whose marriage had been invalidated).

An immediate family member might also be barred from recovery for intentional infliction of emotional distress if consent to the treatment was provided by the patient's lawful surrogate.[145]

**Other Third Parties.**   The rule of the *Restatement* is that if the plaintiff is not an immediate family member—for example, a more distant family member or a friend of the patient—recovery for intentional infliction of emotional distress is not possible unless the plaintiff is physically present and there is *bodily* harm as well as severe emotional distress.[146]

Individuals other than family members can suffer severe emotional distress from witnessing the administration of unwanted life-sustaining medical treatment to a patient. Recovery by a family member will be difficult enough, and recovery by another third party could prove to be almost impossible. The closer the individual is to occupying the role of a family member, the greater the claim that that individual should have to recover if a family member could recover. A non-family member appointed by the patient to act as surrogate should have the strongest claim to being treated the same as a family member. Individuals who live in the patient's household, such as unmarried domestic partners and stepchildren, should be similarly treated.[147] In addition, third parties other than family members must demonstrate that they suffered bodily harm.[148]

### Outrageous Conduct to the *Third Party* Resulting in Harm to Third Party

An action for recovery of damages for emotional distress may be brought by a third party based on outrageous conduct to that party, rather than to the patient. According to the New Jersey Supreme Court in *Strachan v. John F. Kennedy*

---

[144] Strickland v. Deaconess Hosp., 735 P.2d 74, 78 (Wash. Ct. App. 1987).

[145] **MI:** *See* Young v. Oakland Gen. Hosp., 437 N.W.2d 321, 326 (Mich. Ct. App. 1989) ("plaintiff [patient's grandson] could not bring a separate suit for intentional infliction of emotional distress" because plaintiff's daughter had consented to treatment).

[146] Restatement (Second) of Torts § 46(2)(b).

  **WA:** *But see* Benoy v. Simons, 831 P.2d 167, 171 (Wash. Ct. App. 1992) (seemingly applying the bodily harm requirement to family members: "The Benoys have not shown their emotional distress was so severe or extreme it was manifested by objective physical symptoms.").

[147] *But see* Strickland v. Deaconess Hosp., 735 P.2d 74 (recovery for intentional infliction of emotional distress for removal of patient's respirator without patient's consent limited to members of immediate family, not including plaintiffs whose mother was no longer married to patient).

[148] Restatement (Second) of Torts § 46(2)(b).

*Memorial Hospital,*[149] if the patient has not suffered emotional distress or is deceased, the patient would have no claim and neither would third parties.[150] Thus, in *Strachan,* the court held that the parents of a patient who was dead on arrival at the hospital could not recover damages for emotional distress that derived from any harm to the patient because the patient could not, in the eyes of the law, suffer any harm. However, they were entitled to recover damages for harm done to them directly.

## § 17.8   Invasion of Privacy

Of all the potential theories of liability for unauthorized treatment, invasion of privacy is the most poorly developed both conceptually and in application. Such an action might take two different forms. First, a cause of action might lie for violation of a constitutional right of privacy for the unauthorized administration of treatment.[151] Second, invasion of privacy might be actionable as a tort.

The tort law of invasion of privacy has developed along the lines suggested by Prosser[152] and adopted by the *Restatement (Second) of Torts,* which recognizes four different torts under the general heading of invasion of privacy—intrusion upon seclusion, appropriation of name or likeness, publicity given to private life, and publicity placing person in a false light.[153] An allegation of unauthorized treatment does not fit comfortably within any of these theories.

By contrast, Harper, James, and Gray use a different classification scheme from that of the *Restatement.* They contend that "the most important interests protected in tort law under the 'privacy' rubric" include "an interest in personal dignity and self-respect."[154] However, this conception of invasion of privacy, as applied in the right-to-die context, is not substantially different from an action for battery and hence what at first glance appears to be a different theory of recovery probably turns out to be no more than a different name for the same theory.

Because invasion of privacy is not a very promising theory of recovery for unauthorized treatment, it has not been pleaded frequently and has not fared well when it has been raised. In *Estate of Leach v. Shapiro,* the Ohio Court of Appeals did not reach the merits of a claim that unauthorized treatment constituted an invasion of privacy because "[t]he right to privacy is a right personal to the

---

[149] 538 A.2d 346 (N.J. 1988).

[150] *Id.* at 352 ("Because Jeffrey was no longer alive, defendants breached no duty owed him by their failure to turn off the respirator. Jeffrey suffered no harm as a result of defendants' negligence. Plaintiffs' distress, therefore, was not the result of witnessing another's injury, but rather the result of a breach of duty owed directly to plaintiffs.").

[151] See § **17.20.**

[152] *See* Prosser, *Privacy,* 48 Cal. L. Rev. 383 (1960).

[153] Restatement (Second) of Torts §§ 652B–652E (1977).

[154] 2 F. Harper et al., The Law of Torts § 9.6, at 633 (1986).

individual asserting it [and] . . . lapses with the death of the person who enjoys it."[155] An action for violation of the right of privacy must therefore be brought either by the patient himself (if competent) or by the surrogate of an incompetent, but still living, patient.[156]

Although the *Leach* court implicitly acknowledged a patient's common-law right of privacy and the right to recover in tort for its violation, it failed to develop the theory, so that it is impossible to know what the elements of the cause of action that it envisioned might be. Furthermore, some of the discussion suggests that the court had in mind nothing more than recovery for lack of informed consent when it spoke of recovery for invasion of privacy.[157] In other places the court suggested that invasion of privacy might be a theory of recovery distinct from battery but did not develop this notion because it held that the facts would not support such a cause of action in any event because of the patient's death.[158]

## § 17.9   Negligence

Negligence is a very broad theory of recovery, and the variety of different kinds of claims all brought under the aegis of negligence reflect this. In principle, negligence in the treatment of hopelessly ill and terminally ill patients is no different from negligence in any other sphere of medical care: A patient harmed by a physician who fails to administer a medically indicated treatment, who administers a medically contraindicated treatment, or who administers the appropriate treatment in a substandard manner, or a patient who is treated or not treated at all or incorrectly because of a substandard diagnostic process may bring an action in negligence to recover damages for the resultant harm. Even if there is no defalcation in treatment or diagnosis, negligence liability may be incurred for inadequate disclosure of information under a theory of informed consent.[159] (If disclosure is adequate but consent is not properly obtained, the action is ordinarily one for battery.[160])

---

[155] Estate of Leach v. Shapiro, 469 N.E.2d 1047, 1054 (Ohio Ct. App. 1984).

[156] Restatement (Second) of Torts § 652I ("Except for the appropriation of one's name or likeness, an action for invasion of privacy can be maintained only by a living individual whose privacy is invaded."). *Contra* Canino v. New York News, Inc., 475 A.2d 528 (N.J. 1984) (holding that action for defamation survives death of defamed party).

[157] Estate of Leach v. Shapiro, 469 N.E.2d at 1052 ("The requirement of informed consent has its roots not only in the patient's right to privacy but also in the nature of the physician-patient relationship. The physician owes his patient a fiduciary duty of good faith and fair dealing which gives rise to certain specific professional obligations. These obligations include not only the duty to exercise due care and skill, but to fully inform the patient of his condition and to obtain the patient's informed consent to the medical treatment.").

[158] *Id.* at 1054–55.

[159] See §§ 17.11–17.12.

[160] DC: *In re* A.C., 573 A.2d 1235, 1243 (D.C. 1990) ("[A] surgeon who performs an operation without the patient's consent may be guilty of a battery . . . or . . . if the surgeon obtains an insufficiently informed consent, he or she may be liable for negligence.").

A discussion of basic principles of liability for professional negligence is beyond the scope of this section. This discussion is confined to special issues of negligence liability that may arise in the provision or discontinuation of life-sustaining treatment. Also outside the scope of this discussion is the "garden variety" negligence that arises from a physician's failure to possess or exercise requisite training and/or skill in determining what diagnostic or therapeutic course to follow in performing diagnosis or therapy.

Apart from garden variety negligence, claims of negligence are most likely to arise out of disagreements concerning how aggressively to treat a dying patient. Although most right-to-die litigation to date, both the cases seeking equitable relief and those seeking damages, has been of the type in which the attending physician wished to provide *more* aggressive treatment than the patient or surrogate deemed desirable, it is not unlikely that situations in which the tables are turned will increase, that is, situations in which the patient—or more likely, the patient's surrogate or family—wishes to have aggressive treatment administered but the physician believes that life support should be terminated or at least that a less aggressive therapeutic regimen be utilized.[161] Some of the litigation alleging negligence in end-of-life decision-making has arisen from allegedly undue haste in terminating treatment. Most of these claims could also be litigated as intentional infliction of emotional distress claims, and some have been. Negligent failure to disclose information or obtain consent (that is, lack of informed consent)[162] might also provide the basis for claims for unauthorized administration of treatment or delay in terminating treatment. In fact, however, battery, intentional infliction of emotional distress, and related theories have been more popular with litigants in such cases.

Unwarranted haste in terminating treatment, and delay in or unauthorized administration of treatment can result in mental distress to conscious patients. In these cases and also in cases of patients who are no longer able to perceive injury, the patients' families might also bring a cause of action for negligent infliction of emotional distress. Recovery for close family members under a theory of negligent infliction of emotional distress is increasingly easier to obtain in many jurisdictions, but recovery by other third parties still seems quite unlikely. Recovery might also be sought for hospital, nursing home, and/or medical costs in the period between the request for the termination of treatment and the actual termination.[163]

---

OH: Anderson v. St. Francis-St. George Hosp., 614 N.E.2d 841 (Ohio Ct. App. 1992) (administration of cardiopulmonary resuscitation after refusal by patient, as documented in do-not-resuscitate order, is actionable as battery).

UT: Lounsbury v. Capel, 836 P.2d 188 (Utah 1992).

[161] See §§ **17.13–17.15** and **Ch. 19.**

[162] See §§ **17.11–17.12.**

[163] **AK:** *See* Alaska Stat. § 18.12.070(a) (provision in living will statute bars "compensation for medical services provided to a qualified patient after [physician's] withdrawal or after transfer should have occurred").

## § 17.10 —Negligence Liability in Administering Treatment

One class of claims of negligence in end-of-life decisionmaking essentially alleges that there was some defect in the decisionmaking process, such as obtaining consent or informed consent from the wrong person (for example, a surrogate rather than a competent patient,[164] or one family member instead of another[165]) or not informing the decisionmaker about the medical options. As such, these claims should ordinarily be brought either under a theory of battery (for lack of consent)[166] or informed consent (for improper disclosure).[167] One case of this sort is *Anderson v. St. Francis-St. George Hospital,*[168] which was tried both as an instance of battery and of negligence. In *Anderson,* the plaintiff's decedent was resuscitated in spite of the fact that he and his physician had agreed to a do-not-resuscitate order. The appeals court concluded that there was evidence that either the hospital or a nurse, or both, were negligent in not preventing the administration of treatment, and it reversed the trial court's entry of summary judgment and remanded for further proceedings.

In one respect, there is nothing particularly ground-breaking about this case. It, in effect, involves a claim that the hospital and its employees failed to use reasonable care in making certain that written orders are followed, which is hardly a novel claim. Yet from the perspective of imposing liability in the context of end-of-life decisionmaking, it is revolutionary for the simple reason that there are so few cases in which courts have permitted such claims to go to trial.[169]

---

**NJ:** *Cf.* Cavagnaro v. Hanover, 565 A.2d 728 (N.J. Super. Ct. Law Div. 1989) (hospital expenses incurred subsequent to confirmation of brain death not compensable under automobile no-fault insurance act providing for payment of all reasonable medical expenses because not reasonable or necessary).

**NY:** *But cf.* Grace Plaza of Great Neck, Inc. v. Elbaum, 623 N.E.2d 513 (N.Y. 1993) (upholding nursing home's claim of entitlement to be paid for care of patient whose husband refused treatment on her behalf between time of refusal and court order permitting treatment to be stopped).

**OH:** *See* Estate of Leach v. Shapiro, 469 N.E.2d 1047 (Ohio Ct. App. 1984).

*Cf.* Kapp, *Enforcing Patient Preferences: Linking Payment for Medical Care to Informed Consent,* 261 JAMA 1935 (1989) (proposing that financial reimbursement be denied to health care providers for treatment rendered without valid consent).

[164] **IN:** *See, e.g.,* Payne v. Marion Gen. Hosp., 549 N.E.2d 1043 (Ind. Ct. App. 1990).

**WV:** *See, e.g.,* Belcher v. Charleston Area Medical Ctr., 422 S.E.2d 827 (W. Va. 1992).

[165] **MI:** *See, e.g.,* Werth v. Taylor, 475 N.W.2d 426 (Mich. Ct. App. 1991).

[166] See §§ **17.2–17.4.**

[167] **IN:** *See, e.g.,* Payne v. Marion Gen. Hosp., 549 N.E.2d 1043. See §§ **17.11–17.12.**

[168] 614 N.E.2d 841 (Ohio Ct. App. 1992) *opinion after remand,* 1995 WL 109128 (Ohio Ct. App. Mar. 15, 1995).

[169] **CA3:** *See, e.g.,* Kranson v. Valley Crest Nursing Home, 755 F.2d 46 (3d Cir. 1985) (governmental immunity barred recovery).

In *Strachan v. John F. Kennedy Memorial Hospital*,[170] the parents of a man who was pronounced dead in the emergency room of a hospital sought to hold the hospital liable for failure to discontinue life-support systems for three days. They alleged that the hospital was negligent in not having a procedure for the determination of brain death, but the court refused to hold that there was a legal duty for hospitals to have such policies.[171]

The reverse of the circumstances in *Anderson* and *Strachan*—namely, the failure to provide treatment based on an alleged failure to consult with a surrogate and obtain consent before making and implementing a decision to forgo life-sustaining treatment—is also actionable as negligence. However, in *Morgan v. Olds*,[172] which involved such circumstances, the court held that a duty was owed the patient to consult the surrogate before forgoing life-sustaining treatment but that no duty was owed to the surrogate (the patient's wife) to consult with her.

The limitations on using a negligence theory for the unwanted administration of treatment are demonstrated by *Clark v. Perry*,[173] a case involving the alleged nonconsensual administration of a blood transfusion to a Jehovah's Witness. The plaintiff's cause of action failed largely because the court insisted that she establish by expert evidence that the standard of care had been violated by the individuals who had participated in the decision to administer blood and administered it, despite the evidence that the plaintiff's decedent (the patient) had refused it.

Some patients have allegedly been harmed by a hospital's not having policies,[174] or having inadequate policies,[175] about forgoing life-sustaining treatment. None of these claims has been successful, though each has failed for a different reason. Only one case actually reached the merits of the claim (which was a claim for administering treatment rather than forgoing it), and held that there was no legal duty on the part of a hospital to have a policy and procedure for determining brain death.[176] Another assumed without deciding that there is a

---

WA: *See, e.g.,* Benoy v. Simons, 831 P.2d 167 (Wash. Ct. App. 1992) (affirmed dismissal of complaint on ground that under Washington law wrongful death and personal injury actions must be brought by personal representative of deceased, no personal representative had been appointed, and plaintiffs were not within class of beneficiaries entitled to recover).

[170] 538 A.2d 346 (N.J. 1988).

[171] **IN:** *But cf.* Payne v. Marion Gen. Hosp., 549 N.E.2d 1043 (assumed without deciding that duty exists to have do-not-resuscitate policy).

[172] 417 N.W.2d 232 (Iowa Ct. App. 1987).

[173] 442 S.E.2d 57 (N.C. Ct. App. 1994).

[174] **IN:** *See, e.g.,* Payne v. Marion Gen. Hosp., 549 N.E.2d 1043 (failure to have do-not-resuscitate policy).

**NJ:** *See, e.g.,* Strachan v. John F. Kennedy Memorial Hosp., 538 A.2d 346 (N.J. 1988) (failure to have policy for establishing brain death and terminating treatment).

[175] **CA3:** *See, e.g.,* Kranson v. Valley Crest Nursing Home, 755 F.2d 46 (3d Cir. 1985) (inadequate do-not-resuscitate policy; defendant immune from liability under governmental liability statute).

[176] **NJ:** *See* Strachan v. John F. Kennedy Memorial Hosp., 538 A.2d 346.

duty to have a do-not-resuscitate policy, but found the defendant/hospital not liable to the plaintiff for not having one because the evidence failed to establish that the defendant had departed from the standard of care.[177]

## § 17.11   —Informed Consent

The cause of action for failure to obtain informed consent protects the right to be advised of appropriate medical options and to choose among them. With one possible exception—namely, proof of damages[178]—it is particularly well suited as a theory of liability for inadequacies in the decisionmaking process about life-sustaining treatment.

The doctrine of informed consent imposes two separate, though related, duties on physicians. The first is the obligation to provide competent patients or the surrogates of incompetent patients with information about therapeutic and/or diagnostic options, and the other is the obligation to obtain consent from the patient or surrogate before administering any therapy. As the Ohio Court of Appeals has put it,

> [n]ot only must a patient consent to treatment, but the patient's consent must be informed consent. . . . The physician owes his patient a fiduciary duty of good faith and fair dealing which gives rise to certain specific professional obligations. These obligations include not only the duty to exercise due care and skill, but to fully inform the patient of his condition and to obtain the patient's informed consent to the medical treatment.[179]

Similarly, if the patient or surrogate *declines* treatment, the physician might be held liable to the patient for any harm that ensues from forgoing treatment if the physician did not provide the patient with adequate information to decide.[180]

The failure to *adequately* inform is generally remediable through an action in negligence, although at least one jurisdiction purports to treat it as battery[181] and another to recognize only a limited cause of action for failure to disclose.[182] Battery is usually the theory that should be used if the physician has *totally* (rather than inadequately) failed to provide material information to the patient

---

[177] **IN:** *See* Payne v. Marion Gen. Hosp., 549 N.E.2d 1043.

[178] See § **17.25.**

[179] Estate of Leach v. Shapiro, 469 N.E.2d 1047, 1052 (Ohio Ct. App. 1984).

[180] **CA:** Truman v. Thomas, 611 P.2d 902 (Cal. 1980); Moore v. Preventive Medicine Medical Group, 223 Cal. Rptr. 859 (Ct. App. 1986).

   **NY:** Crisher v. Spak, 471 N.Y.S.2d 741 (Sup. Ct. N.Y. County 1983).

[181] **PA:** *See* Moure v. Raeuchle, 604 A.2d 1003 (Pa. 1992) (surgical operation is technical assault if performed without consent).

[182] **GA:** *See* Young v. Yarn, 222 S.E.2d 113 (Ga. Ct. App. 1975) (holding Medical Consent Law, Ga. Code Ann. § 31-9-6, requires physician to inform patient of general terms of treatment but provides no duty to disclose risks of treatment).

or has failed to obtain consent to treatment whether the prior disclosure of information was adequate or not.[183]

Despite the paucity of reported litigation, if it were not for the difficult problem of establishing damages,[184] the risk of liability for inadequate disclosure in the context of decisionmaking about life-sustaining treatment would be great. This risk results largely from the aversion of so many people—health care professionals included—to openly confront and discuss death and issues closely related to it. To the extent that physicians find it less unsettling to make decisions for hopelessly or terminally ill patients without informing patients and their families of the therapeutic options, without attempting to elicit information about the goals and values that the patient wishes or might wish to have guide treatment decisions and the patient's preferences, or to explain that certain theoretical options are not practical options because of their very low likelihood of providing benefit to the patient, the risk of liability for the failure to obtain informed consent is markedly increased. In fact, because of the fiduciary nature of the doctor-patient relationship and "[b]ecause the importance of adequate disclosure increases as the patient is placed at a greater informational disadvantage," the "[f]ailure to disclose material information concerning a patient's condition may be actionable not only as malpractice, but under the appropriate circumstances may be an actionable misrepresentation as well."[185]

There are practical difficulties in prosecuting informed consent actions outside the right-to-die context that will prove troublesome in this context too. They include

1.  the necessity, in better than half the jurisdictions,[186] for the plaintiff to establish by expert testimony that the defendant failed to conform to a professional standard of disclosure—that is, that a reasonably prudent physician would have disclosed that information which in fact was not disclosed; and

2.  the necessity of establishing causation in accordance with an objective standard—namely, that a reasonably prudent person would have made a

---

[183] **DC:** *In re* A.C., 573 A.2d 1235, 1243 (D.C. 1990) ("[A] surgeon who performs an operation without the patient's consent may be guilty of a battery . . . or . . . if the surgeon obtains an insufficiently informed consent, he or she may be liable for negligence.").

**OH:** Anderson v. St. Francis-St. George Hosp., 614 N.E.2d 841 (Ohio Ct. App. 1992) (administration of cardiopulmonary resuscitation after refusal by patient, as documented in do-not-resuscitate order, is actionable as battery).

**UT:** Lounsbury v. Capel, 836 P.2d 188 (Utah 1992).

[184] See § **17.25.**

[185] **OH:** Estate of Leach v. Shapiro, 469 N.E.2d 1047, 1054 (Ohio Ct. App. 1984). See § **17.17.**

[186] Frantz, Annotation, *Modern Status of Views as to General Measure of Physician's Duty to Inform Patient of Risks of Proposed Treatment*, 88 A.L.R.3d 1008 (1978).

choice different from the one the plaintiff in fact made had disclosure been adequate—in all but a very small number[187] of jurisdictions.

In addition to these ordinarily troublesome requirements, plaintiffs in informed consent cases arising from end-of-life decisionmaking might also have difficulty proving damages. In some cases, damages will not be difficult to establish, such as when the patient is conscious and suffers physically and/or mentally as a consequence of the treatment that the patient would have refused if adequate information had been disclosed.[188] But when the patient is not conscious, there will be no physical or mental harm, and recovery for dignitary damages under a theory of informed consent is highly unlikely.[189] Furthermore, the plaintiff is obligated to prove that any damages suffered were caused by the physician's failure to provide adequate information. Thus, the plaintiff must prove that if adequate information had been provided, a reasonable person in the patient's position would have decided differently about treatment.[190] In addition, there must be proof that had the treatment been rendered, the patient's condition would have been ameliorated. For example, the failure to demonstrate that an anencephalic baby would have survived if treated defeated a cause of action for lack of informed consent.[191]

## § 17.12 ——Application to Right-to-Die Cases

Courts have shown a slightly greater receptivity to claims based on lack of informed consent to end-of-life decisionmaking than to any other theory of liability. Perhaps the most receptive court was the Indiana Court of Appeals in *Payne v. Marion General Hospital,*[192] in which a trial court's grant of summary judgment for the defendants was reversed and remanded.

The complaint alleged that the patient was admitted to the hospital "suffering from a variety of maladies, including malnutrition, uremia, hypertensive cardiovascular disease, chronic obstructive lung disease, non-union of a previously fractured left humerus, and congenital levoscoliosis of the lumbar spine."[193] His

---

[187] **AK:** *See, e.g.,* Patrick v. Sedwick, 391 P.2d 453, 458 (Alaska 1964) (applying subjective test of causation based on Alaska Stat. § 9.55.956(a)).

**OK:** *See, e.g.,* Scott v. Bradford, 606 P.2d 554 (Okla. 1979) (applying subjective test of causation).

[188] See § **17.25.**

[189] Meisel, *A "Dignitary Tort" as a Bridge Between the Idea of Informed Consent and the Law of Informed Consent,* 16 Law, Med. & Health Care 210 (1988).

[190] *See, e.g.,* Canterbury v. Spence, 464 F.2d 772, 790 (D.C. Cir.), *cert. denied,* 409 U.S. 1064 (1972).

[191] **CA10:** Johnson v. Thompson, 971 F.2d 1487, 1499 (10th Cir. 1992).

**WA:** *See also* Benoy v. Simons, 831 P.2d 167 (Wash. Ct. App. 1992).

[192] 549 N.E.2d 1043 (Ind. Ct. App. 1990).

[193] *Id.* at 1044.

condition began to deteriorate and on the fourth day of hospitalization he experienced increased difficulty breathing. The attending physician contacted his sister who came to the hospital, and "[a]fter observing Payne for several minutes, . . . informed the nurse she did not want Payne resuscitated if he began to die. . . . After consulting with the nurse and talking to Payne's sister, Dr. Donaldson then authorized the entry of a 'no code' on Payne's chart, after verifying his order with another nurse pursuant to the Hospital's policy."[194] Thereafter, supportive care was continued, but the patient's condition worsened and he died the next day without CPR being attempted.

The basis of the informed consent claim was that Payne was competent when the do-not-resuscitate order was entered and that the attending physician should have obtained his informed consent rather than his sister's. Because of the allegations and evidence in the depositions from a nurse who testified that "Payne was conscious, alert, and able to communicate when the 'no code' was entered, and that he remained competent until shortly before his death,"[195] the court concluded that a jury could find that he was capable of giving informed consent, and it remanded for trial. The court implied that to obtain recovery under a theory of informed consent, the plaintiff would have to establish causation and damages—namely, that, more probably than not, resuscitation would have been successful had it been attempted.[196] The court failed to consider, however, whether the patient would have consented to a DNR order had he been asked, for if he would have agreed to the order as his sister did, an action for lack of informed consent should not succeed.

The court also overlooked two other important issues. First, if the physician's error in this case was relying on the consent of the patient's sister rather than of the patient, the fault was not one concerning inadequate disclosure but complete lack of consent because consent was given by one not having the legal authority to do so. In that case, the proper remedy is arguably battery, not negligence.[197]

---

[194] *Id.*

[195] *Id.* at 1046 (recounting evidence in substantial detail).

[196] *Id.* at 1050.

[197] **DC:** *See, e.g., In re* A.C., 573 A.2d 1235, 1243 (D.C. 1990) ("[A] surgeon who performs an operation without the patient's consent may be guilty of a battery . . . or . . . if the surgeon obtains an insufficiently informed consent, he or she may be liable for negligence.").

**ME:** *See, e.g., In re* Gardner, 534 A.2d 947, 951 (Me. 1987) (Although lack of informed consent is actionable as negligence, "we have continued to recognize the validity of a battery analysis, with its focus on the patient's right to be free from nonconsensual invasions of his bodily integrity, when the treatment applied by the doctor 'is either against the patient's will or substantially at variance with the consent given.' [Citations omitted.] Thus when a competent patient has expressly refused to receive some form of medical care, a doctor would be acting tortiously if he insisted on providing the treatment against his patient's will.").

**OH:** *See, e.g.,* Anderson v. St. Francis-St. George Hosp., 614 N.E.2d 841 (Ohio Ct. App. 1992) (administration of cardiopulmonary resuscitation after refusal by patient, as documented in do-not-resuscitate order, is actionable as battery).

**UT:** *See, e.g.,* Lounsbury v. Capel, 836 P.2d 188 (Utah 1992).

However, a battery claim should prevail only in situations in which there is a touching, so that although the administration of CPR based on permission given by one who has no legal authority to do so is a battery, the forgoing of CPR cannot be a battery because there is no "touching" of the patient. Consequently, negligence is arguably the appropriate cause of action, though not a negligence action for lack of informed consent because that remedy is appropriate only for inadequate disclosure, not for total lack of disclosure or lack of consent. The essence of the cause of action was that the physician failed to use reasonable care in determining who had the legal authority to consent, and the failure to do so caused harm to the patient.[198]

A second issue overlooked in *Payne* is that even if the patient was incompetent and the sister was the proper decisionmaker so that a claim for unauthorized treatment should not succeed, a duty was owed the patient to be sure that the surrogate had been given appropriate information with which to make an informed decision, so that a claim for lack of informed consent might then be successful.[199]

A similar case is *Belcher v. Charleston Area Medical Center,*[200] a wrongful death action brought against several physicians by the parents of a 17-year-old who died as the result of the withholding of cardiopulmonary resuscitation. The boy, who suffered from muscular dystrophy, was taken by ambulance to the hospital after he stopped breathing and was revived by his father. After being placed on and then taken off a ventilator, the physicians obtained his parents' refusal of cardiopulmonary resuscitation or reintubation in the event of respiratory failure. He subsequently suffered an arrest, was not resuscitated or reintubated, and died.

His father, as administrator of the estate, brought suit on the ground that the boy was a mature minor and informed consent to withhold treatment should have been obtained from him rather than from his parents. The West Virginia Supreme Court reversed a jury verdict for the defendant physician and remanded for the trial court to resubmit the case to a jury with a proper instruction on whether or not the patient was a mature minor and therefore whether consent to withhold cardiopulmonary resuscitation should have been sought from him rather than from his parents.

Perhaps the leading case employing a theory of informed consent in end-of-life decisionmaking is *Estate of Leach v. Shapiro,*[201] the first appellate court to make clear that the general principles of informed consent apply in end-of-life decisionmaking. The court also held that when a patient lacks decisionmaking capacity, the physician is obligated to make disclosure and obtain consent from the patient's lawful surrogate. In *Leach,* the court reversed the dismissal of a complaint that alleged, among other things, that the defendants failed to inform

---

[198] See §§ 17.13–17.15.

[199] **OH:** *See* Estate of Leach v. Shapiro, 469 N.E.2d 1047 (Ohio Ct. App. 1984).

[200] 422 S.E.2d 827 (W. Va. 1992).

[201] 469 N.E.2d 1047 (Ohio Ct. App. 1984).

the patient's family of her true condition for a period of two months after she was placed on life support, failed to apprise the family of her course of treatment during this period, and administered experimental drugs without the family's consent.

Mrs. Leach had suffered cardiopulmonary arrest, was resuscitated, and thereafter remained in a "chronic vegetative condition." The plaintiff did not allege that the resuscitation was unlawful. The subsequent placement on a "life support system" was alleged to be unlawful, but as the court correctly observed, if Mrs. Leach was put on life support as part of a properly authorized treatment (that is, cardiopulmonary resuscitation), the trial court was correct in determining that this too was not wrongful.

However, the court went further, stating that all subsequent treatment would be proper because

> [i]n Ohio, at this time, the court system provides the only mechanism which can protect the interest of the doctor, the hospital, the patient, the family and the state, which can objectively weigh the competing interests in an emotionally charged situation, and which can insulate the participants from civil and criminal liability. Until such time as the legislature provides some more efficient means of protecting the rights of patients in Mrs. Leach's condition, we join those courts that require judicial authority for the termination of life-prolonging treatment of an incompetent patient.[202]

This reasoning would not hold in the overwhelming majority of jurisdictions that do not require "judicial authority" to forgo life-sustaining medical treatment.[203] Further, it is not clear that a court order *is* required in Ohio,[204] or that it is required by other divisions of the Ohio Court of Appeals.[205]

The court continued by observing that if the facts demonstrated that Mrs. Leach had personally refused the treatment that was administered, a suit for lack of informed consent might be successfully prosecuted. The court, in effect, recognized as valid an oral advance directive but required that a very high standard be met before the refusal would be considered valid:

> [T]his refusal . . . must satisfy the same standards of knowledge and understanding required for informed consent. A terminally ill patient fully advised of an impending crisis might then be able to refuse treatments which would only prolong suffering, while a patient afflicted with a disease which would be terminal in several years and who had generally expressed the desire to die peacefully would not be denied treatment for injuries sustained in an automobile crash. Both doctor

---

[202] *Id.* at 1052–53.

[203] See § **5.26.**

[204] *See In re* McInnis, 584 N.E.2d 1389, 1390 (P. Ct. Stark County, Ohio 1991) ("spouse, individually and without the intervention of the court, without the appointment of a guardian, has such authority under the common law" and court "will not appoint guardians for the sole purpose to continue or withhold life-sustaining treatment").

[205] *See, e.g.,* Anderson v. St. Francis-St. George Hosp., 614 N.E.2d 841 (Ohio Ct. App. 1992).

and patient would then be protected from statements not made in contemplation of the specific circumstances and the specific medical treatment required.[206]

The court did not, however, appear to be requiring the application of a subjective standard[207] if it turned out that the patient had not given such an "informed refusal," because it concluded that "[g]eneral statements by the patient could still be considered by a court . . . in determining the wishes of a patient in a chronic vegetative condition" if a judicial order was sought.[208]

The court's requirement of "informed refusal" is not consistent with what most other courts have required for the implementation of an advance directive, whether oral or written, and it is not what is contemplated by advance directive statutes, including the subsequently enacted Ohio living will and health care power of attorney statutes.[209] The only other courts to have required that, for a patient's refusal of treatment to be binding on a physician, the patient must have been as fully informed as if she had consented to treatment, involve patients of the Jehovah's Witness faith who have refused blood transfusions. Courts have sometimes held that the prior refusal of treatment by these patients was not binding because the refusal was not made in contemplation of the circumstances that actually arose.[210]

The holdings in these cases are questionable, but in any event the blood transfusion cases are distinguishable from *Leach* in that the patients were not terminally ill, and it was reasonably foreseeable that if treated their health could be restored to the status quo ante. Other courts have not held Jehovah's Witnesses who have refused blood transfusions to such exacting standards. For example, the federal district court in *Holmes v. Silver Cross Hospital,*[211] in discussing the Illinois Supreme Court's *Brooks*[212] decision, stated that

> even when approaching death has so weakened the mental and physical faculties of a theretofore competent adult without minor children that she may properly be said to be legally incompetent, she may not be compelled by a state appointed

---

[206] **OH:** Estate of Leach v. Shapiro, 469 N.E.2d 1047, 1053 (Ohio Ct. App. 1984).

  **MI:** *Accord* Werth v. Taylor, 475 N.W.2d 426 (Mich. Ct. App. 1991).

  **NJ:** *Accord In re* Hughes, 611 A.2d 1148 (N.J. Super. Ct. App. Div. 1992).

[207] See §§ **7.4–7.6.**

[208] Estate of Leach v. Shapiro, 469 N.E.2d at 1053.

[209] *See* Ohio Rev. Code Ann. §§ 2133.01–.15 (living will statute); Ohio Rev. Code Ann. §§ 1337.11–.17 (health care power of attorney statute).

[210] **MI:** *See* Werth v. Taylor, 475 N.W.2d 426.

  **NJ:** *See In re* Hughes, 611 A.2d 1148.

  **OH:** *See* University of Cincinnati Hosp. v. Edmond, 506 N.E.2d 299 (C.P. Hamilton County, Ohio 1986).

  **PA:** *See In re* Estate of Dorone, 534 A.2d 452 (Pa. 1987).

[211] 340 F. Supp. 125 (N.D. Ill. 1972).

[212] *In re* Estate of Brooks, 205 N.E.2d 435 (Ill. 1965).

conservator to accept treatment of a nature which will probably save her life, but which is forbidden by her religious convictions and which she has steadfastly held even though aware that death may result from her refusal to accept such treatment.[213]

Further, the cases requiring a high level of understanding by the patient of the consequences of the refusal are wrongly decided on the basis of the informed consent doctrine because they turn informed consent from a patient's shield into a doctor's sword. The purpose of the requirement of informed consent is to provide the patient with information adequate to make an intelligent decision whether to undergo or forgo treatment. The requirement is for the patient's benefit, not the physician's, which is why a patient may waive disclosure, consent, or both.[214]

In these cases, the patients were not complaining of their physicians' failure to disclose and seeking to recover for the resultant harm from their refusals of treatment. Rather, the gist of the complaints was battery, not negligence. The patients in these cases were not alleging inadequate information to make a decision and that the decision would have been different had adequate information been provided, as was the situation in the classic "informed refusal case," *Truman v. Thomas*.[215] Rather, the patients were complaining that they were treated at all. The courts permitted doctors to escape liability on the ground that the patients were not adequately informed of the consequences of refusal, but the irony is that the *patients* were not complaining about that. The claim that a patient was not fully informed should not serve as a *defense* for a physician, but if anything as an additional ground for liability because it is the very same physician who breached a duty *to inform*.

Other cases have been brought alleging failure to obtain informed consent to initiate or forgo life-sustaining treatment, but they are less significant because they either provide little analysis or were not decided on the merits. The Washington Supreme Court in *Benoy v. Simons* considered a claim that the defendant/physician initiated ventilatory support for a low-birth-weight baby without informed consent. The court affirmed the dismissal of this claim because a suit for damages based on lack of informed consent requires that the plaintiff prove that the patient suffered bodily injury as a result of the physician's inadequate disclosure, and the plaintiffs failed to do so.[216] Again, however, the complaint sounds more in battery than negligence in that it was the physician's failure to obtain consent, rather than to make disclosure, that was at the heart of the plaintiffs' claim.

---

[213] Holmes v. Silver Cross Hosp., 340 F. Supp. at 130.

[214] See §§ **3.25–3.26.**

[215] 611 P.2d 902 (Cal. 1980).

[216] Benoy v. Simons, 831 P.2d 167, 170 (Wash. Ct. App. 1992) (dismissal also affirmed on informed consent claim because under Washington law wrongful death and personal injury actions must be brought by personal representative of deceased, no personal representative had been appointed, and plaintiffs were not within class of beneficiaries entitled to recover).

In another Washington case, *Strickland v. Deaconess Hospital*,[217] the court of appeals affirmed a grant of summary judgment for the defendant hospital and physicians based on an allegation that the physician had entered a DNR order without consent. The basis for the affirmance on most of the counts of the complaint was that they were barred by the survival statute. Although it is not clear that this was also the basis for the affirmance of summary judgment on the informed consent claim, no other basis was given.

## § 17.13 —Negligence Liability for Not Treating ("Futility" Cases)

In most cases involving the termination of life-sustaining treatment that have resulted in litigation, competent patients or the surrogates of incompetent patients have sought to terminate treatment and the attending physician or health care institution has objected on medical, moral, or legal grounds. As previously discussed, this fact pattern might give rise to a variety of intentional torts and perhaps to a claim grounded in negligence.[218]

An opposite set of circumstances could also give rise to an action against health care providers: namely, one in which the attending physician or health care institution wishes to terminate or limit treatment, but the patient or surrogate wants the status quo maintained or even wants treatment to be more aggressively administered. As pressures to control the costs of medical care continually increase, physicians will find themselves under increased pressure to urge the termination of life-sustaining treatment when it appears that there is no hope for recovery.

Regardless of whether the physician's motive for recommending forgoing treatment is economic or otherwise, these are commonly referred to as "futility" cases because the physician determines that further medical treatment would be futile.[219] To date, only a small number of litigated cases have involved situations in which health care providers have sought to withdraw life-sustaining medical treatment, and even fewer in which there has been a claim for damages.[220]

---

[217] 735 P.2d 74 (Wash. Ct. App. 1987).

[218] See §§ **17.2–17.12.**

[219] See **Ch. 19.**

[220] **CA3:** *See* Kranson v. Valley Crest Nursing Home, 755 F.2d 46 (3d Cir. 1985) (claim for damages for not administering cardiopulmonary resuscitation barred by governmental immunity).

**IA:** *See* Morgan v. Olds, 417 N.W.2d 232 (Iowa Ct. App. 1987) (claim by spouse of patient for allegedly removing patient from ventilator without consent).

**WA:** Strickland v. Deaconess Hosp., 735 P.2d 74 (Wash. Ct. App. 1987) (unsuccessful claim for damages for nonconsensual withholding of treatment).

Another area of potential risk for liability for not treating is the provision of inadequate palliative care, although there is no reported litigation to date.[221] The failure to provide adequate analgesia to sensate patients—for example, when a ventilator is disconnected or artificial nutrition and hydration is withdrawn[222]—may inflict physical pain on the patient and emotional distress on the patient and/or the patient's family. There is mounting evidence that many physicians are inadequately knowledgeable about the appropriate use of medications for the relief of pain or are knowledgeable but unwilling to administer adequate doses out of fear of causing the patient's death or addicting the patient.[223]

## § 17.14  —Abandonment

A theory of recovery for harm done to a patient by a physician, referred to as abandonment, might be adaptable to end-of-life decisionmaking. *Abandonment* is a term that refers to a number of different kinds of conduct, which share the characteristic that the physician failed to provide treatment to a patient, which the patient alleges resulted in physical or emotional harm or both. In their treatise on the law of medical malpractice, Louisell and Williams define *abandonment* as

> a failure by the physician to continue to provide service to the patient when it is still needed in a case for which the physician has assumed responsibility and from which he has not been properly relieved.[224]

There must be proof that the physician unilaterally and completely severed the relationship.[225] However, even if consent to severance of the doctor-patient relationship is absent, the abandonment is still not necessarily actionable. Under state law, a physician may unilaterally terminate treatment without risk of liability if notice is given to the patient sufficient to permit the patient

---

[221] *See* Roark, *How Much Painkiller Is Enough?—Health Care Workers Are Often on Guard Against Giving Too Much Medication; A Landmark Case Against a Nursing Home Has Sent a Warning Not to Provide Too Little,* L.A. Times, Dec. 10, 1991, at A-1 (home ed.) (discussing award of $15 million to estate of patient who was undermedicated for pain from cancer). *Cf.* Casswell, *Rejecting Criminal Liability for Life-Shortening Palliative Care,* 6 J. Contemp. Health L. & Pol'y 127–44 (1990).

[222] **GA:** *Cf.* State v. McAfee, 385 S.E.2d 651 (Ga. 1989) (conscious patient has right to have sedative administered when ventilator is removed).

[223] See §§ **9.38** and **18.18.**

[224] 1 D. Louisell & H. Williams, Medical Malpractice ¶ 8.07, at 8-105 (1993).

[225] 61 Am. Jur. 2d *Physicians, Surgeons and Other Healers* § 236, at 366 n.34 (1981); Annotation, *Liability of Physician Who Abandons Case,* 57 A.L.R.2d 432 (1958).

opportunity to secure alternate comparable arrangements for treatment.[226] It is possible, however, that such conduct will give rise to liability under federal statutory law.[227]

Louisell and Williams suggest three different general types of abandonment cases:

(1)  A bald refusal to treat the patient further or to treat him at a crucial time, regardless of the feasibility of getting another physician's services. . . .

(2)  A withdrawal from the case without the consent or knowledge of the patient.

(3)  An error in judgment as to the need for further care.[228]

However, because liability for abandonment is very fact-specific, such general descriptions are not as helpful in understanding abandonment as are specific examples, such as the following:

- "an express declaration or statement by the physician to the effect that he completely withdraws from the case";
- "unqualified refusal to further attend to the patient";
- "leaving the patient during or immediately after an operation while his presence is still necessary";
- "failure to attend to the patient despite his promise to do so";
- "unexplained failure to continue to attend to the patient, even though there was no express promise on his part to do so";
- "refusal to treat the patient at a certain time or at a certain location";
- "the premature discharge of the patient by the physician";
- "the premature removal or dismissal of a patient from a hospital on the physician's orders";
- "the physician's failure to give proper instructions before discharging the patient."[229]

**Duty to Provide Treatment.**  The threshold element of proof is the existence of a duty on the part of the physician to provide treatment. Although a physician is ordinarily under no obligation to enter into a contract to treat a patient, when a physician does enter into such an agreement, the physician is obligated to provide treatment, exercising reasonable care and skill, until discharged by the patient or until the physician gives adequate notice to the patient or surrogate of the severance of the relationship. The existence of a contract is usually

---

[226] 3 Am. Jur. Proof of Facts 2d § 3-117, at 124 (1974); 61 Am. Jur. 2d *Physicians, Surgeons, and Other Healers* § 235, at 366 (1981); McIntire, Comment, *The Action of Abandonment in Medical Malpractice Litigation,* 36 Tulane L. Rev. 834, 836 (1962).

[227] See §§ **17.15** and **19.17.**

[228] 1 D. Louisell & H. Williams, Medical Malpractice ¶ 8.07, at 8-106 to -107 (1993).

[229] 61 Am. Jur. 2d *Physicians and Surgeons* § 237, at 367–68 (1991 & Supp. 1994).

established by showing the existence of a doctor-patient relationship at the time of the alleged unauthorized nontreatment because, absent such a relationship, a physician is generally under no duty to provide treatment.[230] This general no-duty rule is subject to some common-law and statutory exceptions, but they are not likely to be relevant in end-of-life decisionmaking cases because in most cases there will be no dispute about the existence of an established doctor-patient relationship.

The "no duty" rule probably does not apply to hospitals.[231] While at one time hospitals might not have been required to accept all patients, hospitals at least have a limited common-law duty to provide treatment to patients who reasonably rely on them to do so.[232] Furthermore, the older common-law rule of no duty to treat has been abrogated, at least in part, by state[233] and federal statutes.[234] In situations in which a physician is a hospital employee rather than an independent contractor, the hospital's duty to treat might be imposed upon the physician as well, although in practice a particular physician might be able to avoid it by transferring the care of the patient to another physician willing to provide the treatment in question.[235] If this is not possible (as it frequently might not be in the most difficult cases[236]) the physician would probably have to terminate his employment in order to terminate the duty to treat the patient.[237]

---

[230] 1 D. Louisell & H. Williams, Medical Malpractice ¶ 8.02, at 8–14 ("Normally, a physician may initially refuse to assume any professional responsibility toward another individual.").

[231] **MA:** *But see* Custody of a Minor, 379 N.E.2d 1053, 1066 (Mass. 1978) (state's interest in integrity of health care professions extends to ensuring that hospitals have "the full opportunity to care for people under their control").

[232] **DE:** *See, e.g.,* Wilmington Gen. Hosp. v. Manlove, 174 A.2d 135 (Del. 1961). *See generally* Purver, Annotation, *Liability of Hospital for Refusal to Admit or Treat Patient,* 35 A.L.R.3d 841 (1971 & Supp. 1994).

[233] *See* Purver, Annotation, *Liability of Hospital for Refusal to Admit or Treat Patient,* 35 A.L.R.3d 841 (1971 & Supp. 1994); 2 M. Macdonald et al., Treatise on Health Care Law § 11.03(2)(b)(vii) & n.102, at 11-28 to 11-30 (1994 & Supp. 1994).

[234] See § **19.17.**

[235] *See, e.g.,* American Thoracic Soc'y, *Withholding and Withdrawing Life-Sustaining Therapy,* 115 Annals Internal Med. 478, 481–82 (1991) ("If the patient or surrogate decision maker disagrees with the decision to limit the intervention, he or she should have opportunity to transfer responsibility for the patient's care to another physician who is willing to provide the disputed intervention in the same or another institution."); Council on Scientific Affairs & Council on Ethical & Judicial Affairs, *Persistent Vegetative State and the Decision to Withdraw or Withhold Life Support,* 263 JAMA 426, 429 (1990). *Cf.* Hastings Ctr., Guidelines on the Termination of Life-Sustaining Treatment and the Care of the Dying 32 (1987) (Part One, II(8)(c)) ("The patient or surrogate should be at liberty to engage another health care professional.").

[236] *See, e.g.,* Miles, *Informed Demand for "Non-Beneficial" Medical Treatment,* 325 New Eng. J. Med. 512, 514 (1991) ("In this case, every provider contacted by the hospital or the family refused to treat this patient with a respirator.").

[237] *But see* American Thoracic Soc'y, *Withholding and Withdrawing Life-Sustaining Therapy,* 115 Annals of Internal Medicine 478, 482 (1991) ("If no such physician can be found, or if a transfer between institutions is not medically or otherwise possible, the intervention may be withheld or withdrawn in accordance with institutional policies and applicable laws.").

**Breach of Duty.** Failure to treat per se is not actionable. To establish abandonment, there must be a failure of the physician to treat the patient when treatment is appropriate. First, assuming for argument's sake that there is a legal duty to provide treatment in general or in a specific case, it is doubtful that this duty obliges them to provide any and all treatments that a patient or surrogate requests.[238] The failure to treat must be unreasonable.[239] Second, there must be "a premature discharge of the patient and consequent termination of the relationship based on a grave and negligent error in judgment as to the patient's need for further care."[240]

Although it is sometimes said that a patient can be abandoned negligently or intentionally,[241] abandonment is predominantly a species of negligence liability. What is frequently meant by the term "intentional abandonment" is that the physician intentionally engages in conduct that constitutes an abandonment of the patient. However, for abandonment to be an intentional tort, it would need to be established that the physician (actually or constructively) intended to cause harm to the patient by engaging in the conduct that constitutes the abandonment. Under some circumstances it would be possible to establish such intent, but the run-of-the-mill abandonment case is more likely to involve conduct by a physician that bespeaks a failure to use reasonable care resulting in harm rather than an intent to harm. If the physician does not completely sever the relationship with the patient, but only terminates or limits some aspect of treatment without proper legal or medical grounds for so doing, this may constitute the failure to possess or exercise reasonable professional skill or training. In such a case, there is no conceptual difference between abandonment and negligence, although there may be some tactical advantages to bringing a cause of action for abandonment as well as negligence because

> the abandonment phraseology accentuates factors within lay appraisal—the time element, the interval of complete lack of attention, the psychology of being left without help while incapacitated—and in fact abandonment cases often go to the jury without expert evidence.[242]

Furthermore, there is no recognized intentional tort known as abandonment, and thus if abandonment is to be prosecuted as an intentional tort, the facts giving rise to it must be fit into some recognized intentional tort. Battery is not a

---

[238] *See, e.g.,* Tomlinson & Brody, *Futility and the Ethics of Resuscitation,* 264 JAMA 1276, 1277 (1990) (Society "recognize[s] the authority of the physician to place at least some limitations on patients' demands for treatment.").

[239] McIntire, Comment, *The Action of Abandonment in Medical Malpractice Litigation,* 36 Tulane L. Rev. 834, 836 (1962) (citations omitted).

[240] *Id.*

[241] 1 D. Louisell & H. Williams, Medical Malpractice ¶ 8.07, at 8-106 (1993).

[242] *Id.* at 8-107.

likely candidate because battery requires a touching, and abandonment ordinarily occurs from an omission that will not satisfy the touching requirement. For similar reasons, assault is also not a likely candidate. Abandonment may result in intentional infliction of emotional distress, but recovery would need to meet all the requirements of that theory, and that is usually difficult in the context of end-of-life decisionmaking.[243] Finally, some instances of abandonment are conceivably actionable as false imprisonment, but they would need to meet the technical requirements of that tort, which seem quite unlikely in the ordinary case.

**Causation.**   In addition to proof of the existence of a duty to provide services and its breach, the plaintiff must establish that the breach of duty was the proximate cause of harm.[244] If an abandoned patient "consults another physician promptly, thus causing minimal delay in necessary treatment and his recovery from his illness is not impeded, damages, except for mental anguish, are usually minimal."[245]

**Damages.**   Under a negligence theory, the plaintiff must also prove damages.[246] If abandonment can be established under an intentional tort theory, damages could be obtained for dignitary harm as well as for actual harm, but the recovery would probably be nominal.[247]

## § 17.15   ——Application to Futility Cases

Despite the fact that there has been no litigation concerning end-of-life decisionmaking alleging abandonment, abandonment provides a potential remedy for damages for litigating so-called futility cases. In such a case, a physician terminates, withholds, or limits treatment in opposition to the decision of a competent patient, or more likely the surrogate of an incompetent patient, on the ground that treatment is "futile," that is, that it will not provide any benefit or any benefit that the physician believes to be worthwhile.

**Duty.**   An obstacle to prevailing on such a claim is that the plaintiff must establish the existence of a legal duty to continue treatment and a breach of that

---

[243] See § **17.6.**

[244] 1 D. Louisell & H. Williams, Medical Malpractice ¶ 8.07, at 8-107; Annotation, *Liability of Physician Who Abandons Case,* 57 A.L.R.2d 432, 437 (1958).

[245] Rosenthal, *Physician's Abandonment of Patient,* 7 N.C. Cent. L.J. 149, 150–51 (1975).

[246] *Id.* ("A mere showing of negligence . . . is not sufficient to sustain the action" if the abandonment causes no injury.).

[247] *See* 3 Am. Jur. Proof of Facts 2d § 3-117, at 133 (1974).

duty. Duty might arise from the implied contractual undertaking creating the doctor-patient relationship; it is also possible that there may be a statutory basis for a duty to treat.[248]

**Breach.** Establishing breach of the duty might not be simple. It might be difficult in end-of-life cases to prove that the physician completely and unilaterally severed the relationship because, even when a physician believes further life-sustaining treatment to be futile,[249] it seems unlikely that the doctor-patient relationship will be totally severed or treatment totally discontinued. For example, if cardiopulmonary resuscitation were to be withheld, other treatments might be continued. Or if antibiotics were to be discontinued, analgesics or fluids or both might be continued for comfort. The withholding of some treatment does not constitute a complete severance of the relationship and thus would probably not constitute abandonment. On the other hand, a court might find that a decision to forgo life-sustaining treatment is "constructive abandonment"—in effect a total discontinuation of treatment even if ancillary treatment is continued because it is intended to bring about the patient's death.

Even in cases in which the physician does completely and unilaterally sever the relationship, to the extent that the physician gives the patient adequate notice of a termination, withholding, or limitation of treatment, and/or arranges or uses reasonable care in attempting to arrange for treatment to be provided by another physician at the same or a different hospital, there is compliance with the standard of care and hence no breach of duty.[250] It is not clear, however, whether a physician really does, in an end-of-life case, discharge his responsibilities even by giving substantial notice. Transfer of care to another physician under such circumstances, and especially to another hospital, is likely to be very difficult[251]

---

[248] **CA4:** *See, e.g., In re* Baby "K," 16 F.3d 590 (4th Cir. 1994), *cert. denied,* 115 S. Ct. 91 (1994) (Emergency Medical Treatment and Active Labor Act ("EMTALA," 42 U.S.C.A. § 1395dd (West 1992))); *In re* Baby "K," 832 F. Supp. 1022 (E.D. Va. 1993) (EMTALA; § 504 of the Rehabilitation Act of 1973, 29 U.S.C.A. § 794 (West 1985 & Supp. 1994); Child Abuse Prevention and Treatment Act, 42 U.S.C.A. §§ 5101–5116(g) (West 1983 & Supp. 1994)).

**GA:** *See, e.g., In re* Doe, 418 S.E.2d 3 (Ga. 1992) (Ga. Code Ann. §§ 31-39-1 to -9).

See §§ **17.21–17.22.**

[249] *See, e.g.,* Task Force on Ethics of the Soc'y of Critical Care Medicine, *Consensus Report on the Ethics of Foregoing Life-Sustaining Treatments in the Critically Ill,* 18 Critical Care Med. 1435, 1437 (1990) ("The removal of life support from a patient should not be regarded as an abandonment of the patient" if medically futile.).

[250] 3 Am. Jur. Proof of Facts 2d § 3-117, at 124 (1974); 61 Am. Jur. 2d *Physicians, Surgeons, and Other Healers* § 235, at 366 (1981); McIntire, Comment, *The Action of Abandonment in Medical Malpractice Litigation,* 36 Tulane L. Rev. 834, 836 (1962) (refusal to render treatment must be "without the patient's consent, without reasonable notice, and at a critical time when medical attention is needed").

[251] *See* Miles, *Informed Demand for "Non-Beneficial" Medical Treatment,* 325 New Eng. J. Med. 512, 514 (1991) ("In this case, every provider contacted by the hospital or the family refused to treat this patient with a respirator.").

because other physicians and hospitals are not likely to be eager to assume responsibility for what is obviously a contentious case,[252] wholly apart from the substantial financial costs that the transferee institution might have to bear. In addition, the logistics of transferring a patient being kept alive by complex medical equipment and medications from one health care institution to another could render transfer a hypothetical, but not a real, possibility.

In the only case that comes close to testing the balance of responsibilities for obtaining alternative care for a patient in a case in which the physician declines to continue to treat, the court held that there was no actionable abandonment where the patient received three written notifications of severance of the doctor-patient relationship over a period of several months, even though she had difficulty arranging alternative treatment. In this case, *Payton v. Weaver,*[253] the defendant refused to continue to provide outpatient hemodialysis to the plaintiff, a treatment that she needed to receive two or three times per week or she would soon die, because of her " 'persistent uncooperative and antisocial behavior over . . . more than . . . three years . . . , her persistent refusal to adhere to reasonable constraints of hemodialysis, the dietary schedules and medical prescriptions . . . , the use of barbiturates and other illicit drugs and because all this resulted in disruption of [the] program at' " the dialysis clinic.[254] The appeals court affirmed the trial court's finding that the defendant gave sufficient notice by providing the patient "with a list of the names and telephone numbers of all dialysis providers in [the area], and it is apparent from the record that nothing would have pleased him more than to find an alternative facility for her, but there is no evidence that there is anything further he could have done to achieve that goal under the circumstances."[255]

**Causation.**   Although proof that the abandonment caused harm to the patient is usually not difficult to establish in an ordinary abandonment case,[256] proof of

---

[252] **CA4:** *See, e.g., In re* Baby "K," 16 F.3d 590 (4th Cir. 1994).

**CA:** *See, e.g.,* Bartling v. Superior Court, 209 Cal. Rptr. 220, 225 n.7 (Ct. App. 1984) (The hospital and physicians "attempted to strike a compromise between their position and the wishes of Mr. and Mrs. Bartling by trying to locate another hospital which would accept Mr. Bartling as a patient. This effort was unsuccessful.").

**NJ:** *See, e.g., In re* Jobes, 529 A.2d 434, 450 (N.J. 1987) (acknowledging extreme difficulty of transferring persistent vegetative state patient to a nursing home that would cooperate with termination of tube-feeding).

**NY:** *See, e.g.,* Grace Plaza of Great Neck, Inc. v. Elbaum, 588 N.Y.S.2d 853 (App. Div. 1992) (nursing homes unwilling to accept persistent vegetative state patient being kept alive by feeding tube for the purpose of terminating tube-feeding).

[253] 182 Cal. Rptr. 225 (Ct. App. 1982).

[254] *Id.* at 227 (ellipses in original).

[255] *Id.* at 229. *See generally* Purver, Liability of Hospital for Refusal to Admit or Treat Patient, 35 A.L.R.3d 841 (1971 & Supp. 1993).

[256] Annotation, *Liability of Physician Who Abandons Case,* 57 A.L.R.2d 432, 437 (1958) ("[I]n most cases in which it has been found that the physician did abandon the patient, it has also been found that a causal relationship existed between the abandonment and the injury.").

causation (and damages) could prove to be problematic in an end-of-life abandonment claim. When life-sustaining treatment is terminated *with* proper authorization, one of the reasons that no civil or criminal liability is incurred by the physician is that the patient's condition, rather than the physician's conduct, is the cause of death. The same is true even if there is no consent. And if, by reference to professional standards, it could be established that it was not incumbent on the defendant physician to provide further treatment because it would only postpone death rather than improve the patient's condition, this should establish a lack of proximate cause.[257] Rather than analyzing this from the perspective of proximate cause, the same result can be reached from viewing the question of whether or not there is a duty to provide treatment believed by the physician or by prevailing medical standards to be "futile."[258]

**Damages.** Finally, in many instances in which an abandonment claim might arise from a physician's forgoing of life-sustaining treatment with notice to, but without authorization from, the patient or surrogate, it is likely that the patient's life expectancy would be brief, and in those cases (and even in the others in which life expectancy might not be brief, for example, persistent vegetative state) it will be extremely difficult to prove any significant element of damages.[259] About the only provable element of damages might be emotional distress. If the claim is that it was intentionally inflicted, the cause of action is for intentional infliction of emotional distress, and establishing such a claim is itself a daunting task in general and with respect to end-of-life decisionmaking in particular.[260] If the claim is for negligent infliction of emotional distress, there must also be proof of bodily harm.[261]

## § 17.16   Defenses to Negligence Claims

There are a few medical decisionmaking cases in which defendants have raised the traditional affirmative defenses to negligence liability of contributory or comparative negligence, and assumption of the risk. They involve the refusal of blood transfusions by Jehovah's Witnesses, rather than end-of-life decision-making per se.[262]

---

[257] See §§ **18.3** and **18.10.**

[258] See **Ch. 19.**

[259] See § **17.25.**

[260] See §§ **17.5–17.7.**

[261] W.P. Keeton et al., Prosser and Keeton on the Law of Torts § 54 (5th ed. 1984).

[262] **CA5:** *But cf.* Munn v. Algee, 924 F.2d 568 (5th Cir. 1991) (under Mississippi doctrine of avoidable consequences, if decedent's refusal of treatment for religious reasons is unreasonable, estate is barred from recovery; reasonableness to be determined by objective standard and application of doctrine does not violate free exercise clause).

**FL:** *Cf.* Rodriguez v. Pino, 634 So. 2d 681 (Fla. Dist. Ct. App. 1994) (physician who honored patient's refusal of lifesaving intubation not liable for patient's death).

In *Shorter v. Drury*,[263] the patient, a Jehovah's Witness, underwent surgery. Beforehand, the defendant/physician explained to the patient and her husband that there was a possibility of bleeding associated with the surgery, but he failed to explain that there were alternative methods of accomplishing the same results that entailed a lesser risk of bleeding. The patient sought a second opinion, and the second physician likewise informed her of the risk of bleeding but not the lesser risks of the alternatives. This physician testified that Mrs. Shorter had responded to the warning about bleeding by saying that "'she had faith in the Lord and that things would work out.'"[264] At the time of admission to the hospital, the patient and her husband signed a waiver form entitled "Refusal to Permit Blood Transfusion," which stated in part,

> I hereby release the hospital, its personnel, and the attending physician from any responsibility whatever for unfavorable reactions or any untoward results due to my refusal to permit the use of blood or its derivatives and I fully understand the possible consequences of such refusal on my part.[265]

A short time after the surgery, Mrs. Shorter began to bleed profusely. Other surgeons performed emergency exploratory surgery which revealed that the defendant had severely lacerated Mrs. Shorter's uterus. While Mrs. Shorter was still coherent, the doctors begged her and her husband to authorize them to administer blood, but they steadfastly refused and Mrs. Shorter bled to death.

Mr. Shorter brought a wrongful death action on the ground that the defendant had negligently performed the surgery and that that was the proximate cause of Mrs. Shorter's death. Expert witnesses for plaintiff and defendant agreed that a transfusion probably would have saved Mrs. Shorter's life. The jury brought back a verdict for the plaintiff, which also found that "Mr. and/or Mrs. Shorter 'knowingly and voluntarily' assumed the risk of bleeding to death and attributed 75 percent of the fault for her death to her and her husband's refusal to authorize or accept a blood transfusion, thus reducing the damages awarded by that proportion."[266] On appeal, the defendant/physician did not contest the jury finding that he had negligently performed the surgery. Rather, he contended that the release or waiver signed by Mrs. Shorter, although not releasing him from liability for his negligence did release him from liability for the consequences of

---

IL: *See* Corlett v. Caserta, 562 N.E.2d 257 (Ill. App. Ct. 1990).

NY: *See* Randolph v. City of N.Y., 507 N.E.2d 298 (N.Y. 1987) (mem.), *aff'g* 501 N.Y.S.2d 837 (App. Div. 1986).

WA: *See* Shorter v. Drury, 695 P.2d 116 (Wash.) (en banc), *cert. denied,* 474 U.S. 827 (1985).

*See generally* Knapp, *Refusal of Medical Treatment on Religious Grounds as Affecting Right to Recover for Personal Injury or Death,* 3 A.L.R.5th 721 (1992).

[263] 695 P.2d 116 (Wash. 1985) (en banc).

[264] *Id.* at 118.

[265] *Id.* at 119.

[266] *Id.*

"Mrs. Shorter's voluntary refusal to accept blood, which in this case was death."[267]

The court held that because the release did not address the issue of Dr. Drury's negligence, there was no waiver of liability as to the consequences of his negligence. (The court declined to address whether, had the form purported to have been a release from liability for negligence, it would have been against public policy to enforce it.) However, the court characterized the document as "more . . . than a simple declaration that the signer would refuse blood only if there was no negligence by Dr. Drury," and construed it instead as being "a specific request that no blood or blood derivatives be administered to Mrs. Shorter."[268] Although the Shorters "were acting under the compulsion of circumstances[, t]he compulsion . . . was created by the[ir] religious convictions . . . not by the tortious conduct of defendant."[269] The court refused, however, to find the release to be a complete bar to recovery, but instead applied principles of comparative negligence to this express assumption of risk by the patient. The court therefore affirmed the jury verdict for the plaintiff and its reduction by the degree of fault attributable to the Shorter's own conduct, namely, refusal of the blood transfusion.

The case of *Corlett v. Caserta*,[270] comes to the same conclusion as *Shorter* on a similar set of facts.

## § 17.17   Other Tort Theories

A number of cases have attempted to allege a variety of other tort theories to recover for unauthorized administration of treatment in the end-of-life context. None of these seem particularly promising, and in any event most overlap substantially with more common theories of recovery such as battery, intentional infliction of emotional distress, and negligence.

**Fraud or Misrepresentation.**   In *Estate of Leach v. Shapiro,* the plaintiffs' central claim was that they were not provided with adequate information about the patient's condition, a claim which was brought under a theory of lack of informed consent. However, the plaintiffs also claimed that this constituted fraud or misrepresentation, and the court agreed that the plaintiffs' allegations stated a cause of action and reversed the trial court's dismissal of the claim. The basis for this cause of action is the fiduciary nature of the doctor-patient relationship, so that "[w]hen the physician has knowledge of a fact concerning the patient's physical condition which is material to the patient, this fiduciary relationship may render the physician's silence fraudulent."[271]

---

[267] *Id.*

[268] *Id.* at 120.

[269] *Id.*

[270] 562 N.E.2d 257 (Ill. App. Ct. 1990).

[271] Estate of Leach v. Shapiro, 469 N.E.2d 1047, 1054 (Ohio Ct. App. 1984).

**Breach of Fiduciary Duty.**  One might also directly claim that the administration of unwanted treatment is a breach of the fiduciary nature of the doctor-patient relationship, as the plaintiffs did in *Bartling*.[272] However, just as a claim for inadequate information overlaps with (and might be indistinguishable from) a cause of action for lack of informed consent, the claim in *Bartling* is indistinguishable from a battery claim. The court did not analyze or even reach the merits of this claim, affirming its dismissal along with several other claims because "respondents were acting in conformance with what they believed to be their professional and religious obligations,"[273] just as it did with the battery claim.[274]

**Wrongful Living/Wrongful Prolongation of Life.**  Two cases have attempted to assert liability under a new theory labeled by one as "wrongful living"[275] and the other as "wrongful prolongation of life."[276] In *Anderson v. St. Francis-St. George Hospital,* a competent patient had informed his physician that he did not wish to be resuscitated if he suffered a cardiopulmonary arrest, and the physician agreed and wrote a DNR order. When he did suffer an arrest, he was successfully resuscitated by hospital employees (presumably without the physician's knowledge) but later died. His estate brought an action against the hospital and its employees for the resuscitation, alleging several different theories of recovery—battery, negligence, and "wrongful living." The appeals court overturned the grant of summary judgment on the battery and negligence claims, but upheld the judgment dismissing the "wrongful living" claim on the ground that added life, which resulted from the defendants' actions, "is not a compensable harm."[277]

The dismissal of this novel cause of action should work no hardship on the plaintiff in terms of establishing liability because the alleged facts state a cause of action for battery, negligence, or both. However, proof of substantial damages can be difficult, if not impossible, when the plaintiff is already close to death.[278] The proposed cause of action for "wrongful living" is intended to evade the restrictions on damages found in these theories of recovery.[279]

The plaintiffs in the other case, *Benoy v. Simons,* parents of an infant suffering from severe respiratory distress syndrome due to his premature birth, brought an action against the physician and hospital who cared for him, alleging that these defendants had provided unwanted treatment to him. In addition to causes of action for negligence, lack of informed consent, and intentional infliction of emotional distress, the plaintiffs brought an action styled as

---

[272] *See, e.g.,* Bartling v. Glendale Adventist Medical Ctr., 229 Cal. Rptr. 360 (Ct. App. 1986).

[273] *Id.* at 364.

[274] See § **17.4.**

[275] Benoy v. Simons, 831 P.2d 167 (Wash. Ct. App. 1992).

[276] Anderson v. St. Francis-St. George Hosp., 614 N.E.2d 841 (Ohio Ct. App. 1992).

[277] *Id.* at 846.

[278] See § **17.25.**

[279] Oddi, *The Tort of Interference with the Right to Die,* 75 Geo. L.J. 625, 637 *et seq.* (1986).

"wrongful prolongation of life." There is so little discussion of this claim in the appellate opinion and what there is so unenlightening that it is virtually impossible to determine what the plaintiffs were seeking damages for, but a plausible inference is that it must have been either for their own emotional distress or for the pain and suffering of the child between the time of birth and its death. It also seems from the opinion, though this is also very unclear, that this claim either overlaps with or is the same as the claim for negligence and/or lack of informed consent.[280] In any event, the attempt to create a new theory of recovery failed along with the attempts to recover under existing theories.

**Vicarious Liability.** Vicarious liability is not a separate theory of tort recovery but a means of imposing liability (ordinarily, for negligence) on one party because of the status relationship between that party and another against whom tort liability has been established. The most common relationship in which vicarious liability applies is the employment relationship, where it is usually referred to as *respondeat superior,* or "let the superior (employer) respond (be liable for damages)." Vicarious liability is often unavailable in end-of-life decisionmaking because many doctors, who are defendants in the lawsuits, do not stand in an employment relationship with the hospital or other health care facility.[281] However, as more physicians become employees of a hospital or some other entity (such as a health maintenance organization) and fewer are independent contractors, the possibility for the imposition of vicarious liability will increase. Vicarious liability might also be imposed on a hospital for the torts of an independent-contractor physician if the patient or surrogate had no choice in the selection of the physician[282] or under the doctrine of apparent or ostensible agency if the hospital represents or holds out the doctor as its agent and the plaintiff justifiably relies on that representation.[283]

Few efforts have actually been made to vicariously impose liability in end-of-life situations, and none appear to have involved physicians. In the *Anderson* case, the court held that the hospital would be vicariously liable for the torts of its nurse/employee for resuscitating a patient despite the existence of a DNR order, but of course only if the nurse were liable.[284] In *Strachan,* the court alluded to the imposition of liability on the hospital for the conduct of the hospital administrator but was not called on to rule on this issue.[285]

---

[280] Benoy v. Simons, 831 P.2d 167, 170 (Wash. Ct. App. 1992) ("On appeal the Benoys urge us to adopt a new cause of action for wrongful prolongation of Dustin's life under the theory of medical negligence or lack of informed consent.").

[281] **OH:** Anderson v. St. Francis-St. George Hosp., 614 N.E.2d 841, 844 (Ohio Ct. App. 1992) ("[U]nder the doctrine of respondeat superior, any person who controls the physician in a principal-agent relationship is liable for unlawful acts by the physician that are within the scope of that relationship.").

[282] **WV:** *See, e.g.,* Belcher v. Charleston Area Medical Ctr., 422 S.E.2d 827, 835 (W. Va. 1992).

[283] *See generally* Hodson, Annotation, *Liability of Hospital or Sanitarium for Negligence of Physician or Surgeon,* 51 A.L.R.4th 235 § 7 (1987).

[284] Anderson v. St. Francis-St. George Hosp., 614 N.E.2d 841 (Ohio Ct. App. 1992).

[285] Strachan v. John F. Kennedy Memorial Hosp., 538 A.2d 346, 348 (N.J. 1988).

**Refusal to Pay for Care.**   Another remedy for the rendition of unwanted treatment is suggested by *Grace Plaza of Great Neck, Inc. v. Elbaum.*[286] This was an action by a nursing home against the husband of a patient who had been treated in the nursing home to recover the costs of the care and treatment that had been provided. The husband defended on the ground that the services had been provided without consent and, indeed, against his express representation that his wife, who was incompetent, did not want them provided; that is, that she did not want to be kept alive by a feeding tube in a persistent vegetative state.

The New York Court of Appeals upheld the reversal of the trial court's judgment against the nursing home. Its reason for doing so was that the law of New York was clear that a surrogate could not make a decision to forgo life-sustaining treatment. Rather, there had to be clear and convincing evidence that the patient herself had decided, before losing the ability to do so, that she did not want to be treated under these circumstances. The court held that "[i]f a provider harbors some uncertainty on the matter [of the patient's own wishes], it acts within the dictates of [the law as established by] *O'Connor* if it refuses to discontinue treatment until the issue is legally determined."[287]

Although the claim failed in *Elbaum,* that does not necessarily foreclose its future application either in New York or elsewhere. However, it would seem as if, as long as a health care institution acts in good faith in demanding a judicial determination to establish the patient's actual or probable wishes or what course of action is in the patient's best interests (where that standard is accepted[288]), this theory will not succeed.

## § 17.18   Contract

While tort theories seem to be the most promising for recovery both for damages for unwanted treatment as well as the failure to provide treatment, breach of contract also holds out possibilities for recovery, albeit limited possibilities. The primary barrier to recovery under a contract theory is that courts are reluctant to honor anything but express contracts in the context of the doctor-patient relationship.[289]

Only a small number of end-of-life cases even mention liability for breach of contract. In one, the court treated the claim as one entirely for intentional infliction of emotional distress, but a concurring judge mentioned that the "amended complaint, in so many words, alleges an agreement respecting her husband's treatment was breached," and concluded that

---

[286] 623 N.E.2d 513 (N.Y. 1993).

[287] *Id.* at 515 (citing *In re* Westchester County Medical Ctr. (O'Connor), 531 N.E.2d 607 (N.Y. 1988)).

[288] See §§ **7.12–7.13.**

[289] **NY:** *See, e.g.,* Nicoleau v. Brookhaven Memorial Hosp. Ctr., 607 N.Y.S.2d 703, 704 (App. Div. 1994) ("well settled that a breach of contract claim in relation to the rendition of medical services by a physician will withstand a test of its legal sufficiency only when based upon an express special promise to effect a cure or to accomplish some definite result").

the law cannot enforce such agreements with respect to the treatment of incompetent individuals. Without the ability to take direction from the patient, the doctor must remain free to prolong life where it appears at that moment to be in the patient's best interest, notwithstanding a previous contrary understanding with guardians or relatives.[290]

The majority opinion in this case diverges significantly from the judicial consensus about forgoing life-sustaining treatment both in California and nationally, which perhaps explains why the California Supreme Court ordered the opinion not to be published.

Another case to mention breach of contract alleged that there was an agreement between the surrogate and the attending physician not to administer a blood transfusion to the patient. The trial court found, however, that the person acting as surrogate was not legally entitled to do so at the time he signed the contract stating the patient was not to receive a blood transfusion.[291] One case alleging a contract theory grew out of a case involving a decision to forgo life-sustaining treatment,[292] but the case seeking damages is really for disclosure of confidential information rather than for damages arising from unwanted treatment.[293]

One other case involving the administration of a purportedly lifesaving blood transfusion to a Jehovah's Witness also resulted in a suit for damages based in part on contract liability. The court found that a cause of action was stated "based on the plaintiffs' allegation that the patient entered into an oral agreement with her attending physician pursuant to which she agreed to retain his services in exchange for his specific promise to deliver her baby without the administration of blood, . . . and that the breach occurred when he administered blood transfusions to her after she gave birth to her child by Cesarian section."[294]

## § 17.19 State Statutory Violations

Liability is theoretically possible under some state statutory enactments, but in practice, suits of this sort have not been successful.

**Consumer Protection Acts.** In *Benoy v. Simon,* the family of a low-birth-weight baby brought suit alleging the unauthorized administration of treatment. In addition to several common-law theories of recovery, the plaintiffs pleaded

---

[290] **CA:** Westhart v. Mule, 261 Cal. Rptr. 640, 646 n.1 (Ct. App. 1989) (Crosby, A.J.P., concurring) (ordered not published).

[291] **MI:** Young v. Oakland Gen. Hosp., 437 N.W.2d 321, 323 (Mich. Ct. App. 1989).

[292] **MA:** *In re* Spring, 405 N.E.2d 115 (Mass. 1980).

[293] **MA:** Spring v. Geriatric Auth., 475 N.E.2d 727 (Mass. 1985).

[294] **NY:** Nicoleau v. Brookhaven Memorial Hosp. Ctr., 607 N.Y.S.2d 703, 704 (App. Div. 1994).

that the treatment violated the state Consumer Protection Act[295] because the defendant/physician "was deceptive and unfair in retaining [the baby] as a patient [and] . . . he led [the family] to believe the care given to [the baby] was required when it actually had no beneficial value."[296] The court affirmed the dismissal of this count of the complaint because, to maintain a claim under the Act, "there must be a showing of a lack of informed consent resulting from dishonest and unfair practices motivated by financial gain,"[297] and there was no evidence to support the claim. Whether or not there is a basis for a claim of this sort is highly dependent on state law, that is, on whether a state has a statute of this sort and whether the statute can be applied to the facts of an end-of-life decision. Another case involving end-of-life decisionmaking to invoke the state Consumer Protection Act is *Spring v. Geriatric Authority.*[298] However, the claim in this case was for invasion of privacy, rather than any default in the decision-making process itself.

**Advance Directive Statutes.**   Every state has an advance directive statute, yet only one reported case has sought to use it as a basis for recovery. The plaintiff in *Camp v. White* alleged, among other things, that life-sustaining treatment had been withheld from the patient without her written consent, as required by the Alabama living will statute. In other words, the allegation was that because the patient did not have a living will authorizing the withholding of the treatment that was in fact withheld, the defendant/physicians had violated their duty toward her. The court rejected this claim on the ground that the statute was "cumulative," that is, that it merely prescribed a means for the forgoing of life-sustaining treatment, but not the sole means.[299] This is consistent with the language of most advance directive statutes and with the judicial gloss that has been applied to such statutes.[300]

Although the court did not raise this matter in *Camp v. White,* it might have easily and, probably, properly concluded that the violation of an advance directive does not give rise to liability under what is often referred to as "negligence per se."[301] The violation of a statute does not automatically give rise to civil liability. For there to be negligence liability for the violation of a statute, a court must determine that the purpose of statute at issue is

(a)   to protect a class of persons which includes the one whose interest is invaded, and

(b)   to protect the particular interest which is invaded, and

---

[295] Wash. Rev. Code Ann. § 19.86.010 (West 1992).

[296] **WA:** Benoy v. Simons, 831 P.2d 167, 172 (Wash. 1992).

[297] *Id.*

[298] **MA:** 475 N.E.2d 727 (Mass. 1985).

[299] **AL:** Camp v. White, 510 So. 2d 166, 169–70 (Ala. 1987).

[300] See § **10.14.**

[301] *See generally* W.P. Keeton et al., Prosser and Keeton on the Law of Torts § 36, at 229–31 (5th ed. 1984).

(c)   to protect that interest against the kind of harm which has resulted, and

(d)   to protect that interest against the particular hazard from which the harm results.[302]

However, in some states, the living will statute expressly provides the basis for a civil cause of action.[303]

# FEDERAL CONSTITUTIONAL AND STATUTORY REMEDIES

## § 17.20   Federal Civil Rights Actions

Many of the cases seeking to impose liability for unwanted medical treatment have been brought as federal civil rights actions either alone or with pendent state law claims. As a rule, they have not been any more successful than state common-law or statutory remedies. Few have survived a motion to dismiss or a motion for summary judgment, and the appellate courts have not been much more receptive. In fact, there do not appear to be any reported cases in which plaintiffs have recovered damages for violation of their federal civil rights in connection with the administration of unwanted lifesaving medical treatment.

A complete discussion of federal civil rights claims is beyond the scope of this chapter.[304] Rather, the effort here is limited to a review of those end-of-life decisionmaking cases that allege civil rights violations, in order to provide some

---

[302] Restatement (Second) of Torts § 286 (1965). *See generally* Gottesman, *Civil Liability for Failing to Provide "Medically Indicated Treatment" to a Disabled Infant,* 20 Fam. L.Q. 61 (1986) (discussing civil liability for violation of Child Abuse Amendments). See **Ch. 16.**

[303] **AK:** Alaska Stat. § 18.12.070.

**IL:** Ill. Ann. Stat. ch. 755, § 35/8(8).

**LA:** La. Rev. Stat. Ann. § 40:1299.58.9(a).

**NE:** Neb. Rev. Stat. § 20-402(1).

**RI:** R.I. Gen. Laws § 23-4.11-9(e).

**SC:** S.C. Code Ann. § 44-77-160(c).

**TN:** Tenn. Code Ann. § 32-11-108(a).

[304] *See generally* I. Bodensteiner & R. Levinson, State and Local Government Civil Rights Liability (1991 & Supp. 1994); Shepard's Editorial Staff, Civil Actions Against State and Local Government, Its Divisions, Agencies, and Officers (2d. ed. 1992); S. Nahmod, Civil Rights and Civil Liberties Litigation: The Law of Section 1983 (3d ed. 1991); National Lawyers Guild Civil Liberties Comm., Civil Rights Litigation and Attorney Fees Annual Handbook (1993); M. Schwartz & J. Kirklin, Section 1983 Litigation: Claims, Defenses, and Fees (2d ed., John Wiley & Sons 1991 & Supp. 1994); S. Steinglass, Section 1983 Litigation in State Courts (1993); Tenth Annual Section 1983 Civil Rights Litigation and Attorneys' Fees: Current Developments (PLI Litig. & Admin. Practice Course Handbook Series No. H-485, 1993).

indication of the kinds of fact situations that arguably give to such violations, and the difficulties that plaintiffs have had in imposing liability. Not all of the cases are end-of-life decisionmaking cases; some involve refusals of blood transfusions by Jehovah's Witnesses whose health was, or almost certainly would have been, restored by the administration of treatment.

### Section 1983 Claims

A federal civil rights claim for damages is generally brought under 42 U.S.C. § 1983, which states that

> [e]very person who, under color of any statute, ordinance, regulation, custom, or usage . . . subjects, or causes to be subjected, any . . . person . . . to the deprivation of any rights, privileges, or immunities secured by the Constitution and laws, shall be liable to the party injured.[305]

In medical decisionmaking cases, plaintiffs have alleged the infringement of a variety of federally protected rights—that is, rights protected by the laws or Constitution of the United States[306]—by the unwanted administration of treatment, including substantive due process,[307] procedural due process,[308] privacy,[309] free exercise of religion,[310] equal protection,[311] and the contract clause.[312] Civil rights actions are also potentially available for the failure to administer desired treatment.[313]

**Color of State Law.**   In order to recover, a plaintiff must prove not merely that the defendant violated a federally protected right, but that the defendant acted

---

[305] 42 U.S.C.A. § 1983 (West 1984).

[306] Ross v. Hilltop Rehabilitation Hosp., 676 F. Supp. 1528, 1535 (D. Colo. 1987).

[307] **CA9:** Niebla v. County of San Diego, 967 F.2d 589, 1992 WL 140250 (9th Cir. 1992) (unpublished).

   **CA11:** Bendiburg v. Dempsey, 909 F.2d 463 (11th Cir. 1990), *cert. denied,* 500 U.S. 932 (1991).

   **DGA:** Novak v. Cobb County-Kennestone Hosp. Auth., 849 F. Supp. 1559 (N.D. Ga. 1994).

[308] **CA9:** Niebla v. County of San Diego, 967 F.2d 589, 1992 WL 140250.

   **CA11:** Bendiburg v. Dempsey, 909 F.2d 463.

   **DGA:** Novak v. Cobb County-Kennestone Hosp. Auth., 849 F. Supp. 1559.

[309] **CA9:** Foster v. Tourtellotte, 704 F.2d 1009 (9th Cir. 1983).

[310] **CA2:** Winters v. Miller, 446 F.2d 65 (2d Cir. 1971).

   **DGA:** Novak v. Cobb County-Kennestone Hosp. Auth., 849 F. Supp. 1559.

   **WA:** Benoy v. Simons, 831 P.2d 167 (Wash. 1992).

   **IL:** Corlett v. Caserta, 562 N.E.2d 257 (Ill. App. Ct. 1990).

[311] **DGA:** Novak v. Cobb County-Kennestone Hosp. Auth., 849 F. Supp. 1559.

[312] **DGA:** Novak v. Cobb County-Kennestone Hosp. Auth., 849 F. Supp. 1559.

[313] **CA3:** *See* Kranson v. Valley Crest Nursing Home, 755 F.2d 46 (3d Cir. 1985).

"under the color of state law" rather than as a private citizen.[314] This requirement is met when the defendant is a state or municipal official or the employee of a state or municipal agency.[315] Municipalities and other local government entities are considered to be persons for § 1983 purposes, but states and counties are not and thus are not amenable to suit under § 1983.[316]

Furthermore, private citizens are deemed to be acting under color of state law and can also be held liable under § 1983 if they act in concert with a person who is acting under color of state law.[317] Thus, in *Bendiburg,* the court held that a number of private institutions and individuals—a nursing home and a nurse employed by it, a homecare nursing service and a homecare nurse supervisor employee, and physicians in private practice—might be held liable (if the plaintiff could establish the necessary elements of the cause of action against them) because they acted in concert with employees of the county department of children and family services.[318]

To establish § 1983 liability of private citizens, the plaintiff must establish that "the alleged infringement of federal rights [by the private citizen] is attributable to the state."[319] The "central inquiry . . . focuses on: (1) the nature of the relationship between the individual and the State; (2) the dependence of the individual on the state for funds; and (3) whether the individual performs a state function."[320] Thus, a private physician who was chief of staff of a state hospital was acting under color of state law,[321] but a private physician who had admitting privileges at a state-owned hospital was not.[322]

---

[314] **CA11:** Bendiburg v. Dempsey, 909 F.2d 463, 468 (11th Cir. 1990).

**DCO:** Ross v. Hilltop Rehabilitation Hosp., 676 F. Supp. 1528, 1535 (D. Colo. 1987).

**DFL:** McKenzie v. Doctors' Hosp. of Hollywood, Inc., 765 F. Supp. 1504, 1506 (S.D. Fla. 1991), *aff'd without opinion,* 974 F.2d 1347 (11th Cir. 1992).

**DGA:** Novak v. Cobb County-Kennestone Hosp. Auth., 849 F. Supp. at 1565.

**CA:** McMahon v. Lopez, 245 Cal. Rptr. 172, 176 (Ct. App. 1988); Bartling v. Glendale Adventist Medical Ctr., 229 Cal. Rptr. 360, 366 (Ct. App. 1986).

**NY:** Nicoleau v. Brookhaven Memorial Hosp. Ctr., 581 N.Y.S.2d 382, 384 (App. Div. 1992).

**SC:** Banks v. Medical Univ., 444 S.E.2d 519 (S.C. 1994).

[315] **CA11:** Bendiburg v. Dempsey, 909 F.2d 463 (county department of children and family services).

**DGA:** Novak v. Cobb County-Kennestone Hosp. Auth., 849 F. Supp. 1559 (employees of county-owned hospital).

**CA:** McMahon v. Lopez, 245 Cal. Rptr. at 178.

[316] **CA:** McMahon v. Lopez, 245 Cal. Rptr. at 177–78 (citing Monell v. New York City Dep't of Social Servs., 436 U.S. 658, 690 (1978)).

[317] **DIL:** *See, e.g.,* Holmes v. Silver Cross Hosp., 340 F. Supp. 125 (N.D. Ill. 1972).

[318] Bendiburg v. Dempsey, 909 F.2d at 467.

[319] Banks v. Medical Univ., 444 S.E.2d 519, 522 (S.C. 1994).

[320] *Id.*

[321] **CA1:** Downs v. Sawtelle, 574 F.2d 1 (1st Cir.), *cert. denied,* 439 U.S. 910 (1978).

[322] **SC:** Banks v. Medical Univ., 444 S.E.2d 519.

Acting under the color of state law can also be established by showing the existence of a conspiracy between private and state actors. "A conspiracy is an agreement between two or more individuals, where one individual acts in furtherance of the objective of the conspiracy, which causes an injury to a person or property, or deprives a person of exercising any right or privilege as a United States citizen."[323] This requirement is likely to be extremely difficult to establish in most medical decisionmaking situations, for the simple reason that in fact very few such situations involve individuals who are agents of the state,[324] as is illustrated by the cases to date.

*Bendiburg v. Dempsey* is one medical decisionmaking case in which this requirement was met. The district court had granted summary judgment for the private defendants because "the record does not reveal the conspiracy which plaintiff alleges or the kind of joint action necessary to support a claim of state action on the part of the private defendants."[325] However, the court of appeals reversed and reinstated the complaint because the district court "wrongfully required [plaintiff] to produce a 'smoking gun' when nothing more than an 'understanding' and 'willful participation' between private and state defendants is necessary to show the kind of joint action that will subject private parties to § 1983 liability."[326]

In this case, the plaintiff had established that the defendants sought and obtained an ex parte judicial order to temporarily remove custody of the plaintiff's minor son, alleged to be in need of medical treatment to which plaintiff withheld consent, and to vest custody in county employees. The appeals court held that the necessary evidence to hold the private parties liable would be established if the plaintiff could show that "the private defendants intentionally exaggerated the emergency nature of [plaintiff's son's] medical problems, and indeed did this for the purpose of supplying the state officials with the necessary facts to obtain ex parte temporary custody on a court order with the implied approval for a consent to the surgical procedures."[327]

In a factually similar case, though not similar enough for the plaintiffs to prevail, *Novak v. Cobb County-Kennestone Hospital Authority,* the court held that there were "significant factual distinctions between this case and *Bendiburg.*"[328] In *Bendiburg,* "to the extent the private defendants may have exaggerated the emergency nature of the child's condition in order to provide the

---

[323] McKenzie v. Doctors' Hosp. of Hollywood, Inc., 765 F. Supp. 1504, 1507 (S.D. Fla. 1991), *aff'd without op.,* 974 F.2d 1347 (11th Cir. 1992).

**CA11:** *Accord* Bendiburg v. Dempsey, 909 F.2d 463, 468 (11th Cir. 1990) (plaintiff "must show that the parties 'reached an understanding' to deny the plaintiff his or her rights").

[324] *See generally* Annotation, *Action of Private Hospital as State Action Under 42 U.S.C.S. § 1983 or Fourteenth Amendment,* 42 A.L.R. Fed. 463 (1979 & Supp. 1994).

[325] Bendiburg v. Dempsey, 909 F.2d at 468.

[326] *Id.* at 469.

[327] *Id.*

[328] 849 F. Supp. 1559, 1579 (N.D. Ga. 1994).

state actor with a reason to seek custody on an *ex parte* basis when they finally acted, a question of fact was presented on the conspiracy issue."[329] However, on the facts of the present case, it concluded that "there simply is no evidence that any of the private defendants planned ahead to seek the appointment of a temporary guardian and then manufactured a medical emergency at the last minute in order to give the state actors a reason to act on an *ex parte* basis."[330]

In *McMahon v. Lopez*, the California Court of Appeal held that neither the fact that a hospital is licensed to operate by the state nor the fact that it receives financial benefit from the state establishes that it is acting under color of state law for § 1983 purposes: " '[A] State normally can be held responsible for a private decision only when it has exercised coercive power or has provided such significant encouragement, either overt or covert, that the choice must in law be deemed to be that of the State.' "[331] The federal district court in *Ross v. Hilltop Rehabilitation Hospital* similarly held that extensive state regulations; licensing by the state; receipt of compensation through Medicare, Medicaid, and Social Security programs; funding, benefits, and authority from city, county, and state sources; and statutory authority concerning care and treatment of the mentally ill did not render a private hospital susceptible to § 1983 liability.[332] *Ross* also rejected the notion that state court holdings in right-to-die cases that had found a private health provider's refusal to terminate or withhold life-sustaining treatment to be state action were either erroneous[333] or were subsequently overruled.[334]

This seems to be the proper result. The many cases that have predicated the right to refuse life-sustaining medical treatment on a constitutional right of

---

[329] Novak v. Cobb County-Kennestone Hosp. Auth., 849 F. Supp. at 1579 (citing Bendiburg v. Dempsey, 909 F.2d at 469).

[330] *Id.*

[331] 245 Cal. Rptr. 172, 177 (Ct. App. 1988) (quoting Blum v. Yaretsky, 457 U.S. 991, 1004 (1982)).

[332] 676 F. Supp. 1528 (D. Colo. 1987). *See generally* Annotation, *Action of Private Hospital as State Action Under 42 U.S.C.S. § 1983 or Fourteenth Amendment,* 42 A.L.R. Fed. 463, 472 (1979 & Supp. 1994). *But see* Holmes v. Silver Cross Hosp., 340 F. Supp. 125, 133 (N.D. Ill. 1972) (receipt of Hill-Burton funds and "state's administration and regulation of its overall hospital and health care program" constitute state action).

[333] **AZ:** *E.g.,* Rasmussen v. Fleming, 741 P.2d 674 (Ariz. 1987).

[334] **NY:** *See* Eichner v. Dillon, 426 N.Y.S.2d 517 (App. Div. 1980).

**IL:** *See also* Estate of Longeway v. Community Convalescent Ctr., 549 N.E.2d 292, 301 (Ill. 1989) ("[I]f the surrogate decisionmaker is a court-appointed guardian, procedural due process questions involving deprivation of life may arise. (U.S. Const., amend. XIV; Ill. Const. 1970, art, 1, § 2.) Although it is uncertain whether sufficient State action is present to invoke the protections of procedural due process, utilizing a court to oversee the guardian's decision as to the termination of artificial nutrition and hydration will forestall any potential constitutional infirmities.").

**WA:** *See also In re* Colyer, 660 P.2d 738 (Wash. 1983) (not followed in part because relied upon superseded *Eichner* decision).

privacy or, more recently, individual liberty,[335] are not likely to assist litigants in prevailing against private parties for the administration of unwanted medical treatment. The reason for this conclusion is that federal constitutional bases for the right to refuse life-sustaining medical treatment are tenuous when the physicians and health care institutions are private parties, and courts are increasingly abandoning them in favor of a common-law basis.[336] The Supreme Court's *Cruzan* decision, which supports the conclusion that both competent and incompetent patients have a constitutionally protected right to be free of unwanted treatment, does not compel a different conclusion for the reason that the patient in that case was being treated in a hospital owned and operated by the state of Missouri, and the treatment was being administered pursuant to state policy.[337]

**Policy or Custom.**   In order to prevail in a civil rights action against governmental defendants, it is necessary to establish that their conduct occurred in execution of a governmental policy or custom "promulgated either by its lawmakers or by those whose edicts or acts may fairly be said to represent official policy."[338] That is, they are not liable simply because a violation of an individual's federally protected rights resulted from the conduct of a governmental official, agent, or employee. If liability is to be imposed upon a governmental entity, it must be because the violation of the plaintiff's federally protected right arose from the existence of a law, policy, or custom.

The policy or custom pursuant to which defendants act need not be a state law or even a written policy:

> According to the Supreme Court, "official policy" often refers to formal rules or understandings—often but not always committed to writing—that are intended to, and do, establish fixed plans of action to be followed under similar circumstances consistently and over time. . . . [However, if] the decision to adopt [a] particular course of action is properly made by that government's authorized decisionmakers, it surely represents an act of official government "policy" as that term is commonly understood. *Pembaur v. Cincinnati*, 475 U.S. 469, 480–81 (1986).[339]

---

[335] See § **2.8.**

[336] See § **2.7.**

[337] *See* Cruzan v. Director, 497 U.S. 261, 281 n.9 (1990) ("Since Cruzan was a patient at a state hospital when this litigation commenced, the State has been involved as an adversary from the beginning.").

[338] **CA:** Bouvia v. County of L.A., 241 Cal. Rptr. 239, 246–47 (Ct. App. 1987).

**CA9:** *Accord* Niebla v. County of San Diego, 967 F.2d 589, 1992 WL 140250, at 3 (9th Cir. 1992) (unpublished).

**DCO:** *Accord* Ross v. Hilltop Rehabilitation Hosp., 676 F. Supp. 1528, 1537 (D. Colo. 1987).

**DGA:** *Accord* Novak v. Cobb County-Kennestone Hosp. Auth., 849 F. Supp. 1559, 1568 n.7 (N.D. Ga. 1994) (court assumed without deciding that defendant acted pursuant to governmental policy or custom "or acted as a policymaker").

[339] Niebla v. County of San Diego, 967 F.2d 589, 1992 WL 140250, at 3 (ellipses in original) (footnote omitted).

Thus, the United States Court of Appeals for the Ninth Circuit held, in an unpublished decision, that where county officials engaged in repeated efforts to obtain ex parte orders to administer blood transfusions to a minor Jehovah's Witness over her and her parents' protests, plaintiffs pleaded sufficient facts to prevent dismissal of their claim on the ground that the defendants did not act pursuant to policy or custom.[340]

**Causation.** For there to be a violation of § 1983, it must be shown that the state or an agent of the state was responsible for the violation of the plaintiff's federally protected rights.[341] For example, in *Novak,* in which a teenage Jehovah's Witness was administered a blood transfusion without parental consent, the failure to summon the parents to the judicial hearing was not actionable under § 1983 because it did not result from the conduct of an employee of a governmentally owned hospital.[342] Similarly, in *McKenzie v. Doctors' Hospital of Hollywood, Inc.,*[343] even though the hospital acted under color of state law in obtaining an ex parte judicial order authorizing it to administer a blood transfusion to plaintiff over her objection, no cause of action was stated because the patient left the hospital before the transfusion could be administered, and therefore any harm that the patient suffered was not caused by the defendants.

**Standard for Constitutional Violation.** Not any deprivation of a federally protected right constitutes a violation of § 1983. The "state action must 'shock [ ] the conscience' of the court."[344] The trial court in *Bendiburg*[345] "held that circumvention of parental authority for a five-day period did not rise to a level sufficiently egregious or shocking to sustain a substantive due process claim with respect to severance of the parent-child relationship."[346] Also, the conduct

---

[340] *Id.*

[341] **DGA:** Bendiburg v. Dempsey, 707 F. Supp. 1318, 1336 (N.D. Ga. 1989) ("§ 1983 liability can only attach to a supervisory official if the requisite causation is established; i.e., that an affirmative link exists between the official's acts and/or omissions and the constitutional deprivation"); Novak v. Cobb County-Kennestone Hosp. Auth., 849 F. Supp. at 1573 ("[P]laintiffs must prove 'an affirmative causal connection between the actions taken by a particular person "under color of state law" and the constitutional deprivation.'").

[342] **DGA:** Novak v. Cobb County-Kennestone Hosp. Auth., 849 F. Supp. at 1574 ("[T]here is no evidence to indicate that he in any way influenced Judge Hines' in the latter's failure to include either of the plaintiffs in the hearing.").

[343] 765 F. Supp. 1504 (S.D. Fla. 1991), *aff'd without opinion,* 974 F.2d 1347 (11th Cir. 1992).

[344] **DGA:** Novak v. Cobb County-Kennestone Hosp. Auth., 849 F. Supp. at 1566. *Accord* Bendiburg v. Dempsey, 849 F. Supp. at 1579 ("The most widely accepted view is that substantive due process is violated by government conduct that 'shocks the conscience' or when the government engages in action 'which offends those canons of decency and fairness which express the notions of justice of English speaking peoples.'").

**CA:** Bartling v. Glendale Adventist Medical Ctr., 229 Cal. Rptr. 360 (Ct. App. 1986).

[345] **DGA:** Bendiburg v. Dempsey, 707 F. Supp. 1318 (N.D. Ga. 1989).

[346] Bendiburg v. Dempsey, 909 F.2d 463, 468 (11th Cir. 1990).

of a hospital, whose commitment "to the preservation of life was sincere and rooted in what they believed were prevailing medical and legal standards," in using soft restraints to treat a competent patient against his will "was not so extreme as to shock the community."[347]

**Survival of Claims.**   An otherwise valid federal civil rights action might be barred by state law governing the survival of tort actions.[348]

### Section 1985(3)

Another remedy for the violation of federal civil rights is § 1985(3), which provides that

> [i]f two or more persons ... conspire ... for the purpose of depriving, either directly or indirectly, any person or class of persons of the equal protection of the laws, or of equal privileges and immunities under the laws whereby another is injured in his person or property, or deprived of having and exercising any right or privilege of a citizen of the United States, the party so injured or deprived may have an action for the recovery of damages occasioned by such injury or deprivation, against any one or more of the conspirators.[349]

The most significant difference between §§ 1983 and 1985(3) is that the latter does not require that the defendant act under color of state law. In other words, it permits liability to be imposed upon purely private actors. However, there are several limitations on § 1985(3) actions that in the end make it a far narrower remedy and more unlikely that it will be applicable to medical decisionmaking.

First, the plaintiff must prove a conspiracy; there is no remedy for civil rights violations perpetrated by a single individual. On the other hand, a conspiracy is inchoate, and consequently for there to be liability, there only needs to be an agreement and an act to violate federally protected rights in furtherance of the conspiracy, not an actual violation of the plaintiff's federally protected rights. Second, it is unsettled as to whether § 1985(3) applies only to federally protected rights or whether it also applies to rights created by state law.[350] Third, it is also unsettled as to whether the remedy applies only to efforts to deny an individual the equal protection of the law or if it applies to conspiracies to deprive other federally protected rights.[351] The plaintiff must also suffer

---

[347] **CA:** Bartling v. Glendale Adventist Medical Ctr., 229 Cal. Rptr. at 363.

[348] *See* Feld, Annotation, *Survivability of Civil Rights Cause of Action Based on 42 U.S.C. § 1983,* 42 A.L.R. Fed. 163 (1979). See **§ 17.25.**

[349] 42 U.S.C.A. § 1985(3) (West 1994).

[350] Civil Actions Against State and Local Government § 8.64, at 797 (2d. ed. 1992 & Supp. 1994).

[351] Civil Actions Against State and Local Government § 8.65, at 799 (2d. ed. 1992 & Supp. 1994).

personal injury, property damage, or a deprivation of another federally protected right. Finally, and perhaps most significantly, reflecting the basic effort to implement equal protection, there must be proof that there is a "'class-based, invidiously discriminatory animus behind the conspirators' action.'"[352] This requirement will prove very difficult to establish in most medical decision-making cases.[353]

## § 17.21  Rehabilitation Act

Section 504 of the Rehabilitation Act of 1973[354] provides another potential basis for the imposition of liability both for providing unwanted medical treatment and for not providing wanted treatment.[355] However, because of the uncertainty about whether the Act provides a private right of action for damages,[356] any remedy that is sought should be brought under the civil rights statutes.[357] There has been very little litigation testing the applicability of the Rehabilitation Act to end-of-life decisionmaking, probably in part because of the perceived difficulties in applying the text of the statute in this context.

Section 504 of the Rehabilitation Act provides in pertinent part that

> [n]o otherwise qualified individual with a disability . . . shall, solely by reason of her or his disability, be excluded from participation in, be denied the benefits of, or be subjected to discrimination under any program or activity receiving Federal financial assistance.[358]

---

[352] **CA:** Bartling v. Glendale Adventist Medical Ctr., 229 Cal. Rptr. 360, 365–66 (Ct. App. 1986) (quoting Griffin v. Breckenridge, 403 U.S. 88, 102 (1971)).

[353] **CA:** *See, e.g.,* Bartling v. Glendale Adventist Medical Ctr., 229 Cal. Rptr. at 366 (patient's "cause of action must fail for want of an invidiously discriminatory animus").

[354] 29 U.S.C.A. § 794 (West 1985 & Supp. 1994).

[355] *See* Meinhardt, *Bioethics and the Law: The Case of Helga Wanglie: A Clash at the Bedside— Medically Futile Treatment v. Patient Autonomy,* 14 Whittier L. Rev. 137 (1993) (discussing applicability of § 504 to request for treatment by patients or surrogate that physicians deem to be futile).

[356] *See generally* B. Tucker & B. Goldstein, Legal Rights of Persons with Disabilities 8:3 (1992 & Supp. Sept. 1993).

[357] **CA9:** *See, e.g.,* Meyerson v. Arizona, 709 F.2d 1235 (9th Cir. 1983) (limitation on private right of action under Rehabilitation Act cannot be circumvented by bringing suit under Civil Rights Act), *cert. granted and opinion vacated,* 465 U.S. 1095 (1984); Rothschild v. Grottenthaler, 716 F. Supp. 796 (S.D.N.Y. 1989) (Rehabilitation Act does not preclude § 1983 action for damages).

**DPR:** Cordero-Martinez v. Aponte-Roque, 685 F. Supp. 314 (D.P.R. 1988) (§ 1983 action could be maintained as Rehabilitation Act not exclusive remedy available to plaintiff).

*See generally* B. Tucker & B. Goldstein, Legal Rights of Persons with Disabilities 8:11 *et seq.* (1992 & Supp. Sept. 1993). See § **17.20.**

[358] 29 U.S.C.A. § 794(a) (West 1985 & Supp. 1994).

The single case, involving an adult patient, analyzing the applicability of section 504 to a physician's refusal to terminate life-sustaining treatment at a patient's request, *Ross v. Hilltop Rehabilitation Hospital,* gave the following explanation of what a claimant would have to prove:

> In order to state a claim under Section 504, plaintiff must prove that (1) [the patient] was handicapped within the meaning of the Rehabilitation Act; (2) that he was "otherwise qualified" for the position or benefit sought; (3) that he was excluded from the position or benefit solely by reason of his handicap; and (4) that the position or benefit exists as part of a program or activity receiving federal financial assistance.[359]

In this case, the patient, Mr. Rodas, had suffered a stroke, resulting in his being in a "locked-in state," but was still capable of rudimentary communication.[360] When he was hospitalized, a gastrostomy tube was inserted. After four months of hospitalization, he communicated to a hospital employee that he wanted the feeding tube removed. He persisted in this wish but the attending physician refused to honor it because of concerns about his decisionmaking capacity. Consequently, a judicial proceeding was initiated to determine whether or not the patient had the capacity to make a decision to forgo life-sustaining treatment. The patient eventually prevailed in the state court proceedings. After his death, suit was brought in federal court alleging, among other things, that the defendant hospital and physician violated the Rehabilitation Act "by failing to follow Mr. Rodas' explicit instructions to remove his gastrostomy tube because of their perception that Mr. Rodas was mentally handicapped."[361] This, plaintiff claimed, discriminated against the patient on the basis of his "handicap by failing to obtain court authorization for the unwanted treatment—treatment he was physically unable to refuse."[362]

The court held that section 504 does not apply to situations of this kind. It characterized the plaintiff's claim as "an extremely expansive view of 'health care', a view we have considered and reject,"[363] in part because it could find no precedent for such a claim, in part because the only prior case raising a somewhat similar claim rejected it,[364] and in part because of its independent analysis of the matter. The court reasoned that

> the Rehabilitation Act does not apply to the medical treatment decisions of a physically handicapped individual, of questionable mental competency, who requests

---

[359] **DCO:** 676 F. Supp. 1528, 1537–38 (D. Colo. 1987).

[360] *Id.* at 1530 ("He responded to yes-or-no questions by movement of his head and communicated in more detail through the use of a letter board.").

[361] *Id.* at 1538.

[362] *Id.*

[363] *Id.*

[364] *See* United States v. University Hosp., 729 F.2d 144 (2d Cir. 1984).

his treating physician and hospital to terminate medical treatment. The application of the "otherwise qualified" requirement of Section 504 does not square with the facts in this case. Mr. Rodas was admitted to Hilltop for the purpose of obtaining medical treatment for his physical and medical handicap; the defendants' decisions on Mr. Rodas' request to terminate gastrostomy feedings were interwoven with their medical decisions regarding Mr. Rodas' treatment. Thus, in these circumstances, Section 504 of the Rehabilitation Act is inapplicable.[365]

The *Ross* court expressly relied on *United States v. University Hospital,*[366] the leading case on the applicability of section 504 to medical decisionmaking, though not a case seeking damages. The *University Hospital* case is also not directly on point because the patient was a handicapped newborn infant. The United States Department of Health and Human Services (DHHS) had promulgated regulations pursuant to the Rehabilitation Act to implement section 504 in the context of decisionmaking about life-sustaining treatment for handicapped newborn infants. In order to determine whether the Act was being violated by not providing treatment to the patient, DHHS sought to inspect the infants' medical records in the possession of the hospital, but the hospital refused. DHHS then brought an action for an order directing the hospital to give it access to the records.

The United States Court of Appeals for the Second Circuit held that a newborn infant suffering numerous birth defects was a "handicapped individual" within meaning of the Act.[367] However, the court concluded that the requirement that the patient be "otherwise qualified" to receive the treatment in question—that is, the child would be qualified to receive the treatment if she were not handicapped—cannot be meaningfully applied to a medical treatment decision. First, the case law makes clear that the "otherwise qualified" requirement "is geared toward relatively static programs or activities such as education [citations omitted] and transportation systems [citation omitted]."[368] It is not possible to use it

> in the comparatively fluid context of medical treatment decisions without distorting its plain meaning. In common parlance, one would not ordinarily think of a newborn infant suffering from multiple birth defects as being "otherwise qualified" to have corrective surgery performed.[369]

That is, the infant would not be qualified to have corrective surgery if she did not have birth defects because it is the birth defects that create the need for the surgery, and therefore she is not *otherwise* qualified. The court explained that this is not like a burn treatment center denying burn treatment to a deaf person

---

[365] Ross v. Hilltop Rehabilitation Hosp., 676 F. Supp. at 1539.

[366] **CA2:** 729 F.2d 144 (2d Cir. 1984).

[367] *Id.* at 155.

[368] *Id.*

[369] *Id.* at 156.

because he is deaf, if it would provide the same treatment to him if he were not deaf. That would be a violation of section 504.

Second, "in arguing that Baby Jane may have been 'subjected to discrimination,'" the court observed that the government "has taken an oversimplified view of the medical decisionmaking process":

> Where the handicapping condition is related to the condition(s) to be treated, it will rarely, if ever, be possible to say with certainty that a particular decision was "discriminatory".... Beyond the fact that no two cases are likely to be the same, it would invariably require lengthy litigation primarily involving conflicting expert testimony to determine whether a decision to treat, or not to treat, or to litigate or not to litigate, was based on a "bona fide medical judgment," however that phrase might be defined.[370]

Finally, the court held that the legislative history revealed that "congress never contemplated that section 504 would apply to treatment decisions of this nature."[371] The *University Hospital* holding was not reviewed by the Supreme Court, but in a related case, *Bowen v. American Hospital Ass'n,*[372] the Court essentially upheld the reasoning in *University Hospital.*[373]

In *Johnson v. Thompson,* another case involving a handicapped newborn infant, the United States Court of Appeals for the Tenth Circuit described the "otherwise qualified" requirement of section 504 as "a formidable obstacle for anyone alleging discrimination in violation of section 504 based upon the failure to receive medical treatment for a birth defect,"[374] especially when considered along with the fact that section 504 also requires proof that discrimination occurred "solely by reason of [the] handicap." The court's description of what must be proved to establish a section 504 violation echoes that provided by the Second Circuit in the *University Hospital* case and is particularly elucidating:

> Such a plaintiff must prove that he or she was discriminatorily denied medical treatment because of the birth defect and, at the same time, must prove that, in spite of the birth defect, he or she was "otherwise qualified" to receive the denied medical treatment. Ordinarily, however, if such a person were not so handicapped, he or she would not need the medical treatment and thus would not "otherwise qualify" for the treatment.[375]

---

[370] *Id.* at 157.

[371] **CA2:** United States v. University Hosp., 729 F.2d at 157.

   **CA10:** *Accord* Johnson v. Thompson, 971 F.2d 1487, 1492 (10th Cir. 1992) ("Whether section 504 applies to 'individual medical treatment decisions involving handicapped infants' is a controversial issue that the Supreme Court has expressly left open. See *Bowen v. American Hosp. Ass'n,* 476 U.S. 610, 624, 106 S.Ct. 2101, 2110, 90 L.Ed.2d 584 (1986) (plurality opinion).").

[372] 476 U.S. 610 (1986) (plurality opinion).

[373] See § **16.8.**

[374] **CA10:** Johnson v. Thompson, 971 F.2d at 1493.

[375] *Id.*

The court thus held that section 504 was not violated if plaintiffs were denied treatment because they were handicapped *and* because of their socioeconomic status, because of the statutory requirement that discrimination on the basis of handicap be the sole cause of the denial of treatment.[376]

Two other cases have involved the Rehabilitation Act. One concluded that the Act does not apply to dead individuals,[377] a conclusion so seemingly obvious that it hardly seems worth mentioning, which is probably why it was relegated to a footnote.

The other case, however, must be taken more seriously. In *In re Baby "K,"*[378] the court considered the legitimacy of a hospital's request to withhold resuscitation efforts and ventilatory support from an anencephalic baby who was periodically transferred to the hospital, from the nursing home where she lived, when she suffered breathing difficulties. The baby's mother claimed that the patient was entitled to be provided with such medical treatment, in part on the basis of the fact that she was a handicapped individual protected by section 504. Citing *Bowen,* the court concluded that the patient was a "handicapped individual" within the meaning of the Rehabilitation Act because she was " 'an infant who is born with a congenital defect.' "[379] However, the court sought to distinguish the *University Hospital* case's holding of the inapplicability of section 504 on the ground that the basis for that holding was that treatment was withheld because the infant's parents refused to consent to treatment. By contrast, Baby K's mother was affirmatively requesting that treatment be administered. The *Baby K* court further concluded that Baby K is "otherwise qualified" to receive ventilatory support and that its threatened denial was based on the baby's handicap, namely, anencephaly.

The *Baby K* court failed to consider, however, that although the holding in *University Hospital* was based in part on the parents' refusal to consent to the treatment the government sought to compel, it ultimately rested on the conclusion that section 504 cannot be meaningfully applied to a medical treatment decision because the patient is not qualified for treatment ("otherwise qualified") in the absence of the handicapping condition.

---

[376] *Id.* ("The word solely provides the key: the discrimination must result from the handicap and from the handicap alone.").

[377] **FL:** *In re* T.A.C.P., 609 So. 2d 588, 593 n.9 (Fla. 1992).

[378] **CA4:** 832 F. Supp. 1022 (E.D. Va. 1993), *aff'd on other grounds,* 16 F.3d 590 (4th Cir.), *cert. denied,* 115 S. Ct. 91 (1994).

[379] *In re* Baby "K," 832 F. Supp. at 1027 (citing Bowen v. American Hosp. Ass'n, 476 U.S. 610, 624 (1986)).

**CA2:** *Accord* United States v. University Hosp., 729 F.2d 144 (2d Cir. 1984).

**CA10:** *Accord* Johnson v. Thompson, 971 F.2d 1487 (10th Cir. 1992).

## § 17.22   Americans With Disabilities Act

The Americans With Disabilities Act (ADA)[380] is another potential basis for claims of discriminatory decisions to treat or not to treat against the wishes of a competent patient or the surrogate of an incompetent patient.[381] However, there is a great deal of debate and no settled law as to whether the ADA applies to cases of medical decisionmaking in general and forgoing life-sustaining treatment in particular.[382]

There is significant overlap between the ADA and section 504 of the Rehabilitation Act, but one of the important differences is that the ADA, unlike the Rehabilitation Act, does not require that the health care institution be the recipient of federal financial assistance for the provisions of the Act to apply. Because of the similarities of the two acts, it is likely that the case law that has developed under the Rehabilitation Act (apart from the requirement of federal financial assistance) will apply to the coverage of the ADA and that the only added benefit of the ADA will be in the broader class of defendants that might be amenable to suit.[383] However, as is the case with the Rehabilitation Act, it is not clear whether the ADA authorizes a private cause of action for damages. The remedies for violation of Title III of the Act, dealing with discrimination in the provision of public services, are prescribed by 42 U.S.C.A. § 12,188. That section says that the remedies available are those set forth in 42 U.S.C.A. § 2000a-3(a), which states that "a civil action for *preventive* relief . . . may be instituted by the person aggrieved and, upon timely application, the court may, in its discretion, permit the Attorney General to intervene."[384] Thus, it does not appear that this section authorizes a cause of action for damages. However, the ADA also provides for enforcement by the Attorney General, and if the Attorney General brings a civil action for enforcement, "the court . . . may award such other relief as the court considers to be appropriate including monetary damages to the person aggrieved when requested by the Attorney General."[385]

---

[380] Pub. L. No. 101-336, 104 Stat. 327 (1990) (codified at 42 U.S.C.A. §§ 12,101–12,213 (West Supp. 1994)).

[381] *See, e.g., In re* Baby "K," 832 F. Supp. 1022 (E.D. Va. 1993). *See generally Medical Treatment Rights of Older Persons and Persons with Disabilities: 1991,* 7 Issues L. & Med. 407, 409–11 (1992).

[382] *See Discrimination Law Clashes with Bioethics Over PVS,* 7 Med. Ethics Advisor 81 (1991); Parmet, *Discrimination and Disability: The Challenges of the ADA,* 18 Law, Med. & Health Care 331, 339–40 (1990).

[383] *See* 42 U.S.C.A. § 12,101(a) (West Supp. 1994). *See generally* McGraw, *Compliance Costs of the Americans with Disabilities Act,* 18 Del. J. Corp. L. 521, 521–22 (1993).

[384] 42 U.S.C.A. § 2000a-3(a) (West Supp. 1994) (emphasis added).

[385] *Id.* § 12,188(b) (West Supp. 1994).

## MISCELLANEOUS

### § 17.23  Conscientious Objection

One reason that health care providers might be unwilling to comply with a request to forgo (or administer) life-sustaining treatment is that they might be morally opposed to doing so.[386] This opposition is sometimes but not always based on an individual's religious beliefs[387] or a health care institution's affiliation with or ownership by a religious organization.[388] It is not clear how large a proportion of all health care providers hold such beliefs in general, although it is likely that many do at least in particular cases.[389]

---

[386] **DCO:** Ross v. Hilltop Rehabilitation Hosp., 676 F. Supp. 1528 (D. Colo. 1987).

**DRI:** Gray v. Romeo, 697 F. Supp. 580 (D.R.I. 1988).

**CA:** Bartling v. Superior Court, 209 Cal. Rptr. 220 (Ct. App. 1984); Bouvia v. Superior Court (Glenchur), 225 Cal. Rptr. 297 (Ct. App. 1986); Morrison v. Abramovice, 253 Cal. Rptr. 530 (Ct. App. 1988).

**FL:** Browning v. Herbert, 543 So. 2d 258 (Fla. Dist. Ct. App. 1989).

**GA:** State v. McAfee, 385 S.E.2d 651 (Ga. 1989).

**IL:** Estate of Longeway v. Community Convalescent Ctr., 549 N.E.2d 292 (Ill. 1989).

**MA:** *In re* Doe, 583 N.E.2d 1263, 1270 n.17 (Mass. 1992); Norwood Hosp. v. Munoz, 564 N.E.2d 1017 (Mass. 1991); Brophy v. New Eng. Sinai Hosp., Inc., 497 N.E.2d 626 (Mass. 1986).

**NJ:** *In re* Jobes, 529 A.2d 434 (N.J. 1987); *In re* Requena, 517 A.2d 869 (N.J. Super. Ct. App. Div. 1986).

**NY:** Grace Plaza of Great Neck, Inc. v. Elbaum, 588 N.Y.S.2d 853 (App. Div. 1992); Elbaum v. Grace Plaza of Great Neck, Inc., 544 N.Y.S.2d 840 (App. Div. 1989); Delio v. Westchester County Medical Ctr., 516 N.Y.S.2d 677 (App. Div. 1987); A.B. v. C., 477 N.Y.S.2d 281, 283 (Sup. Ct. Schenectady County 1984) (doctor's "moral ethics would dictate that . . . he would of necessity be required to provide [patient] with continuing life-saving medical treatment").

[387] *See, e.g.,* Farnam v. CRISTA Ministries, 807 P.2d 830 (Wash. 1991).

[388] **CA:** *See, e.g.,* Bartling v. Superior Court, 209 Cal. Rptr. at 225 ("Glendale Adventist, which submitted a declaration to the effect that it is a Christian, pro-life oriented hospital, the majority of whose doctors would view disconnecting a life-support system in a case such as this one as inconsistent with the healing orientation of physicians").

**NJ:** *See, e.g., In re* Requena, 517 A.2d at 888 (response of hospital, controlled by Roman Catholic religious order of sisters, to request of competent patient to terminate artificial nutrition and hydration was that it "conflicted with its 'pro-life' values").

[389] *But cf.* Solomon et al., *Decisions Near the End of Life: Professional Views on Life-Sustaining Treatments,* 83 Am. J. Pub. Health 14, 14 (1993) ("[C]hanges in the care of dying patients may not have kept pace with national recommendations, in part because many physicians and nurses disagreed with and may have been unaware of some key guidelines, such as the permissibility of withdrawing treatments.").

This section discusses the legitimacy of conduct of health care providers undertaken on the basis of such beliefs—referred to as "conscientious objection"[390]—and more specifically, whether conscientious objection constitutes a valid legal defense to continuing to provide treatment without the consent of the patient or surrogate. (Health care providers might also conscientiously object to the *administration* of treatment in particular cases, and whether such objection provides a valid defense to the withholding or withdrawing of treatment is even more uncertain.[391])

Conscientious objection needs to be distinguished from more widespread professional views of what is morally proper. An unwillingness to abide by the choices of a competent patient or an incompetent patient's surrogate for reasons of conscience is ordinarily not based on generally accepted professional standards of conduct but on one's own personal beliefs about what is morally permissible or impermissible,[392] which might (or might not) be consistent with the beliefs of some larger group (such as a religion). Although a patient or surrogate "has no right to compel a health-care provider to violate *generally accepted* professional standards,"[393] that does not settle the question of whether a health care provider adhering to views that are not generally accepted within the health care professions may be compelled to take actions in conflict with his, her, or its beliefs. However, professional standards, themselves, sometimes acknowledge that it is acceptable for a physician to act on reasons of conscience.[394]

The conscientious objection to forgoing treatment has arisen in reported cases primarily involving the termination of artificial nutrition and hydration. For example, in *Brophy v. New England Sinai Hospital,* health care providers raised no objection to the entry of a DNR order for a man in a persistent vegetative state but refused to honor the surrogate's request to terminate artificial nutrition and hydration.[395] The basis for the objection to forgoing artificial nutrition and hydration is that some believe that it is not a treatment but constitutes basic sustenance that must be provided all persons and believe that withholding or

---

[390] *See generally* Childress, *Civil Disobedience, Conscientious Objection, and Evasive Noncompliance: A Framework for the Analysis and Assessment of Illegal Actions in Health Care,* 10 J. Med. & Phil. 63 (1985).

[391] *See, e.g.,* Warthen v. Toms River Community Memorial Hosp., 488 A.2d 229 (N.J. Super. Ct. App. Div. 1985). See § **19.12.**

[392] Daar, *A Clash at the Bedside: Patient Autonomy v. A Physician's Professional Conscience,* 44 Hastings L.J. 1241 (1993).

[393] *In re* Farrell, 529 A.2d 404, 412 (N.J. 1987) (emphasis added). See § **8.18.**

[394] *See, e.g.,* American College of Physicians, Ethics Manual 37 (2d ed. 1989) ("For reasons of conscience, the physician may elect to withdraw from the case" if the physician's judgment about the advisability of CPR differs from the competent patient's.).

[395] 497 N.E.2d 626, 629 (Mass. 1986).

withdrawing it means that they are morally complicit in starving the patient to death.[396]

Sometimes the assertion is made that it is particular health care personnel who are morally opposed to the forgoing of life-sustaining treatment;[397] sometimes it is asserted that forgoing life-sustaining treatment would violate the policy of the health care institution;[398] and in other situations, the objection to forgoing treatment is that it violates both the policy of the health care institution and the moral beliefs of individual health care professionals.[399]

## Conscientious Objection in the Courts

For the most part, the courts have tried to satisfy all parties in such situations. In all reported cases, the courts have recognized the patient's right to be free of unwanted life-sustaining medical treatment, but they usually have tried to refrain from forcing either individual health care professionals or a health care institution to take actions that would violate their conscientiously held beliefs and policies. The means by which they have accommodated these conflicting forces has usually been to require the health care institution to transfer the patient to the care of a physician who—and if necessary another health care institution which—is willing to honor the request to terminate treatment.[400]

---

[396] **DRI:** *See, e.g.,* Gray v. Romeo, 697 F. Supp. 580, 583 (D.R.I. 1988) ("denying . . . nutrition and hydration because . . . is tantamount to euthanasia").

**MA:** Brophy v. New Eng. Sinai Hosp., Inc., 497 N.E.2d 626, 632 (Mass. 1986) ("Doctor Lajos Koncz, Brophy's attending physician, refused to carry out Patricia Brophy's request because it is his belief that he would wilfully be causing Brophy's death. Dr. Koncz discussed the matter with the medical and nursing staff at the hospital, who essentially agreed with his opinion. Dr. Richard Field, physician-in-chief at the hospital, took the position that he could not, personally or officially, comply with the request because it would constitute a harmful act which would deliberately produce death. The medical executive committee and the board of directors of the hospital indorsed the position of Drs. Field and Koncz.").

See § **9.39.**

[397] *See, e.g.,* Morrison v. Abramovice, 253 Cal. Rptr. 530 (Ct. App. 1988) ("staff's personal moral objections to removing the tube").

[398] *See, e.g.,* Grace Plaza of Great Neck, Inc. v. Elbaum, 588 N.Y.S.2d 853 (App. Div. 1992) (nursing home).

[399] **DRI:** *See, e.g.,* Gray v. Romeo, 697 F. Supp. at 583 ("hospital as an institution"; "professional health care personnel").

**MA:** *See, e.g.,* Brophy v. New Eng. Sinai Hosp., Inc., 497 N.E.2d at 632 (attending physician, medical and nursing staff, medical executive committee, hospital board of directors).

**NJ:** *See, e.g., In re* Jobes, 529 A.2d 434 (N.J. 1987); *In re* Requena, 517 A.2d 869, 870 (N.J. Super. Ct. App. Div. 1986) ("[t]he subverting of hospital policy and offending the sensibilities of hospital administrators and staff").

[400] **CA:** Morrison v. Abramovice, 253 Cal. Rptr. 530, 534 (Ct. App. 1988) ("In such cases as this no physician should be forced to act against his or her personal moral beliefs if the patient can be transferred to the care of another physician who will follow the conservator's direction.").

In a few cases, the courts have either required the health care providers to comply with the patient's or surrogate's request to terminate treatment[401] or have suggested that they would do so if no other health care provider could readily be found who would terminate treatment.[402]

Without question, the most far-reaching cases are two New Jersey cases, *Jobes* and *Requena,* both of which required the health care providers to comply with the request to terminate life-sustaining medical treatment and refused, as an alternative, to permit the patient to be transferred. The rationale for the similar holdings are different, but complementary. Mrs. Jobes had been in a persistent vegetative state in a nursing home for five years. Her husband and parents requested that the nursing home withdraw the feeding tube, but its management "refused on moral grounds."[403] The trial court concluded that the requisite decisionmaking standard for forgoing life-sustaining treatment from an incompetent patient had been met and therefore authorized the removal of the feeding tube under the supervision of a licensed physician. However, the court held that

---

**MA:** *In re* Doe, 583 N.E.2d 1263, 1270 n.17 (Mass. 1992) ("Medical personnel or Wrentham staff members who disagree with the withdrawal of the nasoduodenal feeding and hydration tube will not be required to care for Doe."): Brophy v. New Eng. Sinai Hosp., Inc., 497 N.E.2d 626 (court ordered hospital to assist guardian in transferring patient either to another facility or home to allow for withdrawal of artificial nutrition and hydration).

**NY:** Grace Plaza of Great Neck, Inc. v. Elbaum, 588 N.Y.S.2d 853, 858 (App. Div. 1992) ("A patient who wishes to abstain from life-saving medical treatment may have the right to do so, but has no right to force a physician to assist, actively or passively, in what the physician himself might regard as the equivalent of suicide."); Delio v. Westchester County Medical Ctr., 516 N.Y.S.2d 677, 693–94 (App. Div. 1987) ("The Medical Center should be directed to either assist in the discontinuance of treatment or to take whatever steps are reasonably necessary to assist in the conservatee's transfer to a suitable facility or to his home where his wishes may be effectuated.").

*See also* Council on Scientific Affairs & Council on Ethical & Judicial Affairs, *Persistent Vegetative State and the Decision to Withdraw or Withhold Life Support,* 263 JAMA 426, 429 (1990) (recommending transfer of patient to another physician).

[401] **CA:** Bouvia v. Superior Court (Glenchur), 225 Cal. Rptr. 297, 307 (Ct. App. 1986) (hospital ordered "forthwith to remove the nasogastric tube from petitioner"). *Cf.* Morrison v. Abramovice, 253 Cal. Rptr. 530 (conservator objected to transfer because of patient's condition, but court required it unless health care provider would voluntarily comply with request to forgo life-sustaining treatment, though suggesting that if transfer were unsafe for patient, it would not be required).

**GA:** State v. McAfee, 385 S.E.2d 651 (Ga. 1989) (requiring physicians to turn off ventilator and administer sedatives).

**NJ:** *In re* Jobes, 529 A.2d 434, 450 (N.J. 1987) ("[W]e recognize that our decision will be burdensome for some of the nursing home personnel. Nevertheless, in view of the immense hardship that would fall on Mrs. Jobes and her family if she were forced out of the nursing home, we are compelled to impose on it for her continued care."); *In re* Requena, 517 A.2d 869 (N.J. Super. Ct. App. Div. 1986).

[402] **GA:** Gray v. Romeo, 697 F. Supp. at 591 (if patient could not be "promptly transferred to a health care facility that will respect her wishes, the [hospital] must accede to her requests").

[403] *In re* Jobes, 529 A.2d 434.

the nursing home was entitled to refuse to participate in the withdrawal of the feeding tube and could keep Mrs. Jobes connected to it until she was transferred to another health care institution.

On appeal, the New Jersey Supreme Court reversed that portion of the trial court order permitting the nursing home to refuse to participate in the termination of life support. Its reason was that the patient's family had no notice at the time of admission to the nursing home that the nursing home had such a policy and consequently that by admitting her there they were "surrendering the right to choose among medical alternatives."[404] The court also observed that

> [t]he nursing home apparently did not inform Mrs. Jobes' family about its policy toward artificial feeding until May of 1985 when they requested that the j-tube be withdrawn. In fact there is no indication that this policy has ever been formalized,[405]

leaving the implication that the nursing home's "policy" might not have been a policy at all or might have been invented for the occasion.

The court refused to hold that if the nursing home had clearly adopted such a policy and given adequate notice of its existence in advance, it would be unenforceable. It instead confined itself to the facts presented and concluded that "in this case . . . it would be wrong to allow the nursing home to discharge Mrs. Jobes," in no small part because "it would be extremely difficult, perhaps impossible, to find another facility that would accept Mrs. Jobes as a patient." Consequently, if the court were "to allow the nursing home to discharge Mrs. Jobes if her family does not consent to continued artificial feeding[, it] would essentially frustrate Mrs. Jobes' right of self-determination."[406]

*Requena* is even more far-reaching because it was established on the record that another health care facility would accept transfer of the patient. In *Requena*, the patient was competent and dying of amyotrophic lateral sclerosis. She requested that artificial nutrition and hydration be withheld when she could no longer swallow and that she be allowed to die. This was not a hasty decision but one that she had contemplated for a long time. The hospital recognized the patient's right not to accept artificial nutrition and hydration but "assert[ed] a strong institutional policy against participating in the withholding of food or fluids from a patient."[407]

Although her physician did not oppose her decision to forgo tube-feeding and was willing to continue to attend her, as soon as she announced her intention, "the Hospital immediately responded that the decision conflicted with

---

[404] *Id.* at 450 (citing N.J. Stat. Ann. § 30:13-5(m) (nursing home residents may not be deprived of constitutional, civil, or legal rights solely by reason of their admission to a nursing home)).

[405] *Id.*

[406] *Id.*

[407] *In re* Requena, 517 A.2d 886, 887 (N.J. Super. Ct. Ch. Div.), *aff'd,* 517 A.2d 869 (N.J. Super. Ct. App. Div. 1986).

its 'pro-life' values."[408] Within two months, the hospital's board of trustees unanimously adopted a resolution stating:

> BE IT RESOLVED by the Board of Trustees that it does hereby reaffirm the policy of the former St. Clare's Hospital that food and water are basic human needs and that such fundamental care cannot be withheld from patients in the Medical Center and that neither the Medical Center nor personnel will participate in the withholding or withdrawal of artificial feeding and/or fluids.[409]

In an unusual move, the hospital asked the patient to leave, which she refused to do, and so brought suit to compel her to leave.

As adamant as the hospital was about evicting Mrs. Requena, she was equally adamant about not leaving. She refused to be transferred to another hospital located 17 miles away, which was somewhat less convenient for her family, "but this [was] not a significant factor because the family members will be able to make travel arrangements and will continue to visit Mrs. Requena frequently."[410] One of her doctors was on the staff of the other hospital and would continue to treat her. Transportation to the hospital would be safe, and it would provide at least equally high quality medical care. Further, the care she would receive "would be supportive and compassionate."[411] The reasons for Mrs. Requena's opposition were that:

> During her 17-month stay at the Hospital, she has received care which is both professionally good and personally compassionate. She has developed trust in and affection for the nurses, the respiratory technicians and the other staff members at the Hospital. She is familiar with the physical surroundings. It would be emotionally and psychologically upsetting to be forced to leave the Hospital. The removal would also have significant elements of rejection and casting out which would be burdensome for Mrs. Requena.[412]

The court acknowledged that requiring the petitioner-hospital to retain Mrs. Requena while she slowly died of the effects of lack of nutrition and hydration would impose serious burdens on the hospital and its employees. Despite the anguish that this would cause them—and that it seemingly caused the trial judge even to contemplate—he concluded that "[i]n the final analysis, it is fairer to ask them to give than it is to ask Beverly Requena to give" because "they are well and whole people. They have full and vibrant lives ahead of them."[413]

---

[408] 517 A.2d at 888.

[409] *Id.* 888–89.

[410] *Id.* at 889.

[411] *Id.*

[412] *Id.* at 893.

[413] *Id.*

If there is a defense to actions for unauthorized treatment (or for the failure to administer desired treatment) based on conscientious objection, it is not necessarily of the same scope for all potential participants in the end-of-life decision-making process. There are good reasons why the defense might be recognized for natural persons (for example, physicians, nurses, and nutrition therapists) but not for health care institutions. "Hospitals are corporations that have no natural personhood, and hence are incapable of having either 'moral' or 'ethical' objections' to actions. And hospitals don't practice medicine, physicians do."[414] On the other hand many health care institutions have a formal statement of their mission that might serve as a basis for their assertion that it is a violation of their conscientiously held beliefs for them to participate in forgoing life-sustaining treatment in general, but more likely in some particular manner (such as the forgoing of artificial nutrition and hydration).[415] There are also reasons for distinguishing private from public health care institutions. Although courts have not confronted this issue directly in the context of end-of-life decisionmaking, in the area of abortion, courts have been unwilling to require hospitals to provide abortions.[416]

As to nonemployee physicians, abandonment law, which seems to have developed with independent contractor/physicians in mind, would be applicable, and the physician would ordinarily satisfy his obligations by giving appropriate notice of termination of the relationship.[417] Such physicians have substantially more latitude within which to follow the dictates of conscience than health care professionals (physicians or nonphysicians) who are employees of hospitals, nursing homes, or other health care institutional providers, which usually cannot decline to attend to a patient even by giving notice.[418]

## Wrongful Discharge

In clinical practice, physicians sometimes write orders to terminate, withhold, or limit life-sustaining medical treatment (or to administer it), but it is other health

---

[414] See generally Annas, *Transferring the Ethical Hot Potato,* 17 Hastings Center Rep. No. 1, at 20, 21 (Feb. 1987).

[415] See generally Miles et al., *Conflicts Between Patients' Wishes to Forgo Treatment and the Policies of Health Care Facilities,* 321 New Eng. J. Med. 48 (1989).

[416] See Wardle, *Protecting the Rights of Conscience of Health Care Providers,* 14 J. Legal Med. 177 (1993); Dresser, *Freedom of Conscience, Professional Responsibility, and Access to Abortion,* 22 J. L., Med. & Ethics 280 (1994). *But see, e.g.,* Doe v. Mundy, 378 F. Supp. 731 (E.D. Wis. 1974) (public hospital); Doe v. Bridgeton Hosp. Ass'n, 403 A.2d 965 (N.J. Super. Ct. App. Div.), *certification denied,* 407 A.2d 1218 (N.J. 1979) (conscience law, which permits hospitals to withhold provision of abortion services or procedures, not applicable to nonsectarian, nonprofit hospitals).

[417] See § **17.14.**

[418] See generally Freedman, *Health Professions, Codes, and the Right to Refuse to Treat HIV-Infectious Patients,* 18 Hastings Center Rep. No. 2, at 20 (Apr.–May 1988).

care professionals (and sometimes other physicians, such as residents[419]) who must implement those orders. For the most part health care professionals have far less latitude in following their consciences than do physicians (or at least those physicians who are independent contractors).[420] There are a few reported cases in which nurses have sought to follow the dictates of their conscience (in some instances by administering treatment, in others by withholding or withdrawing it). In each, the nurse has been discharged and has sued for reinstatement on the ground that such discharge violated public policy.

In the first reported case[421] to raise this issue, *Warthen v. Toms River Community Memorial Hospital*,[422] a nurse was discharged because of her refusal to *administer* kidney dialysis to an incompetent patient. She claimed that she had "'moral, medical and philosophical objections'"[423] to administering dialysis "because the patient was terminally ill and, she contended, the procedure was causing the patient additional complications."[424] The attending physician told the nurse that "the patient's family wished him kept alive through dialysis and that he would not survive without it."[425] After repeated warnings that she would be dismissed if she did not comply, the nurse refused to do so and was discharged. She then sued the hospital, relying on the "public policy" exception to the employment at-will doctrine, claiming that the discharge was wrongful because it violated public policy as expressed in the American Nurses Association's Code for Nurses, a code of ethics.

The New Jersey Superior Court affirmed the grant of summary judgment in favor of the hospital. It recognized that an infraction of professional ethics could constitute a violation of public policy. However, it viewed the plaintiff's actions as neither compelled by the Code for Nurses nor, in fact, motivated by

---

[419] *See* Winkenwerder, *Ethical Dilemmas of the House Staff Physician—The Care of Critically Ill and Dying Patients,* 254 JAMA 3454, 3455 (1985) ("Little attention has been paid to the issue of whether residents are always bound to the decisions of their attending physicians, and whether it may ever be appropriate for residents to decline to participate in the life-sustaining care of patients on the basis of ethical grounds.").

[420] *See* Hastings Ctr., Guidelines on the Termination of Life-Sustaining Treatment and the Care of the Dying 32–33 (1987) (Part One (II)(8)(e)).

[421] *See* Gianelli, *Nurse Who Challenged MDs' Action Wins Case,* Am. Med. News, Sept. 9, 1988, at 10 (nurse who reported termination of tube-feeding by physicians, resulting in their prosecution in Barber v. Superior Court, 195 Cal. Rptr. 484 (Ct. App. 1983), awarded $114,000 damages for being forced to resign).

[422] 488 A.2d 229 (N.J. Super. Ct. App. Div. 1985).

[423] *Id.* at 230.

[424] **NJ:** Warthen v. Toms River Community Memorial Hosp., 488 A.2d at 230.

GA: *Accord In re* Doe, Civ. Action No. D-93064, slip op. at 8–9 (Super. Ct. Fulton County, Ga. Oct. 17, 1991) (Health care professionals believed that "the treatment they are providing . . . is inhumane and undignified. Some of the nurses . . . indicated that they had grave reservations about participating in a course of treatment that could be painful . . . with no hope of any real benefit to Jane."), *aff'd,* 418 S.E.2d 3 (Ga. 1992).

[425] Warthen v. Toms River Community Memorial Hosp., 488 A.2d at 230.

professional nursing ethics.[426] The court construed the provision of the Code cited by the plaintiff as requiring a nurse to preserve human dignity but "not . . . at the expense of the patient's life or contrary to the family's wishes."[427] The court seemed to view the plaintiff's conduct as *against* public policy, rather than in furtherance of it, because "[t]he position asserted by plaintiff serves only the individual and the nurses' profession while leaving the public to wonder when and whether they will receive nursing care."[428]

*Farnam v. CRISTA Ministries,* is similar in outcome to *Warthen,* though the facts are quite different. The plaintiff was a nurse employed by the defendant/nursing home. She objected to the fact that feeding tubes were sometimes (lawfully) removed from some of the nursing home residents and they were allowed to die. Consequently, she undertook several activities—sending a letter to the nursing home's board of trustees, speaking with the state's long-term care ombudsman, and contacting a newspaper, which resulted in a front-page article describing the nursing home "as having permitted 'death by starvation' "[429]—all of which were aimed at ending the nursing home's willingness to permit the forgoing of artificial nutrition and hydration because of her belief that it was inconsistent with the nursing home's (and her own) religious beliefs.

The nursing home's management eventually discharged the plaintiff. They testified that her work performance was deteriorating, which they attributed to her "spending too much time on the feeding tube controversy by organizing meetings, discussing it with others during business hours, and making personal phone calls"[430] but did not discharge her specifically on that basis. Rather, they discharged her after her nursing license expired and she was told to leave work until her new license arrived, but she considered herself discharged and did not return to work.

Like Warthen, Farnam sued claiming that she was wrongfully discharged in violation of public policy, but as set forth in the state's patient abuse reporting statute. The jury returned a verdict for $100,000 in her favor, which the trial court left standing on a judgment notwithstanding the verdict. On appeal, the Washington Supreme Court reversed.

The statute in question—the Washington patient abuse reporting statute—requires that

> any employee of a nursing home who has reasonable cause to believe that a nursing home patient has suffered abuse or neglect "shall report such incident, or cause a report to be made, to either a law enforcement agency or to the [Department of

---

[426] *Id.* at 234 (The plaintiff "makes no assertion that she ever referred to her obligations and entitlements pursuant to her code of ethics. In addition, the very basis for plaintiff's reliance on the Code for Nurses is that she was personally opposed to the dialysis procedure.").

[427] *Id.* at 233.

[428] *Id.* at 234.

[429] 807 P.2d 830, 832 (Wash. 1991).

[430] *Id.*

Social and Health Services]." . . . Failure to make a report is a misdemeanor, RCW 70.124.070, and it is an unfair practice under RCW 49.60 to dismiss an employee for reporting suspected abuse. RCW 70.124.060.[431]

Consequently, the court concluded that

Farnam twice, while still an employee at CRISTA, stated in writing that she believed CRISTA had the legal right to remove NG tubes. . . . A narrow public policy exception intended to protect employees who report employer wrongdoing should not be extended to an employee who has twice told her employer that she believed the actions taken were legally protected.[432]

In addition, the court affirmed for a reason similar to that in the *Warthen* case, namely, that the action was not undertaken by the employee to further the public good but to serve a personal interest of the employee.[433] Finally, the court rested its holding on the manner in which Farnham reported and tried to remedy the situation to which she objected. Voicing her objections to her employer and to the ombudsman were acceptable, but going to the media turned this into a public controversy "despite having acknowledged that she believed that CRISTA acted within the law."[434]

Another case of this kind, *Free v. Holy Cross Hospital,* was also unreceptive to a claim of wrongful discharge. Free, a nurse, was discharged because she refused to carry out a hospital administrator's order to evict a bedridden patient from the hospital, an order given because the patient had been arrested for possession of a handgun and which was opposed by the patient's attending physician.

Free brought suit claiming that the discharge violated the Illinois Right of Conscience Act, which expresses the public policy

to respect and protect the right of conscience of all persons who are engaged in, the delivery of medical services and medical care whether acting individually, corporately, or in association with other persons; and to prohibit all forms of discrimination, disqualification, coercion, disability or imposition of liability upon such persons or entities by reason of their refusing to act contrary to their conscience or conscientious convictions in refusing to obtain, receive, accept or deliver medical services and medical care.[435]

---

[431] *Id.* at 835.

[432] *Id.*

[433] *Id.* at 836 ("Farnam's . . . concern appears to be directed at urging Christian health care providers to adopt her view rather than furthering the public good.").

[434] *Id.*

[435] Free v. Holy Cross Hosp., 505 N.E.2d 1188, 1189–90 (Ill. App. Ct. 1987) (citing Ill. Rev. Stat. 1985, ch. 111 1/2, para. 5302).

According to the court, this statute is designed to apply to "morally controversial issues such as euthanasia, sterilization or abortion."[436] Nonetheless, the court affirmed the dismissal of this claim because Free did not allege that her discharge "would conflict with her moral convictions arising from what are traditionally characterized as religious beliefs."[437] Her own ethical concerns not arising from religious beliefs are not protected by the Act. This portion of the holding might be subject to challenge on equal protection grounds.[438]

## Legislative Treatment of Conscientious Objection

Most advance directive statutes have provisions recognizing the right of health care providers not to comply with a patient's instructions given in a living will[439] or the instructions of a surrogate appointed by a health care power of attorney.[440] The same is true of DNR statutes.[441] Not all require that the objection be based on conscience.[442] Some of these provisions apply only to physicians, others to all health care personnel, and still others also include institutional health care providers. If a health care provider wishes not to comply with a patient's or surrogate's wishes, "reasonable efforts" must first be made to transfer the

---

[436] **IL:** Free v. Holy Cross Hosp., 505 N.E.2d at 1190.

> **DRI:** *Accord* Gray v. Romeo, 697 F. Supp. 580, 589 (D.R.I. 1988) (state statute conferring on person associated with health care facility right on moral or religious grounds to refuse to participate in abortion or sterilization procedure limited to such procedures and does not apply to forgoing life-sustaining treatment; 42 U.S.C. § 300a-7(d), providing that "[n]o individual shall be required to perform or assist in the performance of any part of a health service program . . . funded in whole or in part under a program administered by the Secretary of Health and Human Services if his performance or assistance in the performance of such part of such program would be contrary to his religious beliefs or moral convictions" inapplicable because provision concerns individual's rights in connection with federally funded health service program or research activity).
>
> **NY:** *Accord* Elbaum v. Grace Plaza of Great Neck, Inc., 544 N.Y.S.2d 840, 847 (App. Div. 1989) (same).
>
> *See generally* Daar, *A Clash at the Bedside: Patient Autonomy v. A Physician's Professional Conscience,* 44 Hastings L.J. 1241, 1275 n.149 (1993) (collecting statutes); Durham et al., *Accommodation of Conscientious Objection to Abortion,* 1982 B.Y.U. L. Rev. 253.

[437] Free v. Holy Cross Hosp., 505 N.E.2d at 1190.

[438] *See* Welsh v. United States, 398 U.S. 333 (1970) (equal protection permits conscientious objection from military service for strongly held moral beliefs not of a formal religious origin).

[439] See § **11.18.**

[440] See § **12.46.**

[441] See § **9.21.**

[442] *See, e.g.,* Ind. Code Ann. § 16-36-4-13(f) ("If the attending physician, after reasonable investigation, finds no other physician willing to honor the patient's declaration, the attending physician may refuse to withhold or withdraw life prolonging procedures.").

patient to a willing health care provider. Only if that is not possible can the instructions be ignored with impunity. It is not clear if these provisions also apply to advance directives not made pursuant to statute (such as oral advance directives or nonstatutory advance directives) or to the instructions given by a surrogate not appointed by a health care power of attorney.[443] The federal Patient Self-Determination Act also contains a provision dealing with conscientious objection. The Act states that it is not to be construed to require the implementation of an advance directive by "any health care provider or any agent of such provider" if state law permits an objection to doing so as "a matter of conscience."[444]

## § 17.24  Immunity

The fear of liability has probably been the single most important factor in precipitating recourse to the courts in right-to-die cases.[445] Although a serious concern and despite the considerable number of attempts to impose civil liability for damages, no health care professional or institution has yet been held liable in damages for administering or forgoing life-sustaining treatment without authorization (though a few have been found liable for attorneys' fees[446]). There is only one reported case in which a criminal prosecution of physicians has

---

[443] See §§ 10.11 and 10.13.

[444] 42 U.S.C.A. § 1396a(w)(3) (West. Supp. 1994). See § 10.21.

[445] **DIN:** *See, e.g.,* Fort Wayne Journal-Gazette v. Baker, 788 F. Supp. 379 (N.D. Ind. 1992).

**DNY:** *See, e.g.,* Deel v. Syracuse Veterans Admin. Medical Ctr., 729 F. Supp. 231 (N.D.N.Y. 1990).

**DRI:** *See, e.g.,* Gray v. Romeo, 697 F. Supp. 580 (D.R.I. 1988).

**CA:** *See, e.g.,* McMahon v. Lopez, 245 Cal. Rptr. 172 (Ct. App. 1988); Bartling v. Superior Court, 209 Cal. Rptr. 220, 226 (Ct. App. 1984).

**DE:** *See, e.g., In re* Severns, 425 A.2d 156, 160 (Del. Ch. 1980).

**FL:** *See, e.g.,* Corbett v. D'Alessandro, 487 So. 2d 368, 370 (Fla. Dist. Ct. App. 1986); St. Mary's Hosp. v. Ramsey, 465 So. 2d 666, 668 (Fla. Dist. Ct. App. 1985); Satz v. Perlmutter, 362 So. 2d 160, 163 (Fla. Dist. Ct. App. 1978).

**IN:** *Cf. In re* Lawrance, 579 N.E.2d 32 (Ind. 1991) (nursing home took no position as to proper outcome, but felt it could be subject to federal and state regulatory violations if it permitted forgoing artificial nutrition and hydration, even if family and physicians were in agreement).

**KY:** *See, e.g.,* DeGrella v. Elston, 858 S.W.2d 698, 701 (Ky. 1993).

**NJ:** *See, e.g., In re* Farrell, 529 A.2d 404, 415 (N.J. 1987); *In re* Quinlan, 355 A.2d 647, 669 (N.J. 1976).

**NY:** *See, e.g., In re* Storar, 420 N.E.2d 64, 69 n.3 (N.Y. 1981).

[446] See § 17.26.

progressed as far as the indictment stage, and it was terminated in favor of the defendant/physicians.[447]

It is axiomatic that if there is a legal right to forgo life-sustaining treatment in a particular case, the exercise of which leads to death, there can be no legal liability, either criminal or civil, accruing to participants in the decisionmaking process.[448] However, for there to be immunity from liability, it is essential that there be a right to forgo life-sustaining treatment in the case in question. Because the courts generally do not insist on an adjudication of the issue prior to the forgoing of treatment,[449] health care professionals necessarily subject themselves to some risk of liability for decisionmaking about life-sustaining treatment in the absence of a court order permitting the forgoing or administration of treatment.

However, even with a court order there is no *absolute* immunity from liability. Although it is sometimes said that judicial review insulates the participants from civil and criminal liability,[450] at best judicial review provides immunity for withholding or administering treatment in *good faith* and with *reasonable care,*[451] even if "a health-care professional's assessment . . . proves to be

---

[447] **CA:** *See* Barber v. Superior Court, 195 Cal. Rptr. 484 (Ct. App. 1983). *See also* McMahon v. Lopez, 245 Cal. Rptr. 172 (Ct. App. 1988).

**NY:** *Compare* Grace Plaza of Great Neck, Inc. v. Elbaum, 588 N.Y.S.2d 853 (App. Div. 1992) (suggesting criminal liability for forgoing life-sustaining treatment without court order) (dictum) *with id.* (Rosenblatt, J., dissenting) (claiming that majority misreads New York precedents).

[448] **CA:** Thor v. Superior Court, 855 P.2d 375, 383 (Cal. 1993) ("The competent adult patient's 'informed refusal' supersedes and discharges the obligation to render further treatment.").

**ME:** *In re* Gardner, 534 A.2d 947, 956 (Me. 1987) ("The [trial] court's ruling that Gardner is entitled to have his own personal decision to refuse life-sustaining procedures carried out in his present condition precludes a finding that anyone who assists the discontinuation of those procedures in a responsible and humane manner could be guilty of either a criminal offense or a breach of due care or professional responsibility,") (citing *In re* Storar, 420 N.E.2d at 71).

[449] *See, e.g., In re* Storar, 420 N.E.2d at 74 ("[I]t is inappropriate for those charged with the care of incompetent persons to apply to the courts for a ruling on the propriety of conduct which might seriously affect their charges. We emphasize, however, that any such procedure is optional."). See § **5.26.**

[450] **NY:** Grace Plaza of Great Neck, Inc. v. Elbaum, 588 N.Y.S.2d 853.

**OH:** Estate of Leach v. Shapiro, 469 N.E.2d 1047, 1052–53 (Ohio Ct. App. 1984).

[451] **CA:** Bouvia v. Superior Court (Glenchur), 225 Cal. Rptr. 297 (Ct. App. 1986) ("No criminal or civil liability attaches to honoring a competent, informed patient's refusal of medical service. We do not purport to establish what will constitute proper medical practice in all other cases or even other aspects of the care to be provided petitioner.") (citing Bartling v. Superior Court, 209 Cal. Rptr. 220 (Ct. App. 1984); Barber v. Superior Court, 195 Cal. Rptr. 484).

**FL:** *In re* Dubreuil, 629 So. 2d 819, 823–24 (Fla. 1993) ("When a health care provider, acting in good faith, follows the wishes of a competent and informed patient to refuse medical treatment, the health care provider is acting appropriately and cannot be subjected to civil or criminal liability.").

wrong."[452] Although courts have not addressed what good faith means in this context, a Florida court explained that a surrogate acts in good faith in making a decision for an incompetent patient if "the decision was made with honesty of intention and in an honest effort to make the decision which the patient, if competent, would make."[453]

In *Thor v. Superior Court,* the California Supreme Court stated that "[w]hen a competent, informed adult directs the withholding or withdrawal of medical treatment, even at the risk of hastening or causing death, medical professionals who respect that determination will not incur criminal or civil liability: the patient's decision discharges the physician's duty."[454] But clearly this is a generalization that, while true in principle, is highly dependent on the facts of particular cases. There is no doubt that if a patient gives informed consent for treatment to be forgone, liability cannot attach to the physician who honors the decision exercising that right. Indeed, there can be liability for *failure* to honor the right, and a physician might have an affirmative obligation to assist the patient in the exercise of the right.[455] The same is true in principle about decisionmaking for incompetent patients, but the potential pitfalls are more numerous. Not only can liability crop up in obtaining informed consent from the surrogate, there are also possibilities for liability in connection with determining whether the patient is incompetent, whether the person acting as surrogate is

---

**NJ:** *In re* Jobes, 529 A.2d 434, 447 (N.J. 1987); *In re* Farrell, 529 A.2d 404, 416 (N.J. 1987) ("[N]o civil or criminal liability will be incurred by any person who, in good faith reliance on the procedures established in this opinion, withdraws life-sustaining treatment at the request of an informed and competent patient who has undergone the required independent medical examination described above."); *In re* Conroy, 486 A.2d 1209, 1242 (N.J. 1985) ("In the absence of bad faith, no participant in the decision-making process shall be civilly or criminally liable for actions taken in accordance with the procedures set forth in this opinion."). *Cf. In re* Quinlan, 355 A.2d 647 (N.J. 1976) (providing complete civil and criminal immunity for guardians, physicians, hospitals, and others).

See §§ **9.26, 10.15, 11.17,** and **12.46.**

[452] *In re* Jobes, 529 A.2d at 447–49.

[453] Browning v. Herbert, 543 So. 2d 258, 274 (Fla. Dist. Ct. App. 1989).

[454] **CA:** Thor v. Superior Court, 855 P.2d 375, 386 (Cal. 1993). *Accord* Bartling v. Superior Court, 209 Cal. Rptr. 220 (Ct. App. 1984); Barber v. Superior Court, 195 Cal. Rptr. 484 (Ct. App. 1983).

**FL:** *Accord In re* Dubreuil, 629 So. 2d 819, 823 (Fla. 1993) (health care provider, acting in good faith and following wishes of competent patient immune from civil or criminal liability).

**GA:** *Accord* Kirby v. Spivey, 307 S.E.2d 538, 540 (Ga. Ct. App. 1983).

**ME:** *Accord In re* Gardner, 534 A.2d 947, 956 (Me. 1987).

**MA:** *Accord* Superintendent of Belchertown State Sch. v. Saikewicz, 370 N.E.2d 417, 427 n.12 (Mass. 1977).

**NV:** *Accord* McKay v. Bergstedt, 801 P.2d 617, 630 (Nev. 1990).

**NJ:** *Accord In re* Farrell, 529 A.2d 404, 415–16 (N.J. 1987).

[455] **GA:** *See, e.g.,* State v. McAfee, 385 S.E.2d 651 (Ga. 1989) (requiring administration of sedative and analgesic medication to patient from whom ventilatory support would be forgone).

legally qualified to do so, and what the patient's actual or probable wishes about treatment are.

There would be no immunity even if a court order were issued permitting the administration or forgoing of life-sustaining treatment, for example, if a physician were negligent in any one of a number of central issues such as making adequate disclosure to a competent patient or to a surrogate, assessing a patient's decisionmaking capacity, determining the patient's wishes, and making a proper diagnosis and prognosis on which the court order was based. The Kentucky Supreme Court has correctly summed up the matter of immunity this way:

> Future criminal sanctions or civil liability turn not on the existence or absence of a court order, but on the facts of the case. . . . No liability attaches to a decision to refuse or withdraw treatment in a case of this nature once the necessary facts are established and carefully documented by the parties involved.[456]

Almost 10 years earlier, the Florida Supreme Court issued a similar ruling that "court approval to terminate extraordinary life support systems was not necessary in this type of case in order to relieve the consenting family members, the attending physicians, and the hospital and its administrators of civil and criminal liability. . . . To be relieved of potential civil and criminal liability," the court held, "guardians, consenting family members, physicians, hospitals, or their administrators need only act in good faith."[457] At best, a physician has a qualified immunity without a court order, but the same is true even if there is a court order.

Immunity from liability can also be conferred by advance directive[458] or surrogate decisionmaking statutes,[459] but this immunity is of the same qualified type as common-law immunity or immunity specifically conferred by a court order. It is likely that immunity conferred by an advance directive statute applies to decisions made pursuant to an advance directive.[460] The immunity conferred by an advance directive statute might apply to nonstatutory advance directives because the statutes generally provide that an advance directive "substantially" in the statutory form complies with the act and thereby acquires immunity. However, it is uncertain how much an advance directive may deviate from the statutory form and still clothe the physician with statutory immunity.[461]

---

[456] **KY:** DeGrella v. Elston, 858 S.W.2d 698, 710 (Ky. 1993).

> **NY:** *Accord In re* Storar, 420 N.E.2d 64, 71 (N.Y. 1981) ("A State which imposes civil liability on a doctor if he violates the patient's right [to decline treatment] cannot also hold him criminally responsible if he respects that right.").

[457] John F. Kennedy Memorial Hosp. v. Bludworth, 452 So. 2d 921, 922, 926 (Fla. 1984).

[458] See §§ **11.15** and **12.46–12.47.**

[459] *See In re* Lawrance, 579 N.E.2d 32, 43 (Ind. 1991). See **Ch. 14.**

[460] See §§ **10.10–10.15.**

[461] See § **10.15.**

## § 17.25  Damages

The law of torts recognizes that "one injured by the tort of another is entitled to recover damages from the other for all harm, past, present and prospective, legally caused by the tort."[462] In lawsuits based on a tort theory, the term *injury* refers to the invasion of a legally protected interest;[463] *harm,* to the loss or detriment suffered by the victim from such an invasion;[464] and *damages,* to the money that may be recovered by the victim from the person legally responsible for the injury.[465] This section deals only with the special issues of damages raised by end-of-life decisionmaking.[466] The full range of issues raised under the aegis of damages is broad enough to require a treatise of its own.[467] Because of paucity of lawsuits arising out of end-of-life decisionmaking and their general lack of success, the law on damages is almost nonexistent.

### Nature of the Causes of Action

**Deceased Patient.**  In the first place, the distinction between survival and wrongful death actions must be noted. End-of-life decisionmaking can give rise to either or both. In a survival action, the basis for the action is injury to the patient while the patient is alive. Under a wrongful death theory, the action is for injury to others occasioned by the patient's death, and consequently under wrongful death statutes, the plaintiffs must have been individuals who were financially dependent on the deceased in a manner specified by the statute. If the plaintiff is related in the manner required by statute, the plaintiff must show that he actually was dependent on the deceased or at least had an expectation of support. The fact that the deceased patient had no earning capacity is not determinative; the loss of retirement benefits may serve as a measure of damages.[468]

In both survival and wrongful death actions, the damages that may be recovered are limited respectively by the statute that provides for the survival of the cause of action or that creates the cause of action for wrongful death. A survival action is intended to compensate the decedent's estate for the harm done

---

[462] Restatement (Second) of Torts § 910 (1979).

[463] *Id.* § 7(1) (1965).

[464] *Id.* § 7(2).

[465] *Id.* § 12A.

[466] *See generally* Gasner, *Financial Penalties for Failing to Honor Patient Wishes to Refuse Treatment,* 11 St. Louis U. Pub. L. Rev. 499 (1992); Miller, *Right-to-Die Damage Actions: Developments in the Law,* 65 Denv. U. L. Rev. 181 (1988); Oddi, *The Tort of Interference with the Right to Die,* 75 Geo. L.J. 625 (1986).

[467] *See generally* E. Martin, Personal Injury Damages Law and Practice (1990); J. Stein, Stein on Personal Injury Damages (2d ed. 1991).

[468] 2 J. Stein, Stein on Personal Injury Damages 259–62 (2d ed. 1991).

by the termination of the decedent's life.[469] Typical damages include the medical expenses incurred prior to the decedent's death, pain and suffering experienced by the decedent as a result of the death-creating injury, and lost past and future earnings.[470] Some states do not permit the recovery of damages for pain and suffering in a survival action.[471] The damages available in a wrongful death action include the medical expenses paid by the beneficiaries of the decedent, the loss of the decedent's financial support, and the loss of the decedent's companionship and services.[472]

**Living Patient.**   If the patient is still alive, of course neither a survival action nor a wrongful death action is available, but the underlying tort theories may still be prosecuted, especially those involving injury to the *patient*. Third parties who would be entitled to bring a wrongful death action if the patient had died (and possibly others) might also have an action for their injuries, primarily under a theory of intentional infliction of emotional distress.[473]

## Elements of Damages

In end-of-life decisionmaking cases, patients who are capable of experiencing suffering may recover damages if the other elements of the cause of action can be established. When the patient is competent and either receives nonconsensual treatment or has treatment withheld or withdrawn that causes actual harm, damages are theoretically recoverable. However, in fact, damages can be difficult to establish. Under intentional tort theories, the patient is also entitled to collect damages for the dignitary harm of being treated without consent, but the damages awarded in such situations are usually nominal.[474] Recovery of damages for dignitary harms based on a negligence theory is ordinarily not possible. For example, in an action for failure to make adequate disclosure to a

---

[469] E. Martin, Personal Injury Damages Law and Practice 154 (1990).

[470] *Id.* at 153–57.

[471] **CA:** *See, e.g.,* Bartling v. Glendale Adventist Medical Ctr., 229 Cal. Rptr. 360, 361, 364 (Ct. App. 1986).

**DC:** *See, e.g., In re* A.C., 573 A.2d 1235, 1242 (D.C. 1990).

**NJ:** *See, e.g.,* Strachan v. John F. Kennedy Memorial Hosp., 538 A.2d 346, 352 (N.J. 1988).

**OH:** *See, e.g.,* Estate of Leach v. Shapiro, 469 N.E.2d 1047, 1052 (Ohio Ct. App. 1984).

**WA:** *See, e.g.,* Strickland v. Deaconess Hosp., 735 P.2d 74 (Wash. Ct. App. 1987).

*See generally* 2 J. Stein, Stein on Personal Injury Damages 390 (2d ed. 1991); Miller, *Right-to-Die Damage Actions: Developments in the Law,* 65 Denv. U. L. Rev. 181, 210–12 (1988); Feld, Annotation, *Survivability of Civil Rights Cause of Action Based on 42 U.S.C. § 1983,* 42 A.L.R. Fed. 163 (1979).

[472] E. Martin, Personal Injury Damages Law and Practice 147–53 (1990).

[473] See §§ **17.5–17.8.**

[474] W.P. Keeton et al., Prosser and Keeton on the Law of Torts § 9, at 40 (5th ed. 1984).

patient (or surrogate), even if inadequate disclosure can be established, there is no liability for the mere failure to disclose.[475] Damages are not available unless the plaintiff can establish that he suffered bodily injury as a result of the inadequate disclosure.[476]

**Economic Loss.** Economic loss is possible in end-of-life cases. However, in most, the patient is no longer working and therefore does not experience any lost income either from the shortening of life from the nonconsensual forgoing of treatment or from the prolongation of hospitalization resulting from the non-consensual administration of treatment. The most likely element of damages in end-of-life cases is added medical expenses from the prolongation of hospitalization from the administration of unwanted treatment.

**Pain and Suffering.** Recovery for pain and suffering can also be difficult to establish. In many cases the patient is unable to experience anything, including pain or suffering. Courts have generally held that for a patient to be awarded damages for pain and suffering, the pain and suffering must be consciously experienced by the patient,[477] but courts seem willing to allow awards of damages to stand on even the slimmest thread of evidence.[478] In many end-of-life cases, even if the patient is able to consciously experience pain or suffering, because the patient is so seriously injured or ill, the actual harms and detriments suffered are often nonexistent or de minimis, regardless of the defendant's conduct in wrongfully providing or forgoing treatment.[479]

Despite the fact that patients in a persistent vegetative state are incapable of experiencing anything, some courts have awarded damages to patients in this condition for pain and suffering.[480] None of these cases, however, are end-of-life decisionmaking cases. In each, the defendant's negligent conduct was the cause

---

[475] Meisel, *A "Dignitary Tort" as a Bridge Between the Idea of Informed Consent and the Law of Informed Consent,* 16 Law, Med. & Health Care 210 (1988).

[476] **CA10:** Johnson v. Thompson, 971 F.2d 1487, 1499 (10th Cir. 1992).

   **WA:** Benoy v. Simons, 831 P.2d 167 (Wash. 1992).

[477] Leebron, *Final Moments: Damages for Pain and Suffering Prior to Death,* 64 N.Y.U. L. Rev. 256, 267 n.50 (1989); E. Martin, Personal Injury Damages Law and Practice 155 (1990); 2 J. Stein, Stein on Personal Injury Damages 391–92 (2d ed. 1991).

[478] Leebron, *Final Moments: Damages for Pain and Suffering Prior to Death,* 64 N.Y.U. L. Rev. 256, 267 n.50 (1989) (if patients are unable to feel external stimuli, their mental processes may continue in a way that their thoughts make them aware of their impending death).

[479] Oddi, *The Tort of Interference with the Right to Die,* 75 Geo. L.J. 625, 637 *et seq.* (1986) (arguing that this requires creation of a new cause of action for "wrongful living"); Sharp & Crofts, *Death with Dignity—The Physician's Civil Liability,* 27 Baylor L. Rev. 86, 104 (1975) ("In most situations, the terminal patient will not have much earning potential and the pecuniary loss to his statutory beneficiaries would be minimal.").

[480] **KS:** *See, e.g.,* Gregory v. Carey, 791 P.2d 1329, 1336 (Kan. 1990) (loss of enjoyment of life is an element of disability, pain, and suffering that may be awarded to a plaintiff in a persistent vegetative state).

of the patient's persistent vegetative state. This probably makes no difference in fact as to whether the patient consciously experiences pain and suffering. Probably because of the defendant's wrongdoing, courts seem inclined to uphold juries' findings of conscious pain and suffering in these cases. These awards have been sustained on the "smallest amount of evidence of pain."[481] In some cases, "the tort victim's moans, groans, cries, or other sounds, or responses to external stimuli, or the testimony of a priest that the decedent responded to him when he administered the last rites have been held sufficient to sustain an award for conscious pain and suffering."[482]

There do not appear to be any cases in which recovery for pain and suffering has been sustained for patients whose persistent vegetative state was not caused by the defendant's negligence, and in the typical situation in end-of-life decisionmaking case, the defendant's conduct was not the cause of the persistent vegetative state. In the *Leach* case, the Ohio Court of Appeals recognized a cause of action involving a patient in a persistent vegetative state, but on remand, the case was settled and there were no further reported proceedings.[483] Consequently, *Leach* provides no conclusive decision as to whether damages for pain and suffering would be available to a patient in a persistent vegetative state not caused by the defendant/physician. It is likely that juries and courts will be less favorably inclined toward recovery for pain and suffering from the wrongful administration or forgoing of treatment than they are when the defendant's wrongful conduct is the cause of the patient being in a persistent vegetative state.

The difficulty in obtaining damages in end-of-life cases under existing tort theories has led to the proposal for the creation of a new cause of action termed "wrongful living" or "wrongful prolongation of life."[484]

## § 17.26   Attorneys' Fees

Litigating right-to-die cases can be expensive. One estimate is that in New York the cost of an uncontested hearing to determine whether there is clear and convincing evidence of the patient's wish to have life support terminated ranges

---

NY: *See, e.g.,* McDonald v. Garber, 563 N.E.2d 372 (N.Y. 1989) (allowing recovery for pain and suffering to patient in persistent vegetative state); Walsh v. Staten Island Obstetrics & Gynecology Assocs., P.C., 598 N.Y.S.2d 17, 19 (App. Div. 1993) (infant plaintiff in malpractice action "who cried when he received a painful stimuli, and smiled and laughed at pleasurable stimuli," although in a vegetative state, "clearly had some level of awareness").

PA: *See, e.g.,* Wagner v. York Hosp., 608 A.2d 496 (Pa. Super. Ct. 1992) (rejecting evidence that patient in persistent vegetative state had absolutely no awareness of his surroundings).

[481] 2 J. Stein, Stein on Personal Injury Damages 393 (2d ed. 1991).

[482] *Id.* at 393–94.

[483] Miller, *Right-to-Die Damage Actions: Developments in the Law,* 65 Denv. U. L. Rev. 181, 189 (1988) (reporting settlement for $50,000).

[484] See § **17.17.**

from $10,000 to $40,000.[485] Even in jurisdictions in which fees might be far less for the simple appointment of a guardian, they can still create a serious burden for some. In a contested case, the fees can be daunting if one is compelled to pursue litigation through one or more appellate courts. Consequently, there is a strong incentive on the part of petitioners to also try to obtain attorneys' fees.

However, the well-accepted general rule in the United States is that attorneys' fees cannot be recovered by either party in litigation. There are several exceptions to this general rule. The private attorney general doctrine allows a plaintiff's attorney in state-court litigation to recover reasonable fees when, as a result of the attorney's efforts, "constitutional rights of societal importance are protected to the benefit of a large number of people."[486]

### Federal Civil Rights Act (42 U.S.C. § 1988)

Barring specific statutory authority, the private attorney general doctrine does not lie within the equitable powers of the federal courts. However, specific statutory authority has been provided by Congress in civil rights cases.[487] The original Civil Rights Act of 1866 provides, in relevant part, that,

> [i]n any action or proceeding to enforce a provision of sections 1981, 1982, 1983, 1985, and 1986 of this title, . . . the court, in its discretion, may allow the prevailing party, other than the United States, a reasonable attorney's fee as part of the costs.[488]

Litigants in a number of treatment refusal cases have sought to recover attorneys' fees under this provision. Most have been unsuccessful for the simple reason that they were unsuccessful—that is, they were not a "prevailing party"—in the underlying civil rights litigation.[489] Another substantial barrier to obtaining an award of attorneys' fees under § 1988 is that in the underlying action, the defendant must have been acting under color of state law if the claim is brought under 42 U.S.C. § 1983 or there must have been a conspiracy to deny plaintiff of his civil rights if brought under § 1985(3).[490] For plaintiffs in many right-to-die cases, this will prove to be an insurmountable barrier.

---

[485] **DRI:** *See* Gray v. Romeo, 709 F. Supp. 325 (D.R.I. 1989).

Gasner, *Financial Penalties for Failing to Honor Patient Wishes to Refuse Treatment,* 11 St. Louis U. Pub. L. Rev. 499, 515 (1992).

[486] 7 Am. Jur. 2d *Attorneys at Law* § 238 (1980).

[487] National Lawyers Guild Civil Liberties Comm., Civil Rights Litigation and Attorney Fees Annual Handbook (1993); Tenth Annual Section 1983 Civil Rights Litigation and Attorneys' Fees: Current Developments (PLI Litig. & Admin. Practice Course Handbook Series No. H-485, 1993).

[488] 42 U.S.C.A. § 1988 (West 1981 & Supp. 1994).

[489] **DGA:** *See, e.g.,* Novak v. Cobb County-Kennestone Hosp. Auth., 849 F. Supp. 1559 (N.D. Ga. 1994).

**CA:** *See, e.g.,* McMahon v. Lopez, 245 Cal. Rptr. 172 (Ct. App. 1988); Bouvia v. County of L.A., 241 Cal. Rptr. 239 (Ct. App. 1987).

[490] See § **17.20.**

However, in a small number of right-to-die cases, courts have granted attorneys' fees to prevailing parties. For example, in *Hoffmeister v. Coler*,[491] the court held that the appellants had prevailed in the underlying litigation and thus were entitled to attorneys' fees under § 1988. In the underlying litigation, the plaintiffs had brought a § 1983 civil rights action to obtain an injunction to prevent the discharge of the patient—who suffered from Alzheimer's disease—from a long-term care facility. The facility threatened to discharge him on the basis of a policy letter of the state Department of Health and Rehabilitative Services requiring discharge if a physician or a family member refused to permit forced feeding. The plaintiffs brought suit to prevent discharge on this basis, and while the litigation was pending the state revised the rule on forced feeding of patients. Based on the new rule, the parties entered into a stipulation for entry of a final declaratory judgment, which prohibited the patient's discharge for refusing forced feedings.

Thereafter, plaintiffs sought to tax costs to the defendants and to recover attorneys' fees under § 1988. The trial court denied the motion, but the appellate court reversed on the basis of *Texas State Teachers Association v. Garland Independent School District*,[492] which permits a party to recover attorneys' fees on the basis of the "any significant issue" standard. This standard permits a party to recover attorneys' fees if the "party succeed[ed] on a significant issue and receive[d] some of the relief sought in the lawsuit."[493] The court found that the plaintiffs did prevail on a "significant issue" because under the stipulation the patient could not be force-fed.

Similarly, in *McMahon v. Lopez*,[494] the patient's family obtained a preliminary injunction directing that an order be written to remove a feeding tube. The order was stayed to allow for an appeal, during which time the patient died. The court held that the plaintiffs were prevailing parties within the meaning of § 1988 because of the issuance of the preliminary injunction. The trial court nevertheless denied an award of attorneys' fees because it found special circumstances, namely, that "'all defendants acted with the intent and purpose of complying with the law.'"[495]

This denial was reversed on appeal. While recognizing that § 1988 confers discretion on a trial court in deciding whether to award attorneys' fees to a prevailing party, "that discretion is narrowly limited."[496] An award of attorneys' fees should ordinarily be made "'unless special circumstances would render such an award unjust.'"[497] The court held that there was no showing of such

---

[491] 544 So. 2d 1067 (Fla. Dist. Ct. App. 1989).

[492] 489 U.S. 782 (1989).

[493] 489 U.S. at 784.

[494] 245 Cal. Rptr. 172 (Ct. App. 1988).

[495] *Id.* at 176 (quoting trial court opinion).

[496] *Id.* (citing Bonnes v. Long, 599 F.2d 1316, 1318 (4th Cir. 1979)).

[497] *Id.* at 176 (quoting Newman v. Piggie Park Enters., Inc., 390 U.S. 400, 402 (1968)).

special circumstances in this case. However, it affirmed the trial court's denial of an award of attorneys' fees on the ground that the defendants were not acting under color of state law.[498]

*Gray v. Romeo*[499] also awarded attorneys' fees to a party who had prevailed in litigation to have a feeding tube removed from a patient in a persistent vegetative state.[500] The court rejected the defendant's contention that fees were not available because the underlying litigation was a declaratory judgment action because "'Section 1988 makes no distinction between actions for damages and suits for equitable relief.'"[501] The only requirement for recovery was that the plaintiff be a prevailing party, which he was because, "in a declaratory judgment action: if the defendant, under pressure of the lawsuit, alters his conduct (or threatened conduct) towards the plaintiff that was the basis for the suit, the plaintiff will have prevailed."[502] The court also addressed the criteria for determining the amount of the award. It disallowed a substantial portion of the plaintiff's claim—such as charges for telephone calls to reporters and to attorneys from the Society for the Right to Die—on the ground that the charges were only "tangentially related to representation" of the plaintiff. The calls to reporters were disallowed because defendants are not obligated to compensate a plaintiff for "the cost of generating publicity," and the calls to attorneys because they were an "educational expense."[503]

## Equal Access to Justice Act

The other federal statute that has been used to seek an award of attorneys' fees in a right-to-die case is the Equal Access to Justice Act,[504] which in relevant part provides that

> [e]xcept as otherwise specifically prohibited by statute, a court shall award to a prevailing party other than the United States fees and other expenses . . . incurred by that party in any civil action (other than cases in tort) . . . brought by or against the United States in any court having jurisdiction of that action, unless that court finds that the position of the United States was substantially justified or that special circumstances make an award unjust.[505]

---

[498] See § **17.20.**

[499] 709 F. Supp. 325 (D.R.I. 1989).

[500] *See* Gray v. Romeo, 697 F. Supp. 580 (D.R.I. 1988).

[501] 709 F. Supp. at 326–27 (quoting Blanchard v. Bergeron, 489 U.S. 87, 95 (1989)).

[502] *Id.* at 326.

[503] *Id.* at 327.

[504] 28 U.S.C.A. § 2412 (West 1978 & Supp. 1994).

[505] *Id.* § 2412(d)(1)(A) (West 1978 & Supp. 1994).

An important limitation of this statute is that the underlying action must have been brought against the United States, so that it is likely to be inapplicable in most right-to-die cases.

In *Foster v. Tourtellotte,* the plaintiff, a patient in a Veterans Administration hospital, obtained an injunction from the federal district court ordering that the respirator being used to sustain his life be disconnected. The trial court denied a fee award on the basis that the government's position was both substantially justified and that the special circumstances of the case made an award unjust.[506] The court of appeals affirmed on the ground that the government's position was substantially justified and therefore did not reach the issue of special circumstances. The appeals court applied a reasonableness test and found that because there was no absolute right to refuse lifesaving treatment, and that even if a conditional right to refuse treatment was assumed to exist, the specific fact situation—that the patient had equivocated in the past and several of members of his family opposed the termination of treatment—made it reasonable for the government to seek judicial guidance before allowing for the termination of life-sustaining medical treatment.[507]

In addition, the government feared that acquiescing in the patient's decision would give rise to criminal liability for assisting suicide and to civil liability for wrongful death because the doctors felt that the medication the patient requested might contribute to his death. The court concluded that this was a reasonable fear on the part of the federal officers because the local district attorney refused to grant a declination of prosecution and because there was no state or federal precedent on the issue of civil or criminal liability under such circumstances.[508]

It is unlikely given the substantial aggregation of case law that has arisen on these issues since the underlying facts in *Foster* (which occurred in 1981) that this basis for denying an award of attorneys' fees would still carry any weight.

## State Law

Some states permit prevailing litigants to recover attorneys' fees if they are acting as a "private attorney general," that is, acting to vindicate an important *public* interest. This is an exception to the "general rule that each party must bear its own attorney fees":

> The doctrine ... rests upon the recognition that privately initiated lawsuits are often essential to the effectuation of fundamental public policies embodied in constitutional or statutory provisions, and that, without some mechanism authorizing the award of fees, private actions to enforce such important policies will, as a practical matter, frequently be infeasible.[509]

---

[506] **CA9:** 704 F.2d 1109, 1111 (9th Cir. 1983).

[507] *Id.* at 1112.

[508] *Id.* at 1112–13. See §§ **9.38** and **18.18.**

[509] **CA:** Bouvia v. County of L.A., 241 Cal. Rptr. 239, 243 (Ct. App. 1987).

In the underlying litigation in the *Bouvia* case,[510] the petitioner was a competent patient who was being force-fed against her will. She brought an action for a preliminary injunction to have the feedings stopped, and when it was denied, she obtained a writ of mandamus from the appellate court ordering the trial court to issue the injunction. Thereafter, she brought an action to recover attorneys' fees, arising from the underlying proceedings, under 42 U.S.C. § 1988 and under the California private attorney general statute.

The application under § 1988 was denied because there was no showing of a government policy or custom required for the underlying 42 U.S.C. § 1983 claim.[511] However, the appellate court held that although its previous decision on the merits reiterated principles articulated in previous California cases[512]— specifically "the absolute right of every competent and informed adult patient, regardless of age, prognosis, or motive, to refuse any medical treatment"[513]— the vindication of existing rights was an important public good because "the declaration of rights in so-called 'landmark' cases would have little, if any, importance if those rights could not be enforced in subsequent litigation."[514] In addition, the court determined that the underlying litigation also went further than the existing precedents "in allaying some apprehensions concerning a doctor's civil liability in acceding to a patient's wishes."[515] Based on the good done for the public, Bouvia's attorney was awarded fees under the California private attorney general provision of the Code of Civil Procedure.[516]

Guardianship statutes might also provide a basis for the award of attorneys' fees. In the *Severns* case,[517] the state appealed from an order that it pay $10,000 in guardian's fees arising from the underlying litigation[518] in which the husband of a patient in a persistent vegetative state instituted an action for the termination of life-sustaining medical treatment. The trial court appointed a guardian ad litem in that litigation, who thereafter sought compensation for his service in that role.

The trial court awarded a fee against the state. It reasoned that the guardian ad litem had opposed the "'apparent desires'" of the patient and thus it would be unfair to order the fees to be paid out of her estate, and because the guardian ad litem had asserted the state's interest in the preservation of life, the state ought to compensate the guardian. The state appealed, and the Delaware Supreme

---

[510] **CA:** Bouvia v. Superior Court (Glenchur), 225 Cal. Rptr. 297 (Ct. App. 1986).

[511] Bouvia v. County of L.A., 241 Cal. Rptr. at 246.

[512] *See* Bartling v. Superior Court, 209 Cal. Rptr. 220 (Ct. App. 1984); Barber v. Superior Court, 195 Cal. Rptr. 484 (Ct. App. 1983).

[513] Bouvia v. County of L.A., 241 Cal. Rptr. at 244.

[514] *Id.*

[515] *Id.* at 245.

[516] Cal. Civ. Proc. Code § 1021.5.

[517] **DE:** Severns v. Wilmington Medical Ctr., Inc., 433 A.2d 1047 (Del. 1981).

[518] *See* Severns v. Wilmington Medical Ctr., Inc., 421 A.2d 1334 (Del.), *opinion on remand,* 425 A.2d 156 (Del. Ch. 1980).

Court, noting that the patient was statutorily entitled to representation by counsel,[519] a function which the guardian ad litem served, held that the statute authorizing the trial court to award "costs"[520] permitted the payment of the guardian ad litem. It reasoned that because the guardian ad litem had represented an important public interest, he should be compensated by the state. However, barring a waiver of sovereign immunity, the court had no authority to order the state to pay those fees, and the guardian ad litem's recourse had to be to obtain relief from the General Assembly.

A Michigan appeals court also recognized that family members of a patient opposing a decision to forgo life-sustaining treatment by the patient's wife, who was her judicially appointed guardian, were entitled to an award of attorneys' fees because the patient is benefited by such a challenge. Even though they did not prevail, these family members were entitled to attorneys' fees because of conflicting facts and the unsettled state of the law. In such a situation, the patient "can be said to derive a benefit from a proceeding designed to ensure that his present capacity to decide his own medical treatment is fully explored and, in the event it is determined that he lacks the requisite decision-making capacity, that his medical treatment preferences or best interests are likewise fully and adequately considered and protected. This is particularly so where an erroneous determination will result in the termination of Michael's life against his wishes or best interests."[521] The trial court has "broad discretion in determining what amount constitutes reasonable compensation for attorney services," and the amount of fees to be awarded depends upon, but is not limited to, the following factors:

> (1) the professional standing and experience of the attorney; (2) the skill, time and labor involved; (3) the amount in question and the results achieved; (4) the difficulty of the case; (5) the expenses incurred; and (6) the nature and length of the professional relationship with the client. Although the actual amount of attorney fees requested may be considered, it is not controlling in itself and an award of reasonable attorney fees is not confined to that amount.[522]

In a similar case in New Jersey, *In re Clark,* the trial court awarded attorneys' fees to a lawyer who had been appointed guardian ad litem in the underlying litigation,[523] and charged the costs to the hospital.[524] The hospital initiated the

---

[519] Severns v. Wilmington Medical Ctr., Inc., 433 A.2d at 1049 (citing Del. Code. Ann. tit. 12 § 3914(b)).

[520] Del. Code. Ann. tit. 10, § 5106.

[521] Martin v. Martin, 517 N.W.2d 749, 756 (Mich. Ct. App. 1994) (quoting Martin v. Martin, 504 N.W.2d 917, 927 (Mich. Ct. App. 1993)).

[522] Martin v. Martin, 517 N.W.2d at 755.

[523] *See In re* Clark, 510 A.2d 136 (N.J. Super. Ct. Ch. Div. 1986).

[524] *In re* Clark, 515 A.2d 276 (N.J. Super. Ct. Ch. Div.), *aff'd,* 524 A.2d 448 (N.J. Super. Ct. App. Div. 1987).

litigation to obtain authorization to provide artificial nutrition and hydration to an incompetent patient who had no family to authorize the treatment. On appeal, the court held that New Jersey civil practice rules authorized the payment of guardian fees and that an award of fees, payable by the hospital, was justified. The appellate court approved the trial court's reasons for requiring the hospital to pay on the ground that

> Cooper Hospital, however reluctant, was the petitioner in this action, seeking the court's guidance in a difficult situation. Cooper had an interest in the outcome of this proceeding, and could not have made a decision as to whether or not to proceed with the surgery without exposing itself to liability. Given these circumstances, and the fact that the previous rule expressly authorized an award of counsel fees against a party, an award against Cooper Hospital in this case would not be unreasonable.[525]

The court did reduce the guardian's compensation because the guardian had originally expected to serve pro bono.

---

[525] 515 A.2d at 280.

## Bibliography

Addlestone, S. "Liability for Improper Maintenance of Life Support: Balancing Patient and Physician Autonomy." *Vanderbilt Law Review* 46 (1993): 1255.

Bradley, G. "Different Viewpoints: Does Autonomy Require Informed and Specific Refusal of Life-Sustaining Medical Treatment?" *Issues in Law and Medicine* 5 (1989): 301.

Dawe, T. "Wrongful Life: Time for a 'Day in Court.'" *Ohio State Law Journal* 51 (1990): 473.

Dooling, R. Comment. "Damage Actions for Nonconsensual Life-Sustaining Medical Treatment." *St. Louis University Law Journal* 30 (1986): 895.

Gasner, R. "Financial Penalties for Failing to Honor Patient Wishes to Refuse Treatment." *St. Louis University Public Law Review* 11 (1992): 499.

Gottesman, M. "Civil Liability for Failing to Provide 'Medically Indicated Treatment' to a Disabled Infant." *Family Law Quarterly* 20 (1986): 61.

Loftus, I. "I Have a Conscience, Too: The Plight of Medical Personnel Confronting the Right to Die." *Notre Dame Law Review* 65 (1990): 699.

Merritt, A. "The Tort Liability of Hospital Ethics Committees." *Southern California Law Review* 60 (1987): 1239.

Miller, D. "Right-to-Die Damage Actions: Developments in the Law." *Denver University Law Review* 65 (1988): 181.

Myers, G. "Health Care Provider Civil Liability for Denying Life-Sustaining Treatment." *Defense Counsel Journal* 55 (1988): 301.

Myers, G. "Health Care Provider Civil Liability for Denying the Patient's Right to Refuse Life-Sustaining (Death-Deferring) Medical Treatment." *Federation of Insurance and Corporate Counsel Quarterly* 38 (1988): 263.

Oddi, S. "The Tort of Interference with the Right to Die." *Georgetown Law Journal* 75 (1986): 625.

Rouse, F. "Different Viewpoints: Does Autonomy Require Informed and Specific Refusal of Life-Sustaining Medical Treatment?" *Issues in Law and Medicine* 5 (1989): 321.

Rouse, F. "Does Autonomy Require Informed and Specific Refusal of Life-Sustaining Medical Treatment?" *Issues in Law and Medicine* 5 (1989): 321.

Rubin, A., and M. Scrupski. Note. "When Ethics Collide: Enforcement of Institutional Policies of Non-Participation in the Termination of Life-Sustaining Treatment." *Rutgers Law Review* 41 (1988): 399.

Sharp, T., and T. Crofts. "Death with Dignity—The Physician's Civil Liability." *Baylor Law Review* 27 (1975): 86.

Wardle, L. "Protecting the Rights of Conscience of Health Care Providers." *Journal of Legal Medicine* 14 (1993): 177.

# CHAPTER 18

# CRIMINAL LIABILITY: ASSISTED SUICIDE AND ACTIVE EUTHANASIA

## § 18.1    Two Types of Potential Criminal Liability: Active and Passive Euthanasia

From the outset, right-to-die litigation has been driven in part by a fear of criminal (and civil) liability when a patient dies as a consequence of the withholding or withdrawal of life-sustaining medical treatment.[1] Physicians, administrators of hospitals and nursing homes, and the attorneys who advise them have frequently refused to forgo life-sustaining medical treatment at the request of both competent patients and the families of incompetent patients because of the fear of liability.[2] This concern has been put to rest as a theoretical matter by unanimity among the courts that if proper standards and procedures are followed, forgoing life-sustaining medical treatment does not give rise to criminal liability. In large part, the basis for this result is that forgoing treatment rests on the distinction between letting patients die and actively killing; the former being licit and the latter clearly not. Despite the clear and repeated enunciation by the courts that forgoing life-sustaining treatment does not, prima facie, give rise to criminal (or civil) liability for the patient's death, and despite the virtual absence of criminal prosecutions for forgoing life-sustaining

---

[1] **DIN:** *Cf.* Fort Wayne Journal-Gazette v. Baker, 788 F. Supp. 379 (N.D. Ind. 1992).

**DNY:** Deel v. Syracuse Veterans Admin. Medical Ctr., 729 F. Supp. 231, 234 (N.D.N.Y. 1990).

**DRI:** Gray v. Romeo, 697 F. Supp. 580 (D.R.I. 1988).

**CA:** McMahon v. Lopez, 245 Cal. Rptr. 172 (Ct. App. 1988); Bartling v. Superior Court, 209 Cal. Rptr. 220, 226 (Ct. App. 1984).

**DE:** Severns v. Wilmington Medical Ctr., Inc., 425 A.2d 156, 160 (Del. Ch. 1980).

**FL:** Corbett v. D'Alessandro, 487 So. 2d 368, 370 (Fla. Dist. Ct. App. 1986); St. Mary's Hosp. v. Ramsey, 465 So. 2d 666, 668 (Fla. Dist. Ct. App. 1985); Satz v. Perlmutter, 362 So. 2d 160, 163 (Fla. Dist. Ct. App. 1978).

**IN:** *Cf. In re* Lawrance, 579 N.E.2d 32 (Ind. 1991) (nursing home took no position as to proper outcome, but felt it could be subject to federal and state regulatory violations if it permitted forgoing artificial nutrition and hydration, even if family and physicians were in agreement).

**KY:** DeGrella v. Elston, 858 S.W.2d 698, 701 (Ky. 1993).

**NJ:** *In re* Farrell, 529 A.2d 404, 415 (N.J. 1987); *In re* Quinlan, 355 A.2d 647, 669 (N.J. 1976).

**NY:** *In re* Storar, 420 N.E.2d 64, 69 n.3 (N.Y. 1981).

[2] See **Ch. 17.**

treatment,[3] in practice fear of liability continues to be an obstacle to end-of-life decisionmaking.[4]

The fear of liability is grounded in the logic that when life-sustaining treatment is withheld or withdrawn, the patient's death results from the acts or omissions of those who have withheld or withdrawn treatment and those who have authorized this conduct. The Washington Supreme Court has summed the reasoning up this way, though rejecting it:

> Under Washington's criminal code, homicide is "the killing of a human being by the act, procurement or omission of another," . . . and it is murder in the first degree when, "[w]ith a premeditated intent to cause the death of another person, [one] causes the death of such person." Thus, the *potential* for criminal liability for withdrawing life sustaining mechanisms *appears* to exist.[5]

Fear of criminal liability—arising either from the forgoing of life-sustaining treatment or from more active interventions to end life—can be broken into distinct but closely related concerns: liability for homicide and liability for assisted suicide. Liability for some kind of crime could conceivably arise when any individual—whether a health care professional or not—takes actions that lead to the death of a patient, either by withholding or withdrawing life-sustaining medical treatment or by administering a lethal agent.

The line between homicide and assisted suicide is particularly hazy when the patient is competent and the means by which death occurs is the forgoing of life-sustaining treatment (that is, "voluntary passive euthanasia"), for example, when a physician ends ventilatory support for a competent patient at that patient's request.[6] If the patient is incompetent, it makes even less sense to conceptualize the resulting death as assisted suicide rather than homicide, unless, perhaps, it occurs pursuant to a patient's request through an advance directive.[7] When the means by which death takes place involves an active intervention, providing the patient with the means of taking his own life is generally denominated assisted suicide, but when a third party actually administers the agent that produces the patient's death, this is generally considered to be active euthanasia.

Although in recent years the debate about criminal liability for forgoing treatment has been largely supplanted by the question of whether actively

---

[3] **CA:** *But see* Barber v. Superior Court, 195 Cal. Rptr. 484 (Ct. App. 1983).

[4] *See* Solomon et al., *Decisions Near the End of Life: Professional Views on Life-Sustaining Treatments,* 83 Am. J. Pub. Health 14 (1993).

[5] *In re* Colyer, 660 P.2d 738, 751 (Wash. 1983) (emphasis added).

[6] **FL:** *See, e.g.,* Satz v. Perlmutter, 379 So. 2d 359 (Fla. 1980).

  **GA:** *See, e.g.,* State v. McAfee, 385 S.E.2d 651 (Ga. 1989).

  **NV:** *See, e.g.,* McKay v. Bergstedt, 801 P.2d 617 (Nev. 1990).

  **PA:** *See, e.g., In re* Doe, 45 Pa. D. & C.3d 371 (C.P. Phila. County 1987).

[7] See §§ **18.8** and **18.16.**

causing the death of a patient can ever be exempt from criminal liability,[8] concern still exists about the possibility of incurring liability from forgoing life-sustaining treatment. This fear is largely misplaced if proper procedures and standards are followed. Early in the development of the right to die, the courts made clear that "passive euthanasia"—forgoing life-sustaining medical treatment described by such locutions as withholding treatment, withdrawing treatment, letting the patient die—would not ordinarily be the basis for the imposition of liability, either civil or criminal, assuming that appropriate standards and procedures were followed. However, the courts have drawn a bright line between "passive" and "active" means of ending life, generally refusing to legitimate the latter. The same is true of legislatures that have acknowledged in advance directive statutes that passive euthanasia is neither suicide nor culpable homicide but have expressly refused to sanction active euthanasia or mercy killing. In fact, so clear has this line been that, regardless of one's views about whether as a matter of law, ethics, or public policy assisted suicide and/or active euthanasia ought to be legalized, one potential danger in attempting to breach the line is that it risks upsetting the consensus that has developed in law, medicine, and public opinion about the termination of life support.[9]

Law's approval of forgoing life-sustaining treatment and its corollary condemnation of more active means of ending life is beginning to disintegrate through judicial rulings[10] and legislative action.[11] The basis for the challenges to this time-honored distinction arises from the perceived inequity to patients who are dying a slow, painful, and agonizing death but whose dying is not being prolonged by any medical treatment that, if terminated, would bring about death.[12] People in this position, their physicians, their families, and those sympathetic to their plight have been instrumental in initiating the litigation and legislation that seeks to abolish or weaken the distinction between forgoing life-sustaining treatment on the one hand and assisted suicide and active euthanasia on the other—or at the least to carve out an exception for death brought about by the active assistance of a physician.

There is significant disagreement among commentators about whether there is any morally relevant distinction between active and passive euthanasia. However, even if there is no morally relevant distinction, or at least not on which a legal distinction might be grounded, there might still be strong reasons of policy as to why a legal distinction between the two should be maintained. One

---

[8] See § **18.18.**

[9] *See* Meisel, *The Legal Consensus About Forgoing Life-Sustaining Treatment: Its Status and Its Prospects,* 2 Kennedy Inst. Ethics J. 309 (1992).

[10] See § **18.22.**

[11] See § **18.23.**

[12] Block & Billings, *Patient Requests to Hasten Death—Evaluation and Management in Terminal Care,* 154 Archives Internal Med. 2039, 2039 (1994) (little systematic data available about patients' desires to hasten death; 2.9% of deaths in Netherlands result from active interventions).

reason frequently proffered is that the acceptance of *voluntary* active means of ending life would inevitably lead down the slippery slope toward nonvoluntary and even involuntary ending of life.[13] The simple response to this is that it is the nature of human reason, as manifested in part through law, to establish and enforce boundaries between acceptable and unacceptable behavior. It is also said that trust in doctors would diminish if people knew that their doctors could "kill" them, and this would serve as a strong deterrent to seeking medical care. But if this is true, it should be equally true with respect to forgoing life-sustaining treatment, but it does not appear that the fact that doctors may withhold or withdraw life-sustaining medical treatment and "allow the patient to die" deters people from seeking treatment. In the latter case, this is because doctors do not unilaterally wield that authority; there must also be legally valid consent. And so it would be with respect to active means of ending life. All of the arguments that would seek to maintain a legal distinction between active and passive euthanasia overlook the fundamental fact that what validates the latter is consent.

## FORGOING TREATMENT AND SUICIDE/ASSISTED SUICIDE

### § 18.2 Suicide and Liability for Assisted Suicide

Concern is sometimes expressed that the refusal of life-sustaining treatment by a competent patient[14] (or by an incompetent patient through a written or oral advance directive,[15] or even by a surrogate not acting pursuant to the patient's

---

[13] See § 18.25.

[14] **FL:** *E.g.,* Satz v. Perlmutter, 362 So. 2d 160, 160–63 (Fla. Dist. Ct. App. 1978).

**NJ:** *See, e.g., In re* Farrell, 529 A.2d 404, 411 (N.J. 1987); *In re* Requena, 517 A.2d 886 (N.J. Super. Ct. Ch. Div. 1986).

[15] **CA:** *See, e.g.,* Bartling v. Superior Court, 209 Cal. Rptr. 220, 225–26 (Ct. App. 1984).

**CT:** *Cf.* McConnell v. Beverly Enters.-Conn., Inc., 553 A.2d 596, 605 (Conn. 1989) (would not be suicide to terminate artificial nutrition and hydration in reliance on oral advance directive).

**ME:** *See, e.g., In re* Gardner, 534 A.2d 947, 955 (Me. 1987).

**MA:** *See, e.g.,* Brophy v. New Eng. Sinai Hosp., Inc., 497 N.E.2d 626, 638 (Mass. 1986).

**NY:** *See, e.g.,* Eichner v. Dillon, 420 N.E.2d 64 (N.Y. 1981); *In re* Lydia E. Hall Hosp., 455 N.Y.S.2d 706, 709, 711 (Sup. Ct. Nassau County 1982); Saunders v. State, 492 N.Y.S.2d 510, 512 (Sup. Ct. Nassau County 1985).

**OH:** *See, e.g.,* Leach v. Akron Gen. Medical Ctr., 426 N.E.2d 809, 815 (C.P. P. Div. Summit County, Ohio 1980).

**PA:** *See, e.g.,* Ragona v. Preate, 11 Fiduc. Rep. 2d 1 (C.P. Lackawanna County, Pa. 1990).

*See* Uniform Rights of the Terminally Ill Act § 11(a), 9B U.L.A. 127 (West Supp. 1994) ("Death resulting from the withholding or withdrawal of life-sustaining treatment pursuant to a declaration and in accordance with this [Act] does not constitute, for any purpose, a suicide or homicide.") [hereinafter 1989 URTIA].

clear instructions to forgo life-sustaining treatment[16]) constitutes suicide. If this is the case, then, so the argument goes, a physician (and possibly other health care personnel) who withholds or withdraws life-sustaining medical treatment is subject to liability for aiding, abetting, or assisting another in committing suicide,[17] or as a conspirator or accessory, or under the law of attempts.

Some contend that because committing suicide is no longer a crime[18]—it was at common law[19] because the king was deprived of a subject,[20] and various forms of punishment were imposed depending on the motive[21]—and, indeed, because no American jurisdiction now even treats *attempted* suicide as a crime,[22] there can be no criminal liability for assisting another to do what is not itself criminal. While that is logical enough, and might even be valid reasoning if one were sought to be prosecuted for the common-law crime of assisted suicide,[23] in many jurisdictions statutes have been enacted specifically making it a crime to

---

[16] *Cf. In re* Conroy, 486 A.2d 1209, 1226 (N.J. 1985) (rejecting artificial feeding is not attempted suicide, as decision would probably be based on wish to be free of medical intervention rather than a specific intent to die, and resulting death would be from underlying medical condition).

[17] W. LaFave & A. Scott, Criminal Law § 7.8(c), at 650–52 (2d ed. 1986). *But cf.* State v. McAfee, 385 S.E.2d 651 (Ga. 1989) (device constructed to permit competent patient to turn off the ventilator himself presumably to avoid any legal or moral complicity for assisted suicide).

[18] **DNY:** *Cf.* Quill v. Koppell, 870 F. Supp. 78 (S.D.N.Y. 1994).

**DOR:** *See* Lee v. State, 869 F. Supp. 1491 (D. Or. 1994).

**MI:** *See* Hobbins v. Attorney Gen., 527 N.W.2d 714, (Mich. 1994) (rejecting argument), *cert. denied sub nom.* Hobbins v. Kelley, 115 S. Ct. 1795 (1995).

[19] **US:** Cruzan v. Director, 497 U.S. 261, 294 (1990) (Scalia, J., concurring) ("a suicide—defined as one who 'deliberately puts an end to his own existence, or commits any unlawful malicious act, the consequence of which is his own death,' 4 W. Blackstone, Commentaries *189—was criminally liable").

*See also* W. LaFave & A. Scott, Criminal Law § 7.8, at 649 (2d ed. 1986).

[20] Shaffer, Note, *Criminal Liability for Assisting Suicide,* 86 Colum. L. Rev. 348, 349 & n.6 (1986) (citing 4 W. Blackstone, Commentaries *188–89).

[21] *Id.* at 349 (forfeiture of land and chattels if motivated by anger or ill will, chattels only if motivated by "'"weariness of life or impatience of pain,"'" and no penalty if resulting from insanity); W. LaFave & A. Scott, Criminal Law § 7.8, at 649 (an ignominious burial and forfeiture of the estate).

[22] **US:** Cruzan v. Director, 497 U.S. 261, 294 *et seq.* (1990) (Scalia, J., concurring) (discussing history of American law of suicide).

*See also* W. LaFave & A. Scott, Criminal Law § 7.8(a), at 649. *See also* 1989 URTIA § 11(a) ("Death resulting from the withholding or withdrawal of life-sustaining treatment does not constitute a suicide.").

[23] **DNY:** Quill v. Koppell, 870 F. Supp. 78 (S.D.N.Y. 1994).

**DOR:** Lee v. State, 869 F. Supp. 1491 (D. Or. 1994).

**MI:** *But see* People v. Kevorkian, 527 N.W.2d 714 (Mich. 1994) (permitting prosecution for common-law crime of assisted suicide), *cert. denied sub nom.* Kevorkian v. Michigan, 115 S. Ct. 1795 (1995).

See § **18.17.**

provide another with the means of taking his own life. See **Table 18–1** in § **18.17.** The Model Penal Code also contains such a provision.[24] The offense of providing another with the means to commit suicide is to be distinguished from the more serious offense of causing (or inciting) another to commit suicide.[25] There is very little case law on the subject in either states with[26] or without statutory prohibitions on assisted suicide.[27]

## § 18.3   Forgoing Treatment Distinguished from Assisted Suicide

Before there can be liability for assisted suicide, the death of the patient must first be capable of being considered a suicide.[28] If the forgoing of life-sustaining treatment is not viewed as suicide, then those health care professionals who withhold or withdraw treatment cannot be held liable for assisted suicide.[29] It is possible that they might be amenable to prosecution for some other crime, though it is not likely.[30]

No court has held that the forgoing of life-sustaining treatment constitutes suicide despite the fact that when a patient seeks to terminate life-sustaining treatment because of a poor quality of life,[31] the termination of treatment results in death. From the dawn of right-to-die litigation, the courts have dealt with this issue in essentially the same way as they have dealt with the argument that forgoing life-sustaining treatment is homicide[32] and have uniformly concluded

---

[24] Model Penal Code § 210.5(2) (1980) ("A person who purposely aids or solicits another to commit suicide is guilty of a felony in the second degree if his conduct causes such suicide or attempted suicide, and otherwise of a misdemeanor.").

[25] *Compare* Model Penal Code § 210.5(2) *with id.* § 210.5(1).

[26] *See, e.g.,* Chanslor v. State, 697 S.W.2d 393 (Tex. Crim. App. 1985) (assisted suicide rather than solicitation to murder applicable in case of husband who purchased poison for wife who had suffered a stroke and was confined to a wheelchair).

[27] *See, e.g.,* People v. Kevorkian, 527 N.W.2d 714 (Mich. 1994), *cert. denied sub nom.* Kevorkian v. Michigan, 115 S. Ct. 1795 (1995). See § **18.17.**

[28] **MA:** *Cf. In re* Doe, 583 N.E.2d 1263, 1270 (Mass. 1992) (not suicide because patient "has no ability to commit a volitional act").

Model Penal Code § 2.06.

[29] **AZ:** Rasmussen v. Fleming, 741 P.2d 674, 685 n.16 (Ariz. 1987).

*See also* Wanzer et al., *The Physician's Responsibility Toward Hopelessly Ill Patients,* 320 New Eng. J. Med. 844, 848 (1989) ("Suicide differs from euthanasia in that the act of bringing on death is performed by the patient, not the physician.").

[30] **MI:** *See* People v. Kevorkian, 527 N.W.2d 714, (Mich. 1994), *rev'g* 517 N.W.2d 293 (Mich. Ct. App. 1994) (upholding prosecution for murder for providing one with means to commit suicide), *and overruling* People v. Roberts, 178 N.W. 690 (Mich. 1920) (same).

[31] Rosebush v. Oakland County Prosecutor, 491 N.W.2d 633, 641 (Mich. Ct. App. 1992) (citing first edition of this treatise).

[32] See § **18.10.**

that the withholding or withdrawal of life-sustaining treatment at the request of a competent patient does not constitute suicide.[33] As the New Jersey Supreme Court remarked in *Quinlan,* there is "a real distinction between the self-infliction of deadly harm and a self-determination against artificial life support or radical surgery, for instance, in the face of irreversible, painful and certain imminent death."[34] (This is also uniformly the legislative position.) About the only serious judicial attention accorded the notion that the forgoing of life-sustaining treatment might be considered suicide is Justice Scalia's concurring opinion in *Cruzan v. Director,*[35] in which no other justice joined.

---

[33] **US:** *But see* Cruzan v. Director, 497 U.S. 261 (1990) (Scalia, J., concurring).

**AZ:** Rasmussen v. Fleming, 741 P.2d at 685.

**CA:** Bouvia v. Superior Court (Glenchur), 225 Cal. Rptr. 297, 306 (Ct. App. 1986); Bartling v. Superior Court, 209 Cal. Rptr. 220, 225–26 (Ct. App. 1984).

**CT:** Foody v. Manchester Memorial Hosp., 482 A.2d 713, 720 (Conn. Super. Ct. 1984).

**FL:** Satz v. Perlmutter, 362 So. 2d 160, 160–63 (Fla. Dist. Ct. App. 1978). *But cf.* Browning v. Herbert, 543 So. 2d 258, 270 (Fla. Dist. Ct. App. 1989), ("[T]he act intuitively seems closer to suicide.").

**MA:** Brophy v. New Eng. Sinai Hosp., Inc., 497 N.E.2d 626, 638 (Mass. 1986); Superintendent of Belchertown State Sch. v. Saikewicz, 370 N.E.2d 417, 426 n.11 (Mass. 1977). *But see* In re Doe, 583 N.E.2d 1263, 1275 (Mass. 1992) (O'Connor, J., dissenting) ("Suicide, the purposeful termination of one's own life, is no less suicide when death is accomplished by inaction than when an affirmative act is employed as the agent of death."); Brophy v. New Eng. Sinai Hosp., Inc., 497 N.E.2d 626, 640 (Mass. 1986) (Nolan, J., dissenting) ("[T]he court today has indorsed euthanasia and suicide."); *id.* at 642–43 (Lynch, J., dissenting) (majority nullify the law against suicide); *id.* at 644–45 (O'Connor, J., dissenting).

**ME:** In re Gardner, 534 A.2d 947 (Me. 1987).

**NV:** McKay v. Bergstedt, 801 P.2d 617 (Nev. 1990).

**NJ:** In re Farrell, 529 A.2d 404, 411 (N.J. 1987); In re Conroy, 486 A.2d 1209, 1224–26 (N.J. 1985); In re Quinlan, 355 A.2d 647, 669–70 (N.J. 1976); In re Requena, 517 A.2d 886 (N.J. Super. Ct. Ch. Div.), *aff'd,* 517 A.2d 869 (N.J. Super. Ct. App. Div. 1986).

**NY:** Fosmire v. Nicoleau, 551 N.E.2d 77, 81–82 (N.Y. 1990) ("[M]erely declining medical care, even essential treatment, is not considered a suicidal act."); Eichner v. Dillon, 426 N.Y.S.2d 517, 544 (App. Div. 1980); Saunders v. State, 492 N.Y.S.2d 510, 512 (Sup. Ct. Nassau County 1985); In re Lydia E. Hall Hosp., 455 N.Y.S.2d 706, 709 (Sup. Ct. Nassau County 1982); In re Storar, 433 N.Y.S.2d 388, 393 (Sup. Ct. Monroe County 1980). *But see* Fosmire v. Nicoleau, 551 N.E.2d at 86 (Simons, J., concurring) ("[I]f competent adults, who are presumed to know the natural and probable consequences of their acts, may reject life-saving treatment without reason the rule condones a method of suicide.").

**OH:** Leach v. Akron Gen. Medical Ctr., 426 N.E.2d 809, 815 (C.P. P. Div. Summit County, Ohio 1980).

**PA:** In re Doe, 45 Pa. D. & C.3d 371 (C.P. Phila. County 1987).

**WA:** In re Ingram, 689 P.2d 1363, 1371 (Wash. 1984); In re Colyer, 660 P.2d 738 (Wash. 1983).

[34] *In re* Quinlan, 355 A.2d 647, 665 (N.J. 1976).

[35] 497 U.S. 261 (1990).

The courts have propounded a number of explanations as to why forgoing life-sustaining medical treatment does not constitute suicide. Sometimes these explanations are used separately, but often they are employed together.[36]

## § 18.4 —Legal Right to Forgo Life-Sustaining Treatment

The most straightforward and satisfactory approach to explaining why death from forgoing life-sustaining treatment does not constitute suicide—but not the one always given—is that the voluntary and informed choice of a competent patient, implementing the individual's freedom from unwanted interferences with his person, legitimates the forgoing of life-sustaining treatment. This is the approach taken by the California Court of Appeal in the celebrated *Bouvia* case involving a competent, nonterminally ill woman suffering from severe cerebral palsy, in whom her doctors had inserted a feeding tube against her will.[37] In holding that the forgoing of artificial nutrition and hydration, and indeed spoon-feeding, would not constitute suicide because the patient "merely resigned herself to accept an earlier death, if necessary, rather than live by feedings forced upon her," the court also stated that "a desire to terminate one's life is probably the ultimate exercise of one's right to privacy."[38]

---

[36] **CT:** *See, e.g.,* Foody v. Manchester Memorial Hosp., 482 A.2d at 720.

**MA:** *In re* Doe, 583 N.E.2d 1263 (Mass. 1992); Superintendent of Belchertown State Sch. v. Saikewicz, 370 N.E.2d 417, 426 n.11 (Mass. 1977).

**NJ:** *In re* Conroy, 486 A.2d at 1224.

**NY:** *In re* Lydia E. Hall Hosp., 455 N.Y.S.2d at 711.

[37] Bouvia v. Superior Court (Glenchur), 225 Cal. Rptr. 297 (Ct. App. 1986).

[38] **CA:** Bouvia v. Superior Court (Glenchur), 225 Cal. Rptr. at 306. *Accord* Thor v. Superior Court, 855 P.2d 375 (Cal. 1993) (prison patient who refused to eat or to have feeding tube implanted was exercising right of self-determination, not committing suicide).

**MA:** *Accord* Norwood Hosp. v. Munoz, 564 N.E.2d 1017, 1022 n.5 (Mass. 1991) ("It is difficult to understand how the court's decision endorses suicide in the absence of any evidence that Ms. Munoz wanted to die. There is a clear distinction between respecting the right of individuals to decide for themselves whether to refuse medical treatment and endorsing the idea that it is acceptable for individuals to take their own lives.").

**NY:** *Accord* Fosmire v. Nicoleau, 551 N.E.2d 77, 81–82 (N.Y. 1990) (While "State will intervene to prevent suicide . . . merely declining medical care, even essential treatment, is not considered a suicidal act.").

**NV:** *Contra* McKay v. Bergstedt, 801 P.2d 617 (Nev. 1990) (Springer, J., dissenting) (termination of life support is not an exercise of the right to be let alone when patient is not terminally ill).

## § 18.5 —Causation

Under the causation rationale, a patient's death *subsequent to* forgoing treatment does not constitute suicide because it is not *caused by* forgoing treatment but by the patient's medical condition for which treatment has been forgone.[39] Suicide is self-inflicted death; under these circumstances, death results from an illness or injury that is not self-inflicted.[40]

The same, of course, could be said about death resulting from any decision not to treat an illness or injury. But this was not the position that the New Jersey Supreme Court took in *John F. Kennedy Memorial Hospital v. Heston*[41] only a few years before *Quinlan*. In its holding that an adult Jehovah's Witness had no right to refuse a blood transfusion in connection with lifesaving surgery, the court suggested that, if treatment were forgone, the patient's death would be considered a suicide and that there was "no constitutional right to choose to die."[42] By contrast, in the *Quinlan* case, the court stated that the patient's death resulting from the decision of a surrogate to forgo treatment "would not be homicide but rather expiration from existing natural causes."[43]

---

[39] **DRI:** Gray v. Romeo, 697 F. Supp. 580 (D.R.I. 1988).

    **FL:** *In re* Browning, 568 So. 2d 4, 14 (Fla. 1990); Satz v. Perlmutter, 362 So. 2d 160 (Fla. Dist. Ct. App. 1978).

    **MA:** Brophy v. New Eng. Sinai Hosp., Inc., 497 N.E.2d 626, 638 (Mass. 1986); Superintendent of Belchertown State Sch. v. Saikewicz, 370 N.E.2d 417, 426 n.11 (Mass. 1977).

    **NV:** McKay v. Bergstedt, 801 P.2d 617, 627 (Nev. 1990).

    **NJ:** *In re* Conroy, 486 A.2d 1209, 1224 (N.J. 1985).

    **NY:** Eichner v. Dillon, 426 N.Y.S.2d 517, 544 (App. Div. 1980).

    **PA:** *In re* Doe, 45 Pa. D. & C.3d 371, 386 (C.P. Phila. County 1987).

    *See* National Ctr. for State Courts, Guidelines for State Court Decision Making in Life-Sustaining Medical Treatment Cases 145 (2d ed. 1992).

[40] **CA:** Donaldson v. Van de Kamp, 4 Cal. Rptr. 2d 59, 62 (Ct. App. 1992); Bouvia v. Superior Court (Glenchur), 225 Cal. Rptr. 297, 306 (Ct. App. 1986) ("allow nature to take its course"); Bartling v. Superior Court, 209 Cal. Rptr. 220, 225 (Ct. App. 1984) ("merely . . . hasten . . . inevitable death by natural causes").

    **NV:** McKay v. Bergstedt, 801 P.2d at 632 ("allow the natural consequences of [the patient's] condition to occur").

    **NY:** *In re* Lydia E. Hall Hosp., 455 N.Y.S.2d 706, 711 (Sup. Ct. Nassau County 1982).

    *See also* Wanzer et al., *The Physician's Responsibility Toward Hopelessly Ill Patients,* 320 New Eng. J. Med. 844, 848 (1989) ("Suicide differs from euthanasia in that the act of bringing on death is performed by the patient not the physician.").

[41] 279 A.2d 670 (N.J. 1971).

[42] *Id.* at 672.

[43] **NJ:** *In re* Quinlan, 355 A.2d 647, 670 (N.J. 1976).

    **CT:** *Accord* Foody v. Manchester Memorial Hosp., 482 A.2d 713, 720 (Conn. Super. Ct. 1984).

    **MA:** *Accord In re* Doe, 583 N.E.2d 1263, 1270 (Mass. 1992) ("'death which occurs after the removal of life sustaining systems is from natural causes, neither set in motion nor intended by the patient'").

The difference between these two holdings can only be reconciled on the basis of the factual differences between the two cases. In *Heston* the treatment in question was capable of restoring the patient to health, whereas the treatment at issue in the *Quinlan* case was not. Thus, the causal explanation of why forgoing treatment does not constitute suicide is premised on the assumption that the treatment to be forgone is incapable of restoring the patient to health or that the patient is going to die regardless of what medical measures are undertaken. Indeed, when the New Jersey Supreme Court revisited this issue in *Conroy*,[44] it restated this conclusion with increased clarity and vigor:

> [D]eclining life-sustaining medical treatment may not properly be viewed as an attempt to commit suicide. Refusing medical intervention merely allows the disease to take its natural course; if death were eventually to occur, it would be the result, primarily, of the underlying disease, and not the result of a self-inflicted injury.[45]

Other courts have reached similar conclusions, though differently phrased. Some have said that death results from "natural causes";[46] others, that the patient's "medical conditions are not self-inflicted";[47] yet others, that the "cessation of [treatment] will do no more than allow nature to run its course,"[48] or that

---

[44] *In re* Conroy, 486 A.2d 1209 (N.J. 1985).

[45] *Id.* at 1224.

[46] **CT:** *See* Foody v. Manchester Memorial Hosp., 482 A.2d at 720.

**FL:** Satz v. Perlmutter, 362 So. 2d 160, 162–63 (Fla. Dist. Ct. App. 1978).

**MA:** Brophy v. New Eng. Sinai Hosp., Inc., 497 N.E.2d 626, 638 (Mass. 1986); Superintendent of Belchertown State Sch. v. Saikewicz, 370 N.E.2d 417, 426 n.11 (Mass. 1977).

[47] **NY:** *In re* Lydia E. Hall Hosp., 455 N.Y.S.2d 706, 711 (Sup. Ct. Nassau County 1982).

**CT:** *Accord* Foody v. Manchester Memorial Hosp., 482 A.2d at 720.

**FL:** *Accord* Satz v. Perlmutter, 362 So. 2d at 162–63.

**WA:** *Accord In re* Colyer, 660 P.2d 738, 743 (Wash. 1983).

[48] **NY:** *In re* Storar, 433 N.Y.S.2d 388, 393 (Sup. Ct. Monroe County 1980).

**DDC:** *Accord* Tune v. Walter Reed Army Medical Hosp., 602 F. Supp. 1452, 1455 n.8 (D.D.C. 1985).

**DNY:** *Accord* Deel v. Syracuse Veterans Admin. Medical Ctr., 729 F. Supp. 231, 234 (N.D.N.Y. 1990) ("cause of . . . death, if it were to occur upon removal of artificial respiration, would be the natural underlying disease").

**AZ:** *Accord* Rasmussen v. Fleming, 741 P.2d 674, 685 (Ariz. 1987).

**CA:** *Accord* Bartling v. Superior Court, 209 Cal. Rptr. 220, 225–26 (Ct. App. 1984).

**CT:** *Accord* McConnell v. Beverly Enters.-Conn., Inc., 553 A.2d 596, 605 (Conn. 1989) ("[T]he removal of a gastrostomy tube is not the 'death producing agent,' set in motion with the intent of causing her own death. In exercising her right of self-determination, Mrs. McConnell merely seeks to be free of extraordinary mechanical devices and to allow nature to take its course. Thus, death will be by natural causes underlying the disease, not by self-inflicted injury.").

**ME:** *Accord In re* Gardner, 534 A.2d 947, 956 (Me. 1987).

**NJ:** *Accord In re* Conroy, 486 A.2d 1209, 1224 (N.J. 1985).

the forgoing of treatment "would merely ... hasten ... inevitable death by natural causes."[49] Moreover, a patient's refusal of treatment that is likely to cure in favor of one that is not as effective does not constitute suicide.[50]

## § 18.6 —Act and Omission

Another explanation, closely related to and intertwined with the causal explanation, is based on the distinction between act and omission.[51] When life-sustaining treatment is forgone, under this explanation it is said that death results from an omission to treat. In a case of "genuine" suicide, death results from the patient's affirmative act to end his life. Assisted suicide involves

> affirmative, assertive, proximate, direct conduct such as furnishing a gun, poison, knife, or other instrumentality or usable means by which another could physically and immediately inflict some death producing injury upon himself. Such situations are far different than the mere presence of a doctor during the exercise of his patient's constitutional rights.[52]

This distinction is intuitively appealing but ultimately troubling. It is unsatisfactory because "forgoings" of life-sustaining treatment can be accomplished either by withholding or by withdrawing, and withdrawing—for instance, the turning off of a ventilator—is no less an act than a self-inflicted shooting, poisoning, wrist slitting, hanging, or even overdose of prescribed medication.

---

**OH:** *Accord* Leach v. Akron Gen. Medical Ctr., 426 N.E.2d 809, 815 (C.P. P. Div. Summit County, Ohio 1980).

**PA:** *Accord* Ragona v. Preate, 11 Fiduc. Rep. 2d 1, 11 (C.P. Lackawanna County, Pa. 1990) (removal of patient's feeding tube "permits her to die from the natural progression of her illness").

**WA:** *Accord In re* Colyer, 660 P.2d at 743.

*See also* President's Comm'n for the Study of Ethical Problems in Medicine & Biomedical & Behavioral Research, Deciding to Forego Life-Sustaining Treatment 38 (1983) [hereinafter President's Comm'n, Deciding to Forego Life-Sustaining Treatment].

[49] **CA:** Bartling v. Superior Court, 209 Cal. Rptr. at 225–26.

**FL:** *Cf.* Satz v. Perlmutter, 362 So. 2d at 162.

[50] **WA:** *In re* Ingram, 689 P.2d 1363, 1371 (Wash. 1984).

[51] *See* Cruzan v. Director, 497 U.S. 261 (1990) (Scalia, J., concurring).

[52] **CA:** Bouvia v. Superior Court (Glenchur), 225 Cal. Rptr. 297, 306 (Ct. App. 1986). *Accord* Donaldson v. Van de Kamp, 4 Cal. Rptr. 2d 59 (Ct. App. 1992) (competent individual suffering from brain tumor has no legal right to have himself subjected to premortem cryogenic suspension by another, which will cause death; such procedure is distinguishable from forgoing life-sustaining treatment).

**IL:** *Cf.* Estate of Longeway v. Community Convalescent Ctr., 549 N.E.2d 292, 298 (Ill. 1989) ("[W]e ... emphatically ... do not condone suicide or active euthanasia.").

Indeed, it is questionable whether any clear dividing line can be enunciated to separate acts from omissions.[53]

In his concurring opinion in *Cruzan,* Justice Scalia expressed the view that it is "unreasonable to draw the line precisely between action and inaction."[54] However, from this equation, he drew the conclusion that because the state traditionally condemned self-inflicted lethal acts, it could also equally condemn self-inflicted lethal omissions, which is, of course, contrary to what virtually every state court has concluded by distinguishing the two. Justice Scalia offered the following illustrations:

> It would not make much sense to say that one may not kill oneself by walking into the sea, but may sit on the beach until submerged by the incoming tide; or that one may not intentionally lock oneself into a cold storage locker, but may refrain from coming indoors when the temperature drops below freezing.[55]

He would dismiss this explanation for the reason that

> the early cases considering the claimed right to refuse medical treatment dismissed as specious the nice distinction between "passively submitting to death and actively seeking it. The distinction may be merely verbal as it would be if an adult sought death by starvation instead of a drug. If the State may interrupt one mode of self-destruction, it may with equal authority interfere with the other."[56]

It is noteworthy that the quotation in this statement is from the *Heston* case, which, as mentioned above, involved a patient whose health could be restored to the status quo ante, and thus was distinguished in subsequent cases involving hopelessly ill patients. It is worth wondering whether Justice Scalia's argument supporting the distinction between active and passive ending of life does not prove too much. If they are legally the same, and if courts have approved—as they have—the passive ending of life, that suggests that they should also approve the active ending of life.

The thinness of the distinction between the two is nicely illustrated by the *McAfee* case, which raised the question whether an otherwise healthy, relatively young, ventilator-dependent quadriplegic man might have his ventilatory

---

[53] *In re* Conroy, 486 A.2d 1209, 1234 (N.J. 1985).

[54] Cruzan v. Director, 497 U.S. at 296 (Scalia, J., concurring).

[55] **US:** Cruzan v. Director, 497 U.S. at 296 (preferring to rest on equally problematic distinction: "the intelligent line does not fall between action and inaction but between those forms of inaction that consist of abstaining from 'ordinary' care and those that consist of abstaining from 'excessive' or 'heroic' measures").

**MA:** *See also In re* Doe, 583 N.E.2d 1263 (Mass. 1992) (O'Connor, J., dissenting).

See § **8.8.**

[56] 497 U.S. at 297 (quoting John F. Kennedy Memorial Hosp. v. Heston, 279 A.2d 670, 672–73 (N.J. 1971)).

support withdrawn. The Georgia Supreme Court granted his petition, which would have allowed him to activate a device, designed at his request by an engineer, that would allow Mr. McAfee to "turn[] off the ventilator himself by way of a timer."[57] There is very little factual difference, and it is doubtful whether there is any important moral difference and that there ought to be any legal difference, between what this engineer and Mr. McAfee requested to do and what a physician who inserts an intravenous line connected to a lethal agent into a patient at the patient's request, leaving it to the patient to turn on the intravenous line or not, does. In the end, the only difference between the two situations is factual causation, but there is no moral and should be no legal distinction between the two because in both the result is legitimated by the patient's consent.


## § 18.7 —Intent


Sometimes courts distinguish death from forgoing treatment from suicide on the basis of the patient's intent. According to this explanation, in cases of genuine suicide, the individual's intent is to bring about his death. A decision to forgo life-sustaining treatment does not constitute suicide because the patient's wish is not to end life. The patient is said to have no specific intent to die[58] or to have as his intent the relief of suffering.[59]

---

[57] State v. McAfee, 385 S.E.2d 651, 651 (Ga. 1989).

[58] **NY:** Fosmire v. Nicoleau, 551 N.E.2d 77, 82 n.2 (N.Y. 1990); Eichner v. Dillon, 426 N.Y.S.2d 517, 544 (App. Div. 1980).

**OH:** Leach v. Akron Gen. Medical Ctr., 426 N.E.2d 809, 815 (C.P. P. Div. Summit County, Ohio 1980).

**WA:** *In re* Colyer, 660 P.2d 738, 743 (Wash. 1983).

[59] **US:** *Contra* Cruzan v. Director, 497 U.S. 261, 295 (1990) (Scalia, J., concurring) ("Suicide was not excused even when committed 'to avoid those ills which [persons] had not the fortitude to endure.'") (quoting 4 Blackstone, Commentaries *189.).

**CA:** Thor v. Superior Court, 855 P.2d 375, 386 (Cal. 1993) ("[W]here life must be sustained artificially and under circumstances of total dependence, the adult's attitude or motive may be presumed not to be suicidal.").

**CT:** Foody v. Manchester Memorial Hosp., 482 A.2d 713, 720 (Conn. Super. Ct. 1984).

**MA:** Superintendent of Belchertown State Sch. v. Saikewicz, 370 N.E.2d 417, 426 n.11 (Mass. 1977).

**NV:** McKay v. Bergstedt, 801 P.2d 617, 627 (Nev. 1990).

**NJ:** *In re* Conroy, 486 A.2d 1209, 1224 & passim (N.J. 1985) ("People who refuse life-sustaining medical treatment may not harbor a specific intent to die . . . rather, they may fervently wish to live, but to do so free of unwanted medical technology, surgery, or drugs, and without protracted suffering.").

**NY:** Eichner v. Dillon, 426 N.Y.S.2d 517, 544 (App. Div. 1980); Saunders v. State, 492 N.Y.S.2d 510, 512 (Sup. Ct. Nassau County 1985).

One difficulty with this argument is that it confuses intent with motive. "'Intent' is the word commonly used to describe the desire to bring about the physical consequences, up to and including the death; the more remote objective which inspires the act is called 'motive.'"[60] If a patient's suffering or evaluation of his quality of life is such that he wishes to end his life, then it is correct to say that his motive is to escape suffering, but the intent is to die because that is the goal he seeks to achieve. Thus, although we might not wish to call such a death a suicide, it is hard to see how this result can be reached by saying that the intent to die is absent.[61]

The use of motive rather than intent to distinguish suicide from death from forgoing life-sustaining treatment has similar difficulties. If we wish to conclude that there is a difference between the two because there is a difference in motive, we will be similarly hard-pressed to identify what that motive is. When a patient is terminally ill and undergoing great physical or emotional suffering, the motive for seeking death is to escape that suffering, but that is not necessarily any different from the otherwise healthy but severely depressed, nonterminally ill person who sees death as the only escape from suffering.

*Satz v. Perlmutter*[62] is one of the few cases to actually apply this view; it involved a decision to forgo treatment by a competent patient, whereas most cases discuss the matter in dictum. In an explanation that combines the intent and causation rationales, the court stated that

> [t]he testimony of Mr. Perlmutter . . . is that he really wants to live, but do so, God and Mother Nature willing, under his own power. This basic wish to live, plus the fact that he did not self-induce his horrible affliction, precludes his further refusal of treatment being classed as attempted suicide.[63]

---

[60] W. Prosser, The Law of Torts § 8, at 31 (4th ed. 1971). *See also* W. LaFave & A. Scott, Criminal Law § 29, at 204 (1972) ("One who intentionally kills another human being is guilty of murder, though . . . his motive is the worthy one of terminating the victim's sufferings even from an incurable and painful disease.").

[61] *See, e.g., In re* Doe, 583 N.E.2d 1263, 1275 (Mass. 1992) (O'Connor, J., dissenting) ("[T]he law should recognize a competent person's right to refuse or withdraw medical treatment when that choice is not motivated by a desire to die but, instead, is reasonably motivated by a desire to avoid procedures that are in themselves, and not simply because they prolong life, physically or emotionally painful. Suicide, however, is a different matter.").

[62] 362 So. 2d 160 (Fla. Ct. App. 1978), *aff'd,* 379 So. 2d 359 (Fla. 1980).

[63] **FL:** 362 So. 2d at 162–63.

**CA:** *Accord* Bartling v. Superior Court, 209 Cal. Rptr. 220, 222 (Ct. App. 1984) (patient stated that he wanted to live but preferred death to his intolerable life on the ventilator).

**NV:** *Compare* McKay v. Bergstedt, 801 P.2d 617, 625 (Nev. 1990) (not suicide because "Kenneth harbored no intent to take his own life, voluntarily or otherwise") *with id.* at 634 (Springer, J., dissenting) ("nothing natural about death [of non-terminally ill patient]; he killed himself" by ending ventilatory support).

Even when there was testimony that a patient had said that "he was suffering so much, he wanted to die," a New York court found that the termination of treatment did not constitute suicide.[64]

In an effort to explain the elusive distinction, the Nevada Supreme Court noted that the "primary factors that distinguish" the termination of life support from genuine suicide are "attitude, physical condition and prognosis."[65] It observed that

> [u]nlike a person bent on suicide, Kenneth sought no affirmative measures to terminate his life; he desired only to eliminate the artificial barriers standing between him and the natural processes of life and death that would otherwise ensue with someone in his physical condition. Kenneth survived artificially within a paralytic prison from which there was no hope of release other than death. But he asked no one to shorten the term of his natural life free of the respirator. He sought no fatal potions to end life or hurry death. In other words, Kenneth desired the right to die a natural death unimpeded by scientific contrivances.[66]

For this court, the patient's medical condition and prognosis made a determinative difference:

> The distinction between refusing medical treatment and the other scenarios presented by Justice Scalia [concurring in *Cruzan*] is the difference between choosing a natural death summoned by an uninvited illness or calamity and deliberately seeking to terminate one's life by resorting to death-inducing measures unrelated to the natural process of dying. . . . If [people are] physically healthy, society's respect for human life demanded that the State prevent, if possible, their deaths by suicide. There [is] no need to present [such] person[s] with life-extending medical options, and [they] enjoyed the prospect of mental rehabilitation that might restore the will to live. There is a significant distinction between an individual faced with artificial survival resulting from heroic medical intervention and an individual otherwise healthy or capable of sustaining life without artificial support who simply desires to end his or her life.[67]

## § 18.8   —Advance Directive Legislation

Another basis for distinguishing between forgoing life-sustaining treatment and suicide is to be found in advance directive legislation. Virtually all, if not all, advance directive statutes specifically provide that the death of a patient

---

[64] *In re* Lydia E. Hall Hosp., 455 N.Y.S.2d 706, 709 (Sup. Ct. Nassau County 1982).

[65] McKay v. Bergstedt, 801 P.2d at 625.

[66] **NV:** McKay v. Bergstedt, 801 P.2d at 625–26.

   **CA:** *Accord* Thor v. Superior Court, 855 P.2d 375, 386 (Cal. 1993) (citing and quoting *McKay v. Bergstedt*).

[67] McKay v. Bergstedt, 801 P.2d at 626.

pursuant to the forgoing of treatment in conformity with an advance directive does not constitute suicide. The Washington legislation[68] is representative. It states "that acts in accordance with a directive are not deemed suicide . . . and the cause of death shall be that which placed the patient in a terminal condition."[69] From this, the Washington Supreme Court concluded that "the same principles should apply when the patient's right to refuse life-sustaining treatment is exercised in accordance with" procedures enunciated by the court as well as in accordance with statutory procedures.[70] While the conclusion is sound, it is of limited applicability because most advance directive statutes by their terms apply only to patients who have executed an advance directive.[71]

# FORGOING TREATMENT AND HOMICIDE

## § 18.9 Liability for Homicide

In practice, the imposition of liability for criminal homicide for forgoing life-sustaining treatment is extremely remote as long as proper standards and procedures are followed. There is only one reported prosecution of physicians for such conduct, the *Barber* case in 1983, and the indictment was ultimately dismissed.[72] There are also very few prosecutions against laypersons for the denial of medical care resulting in death, and those too have ended without the

---

[68] Wash. Rev. Code Ann. §§ 70.122.010–.105.

[69] *In re* Colyer, 660 P.2d 738, 751 (Wash. 1983).

*Cf.* 1989 URTIA § 11(a), 9B U.L.A. 96, 113 (Supp. 1992) ("Death resulting from the withholding or withdrawal of life-sustaining treatment pursuant to a declaration and in accordance with this [Act] does not constitute, for any purpose, a suicide or homicide.").

[70] **WA:** *In re* Colyer, 660 P.2d at 751.

**CT:** *Accord* McConnell v. Beverly Enters.-Conn., Inc., 553 A.2d 596, 605 (Conn. 1989) ("Because we hold that the legislature in enacting the Removal of Life Support Systems Act sought to establish a workable mechanism by which individuals may implement their common law and constitutional rights, it follows that by exercising these rights, the individual cannot become criminally liable.").

[71] See §§ **10.10–10.13.**

[72] **CA:** *See* Barber v. Superior Court, 195 Cal. Rptr. 484 (Ct. App. 1983).

**OH:** *Cf. In re* Myers, 610 N.E.2d 663, 668 (P. Ct. Summit County, Ohio 1993) ("removal [of nutrition and hydration] is not a violation of either civil or criminal law").

*See also* 1989 URTIA, § II (a) ("Death resulting from the withholding or withdrawal of life-sustaining treatment . . . does not constitute . . . homicide."); Uniform Rights of the Terminally Ill Act § 10(a), 9B U.L.A. 609, 620 (1987) ("Death resulting from the withholding or withdrawal of life-sustaining treatment pursuant to a declaration and in accordance with this [Act] does not constitute, for any purpose, a suicide or homicide.") [hereinafter 1985 URTIA].

imposition of criminal liability[73] (except when the patient was a child[74]). Indeed, so remote is the likelihood of criminal liability that when efforts are made to join criminal prosecutors in right-to-die litigation seeking equitable relief, they have sometimes[75] (though not always[76]) declined to participate. Perhaps this is because prosecutors agree with the observation of the California Court of Appeal in *Barber* that " 'a murder prosecution is a poor way to design an ethical and moral code for doctors who are faced with decisions concerning the use of costly and extraordinary "life support" equipment.' "[77] What the Massachusetts Supreme Judicial Court stated in 1977 at the dawn of right-to-die litigation still holds true with respect to forgoing life-sustaining treatment, at least if the patient is competent or, if incompetent, there is a proper surrogate who follows the applicable substantive standard:

> [L]ittle need be said about criminal liability; there is precious little precedent, and what there is suggests that the doctor will be protected if he acts on a good faith judgment that is not grievously unreasonable by medical standards.[78]

Despite the paucity of criminal prosecutions and the reassurances by appellate courts that the forgoing of life-sustaining treatment is not grounds for the imposition of criminal liability, there is still some cause for concern.[79] The

---

[73] **NY:** *See, e.g.,* People v. Robbins, 443 N.Y.S.2d 1016 (App. Div. 1981).

**PA:** *See, e.g.,* Commonwealth v. Konz, 450 A.2d 638 (Pa. 1982).

[74] **MA:** *See, e.g.,* Twitchell v. Commonwealth, 617 N.E.2d 609 (Mass. 1993).

**PA:** *See, e.g.,* Commonwealth v. Barnhart, 497 A.2d 616 (Pa. Super. Ct. 1985).

*See generally* Barrett, Annotation, *Homicide: Failure to Provide Medical or Surgical Attention,* 100 A.L.R.2d 483 (1965).

[75] **NY:** *See, e.g.,* Delio v. Westchester County Medical Ctr., 516 N.Y.S.2d 677, 681 (App. Div. 1987) ("The District Attorney has declined active participation in this proceeding and has adopted the position that the application concerns a family matter under the supervision of the court.").

**PA:** *See, e.g.,* Ragona v. Preate, 11 Fiduc. Rep. 2d 1 (C.P. Lackawanna County, Pa. 1990) (district attorney assured parties he would not prosecute for termination of life support in conformity with court's order); *In re* Doe, 45 Pa. D. & C.3d 371 (C.P. Phila. County 1987).

**OH:** *Cf. In re* Myers, 610 N.E.2d at 665 (upon inquiry of court, prosecutor "stated that neither the state nor the county would find any criminal liability if removal of the hydration and nutrition was accomplished").

[76] **MI:** *See, e.g.,* Rosebush v. Oakland County Prosecutor, 491 N.W.2d 633 (Mich. Ct. App. 1992) (county prosecutor obtained preliminary injunction against termination of life support).

**NJ:** *In re* Quinlan, 355 A.2d 647 (N.J. 1976).

[77] Barber v. Superior Court, 195 Cal. Rptr. 484, 486 (Ct. App. 1983).

[78] *In re* Spring, 405 N.E.2d 115, 121 (Mass. 1980) (citing Collester, *Death, Dying and the Law: A Prosecutorial View of the* Quinlan *Case,* 30 Rutgers L. Rev. 304, 310–11 (1977)).

[79] *See* Grace Plaza of Great Neck, Inc. v. Elbaum, 623 N.E.2d 513, 517 (N.Y. 1993) (Hancock, J., concurring) ("[A]n Assistant District Attorney had announced that if life support were withdrawn from Mrs. Elbaum without court permission, the facility risked criminal prosecution.").

removal of life-sustaining medical treatment is an act that brings about the patient's death, and under general principles of criminal law there is a prima facie case of homicide of some degree. Furthermore, the omission to act when there is a duty to act can also be the basis for criminal liability,[80] so that the withholding of life-sustaining medical treatment is, prima facie, no less culpable. And plainly, a physician or other health care professional who, without following proper procedures and standards, proceeds to terminate life support, is likely to be guilty of criminal homicide. Thus, it is necessary to determine what it is about the run-of-the-mill right-to-die case that absolves a physician from what would otherwise be a criminal act or omission.

## § 18.10 Forgoing Treatment Distinguished from Homicide

Courts have provided a number of explanations for the conclusion that forgoing life-sustaining treatment does not result in criminal (or civil) liability. However, all of them except one—that forgoing life-sustaining treatment constitutes an exercise of the patient's legal right to refuse treatment—leave much to be desired, and even that one is usually presented in a less than wholly satisfactory way. In the final analysis, in the case of a competent patient, it is the patient's right to freedom from unwanted interferences with his person, implemented through a voluntary and informed choice to withhold or withdraw treatment, and for an incompetent patient, it is the decision of a legally authorized surrogate, that legitimates the forgoing of life-sustaining treatment. It is for this same reason that the physician or other health care professional who withholds or withdraws life-sustaining treatment is not subject to liability for homicide. The same is true in the case of an incompetent patient, only here it is the voluntary and informed choice of one legally authorized to speak for the patient (that is, the surrogate) that legitimates the forgoing of life-sustaining treatment.

## § 18.11 —Legal Right to Forgo Life-Sustaining Treatment

Among the several reasons given by courts for not imposing liability is that death results from the exercise of the patient's legal right to refuse treatment if competent or for a surrogate do so if the patient cannot, assuming that the requisite substantive standard has been met. In such a situation, forgoing life-sustaining treatment is not unlawful homicide because it "does not amount to criminal agency because the decision and its implementation are authorized

---

[80] *See* Barber v. Superior Court, 195 Cal. Rptr. 484.

under the common law,"[81] or the constitution.[82] Although this explanation might appear to run head-on into the black-letter law that consent to a crime is not a defense,[83] this is not the case. What the courts seem to be saying—and correctly so, though not always as clearly as one might like—is that when there is voluntary and informed consent from a competent patient (or the surrogate of an incompetent patient), there is not even a prima facie case of homicide.

Perhaps the reticence of courts to be too clear about the fact that it is the patient's voluntary and informed decision to forgo life-sustaining treatment that legitimizes its withholding or withdrawal results from their realization that, if they were to do so do, it increases the difficulty of maintaining the carefully crafted distinction between active and passive euthanasia and the criminality of the former. If, as Justice Scalia wrote in *Cruzan,* it is true that "[s]tarving oneself to death is no different from putting a gun to one's temple as far as the common-law definition of suicide is concerned,"[84] then if forgoing artificial nutrition and hydration by a competent patient is a legally protected right, as all courts to have considered the question have held,[85] then it is hard to see how the same person's putting a gun to his head can be said not to be.[86] And if such

---

[81] **MI:** Rosebush v. Oakland County Prosecutor, 491 N.W.2d 633, 641 (Mich. Ct. App. 1992).

**US:** *Contra* Cruzan v. Director, 497 U.S. 261, 298 (1990) (Scalia, J., concurring) (The argument "that frustrating Nancy Cruzan's wish to die in the present case requires interference with her bodily integrity . . . is . . . inadequate, because such interference is impermissible only if one begs the question whether her refusal to undergo the treatment on her own is suicide.").

**NJ:** *Accord In re* Quinlan, 355 A.2d 647, 670 (N.J. 1976).

**NY:** *Accord* Eichner v. Dillon, 420 N.E.2d 64, 71 (N.Y. 1981). *Cf.* People v. Robbins, 443 N.Y.S.2d 1016, 1018–19 (App. Div. 1981) (There is no criminal liability for failure to summon medical assistance for someone who has refused life-sustaining treatment because such failure "was unquestionably the consequence of [her] conscious choice to rely on her faith and forego medical interference. . . . In New York such a rationale would be in direct conflict with the related rule that a competent adult has a right to determine whether or not to undergo medical treatment.").

**WA:** *Accord In re* Colyer, 660 P.2d 738, 751 (Wash. 1983).

*Cf.* 1989 URTIA § 11(a) ("Death resulting from the withholding or withdrawal of life-sustaining treatment pursuant to a declaration and in accordance with this [Act] does not constitute, for any purpose, a suicide or homicide.").

[82] See § **2.8.**

[83] *See* W. LaFave & A. Scott, Criminal Law § 5.11, at 477 (2d ed. 1986); Shaffer, Note, *Criminal Liability for Assisting Suicide,* 86 Colum. L. Rev. 348, 351 (1986); Model Penal Code § 2.11 (1962).

[84] Cruzan v. Director, 497 U.S. at 296 (Scalia, J., concurring).

[85] **CA:** *See* Thor v. Superior Court, 855 P.2d 375 (Cal. 1993); Bouvia v. Superior Court (Glenchur), 225 Cal. Rptr. 297 (Ct. App. 1986).

**FL:** *See* Browning v. Herbert, 568 So. 2d 4 (Fla. 1990) (competent patient authorizing forgoing of artificial nutrition and hydration by living will).

[86] See §§ **18.22–18.23.**

suicide is a legally protected right, it is only a very small step to concluding that one can legitimately authorize another to do what one cannot do for oneself.[87]

## § 18.12    —No Duty

One of the better explanations for not attaching criminal penalties to the forgoing of treatment is the one given in *Barber,*[88] which reflected the thinking of the President's Commission in its report *Deciding to Forego Life-Sustaining Treatment.*[89] For the *Barber* court, the crux of the issue was the nature of the legal duties that physicians owe to patients. The first such duty relevant here is not to affirmatively take the life of a patient—for example, by the injection of a lethal substance.[90] Regardless of the nature of a physician's motives, such an act would show criminal intent and would therefore constitute murder.[91]

This is the simple case; conventional right-to-die cases involving the withholding or withdrawal of life-sustaining medical treatment do not involve conduct that is so clearly criminal. Rather, the cases dealing with the forgoing of treatment often involve an omission to treat. Although it is sometimes said that only an act, not an omission, can constitute the basis of legal liability (either criminal or civil), this is not so. The characterization of a physician's conduct as an omission does not avoid criminal liability. What is determinative is whether or not the physician was under a duty to provide the care that was withdrawn or withheld. If such a duty was breached, then criminal liability may be imposed for an omission, but not otherwise.[92] For the *Barber* court there was no breach

---

[87] **DNY:** *But see* Quill v. Koppell, 870 F. Supp. 78 (S.D.N.Y. 1994).

　　**DOR:** *But see* Lee v. State, 869 F. Supp. 1491 (D. Or. 1994) (opinion on preliminary injunction).

　　**CA:** *See* Bouvia v. Superior Court (Glenchur), 225 Cal. Rptr. at 307 (Compton, J., concurring) ("The right to die is an integral part of our right to control our own destinies so long as the rights of others are not affected. That right should, in my opinion, include the ability to enlist assistance from others, including the medical profession, in making death as painless and quick as possible.").

　　**MI:** *But see* People v. Kevorkian, 527 N.W.2d 714 (Mich. 1994), *cert. denied sub nom.* Kevorkian v. Michigan, 115 S. Ct. 1795 (1995).

　　See § **18.25.**

[88] Barber v. Superior Court, 195 Cal. Rptr. 484 (Ct. App. 1983).

[89] President's Comm'n, Deciding to Forego Life-Sustaining Treatment (1983).

[90] See § **18.18.**

[91] **CA:** Barber v. Superior Court, 195 Cal. Rptr. at 488.

　　**MA:** *In re* Doe, 583 N.E.2d 1263, 1275 (Mass. 1992) (O'Connor, J., dissenting) ("[T]he law should recognize a competent person's right to refuse or withdraw medical treatment when that choice is not motivated by a desire to die but, instead, is reasonably motivated by a desire to avoid procedures that are in themselves, and not simply because they prolong life, physically or emotionally painful. Suicide, however, is a different matter.").

[92] Barber v. Superior Court, 195 Cal. Rptr. at 490.

of duty in omitting the continuance of life-sustaining medical treatment because doctors are not obligated always to provide treatment, but only to provide it when it is "proportionate," that is, when treatment provides benefits to the patient in excess of its burdens.[93]

# § 18.13   —Causation

Courts sometimes reason that forgoing life-sustaining treatment is not the basis for criminal (or civil) liability because when treatment is forgone and a patient dies, the cause of death is the patient's underlying illness rather than the conduct of the physician in withholding or withdrawing treatment.[94] Thus, there is no homicide, let alone culpable homicide. For instance, when a ventilator-dependent patient with a disease that prevents him from breathing—for example, amyotrophic lateral sclerosis—dies after the termination of ventilation, the cause of death for legal purposes is said to be the patient's disease rather than the conduct of the physician.[95] This reasoning is not entirely consistent with standard explanations of legal causation ordinarily employed in criminal and tort law, which courts conveniently ignore in right-to-die cases.[96]

What really validates the forgoing of life-sustaining treatment is the patient's voluntary and informed decision to forgo treatment. That this is so can be seen by considering the situation in which a physician disconnects a ventilator from

---

[93] *Id.* at 491. See § **7.15.**

[94] **DNY:** *See* Deel v. Syracuse Veterans Admin. Medical Ctr., 729 F. Supp. 231, 234 (N.D.N.Y. 1990).

**ME:** *See In re* Gardner, 534 A.2d 947, 955 (Me. 1987).

**MA:** *See In re* Doe, 583 N.E.2d 1263, 1270 (Mass. 1992) ("Canavan's disease, not the removal of the feeding and hydration tube, would be the death producing agent if the tube is removed.").

**MI:** *See* Rosebush v. Oakland County Prosecutor, 491 N.W.2d 633, 641 (Mich. Ct. App. 1992) ("[D]iscontinuance of life-support measures merely allows the patient's injury or illness to take its natural and inevitable course.").

**NJ:** *See In re* Quinlan, 355 A.2d 647, 670 (N.J. 1976) ("expiration from existing natural causes").

**WA:** *See In re* Colyer, 660 P.2d 738, 751 (Wash. 1983).

**WI:** *See* L.W. v. L.E. Phillips Career Dev. Ctr., 482 N.W.2d 60, 71 (Wis. 1992).

*See also* National Ctr. for State Courts, Guidelines for State Court Decision Making in Life-Sustaining Medical Treatment Cases 145 (2d ed. 1992).

[95] *See, e.g.,* Satz v. Perlmutter, 362 So. 2d 160, 162 (Fla. Dist. Ct. App. 1978).

[96] *See, e.g., In re* Doe, 583 N.E.2d at 1277 (O'Connor, J., dissenting) ("The court states . . . that 'Canavan's disease, not the removal of the feeding and hydration tube, would be the death producing agent if the tube is removed.' . . . That surely [meets the definition of a legal fiction, namely,] . . . '[a] situation contrived by the law to permit a court to dispose of a matter.' The court employs a device, a pretense, contrived for the purpose of authorizing the termination of Jane Doe's life. It is clear that, but for removal or non-use of the nasoduodenal tube, Jane Doe will live for the indefinite, perhaps considerable, future. Without it she will promptly die. That is proximate causation according to any recognized definition of that term.").

a competent patient whose life depends on it without the patient's consent (or from an incompetent patient without the proper authorization of one legally authorized to provide it). There is no gainsaying that, in such a case, the physician would be criminally liable for the patient's death. Thus, the true explanation for nonculpability is the existence of legally valid consent rather than an absence of causation.

The causation rationale is used not only to legitimate the forgoing of life-sustaining treatment but also to reinforce the distinction between passive euthanasia and active euthanasia and unequivocally condemn the latter. As one commentator explains, "'As a reality of nature . . . killing and letting die are causally different. . . . There must be an underlying fatal pathology if allowing to die is even possible. Killing, by contrast, provides its own fatal pathology."[97] Whether this distinction ultimately proves to be viable in the face of constitutional challenge remains to be seen.[98]

## § 18.14   —Intent

In cases involving the forgoing of life-sustaining treatment, the intent of the attending physician or other health care professional who withdraws or withholds life-sustaining treatment is different from that of someone who acts with the cold-blooded intent usually associated with murder, the passion associated with voluntary manslaughter, or the neglect associated with involuntary manslaughter.[99] For example, in the *Barber* case, a prosecution of physicians for terminating tube-feeding from a patient in a persistent vegetative state, the magistrate concluded at the probable cause hearing that

> there is . . . no evidence in the record to show that the defendants were acting either in a malignant, selfish, or foolhardy manner in the care and treatment of the patient . . . or in an intentional manner to take the life of another.
>
> [I]n this case, we do not have a willful starvation as the proximate cause of the patient's death. To say that the attending physicians sat back and watched a person starve to death is to ignore the state of bad health of Mr. Herbert.[100]

Despite the strong temptation to attempt to distinguish death from the forgoing of life-sustaining treatment from culpable homicide by virtue of the differential intent, this is not a particularly promising tack. Although upholding

---

[97] *See* Kamisar, *Are Laws Against Assisted Suicide Unconstitutional?*, 23 Hastings Center Rep. 32, 33 (May–June 1993) (quoting Callahan, *The Troubled Dream of Life* ch. 2 (1993)). *But see* Cruzan v. Director, 497 U.S. 261 (1990) (Scalia, J., dissenting) (equating forgoing life-sustaining treatment by a competent person with suicide).

[98] See §§ **18.22–18.23.**

[99] *See, e.g.,* People v. Barber, No. A025586, slip op. at 260 (L.A. Mun. Ct. Mar. 9, 1983) ("The usual presumptions of unlawfulness and willfulness arising from the horrific conduct of a murderer simply do not apply in the context of these doctors' actions.").

[100] *Id.* at 260–61. *See also* Barber v. Superior Court, 195 Cal. Rptr. 484, 487 (Ct. App. 1983).

the magistrate's dismissal of the indictment, the California Court of Appeal in *Barber* rejected his reasoning. In effect, the magistrate had made the error of confusing motive and intent and failed to recognize that motive is irrelevant to liability for homicide.[101] Consequently, if the attending physicians "intentionally killed Mr. Herbert, the malice could be presumed regardless of their motive."[102]

## § 18.15 —Passive Euthanasia

Forgoing life-sustaining treatment, despite the occasional judicial denials that it is euthanasia,[103] is sometimes said to be permissible because it is *passive* euthanasia[104] rather than an active "killing" of the patient. Despite the plethora of judicial rulings permitting the forgoing of life-sustaining treatment and thus approving passive euthanasia in all but name, there is still a strong judicial aversion to employing the term, except as one of criticism. Further, there is significant controversy over whether passive euthanasia is any different in principle from active euthanasia. An important issue is the difficulty in developing principled rules for distinguishing between an act and an omission,[105] a problem which also overlaps the issue of causation. This is graphically illustrated in the controversy over the legitimacy of withholding artificial nutrition and hydration from terminally ill incompetent patients,[106] which has been described by one judge as "pure, unadorned euthanasia."[107]

---

[101] **CA:** Barber v. Superior Court, 195 Cal. Rptr. at 487 ("While the law is settled that motive is irrelevant to a determination of whether a killing amounts to murder, the lack of precision in defining malice often makes it difficult to disentangle motive from a determination of what constitutes malice.").

**NY:** *But cf.* Saunders v. State, 492 N.Y.S.2d 510, 517 (Sup. Ct. Nassau County 1985) ("For [physicians, hospitals, or their administrators] . . . to be held civilly or criminally liable, there must be a showing that their actions were not in good faith, but were intended to harm the patient.").

[102] Barber v. Superior Court, 195 Cal. Rptr. at 487.

[103] **WA:** *See, e.g., In re* Grant, 747 P.2d 445, 454 (Wash. 1987) ("We emphasize that we are not endorsing suicide or euthanasia.").

[104] **KY:** DeGrella v. Elston, 858 S.W.2d 698, 706 (Ky. 1993) (prohibition on "mercy killing, euthanasia, or . . . any affirmative or deliberate act to end life other than to permit the natural process of dying" does not prohibit the termination of life support).

**WA:** *In re* Grant, 747 P.2d at 461 (Goodloe, J., dissenting) ("The majority opinion is the most recent in a series of decisions in which this court judicially moves toward and authorizes passive euthanasia.").

[105] See §§ **8.5** and **18.12.**

[106] See § **9.39.**

[107] **WA:** *In re* Grant, 747 P.2d at 458 (Andersen, J., concurring in part and dissenting in part).

**MD:** *Accord* Mack v. Mack, 618 A.2d 744 (Md. 1993) (Chasanow, J., concurring and dissenting) ("I do not, however, subscribe to the passive euthanasia implication" of the majority opinion.).

**MA:** *Accord* Brophy v. New Eng. Sinai Hosp., Inc., 497 N.E.2d 626, 640 (Mass. 1986) (Nolan, J., dissenting) ("court today has indorsed euthanasia"); *id.* at 644–45 (O'Connor, J., dissenting).

One viewpoint contends that it is either the act of health care professionals in removing artificial nutrition and hydration apparatus or their omission in failing to provide additional nutrition or hydration once the current supply is exhausted, and not the patient's condition, that causes death. The opposing view, which has so far almost unanimously prevailed in the courts, is that a patient who dies when artificial nutrition and hydration are forgone does so because the illness from which he is suffering has resulted in the loss of the ability to swallow or to swallow without choking. Consequently, forgoing artificial nutrition and hydration is the functional equivalent of forgoing ventilatory support, in which case death also results from the underlying disease process which no longer permits normal respiration.[108]

## § 18.16   —Advance Directive Legislation

Perhaps the weakest, and least frequently cited, judicial rationale for not imposing criminal sanctions for forgoing treatment is based on advance directive legislation. The Washington Supreme Court explained as follows:

> Washington's Natural Death Act excludes from criminal liability those who act in good faith and in accordance with a directive complying with the statutory requirements. It further states that acts in accordance with a directive are not deemed suicide ... and the cause of death shall be that which placed the patient in a terminal condition.... We believe the same principles should apply when the patient's right to refuse life-sustaining treatment is exercised in accordance with this opinion.[109]

This is certainly an acceptable rationale when the forgoing of life-sustaining treatment is based on an advance directive that complies with the applicable statute, in Washington or any other state. However, this reasoning is extremely weak[110] and plainly unnecessary as a basis for excusing criminal (or civil) liability when the forgoing of life-sustaining treatment is not based on an advance directive. The latter situation is an analogy to the reasoning that excuses the forgoing of life-sustaining medical treatment from criminal liability on the basis that the patient has a legal right to refuse treatment.[111] That is a far more straightforward and satisfying way of approaching the matter than by analogy.

---

[108] See § **9.53.**

[109] *In re* Colyer, 660 P.2d 738, 751 (Wash. 1983). *Cf.* 1985 URTIA § 11(a) ("Death resulting from the withholding or withdrawal of life-sustaining treatment pursuant to a declaration and in accordance with this [Act] does not constitute, for any purpose, a suicide or homicide."). See §§ **11.17** and **12.46.**

[110] See § **18.18.**

[111] See § **18.4.**

## § 18.17   What Constitutes Assisted Suicide and Homicide

When a physician (or any other person) engages in an active intervention that ends a patient's life, for example by the injection of a lethal overdose of morphine, the physician has engaged in active euthanasia (sometimes called *mercy killing*), which might subject him to liability for some degree of criminal homicide.[112] Can this liability be avoided if the physician provides a competent patient with the means of ending his own life but stops short of actually administering the instrumentality of death? Although the removal of life support is not considered criminal homicide or assisted suicide,[113] this does not resolve the issue of whether or not one who provides a person with some instrumentality that the person then employs to take his own life, by means other than refusing to have treatment administered or continued, is subject to liability for assisted suicide or homicide.

Very little judicial attention has been accorded this question because the practice rarely comes to the attention of the authorities. One reason is the secretiveness of the manner in which it is practiced in the medical context. Another possible reason is that not all jurisdictions have statutes making assisted suicide a crime (see **Table 18–1**), and the status of a common-law crime of assisted suicide is uncertain.[114] Finally, even if the commission of physician-assisted suicide is brought to the attention of the authorities, the pervasive exercise of discretion by a variety of actors in the criminal process (coroners, district attorneys, judges, juries) can prevent the occurrence of the necessary steps (investigation, indictment, trial, and conviction) to bring the practice to the attention of appellate courts.[115] One such example is a New York physician who

---

[112] See § **10.10.**

[113] See §§ **18.10–18.16.**

[114] Shaffer, Note, *Criminal Liability for Assisting Suicide,* 86 Colum. L. Rev. 348, 351 & n.27 (1986).

[115] *See* Shaffer, Note, *Criminal Liability for Assisting Suicide,* 86 Colum. L. Rev. 348, 369–71 (1986); Oelsner, *Few Mercy Killers Draw Full Penalties,* N.Y. Times, June 26, 1973, at 49. *See, e.g.,* Altman, *Jury Declines to Indict a Doctor Who Said He Aided in a Suicide,* N.Y. Times, July 27, 1991, at 1 (nat'l ed.); Brahams, *Euthanasia: Doctor Convicted of Attempted Murder,* 340 Lancet 782, 783 (1992) (prosecutor offered no evidence in prosecution of physician for killing a terminally ill cancer patient with a lethal injection, for whom high doses of heroin had been unable to relieve pain); *Doctor Freed; No One Mentions Euthanasia,* N.Y. Times, Feb. 10, 1974, § 4, at 6; Ellis, *Doctor's Murder Trial Begins in Clayton,* Atlanta J./Constitution, Oct. 24, 1994, at A-1; Gianelli, *Doctor Who Aided Suicide Not to Be Prosecuted,* Am. Med. News, May 6, 1991, at 8; Gianelli, *Death by Injection Ruled "Homicide," But Prosecutor Opts Not to Charge MDs,* Am. Med. News. Jan. 19, 1990, at 2; Lelyveld, *1936 Secret Is Out: Doctor Sped George V's Death,* N.Y. Times, Nov. 28, 1986, at 1 (nat'l ed.); Narvaez, *Jersey Physician Is Spared Prison Sentence for Mercy Killing,* N.Y. Times, Dec. 12, 1986, at 10 (nat'l ed.); *Nurse, on Trial for Murder, Called Compassionate,* N.Y. Times, Mar. 14, 1979, at A17 (city ed.); *Physician Gets Probation in Mercy Death,* Am. Med. News, Jan. 9, 1987, at 2; *Testimony to Begin in Trial of Nurse in Death of Patient,* N.Y.

published an article in the *New England Journal of Medicine* recounting the case of a patient who refused treatment for cancer and for whom he prescribed a lethal amount of barbiturates at the patient's request, so that she might take the medication to end her suffering.[116] The authorities originally declined to attempt to prosecute the physician because the body of the deceased could not be located.[117] However, when it was, the grand jury refused to indict.[118]

The only contemporary attention to the question by an appellate court has occurred in the instance of a physician, Dr. Jack Kevorkian, who has openly aided terminally or hopelessly ill patients to commit suicide.[119] Beginning in 1991, Dr. Kevorkian provided numerous people in the state of Michigan—a state without a statutory prohibition on assisted suicide at that time—with various types of devices to permit them to commit suicide, earning him the title of the "serial mercy killer."[120] After the first use of his "suicide machine," he was indicted for murder, but the indictment was dismissed.[121] Subsequently, after a civil proceeding was initiated against Dr. Kevorkian to confiscate the suicide device to prohibit him from constructing another or assisting anyone else in constructing another, an injunction was granted barring him from using the device.[122] After the second and third uses of the device, the Michigan Board of

---

Times, Sept. 14, 1981, at A22 (city ed.); Wanzer et al., *The Physician's Responsibility Toward Hopelessly Ill Patients,* 320 New Eng. J. Med. 844, 848 (1989) (citing Glantz, *Withholding and Withdrawing Treatment: The Role of the Criminal Law,* 15 Law, Med. & Health Care 231 (1987–1988) ("no physician . . . has ever been prosecuted in the United States for prescribing pills in order to help a patient commit suicide").

[116] *See* Quill, *Death and Dignity: A Case of Individualized Decision Making,* 324 New Eng. J. Med. 691 (1991). *See also* Altman, *Doctor Says He Agonized, But Gave Drug for Suicide,* N.Y. Times, Mar. 7, 1991, at A1 (nat'l ed.).

[117] Gianelli, *Doctor Who Aided Suicide Not to Be Prosecuted,* Am. Med. News, May 6, 1991, at 8.

[118] Altman, *Jury Declines to Indict a Doctor Who Said He Aided in a Suicide,* N.Y. Times, July 27, 1991, at 1 (nat'l ed.).

[119] See § **18.2.**

[120] *See* Belkin, *Doctor Tells of First Death Using His Suicide Device,* N.Y. Times, June 6, 1990, at A1 (nat'l ed.) (describing device invented by Dr. Jack Kevorkian and its use by Janet Adkins); *Michigan Charging Murder After a 2d Assisted Suicide,* N.Y. Times, Aug. 20, 1990, § 1, at 16 (nat'l ed.) (California man who had brought his wife, terminally ill with cancer, to Michigan and assisted in her suicide, charged with murder); *Murder Trial Is Ordered for Man Who Helped Wife Commit Suicide,* N.Y. Times, Sept. 8, 1990, at 10 (late ed.); Wilkerson, *Rage and Support for Doctor's Role in Suicide,* N.Y. Times, Oct. 25, 1991, at A1 (nat'l ed.). *See also Inventor of Suicide Machine Tied to Death of Dentist in California,* N.Y. Times, Feb. 13, 1992, at A13 (nat'l ed.).

[121] Lewin, *Judge Clears Doctor of Murdering Woman with a Suicide Machine,* N.Y. Times, Dec. 14, 1990, at A1 (nat'l ed.); Williams, *Murder Charge Against Dr. Kevorkian Dropped,* Am. Med. News, Dec. 28, 1990, at 4.

[122] State *ex rel.* Thompson v. Kevorkian, No. 90-390963-AZ (Oakland County, Mich. Feb. 5, 1991), *reprinted in* 7 Issues L. & Med. 107 (1991). *See also Michigan Court Bars Doctor from Using His Suicide Machine,* N.Y. Times, Feb. 6, 1991, at A13 (late ed.).

Medicine suspended Kevorkian's license to practice medicine,[123] and he was again indicted for murder. After a preliminary hearing, the charges were again dismissed because the judge found that Dr. Kevorkian had not activated the suicide machines. At most, he had participated in assisted suicide, which was not then a crime in Michigan.[124]

After his license to practice medicine was suspended and he could no longer obtain access to prescription medications, Dr. Kevorkian continued to assist terminally or seriously ill patients in ending their lives by providing them with carbon monoxide gas, which does not require a medical license to obtain. Using this method, he aided a number of other suicides, prompting the Michigan legislature to enact a temporary statute criminalizing assisted suicide, with the ban to be repealed six months after the date that a commission, established under the same legislation, made its recommendations about what the state's policy should be on assisted suicide.[125] As the effective date of the legislation approached, the pace of Dr. Kevorkian's activity increased substantially.[126] Consequently, the Michigan legislature made the legislation effective immediately. Dr. Kevorkian ignored the statutory prohibition, and he was indicted for assisting in the death of a 30-year-old man suffering from amyotrophic lateral sclerosis.[127]

Some of the prosecutions of Dr. Kevorkian led to appeals from the dismissal of indictments for murder and thus to the first judicial opinions discussing the kind of conduct necessary to convict a physician of assisted suicide. Because of the absence of a statutory prohibition on assisted suicide at the time that his conduct occurred, Dr. Kevorkian was indicted for murder. The trial courts dismissed the indictments, but the court of appeals reinstated them, based on a 1920 precedent, *People v. Roberts*.[128] Roberts had been convicted of murder for providing his wife, suffering from multiple sclerosis, with a poison that she administered to herself. This holding had been questioned by the Michigan Court of Appeals in 1983 in *People v. Campbell*,[129] which was affirmed per

---

[123] *See Michigan Board Suspends License of Doctor who Aided in Suicides,* N.Y. Times, Nov. 21, 1991, at D22 (late ed.).

[124] *Murder Charges Against Kevorkian Are Dismissed,* N.Y. Times, July 22, 1992, at A12 (late ed.). *But see* People v. Kevorkian, 527 N.W.2d 714 (Mich. 1994) (holding that defendant could be prosecuted for common-law crime of assisted suicide), *cert. denied sub nom.* Kevorkian v. Michigan, 115 S. Ct. 1795 (1995).

[125] *See* Mich. Pub. Act 270 of 1992, 1992 Mich. Legis. Serv. P.A. 270 (H.R. 4501).

[126] *Kevorkian Aids in 2 More Suicides; Total Is at 15,* N.Y. Times, Feb. 19, 1993, at A10 (late ed.).

[127] Terry, *As He Hoped, Kevorkian Is Charged in a Suicide,* N.Y. Times, Aug. 18, 1993, at A7 (nat'l ed.).

[128] 178 N.W. 690 (Mich. 1920).

[129] 335 N.W.2d 27 (Mich. Ct. App. 1983).

curiam and without an opinion by the Michigan Supreme Court.[130] In *People v. Kevorkian,*[131] the court of appeals distinguished *Campbell* as a case of inciting to commit suicide, rather than assisting in committing suicide, and concluded that in any event, *Roberts* was still good law because "[a] decision of the [Michigan] Supreme Court is binding until the Supreme Court overrules itself," which it had not done by a per curiam affirmance.[132]

On appeal to the Michigan Supreme Court, the court overruled *Roberts,* holding that one could not be prosecuted for murder for assisting another to commit suicide unless the defendant "participates in the final overt act that causes death, such as firing a gun or pushing the plunger on a hypodermic needle."[133] Indeed, in common parlance, it is at least questionable whether such a death would be considered suicide as opposed to voluntary active euthanasia. The court's holding brought Michigan in line with the modern trend. As the court observed, "[i]n the years since 1920, when *Roberts* was decided, inter-pretation of causation in criminal cases has evolved in Michigan to require a closer nexus between an act and a death than was required in *Roberts.*"[134] In addition, although "[e]arly decisions indicate that a murder conviction may be based on merely providing the means by which another commits suicide . . . few jurisdictions, if any, have retained the early common-law view that assisting in a suicide is murder."[135]

However, rather than dismissing the prosecutions, the court held that assisted suicide is a separate common-law offense that can be prosecuted in the absence of a statute under the criminal code's saving clause, which prescribes a punish-ment of imprisonment for not more than five years and a fine not to exceed $10,000 per offense.[136] The court also held that such a prosecution would not violate the constitutional prohibition on ex post facto laws because "[o]ur reinterpretation of the common law does not enlarge the scope of criminal liability for assisted suicide, but rather reduces liability where a defendant merely is involved in the events leading up to the suicide, such as providing the means."[137]

---

[130] People v. Campbell, 342 N.W.2d 519 (Mich. 1984).

[131] 517 N.W.2d 293 (Mich. Ct. App. 1994).

[132] People v. Kevorkian, 517 N.W.2d at 297.

[133] People v. Kevorkian, 527 N.W.2d 714, 738 (Mich. 1994), *cert. denied sub nom.* Kevorkian v. Michigan, 115 S. Ct. 1795 (1995).

[134] *Id.*

[135] *Id.* at 736.

[136] *Id.* at 739 (citing Mich. Comp. Laws § 750.505; Mich. Stat. Ann. § 28.773).

[137] *Id.*

**Table 18–1**

| (A) Assisted Suicide Statutes |
| --- |

| | |
| --- | --- |
| **AK:** | Alaska Stat. § 11.41.120 |
| **AZ:** | Ariz. Rev. Stat. Ann. § 13-1103(A)(3) |
| **AR:** | Ark. Code Ann. § 5-10-104(a)(2) |
| **CA:** | Cal. Penal Code § 401 |
| **CO:** | Colo. Rev. Stat. § 18-3-104 |
| **CT:** | Conn. Gen. Stat. Ann. § 53a-56 |
| **DE:** | Del. Code Ann. tit. 11, § 645 |
| **FL:** | Fla. Stat. Ann. § 782.08 |
| **GA:** | Ga. Code Ann. § 16-5-5(b) |
| **HI:** | Haw. Rev. Stat. § 707-702 |
| **IL:** | Ill. Ann. Stat. ch. 720, § 5/12-31 |
| **IN:** | Ind. Code Ann. § 35-42-1-2 |
| **KS:** | Kan. Stat. Ann. § 21-3406 |
| **KY:** | Ky. Rev. Stat. Ann. § 216.302 |
| **ME:** | Me. Rev. Stat. Ann. tit. 17-A, § 204 |
| **MI:** | Mich. Comp. Laws. § 752.1027 |
| **MN:** | Minn. Stat. Ann. § 609.215 |
| | Minn. Stat. Ann. §§ 147.09(W), 151.06(a)(7)(xii) |
| **MS:** | Miss. Code Ann. § 97-3-49 |
| **MO:** | Mo. Ann. Stat. § 565.023 |
| **MT:** | Mont. Code Ann. § 45-5-105 |
| **NE:** | Neb. Rev. Stat. § 28-307 |
| **NH:** | N.H. Rev. Stat. Ann. § 630:4 |
| **NJ:** | N.J. Stat. Ann. § 2C:11-6 |
| **NM:** | N.M. Stat. Ann. § 30-2-4 |
| **NY:** | N.Y. Penal Law § 120.30 |
| **ND:** | N.D. Cent. Code § 12.1-16-04 |
| **OK:** | Okla. Stat. Ann. tit. 21, §§ 813–818 |
| **OR:** | Or. Rev. Stat. § 163.12(1)(b) |
| **PA:** | Pa. Stat. Ann. tit. 18, § 2505 |
| **SC:** | S.C. Code Ann. § 16-1-10 |
| **SD:** | S.D. Codified Laws Ann. §§ 22-16-37, -38 |
| **TN:** | Tenn. Code Ann. § 39-13-216 |
| **TX:** | Tex. Penal Code Ann. § 22.08 |
| **WA:** | Wash. Rev. Code Ann. § 9A.36.060 |
| **WI:** | Wis. Stat. Ann. § 940.12 |

| (B) Assisted Suicide Prohibited as a Common-Law Crime |
| --- |

| | |
| --- | --- |
| **AL:** | Ala. Code § 1-3-1 |
| **DC:** | D.C. Code Ann. § 22-107 |
| **ID:** | Idaho Code § 18-303 |
| **MD:** | Md. Code Ann., Const. art. 5 |
| **NV:** | Nev. Rev. Stat. Ann. § 192.050 |
| **RI:** | R.I. Gen. Laws § 11-1-1 |
| **SC:** | S.C. Code Ann. § 16-1-10 |
| **VT:** | Vt. Stat. Ann. tit. 1, § 271 |

## ACTIVE INTERVENTIONS TO END LIFE

## § 18.18   Criminal Liability for "Active" Interventions to End Life

Although offering a variety of reasons, some less satisfactory than others, the courts have been steadfastly unwilling to conclude that "forgoing" life-sustaining medical treatment—that is, withholding or withdrawal—constitutes any kind of crime if proper procedures and standards are followed.[138] However, the same cannot be said when the death of a person, regardless of his medical condition, is brought about by some affirmative act that goes beyond the act necessary to terminate medical treatment. A bedrock assumption on which the judicial consensus about forgoing life-sustaining treatment is grounded is that there is a fundamental distinction between a patient's death from withholding or withdrawing treatment and an act that ends life. The courts have manifested an unflagging insistence on establishing and maintaining a bright line between active euthanasia and passive euthanasia even when it seriously strains reasoning to do so.[139] Active euthanasia is almost universally condemned in American statutory and judicial law.[140]

In the absence of the two recognized exceptions to criminal liability for homicide, justification or excuse,[141] defenses that are unlikely to be applicable to the doctor-patient relationship,[142] Anglo-American law has always harshly

---

[138] See §§ 18.10–18.16.

[139] *See* DeGrella v. Elston, 858 S.W.2d 698, 715 (Ky. 1993) (Wintersheimer, J., dissenting) ("There is a very fine line in allowing death because of natural circumstances when assistance is abandoned and actively participating in the onset of death by withdrawal of support."). *See also* Rachels, *Active and Passive Euthanasia,* 292 New Eng. J. Med. 78 (1975).

[140] **CA:** *But see* Bouvia v. Superior Court (Glenchur), 225 Cal. Rptr. 297, 307 (Ct. App. 1986) (Compton, J., concurring) (That the patient "is forced to suffer the ordeal of self-starvation to achieve her objective is in itself inhumane" and therefore right to die should "include the ability to enlist assistance from others, including the medical profession, in making death as painless and quick as possible . . . [and] should not be hampered by the state's threat to impose penal sanctions on those who might be disposed to lend assistance.").

**FL:** *See In re* Browning, 568 So. 2d 4, 13 (Fla. 1990) ("Euthanasia is a crime in this state.").

**IL:** *See* Estate of Longeway v. Community Convalescent Ctr., 549 N.E.2d 292, 298 (Ill. 1989) ("[W]e . . . emphatically . . . do not condone suicide or active euthanasia.").

**KY:** *See* DeGrella v. Elston, 858 S.W.2d 698, 702 (Ky. 1993) ("Nothing in this Opinion should be construed as sanctioning or supporting euthanasia, or mercy killing.").

Annotation, *Criminal Liability for Death of Another as Result of Accused's Attempt to Kill Self or Assist Another's Suicide,* 40 A.L.R.4th 702 (1985); Annotation, *Homicide as Affected by a Humanitarian Motive,* 25 A.L.R. 1007 (1923). *See also* 1989 URTIA § 11(g) ("This [Act] does not condone, authorize, or approve mercy-killing or euthanasia.").

[141] *See generally* W. LaFave & A. Scott, Criminal Law §§ 5.1–5.11 (2d ed. 1986).

[142] *See* Barber v. Superior Court, 195 Cal. Rptr. 484, 487 (Ct. App. 1983).

penalized the intentional taking of human life.[143] The taking of the life of another person by some affirmative act such as the injection of a lethal substance, regardless of the fact that the motive may be the relief of suffering, is culpable homicide—that is, either manslaughter or, more likely, murder. The motive of the killer does not legitimate otherwise illegitimate taking of life.[144] One who acts for merciful reasons is no less guilty of murder,[145] though account of motive is sometimes informally taken into account by prosecutors, judges, juries, and parole boards.

In addition to criminal liability, a physician who assists a patient in committing suicide may also be guilty of "unprofessional conduct,"[146] which can be the basis for disciplinary action, including the loss of one's license to practice medicine.[147] In Minnesota, such legislation also applies to pharmacists.[148] However, the statute explicitly legitimates the principle of *double effect,*[149] by providing that the administration, prescription, or dispensation of "medications or procedures to relieve another person's pain or discomfort, even if the medication or procedure may hasten or increase the risk of death," is not abetting or aiding suicide "unless the medications or procedures are knowingly administered, prescribed, or dispensed to cause death."[150]

Despite its formal illegality, the covert practice of physician-assisted suicide and active euthanasia has occurred throughout history.[151] In recent times, although there are news accounts of physicians (and nonphysicians) who have been investigated by criminal and/or regulatory authorities for administering lethal doses of medications to terminally ill patients, there are few prosecutions.[152]

---

[143] Cruzan v. Director, 497 U.S. 261, 280 (1990) ("As a general matter, the States—indeed, all civilized nations—demonstrate their commitment to life by treating homicide as a serious crime.").

[144] Barber v. Superior Court, 195 Cal. Rptr. at 488. *See generally* W. LaFave & A. Scott, Criminal Law § 3.6(a), at 227–31 (2d ed. 1986).

[145] *Cf.* United States v. Repouille, 165 F.2d 152 (2d Cir. 1947) (alien who performed euthanasia on son denied citizenshp as not being person of "good moral character").

[146] *See, e.g.,* Minn. Stat. Ann. § 147.091(w).

[147] *See id.* §§ 147.36, 147.261(18), 150A.08(14).

[148] *See id.* § 151.06(a)(7)(xii).

[149] See § **8.7.**

[150] **MN:** Minn. Stat. Ann. § 609.215(a).

**FL:** *Accord* Fla. Stat. Ann. § 458.326(3) ("physician may prescribe or administer any controlled substance . . . to a person for the treatment of intractable pain" in accordance with generally accepted medical standards).

**TN:** *Accord* Tenn. Code Ann. § 39-13-216(b)(2) (same).

**TX:** *Accord* Texas Intractable Pain Act, Tex. Rev. Civ. Stat. Ann. art. 4495(c).

*See generally* Caswell, *Rejecting Criminal Liability for Life-Shortening Palliative Care,* 6 J. Contemp. Health L. & Pol'y 127 (1990) (discussing proposals of Law Reform Commission of Canada that would in part recognize principle of double effect).

[151] Emanuel, *Euthanasia—Historical, Ethical, and Empiric Perspectives,* 154 Archives Internal Med. 1890 (1994).

[152] *See, e.g.,* Slovin, *County Attorney Calls Deaths Homicide, But He Won't Prosecute,* Minneapolis Star-Trib., Apr. 25, 1990, at 1B; Gianelli, *Death by Injection Ruled "Homicide," But Prosecutor Opts Not to Charge MDs,* Am. Med. News. Jan. 19, 1990, at 2.

There are even fewer reported cases of it,[153] especially involving physicians, despite the fact that, judging from the news accounts[154] and self-reported physician behavior,[155] they occur with some frequency. The reasons for the paucity of reported cases may be that appeals of such convictions are few or that, by dint of pervasive discretion in the criminal justice system, perpetrators are not indicted, indictments are dismissed, juries refuse to convict even when the evidence of guilt is quite clear, judges are lenient in sentencing, parole boards grant parole, and governors grant pardons. All of this probably results from the fact that motive is the humane one of relieving the suffering of a dying person,

---

[153] **FL:** *See, e.g.,* Gilbert v. State, 487 So. 2d 1185 (Fla. Dist. Ct. App.), *review denied,* 494 So. 2d 1150 (Fla. 1986).

**MI:** *See, e.g.,* People v. Roberts, 178 N.W. 690 (Mich. 1920), *overruled,* People v. Kevorkian, 527 N.W.2d 714 (Mich. 1994).

**MT:** *Cf.* Brackman v. Board of Nursing, 851 P.2d 1055 (Mont. 1993) (disciplinary proceedings against hospice nurses for stockpiling narcotics for use by patients when their needs exceeded prescribed amounts), *discussed in* Duignan-Cabrera, *Montana's "Angels of Mercy,"* Newsweek, June 10, 1991, at 24.

[154] *See* Glantz, *Withholding and Withdrawing Treatment: The Role of the Criminal Law,* 15 Law, Med. & Health Care 231 (1987–1988) (collecting 19 unreported American cases between 1939 and 1981). *See, e.g., Acquittal in Aided Suicide,* N.Y. Times, Feb. 15, 1992, at A5 (nat'l ed.); Fein, *Loving Father to Death, or Manslaughter?,* N.Y. Times, Nov. 7, 1994, at A1 (nat'l ed.); *Doctor Cleared of Murder Charge in Helping Cancerous Wife to Die,* New York Times, Dec. 2, 1988, at A11; *Husband Acquitted by Jury in Mercy Death,* 2 BioLaw § 12-1, at U:1243 (Feb. 1989); *Man Cleared of Murder in Aiding Wife's Suicide,* N.Y. Times, May 11, 1991, at 8 (nat'l ed.); *Man, 77, Killed His Wife Out of Love, Judge Rules,* N.Y. Times, Oct. 6, 1985 (nat'l ed.); *Man Who Killed Ill Wife Is Given Year's Work,* N.Y. Times, Dec. 12, 1985, at 12 (nat'l ed.); *"Mercy Killer" Acquitted on Insanity Plea,* N.Y. Times, Nov. 11, 1973, at 1; *Mercy Slaying Brings Probation in California,* N.Y. Times, Jan. 8, 1986, at 8 (nat'l ed.); *Murder Charge Dropped in Death of Ill Wife,* N.Y. Times, Sept. 20, 1986, at 7 (nat'l ed.); *cf.* Barron, *Hospital Death Ruled Accidental; Man's Children Won't Be Charged,* N.Y. Times, Jan. 26, 1990, at A13 (nat'l ed.) (district attorney did not prosecute family who turned off critically ill father's ventilator because "'[l]egally, there's no way a criminal charge could be sustained here'"); *Probation in Mercy Killing,* N.Y. Times, July 19, 1983, at 11 (city ed.); *but see Father Who Shot Ill Girl Gets Life Sentence,* N.Y. Times, Dec. 22, 1985, at 10 (nat'l ed.).

[155] *See Poll Shows That 1 in 5 Internists Has Helped a Patient Die,* Am. Med. News, Mar. 16, 1992, at 9 (informal survey conducted by the American Society of Internal Medicine found that one in five physicians admitted to taking deliberate actions to end the life of a terminally ill patient, and one in four reported that they had been asked by a terminally ill patient for assistance in committing suicide); Emanuel, *Euthanasia—Historical, Ethical, and Empiric Perspectives,* 154 Archives Internal Med. 1890 (1994). *See also* Simons, *Dutch Move to Enact Law Making Euthansia Easier,* N.Y. Times, Feb. 9, 1993, at A1, A7 (nat'l ed) ("Dutch doctors say their colleagues from France, Britain, Scandinavia and elsewhere, frequently tell them that they also intervene in a number of ways to speed up the death of a terminally ill and suffering patient, but that the Dutch are more open about it."); Altman, *Jury Declines to Indict a Doctor Who Said He Aided in a Suicide,* N.Y. Times, July 27, 1991, § 1, at 1 (late ed.) (reporting that Dr. Timothy Quill, who published an article admitting that he had aided a terminally ill patient in committing suicide—*see* Quill, *Death and Dignity: A Case of Individualized Decision Making,* 324 New Eng. J. Med. 691 (1991)—heard from numerous other physicians that they had acted similarly but had not revealed their conduct); Morain, *Out of the Closet on the Right to Die,* Am. Med. News, Dec. 12, 1994, at 13.

which although irrelevant in the formal criminal process, can be given effect in less formal legal processes.

The ending of the life of another in order to end that patient's suffering is usually referred to as active euthanasia (or mercy killing) or, depending on the mechanism by which death occurs, assisted suicide.[156] More recently, the phrase "aid in dying" has begun to be used to encompass both practices. The term *euthanasia,* from the Greek for "good death," generally refers to the ending of an individual's life for the relief of that individual's suffering from a painful and incurable disease.[157] The use of the unmodified term *euthanasia* runs the risk of confusion with passive euthanasia. While the better term is little used by courts, because the practice is synonymous with forgoing life-sustaining treatment it is generally approved under appropriate circumstances.

Confusion of another sort also pervades the discussion of the difference between active and passive euthanasia. When life-sustaining medical treatment is forgone, this may occur either by a withholding of treatment or by a withdrawing of treatment;[158] put another way, it can be accomplished by an act or by an omission.[159] When it is accomplished by an act—for example, removing a ventilator from a ventilator-dependent patient—although some person must perform the "act" for the ventilatory support to be terminated, this is still regarded as passive euthanasia because the actor's conduct is only a "condition" necessary for the "true" cause, the patient's inability to breathe spontaneously, to bring about death; or if a cause, it is considered an "indirect" rather than a "direct" cause of death, and thus not the legally responsible cause.[160] So intent have the courts been on maintaining this distinction that they have usually eschewed the use of the term "euthanasia." Out of fear of confusing active and passive euthanasia, or because the unmodified term "euthanasia" has for some people acquired the negative connotations associated with active euthanasia, involuntary euthanasia, or both, courts ordinarily avoid the term "euthanasia" (even modified by "passive") and refer to passive euthanasia as forgoing

---

[156] See § **18.19.**

[157] *In re* Grant, 747 P.2d 445, 458 (Wash. 1987) ("'Euthanasia' has been defined as 'the act or practice of painlessly putting to death persons suffering from incurable conditions or diseases.'") (Andersen, J., concurring and dissenting) (citing Webster's Third New International Dictionary 786 (1971)).

[158] See § **8.6.**

[159] See §§ **8.5** and **18.12.**

[160] *See, e.g.,* DeGrella v. Elston, 858 S.W.2d 698, 702 (Ky. 1993) ("The withdrawal of nutrition and hydration from a person in Sue DeGrella's state, irreversible brain damage and a prolonged period in a persistent vegetative state, is medically recognized as fitting the definition of 'permit[ting] the natural process of dying' as documented by the evidence in the record before us") (citing National Ctr. for State Courts, Guidelines for State Court Decision Making in Life-Sustaining Medical Treatment Cases 143–45 (2d ed. 1992)). See §§ **18.5–18.6, 18.13,** and **18.15.**

life-sustaining treatment or terminating life support or refusing treatment, and to active euthanasia as killing or mercy killing.[161]

In active euthanasia, the actor's conduct—such as the administration of a lethal dose of a medication with the intent to bring about death—is said to be the cause, or direct cause, of the patient's death. Consequently, a physician—indeed, anyone—who administers a lethal dose of a medication regardless of whether the purpose is part of a palliative care plan to relieve pain or to end life,[162] is subject to criminal liability in theory.[163] If the medication is one that is used in the treatment of the patient, such as morphine, but is inadvertently given in a large enough dose to produce death—referred to as the principle of *double effect*[164]—this is generally not treated by prosecutors who become aware of it as active euthanasia. However, in theory, one might be subject to liability for murder or negligent homicide.[165]

The rigidity of the formal rules of criminal liability for killing is manifested in other ways besides the lack of allowance for motive. It is equally well accepted that consent to any crime, not just killing, is not a defense (unless the

---

[161] *In re* Storar, 420 N.E.2d 64, 75 n.2 (N.Y. 1981) (Jones, J., dissenting) ("Because 'euthanasia' can have two meanings, to avoid any possible misunderstanding I explicitly disclaim any intention, expressly or by implication, to invite consideration of 'active' euthanasia the deliberate use of a life shortening agent for the termination of life.").

[162] *See* American Medical Ass'n, Current Opinions of the Council on Ethical & Judicial Affairs, Code of Medical Ethics § 2.20, at 14 (1992) ("For humane reasons, with informed consent, a physician may do what is medically necessary to alleviate severe pain, or cease or omit treatment to permit a terminally ill patient to die when death is imminent. However, the physician should not intentionally cause death."). *But cf.* Quill, *The Ambiguity of Clinical Intentions,* 329 New Eng. J. Med. 1039 (1993) (intentions are clear and distinct in ethical theory but not in clinical practice).

[163] *See, e.g.,* Dyer, *Rheumatologist Convicted of Attempted Murder,* 305 Brit. Med. J. 731 (1992) (conviction and 12-month suspended sentence for attempted murder rather than for murder, because body had been cremated, of "long time sufferer from rheumatoid arthritis, [who] had developed ulcers and abscesses on her arms and legs, a rectal sore penetrating to the bone, fractured vertebrae, deformed hands and feet, swollen joints, and gangrene. . . . 'She howled and screamed like a dog' when anybody touched her, a nurse told the court."). *See generally* Caswell, *Rejecting Criminal Liability for Life-Shortening Palliative Care,* 6 J. Contemp. Health L. & Pol'y 127 (1990).

[164] See § **8.7.**

[165] *See generally* Caswell, *Rejecting Criminal Liability for Life-Shortening Palliative Care,* 6 J. Contemp. Health L. & Pol'y 127 (1990). *But see* Brophy v. New Eng. Sinai Hosp., Inc., 497 N.E.2d 626, 640 (Mass. 1986) (Nolan, J., dissenting) (Ethical principle of double effect is "totally inapplicable" to the facts because the patient "will not die from the aneurysm which precipitated loss of consciousness, the surgery which was performed, the brain damage that followed or the insertion of the G-tube. He will die as a direct result of the refusal to feed him.") (citing Bannon, *Rx: Death by Dehydration,* 12 Human Life Rev. No. 3, at 70 (1986)).

absence of consent is a part of the definition of the crime).[166] Nor does the fact that the individual whose life is ended is near death make any difference.[167]

Consequently, at first glance at least, it would seem that there is little likelihood that active interventions to hasten death, even of those who are close to death or leading a life of great pain and suffering occasioned by an illness or injury, could ever be accepted as legitimate. However, that rather well-accepted line of thinking is undergoing considerable challenge on several fronts. One is the direct tactic of legislative change,[168] and a second is an effort to declare unconstitutional these age-old prohibitions, at least as applied to the dying.[169] The reason for these challenges is the perceived inequity in allowing some terminally ill individuals—those being kept alive by medical treatment—to end their suffering through the withholding or withdrawing treatment, while forcing others—those whose terminal illnesses do not require any medical means to support life—to endure their suffering either until they die naturally or until such time as they too require medical treatment to continue to live, which could then legitimately be withheld.

More fundamentally, however, is the realization that what truly legitimates the forgoing of treatment is consent. All of the other rationales provided by the courts for recognizing the legitimacy of life-sustaining medical treatment to be withheld or withdrawn[170] are ultimately incomplete and unsatisfactory explanations. Take, for example, the rationale based on causation. When ventilatory support is withdrawn, the rhetoric of the right-to-die cases is not that the patient was killed by the physician who turned off the ventilator but that the patient was "allowed to die," that "nature took its course," or that the "cause" of death was not turning off the ventilator but the patient's inability to breath unassisted because of his illness or injury. But surely if the very same physician were to turn off a ventilator under a variety of other circumstances, it would not necessarily be licit.

What makes forgoing life-sustaining treatment licit in the right-to-die cases? It is not the fact that the patient is terminally ill, because it is clear that the right to have life-sustaining medical treatment withheld or withdrawn does not inure only to the terminally ill.[171] What legitimates the withdrawal of ventilatory support (or other life-sustaining medical treatment) is *consent,* either the consent of the patient or one authorized by law to give consent for the patient.

---

[166] W. LaFave & A. Scott, Criminal Law § 5.11(a), at 477–80 (2d ed. 1986).

[167] *Cf.* Barber v. Superior Court, 195 Cal. Rptr. 484, 487 (Ct. App. 1983).

[168] See § **18.23.**

[169] See § **18.22.**

[170] See §§ **18.4–18.8** and **18.11–18.17.**

[171] **CA:** Thor v. Superior Court, 855 P.2d 375 (Cal. 1993); Bouvia v. Superior Court (Glenchur), 225 Cal. Rptr. 297 (Ct. App. 1986).

    **GA:** State v. McAfee, 385 S.E.2d 651 (Ga. 1989).

    **NV:** McKay v. Bergstedt, 801 P.2d 617 (Nev. 1990).

    See §§ **8.2** and **9.3.**

    This is so well accepted that it should not require explanation. But perhaps the
fact that it is so well accepted means that we are prone to overlook the crucial
role that consent plays. If the physician were motivated by the same merciful
impulses in turning off the ventilator for a competent patient who had not
consented or for an incompetent patient whose surrogate had not done so, we
would not doubt for a second that the physician would be subject to criminal
liability. Even if a physician's motives were not so pure—suppose, for example,
that he wished to reduce the hospital's electric bill by turning off ventilators—
he would also be subject to liability, and the fact that the cause of death was
the forgoing of treatment or the patient's inability as a result of illness or injury
to breathe unassisted would be completely irrelevant. Why? Because legally
authorized consent was lacking.
    It was inevitable that, sooner or later, the fundamental role that consent plays
in legitimating the forgoing of life-sustaining treatment would be rediscovered
and that attempts would be made to apply it to active interventions—assisted
suicide and active euthanasia—to end life. That is what is now beginning to
occur through legislative efforts to affirmatively permit assisted suicide or to
repeal existing statutory prohibitions on it and through efforts through the courts
to declare unconstitutional those existing statutory prohibitions.


## § 18.19  Terminology: Assisted Suicide and
## Active Euthanasia

Voluntary[172] active interventions to end life take two forms. They are commonly
referred to as *assisted suicide* and *active euthanasia*.[173] (The latter is sometimes
referred to as *mercy killing*.) Unlike the difference between the two different
forms of forgoing life-sustaining treatment—namely, withholding and withdrawing treatment, which are recognized as having no moral or legally determinative distinction,[174] there is an important difference between assisted suicide
and active euthanasia.[175]

---

[172] See § **18.25.**

[173] *See, e.g.,* CeloCruz, *Aid-in-Dying: Should We Decriminalize Physician-Assisted Suicide and
Physician-Committed Euthanasia?,* 18 Am. J. L. & Med. 369 (1992); Emanuel, *Euthanasia—
Historical, Ethical, and Empiric Perspectives,* 154 Archives Internal Med. 1890, 1891 (1994)
(Table 1) (distinguishing among different forms of ending of life); American Medical Ass'n,
Council on Ethical & Judicial Affairs, Code of Medical Ethics § 2.21, at 50 (1994) ("Eutha-
nasia is the active administration of a lethal agent by another person to a patient for the
purpose of relieving the patient's intolerable and incurable suffering."), § 2.211, at 51
("Physician assisted suicide occurs when a physician facilitates a patient's death by
providng the necessary means and/or information to enable the patient to perform the
life-ending act.").

[174] See § **8.6.**

[175] *But see* Shaffer, Note, *Criminal Liability for Assisting Suicide,* 86 Colum. L. Rev. 348, 363
(1986) ("distinction between these forms of behavior is so negligible as to be almost illusory").

In the practice of both assisted suicide and active euthanasia, one person provides the person seeking to end his life (the "patient") with the instrumentality of death, for example, an overdose of barbiturates. This is ordinarily done because the patient is, by virtue of the very illness or injury from which relief is sought, physically incapable of obtaining an instrumentality of death himself. Or the patient might lack the means for obtaining a particular instrumentality of death, for example, the ability to obtain a prescription medication without the assistance of a physician.

The important difference between the two arises from the administration of the lethal agent, not from its procurement. In *assisted suicide,* once the instrumentality of death is obtained, the patient administers it to himself. By contrast, in active euthanasia (at least when it is voluntary and with the consent of the patient), another person (it might be the person who procured the lethal agent or yet another) administers the lethal agent either because the patient is physically unable to do so or because the patient does not wish to do so and requests this person to do so.

If there is a moral and legal difference between the two, it arises from the fact that the complicity of another person in bringing about the patient's death is greater in active euthanasia than in assisted suicide. In assisted suicide the patient retains complete and final control over whether he in fact will die from the administration of a lethal agent. The patient decides when and ultimately whether to end his life, and the patient is the last human agent in bringing about death. By contrast, with active euthanasia, another person retains final control, is the last actor in the sequence of events, and retains ultimate control over when and whether the patient's life in fact will be ended. From a practical perspective, in assisted suicide, the patient retains greater ability to change his mind and to ensure that death will not occur without his voluntary consent.

Yet it is possible that thcsc are distinctions without any important theoretical difference. That is because the legitimacy (if they are legitimate) of both assisted suicide and active euthanasia ultimately turns on the assumption that the ending of life is the *free choice* of the person whose life is ended. In the absence of free choice—that is, voluntary and informed consent—neither can be considered legitimate under any of the existing proposals for legitimation. As of yet, this distinction has not played an important role in the debate about legalizing active interventions to end life, but it is more than a minor possibility that it will in the future. It is far more likely that the road to the decriminalization of assisted suicide will be far less difficult to travel.

The acceptance of passive euthanasia—by lawmaking institutions, by those in the health professions, and by the public—has been facilitated in no small part by the terminology that has been used to describe the practice. Indeed, the term "passive euthanasia" has been almost entirely avoided by those who have sought to confer legitimacy on it, leaving its use primarily to those who have condemned it. We speak, instead, of forgoing life-sustaining treatment, withdrawing life support, letting nature take its course, natural death, and similarly sanitized locutions that have made it easier to understand, accept, and implement the distinction between passive and active euthanasia.

The process of legitimizing active euthanasia will probably need to undergo a similar sanitization of rhetoric. The emotive impact of terms like *suicide* and *killing,* even prefaced by *mercy,* are immense. Perhaps that is why some of the proponents of assisted suicide and mercy killing have begun to utilize the term "aid in dying," and such a strategy might well ease the acceptance of these practices.

## § 18.20  Public's Attitudes Toward Active Euthanasia and Assisted Suicide

Public opinion polls reveal that the majority of people surveyed are in favor of permitting active euthanasia and assisted suicide, and that this support is increasing over time. To the question asked by the National Opinion Research Center, "When a person has a disease that cannot be cured, do you think doctors should be allowed by law to end the patient's life by some painless means if the patient and his family request it?," the rate of positive response increased from 37 percent in 1947, to about 50 percent in 1973, to 63 percent in 1983.[176] In a survey by the Times Mirror Center for the People and the Press in 1990, only 20 percent stated that it was never justified for a husband or wife to kill a spouse "suffering terrible pain from a terminal disease."[177] This survey also found that between 29 and 55 percent agreed that "a person has a moral right to end his or her own life" under varying sets of circumstances,[178] figures that showed significant increases from a 1975 poll asking the same questions. However, only 28 percent said that they could imagine killing a spouse who was suffering terrible pain from a terminal disease.[179]

But as is the case with forgoing life-sustaining treatment,[180] there is a gap between opinion and even the limited behavior of voting, let alone actually taking action to assist another in dying or actively ending another's life. Although surveys indicate that a majority favors physician-assisted suicide,[181] referenda in California and Washington that would have legalized the practice were

---

[176] Shaffer, Note, *Criminal Liability for Assisting Suicide,* 86 Colum. L. Rev. 348, 367–68 n.114 (1986). *See also Euthanasia Favored in Poll,* N.Y. Times, Nov. 4, 1991, at A9 (nat'l ed.) (64% favored physician-assisted suicide for terminally ill patients who request it).

[177] Times Mirror Ctr. for the People & the Press, Reflections of the Times: The Right to Die 8 (1990) (nationwide survey of 1213 adults).

[178] *Id.* at 9 (48% if the person has an incurable disease; 55% if the person is "suffering great pain and has no hope of improvement"; 29% "when this person is an extremely heavy burden on his or her family").

[179] *Id.* at 13.

[180] See § 1.5.

[181] Blendon et al., *Should Physicians Aid Their Patients in Dying?,* 267 JAMA 2658 (1992).

defeated.[182] After these two defeats, Oregon did enact a statute by referendum, but its provisions are so narrowly drawn—in order to win voter approval—that it is likely that the statute will be difficult to use and have minimal impact if it survives constitutional challenge.[183] Bills to legalize physician-assisted suicide and/or mercy killing have been introduced in several states,[184] but none have been enacted through the representative legislative process. Even if formal legitimation of physician-assisted suicide or mercy killing is difficult to achieve, the record of prosecuting physicians or laypersons who engage in such activities shows a high level of unwillingness to prosecute or convict.[185]

## § 18.21  Physicians' Attitudes Toward Active Euthanasia and Assisted Suicide

Both active euthanasia by physicians and aiding patients in committing suicide remain highly controversial in the United States[186] and, regardless of their legal status, are said to violate the tradition and ethics of the medical profession.[187] Nonetheless, euthanasia was practiced by ancient Greek physicians, the views of Hippocrates to the contrary notwithstanding.[188] Physician-assisted suicide

---

[182] *See* Gross, *Voters Turn Down Legal Euthanasia,* N.Y. Times, Nov. 7, 1991, at A10 (nat'l ed.) (Washington state initiative to legalize administration of lethal injections by physicians to "adult patients who are in a medically terminal condition" at the patients' request defeated by 56-to-44% margin); Gianelli, *Euthanasia Measure Fails, But Backers Vow Renewed Push,* Am. Med. News, Nov. 23 and 30, 1992, at 30 (California proposal to legalize euthanasia and physician-assisted suicide defeated by 56-to-44% margin).

[183] *See* Lee v. State, 869 F. Supp. 1491 (D. Or. 1994).

[184] *Compare* Gianelli, *States Weigh Assisted Suicide—AMA Launches More Aggressive Action to Fight Trend,* Am. Med. News, Feb. 27, 1995, at 1 (subsequent to passage of initiative in Oregon legalizing assisted suicide, at least 12 other states have introduced similar legislation) *with* Choice in Dying, The Right-to-Die Law Digest (Sept. 1994) ("Legislation Update" section) (collecting citations to bills in six states prior to enactment of Oregon initiative). *See also* Schanker, Note, *Of Suicide Machines, Euthanasia Legislation, and the Health Care Crisis,* 68 Ind. L.J. 977, 998–1003 (1993).

[185] See §§ 18.17–18.18.

[186] *See* McCarrick, *Active Euthanasia and Assisted Suicide* 2 Kennedy Inst. Ethics J. 80 (1992) (scope note 18) (annotated bibliography).

[187] *See* Hastings Ctr., Guidelines on the Termination of Life-Sustaining Treatment and the Care of the Dying 128 (1987) (Part Six, 1) ("Medical tradition and customary practice distinguish in a broadly acceptable fashion between the refusal of medical interventions and intentionally causing death or assisting suicide."); American Medical Ass'n, Council on Ethical & Judicial Affairs, *Decisions Near the End of Life,* 267 JAMA 2229, 2233 (1992) (despite ethically relevant distinction between active euthanasia and assisted suicide that makes the latter "an ethically more attractive option, . . . the ethical objections to physician assisted suicide are similar to those of euthanasia since both are essentially interventions intended to cause death.").

[188] Emanuel, *Euthanasia—Historical, Ethical, and Empiric Perspectives,* 154 Archives Internal Med. 1890, 1891 (1994).

and active euthanasia have been debated throughout history, and as recently as the end of the nineteenth century "had become a topic of speeches at medical meetings and editorials in British and American medical journals."[189]

The traditional and current opposition of contemporary organized medicine[190]—though it might be beginning to soften[191]—is consistent with the formal criminal law. A number of objections to active euthanasia and physician-assisted suicide are given. First, "[i]f euthanasia by physicians were to be condoned, the fact that physicians could offer death as a medical treatment might undermine public trust in medicine's dedication to preserving the life and health of patients." Second, patients might not "feel free to resist the suggestion that euthanasia may be appropriate for them." Third, if euthanasia were permissible, it might create an incentive for physicians to devote less energy and time to the treatment of difficult cases. Finally, "the increasing pressure to reduce health care costs may serve as another motivation to favor euthanasia over longer-term comfort care."[192]

---

[189] *Id.* at 1892.

[190] *See* American Geriatrics Soc'y Public Policy Comm., *Voluntary Active Euthanasia Position Statement,* 39 J. Am. Geriatrics Soc'y 826 (1991); American Medical Ass'n, Council on Ethical & Judicial Affairs, Code of Medical Ethics § 2.21, at 50, § 2.211, at 51 (1994); American Medical Ass'n, Council on Ethical & Judicial Affairs, *Decisions Near the End of Life,* 267 JAMA 2229, 2233 (1992) (despite ethically relevant distinction between active euthanasia and assisted suicide that makes the latter "an ethically more attractive option, . . . the ethical objections to physician assisted suicide are similar to those of euthanasia since both are essentially interventions intended to cause death."). *Cf.* Hastings Ctr., Guidelines on the Termination of Life-Sustaining Treatment and the Care of the Dying 128 (1987) (Part Six, 1) ("Medical tradition and customary practice distinguish in a broadly acceptable fashion between the refusal of medical interventions and intentionally causing death or assisting suicide.").

[191] *See, e.g.,* Gianelli, *Michigan "Neutral" on Suicide,* Am. Med. News, May 24 and 31, 1993, at 2 ("[A]fter more than a year of contentious debate, [the Michigan State Medical Society has] come down 'firmly ambivalent' on the issue of physician-assisted suicide," rejecting its previous opposition in favor of an official position of " 'no position.' ").

[192] American Medical Ass'n, Council on Ethical & Judicial Affairs, Code of Medical Ethics § 2.20, at 50, § 2.211, at 51 (1994) ("[P]ermitting physicians to engage in euthanasia would ultimately cause more harm than good, . . . would be difficult to impossible to control, and would pose serious societal risks."). *See also* American Medical Ass'n, Council on Ethical & Judicial Affairs, *Decisions Near the End of Life,* 267 JAMA 2229, 2232 (1992); Emanuel, *Euthanasia—Historical, Ethical, and Empiric Perspectives,* 154 Archives Internal Med. 1890, 1892–96 (1994) (summarizing arguments for and against euthanasia); Gianelli, *Die Sooner, Save Money?,* Am. Med. News, Nov. 8, 1993, at 8 (reporting reactions of opponents of euthanasia to an article suggesting that "managed care" programs provide discounts for Medicare beneficiaries who execute a living will"); *Institute of Medical Ethics Working Party on the Ethics of Prolonging Life and Assisting Death,* 336 Lancet 610 (1990); Newman, *Euthanasia: Orchestrating "The Last Syllable of . . . Time,"* 53 U. Pitt. L. Rev. 153, 167–91 (1991) (summarizing arguments for and against euthanasia); Quill et al., *Proposed Clinical Criteria for Physician-Assisted Suicide,* 327 New Eng. J. Med. 1380 (1992); Singer & Siegler, *Euthanasia—A Critique,* 322 New Eng. J. Med. 1881 (1990).

Despite the position of official medical organizations, there is a not insubstantial amount of support for these practices among individual physicians.[193] There is some evidence that a significant number of physicians do help patients to die,[194] but few physicians have been willing to admit to it publicly[195] or openly advocate it.[196] An article in the *New England Journal of Medicine* by a group of prominent physicians, which came very close to supporting physician-assisted suicide, still drew back from supporting active euthanasia.[197] Even among those physicians who have engaged in physician-assisted suicide or mercy killing, there is a great deal of discomfort about it[198] and some are opposed to legalizing it on the ground that it would then become too easy for doctors to kill patients.

Assisted suicide and active euthanasia have been open secrets in the medical profession for a long time, but they have traditionally been considered taboo even for discussion. One judge has observed, in one of the few cases to discuss physician-assisted suicide, that "[s]uicides by terminally ill persons have occurred throughout our history and indeed have often taken place with the quiet and

---

[193] *See, e.g.*, Bachman et al., *Assisted Suicide and Euthanasia in Michigan*, 331 New Eng. J. Med 812 (1994) (67% of physicians favored enactment of legislation to legalize physician-assisted suicide for terminally ill adult patients "suffering unacceptable pain"); Cohen et al., *Attitudes Toward Assisted Suicide and Euthanasia Among Physicians in Washington State*, 331 New Eng. J. Med. 89 (1994) (52% believed euthanasia should be legal in some situations, but only 33% would be willing to perform it; 53% believed assisted suicide should be legal in some situations, but only 40% would be willing to provide assistance); Emanuel, *Euthanasia—Historical, Ethical, and Empiric Perspectives*, 154 Archives Internal Med. 1890, 1898–99 (1994) (Table 3, collecting results of other studies); Stevens & Hassan, *Management of Death, Dying and Euthanasia: Attitudes and Practices of Medical Practitioners in South Australia*, 20 J. Med. Ethics 41 (1994) (19% of "medical practitioners" reported having taken active steps to bring about patients' deaths; 45% support legalization of active euthanasia under some circumstances).

[194] *See* Colen, *Doctors Who Help Patients Die*, Long Island Newsday, Sept. 29, 1991, § 1, at 5; Emanuel, *Euthanasia—Historical, Ethical, and Empiric Perspectives*, 154 Archives Internal Med. 1890, 1898–99 (1994) (Table 3, collecting results of other studies); *Poll Shows That 1 in 5 Internists Has Helped a Patient Die*, Am. Med. News, Mar. 16, 1992, at 9 ("non-scientific survey" of members of American Society of Internal Medicine).

[195] *See, e.g.*, Quill, *A Case of Individualized Decision Making*, 324 New Eng. J. Med. 691 (1991).

[196] *See, e.g.*, Brody, *Assisted Death—A Compassionate Response to a Medical Failure*, 327 New Eng. J. Med. 1384 (1992); Cassel & Meier, *Morals and Moralism in the Debate over Euthanasia and Assisted Suicide*, 323 New Eng. J. Med. 750 (1990); Quill et al., *Care of the Hopelessly Ill—Proposed Clinical Criteria for Physician-Assisted Suicide*, 327 New Eng. J. Med. 1380, 1381 (1992).

[197] *See* Wanzer et al., *The Physician's Responsibility Toward Hopelessly Ill Patients*, 320 New Eng. J. Med. 844, 849 (1989); *but see* Singer & Siegler, *Euthanasia—A Critique*, 322 New Eng. J. Med. 1881 (1990). For an annotated bibliography on active euthanasia, see McCarrick, *Active Euthanasia and Assisted Suicide*, 2 Kennedy Inst. Ethics J. 80 (1992) (scope note 18).

[198] Colen, *"I Gave Him All the Morphine . . . In My Bag. It Wasn't Easy,"* Long Island Newsday, Sept. 29, 1991, § 1, at 5. *See also* Miles, *Physicians and Their Patients' Suicides*, 271 JAMA 1786 (1994).

unpublicized assistance of treating physicians and family members."[199] For example, 50 years passed before the fact was revealed in 1986 that the physicians attending King George V of Great Britain, who was dying of cancer, hastened his death with morphine.[200] The ending of a patient's life by active means (as well as the more conventional and widely accepted forgoing of life-sustaining treatment) is frequently negotiated privately between the patient and/or the patient's family, and the physician.[201]

Because of the secretive nature of the assisted suicide (and active euthanasia), little is known about it. One estimate is that "[a]pproximately 6000 deaths per day in the United States are said to be in some way planned or indirectly assisted, probably through the 'double effect' of pain-relieving medications that may at the same time hasten death or the discontinuation of or failure to start potentially life-prolonging treatments."[202] The problem with this estimate is that it also includes instances of forgoing life-sustaining treatment, which probably strongly predominate. Its authors also observe, "From 3 to 37 percent of physicians responding to anonymous surveys reported secretly taking active steps to hasten a patient's death, but these survey data were flawed by low response rates and poor design."[203]

There are at least two serious problems with this "open secret" approach to "negotiated death." The first is that it is arbitrary and discriminatory, and the second, that it is subject to potentially grave abuse. While its availability is not limited exclusively to royalty, it is discriminatory because it favors those who have the sophistication, the financial resources, the connections, and the time

---

[199] Hobbins v. Attorney Gen., 518 N.W.2d 487, 495 (Mich. Ct. App. 1994) (Shelton, J., dissenting in part). *See also* Shaffer, Note, *Criminal Liability for Assisting Suicide,* 86 Colum. L. Rev. 348, 369 (1986) (A judicial interpretation of homicide and assisted suicide statutes so as "to permit suicide assistance under any but the most tightly circumscribed conditions leads to circumvention of the law. . . . One reporter, . . . [b]ased upon 'scores of interviews around the country,' . . . concluded that due to the advance of medical technology, 'such arranged deaths are not rare,' though they are little discussed because of the fear of criminal liability.") (citing Malcolm, *To Suffer a Prolonged Illness or Elect to Die: A Case Study,* N.Y. Times, Dec. 16, 1984, § 1, at 1).

[200] *See, e.g.,* Lelyveld, *1936 Secret Is Out: Doctor Sped George V's Death,* N.Y. Times, Nov. 28, 1986, at 1 (nat'l ed.).

[201] *See Negotiated Death: An Open Secret,* N.Y. Times, Dec. 16, 1984, at 18 (nat'l ed.); Malcolm, *To Suffer a Prolonged Illness or Elect to Die: A Case Study,* N.Y. Times, Dec. 16, 1984, § 1, pt. 1, at 1 (late city final ed.) (Negotiated deaths "happen every single day. [They] have become a fact of American life."); Klemesrud, *A Daughter's Story: Aiding Mother's Suicide,* N.Y. Times, Sept. 9, 1985, at 17 (reviewing a book by a television reporter describing her mother's "negotiated death"); Colen, *Doctors Who Help Patients Die,* Long Island Newsday, Sept. 29, 1991, § 1, at 5.

[202] Quill et al., *Care of the Hopelessly Ill—Proposed Clinical Criteria for Physician-Assisted Suicide,* 327 New Eng. J. Med. 1380, 1381 (1992) (citing Malcolm, *Giving Death a Hand: Rending Issue,* N.Y. Times, June 14, 1990, at A6).

[203] *Id.*

and energy to find a cooperative doctor, but sometimes it favors those who are just plain lucky to be able to find the doctor they need. The other problem is that there is no guarantee that a willing doctor will necessarily await the request of the dying patient. How many people (King George included?) would rather have suffered to the end than go swiftly into the night will never be known. More than a few must have been unknowingly and possibly unwillingly assisted to die. In part this unilateral decisionmaking occurs because of doctors' fears of opening up the topic for discussion and in part because of the tradition of medical paternalism applied to all medical practices, illicit as well as licit.

The publication in 1988 of an essay, "It's Over, Debbie," in the *Journal of the American Medical Association*[204] of what might have been a fictional account (although it was not presented as such) of physician-administered active euthanasia, the publication of an article[205] documenting a doctor's providing a terminally ill patient with a lethal dose of medication, the publication of a book which became a national best-seller—*Final Exit*, by the director of the Hemlock Society—providing explicit instructions about various ways of committing suicide,[206] and most important of all the activities of Dr. Jack Kevorkian, who has openly solicited patients who wish him to assist their suicide,[207] have focused public debate on physician-assisted suicide and active euthanasia and have created an impetus to more open discussion in both the professional and lay presses about the propriety of physician-assisted suicide and active euthanasia and the conditions under which they might be considered acceptable.[208] They have also increased discussion of the fact that many physicians use inadequate pain relief for the treatment of terminally ill patients, thereby providing a reason for patients to seek death by active euthanasia, assisted suicide, or suicide when measures might be available to eliminate or reduce pain to levels that more people would find tolerable.[209] These efforts have led to increasing discussion in the medical and lay literature about the need for physicians to become better acquainted with adequate measures for controlling the pain of some terminal diseases,[210] and have created an impetus to provide terminally ill patients with

---

[204] *See It's Over, Debbie,* 249 JAMA 272 (1988).

[205] *See* Quill, *A Case of Individualized Decision Making,* 324 New Eng. J. Med. 691 (1991).

[206] *See* Altman, *A How-to Book on Suicide Surges to Top of Best-Seller List in Week,* N.Y. Times, Aug. 9, 1991, at 1, (nat'l ed.).

[207] See § **18.17.**

[208] *See, e.g.,* Cassel & Meier, *Morals and Moralism in the Debate over Euthanasia and Assisted Suicide,* 323 New Eng. J. Med. 750 (1990).

[209] See § **9.38.**

[210] *See, e.g.,* American Medical Ass'n, Council on Ethical & Judicial Affairs, *Decisions Near the End of Life,* 267 JAMA 2229, 2231 (1992) ("[M]any physicians are not informed about the appropriate doses, frequency of doses, and alternate modalities of pain control for patients with severe chronic pain.") (citing Rhymes, *Hospice Care in America,* 264 JAMA 369 (1990)). *See also* Collins, *Despite Gains, Pain Management Still Not Under Control,* Am. Med. News, Oct. 14, 1991, at 20.

other services needed by some, such as treatment for depression, psychotherapy, and/or nursing, and social supports, such as homecare or hospice care. Finally, they have been instrumental in bringing these questions not only to the public's view but also to the courts.

For a number of reasons, just what conduct by physicians constitutes assisting suicide has received little attention from the courts. First, it is possible that this practice occurs relatively infrequently. If a patient wishes to die and the physician wishes to assist the patient, simply administering a dose of morphine larger than necessary to relieve the patient's pain, or administering successively larger doses of morphine until the patient dies, in some cases creates less evidence of assisting the patient to die than does providing the patient with the means to do so himself. Second, even when a physician does provide a patient with the means for ending his own life, it is usually done in a secretive manner to escape detection and prosecution.[211] Also, the desire for suicide by dying patients might be relatively low, for "[i]f care is administered properly at the end of life, only the rare patient should be so distressed that he or she desires to commit suicide."[212] However, in fact, there is ample evidence that many physicians practice inadequate palliative care, thereby providing a reason for patients to seek death by active euthanasia, assisted suicide, or suicide when measures might be available to eliminate or reduce pain to levels that more people would find tolerable.[213]

### § 18.22   Constitutionality of Statutory Prohibitions on Assisted Suicide

Aiding another in committing suicide is a statutory crime in many jurisdictions. See **Table 18–1** in § **18.17.** In others, there is the possibility for prosecution for aiding another in committing suicide as a common-law crime, and in yet others, it might be possible to convict one who aids another in committing suicide of murder.[214] However, the constitutionality of statutes proscribing assisted suicide is open to question on both due process and equal protection

---

[211] *See, e.g.,* Altman, *Jury Declines to Indict a Doctor Who Said He Aided in a Suicide,* N.Y. Times, July 27, 1991, §1, at 1 (late ed.) (physician who publicized fact that he provided lethal overdose to terminally ill patient reported that he had heard from numerous other physicians that they had acted similarly but had not revealed their conduct). *But see, e.g.,* Quill, *Death and Dignity: A Case of Individualized Decision Making,* 324 New Eng. J. Med. 691 (1991) (physician reporting his providing lethal dose of medication to terminally ill patient).

[212] *See* Wanzer et al., *The Physician's Responsibility Toward Hopelessly Ill Patients,* 320 New Eng. J. Med. 844, 847 (1989). *But see* Rosenblum & Forsythe, *The Right to Assisted Suicide: Protection of Autonomy or an Open Door to Social Killing?,* 6 Issues L. & Medicine 3 (1990).

[213] See § **9.38.**

[214] *See* People v. Roberts, 178 N.W. 690 (Mich. 1920) *overruled* by People v. Kevorkian, 527 N.W.2d 714 (Mich. 1994).

grounds.[215] Although only a few challenges have been mounted to date,[216] it can be expected that they will continue to grow as the subject of assisted suicide, and especially physician-assisted suicide, is increasingly a topic for debate in mainstream society. Ultimately, perhaps, greater success will lie in legislative change than in judicial change, although the single instance of legislative change has also been stymied, though perhaps only temporarily, in the courts.[217] Nonetheless, it is possible that courts will be more likely to uphold legislation legalizing active interventions to end life than they will be to find unconstitutional statutes that prohibit the active ending of life if they exhibit the same high degree of deferentiality to the validity of legislative enactments.

Regardless of the future of challenges to the constitutionality of statutory or common-law prohibitions on assisted suicide, challenges might also be brought on the basis of state constitutional provisions. The most plausible bases would be privacy, due process, and equal protection clauses.[218] A few courts have premised the right to forgo life-sustaining medical treatment on such provisions in whole[219] or in part,[220] and their application to more active means of ending life seems virtually inevitable, especially in those jurisdictions that have found the withholding/withdrawing[221] and act/omission[222] distinctions seriously wanting in the forgoing of life-sustaining treatment, which is virtually all jurisdictions.

### Compassion in Dying v. Washington

The leading case is *Compassion in Dying v. Washington*,[223] filed by terminally ill patients, physicians, and the organization, Compassion in Dying, described

---

[215] *See* Sedler, *The Constitution and Hastening Inevitable Death,* 23 Hastings Center Rep. 20 (Sept.–Oct. 1993); Sullivan, *A Constitutional Right to Suicide, in* Suicide: The Philosophical Issues (M. Battin & T. Mayo eds. 1980); Pletcher, *Assisted Suicide for the Terminally-Ill: The Inadequacy of Current Legal Models to Rationally Analyze Voluntary Active Euthanasia,* 13 Crim. Just. J. 303–17 (1992); Risley, *Ethical and Legal Issues in the Individual's Right to Die,* 20 Ohio N. U. L. Rev. 597 (1994). *But see* Bopp, *Is Assisted Suicide Constitutionally Protected?,* 3 Issues L. & Med. 113 (1987); Kamisar, *Are Laws Against Assisted Suicide Unconstitutional?,* 23 Hastings Center Rep. 32 (May–June 1993).

[216] **DNY:** *See* Quill v. Koppell, 870 F. Supp. 78 (S.D.N.Y. 1994).

**DWA:** *See* Compassion in Dying v. Washington, 850 F. Supp. 1454 (W.D. Wash. 1994), *rev'd,* 49 F.3d 586 (9th Cir. 1995).

**MI:** *See* Hobbins v. Attorney Gen., 527 N.W.2d 714 (Mich. 1994), *cert. denied sub nom.* Hobbins v. Kelley, 115 S. Ct. 1795 (1995).

[217] **DOR:** Lee v. State, 869 F. Supp. 1491 (D. Or. 1994). See § **18.23.**

[218] *See generally* Gormley & Hartman, *Privacy and the States,* 65 Temple L. Rev. 1279 (1992); Eaton & Larson, *Experimenting with the "Right to Die" in the Laboratory of the States,* 25 Ga. L. Rev. 1253, 1262–68 (1991).

[219] **FL:** *See, e.g.,* Browning v. Herbert, 568 So. 2d 4 (Fla. 1990).

[220] See § **2.8.**

[221] See § **8.6.**

[222] See § **8.5.**

[223] 850 F. Supp. 1454 (W.D. Wash. 1994), *rev'd,* 49 F.3d 586 (9th Cir. 1995).

in the opinion as providing "support, counseling and assistance to mentally competent, terminally ill adults considering suicide,"[224] and alleging that the Washington statute's[225] total prohibition on assisted suicide violated the due process and equal protection clauses of the Fourteenth Amendment to the United States Constitution. The court granted the motion for summary judgment of the terminally ill plaintiffs on both due process and equal protection grounds, but denied the motions of Compassion in Dying and the physician/plaintiffs (except to the extent that they asserted claims of the terminally ill plaintiffs rather than their own claims). For the court, the underlying constitutional issue was "whether the State of Washington can resolve the profound spiritual and moral questions surrounding the end of life in so conclusive a fashion as to deny categorically any option for a terminally ill, mentally competent person to commit physician-assisted suicide."[226]

**The Due Process Claim.**   In resolving this issue under the due process clause, the court drew on the United States Supreme Court's decisions in *Planned Parenthood v. Casey*[227] and *Cruzan v. Director*[228] to find that there was a constitutionally protected liberty interest of terminally ill persons to decide to commit suicide. The court first reasoned that such decisions, like decisions about abortion, "'involv[e] the most intimate and personal choices a person may make in a lifetime, choices central to personal dignity and autonomy, [and] . . . central to the liberty protected by the Fourteenth Amendment.'"[229] The fundamental purpose of the Fourteenth Amendment's protection of liberty "'is the right to define one's own concept of existence, of meaning, of the universe, and of the mystery of human life.'"[230] The court thus concluded "that the suffering of a terminally ill person cannot be deemed any less intimate or personal, or any less deserving of protection from unwarranted governmental interference, than that of a pregnant woman. Thus, consonant with the reasoning in *Casey,* such an intimate personal decision falls within the realm of the liberties constitutionally protected under the Fourteenth Amendment."[231]

It drew a similar lesson from *Cruzan.* Nancy Cruzan was not a competent patient, and thus what the Court had to say about competent patients was dictum.

---

[224] 850 F. Supp. at 1456. *See also* Belkin, *There's No Such Thing As Simple Suicide,* N.Y. Times, Nov. 14, 1993, § 6 (Magazine), at 48 (describing Compassion in Dying's activities); *New Washington Group Offers Suicide "Assistance,"* Am. Med. News, June 14, 1993, at 31 (same); *New Group Offers to Help the Ill Commit Suicide,* N.Y. Times, June 13, 1993, § 1, at 15 (nat'l ed.).

[225] Wash. Rev. Code Ann. § 9A.36.060.

[226] Compassion in Dying v. Washington, 850 F. Supp. at 1460.

[227] 505 U.S. ____, 112 S. Ct. 2791, 2807 (1992).

[228] 497 U.S. 261 (1990).

[229] Compassion in Dying v. Washington, 850 F. Supp. at 1459 (quoting Planned Parenthood v. Casey, 505 U.S. ____, 112 S. Ct. at 2807).

[230] *Id.*

[231] *Id.* at 1460.

In *Cruzan,* the Court observed that the right of a competent patient to decline life-sustaining treatment "may be inferred from our prior decisions,"[232] and that "the logic of the cases . . . would embrace such a liberty interest."[233] It also assumed for purposes of deciding *Cruzan* "that the United States Constitution would grant a competent person a constitutionally protected right to refuse lifesaving hydration and nutrition."[234] Thus, the district court was "confident" that if "squarely faced with the issue, the Supreme Court would reaffirm Justice Rehnquist's tentative conclusion in *Cruzan* that a competent person has a protected liberty interest in refusing unwanted medical treatment, even when that treatment is life-sustaining and refusal or withdrawal of the treatment would mean certain death."[235]

But this did not resolve the question of whether the Constitution protects a right of terminally ill patients to commit suicide. "In other words," the court asked, "is there a difference for purposes of finding a Fourteenth Amendment liberty interest between refusal of unwanted treatment which will result in death and committing physician-assisted suicide in the final stage of life?"[236] The court concluded that there was not because the Fourteenth Amendment protects *choice,* specifically, choice about matters "essential to personal autonomy and human dignity," such as physician-assisted suicide. Therefore, "[f]rom a constitutional perspective, [no] . . . distinction can be drawn between refusing life-sustaining medical treatment and physician-assisted suicide by an uncoerced, mentally competent, terminally ill adult."[237]

Having found that the protection accorded by the Fourteenth Amendment pertains to a decision by a terminally ill person to end life by suicide, the court proceeded to determine what the standard of review was, that is, for determining whether a challenged statute violates this liberty interest. Following the lead of some, but not all federal courts of appeal, it applied the "undue burden" standard set forth in *Casey,* rather than the older *Salerno* standard.[238] The undue burden test is the means by which to reconcile the state's interest with the constitutionally protected liberty interest.[239] Under the undue burden test, to establish a violation of the due process clause plaintiffs must show that the challenged statute would "operate as a substantial obstacle" to the exercise of a constitutional right.[240] The court proceeded to apply Justice Stevens's view in *Casey,*

---

[232] Cruzan v. Director, 497 U.S. 261, 278 (1990).

[233] *Id.* at 279.

[234] *Id.*

[235] Compassion in Dying v. Washington, 850 F. Supp. 1454, 1461 (W.D. Wash. 1994).

[236] *Id.*

[237] *Id.*

[238] *See* United States v. Salerno, 481 U.S. 739 (1987) (under which the plaintiff must show that no set of circumstances exists under which the challenged statute would be valid).

[239] Compassion in Dying v. Washington, 850 F. Supp. at 1462 (citing Planned Parenthood v. Casey, 112 S. Ct. at 2820).

[240] *Id.* (quoting Planned Parenthood v. Casey, 112 S. Ct. at 2830).

that a burden is "undue" either because it is "too severe or because it lacks a legitimate, rational justification."[241]

To do so, it examined the two justifications the state gave for the total ban on assisted suicide. The court found that the state has a strong and legitimate interest in the first—an interest in deterring suicide itself—but only in "young people and others with a significant natural life span ahead of them," but that "this case is not about people for whom suicide would abruptly cut life short." Rather, this case is "about people suffering through the final stage of life with no hope of recovery." For them, deterring or preventing suicide results in the prolongation of suffering, "an aim in which the State can have no interest."[242] No legitimate state interest is impeded if members of the class to whom plaintiffs belong—mentally competent, terminally ill patients—enlist the assistance of a physician to freely and voluntarily commit suicide.

The state's other articulated interest—preventing undue influence and abuse—is unquestionably legitimate, but it too is not abrogated by permitting individuals to avail themselves of physician-assisted suicide if they make a knowing and voluntary choice to do so without undue influence.[243] Overlapping with the discussion of the equal protection claim, the court observed that the same problem exists with the withholding or withdrawal of life-sustaining medical treatment—indeed, it is potentially more serious because surrogates make decisions for incompetent patients—yet no court has held that to be a constitutionally legitimate barrier to such practices. Furthermore, procedures can be legislatively established for protecting against abuse, coercion, and undue influence, much as legislatures have done in other areas.[244] The constitutionally acceptable solution is for the legislature to narrowly tailor the statute, rather than to enact a complete ban.[245]

**The Equal Protection Claim.** The plaintiffs also claimed that the statutory prohibition on assisted suicide unconstitutionally distinguishes between those terminally ill patients being kept alive by life-sustaining medical treatment and those that are not (including the plaintiffs themselves). The state asserted that the distinction is a valid one because "the removal of life support systems is 'natural' and death resulting from medical assistance other than removal of life support is 'artificial.'"[246] This is an argument that had been made and rejected for two decades in the forgoing of life-sustaining treatment since the *Quinlan* case, though sometimes cast in terms of "ordinary" and "extraordinary" or

---

[241] Planned Parenthood v. Casey, 112 S. Ct. at 2843 (Stevens, J., concurring).

[242] Compassion in Dying v. Washington, 850 F. Supp. at 1464.

[243] *Id.* at 1465.

[244] *Id.* at 1465 n.10.

[245] *Id.* ("[T]he legislature can devise regulations which will define the appropriate boundaries of physician-assisted suicide for terminally ill individuals, and at the same time give due recognition to the important public policy concerns regarding the prevention of suicide.").

[246] *Id.* at 1467.

"heroic" treatment. It is also an argument that has been used and consistently rejected to distinguish the forgoing of "artificial" nutrition and hydration from other forms of life-sustaining medical treatment. Given the consistent rejection of this and related distinctions in the development of the law about forgoing life-sustaining treatment, it is difficult to imagine the state of Washington making this claim with a straight face, and the court summarily rejected it:

> This court is not persuaded that the distinction between "natural" and "artificial" death justifies disparate treatment of these similarly situated groups. . . . Both patients may be terminally ill, suffering pain and loss of dignity and subjected to a more extended dying process without some medical intervention, be it removal of life support systems or the prescription of medication to be self-administered.[247]

The Washington statute makes such a distinction, and thereby "creates a situation in which the fundamental rights of one group are burdened while those of a similarly situated group are not. . . . Such a distinction is not a narrowly-drawn classification tailored to serve a compelling state interest," and is therefore unconstitutional.[248]

The future of the holding in the *Compassion in Dying* case is by no means certain, as the state has appealed the case to the Ninth Circuit.[249] There is a serious question about whether the court applied the proper standard of review, which the court acknowledged in its opinion. To the extent that the holding on due process is also based on *Cruzan,* its strength is also uncertain because the *Cruzan* opinion proceeded on *assumptions,* not holdings, about the rights of competent patients. To the extent that the holding is based on *Casey,* it is also on potentially weak ground because colorable questions can be raised as to whether the analogy to abortion is as sound as the court made it appear to be.[250]

### Hobbins v. Attorney General (People v. Kevorkian)

*Hobbins v. Attorney General* was a suit brought to declare unconstitutional the then newly enacted Michigan statutory prohibition on assisted suicide. There were various groups of plaintiffs, including some suffering from terminal cancer, a friend of one of them, and seven health care professionals. The trial court held the statute to be unconstitutional on various technical Michigan constitutional provisions, and also held it unconstitutional as violating some of the plaintiffs' federal due process rights.[251]

---

[247] *Id.*

[248] *Id.*

[249] *See* Compassion in Dying v. Washington, 49 F.3d 586 (9th Cir. 1995).

[250] *See* Quill v. Koppell, 870 F. Supp. 78, 83 (S.D.N.Y. 1994) (refusing to invalidate prohibition on assisted suicide and noting that "The Supreme Court has been careful to explain that the abortion cases, and other related decisions on procreation and child rearing, are not intended to lead automatically to the recognition of other fundamental rights on different subjects").

[251] Hobbins v. Attorney Gen., No. 93-306-178 CZ, 1993 WL 276833 (Mich. Cir. Ct. May 20, 1993).

The attorney general appealed, and the case was consolidated with two prosecutions of Dr. Jack Kevorkian for assisted suicide.[252] The Michigan Court of Appeals affirmed on the technical state constitutional basis.[253] The court could have ended the discussion there, but in anticipation of review by the Michigan Supreme Court, it undertook an analysis of the constitutionality of the statutory prohibition on assisted suicide under the due process clause of the Fourteenth Amendment, which had been one of the bases for the holding of unconstitutionality by the trial court.

Like the federal district court in the *Compassion in Dying* case, the court began by citing *Casey*.[254] This time, however, the citation was to the Fourteenth Amendment's protection of life, rather than liberty.[255] The court concluded that under either a liberty analysis[256] or a privacy analysis,[257] there is not even, prima facie, a constitutionally protected right to commit suicide. It summarized its discussion by noting that "[l]iberty and justice will not cease to exist if a right to commit suicide is not recognized."[258]

Also like the court in *Compassion in Dying,* the Michigan court next turned to consider the petitioner's argument based on *Cruzan,* namely, that the liberty interest recognized therein contains the basis for a broad principle of self-determination that encompasses a right to be assisted in committing suicide. Rather than extrapolating from the dicta in *Cruzan* as the *Compassion in Dying* court did, the Michigan court read *Cruzan* narrowly, citing the United States Supreme Court's own caution to "follow the judicious counsel . . . 'not to attempt, by any general statement, to cover every possible phase of the subject.'"[259] Thus, it viewed *Cruzan* as recognizing a right "only to refuse unwanted medical treatment and passively die a natural death, not to actively intervene so as to hasten one's death."[260]

A dissent by Judge Shelton tracks the reasoning in *Compassion in Dying*. He, too, read the protection afforded by the due process clause to include the interest in individual liberty, and although not mentioning it specifically, he essentially made an argument for a right to assisted suicide based on equal protection:

---

[252] See § **18.17.**

[253] Mich. Const. art. 4, § 24.

[254] Hobbins v. Attorney Gen., 518 N.W.2d 487, 492 n.7 (Mich. Ct. App. 1994) (citing Planned Parenthood v. Casey, 112 S. Ct. 2791, 2816, 2838, 2866, 2874) (1992).

[255] *Id.* at 492 ("The constitutionality of legislative enactments to protect life is clearly established in our law.").

[256] *Id.* ("The scope of rights encompassed by the concept of ordered liberty does not include the right to commit suicide, much less the right to assisted suicide.").

[257] *Id.* ("The 'guarantee of personal privacy' has been 'exten[ded] to activities relating to marriage, procreation, contraception, family relationships, and child rearing and education.' *Roe, supra* 410 U.S. at 152–153, 93 S. Ct. at 726 (citations omitted). Judicial discovery of a right to terminate one's life is not a logical extension of this catalog of rights.").

[258] *Id.* at 492–93.

[259] *Id.* at 493 (quoting Cruzan v. Director, 497 U.S. 261, 277–78 (1990)).

[260] Hobbins v. Attorney Gen., 518 N.W.2d at 493.

If a terminally ill person can lawfully end her life by disconnecting a life-sustaining machine (*Cruzan*), why cannot she end that same life by connecting a life-ending machine? . . . Does the state have a right to totally prevent a terminally ill person from ending her life by charging the doctor who assists her with a felony punishable by four years' imprisonment, or even with murder? If a doctor (or even a nurse or medical assistant) can lawfully end a patient's life by disconnecting a life-sustaining machine (*Cruzan*), why cannot a doctor do the same by connecting a life-ending machine?[261]

The Court of Appeals's opinion does point up the potential conflict between the protection afforded by the Fourteenth Amendment to life and that afforded to liberty. However, when all is said and done, in the case of a competent person seeking to assert the right to be assisted in committing suicide, the right to life should be considered either not to be implicated at all or to be waived when there is voluntary and informed consent given by the individual whose life will be ended. Whatever protection the Constitution offers to the interest in life is afforded only to those (or at least to those who are competent adults) who seek that protection; to impose the "protection" on those who do not wish it is to violate the equally important interest in liberty. In other words, the constitutional interest in protection of life is subject to waiver.[262] Judge Shelton alluded to this in his observation that the choice by a competent person of assisted suicide is more deserving of constitutional protection and less susceptible to abuse than the forgoing of treatment, resulting in the death of an incompetent patient. Yet we have long honored the latter while refusing to recognize the legitimacy of the former.[263]

The Michigan Supreme Court affirmed the Court of Appeals's reversal of the trial court's holding of unconstitutionality on both the state technical and federal constitutional claims. It distinguished *Cruzan* largely on the ground that if it gave constitutional approval to anything, it was to *passive* conduct that results in death. In so doing, however, the Michigan court tried to have it both ways. That is, it wanted to be able to claim—as have all the appellate courts that have decided right-to-die cases—that there is an important distinction between killing and letting die that legitimates the latter and condemns the former. In so doing, however, it had to revive the long discredited act/omission distinction, claiming that letting die is an omission and therefore nonculpable, but an act that causes death is murder.

---

[261] *Id.* at 496–97 (Shelton, J., dissenting in part).

[262] *See* Lee v. State, 869 F. Supp. 1491, 1498 (D. Or. 1994) (opinion on preliminary injunction) (raising, but not answering, question of whether waiver must be voluntary and informed). See § 18.23.

[263] Hobbins v. Attorney Gen., 518 N.W.2d at 498 (Shelton, J., dissenting in part) ("If anything, the intent is less onerous in these instances [of physician-assisted suicide] because, at least as compared to Ms. Quinlan and other incompetent patients, these patients [assisted by Dr. Kevorkian] made the final personal decision and took the final personal action for themselves.").

But not all omissions are nonculpable; what makes them so, if anything does, is the absence of a *duty* to continue treatment.[264] And what negates the existence of a duty that would otherwise exist is legally valid consent (of the patient or surrogate) in combination with the judgment of the attending physician that further treatment is futile. Thus not all omissions are nonculpable. There is also the problem of correctly labeling conduct as an act or as an omission, a difficulty (if not impossibility) that the New Jersey Supreme Court pointed out in *Conroy* as early as 1985.[265] Many "omissions" to treat require an "act," such as removing a patient from a ventilator.

The Michigan Supreme Court also analyzed the argument for the unconstitutionality of the criminalization of assisted suicide based on *Casey.* In order to determine the existence of a substantive due process right, the court concluded that it "must determine whether the asserted right to commit suicide arises from a rational evolution of tradition, or whether recognition of such a right would be a radical departure from historical precepts." The court found no historical "indication of widespread societal approval" of suicide. It pointed to the facts that at common law, suicide was a "criminal offense, with significant stigmatizing consequences." The reason that it was not criminalized or that it has been decriminalized reflects a legislative recognition of "the futility of punishment and the harshness of property forfeiture and other consequences"[266] rather than a desire to give express approval to suicide. In fact, the strong societal objection to suicide and desire to deter it are demonstrated by the widespread (though by no means unanimous) criminalization of assisted suicide, the existence of statutes permitting the involuntary psychiatric hospitalization of the mentally ill who attempt or threaten suicide, and the disapproval of suicide and mercy killing in living will and health care power of attorney statutes.[267] Thus, the court observed that

> [i]t is . . . incorrect to conclude, on the basis of the absence of criminal penalties for an act of suicide itself and the existence of a pragmatic capacity to commit suicide, that there is a constitutional right to commit suicide. Such a right is not expressly recognized anywhere in the United States Constitution or in the decisions of the United States Supreme Court, and cannot be reasonably inferred. In fact, as we observed earlier in this opinion, those courts that have found a right to refuse to

---

[264] Barber v. Superior Court, 195 Cal. Rptr. 484 (Ct. App. 1983). See **§ 18.12.**

[265] *In re* Conroy, 486 A.2d 1209, 1234 (N.J. 1985) ("Characterizing conduct as active or passive is often an elusive notion, even outside the context of medical decision-making.").

[266] Hobbins v. Attorney Gen., 527 N.W.2d 714, 731 (Mich. 1994), *cert. denied sub nom.* Hobbins v. Kelley, 115 S. Ct. 1795 (1995).

[267] *See, e.g.,* Uniform Health-Care Decisions Act § 13(c), 9 U.L.A. pt. I at 93 (West Supp. 1994). ("This [Act] does not authorize mercy killing, assisted suicide, euthanasia, or the provision, withholding, or withdrawal of health care, to the extent prohibited by other statutes of this State.").

begin or to continue life-sustaining medical treatment have done so only after
concluding that such refusal is wholly different from an act of suicide. . . .

. . . On the basis of the foregoing analysis, we would hold that the right to commit
suicide is neither implicit in the concept of ordered liberty nor deeply rooted in this
nation's history and tradition. It would be an impermissibly radical departure from
existing tradition, and from the principles that underlie that tradition, to declare
that there is such a fundamental right protected by the Due Process Clause.[268]

The court summarily dismissed the equal protection claim on the ground that
"the two situations"—forgoing life-sustaining treatment and assisted suicide—
"are not the same for purposes of constitutional analysis."[269]

## Quill v. Koppell

Quill v. Koppell,[270] like Compassion in Dying and Hobbins, was an action
brought by physicians and patients to invalidate a state's (New York's) statutory
prohibition on assisted suicide, as applied to physicians and terminally ill
patients. The plaintiffs claimed that the prohibition was constitutionally infirm
under the due process and equal protection clauses. The court rejected both
claims and declined to hold the statute unconstitutional.

The court explained, drawing on familiar United States Supreme Court
precedents, that the source of substantive due process rights not expressly found
in the Constitution must either "be implicit in the concept of ordered liberty so
that neither liberty nor justice would exist if they were sacrificed," or they must
be "liberties that are deeply rooted in the nation's history and traditions."[271]
After recounting the history of the criminalization and decriminalization of
suicide, it reached the same conclusion that the Hobbins court did: there is
"nothing in the historical record to indicate that . . . [physician-]assisted suicide
has been given any kind of sanction in our legal history which would help
establish it as a constitutional right."[272]

The court gave even shorter shrift to the equal protection claim. Although it
recognized that there is a right of competent persons under New York law to die
by refusing treatment, the court was unconvinced by the plaintiff's assertion that
the refusal of such treatment "is essentially the same thing as committing suicide
with the advice of a physician."[273] Rather, the court concluded that there is a
reasonable and rational basis for distinguishing the two.

There are at least two problems with the equal protection analysis. First, the
court justified its conclusion that there is a rational distinction between forgoing

---

[268] People v. Kevorkian, 527 N.W.2d at 732–33.

[269] Id. at 732.

[270] 870 F. Supp. 78 (S.D.N.Y. 1994).

[271] Id. at 83 (citing Bowers v. Hardwick, 478 U.S. 186, 191 (1986)).

[272] Id. at 84.

[273] Id.

treatment and assisted suicide by recourse to the state's "obvious legitimate interests in preserving life, and in protecting vulnerable persons."[274] As to "preserving life," it is equally obvious that life is no more or no less preserved if it is ended "passively" or "actively." Further, as courts have almost unanimously recognized in cases involving the forgoing of life-sustaining treatment, it is not mere biological existence that is relevant, but the patient's subjective experience of his own quality of life.[275]

The protection of vulnerable persons is not a trivial concern in end-of-life decisionmaking, but the court pointed to no evidence that vulnerability is any greater an issue in assisted suicide than in forgoing life-sustaining treatment.[276] Patients can be unduly influenced regardless of the means by which life is to end. If vulnerability is to be a concern with respect to assisted suicide, it is of equal concern with respect to forgoing life-sustaining treatment. The remedy is not to prohibit either, but to erect adequate safeguards to guard against abuse, as has been done with forgoing life-sustaining treatment. Consequently, the statutory prohibition on assisted suicide should be viewed as overbroad, because it is not tailored to achieve the state's legitimate interest without at the same time intruding on individual interests.

This brings us to the second problem with the decision. The court analyzed the equal protection claim under a minimal scrutiny test. However, the right at stake—described by the *Compassion in Dying* court as "'involving the most intimate and personal choices a person may make in a lifetime, choices central to personal dignity and autonomy, [and] . . . central to the liberty protected by the Fourteenth Amendment'"[277]—is not merely a legitimate one, it is a fundamental one. As such, infringing on it must be justified not merely by a legitimate state interest but by a compelling state interest.

### *Bouvia v. Superior Court (Glenchur)*

Although not discussing the constitutionality of prohibitions on assisted suicide as such, a concurring opinion in the case of *Bouvia v. Superior Court*

---

[274] *Id.*

[275] See §§ **7.22** and **8.2.**

[276] **DNY:** Quill v. Koppell, 870 F. Supp. at 84.

**DWA:** *See* Compassion in Dying v. Washington, 850 F. Supp. 1454, 1465 (W.D. Wash. 1994), *rev'd,* 49 F.3d 586 (9th Cir. 1995).

**MI:** Hobbins v. Attorney Gen., 518 N.W.2d 487, 498 (Mich. Ct. App. 1994) (Shelton, J., dissenting in part) ("If anything, the intent is less onerous in these instances [of physician-assisted suicide] because, at least as compared to Ms. Quinlan and other incompetent patients, these patients [assisted by Dr. Kevorkian] made the final personal decision and took the final personal action for themselves.").

[277] Compassion in Dying v. Washington, 850 F. Supp. at 1459 (quoting Planned Parenthood v. Casey, 112 S. Ct. 2791, 2807 (1992)).

*(Glenchur)*[278] strongly suggested, though without any analysis, that there was
such a right. Justice Compton, in concurring in a opinion permitting the forgoing
of tube-feeding by a nonterminally, but incurably, ill woman with cerebral palsy,
observed that because she had the right to forgo life-sustaining treatment and
because she was physically incapable of committing suicide, she should have a
right to be provided with the assistance needed. He noted that "[t]he right to die
is an integral part of our right to control our own destinies so long as the rights
of others are not affected."[279] Just as that right, which can be effectuated by
some by forgoing treatment cannot be "hampered by the state's threat to impose
penal sanctions on those who might be disposed to lend assistance," so too "that
right should . . . include the ability to enlist assistance from others, including the
medical profession, in making death as painless and quick as possible."[280]

### *Donaldson v. Van de Kamp*

The only other case to come close to grappling with the issue of the constitutionality of assisted suicide is *Donaldson v. Van de Kamp,* but its facts are
so unusual that they could not but have helped to shape the court's view that the
prohibition on assisted suicide was not unconstitutional. Donaldson, who suffered from an incurable brain tumor, sought to subject himself to "premortem
cryogenic suspension," a procedure that he hoped would freeze his "body to be
later reanimated when curative treatment exists for his brain cancer. Following
cryogenic suspension, [he would] suffer irreversible cessation of circulatory and
respiratory function and irreversible cessation of all brain function," that is,
death.[281]

He brought an action for declaratory and injunctive relief to prevent those
who would perform the procedure from being prosecuted for assisted suicide
and so that the coroner would not perform an autopsy on his body and interfere
with the possibility of reanimation. In refusing to grant the requested relief, the
court concluded that what was sought was tantamount to assisted suicide and
was distinguishable from the forgoing of life-sustaining treatment. The court
held that the state was not constitutionally forbidden, in the interest of promoting individual autonomy, to legislate against assisting another in ending his life.

The court announced three justifications for a statutory prohibition on assisted
suicide, none of which is especially strong. First, the court explained that
such a ban deters "those who might encourage a suicide to advance personal
motives."[282] However, as previously mentioned, the legislature could prescribe

---

[278] 225 Cal. Rptr. 297 (Ct. App. 1986).

[279] *Id.* at 307.

[280] *Id.*

[281] Donaldson v. Van de Kamp, 4 Cal. Rptr. 2d 59, 61 (Ct. App. 1992). *See also* Mitchell v. Roe,
9 Cal. Rptr. 2d 572 (Ct. App. 1992) (requiring state department of health services to provide
cryogenic business with death certificates and permits to dispose of bodies).

[282] 4 Cal. Rptr. at 65.

procedures for ensuring that the decision to end one's life (whether actively or by forgoing treatment) was freely made on the basis of relevant knowledge. Second, the state's interest in the sanctity of life "is threatened by one who is willing to participate in taking the life of another, even at the victim's request."[283] If that is so, the court needs to explain why this is more compelling a state interest than when one ends life by a decision to withhold or withdraw life-sustaining treatment. Finally, the court stated that "although the suicide victim may be mentally ill in wishing his demise, the aider is not necessarily mentally ill."[284] This assertion is founded on an assumption that is sometimes but not always true—that the person requesting suicide is mentally ill. Again, the prescription for such a concern, which is undoubtedly a valid one, is to institute procedures for determining the patient's competency, just as is done in the forgoing of life-sustaining treatment.

### *Rodriguez*

*Rodriguez*[285] illustrates that Canadian law is "leap-frogging" American law. The first case, *Nancy B. v. L'Hotel-Dieu de Quebec,*[286] decided not quite two years earlier, was a conventional right-to-die case involving the termination of a ventilator from a competent patient. In *Rodriguez*, the Supreme Court of Canada was faced with a request from a competent patient suffering from amyotrophic lateral sclerosis (Lou Gehrig's disease) that she be permitted to enlist the assistance of a physician in committing suicide.

Assisting another in committing suicide is a violation of § 241(b) of the British Columbia Criminal Code. Without a judicial declaration that this provision was void as applied to this patient, the physician would have been subject to criminal prosecution. The patient claimed that various provisions of the Charter of Rights—(1) the protection of § 7 accorded to security of the person, encompassing notions of personal autonomy with respect to the right to make choices concerning one's body, control over one's physical and psychological integrity free from state interference, and basic human dignity; (2) the protection of § 12 against cruel and unusual treatment or punishment; and (3) the protection of § 15(1) according equality and freedom from discrimination on the basis of physical handicap—would render such a criminal prohibition unconstitutional. The Supreme Court of British Columbia dismissed the petition, and the Court of Appeal and the Supreme Court of Canada (by a 5-4 vote) affirmed the judgment.

The Supreme Court concluded that any infringement of these rights that the prohibition on assisted suicide might impose cannot be divorced from the sanctity of life, which is also protected by § 7 of the Charter. It also held that

---

[283] *Id.*

[284] *Id.*

[285] Rodriguez v. Attorney Gen. of Can. & Attorney Gen. of B.C., 107 D.L.R.4th 342 (1993).

[286] [1992] R.J.Q. 361 (C.S.).

fundamental justice requires that a fair balance be struck between the interests of the state and those of the individual. The court acknowledged that distinctions between passive and active forms of intervention in the dying process continue to be drawn, and concluded that there is no consensus in favor of the decriminalization of assisted suicide. In fact, the court observed, to the extent there is a consensus, it is that human life must be respected, thus striking the balance against the patient's claim that she had a right to actively terminate her life.

The juxtaposition of the Canadian and American opinions, especially *Quill* but also *Lee*,[287] indicate not merely that the conflict between the legal protections accorded to life and to liberty arise as artifacts of the structure of the United States Constitution but also that the conflict is more fundamentally rooted. It is more than a conflict between two statutory provisions, albeit statutes of the most fundamental kind. Regardless of the text of the constitutional provisions or the nature of the constitutional tools employed to analyze them, an important residue of these conflicts will remain long after the litigation is resolved.

## § 18.23 Constitutionality of Statutes Legalizing Assisted Suicide

Voter initiatives to legalize physician-assisted suicide began to occur in the early 1990s,[288] and legislation is being introduced in a few state legislatures to legalize aid-in-dying.[289] In New York, as one of its several studies of the need to legislate in the area of medical decisionmaking, the State Task Force on Life and the Law undertook a study of physician-assisted suicide and active euthanasia, and ultimately recommended, unanimously, that the New York statute prohibiting assisted suicide and active euthanasia remain unchanged. The reasons given for so doing are representative of the arguments generally put forward by opponents of these practices:

> Assisted suicide and euthanasia would carry us into new terrain—American society has never sanctioned assisted suicide or mercy killing. We believe that the practices would be profoundly dangerous for large segments of the population, especially in light of the widespread failure of American medicine to treat pain adequately or to

---

[287] Lee v. State, 869 F. Supp. 1491 (D. Or. 1994).

[288] Blendon et al., *Should Physicians Aid Their Patients in Dying?—The Public Perspective*, 267 JAMA 2658, 2658 (1992) ("similar initiatives can be found in at least 20 states").

[289] *Compare* Gianelli, *States Weigh Assisted Suicide—AMA Launches More Aggressive Action to Fight Trend*, Am. Med. News, Feb. 27, 1995, at 1 (subsequent to passage of initiative in Oregon legalizing assisted suicide, at least 12 other states have introduced similar legislation) *with* Choice in Dying, The Right-to-Die Law Digest (Sept. 1994) ("Legislation Update" section) (collecting bills to legalize physician-assisted suicide). *See also* Schanker, Note, *Of Suicide Machines, Euthanasia Legislation, and the Health Care Crisis*, 68 Ind. L.J. 977, 998–1003 (1993).

diagnose and treat depression in many cases. The risks would extend to all individuals who are ill. They would be most severe for those whose autonomy and well-being are already compromised by poverty, lack of access to good medical care, or membership in a stigmatized social group. The risks of legalizing assisted suicide and euthanasia for these individuals, in a health care system and society that cannot effectively protect against the impact of inadequate resources and ingrained social disadvantage, are likely to be extraordinary.[290]

Others, however, take the view, which is likely in the long run to prevail, that because in some, probably small, proportion of cases, there is nothing that physicians can do to relieve the unbearable pain and suffering of some terminal illness,[291] the only merciful course of action remaining is to assist patients in ending their lives and to end the lives of those patients who request it but are unable to do so themselves. This is not a new realization; it is well-known that some physicians already practice assisted suicide and/or active euthanasia[292] either overtly or under the shelter provided by the principle of double effect (or by other euphemisms)[293] by providing medication for the relief of pain to such an extent that they know that the patient will die.[294] Rather than practice covertly, some believe that it is better to formally legalize these practices so that they can also be regulated.[295]

The first two efforts at legalization and regulation were referenda in Washington in 1991[296] and California in 1992,[297] which were defeated by identical 56-to-44

---

[290] New York State Task Force on Life & the Law, When Death Is Sought—Assisted Suicide and Euthanasia in the Medical Context vii–viii (1994). *But cf.* Editorial, *Mercy for the Dying,* N.Y. Times, May 28, 1994, at A18 ("the best approach to assisted suicide is to do it openly, requiring doctors to follow codes of conduct designed to minimize mistakes and abuses" rather than permitting it to continue covertly as "a strictly amateur affair"). *See also Institute of Medical Ethics Working Party on the Ethics of Prolonging Life and Assisting Death,* 336 Lancet 610 (1990).

[291] See § **9.38.**

[292] See § **18.21.**

[293] *See* Colen, *Doctors Who Help Patients Die,* Long Island Newsday, Sept. 29, 1991, § 1, at 5 (glossary of "euphemisms and euthanasia" including "snowing a patient," which means providing "increasing levels of painkillers to such a degree that the patient loses consciousness and, because the respiration is depressed by the narcotics, dies far more rapidly than would otherwise by the case").

[294] *See, e.g.,* Preston, *Killing Pain, Ending Life,* N.Y. Times, Nov. 1, 1994, at A15 ("I have never found a colleague who thinks a morphine drip is wrong if the patient is dying."). See §§ **8.7** and **9.38.**

[295] *See, e.g.,* Miller et al., *Regulating Physician-Assisted Death,* 331 New Eng. J. Med. 119 (1994).

[296] *See* Gross, *Voters Turn Down Legal Euthanasia,* N.Y. Times, Nov. 7, 1991, at A10 (nat'l ed.). *See also* Special Supplement, *Euthanasia: Washington State Initiative 119,* 406 Commonweal 465–80 (Aug. 1991) (including Jonsen, *What Is at Stake?;* Gomez, *Consider the Dutch;* Kass, *Why Doctors Must Not Kill;* Callahan, *"Aid-in-Dying": The Social Dimensions*).

[297] *See* Gianelli, *Euthanasia Measure Fails, But Backers Vow Renewed Push,* Am. Med. News, Nov. 23 and 30, 1992, at 30 (would also have legalized mercy killing by physicians). *See also* Special Supplement, 19 Hastings Center Rep. (Jan.–Feb. 1989).

percent margins. However, Oregon voters approved a referendum legalizing physician-assisted suicide in the November 1994 election. Known as the Oregon "Death with Dignity Act" or Measure 16,[298] it is so carefully crafted, so narrowly drawn, and so laden with procedural safeguards that it may well demand more energy and fortitude to comply with it than some terminally ill people who nominally qualify are likely to have.

To qualify for physician-assisted suicide, a person must be an Oregon resident,[299] over age 18,[300] "capable"[301] (that is, in possession of decisionmaking capacity),[302] and suffering from a terminal disease that will lead to death within six months.[303] He must make one written[304] and two oral requests[305] for medication to end his life, the written one "substantially in the form" provided in the Act, signed, dated, witnessed by two persons, in the presence of the patient, who attest that the patient is "capable, acting voluntarily, and not being coerced to sign the request,"[306] and there are stringent qualifications as to who may act as a witness.[307] The patient's decision must be an "informed" one,[308] and the attending physician is therefore obligated to provide the patient with information about the diagnosis, prognosis, potential risks and probable consequences of taking the medication to be prescribed, and alternatives, "including but not limited to, comfort care, hospice care and pain control."[309] There must be a confirmation of the diagnosis, the patient's decisionmaking capacity, and the patient's voluntariness by another physician.[310] There are requirements for counseling if the patient is thought to be suffering from a mental disorder,[311] for documentation in the patient's medical record,[312] for a waiting period,[313] for notification of the patient's next of kin,[314] and for reporting to state

---

[298] Oregon Death with Dignity Act, Measure No. 16 (enacted Nov. 8, 1994; effective Dec. 8, 1994; *implementation stayed,* Lee v. State, 869 F. Supp. 1491 (D. Or. 1994)).

[299] *Id.* §§ 2.01, 3.18.

[300] *Id.* §§ 2.01, 1.01(1).

[301] *Id.* § 2.01.

[302] *Id.* § 1.01(6).

[303] *Id.* §§ 2.01, 1.01(12).

[304] Oregon Death with Dignity Act §§ 2.02(1), 3.06.

[305] *Id.* §§ 3.06, 6.01 (form).

[306] *Id.* § 2.02(1).

[307] *Id.* § 2.02(2)–(4).

[308] *Id.* §§ 3.01(2), 3.04.

[309] *Id.* § 3.01(2).

[310] Oregon Death with Dignity Act § 3.02.

[311] *Id.* § 3.03.

[312] *Id.* § 3.09.

[313] *Id.* § 3.08.

[314] *Id.* § 3.05.

authorities.[315] The patient has a right to rescind the request for medication to end his life at any time.[316]

Having complied with these requirements, the person requesting to die is entitled only to a prescription for medication to end life. The Act does not "authorize a physician or any other person to end a patient's life by lethal injection, mercy killing or active euthanasia."[317] In other words, the statute accepts physician-assisted suicide but rejects active euthanasia. What this is likely to mean in practice is that there are will be some situations in which patients are not able to administer the medication to themselves by the time they meet all the statutory requirements. Or there will be tragic and unaesthetic instances in which patients are able to take some but not all of the medication (or too little is prescribed) and fall short of their desired end, making themselves nauseated or waking up.[318] At least some patients who are able to comply with the Act are probably also capable of hoarding enough pills to end their lives without a doctor's help, and for them the Act will provide little or no advantage.

Before the Oregon "Death with Dignity Act" could take effect, a proceeding was brought in federal court, *Lee v. State,* to enjoin it, and a preliminary injunction was granted postponing "the implementation of the legislation until the constitutional concerns are fully heard and analyzed."[319] The plaintiffs in *Lee* were "two physicians, four terminally ill or potentially terminally ill patients, a residential care facility, and individual operators of residential care facilities."[320] They claimed that the Death with Dignity Act violated the due process and equal protection clauses, the First Amendment protection accorded association and the free exercise of religion, and the Americans With Disabilities Act.

The due process claim is in some respects the reverse of that alleged in the challenges to the constitutionality of state statutes *prohibiting* assisted suicide. In those cases, the plaintiffs sought to establish that the statutes infringed on their interest in *liberty;* here the plaintiffs claimed that the statute loosening the prohibition on assisted suicide denied them constitutional protection to their interest in *life.* As suggested in the discussion of the Michigan Court of Appeals's decision in *Hobbins,*[321] these two different but related interests protected by the Fourteenth Amendment are potentially on a collision course with each other. *Lee* makes that manifest. Just as it is arguable that statutes

---

[315] *Id.* § 3.11.

[316] Oregon Death with Dignity Act § 3.07.

[317] *Id.* § 3.14.

[318] *See, e.g.,* Selzer, *A Question of Mercy,* N.Y. Times, § 6 (Magazine), at 32, Sept. 22, 1991 (physician's account of failed suicide attempt which he half-heartedly assisted).

[319] Lee v. State, 869 F. Supp. 1491 (D. Or. 1994).

[320] *Id.* at 1493.

[321] See § **18.22.**

prohibiting assisted suicide prima facie infringe on the constitutionally protected interest in liberty, it is equally arguable that statutes permitting the same practice prima facie infringe on the constitutionally protected interest in life. The plaintiffs also alleged, however, that the legislation infringed on their liberty interest by not sufficiently guaranteeing that the choice to end life would be informed and voluntary.

The court's opinion in granting the preliminary injunction is highly abbreviated. It does little more than raise questions, primarily the questions that the plaintiffs raised. However, one of the footnotes gives some reason to believe that the court will ultimately rule against the constitutionality of the statute. Footnote 3 contains a relatively long recital of information suggesting that many people seeking to commit suicide are suffering from a psychiatric disorder, and thus that the decision is not necessarily voluntary or informed.[322]

It might well turn out that courts will be more willing to uphold the constitutionality of legislation, such as Oregon's, that partially decriminalizes assisted suicide, if that legislation is narrowly drafted and contains adequate protections, than they are to hold unconstitutional statutes that criminalize assisted suicide. So doing would exhibit the kind of deference to democratic values and to the limited role of the courts—especially when the partial decriminalization legislation is enacted by referendum—that courts almost reflexively invoke when hesitating to hold statutes unconstitutional.

## § 18.24   Active Euthanasia in the Netherlands

The introduction of active euthanasia into the realm of acceptable medical practice began in the Netherlands in 1969. A book by Professor J.H. van den Berg proposed a "new ethic" in regard to halting the unwanted prolongation of life-sustaining medical treatment.[323] He proposed that the unwanted prolongation of the dying process could be ended by physicians by withholding or stopping life-sustaining treatment, or by actively intervening to end a terminally ill patient's life. Although the initial impact of this book was small, within four years of its publication the Dutch medical community, legislators, and courts

---

[322] *See* Brown et al., *Is It Normal for Terminally Ill Patients to Desire Death?*, 143 Am. J. Psychiatry 208 (1986) ("Suicidal thoughts and desire for death appear in our patient group to be linked exclusively to the presence of mental disorder. If this finding can be generalized, it would appear that patients with terminal illness who are not mentally ill are no more likely than the general population to wish for premature death."). *But see* Conwell & Caine, *Rational Suicide and the Right to Die: Reality and Myth,* 325 New Eng. J. Med. 1100, 1101–02 (1991) ("The distinction between the depressed mood or sadness that develops as a natural response to serious illness and the clinical depressive syndrome for which treatment is warranted is a subtle one that should be made by a" psychiatrist.).

[323] Pollard, *Medical Aspects of Euthanasia,* 154 Med. J. Austl. 613 (1991).

were engaged in a debate that would ultimately change the landscape of treating terminally ill patients.

The year 1973 witnessed three important events. First, a commission established by the State Secretary of Social Health issued a report concerning active and passive euthanasia. The commission reported that "active euthanasia is not allowed, because it is and must remain forbidden; but that passive euthanasia must become permissible in certain circumstances."[324] Second, the Royal Dutch Medical Association issued a statement providing support for the practice. It said in part that "legally euthanasia should remain a crime, but that if a physician, after having considered all the aspects of the case, shortens the life of a patient who is incurably ill and in the process of dying, the court will have to judge whether there was a conflict of duties which could justify the act of the physician."[325]

Finally, the courts took a major step in permitting the practice of euthanasia by the ruling in the *Leeuwarden* case. This case involved a physician charged with killing her 78-year-old mother, who was partly paralyzed after suffering a stroke. Although the physician was convicted, she received a suspended jail sentence of only one week,[326] despite the fact that article 293 of the Dutch penal code provides that anyone who "takes another person's life even at his explicit and serious request, will be punished by imprisonment of at most 12 years or a fine of the fifth category."[327] This decision established a set of conditions in which medical mercy killing would not be prosecuted:

1.  the disease is incurable;
2.  the patient's suffering is unbearable;
3.  the patient's condition is terminal;
4.  the patient requests death.[328]

During the ensuing decade, these rules governed active euthanasia in the Netherlands.

---

[324] Dreisse et al., *Euthanasia and the Law in the Netherlands,* 3 Issues L. & Med. 385, 393 (1988).

[325] de Wachter, *Active Euthanasia in the Netherlands,* 262 JAMA 3316, 3317 (1989).

[326] Pollard, *Medical Aspects of Euthanasia,* 154 Med. J. Austl. 613, 613 (1991); Emanuel, *Euthanasia—Historical, Ethical, and Empiric Perspectives,* 154 Archives Internal Med. 1890, 1896 (1994); Kuhse, *Voluntary Euthanasia in the Netherlands,* 147 Med. J. Austl. 394, 394 (1987).

[327] de Wachter, *Active Euthanasia in the Netherlands,* 262 JAMA 3316, 3317 (1989) (fine of fifth category roughly equivalent to $60,000).

[328] Jecker, *Physician-Assisted Death in the Netherlands and the United States; Ethical and Cultural Aspects of Health Policy Development,* 42 J. Am. Geriatrics Soc'ty 627, 627–28 (1994).

In 1984, the Royal Dutch Medical Association issued "Guidelines for Euthanasia," containing five similar requirements:

1.  voluntariness on the patient's part;
2.  a well-considered request;
3.  stability of desire;
4.  unacceptable suffering; and
5.  collegial consultation.[329]

These judicial and medical guidelines provided physicians with a mechanism for engaging in active euthanasia while avoiding prosecution.

The jurisprudential basis for the acceptance by courts of physician-performed active euthanasia is the concept of *force majeure,* defined as a situation "in which the physician's professional duty to alleviate suffering prevails over the duty to preserve life."[330] Thus, "[l]egally speaking, there is no question that these cases should be seen as anything but murder,"[331] but the courts will almost certainly excuse them under the force majeure defense.

Although active euthanasia technically remains a crime under article 293, in 1993 the Dutch Parliament enacted legislation explicitly granting physicians immunity from prosecution if they abide by the requirements for justifiable euthanasia,[332] including notification of "the coroner of any death they have deliberately brought on and [provision of] a detailed account of the circumstances based on an official checklist."[333] This legislation does not decriminalize active euthanasia, but it does permit physicians to escape prosecution through a grant of immunity.[334]

For a number of reasons, the statistics on the frequency of active euthanasia in the Netherlands are uncertain. The most significant is thought to be that physicians falsify records. Although physicians are not being prosecuted for murder, many are still fearful of this possibility. As a result, they sometimes report to the coroner that the person died from natural causes and hope that there is no investigation. Another reason for the variance is that there is not a clear

---

[329] Keown, *On Regulating Death,* 22 Hastings Center Rep. 39, 40 (Mar.–Apr. 1992).

[330] de Wachter, *Euthanasia in the Netherlands,* 22 Hastings Center Rep. 23, 26 (Mar.–Apr. 1992).

[331] van Delden et al., *The Remmelink Study—Two Years Later,* 23 Hastings Center Rep. 24, 25 (Nov.–Dec. 1993).

[332] Emanuel, *Euthanasia—Historical, Ethical, and Empiric Perspectives,* 154 Archives Internal Med. 1890, 1897 (1994).

[333] Simons, *Dutch Move to Enact Law Making Euthansia Easier,* N.Y. Times, Feb. 9, 1993, at A1 (nat'l ed.). *See also* Fenigsen, *New Regulations Concerning Euthanasia,* 9 Issues L. & Med. 167, 172–73 (reprinting checklist).

[334] Fenigsen, *New Regulations Concerning Euthanasia,* 9 Issues L. & Med. 167, 167 (1993).

definition of euthanasia. Furthermore, "physicians do not clearly and carefully maintain the distinction between euthanasia . . . and other medical decisions concerning the end of life."[335]

Depending on the definition, anywhere from 2,000 to 20,000 mercy killings are performed annually in the Netherlands. A committee headed by the Attorney General of the Supreme Court, Remmelink, commissioned a study of euthanasia in the Netherlands.[336] This study found that approximately 2,300 cases of active euthanasia occurred, with 400 being ruled physician-assisted suicide.[337] The total number of deaths in the Netherlands at that time was about 130,000 per year, in 49,000 of which there was some physician involvement in a decision to end life either passively or actively.[338] According to this study, when applying a "liberal" definition of voluntary euthanasia, the incidence rate rises to 25,306 per year. Terminally ill cancer patients are the most likely to ask for euthanasia to be performed on them, and the persons who request euthanasia tend to be male and over the age of 65.[339]

The Remmelink Committee and other commentators have raised questions about whether active euthanasia is being abused. The most general concern arises from the increased number of mercy killings. There were 400 cases in 1990 and 1,318 in 1992.[340] Critics charge that this is the result of "trigger-happy" physicians, but others argue that this is merely the consequence of patients being made more aware of their rights and medical options,[341] while others have argued that there is merely greater compliance with reporting requirements.[342] A major concern is whether patients are being subjected to

---

[335] de Wachter, *Euthanasia in the Netherlands,* 22 Hastings Center Rep. 23, 23 (Mar.–Apr. 1992). *See also* Keown, *On Regulating Death,* 22 Hastings Center Rep. 39, 40 (Mar.–Apr. 1992) (citing C. Gomez, Regulating Death: Euthanasia and the Case of the Netherlands 96–97 (1991)).

[336] *See* van der Maas et al., *Euthanasia and Other Medical Decisions Concerning the End of Life,* 338 Lancet 669 (1991).

[337] van der Maas et al., *Euthanasia and Other Medical Decisions Concerning the End of Life,* 338 Lancet 669, 671 (1991). *See also* van der wal et al., *Euthanasia & Assisted Suicide: I. How Often Is It Practised by Family Doctors in the Netherlands?,* 9 Fam. Prac. 130 (1992) (approximately 2,000 active euthanasias per year).

[338] ten Have & Welie, *Euthanasia: Normal Medical Practice?,* 22 Hastings Center Rep. 34, 34 (Mar.–Apr. 1992).

[339] van der Maas et al., *Euthanasia and Other Medical Decisions Concerning the End of Life,* 338 Lancet 669, 671 (1991).

[340] Simons, *Dutch Parliament Approves Law Permitting Euthanasia,* N.Y. Times, Feb. 10, 1993, at A5 (nat'l ed.).

[341] *See* Simons, *Dutch Parliament Approves Law Permitting Euthanasia,* N.Y. Times, Feb. 10, 1993, at A5.

[342] van Delden et al., *The Remmelink Study—Two Years Later,* 23 Hastings Center Rep. 24, 25 (Nov.–Dec. 1993).

*nonvoluntary* active euthanasia, that is, euthanasia that is not requested by the patient.[343] Under the Committee's "liberal" definition of mercy killing, between 14,000 and 15,000 deaths per year would be classified as *nonvoluntary* active euthanasia. The Remmelink Committee, however, reported that only 1,000 of these deaths involve "deliberate action to terminate the patient's life without the explicit request of the patient."[344] By contrast, there is a 1986 estimate that nonvoluntary active euthanasia is between two and five times more frequent than voluntary.[345] In addition, there is evidence that doctors use inconsistent standards for the determination of voluntariness.[346] However, another study reports that life-terminating acts without the request of the patient occur in only 0.8 percent of all deaths, that in 41 percent discussion with the patient was no longer possible, that the physician knew the patient for a number of years, that in 83 percent the physician discussed the decision with relatives, and that in nearly all cases the physician determined that the patient was suffering unbearably, there was no chance of improvement, and palliative treatment was not working.[347]

Another problem is the failure of physicians to follow the proper procedures, including failing to require patients to give persistent "death wishes."[348] Physicians rely on oral requests in a large majority of cases. One survey found that there was only a single request for euthanasia in 22 percent of the cases, and that the interval between the first and last requests was between an hour and a week in 30 percent of the cases.[349] Physicians frequently do not properly report death from euthanasia. Required reports to the authorities are made in less than 20 percent of the cases, possibly because of the uncertainty about

---

[343] See Gevers, Legislation on Euthanasia: Recent Developments in the Netherlands, 18 J. Med. Ethics 138, 140 (1992) (arguing that distinction between voluntary and nonvoluntary euthanasia must be maintained). *See also* Muller et al., *Voluntary Active Euthanasia and Physician-Assisted Suicide in Dutch Nursing Homes: Are the Requirements for Prudent Practice Properly Met?*, 42 J. Am. Geriatrics Society 624 (1994) (85% of nursing home physicians state that patient first broached subject of active euthanasia or physician-assisted suicide). *But see* van Delden et al., *The Remmelink Study—Two Years Later,* 23 Hastings Center Rep. 24, 25 (Nov.–Dec. 1993) (suggesting other reasons for seeming increase in unrequested euthanasia).

[344] Fenigson, *The Report of the Dutch Governmental Committee on Euthanasia,* 7 Issues L. & Med. 339, 340 (1991).

[345] Pollard, *Medical Aspects of Euthanasia,* 154 Med. J. Austl. 613, 615 (1991).

[346] *See also* Keown, *On Regulating Death,* 22 Hastings Center Rep. 39, 40 (Mar.–Apr. 1992).

[347] Pijnenborg et al., *Life-Terminating Acts Without Explicit Request of Patient,* 341 Lancet 1196 (1993).

[348] *See, e.g.,* Muller et al., *Voluntary Active Euthanasia and Physician-Assisted Suicide in Dutch Nursing Homes: Are the Requirements for Prudent Practice Properly Met?*, 42 J. Am. Geriatrics Soc'y 624 (1994) (study found that nursing home physicians observed all requirements in 41% of cases, but a variety of departures occurred in majority of cases).

[349] Keown, *On Regulating Death,* 22 Hastings Center Rep. 39 (Mar.–Apr. 1992). *See also* Muller et al., *Voluntary Active Euthanasia and Physician-Assisted Suicide in Dutch Nursing Homes: Are the Requirements for Prudent Practice Properly Met?*, 42 J. Am. Geriatrics Soc'y 624 (1994) (period between first discussion of subject and administration ranged from less than a day to more than a year).

prosecution.[350] Death certificates are also not accurately completed; in 75 percent of cases that were euthanasias, physicians gave "death from natural causes" as the reason on the death certificate "to avoid the fuss and possibility of prosecution."[351]

Finally, a ruling by the Supreme Court of the Netherlands suggests that the currently accepted standards for providing physician-assisted suicide or active euthanasia will be expanded. In this case, a psychiatrist provided a physically healthy but severely depressed woman with a fatal dose of sleeping pills. Although he was found guilty, the court held that he should not be punished.[352]

## § 18.25   Nonvoluntary and Involuntary Active Euthanasia

When a request for forgoing of life-sustaining treatment comes from a competent patient, it should be referred to as *voluntary* passive euthanasia if it meets the requirements for informed consent. Most litigated right-to-die cases, however, have involved incompetent patients and therefore the requests, of necessity, have been made by others on their behalf. When the basis for granting the request to forgo life-sustaining treatment is an advance directive of the incompetent patient, this should also be viewed as being voluntary passive euthanasia.

When a patient is incompetent and has been silent on the matter of forgoing treatment prior to losing decisionmaking capacity and authorization to forgo life-sustaining treatment is given by a surrogate, the practice is more appropriately denominated *nonvoluntary* passive euthanasia, because the decision to forgo life-sustaining treatment is made without actual or presumed knowledge of the patient's will. Only if forgoing life-sustaining treatment were to be undertaken against the patient's actual or probable wishes or over the refusal of a surrogate should it be referred to as *involuntary* passive euthanasia.

The current debates about physician-assisted suicide and active euthanasia contemplate that it will be *voluntary*—but that it will be voluntary *active* euthanasia rather than the voluntary *passive* euthanasia that has been at the center of the debate since the *Quinlan* case. If the law comes to accept—through legislation, judicial decisions, or both—assisted suicide and active euthanasia for competent patients, efforts will undoubtedly occur to extend the scope of permissible active euthanasia. It does not take a great deal of foresight to imagine that such extensions might occur along lines similar to those that have occurred in the development of the law governing forgoing life-sustaining treatment.

---

[350] van Delden et al., *The Remmelink Study—Two Years Later,* 23 Hastings Center Rep. 24, 25 (Nov.–Dec. 1993).

[351] Emanuel, *Euthanasia—Historical, Ethical, and Empiric Perspectives,* 154 Archives Internal Med. 1890, 1897 (1994). *See also* Muller et al., *Voluntary Active Euthanasia and Physician-Assisted Suicide in Dutch Nursing Homes: Are the Requirements for Prudent Practice Properly Met?,* 42 J. Am. Geriatrics Soc'y 624 (1994).

[352] *Dutch Doctor Unpunished in Aided Suicide,* N.Y. Times, June 22, 1994, at A10 (late ed.).

In the latter realm, there was a long- and well-established right of individuals, protected by the common law through actions for battery, not to be subjected to medical treatment without consent. This right developed in the context of situations in which there was little chance that the refusal of treatment would lead to death. It was then extended to situations in which forgoing treatment would certainly or almost certainly lead to death. Further extensions permitted others to make such decisions on behalf of individuals who were no longer personally able to do so, and permitted individuals to make their own decisions anticipatorily through advance directives. It is likely that efforts will be made to implement a similar pattern in the context of active interventions to end life might. This pattern—or as some would call it, descent down the slippery slope[353]—might proceed along the following lines:

(1)  *Application to Competent Nonterminally Ill Patients.* The smallest step in the extension of physician-assisted suicide and active euthanasia beyond terminally ill patients would be to nonterminally ill, but very seriously ill or injured, competent patients. This has already happened in the realm of forgoing life-sustaining treatment. Although the first cases among competent patients were those who were terminally ill,[354] courts have had little difficulty in abolishing this limitation for which no strong state interest has been advanced.[355] Thus, courts have ruled that individuals with potentially long life expectancies but who are dependent for continued life on life-sustaining medical treatment such as feeding tubes[356] or ventilators,[357] and who have determined for themselves that their quality of life under such conditions is unacceptable have the right to have treatment withheld or withdrawn. The more favorable attitude of courts to the forgoing of lifesaving blood transfusions by members of the Jehovah's Witness faith[358] represents a further extension and application of the abolition of the terminal-illness limitation on refusal of treatment.

Individuals who are seriously disabled but not being kept alive by any form of life-sustaining medical treatment, and thus cannot die by having such treatment

---

[353] *In re* Grant, 747 P.2d 445, 458 (Wash. 1987), *modified,* 757 P.2d 534 (Wash. 1988) (forgoing of artificial nutrition and hydration from never-competent patient "is pure, unadorned eutha-nasia. It is a step upon a slippery slope, one that I would not take.").

[354] **FL:** *See, e.g.,* Satz v. Perlmutter, 379 So. 2d 359 (Fla. 1980).

   **OH:** *See, e.g.,* Leach v. Akron Gen. Medical Ctr., 426 N.E.2d 809 (P. Ct. Summit County, Ohio 1980).

[355] See **Ch. 8.**

[356] **CA:** *See, e.g.,* Bouvia v. Superior Court (Glenchur), 225 Cal. Rptr. 297 (Ct. App. 1986).

[357] **CA:** Thor v. Superior Court, 855 P.2d 375 (Cal. 1993).

   **GA:** *See, e.g.,* State v. McAfee, 385 S.E.2d 651 (Ga. 1989).

   **NV:** *See, e.g.,* McKay v. Bergstedt, 801 P.2d 617 (Nev. 1990).

[358] See § **9.3.**

withheld or withdrawn, will undoubtedly assert that they should have the right to end their lives, if they find their quality unacceptable, either by assisted suicide or by having someone else actively end their life if they are unable to do so themselves and if there is such a willing person. This is also true of individuals suffering no injury or physical illness, but who are experiencing severe psychic pain either on an acute or chronic basis.[359] Yet another variation on this theme would be the attempted application of the right to aid-in-dying for individuals who are not physically ill, but who suffer from serious mental illnesses that cause them to experience a subjectively unacceptable quality of life but do not deprive them of decisionmaking capacity.

(2) *Application to Terminally Ill, Incompetent Patients Through Written Advance Directives.* Individuals wishing to have their lives actively ended if they became terminally ill and incompetent could execute advance directives requesting such procedures. This might be done either by writing a living will that specifically requests active euthanasia under specified circumstances or by executing a health care power of attorney empowering a proxy to authorize active euthanasia either under specified circumstances or at the proxy's own discretion. Existing advance directive statutes specifically preclude the implementation of such advance directives. However, if the prohibition on assisted suicide and/or active euthanasia is unconstitutional, it is likely that these provisions of advance directive statutes would be unconstitutional on the basis of similar reasoning (specifically, the violation of due process and/or equal protection). Of course, the statutes might also be amended by legislation or by voter initiative as is beginning to happen with prohibitions on assisted suicide. Finally, one might seek to evade the exclusion of physician-assisted suicide and active euthanasia in advance directive statutes by drafting an advance directive based on common-law or constitutional rights of self-determination rather than on the basis of the statute,[360] but it is not likely that a physician would implement such a directive in the absence of a judicial ruling that it is permissible to do so.

One potentially important difference between using an advance directive to authorize active euthanasia and a contemporaneous request for active euthanasia or assisted suicide is that with an advance directive there is a significantly reduced opportunity to evaluate the patient's competence, voluntariness, and steadfastness in comparison with a contemporaneous request. However, this is no different from the forgoing of life-sustaining treatment on the basis of an advance directive in comparison with the contemporaneous decision by a competent patient. Thus, if the legitimacy of active euthanasia and physician-assisted suicide is a given, the use of advance directives to request them does not

---

[359] *See, e.g.,* Ogilvie & Potts, *Assisted Suicide for Depression: The Slippery Slope in Action?— Learning from the Dutch Experience,* 309 Brit. Med. J. 492 (1994).

[360] See §§ **10.10–10.13.**

appear to introduce any reasons for concern greater than or different from those attendant upon the use of advance directives to withhold or withdraw life-sustaining medical treatment.

(3) *Application to Nonterminally Ill, Incompetent Patients Through Advance Directives.* Combining the first two fact situations, individuals not only might wish to execute advance directives that authorize active euthanasia if they are terminally ill but also might wish to authorize it if they are not terminally ill but in some condition that they find unacceptable, such as permanent unconsciousness. This is precisely what has occurred with many advance directive statutes in the context of withholding or withdrawing life-sustaining treatment. Some statutes that were originally limited to terminally ill patients were amended to include patients who were permanently unconscious. As has also occurred in the case of conventional advance directives, it is likely that there will be some who would wish to authorize active euthanasia in situations other than terminal illness or permanent unconsciousness, such as dementia.

(4) *Application to Incompetent Patients with Oral Advance Directives.* Circumstances would undoubtedly arise, as they do when consideration is being given to forgoing life-sustaining treatment, to the use of oral advance directives when there is no written one. Assuming that active euthanasia is itself legal, the use of oral advance directives to administer active euthanasia does not seem to present any problems different from those that currently arise in their use to withhold or withdraw treatment. The same problems of veracity and motive of those who report the patient's wishes would exist.

(5) *Application to Incompetent Patients Without Advance Directives ("Non-voluntary" Active Euthanasia).* An extension of active euthanasia differing substantially in kind from the previous types is its administration to an incompetent patient who has not executed an instruction directive requesting active euthanasia or a durable power of attorney expressly empowering a proxy to authorize it, and who has not even made advance oral statements requesting it sufficient to satisfy the subjective standard for decisionmaking for incompetent patients.[361] Currently with respect to forgoing life-sustaining treatment, in situations in which the subjective standard cannot be met, the overwhelming number of jurisdictions that have considered the issue permit the use of the more hypothetical substituted judgment standard, in which decisions are based on the patient's presumed wishes rather than the patient's actual wishes.

Undoubtedly, if the use of advance directives to authorize active euthanasia were to become legal, pressure would grow for its use even in the absence of an advance directive if a patient's wish for it could be inferred—that is, if the substituted judgment standard could be met—as has been the case with withholding and withdrawing life-sustaining medical treatment. And there is little

---

[361] See §§ 7.4–7.6.

reason to believe that if there were insufficient probative evidence of a patient's probable wish for active euthanasia, efforts would not be made to apply the best interests standard, again as has been done in the case of forgoing life-sustaining treatment. Justice O'Connor, of the Massachusetts Supreme Judicial Court, writing in a case involving the forgoing of life-sustaining treatment from a never-competent patient, made the following apt observation:

> Can it reasonably be doubted that legal acceptance of suicide, assisted suicide, and voluntary euthanasia presents a serious risk that acceptance of involuntary euthanasia (mercy killing not chosen by the affected individual) is soon to follow? Today's decision is most instructive. Indeed, it is a case in point. By a process of substituted judgment, a Probate and Family Court judge, affirmed by this court, attributed to Jane Doe, a woman who has been profoundly retarded since infancy and exists in a persistent vegetative state, a choice to discontinue the tube-feeding and hydration necessary to her survival. This attribution of choice was made and affirmed although Doe, never having had an ability to commit volitional acts, and showing no response to stimuli calculated to cause pain in a conscious individual, could not possibly have sought to be free from physically or emotionally painful treatment. Nevertheless, the choice made for, and attributed to, Doe is said to have been predicated on the judge's decision, based on the preponderance of the evidence, that Jane Doe, were she competent, would have preferred death over life as she was living it, and would have requested that her choice to end her life would be honored. On the basis of an assessment of the quality of life accessible to Doe, the judge authorized the withholding of food and water in order that Doe, who actually had no say in the matter, might "go in peace." If this is not involuntary euthanasia, or worse, it is hard to know what is.[362]

However, the arguments to be made in favor of relaxing (or not relaxing) the standard for administering active euthanasia to incompetent patients do not seem to be any different, nor any more or less sound, than they are in the case of forgoing treatment.

(6) *Application to Protesting Patients ("Involuntary" Active Euthanasia).* In some of the foregoing discussions of potential extensions of active euthanasia, the patients were, by hypothesis, incompetent and thus the request was made through the use of an advance directive. Also, in all of these possible extensions the patient either voluntarily requested active euthanasia or left no record of opposition to it, so that even if the active euthanasia was not voluntary, neither was it involuntary.

Situations can readily be imagined in which an individual specifically did not want active euthanasia and said so either orally or in writing. Just as advance directives can be used to request that treatment be administered rather than forgone, if an advance directive can be used to authorize active euthanasia, there

---

[362] *See, e.g., In re* Doe, 583 N.E.2d 1263, 1272 (Mass. 1992) (O'Connor, J., dissenting).

is no logical reason why it might not be used to forbid active euthanasia. Further, just as most advance directive statutes provide that no inference about a patient's wishes are to be drawn from the failure to execute an advance directive, the same conclusion should be reached about a patient's failure to issue a written or an oral advance directive forbidding active euthanasia. That is, the failure to do so should not give rise to an assumption that the individual did want active euthanasia. In such a situation, if active euthanasia were to occur, it should properly be termed *involuntary,* as opposed to *nonvoluntary,* the latter term being the one used when euthanasia is administered in the absence of a specific contemporaneous or advance request by the patient.

That advance directives *can* be drafted so as to forbid active euthanasia (or request treatment, as the case may be) does not necessarily mean that physicians will be required to abide by them. An advance directive forbidding active euthanasia is likely to be, in effect, a demand that treatment continue to be provided. We are just now beginning to grapple—under the commonly used term "futility cases"—with the problem of how to respond to demands by surrogates for treatment, treatment that is considered by physician to be inappropriate for the patient.[363]

Certainly no legal consensus—and probably no consensus in public opinion, among health care professionals, or among medical ethicists—has been reached about whether such demands must be honored; and if so, under what circumstances. But if they are not honored—that is, if a demand for life-sustaining treatment is rejected—and the patient's death results, then surely the result should be denominated involuntary, from the perspective of a competent patient or an incompetent patient with an advance directive requesting treatment under such circumstances, or from the perspective of the surrogate deciding for the patient.

The intersection of the issues of involuntary ending of life and futility ought now to be clear. Regardless of the nomenclature, if life-sustaining treatment is forgone against the wishes of the surrogate (or against the wishes of a competent patient), this is surely a case of involuntary passive euthanasia. If it ultimately becomes acceptable, it is only a short step to involuntary *active* euthanasia, that is, the acceptance of active euthanasia in the face of prior objections from a patient contained in an advance directive or in contemporaneous objections from a surrogate.

It is sometimes said that we should not legitimate physician-assisted suicide or active euthanasia even in the most compelling cases—for example, a competent terminally ill person dying of an extremely painful illness for which there is not only no known cure but also no adequate relief from pain who requests that his life be ended and whose request is unquestionably freely given—because to do so is to start a descent down a slippery slope (or to continue the descent

---

[363] See **Ch. 19.**

already begun if one believes that forgoing life-sustaining treatment—passive euthanasia—should not be permissible).[364] What is at the bottom of the slope is sometimes left unstated, but sometimes it is described by comparison with the euthanasia program in Nazi Germany in the 1930s,[365] and occasionally the implication or an express statement is made that allowing physician-assisted suicide or active euthanasia even in the most compelling case is merely the first step on the road to genocide of the "socially undesirable." Rather than the socially undesirable being Gypsies, homosexuals, Jews, Poles, and other religious or ethnic groups as was the case in Nazi Germany, the undesirables at the bottom of this particular slippery slope are the seriously ill, the physically disabled, the mentally disabled, and others whose lives society is said to devalue, perhaps on economic and aesthetic grounds.

There is some evidence that the practice of active euthanasia in the Netherlands, which began as voluntary active euthanasia, has experienced some departure from the strict requirements originally set forth and subsequently reiterated by courts, the parliament, and medical societies. In sum, there is evidence that active euthanasia is being administered to patients who are no longer capable of making a request for it and did not make such a request before losing the capacity to do so.[366] Consequently, there is some empirical basis for believing that the same could happen if American law were to follow a similar path. Nonetheless, these clearly undesirable outcomes do not appear to be any more likely to occur from the proposed practice of active euthanasia than from the long-accepted practice of passive euthanasia.

---

[364] *See, e.g.,* Kamisar, *When Is There a Constitutional "Right to Die"? When Is There No Constitutional "Right to Live"?,* 25 Ga. L. Rev. 1203 (1991); Kamisar, *Are Laws Against Assisted Suicide Unconstitutional?,* 23 Hastings Center Rep. 32, 36 (May–June 1993) (no principled way to confine assisted suicide to the terminally ill); Newman, *Euthanasia: Orchestrating "The Last Syllable of . . . Time,"* 53 U. Pitt. L. Rev. 153, 167–70 (1991) (rejecting slippery slope arguments); Singer & Siegler, *Euthanasia—A Critique,* 322 New Eng. J. Med. 1881 (1990).

[365] *See* R. Lifton, The Nazi Doctors: Medical Killing and the Psychology of Genocide (1986).

[366] *But see* van Delden et al., *The Remmelink Study—Two Years Later,* 23 Hastings Center Rep. 24, 25 (Nov.–Dec. 1993) ("[N]o empirical data can be marshalled to support the slippery slope argument against the Dutch."). See § **18.24.**

## Bibliography

Admiraal, P. "Euthanasia in the Netherlands—Justifiable Euthanasia." *Issues in Law and Medicine* 3 (1988): 361.

American Geriatrics Society Policy Committee. "Voluntary Active Euthanasia." *Journal of the American Geriatrics Society* 39 (1991): 826.

Annas, G. "Killing Machines." *Hastings Center Report* 21 (January–February 1991): 33.

Battin, M. "Voluntary Euthanasia and the Risks of Abuse: Can We Learn Anything from The Netherlands?" *Law, Medicine and Health Care* 20 (1992): 133.

Battin, M., and D. Mayo, eds. *Suicide: The Philosophical Issues.* New York: St. Martin's Press, 1980.

Brody, B., ed. *Suicide and Euthanasia: Historical and Contemporary Themes.* Dordrecht: Kluwer Law Book Publishers, 1989.

Beauchamp, T. "A Reply to Rachels on Active and Passive Euthanasia." In *Ethical Issues in Death and Dying,* edited by T. Beauchamp & S. Perlin. Englewood Cliffs, N.J.: Prentice-Hall, 1978.

Bender, L. "A Feminist Analysis of Physician-Assisted Dying and Voluntary Active Euthanasia." *Tennessee Law Review* 59 (1992): 519.

Bleich, D. "Life as an Intrinsic Rather Than Instrumental Good: The "Spiritual" Case Against Euthanasia." *Issues in Law and Medicine* 9 (1993): 139.

Bopp, J. "Is Assisted Suicide Constitutionally Protected?" *Issues in Law and Medicine* 3 (1987): 113.

Brock, D. "Voluntary Active Euthanasia." *Hastings Center Report* 22 (March–April 1992): 10.

Browne, A. "Assisted Suicide and Active Voluntary Euthanasia." *Canada Journal of Law and Jurisprudence* 2 (1989): 35.

Callahan, D. "Ad Hominem Runs Amok: A Response to John Lachs." *Journal of Clinical Ethics* 5 (1994): 13.

Callahan, D. "Can We Return Death to Disease?" *Hastings Center Report* 19 (January–February 1989) (special supplement): 4.

Campbell, C. "'Aid-in-Dying' and the Taking of Human Life." *Journal of Medical Ethics* 18 (1992): 128.

Caplan, A. "Bioethics on Trial." *Hastings Center Report* 21 (March–April 1991): 19.

Cassel, C., and D. Meier. "Morals and Moralism in the Debate over Euthanasia and Assisted Suicide." *New England Journal of Medicine* 323 (1990): 750.

Caswell, D. "Rejecting Criminal Liability for Life-Shortening Palliative Care." *Journal of Contemporary Health Law and Policy* 6 (1990): 127.

CeloCruz, M. "Aid-in-Dying: Should We Decriminalize Physician-Assisted Suicide and Physician-Committed Euthanasia?" *American Journal of Law and Medicine* 18 (1992): 369.

de Wachter, M. "Active Euthanasia in the Netherlands." *JAMA* 262 (1989): 3316.

de Wachter, M. "Euthanasia in the Netherlands." *Hastings Center Report* 22 (March–April 1992): 23.

Dickey, N. "Euthanasia: A Concept Whose Time Has Come?" *Issues in Law and Medicine* 8 (1993): 521.

Doherty, D. "Physician-Assisted Suicide: What Constitutes Assistance?" *Wisconsin Lawyer* 65 (1992): 20.

Driesse, M. et al. "Euthanasia and the Law in the Netherlands." *Issues in Law and Medicine* 3 (1988): 385.

Eaton, T., and E. Larson. "Experimenting with the 'Right to Die' in the Laboratory of the States." *Georgia Law Review* 25 (1991): 1253.

Emanuel, E. "Euthanasia—Historical, Ethical, and Empiric Perspectives." *Archives of Internal Medicine* 154 (1994): 1890.

Feinberg, J. "Voluntary Euthanasia and the Inalienable Right to Life." In *Medicine and Moral Philosophy,* edited by M. Cohen et al. Princeton: Princeton University Press, 1981.

Fenigsen, R. "Euthanasia in the Netherlands." *Issues in Law and Medicine* 6 (1990): 229.

"Final Report of the Netherlands State Commission on Euthanasia: An English Summary." *Bioethics* 1 (1987): 163.

Foley, K. "The Relationship of Pain and Symptom Management to Patient Requests for Physician-Assisted Suicide." *Journal of Pain and Symptom Management* 6 (1991): 289.

Fuller, M. "Just Whose Life Is It?: Establishing a Constitutional Right for Physician-Assisted Euthanasia." *Southwestern University Law Review* 23 (1993): 103.

Gaylin, W., et al. "Doctors Must Not Kill." *JAMA* 259 (1988): 2139.

Gilbreath, V. "The Right of the Terminally Ill to Die, With Assistance If Necessary." *Criminal Justice Journal* 8 (1986): 403.

Gillon, R. "Euthanasia, Withholding Life-Prolonging Treatment, and Moral Differences Between Killing and Letting Die." *Journal of Medical Ethics* 14 (1988): 115.

Glantz, L. "Withholding and Withdrawing Treatment: The Role of the Criminal Law." *Law, Medicine and Health Care* 15 (1987–1988): 231.

Gleicher, E. "Legalized Physician-Assisted Suicide." *Michigan Bar Journal* 73 (1994): 184.

Gomez, C. *Regulating Death: Euthanasia and the Case of the Netherlands.* New York: Free Press, 1991.

Gostin, L. "Drawing a Line Between Killing and Letting Die: The Law, and Law Reform, on Medically Assisted Dying." *Law, Medicine and Ethics* 21 (1993): 94.

Hoberman, H. "The Impact of Sanctioned Assisted Suicide on Adolescents." *Issues in Law and Medicine* 4 (1988): 191.

Howe, E. "Clinical Dilemmas When Patients Want Assistance in Dying." *Journal of Clinical Ethics* 5 (1994): 3.

Humphry, D. *Final Exit.* Los Angeles: Hemlock Society, 1991.

Humphry, D. *Lawful Exit.* Junction City, Or.: Norris Lane Press, 1993.

Institute of Medical Ethics Working Party on the Ethics of Prolonging Life and Assisting Death. "Assisted Death." *Lancet* 336 (1990): 610.

Jecker, N. "Giving Death a Hand: When the Dying and the Doctor Stand in a Special Relationship." *Journal of the American Geriatrics Society* 39 (1991): 831.

Jecker, N. "Physician-Assisted Death in the Netherlands and the United States; Ethical and Cultural Aspects of Health Policy Development." *Journal of the American Geriatrics Society* 42 (1994): 627.

Johnson, M. "Voluntary Active Euthanasia: The Next Frontier?" *Issues in Law and Medicine* 8 (1992): 343.

Jonsen, A. "Living with Euthanasia: A Futuristic Scenario." *Journal of Medicine and Philosophy* 18 (1993): 241.

Kadish, S. "Letting Patients Die: Legal and Moral Reflections." *California Law Review* 80 (1992): 857.

Kamisar, Y. "Active v. Passive Euthanasia: Why Keep the Distinction." *Trial* 29 (1993): 32.

Kamisar, Y. "Are Laws Against Assisted Suicide Unconstitutional?" *Hastings Center Report* 23 (May–June 1993): 32.

Kamisar, Y. "Some Non-Religious Views Against Proposed 'Mercy-Killing' Legislation." *Minnesota Law Review* 42 (1958): 969.

Kamisar, Y. "When Is There a Constitutional 'Right to Die'? When Is There No Constitutional 'Right to Live'?" *Georgia Law Review* 25 (1991): 1203.

Keown, J. "On Regulating Death." *Hastings Center Report* 22 (March–April 1992): 39.

Klagsbrun, S. "Physician-Assisted Suicide: Double Dilemma." *Journal of Pain and Symptom Management* 6 (1991): 325.

Kline, T. "Suicide, Liberty and Our Imperfect Constitution: An Analysis of the Legitimacy of the Supreme Court's Entanglement in Decisions to Terminate Life-Sustaining Medical Treatment." *Campbell Law Review* 14 (1991): 69.

Kohl, M. "Altruistic Humanism and Voluntary Beneficent Euthanasia." *Issues in Law and Medicine* 8 (1992): 331.

Kuhse, H. "The Case of Active Voluntary Euthanasia." *Law, Medicine and Health Care* 14 (1986): 145.

Kuhse, H. "Voluntary Euthanasia in the Netherlands." *Medical Journal of Australia* 147 (1987): 394.


Lachs, J. "When Abstract Moralizing Runs Amok." *Journal of Clinical Ethics* 5 (1994): 10.

Law Reform Commission of Canada. *Euthanasia, Aiding Suicide, and Cessation of Treatment.* Ottawa: Law Reform Commission of Canada, 1982 and 1983.


Matthews, M. "Suicidal Competence and the Patient's Right to Refuse Life-saving Treatment." *California Law Review* 75 (1987): 707.

Mayo, T. "Constitutionalizing the 'Right to Die.'" *Maryland Law Review* 49 (1990): 103.

Miller, F. "Is Active Killing of Patients Always Wrong?" *Journal of Clinical Ethics* 2 (1991): 130.

Misbin, R. "Physicians' Aid in Dying." *New England Journal of Medicine* 325 (1991): 1307.

Morgan, R., et al. "The Issue of Personal Choice: The Competent Incurable Patient and the Right to Commit Suicide?" *Missouri Law Review* 57 (1992): 1.


Neeley, G. *The Constitutional Right to Suicide: A Legal and Philosophical Examination.* New York: Peter Lang, 1994.

Neeley, G. "The Constitutional Right to Suicide, the Quality of Life, and the 'Slippery Slope': An Explicit Reply to Lingering Concerns." *Akron Law Review* 28 (1994): 53.

New York State Task Force on Life and the Law. *When Death Is Sought: Assisted Suicide and Euthanasia in the Medical Context.* New York: New York State Task Force on Life and the Law, 1994.

Newman, S. "Euthanasia: Orchestrating "The Last Syllable of . . . Time." *University of Pittsburg Law Review* 53 (1991): 153.

Note. "Physician-Assisted Suicide and the Right to Die with Assistance." *Harvard Law Review* 105 (1992): 2021.

Orentlicher, D. "Physician Participation in Assisted Suicide: From the Office of the General Counsel." *JAMA* 262 (1989): 1844.

Pletcher, R. "Assisted Suicide for the Terminally-Ill: The Inadequacy of Current Legal Models to Rationally Analyze Voluntary Active Euthanasia." *Criminal Justice Journal* 13 (1992): 303.

Potter, C. "Will the 'Right to Die' Become a License to Kill? The Growth of Euthanasia in America." *Journal of Legislation* 19 (1993): 31.

Preston, T. "Professional Norms and Physician Attitudes Toward Euthanasia." *Journal of Law, Medicine and Ethics* 22 (1994): 36.

Pugliese, J. "Don't Ask—Don't Tell: The Secret Practice of Physician-Assisted Suicide." *Hastings Law Journal* 44 (1993): 291.

Quill, T. "A Case of Individualized Decision Making." *New England Journal of Medicine* 324 (1991): 691.

Quill, T. "Risk Taking by Physicians in Legally Gray Areas." *Albany Law Review* 57 (1994): 693.

Rachels, J. "Active and Passive Euthanasia." *New England Journal of Medicine* 292 (1975): 78.

Risley, R. "Ethical and Legal Issues in the Individual's Right to Die." *Ohio Northern University Law Review* 20 (1994): 597.

Risley, R. Voluntary Active Euthanasia: The Next Frontier—Impact on the Indigent." *Issues in Law and Medicine* 8 (1992): 361.

Rosenblum, V., and C. Forsythe. "The Right to Assisted Suicide: Protection of Autonomy or an Open Door to Social Killing?" *Issues in Law and Medicine* 6 (1990): 3.

Schanker, D. Note. "Of Suicide Machines, Euthanasia Legislation, and the Health Care Crisis." *Indiana Law Journal* 68 (1993): 977.

Sedler, R. "The Constitution and Hastening Inevitable Death." *Hastings Center Report* 23 (September–October 1993): 20.

Shaffer, C. "Criminal Liability for Assisting Suicide." *Columbia Law Review* 86 (1988): 348.

Singer, P., and M. Siegler. "Euthanasia—A Critique." *New England Journal of Medicine* 322 (1990): 1881.

Smith, G. "All's Well That Ends Well: Toward a Policy of Assisted Rational Suicide or Merely Enlightened Self-Determination?" *University of California at Davis Law Review* 22 (1989): 275.

Sneideman, B. "Why Not a Limited Defence? A Comment on the Proposals of the Law Reform Commission of Canada on Mercy-Killing." *Manitoba Law Journal* 15 (1985): 85.

Teno, J., and J. Lynn. "Voluntary Active Euthanasia: The Individual Case and Public Policy." *Journal of the American Geriatrics Society* 39 (1991): 827.

Thomasma, D., and G. Graber. *Euthanasia: Toward an Ethical Social Policy.* New York: The Continuum Publishing Company, 1990.

van Delden, J., et al. "The Remmelink Study—Two Years Later." *Hastings Center Report* 23 (November–December 1993): 24.

van der Maas, P., et al. "Euthanasia and Other Medical Decisions Concerning the End of Life." *Lancet* 338 (1991): 669.

Vaux, K. "The Theological Ethics of Euthanasia." *Hastings Center Report* 19 (January–February 1989) (special supplement): 19.

Wanzer, S., et al. "The Physician's Responsibility Toward Hopelessly Ill Patients." *New England Journal of Medicine* 320 (1989): 844.

Weigand, W. "Has the Time Come for Doctor Death: Should Physician-Assisted Suicide Be Legalized?" *Journal of Law and Health* 7 (1992–1993): 321.

Weir, R. "The Morality of Physician-Assisted Suicide." *Law, Medicine and Health Care* 20 (1992): 116.

Williams, G. "Mercy-Killing Legislation—A Rejoinder." *Minnesota Law Review* 43 (1958): 1.

Wolf, S. "Final Exit—The End of Argument." *Hastings Center Report* 22 (January–February 1992): 30.

Wolf, S. "Holding the Line on Euthanasia." *Hastings Center Report* 19 (January–February 1989) (special supplement): 16.

# CHAPTER 19

# THE PROBLEM OF "FUTILE" MEDICAL TREATMENT

## § 19.1   Nature of "Futility Cases"; Relationship to "Conventional" Right-to-Die Cases

There is a substantial and ever-growing debate among physicians and medical ethicists about the existence of an obligation to provide "futile" medical treatment. The debate is over the question of whether patients (or surrogates) may compel a physician to provide treatment that the physician deems to be "futile," or, to put it the other way, whether a physician is morally and/or legally obligated to provide such treatment. "The futility debate is the recognition that aggressive intervention does not mean therapeutic success."[1]

The fundamental legal question in the futility debate is whether the right of self-determination encompasses a "positive" legal right to compel the provision of treatment or whether it is limited to the long-standing "negative" right to be free from unwanted interferences with bodily integrity.[2] It is now relatively clear that there is no broad constitutional basis for such a claim[3] and that the general common-law precedents for positive rights range from mixed to weak.[4] Given the current climate of health care cost control, it is possible that third-party payors will make efforts to relieve themselves contractually of obligations to provide care deemed by the attending physician (possibly with a second opinion) to be futile, perhaps under the existing language in most health insurance contracts that coverage is limited to "medically necessary" treatment.[5]

This debate, which is just beginning to be played out in the courts, is likely to occupy as much, if not more, judicial effort in the coming years as conventional right-to-die cases have in the last two decades unless legislation cuts it short. Given the highly emotional nature of the debate and the serious implications for individual well-being of how it is resolved, it is questionable whether enough of a consensus can be achieved for legislation to be enacted. And, if it is, like advance directive legislation it could easily raise as many questions as it answers.

In a conventional right-to-die case, the patient or family seeks to withhold or withdraw life-sustaining medical treatment, because they have concluded that in some sense further treatment is futile. However, the physician will not acquiesce

---

[1] Jonsen, *Intimations of Futility,* 96 Am. J. Med. 107, 107 (1994). *See also* Mitchell et al., *Medical Futility, Treatment Withdrawal and the Persistent Vegetative State,* 19 J. Med. Ethics 71, 73 (1993); Tomlinson & Brody, *Futility and the Ethics of Resuscitation,* 264 JAMA 1276, 1278 (1990) ("[E]veryone recognizes that there comes a time, short of physical exhaustion, when hope for success is no longer reasonable and when the physician may stop, regardless of what the patient or family might have demanded."); Jecker & Pearlman, *Medical Futility: Who Decides,* 152 Archives Internal Med. 1140 (1992) (review and critique of futility literature).

[2] See § **19.9.**

[3] See § **19.10.**

[4] See §§ **19.11–19.15.**

[5] *See* Callahan, *Medical Futility, Medical Necessity: The-Problem-Without-A-Name,* 21 Hastings Center Rep. 30 (July–Aug. 1991).

in that request because of the belief that treatment is *not* futile or because also believing it to be futile, he nonetheless fears the imposition of liability if treatment is not administered and/or believes that the forgoing of life-sustaining treatment is immoral. As a result, a judicial resolution might ultimately need to be sought to resolve the impasse. Lawsuits that have arisen from such situations have virtually always led to the issuance of a decree allowing the forgoing of such "futile" treatment. These are the garden-variety right-to-die cases from which the consensus about forgoing life-sustaining treatment has evolved.

As the right to die has evolved, it has become increasingly clear that "reverse" right-to-die cases would arise. In a reverse right-to-die case—or a *futility* case, as they have come to be known—the physician recommends to the patient, or more likely to the surrogate of an incompetent patient, that treatment be withheld or withdrawn, because the physician has concluded that further treatment is futile. As physicians increasingly act on the lessons of the right-to-die cases by recommending that life support be terminated or that no new aggressive measures (such as cardiopulmonary resuscitation) be instituted when there is no hope of recovery from a terminal or hopelessly critical condition (such as a persistent vegetative state) requiring the indefinite use of life-support systems, surrogates, families, and competent patients sometimes resist the suggestion, claiming that they want "everything possible" done.[6] In a sense, futility is a *physician's* right to refuse (to provide) treatment, and just as litigation arose from the uncertainty about a patient's or a surrogate's right to refuse life-sustaining medical treatment beginning in the 1970s and continuing to this time, litigation is sure to ensue around this parallel issue.

The focus of this and the following sections is on the *law* of futile medical treatment. Although this debate has gone on since at least 1980 in the medical and medical ethics literature[7] and in the popular press,[8] it received scant legal

---

[6] *See, e.g.,* Morgan v. Olds, 417 N.W.2d 232 (Iowa Ct. App. 1987) (wife of patient who had suffered three cardiac arrests within short period of time and ensuing brain damage from lack of oxygen and was diagnosed as being in a "vegetative state" claimed in malpractice action that she refused to allow withholding of life-sustaining treatment).

[7] Jonsen, *Intimations of Futility,* 96 Am. J. Med. 107, 107 (1994) ("A medline search from 1983 through 1987 turned up not a single example of futility as a keyword, but in a search from 1988 through June 1992, 41 references appeared."). *See, e.g.,* Paris et al., *Physician's Refusal of Requested Treatment—The Case of Baby L,* 322 New Eng. J. Med. 1012 (1990). *See also* Brett & McCullough, *When Patients Request Specific Interventions—Defining the Limits of the Physician's Obligation,* 315 New Eng. J. Med. 1347 (1986) (reporting clinical cases).

[8] *See, e.g.,* Kolata, *Battle over a Baby's Future Raises Hard Ethical Issues,* N.Y. Times, Dec. 27, 1994, at A1 (nat'l ed.). Twedt, *Should Comatose Boy Live? Hospital, Dad Differ,* Pittsburgh Press, June 3, 1990, at A1; Weiser, *A Question of Letting Go: Child's Trauma Drives Doctors to Reexamine Ethical Roles,* Wash. Post, July 14, 1991, at A1 (describing 1988 case of severely brain-damaged two-month-old child); Reid, *Judge Rejects Proposal to Let Revere Man Die,* Boston Globe, July 12, 1991, at 55; Reid, *After Transplant, A Fight over Care,* Boston Globe, June 23, 1991, at 21 (trial court granted hospital's petition to discharge severely brain-damaged patient because of costs in excess of $375,000 but ordered hospital to pay for care at home).

attention until 1990—although some judges had acknowledged that such a case might arise[9]—even if one counts the reported cases in which family members have insisted on the continuation of life support when the patient was brain dead.[10] In 1990, litigation was instituted in the *Wanglie* case,[11] followed by the *Doe*[12] and *Baby K*[13] cases in 1991 and 1993, respectively. Even the law reviews have been relatively silent on this topic.[14]

## § 19.2  Current State of the Law

Currently, no legal consensus has evolved about how futility cases should be resolved.[15] Unlike conventional right-to-die cases, in which consensus evolved rather rapidly based on common-law principles, a variety of conflicting common-law and statutory arguments have been invoked in the futility debate, and no consensus about the law is in sight. While the litigated cases point in the direction of not permitting physicians to withhold or withdraw life-sustaining medical treatment without the consent of the patient or surrogate, the body of common-law precedents in the larger body of medical decisionmaking cases can (though they need not necessarily) be read to suggest the opposite conclusion,[16] as do some statutory enactments.[17] About the only certainty concerning the obligation of health care providers to provide—or the correlative right of patients or surrogates to demand—futile medical treatment is that treatment

---

[9] *See* Cruzan v. Harmon, 760 S.W.2d 408 (Mo. 1988) (Blackmar, J., dissenting) ("I do not place primary emphasis on the patient's expressions, except possibly in the very unusual case, of which I find no example in the books, in which the patient expresses a view that all available life supports should be made use of.").

[10] **CA:** *E.g.,* Dority v. Superior Court, 193 Cal. Rptr. 288 (Ct. App. 1983).

**NY:** *E.g.,* Alvarado v. New York City Health & Hosps. Corp., 547 N.Y.S.2d 190 (Sup. Ct. N.Y. County 1989), *vacated and dismissed sub nom.* Alvarado v. City of N.Y., 550 N.Y.S.2d 353 (App. Div. 1990).

[11] *In re* Wanglie, No. PX-91-283 (Minn. 4th Dist. Ct. Hennepin County July 1, 1991). See § **19.3.**

[12] *In re* Doe, 418 S.E.2d 3 (Ga. 1992).

[13] *In re* Baby "K," 832 F. Supp. 1022 (E.D. Va. 1993), *aff'd,* 16 F.3d 590 (4th Cir.), *cert. denied,* 115 S. Ct. 91 (1994).

[14] *See* Daar, *A Clash at the Bedside: Patient Autonomy v. A Physician's Professional Conscience,* 44 Hastings L.J. 1241 (1993); Marsh & Staver, *Physician Authority for Unilateral DNR Orders,* 12 J. Legal Med. 115, 138 (1991); Meinhardt, *Bioethics and the Law: The Case of Helga Wanglie: A Clash at the Bedside—Medically Futile Treatment v. Patient Autonomy,* 14 Whittier L. Rev. 137 (1993); Stell, *Stopping Treatment on Grounds of Futility: A Role for Institutional Policy,* 11 St. Louis U. Pub. L. Rev. 481 (1992).

[15] National Ctr. for State Courts, Guidelines for State Court Decision Making in Life-Sustaining Medical Treatment Cases 147 (2d ed. 1992).

[16] See §§ **19.5–19.7.**

[17] See §§ **19.16–19.20.**

need not be administered when it is of absolutely no physiologic value, such as the continued ventilation of a brain-dead person.[18]

However, the current debate about futility does not involve exclusively cases of this kind, or it would have been resolved long ago and without much fanfare. The cases that are being debated in the medical and medical ethics literature under the aegis of futility and that have been litigated to date involve situations in which the treatment being provided definitely or probably affords the patient some physiologic benefit but offers no prospect or no reasonable prospect of recovery. These cases are also instances in which providing the treatment to the patient does not deny it to any other identifiable person and perhaps to no other person at all. These cases do not involve requests for treatments of unproved benefit. Rather, they have involved requests to continue to provide a treatment that is already being provided, such as ventilation, and related therapies such as antibiotics and pressors, or artificial nutrition and hydration, or a treatment that has been provided in the past and for which a need might recur, such as cardiopulmonary resuscitation. The litigated cases have involved treatments that were medically indicated when they were initiated, and at the time that termination of treatment is contemplated, they are providing the same physiologic benefit as when they were initiated. The only thing that has changed is the passage of time and the consequent confirmation that there is virtually no possibility for the patient's recovery—based on physicians' similar experiences with similar patients and the same treatment, and from the failure of the treatment to improve this patient's condition.

## § 19.3   —The Prototypical Futility Case: The *Wanglie* Case

The case of *In re Wanglie*[19] illustrates the kind of case around which the futility debate centers. The patient was an 87-year-old woman who was ventilator-dependent as a result of emphysema and was in a persistent vegetative state. The

---

[18] **CA:** *See, e.g.,* Dority v. Superior Court, 193 Cal. Rptr. 288 (Ct. App. 1983).

**NY:** *Cf.* Alvarado v. New York City Health & Hosps. Corp., 547 N.Y.S.2d 190 (Sup. Ct. N.Y. County 1989), *vacated and dismissed sub nom.* Alvarado v. City of N.Y., 550 N.Y.S.2d 353 (App. Div. 1990).

*But see Brain-Dead Florida Girl Will Be Sent Home on Life Support,* N.Y. Times, Feb. 19, 1994, at 7 (nat'l ed.) (parents of 13-year-old girl who doctors diagnosed as dead by brain-death criteria insisted that she was alive and that life-sustaining medical treatment be continued; hospital agreed to continue life support at its expense in parents' home because "'the nursing staff is wrung out'"); *Hospital Fights Parents' Wish to Keep Life Support for a "Brain Dead" Child,* N.Y. Times, Feb. 12, 1994, at 6 (nat'l ed.); *Public Hospital to Finance Home Care of Brain-Dead Teenager,* 3 BNA's Health L. Rep. 287 (1994).

[19] No. PX-91-283 (Minn. 4th Dist. Ct. Hennepin County July 1, 1991), *reprinted in* 2 BioLaw U:2161 (Aug.–Sept. 1991). *See also Helga Wanglie's Ventilator,* 21 Hastings Center Rep. 23 (July–Aug. 1991) (recounting underlying facts of *Wanglie* case.).

attending physician and consultant physicians had repeatedly recommended to the patient's husband and children over the course of many months that Mrs. Wanglie's ventilatory support be discontinued and that she be permitted to die because there was no hope of recovery.

The patient's family did not share the belief of her physicians that there was no hope of recovery, and they did not share the physicians' evaluation that the quality of life characteristic of a persistent vegetative state did not warrant the continuation of treatment. This is not an atypical reaction from families, who sometimes hold out hope that the doctor is wrong and that a miracle will occur,[20] and who might hold a vitalist position that human life in whatever form is worthy of preservation and protection.[21] Thus, the patient's husband, who was her judicially appointed guardian, and their children resisted the doctors' entreaties, claiming that if she were able to express her views, Mrs. Wanglie would want treatment continued. When it became clear after an extended period of time that permission would not be forthcoming to terminate life support and that the only health care facility that would accept the transfer of a ventilator-dependent patient was not acceptable to the family, the hospital administration, with the approval of the governing body of the hospital (which was the County Board of Commissioners), initiated litigation to break the impasse.[22]

Rather than seeking an order authorizing the patient's attending physician to turn off the ventilator or to transfer the patient, the hospital authorities took the more indirect route of filing a petition asserting that the patient's husband was not acting in her best interests and seeking to appoint an independent conservator. The probate court declined to do so, finding that Mr. Wanglie "is dedicated to promoting his wife's welfare."[23] Mrs. Wanglie died four days after the issuance of the court order, still connected to the ventilator.[24] Thus, *Wanglie* offers virtually no guidance for other cases, apart from the lesson that asking the wrong question can generate an unhelpful answer.[25]

---

[20] *See* Morreim, *Profoundly Diminished Life: The Casualties of Coercion,* 24 Hastings Center Rep. 33 (Jan.–Feb. 1994) (referring to "Baby Rena" case, described in Weiser, *A Question of Letting Go: Child's Trauma Drives Doctors to Reexamine Ethical Roles,* Wash. Post, July 14, 1991, at A1; Weiser, *While Child Suffered, Beliefs Clashed,* Wash. Post, July 15, 1991, at A1).

[21] *See, e.g.,* Cruzan v. Harmon, 760 S.W.2d 408, 420 (Mo. 1988) ("[T]he state's interest is not in quality of life. . . . [T]he state's interest is in life; that interest is unqualified.").

[22] *See* Cranford, *Helga Wanglie's Ventilator,* Hastings Center Rep. 23 (July–Aug. 1991).

[23] *In re* Wanglie, slip op. at 5 (finding of fact no. 4).

[24] N.Y. Times, July 6, 1991, at 8, col. 1 (nat'l ed.).

[25] *See* Mishkin, *The Next* Wanglie *Case: The Problems of Litigating Medical Ethics,* 2 J. Clinical Ethics 282 (1991).

## § 19.4   Nature of the Debate About Futility; Meaning of Futility

At its core, what the dispute in futility cases is about is quality of life—who decides what it is and when it justifies the administration or forgoing of life-sustaining medical treatment.[26] Thus, it is also possible that the futility debate will not easily be resolved, but will, like the abortion debate, continue to generate fierce political, judicial, and bedside clinical battles for many years because it "revolves around fundamentally irresolvable moral conflicts concerning our most deeply held beliefs about the value of life, especially profoundly diminished life."[27]

As actually used in medical practice, futility has a "variety of meanings . . . including the narrow sense—physiologic inefficacy and inability to postpone death—and a broader sense—inability to prolong life for a time, inability to maintain an acceptable quality of life, very low probability of achieving any one of the foregoing."[28] Consequently, "[r]ather than being a discrete and definable entity, futile therapy is merely the end of the spectrum of therapies with very low efficacy."[29] Virtually all participants in the debate about whether or not physicians are obligated to provide treatment to patients that they believe to be futile—regardless of the meaning of futility—agree that it is important to openly communicate with competent patients or the surrogate of an incompetent patient. If a treatment is one that a patient or surrogate might reasonably expect to be employed—such as cardiopulmonary resuscitation—most authorities agree that the physician should explain that the treatment is going to be withheld.[30]

---

[26] Tomlinson & Brody, *Futility and the Ethics of Resuscitation,* 264 JAMA 1276, 1278 (1990) ("The real question can no longer be *whether* value judgments can be made concerning the provision of CPR or other medical techniques; rather, the question is *which* value judgments physicians may use in deciding whether to meet patients' demands. Certain likelihoods of success must be judged worth pursuing, and others not. Certain kinds of symbolic values must be judged worth recognizing, and others not. This change in direction signifies a turn away from *individual* conceptions toward *social* conceptions of reasonableness and of the worthy ends of medicine.") .

[27] Morreim, *Profoundly Diminished Life: The Casualties of Coercion,* 24 Hastings Center Rep. 33, 33 (Jan.–Feb. 1994).

[28] Youngner, *Who Defines Futility?,* 260 JAMA 2094, 2095 (1988). *Accord* Council on Ethical & Judicial Affairs, American Medical Ass'n, *Guidelines for the Appropriate Use of Do-Not-Resuscitate Orders,* 265 JAMA 1868, 1870 (1991) ("[J]udgments of futility are subject to a wide variety of interpretations."). *See also* Jecker & Pearlman, *Medical Futility: Who Decides,* 152 Archives Internal Med. 1140, 1140 (1992) (summarizing different meanings of futility). Solomon, *"Futility" as a Criterion in Limiting Treatment,* 327 New Eng. J. Med. 1239 (1992) ("physicians used the concept of futility and the word itself in multiple and contradictory ways").

[29] Lantos et al., *The Illusion of Futility in Clinical Practice,* 87 Am. J. Med. 81, 81 (1989).

[30] See §§ **9.4–9.6.**

Those who would allow the withholding or withdrawal of life-sustaining medical treatment on the basis of a medical judgment, without requiring the informed consent of the patient or surrogate, base their position on one or more of three arguments: that the treatment in question provides no benefit to the patient, that it imposes suffering on the patient and is therefore cruel, or that it is wasteful,[31] and thus physicians are not morally and should not be legally obligated to provide nonbeneficial treatment.

The opposing point of view narrowly circumscribes the concept of futile medical treatment. In this view, a medical treatment is to be defined as futile in *physiologic* terms, that is, a treatment is futile only if it is unable to accomplish the physiologic goal for which it is applied. For example, the New York statute governing decisionmaking about cardiopulmonary resuscitation defines "medically futile" in physiologic terms as resuscitation that "will be unsuccessful in restoring cardiac and respiratory function. . . ."[32] In this understanding of futility, only if treatment is physiologically futile may it be fogone unilaterally by the physician without the patient's or surrogate's authorization.

Established law supports this position to the extent that when there is no physiologic benefit from a treatment—to take for example the clearest case, the continued ventilation of an individual who is dead by "brain death" standards[33]— there is no general legal obligation on the part of the physician to continue treatment. The same is probably true even if a treatment provides physiologic benefit but little or no chance of recovery.[34] However, what is not certain is whether the law permits the unilateral forgoing of treatment by a physician under a broader concept of futility.

The physiologic view of futility takes the position that if futility is defined more broadly—that treatment is unable to prolong life for a time or is unable to maintain an acceptable quality of life, or that there is a very low probability of prolonging life or maintaining an acceptable quality of life—it is based on a value judgment about whether it is worthwhile to provide the treatment and

---

[31] Morreim, *Profoundly Diminished Life: The Casualties of Coercion,* 24 Hastings Center Rep. 33, 34 (Jan.–Feb. 1994).

[32] **NY:** N.Y. Pub. Health Law § 2961(9).

**GA:** *Accord* Ga. Code Ann. § 31-39-2(4)(C).

[33] **CA:** *See, e.g.,* Dority v. Superior Court, 193 Cal. Rptr. 288 (Ct. App. 1983) (no obligation to continue ventilation of brain-dead patient).

**NY:** *Cf.* Alvarado v. New York City Health & Hosps. Corp., 547 N.Y.S.2d 190 (Sup. Ct. N.Y. County 1989), *vacated and dismissed sub nom.* Alvarado v. City of N.Y., 550 N.Y.S.2d 353 (App. Div. 1990) (if patient were brain dead, there would be no obligation to continue ventilation).

[34] **GA:** Ga. Code Ann. § 31-39-2(4)(C).

**NY:** *See, e.g.,* N.Y. Pub. Health Law § 2961(9) (considers CPR to be futile if as a result of administration of CPR, "the patient will experience repeated arrest in a short time period before death occurs").

about the worth of the particular patient's life.[35] As such it is the province of the patient or the surrogate, not the physician, to determine whether and when treatment is futile.[36] In this view, the broad use of "futility judgments" based on physicians' values and as a basis for physicians' forgoing treatment without the consent of the patient or surrogate signal a return to the paternalistic ways of yesteryear.[37]

## § 19.5  Meaning of Common-Law Right to Self-Determination and Relationship to Futility

Most litigated right-to-die cases have raised the question of whether, on the given facts, it was permissible to terminate life support without incurring legal liability therefor. The overwhelmingly (though not unanimously) affirmative answer to that question stands for the proposition that it *is* permissible to terminate medically futile treatment. Perhaps the clearest enunciation of that conclusion is in *Barber v. Superior Court,* which both speaks in the language of futility and is the only case involving a criminal prosecution for the termination of life-sustaining treatment. In dismissing the indictment, the court explained that

> [a] physician has no duty to continue treatment, once it has proved to be ineffective. Although there may be a duty to provide life-sustaining machinery in the immediate aftermath of a cardio-respiratory arrest, there is no duty to continue its use once it has become futile in the opinion of qualified medical personnel.

---

[35] Truog et al., *The Problem with Futility,* 326 New Eng. J. Med. 1560, 1563 (1992) (such "assertions of futility may camouflage judgments of comparative worth that are implicit in debates about the allocation of resources"). *Accord* Cranford & Gostin, *Futility: A Concept in Search of a Definition,* 20 Law, Med. & Health Care 307, 308 (1992) ("The term 'futility' allows the profession to medicalize a difficult personal, familial, and social decision.").

[36] *See, e.g.,* American Medical Ass'n, Current Opinions of the Council on Ethical and Judicial Affairs § 2.22, at 15 (1992) ("Physicians should not permit their personal value judgments about the quality of life to obstruct the implementation of a patient's preferences regarding the use of CPR."); American College of Physicians, Ethics Manual 37 (2d ed. 1989) ("In cases of conflict between the competent patient and the physician, the patient's wishes should prevail."); Farber, *Ethics of Life Support and Resuscitation,* 218 New Eng. J. Med. 1757 (1988) (spokesman for American College of Physicians); Hastings Ctr., Guidelines on the Termination of Life-Sustaining Treatment and the Care of the Dying 32 (1987) (Part One, II(8)(c)); Schiedermayer, *The Decision to Forego CPR in the Elderly Patient,* 260 JAMA 2096 (1988); Youngner, *Who Defines Futility?,* 260 JAMA 2094 (1988) ("Physicians should not offer treatments that are physiologically futile or certain not to prolong life, and they could ethically refuse patient and family requests for such treatments. Beyond that, they run the risk of 'giving opinions disguised as data.'"); Zawacki, *Tongue-Tied in the Burn Intensive Care Unit,* 17 Critical Care Med. 198 (1989).

[37] *See, e.g.,* Youngner, *Who Defines Futility?,* 260 JAMA 2094, 2095 (1988) ("lapse back into an outdated (but perhaps yearned for) notion of paternalism").

> "A physician is authorized under the standards of medical practice to discontinue a form of therapy which in his medical judgment is useless . . . without fear of civil or criminal liability. By useless is meant that the continued use of the therapy cannot and does not improve the prognosis for recovery."[38]

However, this conclusion must be understood in the context of the cases giving rise to it. In every such case holding permissible the forgoing of life-sustaining treatment, there was legally valid consent from the patient either contemporaneously or through an advance directive or from a surrogate to do so. Indeed, the earliest right-to-die cases—and possibly the current ones as well—are litigated precisely because there is a question about whether forgoing life-sustaining treatment is lawful if there is appropriate consent. The answer has almost uniformly been in the affirmative, and the existence of such consent is what makes forgoing of treatment lawful.

Thus, a more accurate description of the right to self-determination that has arisen from the corpus of conventional right-to-die cases is that it is permissible to forgo life-sustaining medical treatment deemed futile by a *competent patient* or by the *surrogate* of an incompetent patient. This conclusion does not *necessarily* answer two correlative questions at the core of the futility debate: (1) whether such treatment *must* be terminated, and (2) whether it may be terminated *unilaterally* by an attending physician without the permission of someone authorized to give it or even in opposition to such a party.

It is not clear whether the answers to these questions can be derived from the broader medical decisionmaking case law of which the right-to-die cases are a part—medical battery cases, informed consent cases, and cases involving the right to refuse medical treatment in other than end-of-life situations—for what the case law stands for is itself open to debate. Does the well-established legal principle enunciated by Cardozo in 1914—that "[e]very human being of adult years and sound mind has a right to determine what shall be done with his body"[39] (and the immense body of law that is its direct descendant)—mean that a patient or one legally authorized to speak for an incompetent patient has the right to demand that treatment be provided? Or is the meaning more restricted—namely, that the case law creates a right to *refuse* treatment but not necessarily a right to compel the provision of treatment? The right to self-determination grounded in the medical decisionmaking cases might envision a broad right to choose that encompasses a right to compel the provision of treatment. Certainly the dicta of the cases can be read that way. However, it is also possible to read the body of medical decisionmaking cases more narrowly as standing for a right

---

[38] Barber v. Superior Court, 195 Cal. Rptr. 484, 490–91 (Ct. App. 1983) (citing Horan, *Euthanasia and Brain Death: Ethical and Legal Considerations,* 315 Annals N.Y. Acad. Sci. 363, 367 (1978), *as quoted in* President's Comm'n, Deciding to Forego Life-Sustaining Treatment 191 n.50).

[39] Schloendorff v. Society of New York Hosp., 105 N.E. 92, 93 (N.Y. 1914).

to choose but only from among those options that sound professional judgment require be made available.

## § 19.6   —Right to Choose Encompasses a Right to Demand Treatment

The argument that patients or surrogates may require the provision of life-sustaining medical treatment even when a physician recommends against its administration is quite simple and straightforward. It is based on the assumption that the medical decisionmaking cases create a broad right of self-determination permitting patients to compel the provision of life-sustaining medical treatment because the right of self-determination would be a very cramped right if it merely accorded patients a right to say no to a physician's treatment recommendations.

Instead, the argument continues, the case law has created a robust right of self-determination in medical decisionmaking that is broader than merely a right to veto medical recommendations. The right of self-determination also encompasses the right to choose what treatment, if any, patients will undergo. They have the right to choose their physician and the right to choose a particular hospital (as long as their physician has privileges in that hospital), and, perhaps most telling, the physician has an obligation under the informed consent doctrine to provide patients with information not merely about the treatment that he recommends but also about alternative treatments.[40] Indeed, the informed consent cases proclaim a right described as "thorough going self-determination,"[41] and with words of that sort, surely the common law confers on patients a right not to have treatment withheld or withdrawn without their agreement.

## § 19.7   —Right to Choose Is Merely a Right to Refuse

The opposing point of view is more complex. It grants that the medical decision-making cases create a right to choose and admits that physicians have an obligation to explain to the patient the medical alternatives to the recommended treatment. However, it denies that patients or surrogates have a right to compel the provision of treatment, if for no other reason, because the precedents giving rise to the right of self-determination must be read and understood in the context from which they arise.

The right to refuse treatment created by the doctrine of informed consent is certainly a more vigorous version of the right to refuse treatment than a simple

---

[40] See § **3.15.**

[41] Natanson v. Kline, 350 P.2d 1093, 1104 (1960).

veto of a doctor's recommended treatment, because that doctrine requires that the physician provide the patient with information adequate to making an intelligent choice about treatment. If, in the physician's professional judgment and in accordance with generally accepted medical standards, a treatment exists for the patient's condition, the physician is obligated to recommend that treatment or incur liability for negligence. In connection with the recommendation, so that the patient might make an intelligent choice about accepting or rejecting the physician's recommendation, the physician must also provide information material to making a decision about the treatment.

One facet of material information besides the risks and benefits of the treatment is alternative treatments and their associated risks and benefits, and physicians are obligated to provide patients with information about them and to allow the patient to decide which, if any, treatment the patient wants. Physicians are not obligated to provide information about all treatments but only about those that are reasonably likely to improve a patient's well-being.[42] In some jurisdictions the scope of required disclosure of information is determined by reference to professional standards and in others by reference to legal standards.[43]

This right of choice has never been held to empower a patient to require a physician to provide a particular form of treatment to a patient but merely to choose from among those that the physician is qualified to offer or that other qualified physicians might offer.[44] Although this choice is not merely an assent to or veto of the treatment recommended by the physician because the physician is obligated to provide the patient with information about "relevant" medical options, it is still essentially a negative right—a right to say no to a recommended treatment; a right to be free from unwanted interferences with one's bodily integrity. To contend that even a right of self-determination described as "thorough going" creates a claim on the part of patients to require that life-sustaining treatment be continued against the will of the physician—in effect, a right on the part of patients or families to dictate to physicians what treatment they will administer—is to read the common-law precedents both out of context and far too broadly.

A physician's obligation to provide treatment—life-sustaining or otherwise—arises not only from patients' wishes (articulated contemporaneously, through

---

[42] *See, e.g.,* Moore v. Baker, 989 F.2d 1129 (11th Cir. 1993) (informed consent doctrine does not impose obligation on physician to inform patient of treatment that was not generally recognized and accepted alternative to treatment recommended by physician); Polikoff v. United States, 776 F. Supp. 1417, 1421 (S.D. Cal. 1991) (under California law, physician under no duty to inform patient as to availability of additional test if test would not ordinarily be recommended).

*See generally* Marsh & Staver, *Physician Authority for Unilateral DNR Orders,* 12 J. Legal Med. 115, 138 (1991).

[43] See § **3.14.**

[44] Miles, *Informed Demand for "Non-Beneficial" Medical Treatment,* 325 New Eng. J. Med. 512, 514 (1991) ("Doctors should inform patients of all medically reasonable treatments, even those available from other providers. Patients can refuse any prescribed treatment or choose among any medical alternatives that physicians are *willing* to prescribe." (emphasis added)).

an advance directive, or through a surrogate) but also from *professional stand-ards,* and these professional standards create the primary, if not the exclusive, basis for determining what treatment must be, or need not be, offered.[45] The American Medical Association has adopted such a standard, which states that

> [p]hysicians are not ethically obligated to deliver care that, in their best profes-sional judgment, will not have a reasonable chance of benefitting their patients. Patients should not be given treatments simply because they demand them.[46]

The difficulty is in articulating and especially in applying professional stand-ards in such a way that "this power can be restrained to assure that physicians' standards of 'reasonableness' are not utterly arbitrary and serve the genuine and significant concerns and needs of patients,"[47] and that physicians do not "lapse back into an outdated (but perhaps yearned for) notion of paternalism."[48] Tomlinson and Brody cogently assert that "[t]he best safeguard against profes-sional arrogance and arbitrariness is not patient arbitrariness, but rather an effective social dialogue, which can ensure that the value judgments that physi-cians must necessarily make have an adequate social warrant."[49] However, this

---

[45] Barber v. Superior Court, 195 Cal. Rptr. 484, 491 (Ct. App. 1983) (decision as to when treatment will have no reasonable benefit to the patient "is essentially a medical one"). *See also* Schneiderman et al., *Medical Futility: Its Meaning and Ethical Implications,* 112 Annals Internal Med. 949, 953 (1990) ("futility is a professional judgment that takes precedence over patient autonomy and permits physicians to withhold or withdraw care deemed to be inappro-priate without subjecting such a decision to patient approval"); Tomlinson & Brody, *Futility and the Ethics of Resuscitation,* 264 JAMA 1276 (1990).

[46] Council on Ethical & Judicial Affairs, American Medical Ass'n, Code of Medical Ethics: Current Opinions with Annotations § 2.035, at 6–7 (1994). *See also* Uniform Health-Care Decisions Act § 13(d) ("This [Act] does not authorize or require a health-care provider or institution to provide health care contrary to generally accepted health-care standards appli-cable to the health-care provider or institution.").

[47] Tomlinson & Brody, *Futility and the Ethics of Resuscitation,* 264 JAMA 1276, 1279 (1990). *Accord* Alpers & Lo, *When Is CPR Futile?,* 273 JAMA 156 (1995) (although unilateral withholding of CPR might be justifiable in theory, in practice "the futility threshold creeps up to include interventions that might be medically reasonable," based on study by Curtis et al., *Use of the Medical Futility Rationale in Do-Not-Attempt-Resuscitation Orders,* 273 JAMA 124 (1995)).

[48] Youngner, *Who Defines Futility,* 260 JAMA 2094, 2095 (1988). *See also* Solomon, *"Futility" As a Criterion in Limiting Treatment,* 327 New Eng. J. Med. 1239 (1992) ("physicians used the concept of futility and the word itself in multiple and contradictory ways . . . to support evaluative judgments based on quality-of-life considerations; only rarely were they used to designate treatments that were medically inefficacious").

[49] Tomlinson & Brody, *Futility and the Ethics of Resuscitation,* 264 JAMA 1276, 1280 (1990). *See also* Youngner, *Futility in Context,* 264 JAMA 1295, 1295 (1990) ("If such value judg-ments are 'socially validated,' they can be used to overrule patient and family demands that are not."). *See also* Council on Ethical & Judicial Affairs, American Medical Ass'n, Code of Medical Ethics: Current Opinions with Annotations § 2.035, at 6–7 (1994) ("Denial of treat-ment should be justified by reliance on openly stated ethical principles and acceptable stand-ards of care . . . not on the concept of 'futility,' which cannot be meaningfully defined."); Uniform Health-Care Decisions Act § 13(d) ("This [Act] does not authorize or require a health-care provider or institution to provide health care contrary to generally accepted health-care standards applicable to the health-care provider or institution.").

is easier said than done, and when it is done—indeed, even when it is well done—it can lead to inconclusive results. As the litigated cases demonstrate, sometimes only litigation can break the impasse between demanding families and resistant health care professionals.

## § 19.8  The Differing Contexts of Right-to-Die and Futility Cases

The argument can be and has been made that the right of self-determination of a competent patient recognized both in the larger body of medical decisionmaking cases and in conventional right-to-die cases, and the right of the family of an incompetent patient to assert and implement that right without recourse to the courts provide a basis for compelling physicians to accede to the demands of patients and surrogates for treatment. However, these cases and the principles enunciated in them arose in different contexts and in response to fundamentally different questions, and therefore they are not determinative of the question of whether a physician may be compelled to provide treatment deemed to be futile.

### Right of Self-Determination as a Basis for Compelling Treatment

The right of medical self-determination has evolved in response to a different question from that being asked in the futility cases. The question in battery, informed consent, and even right-to-die cases has always been whether it is legally permissible for a physician to *administer* treatment to a patient without the consent of the patient or someone legally authorized to speak for the patient. When the courts say that patients have a right of self-determination, it is in response to this question that they have virtually uniformly answered in the affirmative.

The question being asked in the futility cases, by contrast, is a completely different one, namely, whether a physician has a right to withhold or withdraw life-sustaining treatment without the consent of the patient or surrogate, or, to put it slightly differently, whether a patient or surrogate has the right to compel the physician to provide treatment. Until recently, no reported case had ever grappled with the question of whether there is a right to compel a physician to provide treatment he has not offered, or would not think appropriate to offer, or one which, although begun, was not in the physician's view appropriate to continue. It is a tremendous conceptual leap to derive a right to compel the provision of treatment (a "positive" right) from a right to refuse treatment (a "negative" right). The answer to the question posed in treatment refusal cases does not necessarily carry over to cases in which a different, though related, question is posed. Furthermore, the notion of a thoroughgoing right of self-determination—whether arising from a battery case, an informed consent case, or a right-to-die case—is obiter dictum. It is not part of the holding in the case because it was not necessary to the decision of the question raised by the case. Thus, the fact that these cases might state that there is a right of self-determination is certainly not dispositive of futility cases if it is even relevant to their resolution at all.

For the same reason, even the statements in right-to-die cases that physicians are under no obligation to provide *futile* treatment are not determinative of, and probably not even relevant to, *futility cases.* Even a statement as clear-cut as that in *Barber* that "[a] physician has no duty to continue treatment once it has become futile in the opinion of qualified medical personnel"[50] does not resolve the question raised in futility cases because the question posed in *Barber* was a different question entirely. The question in *Barber* was whether a physician could be held criminally liable for terminating life-sustaining treatment and allowing a permanently unconscious patient to die, *with the consent of the patient's family.* In a futility case, such consent is lacking. Therefore, the statement in *Barber* that a physician has no obligation to provide futile treatment only means that a physician is under no obligation to provide futile treatment when the physician and family both agree that it is futile. *Barber* stands for the same conclusion as other right-to-die cases, namely, that a physician and surrogate may enter into an agreement to forgo life-sustaining treatment without fear of liability (as long as certain other criteria are met), but it simply does not address the question of whether the patient or family may compel the provision of treatment by an unwilling physician. That question was not posed by the facts of the case.

Similarly, the *Dinnerstein* case,[51] which addressed the forgoing of cardio-pulmonary resuscitation, the form of treatment that sparked the debate about futile medical treatment, is not determinative. In *Dinnerstein,* the patient, who was suffering from Alzheimer's disease, had had a massive stroke and was in "an essentially vegetative state."[52] Her attending physician recommended to her family that resuscitation not be attempted in the event of a cardiac or respiratory arrest, and the family agreed. Because of the existence of judicial precedent in Massachusetts (the *Saikewicz* case)[53] suggesting that judicial approval was always necessary to forgo life-sustaining treatment, the family, physician, and hospital joined in petitioning for an order to withhold CPR.

The court held that a judicial order was not required to withhold CPR. It justified this conclusion with the reasoning that judicial approval to forgo life-sustaining treatment was required by *Saikewicz* only in situations in which the treatment "presented a substantial question of choice . . . of a treatment offering hope of restoration to normal, integrated, functioning, cognitive existence."

---

[50] Barber v. Superior Court, 195 Cal. Rptr. 484, 491 (Ct. App. 1983).

[51] *In re* Dinnerstein, 380 N.E.2d 134 (Mass. App. Ct. 1978).

[52] *Id.* at 135.

[53] Superintendent of Belchertown State Sch. v. Saikewicz, 370 N.E.2d 417 (Mass. 1977).

However, "[t]hat is not the situation that presents itself in this case, or in the case of any patient in the terminal stages of an unremitting, incurable mortal illness."[54] The court continued by observing that professional guidelines for the use of CPR state that CPR is indicated to prevent "sudden, unexpected death," but not

> in certain situations, such as in cases of terminal irreversible illness where death is not unexpected or where prolonged cardiac arrest dictates the *futility* of resuscitation efforts. Resuscitation in these circumstances may represent a positive violation of an individual's right to die with dignity. When CPR is considered to be contraindicated for hospital patients, it is appropriate to indicate this in the patient's progress notes. It also is appropriate to indicate this on the physician's order sheet for the benefit of nurses and other personnel who may be called upon to initiate or participate in cardiopulmonary resuscitation.[55]

The facts of *Dinnerstein* take it out of the situations in which CPR is medically indicated because it is "clear that the case is hopeless and that death must come soon, probably in the form of cardiac or respiratory arrest. Attempts to apply resuscitation, if successful, will do nothing to cure or relieve the illnesses which will have brought the patient to the threshold of death."[56] While seeming to say that futile treatment need not be administered, what the court held, as opposed to its dicta, was that futile treatment need not be administered when there was *agreement* between the patient's physician and surrogate to withhold it. The facts of the case simply did not present the question of whether CPR could be withheld if the physician believed it to be futile but the patient or surrogate did not.

Another case relevant on its face, but the relevance of which weakens on closer examination, is *Morgan v. Olds*. The Iowa Court of Appeals stated that "[w]e hold . . . that the doctor, as part of his duty to the incompetent patient, must consult with the incompetent patient's surrogate decision-maker before implementing a course of treatment."[57] The case involved the *withholding* of treatment, so that the use of the phrase "implementing a course of treatment" might be read as also requiring such consultation when a physician proposes to withhold treatment as well as administer it. However, because the case involved a suit for damages by the patient's wife for emotional harm to her, the court was not confronted with the question of whether, had the physician not consulted with the surrogate before withholding treatment, there would be liability to the *patient* (or the patient's estate), and thus the court's statement is not clearly applicable to such a situation.

---

[54] *In re* Dinnerstein, 380 N.E.2d at 138.

[55] *Id.* at 139 n.10 (quoting National Conference on Standards for Cardiopulmonary Resuscitation & Emergency Cardiac Care, *Standards for Cardiopulmonary Resuscitation (CPR) and Emergency Cardiac Care (ECC)*, 227 JAMA 837, 864 (1974) (emphasis added)).

[56] *Id.* at 138–39.

[57] Morgan v. Olds, 417 N.W.2d 232, 236 (Iowa Ct. App. 1987).

### The Family's Authority as Decisionmaker as a Basis for Compelling Treatment

There is another reason sometimes offered as to why the medical decision-making cases—and especially right-to-die cases—stand for the proposition that physicians are not entitled to withhold or withdraw life-sustaining medical treatment without the consent of the patient or surrogate. Many right-to-die cases hold that families are the proper surrogates for incompetent patients and as such are entitled to make decisions for them, and to do so without having been judicially appointed as guardians. From this statement of the law has arisen the notion that families "make decisions." To the extent that this is true,[58] it too has arisen in response to a question different from that posed by futility cases.

The question to which this statement responds is whether, when making decisions about life-sustaining treatment for incompetent patients, a surrogate has the authority to decide (consistent with the substantive standards for making decisions for incompetent patients[59]) or whether a court must make the decision. The predominant answer is that there is no need to take end-of-life decision-making cases to court but instead that "families decide." The question in futility cases is a different one: whether physicians may make unilateral decisions to withhold or withdraw treatment or whether consent of the patient or surrogate is required. Therefore, the answer to the first question is not dispositive of the second one.

In summary, the view that the right to self-determination enunciated in conventional right-to-die cases encompasses a right to compel a physician to provide treatment and the view that a surrogate's authority to make decisions for an incompetent patient encompasses a like right have arisen from asking different questions than those posed by futility cases. The specific questions and answers of the medical decisionmaking cases are as follows: (1) When a physician proposes a treatment that he believes is medically appropriate, is the patient obliged to undergo it? Answer: No, the patient may refuse. (2) When patients are unable to decide, should decisions be made by courts? Answer: No, they should be made by families in collaboration with physicians. The unarticulated premise in both situations is that the physician had already offered or recommended or, indeed, instituted a treatment, but one which the patient or surrogate does not want, or no longer wants, administered. That is all that the case law on medical decisionmaking has recognized in enunciating a legal right of self-determination: a negative right; a right to refuse.

---

[58] See §§ 5.10 and 5.12–5.14.

[59] See Ch. 7.

## § 19.9  Negative and Positive Rights

There is another, more fundamental difficulty with the argument that the right of self-determination encompasses not only a right to refuse treatment but a right to compel the provision of treatment. This objection is based on the distinction between negative and positive rights and the very meager support that positive rights have in common and constitutional law.

A *negative* right embodies the freedom to do what one wants without interference from others. The right to refuse medical treatment is such a right. It is a right to live one's life without being imposed upon by physicians who, for their own reasons and based on their own values (however benevolent), might wish to compel an individual to receive treatment that that individual does not want.

The right being asserted in the futility cases, by contrast, is a *positive* right. Like a negative right, a positive right envisions that one should be free to do what one wants, but rather than envisioning a freedom *from*—specifically, freedom from interference by others—it envisions a freedom *to*—specifically, freedom to make the most of one's life with the resources that one can legitimately superintend without entrenching on others' freedom to be free from unwanted interference.[60] In the context of medical decisionmaking, it is the freedom to have whatever medical treatment one might wish.[61]

The concept of negative and positive rights is central in determining what legal duties are owed individuals by both the state and private actors. Law traditionally takes a very narrow view of the scope of positive legal rights—that is, the scope of the duty of either private individuals or the state to act for the benefit of individuals by providing them with particular goods or services.

## § 19.10  —Positive Constitutional Rights: Claims Against the State

When actions have been brought against the *state* claiming that the petitioner is entitled to be provided with certain services—such as a public education[62] or protection from child abuse[63]—the United States Supreme Court has refused to recognize such entitlements. Such claims have been brought (and rejected) under both the due process and the equal protection clauses. A claim for services brought under the due process clause will not prevail because "the Due Process Clauses generally confer no affirmative right to governmental aid, even where

---

[60] *See generally* I. Berlin, *Two Concepts of Liberty, in* Four Essays on Liberty 118, 122–34 (1969).

[61] *See generally* Chervenak & McCullough, *Justified Limits on Refusing Intervention,* 21 Hastings Center Rep. 12 (Mar.–Apr. 1991).

[62] San Antonio Indep. Sch. Dist. v. Rodriguez, 411 U.S. 1 (1973).

[63] DeShaney v. Winnebago County Dep't of Social Servs., 489 U.S. 189 (1989).

such aid may be necessary to secure life, liberty, or property interests of which the government itself may not deprive the individual."[64] If the individuals denying the service are employees or agents of the state and provide the service on an unequal basis, a claim for the service brought under the equal protection clause will fail unless the service in question is "regarded as fundamental" or unless the basis for the unequal distribution of the service is a suspect classification such as race, religion, national origin or sex.[65]

Like public education, health or medical care has never been held to be a fundamental right. However, there is a line of cases holding that individuals are entitled to be provided with services by the state if the state has imposed limitations on their "freedom to act on [their] own behalf—through incarceration, institutionalization, or other similar restraint of personal liberty—which is the 'deprivation of liberty' triggering the protections of the Due Process Clause."[66] These cases involved individuals who were involuntarily in state custody in prisons[67] or state psychiatric hospitals.[68] The obligation to provide treatment that exists in such circumstances is not an absolute one. Whether or not the obligation has been satisfied is to be measured by reference to professional standards and professional judgment.[69]

There is considerable doubt that a patient in a hospital—even a totally helpless patient dependent on others for basic needs—meets these requirements. In cases of end-of-life decisionmaking, very few patients are in state institutions,[70] and none are hospitalized involuntarily, at least not in the sense that they have been committed to the institution by operation of law as is the case with prisoners and involuntary psychiatric patients.

## § 19.11   —Positive Common-Law Rights: Claims Against Private Parties

The common law is as inhospitable to claims of entitlement to resources by one private individual against another as the constitution is to claims of entitlement to resources by an individual against the state. The common law does, of course, recognize through tort remedies that individuals possess a *negative* right against— that is, a right to be from—interference by private parties. Thus, one who intentionally or negligently interferes with the person or property of another can

---

[64] *Id.* at 196.

[65] San Antonio Indep. Sch. Dist. v. Rodriguez, 411 U.S. 1 (1973).

[66] DeShaney v. Winnebago County Dep't of Social Servs., 489 U.S. at 200.

[67] *See, e.g.,* Whitley v. Albers, 475 U.S. 312 (1986); Hughes v. Rowe, 449 U.S. 5 (1980).

[68] *See, e.g.,* Youngberg v. Romeo, 457 U.S. 307 (1982); Vitek v. Jones, 445 U.S. 480 (1980).

[69] Youngberg v. Romeo, 457 U.S. at 321–22.

[70] *But see, e.g.,* Cruzan v. Harmon, 760 S.W.2d 408 (Mo. 1988), *aff'd sub nom.* Cruzan v. Director, 497 U.S. 261 (1990).

be held liable for damages for the harm occasioned thereby. However, individuals generally have no right to compel others to act to benefit them. Under the common law, no one is generally obligated to rescue another. That is, there is no *general* positive right to appropriate efforts or possessions of other private individuals for one's own use.[71] An application of this principle in the health care context is that no one may ordinarily compel a physician to provide medical services.[72]

There are, however, some important exceptions to the "no duty" rule. First, one can create a duty to provide services—to "rescue," as it were—through the mutual agreement of the parties, that is, by contract.[73] The physician-patient relationship is a contractual one, but it is not clear to what extent the mere existence of that relationship compels a physician to continue to provide treatment he believes to be unnecessary, or even for other reasons. A related exception arises when one *relies* on another to rescue.[74] Both of these exceptions fall under the heading of "abandonment," which is discussed in §§ **17.14** and **17.15.** Finally, the common-law no-duty rule has been modified by statute and to some extent by case law in the context of the provision of health care services. For the most part, however, these modifications apply to the provision of health care on an emergency basis.[75]

## § 19.12    ——Conscientious Objection

The difficulty with implementing positive legal rights in general is the one that makes it especially problematic in the context of medical decisionmaking—namely, that for a patient to have whatever treatment he might request would impose on the freedom of physicians, especially on their freedom to practice their calling in accordance with their own conscientiously held beliefs and standards of what constitutes appropriate medical practice. This problem also exists with respect to the refusal of treatment,[76] though to a far lesser degree. Brett and McCullough explain the difference this way:

---

[71] W.P. Keeton et al., Prosser and Keeton on the Law of Torts §§ 53, 56 (5th ed. 1984). *Cf.* Barber v. Superior Court, 195 Cal. Rptr. 484, 490 (Ct. App. 1983) (failure to feed infant distinguishable from doctor's termination of artificial nutrition and hydration because parent has "a clear duty to feed an otherwise healthy child").

[72] Hurley v. Eddingfield, 59 N.E. 1058 (Ind. 1901). *See generally* Purver, Annotation, *Liability of Hospital for Refusal to Admit or Treat Patient,* 35 A.L.R.3d 841 (1971 & Supp. 1994).

[73] See § **17.18.**

[74] W.P. Keeton et al., Prosser and Keeton on the Law of Torts § 56, at 376–78 (5th ed. 1984).

[75] *See, e.g.,* Wilmington Gen. Hosp. v. Manlove, 174 A.2d 135 (Del. 1961). *See generally* Purver, Annotation, *Liability of Hospital for Refusal to Admit or Treat Patient,* 35 A.L.R.3d 841 (1971 & Supp. 1994).

[76] See § **17.23.**

If a competent patient refuses to comply with a recommended intervention, the physician has not acted contrary to his or her own moral principles but has merely failed to convince the patient to undergo the intervention. However, if the physician facilitates the patient's request for an unnecessary or harmful intervention to satisfy a principle of respect of patient autonomy, the action reciprocally undermines the physician's autonomy.[77]

While there is generally no legal bar to patients seeking and obtaining medical treatment of questionable utility from a *willing* physician (with certain exceptions such "quack" or illegal medications, or those with harmful side effects, such as steroids for athletes[78]) neither is there, generally speaking, a right to compel an unwilling health care provider to administer *any* medical treatment, proven or unproven,[79] even if the treatment has no harmful side effects (such as antibiotics for the common cold),[80] or no known side effects (such as human growth hormone for children whose parents wish for them to be taller but who are not suffering from a natural deficiency of this hormone).

It has been argued that the widespread judicial recognition of the state interest in the ethical integrity of the medical profession[81] confers on physicians a right to withhold or withdraw medical treatment that they believe to be futile.[82] This

---

[77] Brett & McCullough, *When Patients Request Specific Interventions—Defining the Limits of the Physician's Obligation,* 315 New Eng. J. Med. 1347, 1349 (1986). *Accord* American College of Physicians, Ethics Manual 37 (2d ed. 1989) ("For reasons of conscience, the physician may elect to withdraw from the case" if the physician's judgment about the advisability of CPR differs from the competent patient's.); American Thoracic Soc'y, *Withholding and Withdrawing Life-Sustaining Therapy,* 115 Annals of Internal Medicine 478, 481 (1991) ("A physician has no ethical obligation to provide a life-sustaining intervention that is judged futile, as defined previously, even if the intervention is requested by the patient or surrogate decision maker. Forcing physicians to provide medical interventions that are clearly futile would undermine the ethical integrity of the medical profession."); Miles, *Informed Demand for "Non-Beneficial" Medical Treatment,* 325 New Eng. J. Med. 512, 514 (1991) ("Respect for [patient] autonomy does not empower patients to oblige physicians to prescribe treatments in ways that are fruitless or inappropriate."); Truog et al., *The Problem with Futility,* 326 New Eng. J. Med. 1560, 1562 (1992) ("[U]nrestrained deference to the wishes of the patient or surrogate conflicts with two other values that do not require a unilateral judgment of the futility of treatment: professional ideals and social consensus.").

[78] *See, e.g.,* Brett & McCullough, *When Patients Request Specific Interventions—Defining the Limits of the Physician's Obligation,* 315 New Eng. J. Med. 1347, 1349 (1986).

[79] *See, e.g.,* Payton v. Weaver, 182 Cal. Rptr. 225 (Ct. App. 1982). *See generally* Purver, *Liability of Hospital for Refusal to Admit or Treat Patient,* 35 A.L.R.3d 841 (1971 & Supp. 1993).

[80] Schneiderman et al., *Beyond Futility to an Ethic of Care,* 96 Am. J. Med. 110, 112 (1994) ("Many have observed (and few have counterargued) that physicians are not obligated to provide useless treatments, such as antibiotics for the common cold.").

[81] See § 8.18.

[82] *See* Daar, *A Clash at the Bedside: Patient Autonomy v. A Physician's Professional Conscience,* 44 Hastings L.J. 1241, 1260–63 (1993); Marsh & Staver, *Physician Authority for Unilateral DNR Orders,* 12 J. Legal Med. 115, 144 (1991).

argument, however, suffers from the same flaw as does the more general argument that because courts have recognized in conventional right-to-die cases that futile treatment need not be administered, physicians may unilaterally withhold or withdraw life-sustaining medical treatment. Both arguments overlook the differing contexts in which conventional right-to-die cases and futility cases arise, specifically, that in conventional right-to-die cases the patient or surrogate has *consented* to the forgoing of life-sustaining treatment, whereas in futility cases, by hypothesis, they have not, and that it is patient or surrogate consent that is what legitimates the forgoing of treatment.

## § 19.13 ——Non-Medically Indicated Treatment

It is undoubtedly the case that a physician is not legally required to offer or provide a treatment that is not medically indicated for a patient's condition, such as an appendectomy for the treatment of stomach ulcers in a person who does not have appendicitis. It is equally true that a physician is not legally obligated to offer or provide a patient with a treatment that is generally considered by other members of the medical profession to be a treatment of demonstrated lack of benefit, such as the treatment of cancer with laetrile. A treatment need not even be a clear-cut form of quackery for there to be no legal obligation to provide it. There are some forms of treatment that are used by some doctors but were never, or are no longer, considered generally accepted by the medical profession or the specialty in which the doctor practices.[83]

## § 19.14 ——Rationing and Triage

Treatments of unproved efficacy or certain lack of efficacy are the easy cases. The more difficult ones are those in which the treatment at issue unquestionably provides physiologic benefit to the patient, but there are strong moral and medical reasons as to why the physician might wish not to provide it. A particular kind of treatment might be a very scarce resource that, if provided to this patient, could not be provided to another patient. Organ transplantation is an obvious example, and hospitals have established guidelines making organ transplantation unavailable to individuals over a certain age because of the extreme scarcity of the resource.[84]

---

[83] *See, e.g.,* Hood v. Phillips, 554 S.W.2d 160 (Tex. 1977) (carotid body surgery for treatment of emphysema "not generally accepted and was in fact highly controversial").

[84] *But cf.* Schneiderman et al., *Beyond Futility to an Ethic of Care,* 96 Am. J. Med. 110, 112 (1994) (distinguishing denial of treatment based on futility from denial of treatment to ration scarce resources or contain costs, but acknowledging possible overlap; "[F]utile treatments ought not to be offered at all, regardless of the economic wealth of a health care system. . . . [W]ith rationing, beneficial services are withheld from one patient or group in order to provide them to other patients or groups whose entitlement is greater.").

Hospitals might develop similar policies for other resources that are, at least in the short run, scarce. For example, a hospital might establish a policy requiring removal of a ventilator-dependent patient from a ventilator if that patient was near death and the ventilator was needed for someone suffering from an acute illness for whom there is a significant chance of recovery if ventilation is provided.[85] The rationale for such a rule is that even though the terminally ill patient is benefiting from the ventilator, by hypothesis the ventilation affords no opportunity for the patient's recovery. However, if the ventilator were provided to the acutely ill patient, there is a substantial chance that it would tide him over an immediate crisis from which he would be almost certain to recover.[86]

Strong arguments can be made for either of the competing positions—namely, that we should employ a first-come, first-served rule for distribution of scarce resources, or alternatively, that we should distribute the scarce resource to the person who can derive the most benefit from it, especially if there is a substantial differential in the benefits to be derived by different patients.

### § 19.15    ——The "Right" to Provide Futile Medical Treatment

Even assuming that there is no legal obligation to do so, there are situations in which physicians might wish to provide treatment that they do not believe offers any or any significant benefit to a patient at least for a brief period.[87] One such situation is the case of sudden and unexpected serious injury or death. In such a case, treatment is sometimes administered to provide the family with additional time to accept the reality of what has occurred, and it is perhaps more accurate

---

[85] *See, e.g.,* American Thoracic Soc'y, *Withholding and Withdrawing Life-Sustaining Therapy,* 115 Annals Internal Med. 478, 482 (1991) ("[A] health care institution has the right to limit a life-sustaining intervention without consent of a patient or surrogate by restricting admission to, or continued care in, a special care unit, such as an intensive care unit, based on the ethical principle of just allocation of scarce resources and the principle of medical triage."); Task Force on Ethics of the Soc'y of Critical Care Medicine, *Consensus Report on the Ethics of Foregoing Life-Sustaining Treatments in the Critically Ill,* 18 Critical Care Med. 1435, 1437 (1990) ("A PVS patient should not be maintained in the ICU to the exclusion of a patient who can derive benefit from ICU care. . . . The healthcare team should make every effort to assist the family of such a patient to appreciate the medical futility of continued ICU treatment and to understand the rationale for transfer to another level of care.").

[86] Society of Critical Care Medicine Ethics Comm., *Consensus Statement on the Triage of Critically Ill Patients,* 271 JAMA 1200 (1994) (recommending that hospitals establish policies to determine which patients should or should not be admitted to intensive care units based on expected benefit to the patient).

[87] Hastings Ctr., Guidelines on the Termination of Life-Sustaining Treatment and the Care of the Dying 32 (1987) (Part One, II(8)(c)) ("Treatment that is physiologically futile may offer psychological benefits and so may be warranted."). *But see* Youngner, *Futility in Context,* 264 JAMA 1295, 1295 (1990) ("[B]y offering life-sustaining treatment that they consider futile, physicians may actually undermine patient and family autonomy. Such offers send a mixed message, implying a real choice when none exists.").

to say that treatment is being provided (to the patient) for the benefit of the family.[88]

Another sort of situation in which treatment might be rendered despite its certain or probable lack of medical benefit occurs when the patient or family has personal, "nonmedical" reasons for wanting the treatment—such as wanting to live a few more days until a loved one can come to visit the patient.[89] In cases such as these, however, treatment is administered not necessarily because the patient has a right to direct that it be—that is, not for reasons of self-determination—but out of concern for the patient's overall well-being,[90] and thus treatment should be administered in such circumstances, if at all, only if it is not unduly burdensome to the patient.[91]

In addition, physicians need to take care about the manner in which they terminate treatment when there is no physiologic benefit being provided so that they do not cause harm or offense to the patient's loved ones, and thus also reduce the risk of incurring liability for intentional infliction of emotional distress[92] or giving such offense to the patient's family as to generate a reason for them to challenge the physician's decision through litigation or otherwise.

## § 19.16  —Positive Statutory Rights

Even if there is no certain constitutional or common-law basis for compelling the provision of medical treatment deemed by the patient's physician to be futile, there may be statutory grounds for such a right. It is well established that legislatures may create claims of entitlement by statutory enactment that would not exist in the absence of such enactments. Of the litigated futility cases, all three have been decided on statutory grounds, with two supporting the claimed right to be treated.

---

[88] Hackler & Hiller, *Family Consent to Orders Not to Resuscitate: Reconsidering Hospital Policy,* 254 JAMA 1281, 1283 (1990) ("We are not suggesting that physicians should ignore the needs of family. Aggressive support of dying patients may be necessary to give families time to accept the inevitable or to allow a relative time to arrive at the bedside.").

[89] *See, e.g.,* Schneiderman et al., *Medical Futility: Its Meaning and Ethical Implications,* 112 Annals Internal Med. 949, 950 (1990).

[90] Tomlinson & Brody, *Futility and the Ethics of Resuscitation,* 264 JAMA 1276, 1279 (1990) ("When a patient or family continues to insist on futile resuscitation, the physician may be justified in honoring the demand, but not out of respect of patient autonomy. . . . Consideration of the patient's welfare . . . may support a decision to meet this need.").

[91] Hackler & Hiller, *Family Consent to Orders Not to Resuscitate: Reconsidering Hospital Policy,* 254 JAMA 1281, 1283 (1990) ("At a certain point . . . respect for the family must give way to concern for the patient. Hospital policy should not force physicians to inflict additional suffering on their patients when surrogates insist on burdensome treatment for unacceptable reasons. It is wrong to inflict pain on one person without chance of significant benefit to satisfy another person or out of slavish adherence to an occasionally misdirected procedural principle.").

[92] See §§ **17.5–17.7.**

## § 19.17  ——Federal Statutory Rights: The *Baby K* Case

The *Baby K* case[93] exemplifies the kind of futility case in which the treatment will bring about recovery from the immediate medical crisis, but the patient will recover to a state of existence that the physician believes not to be sufficiently improved as to warrant the treatment in question. Indeed, the administration of treatment is not merely contrary to the beliefs of the physicians involved in the treatment of this patient, but also contrary to prevailing professional standards unanimously accepted for the treatment of all patients in this particular condition.

Baby K was born in October 1992 with a condition known as anencephaly. In the words of the United States Court of Appeals for the Fourth Circuit, anencephaly is "a congenital malformation in which a major portion of the brain, skull, and scalp are missing. While the presence of a brain stem does support her autonomic functions and reflex actions, because Baby K lacks a cerebrum, she is permanently unconscious. Thus, she has no cognitive abilities or awareness. She cannot see, hear, or otherwise interact with her environment,"[94] nor can she experience pain.[95]

Anencephalic babies usually die within days, or weeks at most, because of "breathing difficulties and other complications,"[96] which go untreated because of the severe and irremediable nature of the condition. Consequently, the doctors attending Baby K explained to her mother that if she suffered breathing difficulties, no mechanical ventilation or resuscitation would be provided, which is the medical standard of care in such instances. The doctors would, however, continue to provide nourishment to the baby and keep her warm, which is also standard procedure though, interestingly, no less futile in terms of the baby's "recovery" than ventilation or resuscitation. Because an anencephalic baby experiences nothing, including hunger or cold if these "comfort measures" were also withheld, they were futile in the narrow physiologic sense as well.

The baby's mother insisted that ventilation and resuscitation be provided, based in part on her "religious conviction that all life is sacred and must be protected."[97] The hospital attempted to transfer Baby K to another hospital, but none with an intensive care unit would accept her, which is further evidence that such treatment is not part of accepted care for anencephalic babies. After several weeks in the hospital, acute hospital care was no longer necessary, and Baby K was transferred to a nursing home. However, she continued to have respiratory difficulties, and each time she did she was transferred back to the hospital in which she was born. After the second such hospitalization, the hospital filed an

---

[93] *In re* Baby "K," 16 F.3d 590 (4th Cir.), *cert. denied,* 115 S. Ct. 91 (1994).

[94] 16 F.3d at 592.

[95] *In re* Baby "K," 832 F. Supp. 1022, 1025 (E.D. Va. 1993).

[96] *In re* Baby "K," 16 F.3d at 592.

[97] *In re* Baby "K," 832 F. Supp. at 1030.

action seeking a declaratory judgment that withholding ventilation over the mother's objection would not violate federal or state law.

The district court held that withholding treatment without the mother's consent would violate three of four federal statutes: the Emergency Medical Treatment and Active Labor Act (EMTALA),[98] section 504 of the Rehabilitation Act of 1973,[99] the Americans With Disabilities Act,[100] and the Child Abuse Act.[101] It also declined to hold that a refusal to provide further treatment would not violate the Virginia Medical Malpractice Act.[102] The court of appeals affirmed on the basis of EMTALA and did not reach the other federal and state statutory claims.

**Purpose of EMTALA.** The appellate court's reasoning closely tracks the text of the statute, yet seems oddly detached from the underlying purpose of the statute. EMTALA was enacted as a response to the fact that some hospitals were refusing to provide emergency medical treatment to patients who were unable to pay.[103] However, courts have held that the statute applies to all patients regardless of their ability to pay.[104] In order to ensure that adequate emergency treatment is available, EMTALA imposes two duties on all hospitals that have emergency departments (and that participate in the Medicare program, which is virtually all hospitals): the duty to provide "appropriate medical screening,"[105] and the duty either to treat or transfer the patient.[106] If the patient is to be transferred, treatment must be provided "to stabilize" the patient's medical condition, and treatment must be provided that will "assure . . . that no material deterioration of the condition is likely to result from or occur during the transfer of the individual from a facility."[107]

---

[98] 42 U.S.C.A. § 1395dd (West 1992 & Supp. 1994).

[99] 29 U.S.C.A. § 794 (West 1992 & Supp. 1994). *Cf.* Johnson v. Thompson, 971 F.2d 1487, 1494 (10th Cir. 1992) ("Section 504 proscribes discrimination between the nonhandicapped and the 'otherwise qualified' handicapped. It does not create any absolute substantive right to treatment. . . . Without a showing that the nonhandicapped received the treatment denied to the 'otherwise qualified' handicapped, the appellants cannot assert that a violation of section 504 has occurred.").

[100] 42 U.S.C.A. §§ 12,101–12,213 (West Supp. 1994) *See generally* Orentlicher, *Rationing and the Americans with Disabilities Act,* 271 JAMA 308, 311 (1994) ("[U]nless a treatment would fall within a narrow, physiological definition of futility (ie, the treatment would not provide any physiological benefit), the eligibility requirement would be satisfied."); National Legal Ctr. Staff, *Medical Treatment Rights of Older Persons and Persons with Disabilities: 1991 Developments,* 7 Issues L. & Med. 407, 409–11 (1992). See § **17.22.**

[101] 42 U.S.C.A. §§ 5101–5119c (West Supp. 1994). See § **19.20.**

[102] Va. Code §§ 8.01-581.1 *et seq.*

[103] *In re* Baby "K", 16 F.3d 590, 593 (4th Cir. 1994).

[104] *Id.* at 593 (citing Brooker v. Desert Hosp. Corp., 947 F.2d 412, 415 (9th Cir. 1991) (holding that EMTALA applies "to any and all patients"); Gatewood v. Washington Healthcare Corp., 933 F.2d 1037, 1040 (D.C. Cir. 1991) (same); Cleland v. Bronson Health Care Group, Inc., 917 F.2d 266, 268 (6th Cir. 1990) (same)).

[105] *See* 42 U.S.C.A. § 1395dd(a).

[106] *Id.* § 1395dd(b)(1).

[107] *Id.* § 1395dd(e)(3)(A).

**Application to Facts.**   The hospital conceded that Baby K's need for ventilation arises on an emergency basis, and therefore the obligations imposed by EMTALA are triggered, and consequently the hospital must stabilize her condition or transfer her. Because no other hospital would accept Baby K, transfer was not an option, which means that the hospital is required to stabilize her condition in a medically appropriate manner, which the hospital admitted in its complaint includes ventilation.[108] The court concluded that "a straightforward application of the statute obligates the Hospital to provide respiratory support to Baby K when she arrives at the emergency department of the Hospital in respiratory distress and treatment is requested on her behalf."[109]

However, the hospital proposed four reasons that it should be exempt from EMTALA's obligations under the circumstances posed by this case, and the court rejected all four.

(1)   *Baby K Was Provided with the Same Treatment Provided Other Anencephalic Babies.*   The hospital argued that it was only required to provide the same treatment to Baby K as would be provided to other anencephalic babies, which was no treatment. This argument is in effect an effort to substantiate the view that physicians are required to provide treatment to a patient only insofar as doing so is consistent with accepted standards of medical practice.[110] However, the court concluded that the baby's condition for which treatment was sought on an emergency basis was not anencephaly but respiratory distress (technically known as bradypnea or apnea) and that the hospital conceded that the medically appropriate treatment for respiratory distress was resuscitation and ventilation. Hence, they had to be provided.

(2)   *Congress Did Not Intend to Require Physicians to Provide Medical Treatment Outside the Prevailing Standard of Medical Care.*   The court rejected the hospital's more direct argument that Congress did not intend to require physicians to provide medical treatment outside the prevailing standard of medical care because "[t]he Hospital has been unable to identify, nor has our research revealed, any statutory language or legislative history evincing a Congressional intent to" make such an exception.[111] Consequently, the court concluded, the proper remedy for the hospital is to seek legislative change, but not to withhold treatment. This is an extremely cramped reading of the legislative history if only because it requires Congress to express an intent as to what it did *not* intend. Proof of a negative is difficult enough, but to expect a legislature to expressly negate something that it most likely could not even foresee is clearly unreasonable.

---

[108] *In re* Baby "K," 16 F.3d at 597.

[109] *Id.* at 594 (footnote omitted).

[110] *See* Council on Ethical & Judicial Affairs, American Medical Ass'n, Code of Medical Ethics: Current Opinions with Annotations § 2.035, at 6–7 (1994).

[111] *In re* Baby "K," 16 F.3d at 596.

(3)   *Virginia Law Permits Physicians to Refuse to Provide Such Care.* The hospital contended that the Virginia advance directive statute (Health Care Decisions Act[112]) specifically precludes requiring a physician to provide any medical treatment he deems to be "medically or ethically inappropriate." Because, the argument continues, the hospital has no physicians who believe it is appropriate to provide ventilation to Baby K, EMTALA does not require it to provide such treatment.

The court rejected this argument for three reasons. First, EMTALA imposes obligations on physicians as well as on hospitals. Second, EMTALA specifically preempts state laws that are in conflict with its requirements.[113] Finally, the Virginia legislature did not intend for the advance directive statute to apply to treatment decisions for infants.[114] As part of the advance directive act, it is not likely that the legislature intended for the provision to apply to any non-declarant, infant or adult. The statute states that "[n]othing in *this article* shall be construed to require a physician to prescribe or render medical treatment to a patient that the physician determines to be medically or ethically inappropriate."[115] The provision continues by explaining that a physician has a duty to make a reasonable effort to transfer a patient for whom treatment is futile, "if the physician's determination is contrary to the terms of *an advance directive* of a qualified patient or the treatment decision of a person designated to make the decision *under this article,*"[116] further emphasizing that the provision is intended to apply only to patients who have made an advance directive.[117]

(4)   *EMTALA Only Applies to Patients Who Are Transferred.* Because EMTALA defines a "stabilizing treatment" as one that is "necessary to assure, within reasonable medical probability, that no material deterioration of the condition is likely to result from or occur during the transfer of the individual,"[118] the hospital argued that the obligation to provide stabilizing treatment applies only to patients who are to be transferred. Because Baby K could not be transferred, there was no obligation to stabilize her condition. The court found this argument to be without merit:

> [Section] 1395dd(b) requires a hospital to provide stabilizing treatment to any individual who comes to a participating hospital, is diagnosed as presenting an emergency medical condition, and cannot be transferred. . . . The use of the word "transfer" to describe the duty of a hospital to provide stabilizing treatment evinces a Congressional intent to require stabilization prior to discharge or that treatment

---

[112] Va. Code Ann. § 54.1-2990.

[113] *See* 42 U.S.C.A. § 1395dd(f).

[114] *In re* Baby "K," 16 F.3d at 597 n.10.

[115] Va. Code Ann. § 54.1-2990 (emphasis added).

[116] *Id.* (emphasis added).

[117] See § **10.13.**

[118] 42 U.S.C.A. § 1395dd(e)(3)(A).

necessary to prevent material deterioration of the patient's condition during transfer. It was not intended to allow hospitals and physicians to avoid liability under EMTALA by accepting and screening a patient and then refusing to treat the patient because the patient cannot or will not be transferred. [Citations omitted.][119]

**Dissent.**   Judge Sprouse wrote a brief dissenting opinion based largely on the legislative purpose and history of EMTALA. He accurately pointed out that the majority's reading of EMTALA would require "the judiciary to superintend the sensitive decision-making process between family and physicians at the bedside of a helpless and terminally ill patient under the circumstances of this case." "Congress," he observed, "even in its weakest moments, would not have attempted to impose federal control in this sensitive, private area."[120]

EMTALA was intended to address a specific abuse, namely, the refusal of hospitals to treat indigent or uninsured patients[121]—what is referred to as "dumping." However, as the brief for the hospital in its petition for certiorari observes, "[u]nfortunately, an imperfect alignment between the language and purpose of the statute has led the lower courts to extend EMTALA's reach well beyond the documented Congressional aim."[122] There was no indication of such an intent or practice on the part of the hospital in this case:

> To the contrary, Baby K's introduction to the hospital was not for emergency treatment—she was born there. She was twice readmitted and after her subsidiary medical condition [*i.e.,* respiratory distress] was stabilized, transferred back to a nursing home. In light of the purposes of the statute and this child's unique circumstances, I would find this case to be outside the scope of EMTALA's anti-dumping provisions.[123]

Furthermore, the statute was not intended to address the kind of continuing emergencies presented by Baby K's condition. It was crafted to prevent the disparate treatment of emergency patients on the basis of their ability to pay. The hospital complied with EMTALA because it has provided Baby K the same attention it would provide any other infant in her condition. The condition that continues to bring her to the hospital is anencephaly, as the hospital contended,

---

[119] *In re* Baby "K," 16 F.3d at 597.

[120] *Id.* at 598.

[121] H.R. Rep. No. 241, 99th Cong., 2d Sess., pt. 1, at 27 (1986), *reprinted in* 1986 U.S.C.C.A.N. 42, 605. *See, e.g.,* Brooks v. Maryland Gen. Hosp. Inc., 996 F.2d 708, 709 (4th Cir. 1993); Baber v. Hospital Corp. of Am., 977 F.2d 872, 880 (4th Cir. 1992).

[122] Brief for Petitioners at 8, Petition for Writ of Certiorari, *In re* Baby "K," 16 F.3d 590 (4th Cir. 1994); *id.* at 9 ("In the eight years since its enactment, lower courts have extended EMTALA's reach to all patients, regardless of indigence, and from emergency rooms to hospital care. A limited federal duty, which was not intended to displace state malpractice laws, has gradually become an alterative to a malpractice action for any claim involving alleged deficiencies in hospital care of patients in crisis.").

[123] *In re* Baby "K," 16 F.3d at 598.

and the respiratory distress is "one of many subsidiary conditions found in a patient with" this condition.[124]

The dissent pointed out that there is a fundamental flaw in the majority's reasoning, namely, the assumption that the baby was being treated for respiratory distress. Of course that was the reason that the baby was periodically transported from the nursing home where she resided to the petitioner/hospital. However, the court failed to see this in the larger context, namely, that the reason she periodically suffered from respiratory distress was because she was anencephalic. Viewing the case in this broader, commonsense fashion leads to an acceptance of the hospital's argument that it was not treating Baby K any differently from any other anencephalic baby and that it was acting in accordance with accepted medical practice.

## § 19.18 ——"DNR" Statutes: The *Doe* Case

Many states have statutes governing the withholding of cardiopulmonary resuscitation.[125] Virtually all require the consent of the patient or surrogate to withhold CPR under most circumstances,[126] which could be interpreted as supporting the proposition that physicians are not permitted unilaterally to withhold or withdraw CPR that they believe to be futile but that the patient or surrogate wants. However, these statutes do not necessarily create a right to have treatment (CPR) provided if they are interpreted as intended to protect individuals against the *administration* of unwanted treatment rather than the withholding of wanted treatment, much the same as the common-law right of self-determination developed to protect patients from unwanted treatment, but not necessarily to empower them to demand treatment from an unwilling physician.[127]

The facts of the *Doe*[128] case bear a resemblance to the *Baby K* case, as does the outcome, but the legal basis for the decision is different and far more limited. The hospital instituted proceedings to limit cardiopulmonary resuscitation for a 13-year-old girl who had "experienced medical problems since birth" and who had been admitted to the hospital "following a mild choking episode." Although the girl's precise diagnosis was uncertain, she was suffering from some type of degenerative neurological condition "with substantial atrophy of the brain and no reasonable possibility of a 'meaningful recovery,' due to the fact that substantial portions of her brain are irreversibly damaged, including the areas which control her cognitive functions, her ability to eat, swallow, and breathe." She had no "self-awareness, self control, capacity to relate to others,

---

[124] *Id.* at 599.

[125] See **Table 9–1** in § **9.8.**

[126] See § **9.9.**

[127] See § **9.5.**

[128] *In re* Doe, 418 S.E.2d 3 (Ga. 1992).

or capacity to communicate or control her existence."[129] According to the trial court, she was not in what it termed a "chronic vegetative state," but her condition certainly resembled that of, and might well have been, a persistent vegetative state, as she was described as being "chronically and irreversibly stuporous."

Her physicians recommended "deescalation" of life support and the entry of a do-not-resuscitate order after a long period in which her condition fluctuated between stupor and coma and her brain stem began to degenerate from neurological disease, and the hospital's ethics committee agreed. Her father refused to authorize a do-not-resuscitate order and her mother "appear[ed] to agree with [hospital] officials with respect to their advice not to resuscitate" but was "reluctant . . . to commit in writing."[130] Eventually the hospital sought a declaratory judgment. Thereafter, the mother's position began to waver, and at the time of trial "both parents opposed deescalation of treatment."[131] The trial court found that the hospital was motivated to commence the action by nothing "but the best of intentions."[132] Specifically, those responsible for treating the patient believed that "the treatment they are providing . . . is inhumane and undignified. Some of the nurses . . . indicated that they had grave reservations about participating in a course of treatment that could be painful . . . with no hope of any real benefit to Jane."[133] However, because of the fundamental right of parents to determine the course of treatment for their children,[134] the inability to know the wishes of the patient,[135] the "presumption in favor of life which arises from the constitutions of the United States and the State of Georgia," and "the finality of a decision to deescalate and/or permit DNR," the court concluded that it "must yield to the presumption in favor of life."[136] Furthermore, in the event of disagreement between the parents, as was the situation in this case at least at times, the court concluded that the presumption in favor of life dictates that treatment not be forgone.[137] The court concluded by directing the attorney general to appeal the case to the state supreme court.

The Georgia Supreme Court reaffirmed its 1984 holding that parents have the authority to forgo life-sustaining treatment on behalf of their minor children,[138] even if death of the child is not imminent, and that they may do so without prior

---

[129] *In re* Doe, Civ. Action No. D-93064, slip op. at 4 (Fulton County, Ga. Oct. 17, 1991).

[130] *Id.* at 7.

[131] *Id.* at 6.

[132] *Id.* at 8.

[133] *Id.* at 8–9.

[134] *Id.* at 12, 17.

[135] *In re* Doe, Civ. Action No. D-93064, slip op. at 15–16.

[136] *Id.* at 18.

[137] *Id.* at 18–19.

[138] *See In re* L.H.R., 321 S.E.2d 716 (Ga. 1984).

judicial approval.[139] From this conclusion, the court reasoned that the parents had the correlative right to consent to treatment on the child's behalf. Had the court stopped there, there would be nothing controversial about its dicta. However, the court concluded, from the fact that the parents had the authority to consent to treatment on behalf of the child, that they also had the right to compel the provision of medical treatment thought to be inappropriate by her attending physicians.

The holding rests on a narrow statutory basis. Because the type of treatment that the physician wished to forgo was cardiopulmonary resuscitation, the matter was governed by the Georgia statute governing decisionmaking about CPR and DNR orders. According to the court, this statute "requires the agreement of both parents, if both parents are present and actively participating in the medical decision-making process for the child."[140] Although the patient's mother consented to the DNR order, "because the father revoked consent, the trial court correctly determined the hospital could not enter a DNR order."[141] Indeed, there was evidence that the mother had also reversed her position and by the time of the hearing "opposed deescalation of treatment."[142]

Because of this narrow statutory basis, the court's reasoning is not necessarily persuasive in any other jurisdiction, and it is not even clear that the court's reasoning would apply to any other treatment administered in Georgia because the statute governs only decisionmaking about cardiopulmonary resuscitation. *Doe* is thus very thin precedent for anything other than the same fact situation in the same jurisdiction.

## § 19.19 ——Advance Directive Statutes

Arguably, another possible source of statutory law for the establishment of a right to require that treatment be provided is advance directive statutes. Some advance directive statutes specifically envision that a living will or a proxy directive may direct the provision of treatment as well as the withholding or withdrawing of treatment, and some living will forms found in a number of living will statutes contain checklists that declarants can use to indicate that they do not—or *do*—want the listed treatments if they are ever in a situation in which the living will goes into effect.

Although the enactment of advance directive statutes was originally motivated by the wish to provide individuals with a vehicle for having treatment withheld or withdrawn when they are no longer contemporaneously able to make such a request, and concomitantly to provide immunity from liability to

---

[139] *In re* Doe, 418 S.E.2d 3, 6 (Ga. 1992).

[140] *Id.* at 7 (citing Ga. Code Ann. §§ 31-39-1 to -9).

[141] *Id.*

[142] *Id.* at 6.

physicians who follow the patient's wishes, a court construing a living will that requests that treatment be administered might find a right to do so based on a statutory provision or checklist even if the statute does not expressly provide for this.

Yet, for two reasons, this might not prove to be a particularly fruitful avenue to pursue. First, advance directive statutes also contain provisions absolving physicians from noncompliance with a directive or with a health care proxy's instructions if the physician makes a reasonable effort to attempt to transfer the patient to the care of another physician who is willing to comply.[143] This is essentially the same result that would occur if one were to attempt to establish that a physician's failure to provide requested treatment were a common-law abandonment.[144] Second, to the extent that advance directive legislation has been held not to create substantive rights but merely to provide a mechanism for the enforcement of rights from constitutional or common-law sources,[145] advance directives are not likely to be construed as creating a right to have treatment administered. The Uniform Health-Care Decisions Act has specifically addressed the possibility of advance directive legislation being used as a basis for patients' or surrogates' demanding health care by specifically including a provision to thwart such demands.[146]

## § 19.20      ——Statutes Protecting Against Abuse of Patients

There are a variety of state and federal statutes and regulations that protect against "abuse" of patients. Some of these statutes define abuse in such a way as to suggest that the provision of medical treatment under some circumstances constitutes abuse or alternatively that the withholding or withdrawing of treatment does not constitute abuse. However, these statutes and regulations are premised on the assumption that the patient or surrogate wishes to forgo life-sustaining treatment, and thus they are subject to the same limitation as are the judicial right-to-die cases in terms of their applicability to situations in which a physician might wish to forgo treatment *against* the wishes of the surrogate.[147]

---

[143] See §§ **11.17** and **12.46.**

[144] See §§ **17.14–17.15.**

[145] See § **10.13.**

[146] Uniform Health-Care Decisions Act § 13(d) ("This [Act] does not authorize or require a health-care provider or institution to provide health care contrary to generally accepted health-care standards applicable to the health-care provider or institution.").

[147] See § **19.5.**

**State and Federal Statutes and Regulations Governing Long-Term Care Facilities.** State and federal statutes and administrative regulations governing long-term care facilities contain provisions defining and prohibiting "abuse" of residents in the facilities.[148] One type of abuse is "'providing to a resident treatment that is not medically indicated.'"[149] "Medically indicated" is further defined as "'treatment that will improve the medical condition of the resident or is necessary to provide palliative care to the resident.'"[150] Consequently, providing a patient with futile treatment—if futile treatment is defined as treatment that does not improve the patient's medical condition or provide palliation— would violate this regulation.

**Child Abuse Statutes and Regulations.** The federal Child Abuse Amendments and regulations issued pursuant to that statute define child abuse to include the withholding or withdrawing of medically indicated life-sustaining treatment.[151] Consequently, it might be concluded that the failure to administer any treatment requested by a surrogate for a handicapped newborn infant, that is not physiologically futile, constitutes child abuse.

However, the regulations also recognize certain exceptions in which the forgoing of life-sustaining treatment does not constitute abuse. Two of the five exceptions permit the forgoing of "futile" medical treatment. Specifically, life-sustaining medical treatment may be withheld or withdrawn if it would "be futile in terms of the survival of the infant"[152] or "virtually futile in terms of the survival of the infant and the treatment itself would be inhumane."[153] The term "futile" is not defined in the statute, final rule, or interpretative guidelines, although the term "virtually futile" is defined in the interpretative guidelines as a treatment that is "highly unlikely to prevent death in the near future."[154] Thus, a treatment should be considered futile if it will *definitely* not prevent death in the near future. Perhaps even more important is that the regulations state on a number of occasions that determinations such as these are to be made by reference to "reasonable medical judgment."[155]

---

[148] *See* Lazarus et al., *Don't Make Them Leave Their Rights at the Door: A Recommended Model State Statute to Protect the Rights of the Elderly in Nursing Homes,* 4 J. Contemp. Health Law & Pol'y 321, 330 n.54 (1988) (collecting statutes).

[149] Gleason v. Abrams, 593 A.2d 1232, 1236 (N.J. Super. Ct. App. Div. 1991) (quoting N.J. Admin. Code tit. 5, § 100-1.2 (1990)).

[150] *Id.* at 1236 n.2 (quoting N.J. Admin. Code tit. 5, § 100-2.2).

[151] See **Ch. 16.**

[152] 45 C.F.R. § 1340.15(b)(2)(ii) (1993).

[153] *Id.* § 1340.15(b)(2)(iii).

[154] 45 C.F.R. pt. 1340 app. at 219 (1987) (interpretative guideline no. 8).

[155] *See, e.g.,* 45 C.F.R. pt. 1340 app. at 217, 218, 219 (1987) (interpretative guideline nos. 6, 7, 8). See §§ **16.17** and **16.19.**

## § 19.21 The Future of Futility

It is possible that the resolution of futility cases will ultimately occur through changes in individual clinical practice rather than through litigation or legislation. Some (and perhaps most) futility cases can be resolved at the bedside, without the necessity of litigation, by acquiescence of one of the parties to the view of the other, or by transfer of the patient to another physician or another health care facility, although transfer in such cases, as is also so in conventional right-to-die cases, can be difficult to achieve.[156] Futility cases often arise because of a lack of mutual understanding between physicians and families of incompetent patients about what are the realistic goals of treatment. Although it is trite, it is probably also true that better communication by physicians about what is medically realistic would lead to more realistic expectations on the part of patients and surrogates and thus to more realistic requests from them—indeed, to more requests and to less demands.[157] Thus, even if physicians are ultimately accorded full or even limited legal authority to unilaterally withhold or withdraw treatments they deem to be futile, this should not excuse them from having discussions with patients or surrogates about what they do and do not believe to be futile and what treatments they are or are not willing to provide.

Yet another extralegal way—or perhaps more correctly, quasilegal way—in which the futility debate might be resolved is through the development of medical professional standards about when it is appropriate and when it is not to provide life-sustaining medical treatment. This process has been going on through the barrage of writings in the medical and medical ethics journals for a decade or more. More recently, formal efforts have been undertaken in a variety of places, with individual hospitals, groups of hospitals or other health care providers, and medical societies drafting "futility guidelines."[158]

---

[156] See § **17.23.**

[157] *See, e.g.,* Schneiderman et al., *Beyond Futility to an Ethic of Care,* 96 Am. J. Med. 110, 111, 112 (1994) ("The crucial element often overlooked, both at the bedside and in public commentary, is the ethical duty of the physician to redirect efforts from life-saving treatments toward the aggressive pursuit of treatments that maximize comfort and dignity for the patient and for the grieving family."); Task Force on Ethics of the Soc'y of Critical Care Medicine, *Consensus Report on the Ethics of Foregoing Life-Sustaining Treatments in the Critically Ill,* 18 Critical Care Med. 1435, 1437 (1990) ("[T]he attention of the healthcare team must . . . be redirected to alleviating the suffering of the patient and his or her family and ensuring that death will occur with dignity" when continued treatment is "medically futile.").

[158] *See, e.g.,* Sadler & Mayo, *The Parkland Approach to Demands for "Futile" Treatment,* 5 HEC Forum 35 (1993). *See also* Council on Ethical & Judicial Affairs, American Medical Ass'n, Code of Medical Ethics: Current Opinions with Annotations § 2.035, at 6–7 (1994) ("Denial of treatment should be justified by reliance on openly stated ethical principles and acceptable standards of care.").

In a sense, the entire corpus of right-to-die cases stands for the proposition that there is no duty to administer treatment deemed to be futile—but, and this is the critical point, so deemed by a *competent patient* or by a *surrogate*. Although there is still significant evidence of physician resistance to forgoing life-sustaining treatment,[159] it has gradually become accepted practice for physicians to recommend to surrogates and families of hopelessly ill incompetent patients that all treatment or aggressive treatment be forgone and that the patient be allowed to die.

Two factors are likely to increase the volume of "futility litigation." First, as physicians continue to learn and absorb the basic principal of *Quinlan* and its progeny—that patients are not automatically nor presumptively obligated to accept life-sustaining medical treatment—they will increasingly act on this information by suggesting that life-sustaining medical treatment be withheld or withdrawn for particular patients for whom they no longer believe it will do much, if any, good.

Second, as the costs of providing medical care become an increasingly important political and social issue, physicians, health care administrators, third-party payors, and government officials will come under increasing pressure to limit or eliminate the costs of treatments that do not provide very much benefit.[160] (It is unclear, however, whether curtailing care thought to be futile near the end of life will result in much cost savings, because of the expense of even "low-technology" palliative care administered outside of hospitals and because of "the unpredictability of death."[161]) As the public becomes more aware of this increased pressure on health care providers to control the costs of medical treatment, patients and their families might increasingly become inclined to add to their list of reasons for resisting a physician's recommendation to forgo treatment the fear that the physician is making the recommendation not because it is in the best interests of the patient to do so but because of financial pressures placed on the physician by others. Regardless of which of these factors is operating—and it is likely that they will frequently operate in tandem—they will come into conflict with patients or surrogates who believe otherwise and who want "everything possible" done or who at least want some treatment or treatments administered that the attending physician believes are not warranted.

---

[159] *See* Solomon et al., *Decisions Near the End of Life: Professional Views on Life-Sustaining Treatments,* 83 Am. J. Pub. Health 14 (1993).

[160] *See* Gianelli, *Getting a Better Fix on Futility: More Providers Seeking Consensus on How to Set Limits,* Am. Med. News, Dec. 5, 1994, at 3; Meyer, *Cost-Conscious Hospitals Set Futile Care Rules,* Am. Med. News, June 28, 1993, at 3, col. 1 (Hospitals are adopting or developing rules, under "growing pressures to control costs" to stop "what they consider futile care."); Truog et al., *The Problem with Futility,* 326 New Eng. J. Med. 1560 (1992). *Cf.* DeGrella v. Elston, 858 S.W.2d 698, 712 (Ky. 1993) ("the ever-present problem of factoring in the economic ingredient of public taxpayer funding of Medicare and medical support for those in nursing homes or in a persistent vegetative state").

[161] Emanuel & Emanuel, *The Economics of Dying: The Illusion of Cost Savings at the End of Life,* 330 New Eng. J. Med. 540, 543 (1994). *But see* Correspondence, *Cost Savings at the End of Life,* 331 New Eng. J. Med. 477 (1994).

## Bibliography

Ackerman, T. "The Significance of a Wish." *Hastings Center Report* 21 (July–August 1991): 27.

Alpers, A., and B. Lo. "Futility: Not Just a Medical Issue." *Law, Medicine and Health Care* 20 (1992): 327.

Angell, M. "The Case of Helga Wanglie—A New Kind of 'Right to Die' Case." *New England Journal of Medicine* 325 (1991): 511.

Blackhall, L. "Must We Always Use CPR?" *New England Journal of Medicine* 317 (1987): 1281.

Blake, D., et al. "Bioethics and the Law: The Case of Helga Wanglie: A Clash at the Bedside—Medically Futile Treatment v. Patient Autonomy." *Whittier Law Review* 14 (1993): 3.

Boozang, K. "Death Wish: Resuscitation Self-Determination for the Critically Ill." *Arizona Law Review* 35 (1993): 24.

Braithwaite, S., and D. Thomasma. "New Guidelines on Foregoing Life-Sustaining Treatment in Incompetent Patients: An Anticruelty Policy." *Annals of Internal Medicine* 104 (1986): 711.

Brennan, T. "Physicians and Futile Care: Using Ethics Committees to Slow the Momentum." *Law, Medicine and Health Care* 20 (1992): 336.

Bresnahan, J. "Medical Futility or the Denial of Death?" *Cambridge Quarterly of Healthcare Ethics* 2 (1993): 213.

Brett, A., and L. McCullough. "When Patients Request Specific Interventions—Defining the Limits of the Physician's Obligation." *New England Journal of Medicine* 315 (1986): 1347.

Callahan, D. "Medical Futility, Medical Necessity: The-Problem-Without-A-Name." *Hastings Center Report* 21 (July–August 1991): 30.

Capron, A. "In re Helga Wanglie." *Hastings Center Report* 21 (September–October 1991): 26.

Chervenak, F., and L. McCullough. "Justified Limits on Refusing Intervention." *Hastings Center Report* 21 (March–April 1991): 12.

Coogan, M. "Medical Futility in Resuscitation: Value Judgement and Clinical Judgement." *Cambridge Quarterly of Healthcare Ethics* 2 (1993): 197.

Cotler M., and D. Gregory. "Futility: Is Definition the Problem?" *Cambridge Quarterly of Healthcare Ethics* 2 (1993): 219.

Council on Ethical and Judicial Affairs. American Medical Association. "Guidelines for the Appropriate Use of Do-Not-Resuscitate Orders." *JAMA* 265 (1991): 1868.

Cranford, R., and L. Gostin. "Futility: A Concept in Search of a Definition." *Law, Medicine and Health Care* 20 (1992): 307.

Daar, J. "A Clash at the Bedside: Patient Autonomy v. A Physician's Professional Conscience." *Hastings Law Journal* 44 (1993): 1241.

Drane, J., and J. Coulehan. "The Concept of Futility: Patients Do Not Have a Right to Demand Medically Useless Treatment." *Health Progress* 74 (1993): 28.

Franklin, C. "Allowing Patients to Decide." *Cambridge Quarterly of Healthcare Ethics* 2 (1993): 205.

Goldworth, A. "Jeremy Bentham and the Patient in Room 326." *Cambridge Quarterly of Healthcare Ethics* 2 (1993): 142.

Grant, E. "Medical Futility: Legal and Ethical Aspects." *Law, Medicine and Health Care* 20 (1992): 330.

Gregory, D., and M. Cotler. "Futility: Are Goals the Problem?" *Cambridge Quarterly of Healthcare Ethics* 3 (1994): 125.

Gregory, D., and M. Cotler. "The Problem of Futility: The Importance of Physician-Patient Communication and a Suggested Guide Through the Minefield." *Cambridge Quarterly of Healthcare Ethics* 3 (1994): 257.

Hackler, C., and F. Charles Hiller. "Family Consent to Orders Not to Resuscitate: Reconsidering Hospital Policy." *JAMA* 264 (1990): 1281.

Hastings Center. *Guidelines on the Termination of Life-Sustaining Treatment and the Care of the Dying.* Briarcliff Manor, N.Y.: Hastings Center, 1987.

Jecker, N. "Knowing When to Stop: The Limits of Medicine." *Hastings Center Report* 21 (May–June 1991): 5.

Jecker, N., and R. Pearlman. "Medical Futility: Who Decides." *Archives of Internal Medicine* 152 (1992): 1140.

Jecker, N., and L. Schneiderman. "Ceasing Futile Resuscitation in the Field." *Archives of Internal Medicine* 152 (1992): 2392.

Jecker, N., and L. Schneiderman. "An Ethical Analysis of the Use of 'Futility' in the 1992 American Heart Association Guidelines for Cardiopulmonary Resuscitation and Emergency Cardiac Care." *Archives of Internal Medicine* 153 (1993): 2195.

Jecker, N., and L. Schneiderman. "Futility and Rationing." *American Journal of Medicine* 92 (1992): 189.

Jecker, N., and L. Schneiderman. "Medical Futility: The Duty Not to Treat." *Cambridge Quarterly of Healthcare Ethics* 2 (1993): 151.

Johnson, D. "Helga Wanglie Revisited: Medical Futility and the Limits of Autonomy." *Cambridge Quarterly of Healthcare Ethics* 2 (1993): 161.

Jonsen, A. "Intimations of Futility." *American Journal of Medicine* 96 (1994): 107.

Koch, K., et al. "Analysis of Power in Medical Decision-Making: An Argument for Physician Autonomy." *Law, Medicine and Health Care* 20 (1992): 320.

Lantos, J., et al. "The Illusion of Futility in Clinical Practice." *American Journal of Medicine* 87 (1989): 81.

Lantos, J., et al. "Survival After Cardiopulmonary Resuscitation in Babies of Very Low Birthweight: Is CPR Futile Therapy?" *New England Journal of Medicine* 318 (1988): 91.

Loewy, E., and R. Carlson. "Futility and Its Wider Implications: A Concept in Need of Further Examination." *Archives of Internal Medicine* 153 (1993): 429.

Mahowald, M. "Futility and Unilateral Decision Making: A Different View." *Cambridge Quarterly of Healthcare Ethics* 2 (1993): 211.

Marsh, F., and A. Staver. "Physician Authority for Unilateral DNR Orders." *Journal of Legal Medicine* 12 (1991): 115.

Miles, S. "Futile Feeding at the End of Life: Family Virtues and Treatment Decisions." *Theoretical Medicine* 8 (1987): 293.

Miles, S. "Informed Demand for 'Non-Beneficial' Medical Treatment." *New England Journal of Medicine* 325 (1991): 512.

Miles, S. "Medical Futility." *Law, Medicine and Health Care* 20 (1992): 310.

Mishkin, D. "The Next Wanglie Case: The Problem of Litigating Medical Ethics." *Journal of Clinical Ethics* 1 (1991): 282.

Mitchell, K., et al. "Medical Futility, Treatment Withdrawal and the Persistent Vegetative State." *Journal of Medical Ethics* 19 (1993): 71.

Morreim, H. "Profoundly Diminished Life: The Casualties of Coercion." *Hastings Center Report* 24 (January–February 1994): 33.

Murphy, D. "Do-Not-Resuscitate Orders: Time for Reappraisal in Long-Term-Care Institutions." *JAMA* 260 (1988): 2098.

Murphy, D. and D. Matchar. "Life-Sustaining Therapy: A Model for Appropriate Use." *JAMA* 264 (1990): 2103.

Paris, J. "Pipes, Colanders, and Leaky Buckets: Reflections on the Futility Debate." *Cambridge Quarterly of Healthcare Ethics* 2 (1993): 147.

Paris, J., and F. Reardon. "Physician Refusal of Requests for Futile or Ineffective Interventions." *Cambridge Quarterly of Healthcare Ethics* 1 (1992): 127.

Paris, J., et al. "Physician's Refusal of Requested Treatment—The Case of Baby L." *New England Journal of Medicine* 322 (1990): 1012.

Rie, M. "The Limits of a Wish." *Hastings Center Report* 21 (July–August 1991): 24.

Schade, S., and H. Muslin. "Do Not Resuscitate Decisions: Discussions with Patients." *Journal of Medical Ethics* 15 (1989): 186.

Schneiderman, L., and N. Jecker. "Futility in Practice." *Archives of Internal Medicine* 153 (1993): 437.

Schneiderman, L., et al. "Beyond Futility to an Ethic of Care." *American Journal of Medicine* 96 (1994): 110.

Schneiderman, L., et al. "Medical Futility: Its Meaning and Ethical Implications." *Annals of Internal Medicine* 112 (1990): 949.

Solomon, M. "How Physicians Talk about Futility: Making Words Mean Too Many Things." *Journal of Law, Medicine and Ethics* 21 (1993): 231.

Stell, L. "Stopping Treatment on Grounds of Futility: A Role for Institutional Policy." *St. Louis University Public Law Review* 11 (1992): 481.

Task Force on Ethics of the Society of Critical Care Medicine. "Consensus Report on the Ethics of Foregoing Life-Sustaining Treatments in the Critically Ill." *Critical Care Medicine* 18 (1990): 1435.

Tomlinson, T., and H. Brody. "Ethics and Communications in Do-Not-Resuscitate Orders." *New England Journal of Medicine* 318 (1988): 43.

Tomlinson, T., and H. Brody. "Futility and the Ethics of Resuscitation." *JAMA* 264 (1990): 1276.

Truog, R., et al. "The Problem with Futility." *New England Journal of Medicine* 326 (1992): 1560.

Veatch, R., and C. Spicer. "Futile Care: Physicians Should Not Be Allowed to Refuse to Treat." *Health Progress* 74 (1993): 22.

Veatch, R., and C. Spicer. "Medically Futile Care: The Role of the Physician in Setting Limits." *American Journal of Law and Medicine* 18 (1992): 15.

Youngner, S. "Futility in Context." *JAMA* 264 (1990): 1295.

Youngner, S. "Who Defines Futility?" *JAMA* 260 (1988): 2094.

# TABLE OF CASES

| *Case* | *Book §* |
|---|---|
| Winthrop Univ. Hosp., *In re,* 490 N.Y.S.2d 996 (Sup. Ct. Nassau County 1985) | § 8.17 |
| Wons v. Public Health Trust, 541 So. 2d 96 (Fla. 1989), *aff'g* 500 So. 2d 679 (Fla. Dist. Ct. App. 1987) | §§ 1.7, 2.4, 2.9, 5.11, 5.40, 8.2, 8.9, 8.10, 8.13, 8.14, 8.15, 8.16, 8.17, 8.18, 8.19, 9.3, 9.55, 10.7 |
| Wood, *In re* Estate of, 553 A.2d 772 (Pa. Super. Ct. 1987) | § 5.4 |
| Wisconsin v. Yoder, 406 U.S. 205 (1972) | § 15.6 |
| Workmen's Circle Home & Infirmary for the Aged v. Fink, 514 N.Y.S.2d 893 (Sup. Ct. Bronx County 1987) | §§ 1.7, 7.7, 8.6, 8.8, 8.10, 8.12, 9.37, 9.39, 10.16, 10.34 |
| Wu v. Spence, 605 A.2d 395 (Pa. Super. Ct. 1992) | § 3.11 |
| Yetter, *In re,* 62 Pa. D. & C.2d 619 (C.P. Northampton County 1973) | §§ 1.7, 4.7, 4.23, 4.31, 9.49, 10.16 |
| Yetzke, *In re,* No. 93-155558 GD (P. Ct. Kent County, Mich. Aug. 12, 1993) | § 1.7 |
| Young, *In re,* No. A 100863 (Super. Ct. Orange County, Cal. Sept. 11, 1979) | § 1.7 |
| Young v. Emory Univ., Civ. Action No. 83-6143-5 (Super. Ct. Dekalb County, Ga. Aug. 10 and 29, 1983) | § 1.7 |
| Young v. Oakland Gen. Hosp., 437 N.W.2d 321 (Mich. Ct. App. 1989) | §§ 5.13, 5.20, 17.1, 17.7, 17.18 |
| Young v. Yarn, 222 S.E.2d 113 (Ga. Ct. App. 1975) | § 17.11 |
| Youngberg v. Romeo, 457 U.S. 307 (1982) | § 19.10 |
| Younts v. St. Francis Hosp. & Sch. of Nursing, Inc., 469 P.2d 330 (Kan. 1970) | § 15.3 |
| Zahn, *In re,* No. 85-3723 (Fla. Cir. Ct. Broward County Nov. 20, 1986) | § 1.7 |
| Zant v. Prevatte, 286 S.E.2d 715 (Ga. 1982) | §§ 2.8, 8.19 |
| Zodin v. Manor, No. 9010821007 (Super. Ct. Cobb County, Ga. Nov. 21, 1990) | § 1.7 |

# INDEX

609